PĀṆINI

A SURVEY OF RESEARCH

PĀṆINI

A SURVEY OF RESEARCH

by

GEORGE CARDONA

University of Pennsylvania

MOTILAL BANARSIDASS

Delhi :: Varanasi :: Patna

First Indian Reprint : Delhi, 1980

ISBN: 978-81-2081-494-3

Also available at:

MOTILAL BANARSIDASS
41 U.A. Bungalow Road, Jawahar Nagar, Delhi 110 007
8 Mahalaxmi Chamber, Warden Road, Mumbai 400 026
120 Royapettah High Road, Mylapore, Chennai 600 004
Sanas Plaza, Subhash Nagar, Pune 411 002
16 St. Mark's Road, Bangalore 560 001
8 Camac Street, Calcutta 700 017
Ashok Rajpath, Patna 800 004
Chowk, Varanasi 221 0011

PRINTED IN INDIA

BY JAINENDRA PRAKASH JAIN AT SHRI JAINENDRA PRESS,
A-45 NARAINA, PHASE I, NEW DELHI 110 028
AND PUBLISHED BY NARENDRA PRAKASH JAIN FOR
MOTILAL BANARSIDASS PUBLISHERS PRIVATE LIMITED,
BUNGALOW ROAD, DELHI 110 007

PREFACE

TO PARTS 1 – 3

PREFACE

This is the first volume (divided for technical reasons, into three sub-volumes) of a projected larger work in which I plan to treat the history and methodology of Indian grammatical thought. Subsequent volumes will include an introduction to Pāṇini's Aṣṭādhyāyī, a survey of commentatorial literature on this work, and studies of non-Pāṇinian works on grammar. The first of these subsequent volumes has been in typescript since 1970, and I hope soon to have it ready for publication.

The present volume is intended as a critical survey of research carried out in the specific area of Pāṇinian grammar, including works by Pāṇinīyas on semantics and philosophy of grammar. Articles and monographs devoted specifically to other Indian schools of grammar and to Prātiśākhyas and the Nirukta have been considered here only in so far as reference to them was required by the specific topic at hand. More detailed bibliographic information on these will appear in subsequent volumes.

I have attempted to read and give serious thought to as many studies as I could in the area of discussion. Yet I have no illusions that the bibliography included here is anywhere near exhaustive. There are quite a few articles and monographs referred to in bibliographies which remain inaccessible to me. Moreover, I could not consult other works due to my own limitations, for example, works in Dravidian languages. In order to get a fuller bibliographic information, the reader is referred to the works noted in sections II. 1 - 3, though even the addition of these does not, I think, exhaust the field. Nevertheless, I hope to have covered enough of the work which has been done to give the reader a fair idea of the scope of the field, of the topics which have attracted and continue to attract the attention of scholars, and of the current state of research in this area. The aim of giving the reader a view of the state of research in this field required, I think, that I carry out two duties. First, that I give as much information as possible. Second, that I consider critically the work done, that is, that I treat the ideas and conclusions of scholars relative to topics which have been deemed important, and that, wherever possible, I sift conflicting views and give what I consider to be reasonable and tenable conclusions warranted by the evidence, refraining from such conclusions where the evidence appears insufficient. This attitude has determined the format of this volume.

The bibliography which constitutes the first part, though not, strictly speaking, fully annotated, gives information on books and monographs which, in my opinion, a reader needs in order to know what an author or editor has done. In the survey, I have attempted to set forth the principal topics of interest and importance, views concerning these, and the evidence for these views. In each case, I have made a serious effort to keep from airing facile opinions or dismissing a given opinion – either favorably or unfavorably – with a mere epithet. Instead, I have attempted to summarize authors' works, where I thought this possible, and the evidence which has led to given conclusions. I am aware that in so doing I have risked serving two possibly irreconcilable masters, the brevity of a survey and the prolixity consequent on discussion of evidence. I hope, nevertheless, that I have been able to strike a balance.

As I said, I view this work as a critical survey of research, not as a history of scholarship in the field. For, to begin with, I do not consider myself a historian. Nevertheless, I hope that the treatment of the topics considered serves to give the reader an idea of changing interests and emphases. And, of course, it is these interests and emphases which have to a great extent dictated the amount of attention devoted to particular topics.

This work was completed in November 1974. Between then and now, there have appeared studies, some, but not all, of which I have been able to incorporate into my work. Others will be included and commented on in subsequent volumes.

It is now my pleasant obligation to thank those who have helped me. I began working on this survey during the year 1971 - 1972, while I was a fellow of the Center for Advanced Study in the Behavioral Sciences, Palo Alto, to the director of which, O. Meredith Wilson, I extend my thanks for the superb working conditions and camaraderie I enjoyed. Many coworkers have also put me in their debt through their generosity. Professors Ashok N. Aklujkar (University of British Columbia), Madhav M. Deshpande (University of Michigan), Hans H. Hock (University of Illinois), Ramanath Sharma (University of Rochester), Wilhelm Rau (Philipps-Universität Marburg), Rosane Rocher (University of Pennsylvania), and Michael Shapiro (University of Washington) helped me to obtain various works and information on dissertations. Many friends and colleagues in India gave me generously of their time in assisting me in obtaining works and information on research being done in their universities: Bhāgīratha Prasāda Tripāṭhī (Vārāṇaseya Saṃskṛta Viśvavidyālaya), Jayashree A. Gune (Deccan College), Dayashankar M. Joshi (Deccan College), Shivram D. Joshi (University of Poona), K. Kunjunni Raja (University of Madras), Pt. Raghunātha Śarmā (retired Professor, Vārāṇaseya Saṃskṛta Viśvavidyālaya), Rāmaprasāda Tripāṭhī (Vārāṇaseya Saṃskṛta Viśvavidyālaya), Satyavrat Shastri (Delhi University), Umakant P. Shah

(Oriental Institute, M. S. University of Baroda), Shiva Narayana Shastri (Kirorimal College, Delhi University), Esther Solomon (Gujarat University). In addition, Professors Rosane Rocher and Wilhelm Rau did me the great favor of reading and commenting on the bibliography and the survey. To all of these friends and colleagues I offer my sincerest thanks. Not for mine but for their sake do I echo Kumārila's words:

> tad vidvāṃso'nugṛhṇantu cittaśrotraiḥ prasādibhiḥ/
> santaḥ praṇayivākyāni gṛhṇanti hy anasūyavaḥ//
> na cātrātīva kartavyaṃ dosadṛṣṭiparaṃ manaḥ/
> doṣo hy avidyamāno'pi taccittānāṃ prakāśate//

Philadelphia, 24 March 1975 GEORGE CARDONA

TABLE OF CONTENTS

PART 1:

BIBLIOGRAPHY

PRELIMINARY REMARKS

The following are to be noted:

(1) Abbreviations do not include specifications such as "humanities section" or "philologisch-historische Klasse" for journals of universities and academies. The reader is to understand that references are to such sections.

(2) For editions which bear titles in English and another language (Sanskrit etc.), both titles are given, one in parentheses. Since the present work is in English, the English title appears first. Information contained in one title and lacking in the other is supplied in square brackets. Entries in Sanskrit, etc., show deletion marks ('...'). I have thereby indicated the omission of authors' names, position, academic affiliation, and titles given on titlepage.

(3) Translations of titles of works written in languages other than English and other commonly known European languages appear in square brackets following the titles. The language in question is also specified within these brackets.

(4) All Festschriften, including "N. N. volumes" and "Mélanges N. N." are listed under "Festschrift ..." in the bibliography.

(5) Articles published in the *Publications of the Centre of Advanced Study in Sanskrit, Class A,* are for the most part stated to be reprints of articles published in the *Journal of the University of Poona.* However, the latter is at times dated later than the former. Therefore, I have listed all such articles first as appearing in the former, followed by "also in ...." within square brackets.

(6) If a book or article has been reprinted without modification, this is indicated in square brackets by the specification "reprint:". If, however, an article has been republished with any modifications, reference is made to the subsequently published article by the mention "see also".

(7) A work which I have not personally consulted is marked by asterisks surrounding the date (e.g., *1950*) if I have not been able to verify its contents. If I have not been able to consult the work

directly but a summary of this has appeared in *Prācī Jyoti* or Dandekar's bibliography (see the bibliography under these), however, no asterisks surround the date. Instead, a reference to the above-mentioned reference works is given in square brackets accompanying the entry.

(8) Many Indian editions are dated according to the vikrama era. If a month is not given either on the title page or in a preface or introduction, I give two A.D. dates. For example, a work published in saṃvat 2014 is listed as published in 1957/8.

ALPHABETICAL LIST OF ABBREVIATIONS OF JOURNALS AND FESTSCHRIFTEN AND COLLECTIVE WORKS

AA:	Acta Asiatica; Bulletin of the Institute of Eastern Culture (Tokyo).
ABORI:	Annals of the Bhandarkar Oriental Research Institute (Poona).
ACIL:	Actes du ... congrès international des linguistes; see *Congrès* (1968).
ACUT:	Acta et communicationes Universitatis Tartuensis.
AGM:	Ādarśa-grantha-mālā (Adarsh Granthmala).
AICL:	All-India Conference of Linguists; see *Conference* (1972b).
AIOK:	Akten des .... internationalen Orientalisten-Kongresses; see *Kongress* (1957).
AIONSL:	Annali, Istituto Orientale di Napoli, sezione linguistica.
AIPHOS:	Annuaire de l'Institut de Philologie et d'Histoire Orientales et Slaves, Bruxelles.
AJGM:	Śrī Ātmānand Jain Grantha-mālā.
AJP:	American Journal of Philology, Baltimore.
AKM:	Abhandlungen für die Kunde des Morgenlandes.
ALB:	Brahmavidyā, The Adyar Library Bulletin, Adyar (Madras).
ALS:	The Adyar Library Series.
AMGG:	Abhandlungen der Marburger Gelehrten Gesellschaft.
AO:	Acta Orientalia, Leiden.
AOR:	Annals of Oriental Research, University of Madras, Sanskrit section.
AOS:	American Oriental Series.
AOSE:	American Oriental Series Essay.
AP:	The Aryan Path, Bombay.
Arch. Or.:	Archiv Orientální, Praha.
ARSHLL:	Acta Regiae Societatis Humaniorum Litterarum Lundensis
AS:	Asian Studies, Quezon City, Philippines.
ASS:	Ānandâśrama Sanskrit Series.
ASVOI:	Annals of the Sri Venateswara Oriental Institute, Tirupati.
AUJ:	Annamalai University Journal, Annamalainagar.
AUS:	Andhra University Series.

AUSt.:	Allahabad University Studies.
AAWLM:	Abhandlungen der Akademie der Wissenschaften und der Literatur, Mainz.
BB:	(Bezzenbergers) Beiträge zur Kunde der indogermanischen Sprachen, Göttingen.
BDCRI:	Bulletin of the Deccan College Research Institute, Poona.
BEFEO:	Bulletin de l'École Française d'Extrême-Orient, Paris.
BEPHE:	Bulletin de l'École Pratique des Hautes Études, Paris.
BGWL:	Berichte über die Verhandlungen der königlichen sächsischen Gesellschaft der Wissenschaften zu Leipzig.
Bhāṣā:	Bhāṣā; Kendriya Hindi Nideśālaya, New Delhi.
BHUSS:	Banaras Hindu University Sanskrit Series.
BhV:	Bhāratīya Vidyā, Bombay.
BI(E)S:	Bulletin of the Institute of Postgraduate (Evening) Studies, Delhi.
BIG:	Bibliothek indogermanischer Grammatiken.
BORI:	Bhandarkar Oriental Research Institute, Poona.
BORIS:	Bhandarkar Oriental Research Institute Post-graduate and Research Series.
BOS:	Bonner Orientalistische Studien.
BoSS:	Bombay Sanskrit Series.
BP:	Buddhi Prakāśa, Ahmedabad.
BPSC:	Bulletin of the Philological Society of Calcutta.
BSOAS:	Bulletin of the School of Oriental and African Studies, London.
BSOS:	Bulletin of the School of Oriental Studies, London.
BSPS:	Bombay Sanskrit and Prakrit Series.
BSS:	Benares Sanskrit Series. [Entries contain both the numbers of works and the numbers of individual fascicles of works.]
BSSM:	Shri Bahadur Singh Singhi Memoirs.
CASS-St.:	Center of Advanced Study in Sanskrit, Studies (= *PCASS-E*)
CLTA:	Cahiers de linguistique théorique et appliquée, București.
COJ:	Calcutta Oriental Journal.
CR:	The Calcutta Review.
CSA:	Cahiers de la Société Asiatique, Paris.
CSCRS:	Calcutta Sanskrit College Research Series.
CSS:	Chowkhamba Sanskrit Series. [Entries contain both the numbers of works and the numbers of individual fascicles of works.]
CSSt.:	Chowkhamba Sanskrit Studies.
CW:	Collected Works.

DAWIO: Deutsche Akademie der Wissenschaften zu Berlin, Institut für Orientforschung.
DCBCS: Deccan College Building Centenary Series.
DCBCSJS: Deccan College Building Centenary and Silver Jubilee Series.
DCDS: Deccan College Dissertation Series.
DCMS: Deccan College Monograph Series.
EVP: Études védiques et pāṇinéennes; see Renou (1955), (1956c), (1961).
EW: East and West, Roma.
FL: Foundations of Language, Dordrecht.
FLSS: Foundations of Language, supplementary series.
GBS: Govind Book Series.
GGA: Göttingische Gelehrte Anzeigen.
GJPM: Gaṅgānātha Jhā Pravacana-mālā [Gaṅgānātha Jhā Lecture Series].
GKP: Gurukula Patrikā, Haridwar.
GOS: Gaekwad's Oriental Series.
GovOS: Government Oriental Series. [The abbreviation is followed by a class letter.]
GSA: Giornale della Società Asiatica Italiana, Roma.
GSPM: Grantha-saṃśodhana-prakāśana-maṇḍala.
GSS: Gurukula Sanskrit Series.
HKNM: Hari-kṛṣṇa-nibandha-maṇi-mālā.
HOS: Harvard Oriental Series.
HSS: Haridas Sanskrit Series.
IA: Indian Antiquary, Bombay.
IA³: Indian Antiquary, third series, Bombay.
IBKW: Innsbrucker Beiträge zur Kulturwissenschaft.
IC: Indian Culture; Journal of the Indian Historical Institute, Calcutta.
IF: Indogermanische Forschungen, Berlin.
IHQ: Indian Historical Quarterly, Calcutta.
IIJ: Indo-Iranian Journal, The Hague.
IJDL: International Journal of Dravidian Linguistics, Trivandrum.
IL: Indian Linguistics; Journal of the Linguistic Society of India, Poona. [The page numbers for volumes 1 - 15 are those of the reprints in three volumes (Poona: Centre for Advanced Study in Linguistics and the Linguistic Society of India); 1: volumes 1 - 4 (1931 - 4), 1966; 2: volumes 5 - 8 (1935 - 44), 1965; 3: volumes 9 - 15 (1944 - 50), 1965].
IndF: Indische Forschungen, Breslau.

IPQ:	International Philosophical Quarterly, New York.
IS:	Indische Studien, Leipzig.
IZAS:	Internationale Zeitschrift für allgemeine Sprachwissenschaft, Heilbronn.
JAHRS:	Journal of the Andhra Historical Research Society, Hyderabad.
JAOS:	Journal of the American Oriental Society, New Haven.
JAs:	Journal Asiatique, Paris.
JASB:	Journal of the Asiatic Society of Bengal, Calcutta.
JASL:	Journal of the Asiatic Society (of Calcutta), Letters.
JBBRAS:	Journal of the Bombay Branch of the Royal Asiatic Society.
$JBBRAS^2$:	Journal of the Bombay Branch of the Royal Asiatic Society, new series.
JDLCU:	Journal of the Department of Letters, Calcutta University. [Papers are numbered and paginated separately; entries show the number of the paper and pages].
JDSDU:	Journal of the Department of Sanskrit, Delhi University.
JGJRI:	Journal of the Gangānātha Jhā Research Institute, Allahabad.
JGJKSV:	Journal of the Gangaṇātha Jhā Kendrīya Sanskrit Vidyāpeeth. [New name for *JGJRI* as of 1971].
JIBS:	Journal of Indian and Buddhist Studies, Tokyo. [Two page entries are shown; the first is the Japanese pagination, to be read in reverse order; the second is to be read in ascending order].
JIP:	Journal of Indian Philosophy, Dordrecht.
JKU:	Journal of the Karnatak University, Dharwar.
JL:	Janua Linguarum; studia memoriae Nicolai van Wijk dedicata.
JLSP:	Janua Linguarum, series practica.
JMSUB:	Journal of the Maharaja Sayajirao University of Baroda.
JMU:	Journal of the Madras University.
JOIB:	Journal of the Oriental Institute, Baroda.
JOR:	Journal of Oriental Research, Madras.
JPMJG:	Jñānapīṭha Mūrtidevī Jaina Grantha-mālā. [Sanskrit volumes].
JRAS:	Journal of the Royal Asiatic Society of Great Britain and Ireland, London.
JSP:	Śrī Jaina Satya Prakāśa, Ahmedabad.
JSVOI:	Journal of the Sri Venkateswara Oriental Institute, Tirupati, Sanskrit section.
JUB:	Journal of the University of Bombay.
JUG:	Journal of the University of Gauhati.
JUP:	Journal of the University of Poona.
JVS:	Journal of Vedic Studies, Lahore.

KSINA: Kratkie soobščenija Instituta naradov Azii AN SSSR, Moskva.
KSS: Kāśī Sanskrit Series.
KSVS: Kendriya Sanskrit Vidyapeetha Series.
KUDSP: Kerala University Department of Sanskrit Publications.
KURJ: Kurukshetra University Research Journal.
KZ: (Kuhns) Zeitschrift für vergleichende Sprachforschung auf dem Gebiete der indogermanischen Sprachen, Göttingen.
LBS: Linguistic Bibliography Series.
LD: Language Dissertation.
LDS: Lalbhai Dalpatbhai Series.
Lg.: Language; Journal of the Linguistic Society of America, Baltimore.
Linguistic Inquiry: Linguistic Inquiry, Cambridge, Massachusetts.
LOS: London School of Oriental and African Studies, London Oriental Series.
LS: Language Sciences, Bloomington, Indiana.
LUAS: Lunds Universitets Årsskrift, N. F. Avd. 1.
MAPS: Memoirs of the American Philosophical Society.
Medhā: Medhā, Government Sanskrit College, Raipur.
MGOMS: Madras Government Oriental Manuscript Series.
MIK: Miscellanea Indologica Kiotiensia, Kyoto.
MO: Mysore Orientalist, Mysore.
MSL: Mémoires de la Société Linguistique de Paris.
MSPS: Mehar Chand Lachman Das Sanskrit and Prakrit Series.
MSS: Münchener Studien zur Sprachwissenschaft, München.
MSUOS: The M[aharaja] S[ayajirao] University Oriental Series.
MSURS: The M. S. University of Baroda Research Series.
MUSS: Madras University Sanskrit Series.
NGGW: Nachrichten von der königlichen Gesellschaft der Wissenschaften zu Göttingen.
NIA: New Indian Antiquary, Bombay.
NPP: Nāgarī Pracāriṇī Patrikā, Nāgarī Pracāriṇī Sabhā, Varanasi.
NTS: Norsk Tidsskrift for Sprogvidenskap, Oslo.
NUJ: Nagpur University Journal.
OH: Our Heritage; Bulletin of the Department of Post-Graduate Training and Research, Sanskrit College, Calcutta.
OLZ: Orientalistische Literaturzeitung, Leipzig.
Oriens: Oriens; Journal of the International Society for Oriental Research, Leiden.
OS: Orientalia Suecana, Uppsala.

OT: Oriental Thought, Nasik.
OU: Occident und Orient, Göttingen.
PAICL: Proceedings of the ... All-India Conference of Linguists; see *Conference* (1970), (1972b).
PAIOC: Proceedings (and Transactions) of the ... All-India Oriental Conference. [The place and date of each conference appear in parentheses following the number of the conference; all page references are to volumes of papers.]
PBS: Prāchya Bhāratī Series.
PCASS: Publications of the Centre of Advanced Study in Sanskrit, University of Poona. [The abbreviation is followed by a class letter and a number.]
PEFEO: Publications de l'École Francaise d'Extrême-Orient, Hanoi, Paris.
PEW: Philosophy East and West, Honolulu.
PICI: Publications de l'Institut de Civilisation indienne, série in-8°.
PICL: Proceedings of the ... International Congress of Linguists; see "Congress (1962)".
PICLMP: Proceedings of the ... International Congress for Logic, Methodology and Philosophy of Science; see "Congress (1960)".
PICO: Proceedings of the ... International Congress of Orientalists; see "Congress (1964b), (1967)".
PIFI: Publications de l'Institut français d'Indologie, Pondichéry.
PO: The Poona Orientalist.
PPMGM: Prajñā Pāṭhashālā Maṇḍala Grantha Mālā.
PWSBS: Princess of Wales Sarasvati Bhavana Studies.
PWSBTS: The Princess of Wales Sarasvati Bhavana Texts Series.
QJMS: Quarterly Journal of the Mythic Society, Bangalore.
RLKTS: Rāma Lāl Kapūr Trust Series.
RSCG: Shri Rajasthan Sanskrit College Granthamala.
RSO: Rivista degli Studi Orientali, Roma.
RUB: Revue de l'Universite de Bruxelles.
Sāg.: Sāgarikā, Sāgar University.
Saṃgamanī: Saṃgamanī; Saṃskṛta Sāhitya Pariṣad, Prayāga (Allahabad).
Saṃvid: Saṃvid, Bhāratīya Vidyā Bhavan, Bombay.
SAO: Studia et Acta Orientalia, Bucureşti.
SAS: Sanskrit Academy Series.
SBAM: Sarasvatī Bhavana Adhyayana-mālā.
SBAW: Sitzungsberichte der preussischen Akademie der Wissenschaften, Berlin.

SBGM:	Sarasvatī Bhavana Grantha-mālā.
SBh.:	Sura-bhāratī; Baroda Sanskrit College.
SBMS:	Sri Balamanorama Series.
SBS:	Sarasvatī Bhavana Studies.
Scientia:	Scientia, Rivista di Scienza; International Review of Scientific Synthesis, Bologna.
SCOM:	Śrī Citrodaya Mañjarī.
SHAW:	Sitzungsberichte der Heidelberger Akademie der Wissenschaften.
SIAL:	Sources of Indo-Aryan Lexicography.
SIL:	Studies in Linguistics.
SJS:	Singhi Jain Series.
SPAIOC:	Summaries of Papers, ... All-India Oriental Conference.
SPISC:	Summaries of Papers, First International Sanskrit Conference; see "Conference (1972a)".
ŚPP:	Śāradā Pīṭha Pradīpa, a bi-annual of the Indological Research Institute, Dwarka.
SS:	Sārasvatī Suṣamā, Varanasi.
SSGM:	Savitarāya-smṛti-rakṣaṇa-grantha-mālā.
ŚSLPM:	Śrī Setu Laksmī Prasāda-mālā.
SSP:	Saṃskṛta Sāhitya Pariṣad, Calcutta.
Svādhyāya:	Svādhyāya, Baroda.
SVPM:	Sanskrit Vidyāpeeth Prakashanmala.
SVS:	Sarasvati Vihar Series.
SVUOJ:	Sri Venkateswara University Oriental Journal, Tirupati.
SWAW:	Sitzungsberichte der kaiserlichen Akademie der Wissenschaften zu Wien.
TAPA:	Transactions of the American Philological Association, Hartford/Cleveland.
TAPS:	Transactions of the American Philosophical Society, new series.
TICO:	Transactions of the ... Congress of Orientalists; see *Congress* (1892).
TPS:	Transactions of the Philological Society, London.
ULBTFPL:	Université Libre de Bruxelles, Travaux de la faculté de philosophie et lettres.
UMS:	Usha Memorial Series.
UPSPS:	University of Poona Sanskrit and Prakrit Series.
UTSS:	University of Travancore Sanskrit Series.
Vāk:	Vāk, Poona.
VAPS:	The late MM Vasudev Shastri Abhyankar Publication Series.

VBSGM:	Vidyābhavana Sanskrit Grantha-mālā.
VIDK:	Verhandlungen des ... internationen Dialektologenkongresses; see "Kongress (1968)".
VIJ:	Vishveshvaranand Indological Journal, Hoshiarpur.
VIS:	Vishveshvaranand Indological Series.
VISUE:	Veröffentlichungen des indogermanischen Seminars der Universität Erlangen.
VKAWA:	Verhandelingen der koninklijke Akademie van Wetenschappen te Amsterdam, Nieuwe Reeks.
VRGM:	Vidyābhavana Rāṣṭrabhāṣā Grantha-mālā.
VS:	Viśva-saṃskṛtam, Hoshiarpur.
VSMV:	Vidarbha Saṃśodhana Maṇḍala Vārṣika, Nagpur.
WZKM:	Wiener Zeitschrift für die Kunde des Morgenlandes, Bombay, Wien.
WZKMUL:	Wissenschaftliche Zeitschrift der Karl-Marx-Universität Leipzig.
WZMLUH:	Wissenschaftliche Zeitschrift der Martin-Luther-Universität Halle-Wittenberg.
WZKSOA:	Wiener Zeitschrift für die Kunde Süd- und Ostasiens und Archiv für indische Philosophie, Wien.
ZDMG:	Zeitschrift der deutschen morgenländischen Gesellschaft, Leipzig, Wiesbaden.
ZII:	Zeitschrift für Indologie und Iranistik, Leipzig.
ZMF:	Zeitschrift für Mundartforschung, Wiesbaden.

BIBLIOGRAPHY

Abegg, Emil

1914 "Die Lehre vom sphoṭa im Sarvadarśanasaṃgraha", *Festschrift Ernst Windisch,* pp. 188-95.

Abhyankar, Kashinath Vasudev

1951 "Date and authorship of the Śabdaratna and the Bṛhat-śabdaratna", *ABORI* 32: 258-62.

1952 "The term *karmadhāraya, ABORI* 33: 238-44.

1954 [See Abhyankar, Vasudev Shastri – Kashinath Vasudev Abhyankar.]

1955 "A short note on paribhāṣā works in Sanskrit grammar", *ABORI* 36: 157-62.

1957 "Short *e (ardha ekāra)* and short *o (ardha okāra)* in Sanskrit". *ABORI* 38: 154-7.

1960 *The Paribhāṣenduśekhara of Nāgojībhaṭṭa, edited and explained by F. Kielhorn.* 2: *translation and notes*[2] [New edition, with preface by K. V. Abhyankar, of Kielhorn (1874a)] [Preface to the second edition, pp. 1-7; Kielhorn's preface, pp. i-xxv; appendix: Paribhāsāṣ contained in Sīradeva's Paribhāṣāvṛtti, pp. 529-37.]

1961 *A dictionary of Sanskrit grammar* (= *GOS* 134) (Baroda: Oriental Institute).

1962 (Ed.,) *The Paribhāṣenduśekhara of Nāgojībhaṭṭa, edited critically with the commentary Tattvādarśa of MM. Vasudev Shastri Abhyankar.* 1 *(Śrīmad-upādhyāyôpanāmaka-śivabhaṭṭa-suta-satī-garbhaja-nāgojībhaṭṭa-kṛtaḥ śrīman-mahāmahôpādhyāya-abhyaṃkarôpāhva-vāsudevaśāstri-viracitayā tattvâdarśâbhidhayā vyākhyayā samavêtaḥ paribhāṣêndu-śekharaḥ, prathamo bhāgaḥ)* (Poona: *BORI*). [New edition, with new Sanskrit commentary, of Kielhorn (1868)] [Introduction by K. V. Abhyankar, pp. 1-40; serial index of paribhāṣās with corresponding numbers of paribhāṣās in Puruṣottama's Paribhāṣā-pāṭha, Vyāḍi's Paribhāṣā-sūcana, Puruṣottama's Paribhāṣā-vṛtti, Sīradeva's Paribhāṣā-vṛtti, and Nīlakaṇṭha's Paribhāṣā-vṛtti, pp. 41-6; alphabetic index of paribhāṣās with corresponding numbers of paribhāṣās in Vyāḍi's, Puruṣottama's (Paribhāṣā-vṛtti), and Sīradeva's collections, pp. 201-06].

1962-72 (Ed.) *The Vyākaraṇa-mahābhāṣya of Patañjali, edited by F. Kielhorn, third edition, revised and furnished with additional readings, references and select critical notes by K. V. Abhyankar,* 3 vol. (Poona: *BORI*). [1: (1962); 2: (1965); 3: (1972)] [Revised edition of Kielhorn (1892-1909); see Kielhorn (1880-85).] [Prefaces to the volumes of the third edition: 1: 7-8; 2: 7-8; 3: 5-6; select critical notes: 1: 561-72.]

1964 "Authorship of the Laghuśabdaratna", *ABORI* 45: 152-8.

1965 "Euphonic combinations of *ṛ* and *ḷ* with *ṛ* and *ḷ*", *Festschrift Sukumar Sen,* pp. 1-7.

1966 "A dissertation on a doubtful passage in the Kāśikāvṛtti on P.I.1.4 and two passages in the Taittirīya Āraṇyaka prapāṭhaka 4", *ABORI* 47: 101 - 3.

1967 (Ed.) *Paribhāṣāsaṁgraha (a collection of original works on vyākaraṇa paribhāṣā), edited critically with an introduction and an index of paribhāṣās (Paribhāṣā-saṃgrahaḥ (vyāḍi-śākaṭāyanâdi-prôkta-paribhāṣā-pāṭhānāṃ tat-praṇīta-vṛttīnāṃ ca saṃgrahaḥ))* (= *BORIS* 7) (Poona: BORI). [Prefatory note, pp. 1-5; introduction, pp. 1-64; alphabetic index, pp. 466-93.] [Contains: Vyāḍi's Paribhāṣā-sūcana (pp. 1-38), Vyāḍi's Paribhāṣā-pāṭha (pp. 39-43), Śākaṭāyana's Paribhāṣā-sūtras (pp. 44-46), Candra's Paribhāṣā-sūtras (pp. 47-48), Durgasiṃha's Kātantra-paribhāṣā-sūtra-vṛtti (pp. 49-66), Bhāvamiśra's Kātantra-paribhāṣā-sūtra-vṛtti (pp. 67-75), Kātantra-paribhāṣā-sūtras (pp. 76-77), Kālāpa-paribhāṣā-sūtras (pp. 78-80), K. V. Abhyankar's Jainendra-paribhāṣā-vṛtti (pp. 81-104), Bhoja's Paribhāṣā-vṛtti (pp. 105-7), Hemacandra's paribhāṣās as collected by Hemahaṃsagaṇi (pp. 108-11), Puruṣottama's Laghu-paribhāṣā-vṛtti (pp. 112-60) and Paribhāṣā-pāṭha (pp. 160a-b), Sīradeva's Bṛhat-paribhāṣā-vṛtti with the Bṛhat-paribhāṣā-vṛtti-ṭippaṇī (Vijayā) of Mānaśarmā (pp. 273-92), Nīlakaṇṭha's Paribhāṣā-vṛtti (pp. 293-316), Haribhāskara Agnihotrī's Paribhāṣā-bhāskara (pp. 317-74), Nāgeśabhaṭṭa's paribhāṣās (pp. 375-77), Śeṣādri's Paribhāṣā-bhāskara (pp. 378-465).]

1969 "Dramatic, pictorial, and verbal representations of past events at the time of Patañjali", *Festschrift Gopinath Kaviraj,* pp. 257-61.

1970 "A brief note on the chronological order of the Phiṭ-sūtras, the Uṇādi-sūtras and the Aṣṭādhyāyī", *JOIB* 19: 331-32.

1971 "Kā nāma vṛttiḥ kati vṛttayas tāḥ" [What is vṛtti and how many vṛttis are there?] *Festschrift Rajeshwar Shastri Dravid*, grammar section, pp. 26-28. [In Sanskrit]

Abhyankar, Kashinath Vasudev – V. P. Limaye

1965 (Eds.) *Vākyapadīya of Bhartṛhari (Bhartṛhari-viracitaṃ vākya-padīyam)* (= *UPSPS* 2) (Poona: University of Poona). [Introduction, pp. i - xv; appendices: 1: index of verses, pp. 166-92; 2: synopsis of the second kāṇḍa by Puṇyarāja, pp. 193-96; 3: verses from the Vākya-padīya cited by various later authors, with the context in which these are cited, pp. 197 - 297; supplement to appendix 3, pp. 297 - 357; 4: verses attributed to Bhartṛhari but not found in this edition, pp. 358 - 68; 5: glossary of important words in the Vākya-padīya, pp. 369 - 408; 6: verses from the Vākya-padīya cited in Haradatta's Pada-mañjarī, pp. 409 - 22; 7: passages from ancient works referred to by Bhartṛhari in the Vākya-padīya and his commentary thereon, pp. 423 - 64.]

1967 *Mahābhāṣya-dīpikā of Bhartṛhari* 1: *āhnikas 1 - 5 (Śrīman-mahôpādhyāya-bhartṛhari-viracitā mahābhāṣya-dīpikā āhnika-pañcâtmakaḥ prathamo bhāgaḥ)* (= *BORIS* 8) (Poona: BORI). [Originally published as supplements to *ABORI* 43 - 47 (1962-66).]

1969 *Mahābhāṣya-dīpikā of Bhartṛhari* 2: *āhnikas 6-7* (= Supplement to *ABORI* 50). [I have supplied the title according to Abhyankar – Limaye (1967).]

Abhyankar, Kashinath Vasudev – Jayadev Mohanlal Shukla

1968 (Eds., tr.) *Patañjali's Vyākaraṇa-mahābhāṣya – (navāhnikī), fasciculus 1 (āhnikas 1 and 2), with English translation and notes (Śrī-bhagavat-patañjali-kṛta-vyākaraṇa-mahābhāṣyam (navâhnikī), khaṇḍaḥ 1 (prathame dve āhnike), āṅglā-bhāṣânuvādena ṭippaṇībhiś ca sahitaḥ)* (= *VAPS* 15) (Poona: Sanskrit Vidyā Parisaṃsthā). [Includes in the notes extensive citations, untranslated, from Bhartṛhari's commentary (edited by Abhyankar – Limaye 1967).]

Abhyankar, Vasudev Shastri – Kashinath Vasudev Abhyankar

1938-54 (Eds., tr.) *Śrīmad-bhagavat-patañjali-viracita-vyākaraṇa-mahābhāṣya, mūḷa āṇi marāṭhī bhāṣântara; bhāṣāntara-kāra mahāmahopādhyāya Vāsudeva Śāstrī Abhyaṅkara, saṃpādaka Kāśīnātha Vāsudeva Abhyaṅkara* [Patañjali's Vyākaraṇa-mahābhāṣya; Sanskrit text and Marathi translation; translated by Vasudev Shastri Abhyankar, edited by K. V. Abhyankar], 7 vols. (Poona: Deccan

Education Society). [1 (1938): adhyāya 1, pādas 1-2; 2 (1941): adhyāya 1, pādas 3-4, adhyāya 2; 3 (1951): adhyāya 3; 4 (1952): adhyāyas 4-5; 5 (1953): adhyāya 6; 6 (1951): adhyāyas 7-8; 7 (1954): prastāvanā, Marathi introduction by K. V. Abhyankar. Contains explanatory footnotes by the translator.]

Ādyā Prasāda Miśra

1966 *Prakriyā-kaumudī-vimarśaḥ* [A study of the Prakriyā-kaumudī, in Sanskrit] (= *SBS* 15) (Varanasi: Vārāṇaseya Saṃskṛta Viśvavidyālaya). [Originally a Vārāṇaseya Saṃskṛta Viśvavidyālaya doctoral dissertation, 1964.]

Agnihotrī, Prabhudayāla [see Prabhudayāla Agnihotrī]

Agrawala, Vasudev Sharan [= Agravāla, Vāsudeva Śaraṇa]

1937 "Patañjali on the kṣudraka-mālavas", *PO* 1.4: 1-7.

1939 "Patañjali and the vāhīka-grāmas", *IC* 6: 129-36.

1940 "Pūrvācārya saṃjñās for lakāras", *NIA* 3: 39-40.

1943 "Sumanottarā", *PO* 7: 197-200.

1945 "Pāṇini, his life and works", *JGJRI* 2: 81-114.

1946 "Food and drink (*annapāna*) in ancient India from Pāṇini's Aṣṭādhyāyī", *JGJRI* 4: 11-33.

1947 "Current proper names (*manuṣyanāma*) in Pāṇini", *Festschrift Mookerji*, pp. 1049-63.

1949 "Pāṇini", *JOR* 19: 124-34.

1950 "Pre-Pāṇinian technical terms", *Festschrift Siddheshwar Varma* 2, pp. 135-37.

1951 "Some chronological considerations about Pāṇini's date", *IHQ* 27: 269-86.

1953a "Geographical data in Pāṇini", *IHQ* 29: 1-34.

1953b "An ancient reference to Menander's invasion", *IHQ* 29: 180-82.

1956-57 "A note on *puṣya-māṇava*", *JOIB* 6: 109-10.

1963a *India as known to Pāṇini (a study of the cultural material in the Aṣṭādhyāyī)*[2] (Varanasi: Prithivi Prakashan). [First edition: (Lucknow, 1953).] [Originally delivered as the Radha Kumud Mookerji lectures for 1952 at the University of Lucknow.] [Preface to first edition, pp. xi-xv. Appendices: 1: Janapadas and the Greek city-state, pp. 479-93; 2: A critical text of the geographical gaṇas, pp. 449-521; 3: Gotras, pp. 522-60; cf. Plate of punch-marked coins, opposite p. 561; key to plate, pp. 561-63. Foldout maps of northwestern India, Panjab, India at the time of Pāṇini].

1963b *Gotras in Pāṇini (an exposition with a critical text of the gotras in the Aṣṭādhyāyī)* (Varanasi: Prithivi Prakashan). [Separate issue of Appendix 3 in Agrawala (1963).]

1969 *Pāṇinikālīna Bhāratavarṣa (Aṣṭādhyāyī kā saṃskṛtika adhyayana)* (= *VRGM* 50) (Varanasi: Chowkhamba). [Hindi translation, by the author, of Agrawala (1963a).]

Aklujkar, Ashok Narhar

1969 "Two textual studies of Bhartṛhari", *JAOS* 89: 547-63.

1970a "Ancient Indian semantics", *ABORI* 51: 11-29.

1970b *The philosophy of Bhartṛhari's Trikāṇḍī.* [Harvard University dissertation, unpublished; bibliography on Bhartṛhari the grammarian, pp. 280-301]

1971a "Nakamura on Bhartṛhari", *IIJ* 13: 161-75.

1971b "Mahābhāṣya-dīpikā or Tripādī? ", *ALB* 35: 159-69.

1971c "The number of kārikās in Trikāṇḍī book 1", *JAOS* 91: 510-13.

1972 "The authorship of the Vākyapadīya-vṛtti", *WZKSOA* 16: 181-98.

1974 "The authorship of the Vākya-kāṇḍa-ṭīkā", *Festschrift Charudeva Shastri*, pp. 165-88.

forthcoming Review of Scharfe (1971a), *OLZ*.

Al-George, Sergiu

1957 "Le sujet grammatical chez Pāṇini", *SAO* 1: 39-47.

1966 "La fonction révélatrice des consonnes chez les phonéticiens de l'Inde antique", *CLTA* 3: 11-15.

1967 "The semiosis of zero according to Pāṇini", *EW* 17: 115-24.

1968 "The extra-linguistic origin of Pāṇini's syntactic categories and their linguistic accuracy", *JOIB* 18: 1-7.

1969 "Sign (lakṣaṇa) and propositional logic in Pāṇini", *EW* 19: 176-93.

1970 "L'Inde antique et les origines du structuralisme", *ACIL* 10. 2: 235-40.

1971 "Lakṣaṇa, grammatical rule", *Festschrift K. C. Chaṭṭopādhyāya*, pp. 213-21.

1972 "Pāṇini and modern thought" *SPISC* 2: 42-43.

Allen, William Sidney

1953 *Phonetics in ancient India* (= *LOS* 1) (London: Oxford University Press). [reprint: (1963)]

1955 "Zero and Pāṇini", *Festschrift S. K. Chatterji* pp. 106-13.

1962 *Sandhi, the theoretical, phonetic, and historical bases of word-junction in Sanskrit* (= Janua Linguarum. Series minor 17) (The Hague: Mouton).

Ananthanarayana, H. S.
1969 "The feminine formation in Pāṇini's grammar", *Festschrift S. M. Katre* 2, pp. 1-12.
1970 "The kāraka theory and case grammar", *IL* 31: 14-27.
1972 "A syntactic classification of verbs in Pāṇini's grammar", *AICL* 3: 30.

Anjaneya Sarma, V.
1965 "The śabda-brahman and the prasthāna-traya", *SVUOJ* 8: 31-35.

Arora, Sudarshan Kumari
1969 *Patañjali as a critic of Kātyāyana and Pāṇini.* [Delhi University dissertation, unpublished]

Aryendra Sharma – Khanderao Deshpande – D. G. Padhye
1969-70 (Eds.) *Kāśikā, a commentary on Pāṇini's grammar by Vāmana and Jayāditya (Śrī-vāmana-jayāditya-viracitā pāṇinīyâṣṭâdhyāyī-sūtra-vṛttiḥ kāśikā),* 2 vol. (= *SAS* 17, 20) (Hyderabad: Sanskrit Academy, Osmania University). [1: adhyāyas 1-4, 2: adhyāyas 5-8] [English introduction, vol. 1: v-vi; subject indices of chapters, vol. 1: x-xvi, vol. 2: v-xvi]

Athalekar, Shripad L.
1974 *Kāśikā-gatāni udāharaṇāni* [Examples in the Kāśikā, in Sanskrit] [University of Poona doctoral dissertation]

Aufrecht, Theodor
1847 *De accentu compositorum sanskritorum* [On the accent of Sanskrit compounds](Bonn: König). [In Latin]
1858 "Die Handschriften der Prauḍhamanoramā in der Bodleyanischen Bibliothek (Codd. Wils. 156. 200. 320. 426)", *IS* 4: 171 - 76.
1859 (Ed.) *Ujjvaladatta's commentary on the uṇādisūtras, edited from a manuscript of the East India House* (Bonn: Marcus). [Preface, pp. v-xxii; notes, pp. 148-63; alphabetic index of sūtras, pp. 164-71; index of suffixes with their markers, pp. 171-76; index of suffixes without their markers, pp. 176-79; list of uṇādi suffixes which actually occur in Sanskrit, pp. 269-78.]
1860 "Zwei Pāṇini zugeteilte Strophen", *ZDMG* 14: 581-83.
1875 "Pāṇini", *IA* 4: 281.
1882 "Beiträge zur Kenntniss indischer Dichter", *ZDMG* 36: 361-83. [365 - 68: Strophen von Pāṇini, 370: Eine Strophe von dem Bhāṣyakāra]
1891a "Über Bhaṭṭojī", *ZDMG* 45: 306-07.
1891b "Jāmbavativijayam", *ZDMG* 45: 308.

Avadh Bihari Mishra
1937 (ed.) *The Vākya Padīya – Brahma Kandam of Bhartri-hari* [sic] *with the Prakash commentary of Pt. Narain Datt Tripathi (Pada-vākya-pramāṇa-pārâvarīṇena śrī-bhartṛhariṇā viracitam vākya-padīya-brahma-kāṇḍam . . . p. nārāyaṇa-datta-śarmma-tripāṭhinā viracitayā prakāśa-ṭīkayā prakāśitam)* (= *GBS* 1) (Varanasi: Swami Dershanand, principal, Shri Chandra College).

Ayachit, S. M.
1959 *Gaṇapāṭha; a critical study*. [Poona University doctoral dissertation, unpublished] [cf. Ayachit (1961)]
1961 "Gaṇapāṭha: a critical study", *IL* 22: 1-63. [cf. Ayachit (1959)]

Bahulikar, Saudamini
1966 "The constructions *stokaḥ pākaḥ* and *stokaṃ pākaḥ*", *PAIOC* 22 (Gauhati, 1965): 93-98.
1972 *Some criteria for determining the insertions in the Aṣṭādhyāyī.* [Harvard University dissertation, unpublished] [See Bahulikar (1973, 1974).]
1973 "Concerning the structure of Pāṇini's Aṣṭādhyāyī", *IL* 34: 75-99. [Chapter 1 of Bahulikar (1972).]
1974 "Use of the particle *ca* in the Aṣṭādhyāyī", *CASS-St.* 2: 67-82. [Chapter 2 of Bahulikar (1972).]

Balasubrahmanyam, M. D.
1961-62 "On the accentuation of the vocative *ṛtāvṛddhau* in RV 1.2.8", *BDCRI* 22: 92-104.
1962-63 "The accentuation of *arya-* in Pāṇini and the Veda", *BDCRI* 23: 94-100. [Reprint: Balasubrahmanyam (1969)]
1965 "An accentual note on *vikaṭa-* in Pāṇini and the Veda", *Festschrift Sukumar Sen* pp. 18-26.
1966a "The three Pāṇinian suffixes *Ṇac, inUṆ,* and *Ktri*", *PCASS-A* 6. [Also in *JUP* 23 (1966): 123-38]
1966b "An accentual problem in Pāṇini and the Veda a propos of the word *hāyana-*", *BDCRI* 25: 43-58.
1966c "Patañjali and the pre-Pāṇinian anubandhas *ṅ* and *c*", *PCASS-A* 11. [Also in *JUP* 25 (1967): 77-82]
1968 "*Amāvasyā:* an accentual study", *JUP* 27: 1-25.
1969a "*Arya-:* an accentual study", *Festschrift R. N. Dandekar,* pp. 112-27.
1969b "The accentuation of *arya-* in Pāṇini and Veda", *PICO* 26: III: 21-24. [See Balasubrahmanyam (1962-63)]
1969c *The accent of kṛt formations.* [University of Poona dissertation, unpublished]

1971 "Vedic *starya-* and Pāṇini 3.1.123", *Festschrift K. C. Chaṭṭopādhyāya,* pp. 21-28.

1972a "Vedic *śriyase* and Pāṇini 3.4.9", *VIJ* 10: 7-10.

1972b "Pāṇini 5.2.28-29", *JGJKSV* 28.3-4: 79-99.

1974 "Pāṇini 6.1.209-210", *Festschrift Charudeva Shastri* pp. 189-93.

Bali, Surya Kant

1971 *Contribution of Bhaṭṭoji Dīkṣita to Sanskrit grammar.* [Delhi University dissertation, unpublished.]

Ballantyne, James R.

1849 (ed.) *The Laghu Kaumudi, a Sanskrit grammar by Varadarāja, with an English version, commentary and references*[3] (Varanasi: E. J. Lazarus). [Reprint: (Delhi: Motilal Banarsidass 1961).] [Indices (after the text): sūtras, pp. i-xxiii; nominal bases, pp. xxiii-xxv; verb roots, pp. xxv-xxvii.]

Ballantyne, James R. and the pandits of the Benares college

1856 (Ed., tr.) *The Mahābhāshya with its commentary the Bhāshya-pradīpa, and the commentary thereon, the Bhāshya-pradīpodyota* 1: *containing the navāhnika with an English version of the opening portion (Mahā-bhāṣyam bhāṣya-pradīpena vivaraṇena ca sahitaṃ kāśyāṃ rājakīya-pāṭhālaye śrīmad-bālanṭain-nāmaka-tad-adhyakṣa-preritais tatratyaiḥ śrī-nārāyaṇa-śāstri-devadatta-durgādatta-śarmabhir vyākaraṇa-paṇḍitaiḥ śrīmac-caturveda-hīrāṇanda-śarmabhir alaṅkāra-paṇḍitaiś ca saṃśodhitam . . .)* (Mirzapore: Orphan School Press). [Pp. 1-40: English translation of small part of the Mahā-bhāṣya, Pradīpa and Uddyota, equivalent to the text in Kielhorn (1880 - 85 1. 1 - 6.7).] [The Sanskrit title identifies the editors as Nārāyaṇa Śāstrī, Devadatta, Durgādatta, Hīrāṇanda Caturveda; the date of publication on the Sanskrit title page is given as 1855.]

Baṃsīlāl, Rājā Govindalāl

1969 *"Liṭ" aur "luṅ" la-kāra kī rūpa-bodhaka sarala-vidhi* [The rules for deriving forms with the L-suffixes *liṭ* and *luṅ*] (Bombay: The author). [In Hindi.]

Barlingay, S. S.

1964 "Theories of language in Indian logic", *IPQ* 4: 94-109.

Belvalkar, Shripad Krishna

1915 *An account of the different existing systems of Sanskrit grammar, being the Vishwanath Narayan Mandlik gold medal prize essay for 1909* (Poona: The author).

Bendall, Cecil

1889 Review of F. Kielhorn, *A grammar of the Sanskrit language*[3]

(Bombay: Government Central Book Depot 1888), *IA* 18: 253-54.

Benfey, Theodor

1852 *Vollständige Grammatik der Sanskritsprache zum Gebrauch für Vorlesungen und zum Selbststudium* (Leipzig: Brockhaus).

1874 *Einleitung in die Grammatik der vedischen Sprache; erste Abhandlung: der Saṃhitā Text* (Aus dem 19. Bande der Abhandlungen der königlichen Gesellschaft der Wissenschaften zu Göttingen) (Göttingen: Dieterich).

Bhāgavat, Vāmana Bālakrishna

1965 *Vākyapadīya kāṇḍa 1* (= *GSPM* 2) (Poona: Tilak Mahārāshtra Vidyāpeeth). [Text and Marathi translation.]

1969 "Pāṇinīya-gaṇa-nirdeśe bahu-vidhatā" [The various ways in which Pāṇini refers to groups of items], *PAIOC* 23 (Aligarh, 1966): 381-82. [In Sanskrit.]

Bhāgīratha Prasāda Tripāṭhī

1965 *Pāṇinīya-dhātupāṭha-samīkṣā* [A critical study of Pāṇini's Dhātupāṭha] (= *SBS* 14) (Varanasi: Vārāṇaseya Saṃskṛta Viśvavidyālaya). [In Sanskrit.] [Originally a Vārāṇaseya Saṃskṛta Visvavidyālaya dissertation (1964).]

1969 *Dhātv-artha-vijñānam* [On the meanings of roots] [Vārāṇaseya Saṃskṛta Viśvavidyālaya dissertation for the degree of vidyāvācaspati] [In Sanskrit.]

1972 "Pāṇinīyāḥ 'abhyāsaḥ', 'āmreḍitam', 'abhystam' cêti śabdāḥ" [The Pāṇinian terms *abhyāsa, āmreḍita,* and *abhyasta*], *Festschrift K. C. Chaṭṭopādhyāya,* pp. 697-99. [In Sanskrit.]

Bhāṇḍāri, Mādhava Śāstrī

1940 "Pāṇinīya-vyākaraṇasya saṃkṣiptam aitihyam" [A brief account of the history of Pāṇinian grammar], *Festschrift Woolner,* pp. 7-16. [In Sanskrit.]

Bhāṇḍāri, Mādhava Śāstrī, Madan Mohan Pāṭhak, Nityānand Panta Parvatīya

1926 (Eds.) *Vaiyākaraṇa Siddhānta Laghu Manjūsha by Mahāmahopādhyāya Śrī Nāgeśa Bhaṭṭa, with two commentaries, i.e., Kuñjikā of Durbalāchārya and Kalā of Bālam Bhaṭṭa (Vaiyākaraṇa-siddhânta-laghu-mañjūṣā mahāmahôpādhyāya-śrī-nāgeśabhaṭṭa-viracitā, śrīmad-durbalâcārya-bālambhaṭṭâbhyāṃ viracita-kuñjikā-kalâhva-ṭīkā-dvaya-saṃvalitā)* (= *CSS* 44: 191 (1913), 192 (1913), 211 (1915), 212 (1915), 213 (1915), 214 (1915), 227 (1916), 228 (1916), 237 (1917), 238 (1917), 253 (1919), 328 333 (1925), 340, 345 (1926)). [The date given is that of the last fascicle; the title page gives 1925 as the date; the title is given as it appears in the third fascicle.]

Bhandarkar, Devadatta Ramakrishna

1934 "Notes on ancient history of India: (3) 'śaka-yavanam'", *IC* 1: 275-80.

Bhandarkar, Ramakrishna Gopal

1868 *Second book of Sanskrit; a treatise on grammar, with excercises.* (22nd edition, revised by S. R. Bhandarkar (Bombay: Karnatak Publishing House 1952). [Reference made here to extracts from preface reprinted in R. G. Bhandarkar (1927-33 2: 415 - 20).]

1871-74 "On the date of the Mahābhārata", *JBBRAS* 10: 81-92. [Reprint: R. G. Bhandarkar (1927-33 1: 79-93), under the title "Consideration of the date of the Mahābhārata", with 1872 given as the date of publication.]

1872a "Pāṇini and the geography of Afghanistan and the Panjab", *IA* 1: 21-23. [Reprint: R. G. Bhandarkar (1927-33 1: 102-07).]

1872b "On the date of Patañjali and the king in whose reign he lived", *IA* 1: 299-302. [Reprint: R. G. Bhandarkar (1927-33 2: 108-14), Staal (1972: 78-81).]

1873a "Note on the above", *IA* 2: 59 - 61. [A note on Weber (1873a)] [Reprint: R. G. Bhandarkar (1927-33 1: 115-20), under the title "A note on Professor Weber's letter".]

1873b "Patañjali's Mahābhāṣya", *IA* 2: 69-71. [Reprint: R. G. Bhandarkar (1927-33 1: 121-24), under the title "Mahābhāṣya of Patañjali".]

1873c "On the interpretation of Patañjali", *IA* 2: 94-96. [Reprint: R. G. Bhandarkar (1927-33 1: 125-9).]

1873d "Reply to Professor Weber's letter", *IA* 2: 238-40. [Reprint: R. G. Bhandarkar (1927-33 1: 130-5).] [Reply to Weber (1873c).]

1874 "Allusions to Kṛṣṇa in Patañjali's Mahābhāṣya", *IA* 3: 14-6. [Reprint: R. G. Bhandarkar (1927-33 1: 209-13).]

1876 "Āchārya, the friend of the student, and the relation between the three āchāryas", *IA* 5: 345-50. [Reprint: R. G. Bhandarkar (1927-33 1: 136-47); partial reprint: Staal (1972: 86).]

1877 "Dr. Goldstücker's theory about Pāṇini's technical terms", *IA* 6: 107-13. [Reprint: R. G. Bhandarkar (1927-33 1: 496-510), under the title "A review of Dr. Goldstücker's 'Pāṇini' and his theory about Pāṇini's technical terms". The original review of Goldstücker (1861) appeared in *Native opinion,* August 21st and 28th 1864.]

1883-85a "The date of Patañjali: A reply to Professor Peterson", *JBBRAS* 16: 199-222. [Reprint: R. G. Bhandarkar (1927-33 1: 157-85), under the title "The date of Patañjali, no. 1: being the first reply to Professor Peterson".] [Reply to Peterson (1883-85); see also R. G. Bhandarkar (1885).]

1883-85b "Development of language and of Sanskrit", *JBBRAS* 16: 245-74 (= *Wilson Philological Lectures of 1877* 1). [Reprint: R. G. Bhandarkar (1927-33 4: 241-74); partial reprint: Staal (1972: 87-93).]

1885 "Date of Patañjali, no. 2: being a second reply to Professor Peterson". [Originally privately published; reprinted in R. G. Bhandarkar (1927-33 1: 186-207). The original was not availlable to me, so that I have given the title and date as they appear in Bhandarkar 1927-33.]

1887a "The Maurya-passage in the Mahābhāṣya", *IA* 16: 156-58. [Reprint: R. G. Bhandarkar (1927-33 1: 148-53).]

1877b "A supplementary note on the Maurya-passage in the Mahābhāṣya", *IA* 16: 172-73. [Reprint: R. G. Bhandarkar (1927-33 1: 154-56).]

1893 "Miscellaneous notes, I: a Buddhist Jātaka story in Patañjali", *TICO* 9: 421 - 23. [Reprint: R. G. Bhandarkar (1927-33 1: 295-97)].

1895 *The early history of the Deccan down to the Mahomedan conquest*[2] (Calcutta: S. Gupta). [Reprint: R. G. Bhandarkar (1927-33 3: 1-198).]

1910 "Vāsudeva of Pāṇini IV.III.98", *JRAS* 1910: 168-70. [Reprint: R. G. Bhandarkar (1927-33 1: 214-16).]

1913 *Vaiṣṇavism, śaivism and minor religious systems* (= *Grundriss der indo-arischen Philologie und Altertumskunde* (ed. H. Lüders – J. Wackernagel) 3.6) (Strassburg: Trübner).

1927-33 *Collected works of Sir R. G. Bhandarkar,* 4 vol. (ed.: Narayana Bapuji Utgikar – Vasudev Gopal Paranjpe) (= GovOS-B 1 - 4) (Poona: BORI). [1: (ed.: the late N. B. Utgikar – V. G. Paranjpe) (1933); 2 - 4: (ed.: N. B. Utgikar) (1928, 1927, 1929)]

Bhāradvāja, Gaṅgādhara Śāstrī: see Gaṅgādhara Śāstrī Bhāradvāja.

Bhāradvāja, Śiva Prasāda: see Śiva Prasāda Bhāradvāja.

Bhārgavaśāstrī Joshi: see Joshi, Bhārgavaśāstrī Bhikājī.

Bhāradvāja, Dāmodara Śāstrī (Ed.)

1897 *Mādhavīyadhātuvṛtti* (Benares: Medical Hall Press).

Bhat, M. S.

1959a "Bhairava Miśra, circa 1780 - 1840 A.D.", *IHQ* 35: 76-78.

1959b "Ācārya Pauṣkarasādi and the date of Pāṇini", *JOIB* 8: 385-88.

1965 "Authorship of Laghuśabdaratna", *Festschrift H. D. Velankar*, pp. 203-05.

1966-67 "The Vedic stem *rātrī-* and Pāṇini", *JBBRAS* 41-42: 8-11.

Bhate, Saroja V.

1968 "Some primary and secondary suffixes known to Yāska", *PCASS-A* 15. [Also in *JUP* 27 (1968): 121-32.]

1971 *Pre-Pāṇinian grammatical elements in Pāṇini's Aṣṭādhyāyī.* [University of Poona dissertation, unpublished.]

Bhatnagar, Veena

1973 *Un-Pāṇinian sandhi and syntax in epic Sanskrit.* [Delhi University dissertation, unpublished.]

Bhattacharjee, Umesh Chandra

1925 "The evidence of Pāṇini on Vāsudeva-worship", *IHQ* 1: 483-89.

1926a "The evidence of Pāṇini on Vāsudeva-worship", *IHQ* 2: 409-10. [Against K. G. Subrahmanyam (1926a).]

1926b [Answer to K. G. Subrahmanyam 1926b], *IHQ* 2: 865. [The answer is printed without a title.]

Bhattacharya, Bhavānīprasāda

1969 "Vaidika-vyākaraṇam (pāṇini-kṛtāyā vaidika-prakriyāyā vivaraṇa-samêtaṃ saṃskaraṇam)" [Vedic grammar (an edition, with commentary, of Pāṇini's rules for Vedic derivations)], *SSP* 51: 244-51; 52: 34-43; 69-71 [Pāṇini's Vedic rules, with original Sanskrit commentary and English paraphrase; incomplete.]

Bhattacharya, Bishnupada

1956a "Philosophical data in Patañjali's Mahābhāṣya", *OH* 4: 51-65.

1956b "Constitution of words: sphoṭa theory and its opponents", *OH* 4: 217-26.

1957 "Connotation of words (a comparative study of the view-points of grammarians, Mīmāṃsakas and Naiyāyikas)", *OH* 5: 147-67.

1958 *Yāska's Nirukta and the science of etymology;* an *historical and critical survey* (Calcutta: Mukhopadhyay).

1962 *A study in language and meaning (a critical examination of some aspects of Indian semantics)* (Calcutta: Progressive Publishers).

Bhattacharya, Biswanath

1970 "Marutvac-chabda-nirvacana-vicāraḥ" [On the explanation of the word *marutvat*]. *JKU* 14: 1-3. [In Sanskrit.]

Bhattacharya, Dinesh Chandra

1922 "Pāṇinian studies in Bengal", *Festschrift Sir Asutosh Mookerjee* (1922-25 1: 189-208).

1943 "Puruṣottamadeva's commentary on the Mahābhāṣya", *IHQ* 19: 201-13.

Bhattacharya, Gaurinath
1937 "A study in the dialectics of sphoṭa", *JDLCU* 29.4: 1-115. [See also Gaurinath Shastri (1959).]

Bhattacharya, Ram Shankar [= Rāma Śaṅkara Bhaṭṭācārya]
1950-52 "Pāṇinian principles of determining the desired import of words", *JAHRS* 21: 133-41 [See also R. S. Bhattacharya (1966w).]
1951 "Some principles of tracing pre-Pāṇinian portions in Pāṇinian works", *JGJRI* 8: 407-18. [See also R. S. Bhattacharya (1966c).]
1952 "Pāṇini's notion of the authoritativeness of the views of his predecessors", *JGJRI* 9: 163-81.
1952-53 "Significance of the examples in the Mahābhāṣya", *JGJRI* 10: 39-48.
1952-55 "Some chief characteristics of Pāṇini in comparison to his predecessors", *JOIB* 2: 165-73; 5: 10-18.
1953a "Senses of *ca*", *PO* 18: 8-10.
1953b "A new *bhrāja* stanza", *PO* 18: 11-12. [See also R. S. Bhattacharya (1966ii).]
1953c "Kinds of agents [*kartā*] as depicted by Pāṇini", *Vāk* 3: 129-33. [See also R. S. Bhattacharya (1966z).]
1953d "Pāṇini kī dṛṣṭi meṃ bhāṣā kā svarūpa" [The character of bhāṣā in Pāṇini's view], *Śodha Patrikā* (Udaipur) 5: 13-22. [In Hindi.]
1954a "One corrupt reading of the Mahābhāṣya", *PO* 19: 2-3.
1954b "A new verse of the Saṁgraha", *PO* 19: 4-5.
1954c "Importance of the first words of the gaṇa-pāṭha-s", *BhV* 15: 29-34.
1954d "Some unknown senses of the plural number as shown by Pāṇini", *JUB* 23.2: 45-48. [See also R. S. Bhattacharya (1966bb).]
1954e "The Mahābhāṣya vs. the Kāśikā", *JSVOI* 15: 61-70.
1954f "Some characteristic expressions of Patañjali", *JSVOI* 15: 139-46.
1954-55 "On the original reading of a Pāṇinian sūtra", *JOIB* 4: 268-69. [On rule 6.1.115.]
1955a "Some characteristics of the ancient vṛttis on the Aṣṭādhyāyī", *IHQ* 31: 168-74. [See also R. S. Bhattacharya (1966b).]
1955b "Kinds of exposition in Sanskrit Literature", *ABORI* 36: 123-32.
1956a "Some objections on the textual order of the Aṣṭādhyāyī and their refutation", *JGJRI* 13: 119-29.
1956b "Some anomalies in the Aṣṭādhyāyī and their justifications", *BhV* 15: 110-19.

1957-58 "Some broad aspects on Indian grammar and the theory of sphoṭa", *JGJRI* 15: 83-92.

1963 "Padakāra ke artha ke viṣaya meṃ eka bhrama" [An error concerning the meaning of the term *padakāra*]. *Śodha Patrikā* (Udaipur) 14: 165-68. [In Hindi.] [*Prācī Jyoti* (1963-72 2: 134-35) see also R. S. Bhattacharya (1966p).]

1966 *Pāṇinīya vyākaraṇa kā anuśīlana* [Studies in Pāṇinian grammar] (Varanasi: Indological Book House). [In Hindi; Collection of papers].

1966a "Aṣṭādhyāyī ke prakaraṇakramoṃ kī saṃgati" [The consistency of the order of sections in the Aṣṭādhyāyī], in: R. S. Bhattacharya (1966) pp. 1-52.

1966b "Aṣṭādhyāyī kī prācīna vṛttiyoṃ kā svarūpa" [The character of ancient vṛttis on the Aṣṭādhyāyī], in: R. S. Bhattacharya (1966), pp. 53-60. [See also R. S. Bhattacharya (1955a).]

1966c "Pāṇini ke granthoṃ se prākpāṇinīya aṃśoddhāra ke upāya" [Means of tracing pre-Pāṇinian portions in Pāṇini's works], in: R. S. Bhattacharya (1966) pp. 61-88. [See also R. S. Bhattacharya (1951).]

1966d "Kyā Pāṇinīya vyākaraṇa aṣṭadhā vyākaraṇa meṃ anyatama hai? " [Is Pāṇini's grammar among those referred to as the eight-fold grammar?], in: R. S. Bhattacharya (1966) pp. 89-95.

1966e " 'Chandovat sutrāṇī bhavanti' kā tātparya" [The import of the statement 'sūtras are Veda-like'], in: R. S. Bhattacharya (1966) pp. 96-100.

1966f "Aṣṭādhyāyī ke nipātanasūtra" [The nipātana rules of the Aṣṭādhyāyī], in: R. S. Bhattacharya (1966) pp. 101-14. [Cf.: "Pāṇinīya-nipātana-sūtrâlocanam" (A survey of Pāṇini's nipātana rules), *SS* 10: 120-30 (in Sanskrit).]

1966g " 'Saṃjñāyām'-pada-ghaṭita sūtroṃ kā tātparya" [The import of rules formed with the term *saṃjñāyām*], in: R. S. Bhattacharya (1966) pp. 115-30. [Cf.: Saṃjñā-niṣpādaka-sūtrâlocanam" (A survey of rules which serve to form terms called saṃjñā) *SS* 12.2: 50-56: 12.3-4: 69-75 (in Sanskrit).]

1966h "Kārakavimarśa" [On kārakas], in: R. S. Bhattacharya (1966) pp. 131-62.

1966i "Aṣṭādhyāyī ke praśaṃsā-pūjādiparak sūtra" [Rules of the Aṣṭādhyāyī involving praise, honoring, etc.], in: R. S. Bhattacharya (1966) pp. 163-71. [Cf.: "Pāṇini ke praśaṃsārthaka tathā pūjarthaka sūtra" (Pāṇini's rules for items connoting praise and honoring) *NPP* 61: 141-49 (in Hindi).]

1966j "Aṣṭādhyāyi ke kṣepa-kutsādiparaka sūtra" [Rules of the Astādhyāyī involving censure, pejoration, etc.], in: R. S. Bhattacharya (1966) pp. 172-83.

1966k "Pāṇinismṛta bhikṣusūtra kā svarūpa" [The character of the bhikṣusūtras noted by Pāṇini], in: R. S. Bhattacharya (1966) pp. 184-90.

1966l "Pāṇini dvārā smṛta śiśukrandīya grantha kā svarūpa" [The character of the work Śiśukrandīya noted by Pāṇini], in: R. S. Bhattacharya (1966) pp. 191-93. [Cf.: "Pāṇini-smṛtasya śiśukrandīya-granthasya svarūpam" *SS* 18. 4: 121-23 (in Sanskrit).]

1966m "Pāṇinīya yavanānī-śabda ke artha ke viṣaya meṃ eka bhrama" [An error concerning the meaning of the Pāṇinian word *yavanānī*], in: R. S. Bhattacharya (1966) pp. 194-97.

1966n "Pāṇinīyasūtrajñāpita ṛgvedīya kaṭhaśākhā kī sattā" [The existence of a Ṛgvedic Kaṭha branch as indicated by a Pāṇinian rule], in: R. S. Bhattacharya (1966) pp. 198-202.

1966o "Adhikṛtya kṛte granthe sūtra evaṃ jyotiṣ śabda" [Rule 4.3.87 and the word *jyotiṣ*], in R. S. Bhattacharya (1966) pp. 203-07.

1966p "Mahābhāṣyokta padakāra ke artha ke viṣaya meṃ eka bhrama" [An error concerning the meaning of the term *padakāra* used in the Mahābhāṣya], in: R. S. Bhattacharya (1966) pp. 208-11. [See also R. S. Bhattacharya (1963).]

1966q "Pāṇinīya dṛṣṭi meṃ vyākaraṇa kī maryādā" [The bounds of grammar in the Pāṇinian view], in: R. S. Bhattacharya (1966) pp. 212-24.

1966r "Pāṇinīya vaiyākaraṇoṃ kī prakṛti-pratyaya-viśleṣaṇa-paraka dṛṣṭi" [The view of Pāṇinian grammarians concerning the analysis of bases and affixes], in R. S. Bhattacharya (1966), pp. 225-37.

1966s "Pāṇinīya matānusāra kavarga kā uccāraṇasthāna" [The point of articulation of velar stops according to the Pāṇinian view], in R. S. Bhattacharya (1966) pp. 238-46.

1966t "Pāṇinīya vaiyākaraṇoṃ kī dṛṣṭi meṃ anabhidhāna kī sahetukatā" [The principle of anabhidhāna: it is justified according to Pāṇinian grammarians], in R. S. Bhattacharya (1966) pp. 247-58.

1966u "Chātrī śabda kā sādhutva" [The word *chātrī*, its correctness], in: R. S. Bhattacharya (1966) pp. 259-65.

1966v "Rāṣṭrīya śabda kī sādhutā" [The word *rāṣṭrīya*, its correctness], in: R. S. Bhattacharya (1966) pp. 266-71.

1966w "Pāṇini ke śabdārthajñāpaka kauśala" [Pāṇini's ways of making known particular meanings of words], in: R. S. Bhattacharya (1966) pp. 272-79. [See also R. S. Bhattacharya (1950-52).]

1966x "Pāṇinīya sampradāya kī dṛṣṭi meṃ lokaprāmāṇyavāda" [The position that normal usage is authoritative, according to the Pāṇinian tradition], in R. S. Bhattacharya (1966) pp. 280-87.

1966y "Aṣṭādhyāyī ke jñānasambaddha śabda" [Words in the Aṣṭādhyāyī connected with knowing], in R. S. Bhattacharya (1966) pp. 288-97. [Cf.: "Aspects of knowing as depicted by Pāṇini", *BhV* 14: 99-108.]

1966z "Aṣṭādhyāyī-varṇita kartṛtvabheda" [Kinds of agents depicted in the Aṣṭādhyāyī], in: R. S. Bhattacharya (1966) pp. 298-302. [See also R. S. Bhattacharya (1953c).]

1966aa "Aṣṭādhyāyīprokta kriyābheda evaṃ utpatti" [Kinds of action and origination as set forth in the Aṣṭādhyāyī], in: R. S. Bhattacharya (1966) pp. 303-14.

1966bb "Bahuvacanajñāpita artha" [Meanings conveyed by the plural], in: R. S. Bhattacharya (1966) pp. 315-21. [See also R. S. Bhattacharya (1954d).]

1966cc "Kāśikokta kucch udāharaṇoṃ kā tātparya" [The import of some examples given in the Kāśikā], in: R. S. Bhattacharya (1966) pp. 322-30.

1966dd "Bhāṣyādi ke kucch pāṭhoṃ kī samīkṣā" [An examination of some readings in the Bhāṣya etc.], in: R. S. Bhattacharya (1966) pp. 331-42.

1966ee "Ācāryanāma evaṃ vibhāṣā-vā-ghaṭita sūtroṃ kā tātparya" [The import of rules in which teachers' names are mentioned and which are formed with the terms *vibhāṣā, vā*], in: R. S. Bhattacharya (1966) pp. 343-59.

1966ff "Aṣṭādhyāyī ke pāṭhāntaroṃ kā vivecana" [A study of variant readings in the Aṣṭādhyāyī], in: R. S. Bhattacharya (1966) pp. 360-76.

1966gg "Pāṇinīyasūtrapāṭhāntarasaṃkalana" [A collection of variant readings of Pāṇinian sūtras], in: R. S. Bhattacharya (1966) pp. 377-96. [Cf.: "Pāṇinīya-sūtra-pāṭhântara-saṃkalanam", *SS* 7. 2: 47-62. (in Sanskrit).]

1966hh " 'Chandobrāhmaṇāni' sūtrastha chandaḥśabda kā artha" [The meaning of the word *chandas* in rule 4.2.66], in: R. S. Bhattacharya (1966) pp. 397-406.

1966ii "Eka lupta bhrāja śloka" [A lost Bhrāja verse], in: R. S. Bhattacharya (1966) pp. 407-09. [See also R. S. Bhattacharya (1953b).]

1966jj "Vākyapadīya kā eka sāṃśayika śloka" [A doubtful verse of the Vākyapadīya], in: R. S. Bhattacharya (1966) pp. 410-12.

Bhattacharya, S.

1963 "A note on Pāṇini", *Bharati* 6: 76-80. [*Prāci Jyoti* (1963-72) 2: 132).]

Bhattacharya, S. P.

1947 "The Bhāgavṛtti and its author", *PAIOC* 12 (Varanasi 1943-44): 273-87.

Bhattacharya, Vidhuśekhar

1921 "Śākapārthiva", *IA* 50: 228.

1933 "Pāṇini's grammar and the influence of Prakrit on Sanskrit", *Festschrift Grierson* 2: 439-41.

Bhave, D. G.

1940 "A note on the 'Ābhīras' in Patañjali", *BDCRI* 2: 137-38.

Bhawe, Shrisrishna Sakharam

1953 "Pāṇini's rules and vedic interpretation", *PAIOC* 17 (Ahmedabad 1953): 231-40. [See also Bhawe (1955).]

1954 "Interpretation of some Rigvedic compounds", *JOIB* 4: 315-29.

1955 "Pāṇini's rules and vedic interpretation", *Festschrift S. K. Chatterji*, pp. 237-49. [See also Bhawe (1953).]

1957-62 *The soma hymns of the Ṛgveda; a fresh interpretation*, 3 vol. (= *MSURS* 3, 5, 6) (Baroda: Oriental Institute).

Bhīmasena Śāstrī

1969 (Ed., commentator) *Srimād-vidvad-vara-kauṇḍabhaṭṭa-viracito vaiyākaraṇa-bhūṣaṇa-sārah bhaimī-bhāṣyôpêtaḥ (dhātv-artha-nirṇayântaḥ)* [Kauṇḍabhaṭṭa's Vaiyākaraṇa-bhūṣaṇa-sāra, with the Bhaimī Sanskrit commentary of Bhīmasena, to the end of the dhātv-artha-nirṇaya section] (Delhi: The author).

1973 "Balamanoramākārasya kānicit skhalitāni" [Some errors by the author of the Bālamanoramā], *Festschrift Charudeva Shastri* pp. 84-89. [In Sanskrit].

Biardeau, Madeleine

1958 (Tr.) *Sphoṭa siddhi (la démonstration du sphoṭa) par Maṇḍana Miśra, introduction, traduction et commentaire par Madeleine Biardeau, texte sanskrit établi par N. R. Bhatt avec la collaboration de T. Ramanujan* (= *PIFI* 13) (Pondichéry: Institut français d'Indologie).

1964a *Théorie de la connaissance et philosophie de la parole dans le brahmanisme classique* (= *Le monde d'outre-mer passé et présent,* Première série, études 23) (Paris - La Haye: Mouton). [La philosophie de la grammaire: Bhartṛhari, pp. 251-449; bibliography, pp. 453 - 61].

1964b (Tr.) *Bhartṛhari, Vākyapadīya brahmakāṇḍa avec la vṛtti de Harivṛṣabha; texte reproduit de l'édition de Lahore; traduction, introduction et notes par M. B.* (= *PIFCI* 24) (Paris: Boccard). [Introduction, pp. 1-21.] [For the Lahore edition see Charudeva Shastri (1934).]

1965 Review of Kunjunni Raja (1963), *IIJ* 8: 228-32. [See Kunjunni Raja (1969).]

Birwé, Robert

1955 "Interpolationen in Pāṇini's Aṣṭādhyāyī", *Festschrift Kirfel*, pp. 27-52.

1958 "Variae lectiones in Adhyāya IV und V der Aṣṭādhyāyī", *ZDMG* 108: 133-54.

1961 *Der Gaṇapāṭha zu den Adhyāya IV und V der Grammatik Pāṇinis: Versuch einer Rekonstruktion* (Wiesbaden: Harrassowitz). [Pp. 45-429: charts of the gaṇas for chapters 4 and 5 as given in *Böhtlingk* (1887a), the Siddhānta-kaumudī, Bhāṣā-vṛtti, Śabda-kaustubha, Prakriyā-kaumudī, Gaṇa-ratna-mahôdadhi, Hemacandra, Bhoja, Śākaṭāyana, Kāśikā, Jainendra, Candra, reconstruction; pp. 430 - 59: charts of gaṇas in vārttikas for chapters 4 and 5. Appendices: 1: the age of the gaṇa-pāṭha which appears in *Böhtlingk* (1887a), the Siddhānta-kaumudī, and the Bhāṣā-vṛtti (pp. 460-62); 2 (pp. 463-65): the gaṇa-pāṭha of Śākaṭāyana; 3 (pp. 466-67): concordance: Pāṇini, Candra, Jainendra, Sākaṭāyana, Bhoja, Hemacandra; 4 (pp. 478-90): remarks on Vardhamāna's Gaṇa-ratna-mahôdadhi; indices: pp. 491-92: gaṇa-initial words; p. 492: initial words of vārttika-gaṇas.]

1966 *Studien zu Adhyaya III der Aṣṭādhyāyī Pāṇinis* (Wiesbaden: Harrassowitz). [Pp. 141-46: Tabellarische Übersicht über die Grundlage und die zugefügten Sutras des Adhyaya III; appendix additions and corrections to Lahiri (1935), pp. 204-7.]

1968 "Ist Candragomin der Verfasser der Candra-Vṛtti? ", *Festschrift Renou*, pp. 127-42.

1971 English introduction to Shambhunath Tripathi (1971): pp. (1-119). [Pp. 5-10: concordance of Śākaṭāyana 2.4.128-239 with Panini's rules and those of other grammars, enlarged from Kielhorn (1894).]

1973 Review of Aryendra Sharma – Khanderao Deshpande – D. G. Padhye (1969-70). vol. 1, *ZDMG* 123: 427-41.

Bloomfield, Leonard

1927 "On some rules of Pāṇini", *JAOS* 47: 61-70. [reprint: Hockett (1970: 157-65), Staal (1972: 266-72).]

1929 Review of Liebich (1928), *Lg.* 5: 267-76. [reprint: Hockett (1970: 219-26).]

1933 *Language* (New York: Henry Holt and Company).

Bodas, Mahadev Rajaram

1918 "Introduction: a historical survey of Indian logic", *Tarka-saṃgraha of Annaṁbhaṭṭa with the author's own Dīpikā and Govardhana's Nyāya-bodhinī, edited with critical and explanatory notes by the late Yashwant Vasudev Athalye by the late Mahadev Rajaram Bodas*[2] (= *BoSS* 55) [Revised and enlarged second impression of the second edition, by A. D. Pusalker; (Poona: BORI, 1963).], pp. ix - lxiii.

Böhtlingk, Otto

1839-40 *Pāṇini's acht Bücher grammatischer Regeln,* 2 vol. (Bonn: König). [1: sūtras and scholia; 2: introduction, pp. iii-lxv; alphabetic index of sūtras, pp. I-LXXXIV; alphabetic gaṇa-pāṭha, pp. LXXXV-CXXV; German comments on rules, pp. 1-399; index of technical terms, with glosses, pp. 401 - 556).]

1844 *Die Uṇādi-Affixe, herausgegeben und mit Anmerkungen und verschiedenen Indices versehen (Aus den Mémoires de l'Académie Impériale des Sciences de St.-Pétersbourg; sciences politiques etc., VIme série, t. VII)* (St. Petersburg: Kaiserliche Akademie der Wissenschaften). [Comments, pp. 72-83; alphabetic index of sūtras, pp. 83-98; alphabetic index of affixes, pp. 99-156.]

1875a "Kātyāyana oder Patañjali im Mahābhāṣya", *ZDMG* 29: 183-90.

1875b "Das Verhalten der drei kanonischen Grammatiker in Indien zu den im Wurzelverzeichniss mit ṣ und ṇ anlautenden Wurzeln", *ZDMG* 29: 483-90.

1885 "Ein Versuch zur Beilegung eines literarischen Streites", *ZDMG* 39: 528-31.

1887a *Pāṇinis Grammatik, herausgegeben, übersetzt, erläutert und mit verschiedenen Indices versehen* (Leipzig: Haessel). [Reprint: (Hildesheim: Olms 1964).] [Indices: alphabetic index of sūtras (pp. 1*-60*); alphabetic index of verb roots (pp. 95*-145*, preceded by the text of the dhātu-pāṭha, pp. 84*-94*, and followed by the text of the gaṇa-pāṭha, pp. 95*-145*); index of nonmeaningful grammatical elements, including markers (pp. 146*-87*); index of suffixes without their markers (pp. 187*-92*); Pāṇini's vocabulary (pp. 193*-296*); subject index (pp. 297*-300*); the vocabulary of the gaṇa-pāṭha (pp. 301*-57*).]

1887b "Noch ein Wort zur Maurya-Frage im Mahābhāṣya", *ZDMG* 41: 175-78.

1887c "Haben *iti* und *ca* bisweilen die Bedeutung von *ādi*?", *ZDMG* 41: 516-20.
1887d "Über die Grammatik Kātantra", *ZDMG* 41: 657-66.
1887e Review of Speijer (1886), *ZDMG* 41: 179-91.
1890 "Versuch, eine jüngst angefochtene Lehre Pāṇini's in Schutz zu nehmen", *BAWL* 42: 79-82.
1893 "Whitney's letzte Angriffe auf Pāṇini", *BGWL* 45: 247-57. [Reprint: Staal (1972: 186-92): against Whitney (1884).]
1897 "Neue Miscellen", *BGWL* 1897: 39-52. [4. Pāṇini's adhikāra. pp. 46-48]
1900 "Kritische Beiträge, II. Rājataraṅgiṇī I, 176", *WZKM* 14: 46-50.

Boudon, Pierre
1938 "Une application du raisonnement par l'absurde dans l'interprétation de Pāṇini (les *jñāpakasiddhaparibhāṣā*)", *JAs* 230: 65-121. [Reprint: Staal (1972: 358-91).]

Brahmadatta Jijñāsu: see Nārāyaṇa Miśra (1969), Śobhita Miśra (1952).

Brahmadatta Jijñasu – Prajña Devı (tr., commentators)
1964-68 *Aṣṭādhyāyī-bhāṣya-prathamāvṛtti,* 3 vol. (= *RLKTS* 32) (Amritsar: Rāma Lāl Kapūr Trust). [Pāṇini's grammar with analysis of sūtras into components, Sanskrit paraphrases, Hindi translation and explanations; volumes 1 - 2 by Brahmadatta Jijñāsu, volume 3 by Prajñā Devī; the whole prepared for oublication by Yudhiṣṭhira Mīmāṃsaka.]

Breloer, B.
1929 "Studie zu Pāṇini", *ZII* 7: 114-35.
1935-36 "Die 14 pratyāhāra-sūtras des Pāṇini", *ZII* 10: 133-91.

Brough, John
1946 "The early history of the gotras", *JRAS* 1946: 32-45.
1951 "Theories of general linguistics in the Sanskrit grammarians", *TPS* 1951: 27-46. [Reprint: Staal (1972: 402-14).]
1952 "Audumbarāyaṇa's theory of language", *TPS* 1952: 73-77.
1953a *"The early brahmanical system of gotra and pravara; a translation of the Gotra-pravara-mañjarī of Puruṣottama-paṇḍita with an introduction* (Cambridge: Cambridge University Press).
1953b "Some Indian theories of meaning", *TPS* 1953: 161-76. [Reprint: Staal (1972: 414-23).]
1973 "I-Ching on the Sanskrit grammarians", *BSOAS* 36: 248-60.

Buddha Prakash
1967 "On Pāṇini's sūtra IV.3.98, *vāsudervārjunābhyāṃ vun*", *KURJ* 1: 1-9. [*Prāci Jyoti* (1963-72) 5: 138-40]
1969 "On Pāṇini's sūtra V. 3, 99", *Festschrift Aditya Nath Jha* 3, pp. 394-404.

1970 "A historical study of the term 'devānāṃpriya-' ", *VIJ* 8: 160-71.

Budruss, Georg (ed.)

1971 *Paul Thieme; Kleine Schriften,* 2 vol. [continuous pagination] (= Glasenapp-Stiftung 5. 1-2. (Wiesbaden: Steiner). [Pp. vii-xv: bibliography of Thieme's writings.]

Bühler, Georg

1864 "Notiz über die Grammatik des Śakaṭāyana", *OU* 2: 691-706.

1878 "Mss. of the Mahābhāṣya from Kaśmīr", *IA* 7: 54-57.

1882 "Über die Erklärung des Wortes *āgama* im Vakyapadīya II.1-6", *ZDMG* 36: 653-55.

1887 "A disputed meaning of the particles *iti* and *ca*", *WZKM* 1: 13-20.

1894 "The roots of the dhātupāṭha not found in literature", *WZKM* 8: 17-42, 122-36. [Reprint: *IA* 23 (1894): 141-54; 250-55; Staal (1972: 194-204).]

Buiskool, Herman E.

1934 *Pūrvatrāsiddham; analytisch onderzoek aangaande het systeem der Tripādī van Pāṇini's Aṣṭādhyāyī* (Amsterdam: Paris). [See Buiskool (1939).]

1939 *The Tripādī; being an abridged English recast of Pūrvatrāsiddham (an analytic-synthetic inquiry into the system of the last three chapters of Pāṇini's Aṣṭādhyāyī)* (Leiden: Brill). [See Buiskool (1934).]

Burnell, A. C.

1875 *On the Aindra school of Sanskrit grammarians, their place in the Sanskrit and subordinate literatures* (Mangalore: Basel Mission Book and Tract Depository).

Burrow, Thomas

1936 "Indian theories on the nature of meaning", *TPS* 1936: 92-93. [Summary of paper.]

1955 *The Sanskrit language* (London: Faber and Faber). [Reprint: (London: Faber and Faber 1959).]

Caland, Willem

1931 "A rhythmic law in language", *AO* 9: 59-68.

Cardona, George

1964 "The formulation of Pāṇini 7.3.73", *JOIB* 14: 38-41.

1965a "On Pāṇini's morphophonemic principles", *Lg.* 41: 225-38.

1965b "On translating and formalizing Pāṇinian rules", *JOIB* 14: 306-14.

1967a Negations in Pāṇinian rules", *Lg.* 43: 34-56.

1967b "Pāṇini's syntactic categories", *JOIB* 16: 201-15.
1967-68 "Anvaya and vyatireka in Indian grammar", *Festschrift V. Raghavan,* pp. 313-52. [Summary of paper: *PICO* 27: 313-14.]
1968a "Pāṇini's definition, description and use of svarita", *Festschrift F. B. J. Kuiper,* pp. 448-61.
1968b Review of Vidya Niwas Misra (1966), *Lg.* 44: 643-49.
1968c Review of S. D. Joshi (1967a), *JOIB* 17: 445-50.
1969 *Studies in Indian grammarians, I: the method of description reflected in the śivasūtras* (= *TAPS* 59. 1) (Philadelphia: American Philosophical Society).
1970a "Some principles of Pāṇini's grammar", *JIP* 1: 40-74.
1970b "A note on Pāṇini's technical vocabulary", *JOIB* 19: 195-212.
1970c Review of Vidya Niwas Misra (1966), *IIJ* 12: 226-32.
1970d Review of Staal (1967), *IIJ* 12: 232-39.
1970e Review of R. Rocher (1968a), *Lingua* 25: 210-22.
1971 "Cause and causal agent: The Pāṇinian view", *JOIB* 21: 22-40. [See also Cardona (1973c.)]
1972a "Pāṇini's use of the term *upadeśa* and the ekānta and anekānta views regarding anubandhas", *SPISC* 4: 23-25.
1972b Review of Mehendale (1968), *Lg.* 48: 171-79.
1972c Review of S. D. Joshi (1969a), *JOIB* 22: 225-32.
1973a "Indian grammarians on adverbs", *Festschrift Kahane,* pp. 85-98.
1973b "On the interpretation of Pāṇini 1. 4. 105-8", *ALB* 37: 1-47.
1973c "Cause and causal agent: the Pāṇinian view", in: Konks – Numerkund – Mäll (1973), pp. 354-81. [Unauthorized publication, see Cardona (1971): 22, note *.]
1973d Review of S. M. Katre (1968-69), *IIJ* 15: 43-56.
1973e Review of Scharfe (1971a), *IIJ* 15: 207-21.
1973f Review of S. D. Joshi (1968), *OLZ* 68: 229-38.
1973g Review of Staal (1972), *LS* 26: 43-48.
1974a "On Pāṇini's metalinguistic use of cases", *Festschrift Charudeva Shastri,* pp. 305-26.
1974b "Pāṇini's kārakas: agency, animation and identity", *JIP* 2: 231-306.
forthcoming
a "Pāṇini's use of the term *upadeśa* and the ekānta and anekānta views regarding anubandhas", *PISC.* [See Cardona (1972a).]
b "On Yāska's etymology of *daṇḍa*", *JOR* golden jubilee volume.
c "Some features of Pāṇinian derivations", *History of linguistic thought and contemporary linguistics* (Ed.: H. Parret) (Berlin: de Gruyter).

d "A note on the formulation of Pāṇini 6.1.67", *AOR* silver jubilee volume.

e "On the Pāṇinian view regarding agency and animation", *Festschrift K. S. Subramania Iyer.*

Cārudeva: see Charudeva Shastri.

Caturveda, Giridharaśarmā: see Giridharaśarmā Caturveda.

Chakravarti, Prabhat Chandra

1925 "The Mahābhāṣya", *IHQ* 1: 703-39.

1926 "Patañjali as he reveals himself in the Mahābhāṣya", *IHQ* 2: 67-76, 262-89, 464-94, 738-60.

1930 *The philosophy of Sanskrit grammar* (Calcutta: Calcutta University). [Revised version of Calcutta University dissertation, 1924.]

1933 *The linguistic speculations of the Hindus* (Calcutta: Calcutta University). [Originally published in *JDLCU* 12 (1925).]

1934 "Spiritual outlook of Sanskrit grammar", *JDCLU* 25.1: 1-11. pp. 1-11.

Chakravarti, Srish Chandra (Ed.)

1918 *The Bhāṣā-vṛtti, a commentary on Pāṇini's grammatical aphorisms excepting those which exclusively pertain to the Veda by Purushottamadeva; edited with annotations (Bhāṣā-vṛttiḥ, mahāmahôpādhyāya-śrī puruṣottamadeva-viracitā, sā ca kevala-veda-viṣayaka-sūtra-vyatirikta-sūtra-vṛttiḥ)* (= *SSGM* 1) (Rajshahi: The Varendra Research Society). [English introduction, pp. 1-21. Appendices: gaṇa-pāṭha, pp. 574-94; dhātu-pāṭha, pp. 595-610; liṅgânuśāsana, pp. 610-12; paribhāṣās, pp. 613-14. The introduction is separately paginated.]

1919 *The Dhātu-pradeepa by Maitreya-rakṣita; edited with annotations (Dhātu-pradīpaḥ, mahāmahôpādhyāya-śrī maitreya-rakṣita-viracitaḥ)* (= *SSGM* 2) (Rajshahi: The Varendra Research Society). [Introduction, pp. 1-3, separately paginated.]

1919-25 *The Kāśikā Vivaraṇa Pañjikā (the Nyāsa), a commentary on Vāmana – Jayāditya's Kāśikā by Jinendra Buddhi; edited with introduction and occasional notes (Kāśikā-vivaraṇa-pañjikā, bodhisattvadeśīyâcārya-jinendrabuddhipāda-viracitā),* 3 vol. (Rajshahi: The Varendra Research Society). [1 (1925): adhyāyas 1-4; 2 (1919): adhyāyas 5-6; 3 (1925): adhyāyas 7-8. Introduction, separately paginated, volume 1, pp. 1-26. In the preface to volume 3, the editor states that publication was begun in 1913. However, the introduction to volume 1 is dated 1925.]

Chanda, Ramaprasad

1929 "Puṣyamitra and the Śuṅga empire", *IHQ* 5: 393-407, 587-613.

Chandrasekharan, T. (Ed.)

1952 *The Vyākaraṇa-mahābhāṣya by Bhagavat-Patañjali, with Pradīpa by Kaiyaṭa and Mahābhāṣya-pradīpoddyotana by Annambhaṭṭa; part II (āhnikas 5 to 9)* (= *MGOMS* 13) (Madras: Government Oriental Manuscripts Library). [English introduction, pp. i-xiv; for part I see P. P. S. Shastri and A. Sankaran.]

1954-55 *Pāṇinisūtravyākhyā (with illustrations from classical works) by Vīrarāghavācārya (Pāṇini-sūtra-vyākhyā (sôdāharaṇa-ślokā) maṇalur-vīrarāghavâcārya-viracitā),* 2 vol. (= *MGOMS* 33, 47) (Madras: Government Oriental Manuscripts Library). [Appendices (separately paginated at end of second volume): 1: index of Pāṇinian rules, pp. 1-35; 2: index of vārttikas, pp. 36-44; 3: index of uṇādi-sūtras, pp. 45-55; 4: index of liṅgânuśāsana rules, pp. 56-59; 5: index of gaṇas, pp. 60-63; 6: index of gaṇa-sūtras, p. 64; 7: index of illustrative verses, pp. 65-119; 8: index of words exemplified, pp. 120-297.]

Charpentier, Jarl

1923 "The name Kambyses (Ka^{n}būǰiya)", *ZII* 2: 140-52.

Charudeva Shastri (Charu Deva Shastri, Cārudeva)

1930 "Bhartṛhari: a critical study with special references to the Vākyapadīya and its commentaries", *PAIOC* 5 (Lahore, 1928): 630-55.

1934 (Ed.) *Bhagavad-bhartṛhari-viracitaṃ vākya-padīyam; tatra hary-upajña-vṛtti-sanāthaṃ vṛṣabhadeva-ṭīkā-saṃkṣepa-saṃyutaṃ prathamaṃ kāṇḍam* [The Vākya-padīya of Bhartṛhari with the autocommentary of Hari and extracts from the commentary on this by Vṛṣabhadeva, first kāṇḍa] (Lahore: Rāma Lāl Kapūr Trust saṃvat 1991). [English preface, pp. 1-8. Sanskrit introduction, pp. 1-26. Indices: (following the text): of verses, pp. 1-3; of particular words in the verses and the vṛtti, pp. 4-6; of citations from other works, pp. 7-9. All paginated separately from the text.]

1939-40 (Ed.) *Vākya-padīyam, Bhartṛhary-upajña-vṛtti-sanāthaṃ puṇyarāja-ṭīkā-saṃyutaṃ dvitīyam kāṇḍam (dvitīya-bhāge prathama-khaṇḍaḥ)* [The Vākya-padīya with Bhartṛhari's autocommentary and the commentary of Puṇyarāja, second kāṇḍa; part 2, section 1] (Lahore: Rāma Lāl Kapūr Trust saṃvat 1996).

1950a "Kim-upakārā upasargāḥ kim-arthakāś ca" [What is the function of preverbs and what meanings do they have?] *SS* 5. 2: 33-39. [In Sanskrit] [See also Charudeva Shastri (1972a).]

1950b "Vāg-vyavahāraḥ" [Sanskrit usage] *SS* 5.4: 69-82. [In Sanskrit.] [Reprint: Charudeva Shastri (1971).]

1953 "Paryāya-vacana-vivekaḥ" [A study of synonyms], *PAIOC* 16 (Lucknow, 1951): 239-50. [In Sanskrit.]

1957-58 "Pāṇinīye dhātu-pāṭhe'rtha-nirdeśaḥ" [The statement of meanings in Pāṇini's dhātu-pāṭha], *JOR* 27: 79-84. [In Sanskrit.]

1963 *Prastāvataraṅgiṇī (a text book of Sanskrit essays)*[2] (= *HSS* 201) (Varanasi: Chowkhamba). [1st edition: 1951.]

1963a "Kiṃ śabdo nitya utânityaḥ" [Is speech eternal or not?], in: Charudeva Shastri (1963), pp. 192-96. [In Sanskrit.]

1963b "Vivakṣātaḥ kārakāṇi bhavanti" [Kāraka classifications depend on what the speaker wishes to express], in: Charudeva Shastri (1963), pp. 213-22. [In Sanskrit.]

1963c "Karotinā sarva-dhātv-arthânuvādaḥ kriyate" [The verb *kṛ* ["do, make"] is used to convey all root meanings], in: Charudeva Shastri (1963), pp. 222-26. [In Sanskrit.]

1967 "Pāṇinīyâṣṭake kāścid vyavahāra-diśaḥ" [Some indications on usage in Pāṇini's grammar], *VS* 4: 107-13. [In Sanskrit]

1968 (Tr.) *Bhagavat-patañjali viracita vyākaraṇa-mahābhāṣya (prathama navāhnika) kā hindī anuvāda tathā vivaraṇa* [The Mahābhāṣya of Patañjali, translated into Hindi with comments: first nine āhnikas] (Delhi: Motilal Banarsidass saṃvat 2025).

1969-73 *Vyākaraṇa-candrodaya,* 5 vol. (Delhi: Motilal Banarsidass). [1: *Kāraka va samāsa* [Kārakas and compounds], 1969; 2: *Kṛt va taddhita* [Kṛt and taddhita affixes] 1970; 3: *Kriyā* [Action] 1971; 4: *Strī-pratyaya* [Feminine affixes] 1972; 5: *Saṃjñā* [Technical terms] 1973.]

1971 "Vāg-vyavahāraḥ", *Festschrift Rajeshwar Shastri Dravid,* grammar section, pp. 89-96. [See Charudeva Shastri (1950b).]

1972 "Kim-upakārā upasargāḥ kim-arthakāś ca", *JDSDU* 1.2: 81-94. [Revised version of Charudeva Shastri (1950a).]

Chatterji, Kshitish (Kshitis) Chandra (Kṣetreśa Chandra Chaṭṭopādhyāya)

1931a "The Bhāgavṛtti", *IHQ* 7: 413-18.

1931b "The authorship of the Anunyāsa" *IHQ* 7: 418-19.

1932 "Kāśakṛtsna", *IHQ* 8: 224-27.

1933a "Pāṇini as a poet", *COJ* 1: 1-24.

1933b "The Mugdhabodha system of grammar", *COJ* 1: 47-56.

1933c "The anubandhas of Pāṇini", *COJ* 1: 100-16.

1933d "More about Pāṇini as a poet", *COJ* 1: 135. [Cf.: K. C. Chatterji (1933a).]

1933e "Some technical terms of Sanskrit grammar", *IHQ* 9: 279-81. [On the terms *sarvanāmasthāna, sārvadhātuka*]

1934a "The śiva sūtras", *JDLCU* 24.2: 1-10.
1934b "The critics of Sanskrit grammar", *JDLCU* 24.3: 1-21. 1-21. [Reprint: Staal (1972): 287-97]
1934c "The sāvarṇya of *ṛ* and *ḷ*", *COJ* 1: 171-72.
1934d "Some grammatical notes, 1. *ehi manye*", *COJ* 1: 177-78.
1935a "Some rules of sandhi", *COJ* 2: 261-68, 3: 9-16.
1935b "The Aṣṭādhyāyī and the Siddhāntakaumudī", *COJ* 3: 1-2.
1935c "A rule of Pāṇini", *COJ* 3: 17-28. [On rule 1.3.3: the texts of the Mahā-bhāṣya, Pradīpa, Uddyota, Kāśikā, Nyāsa, Pada-mañjarī, Śabda-kaustubha, and Jagannātha's Manoramā-kuca-mardinī on the pertinent portion of the Mahā-bhāṣya discussion of this rule appear in an appendix, pp. 24-28.]
1935d "Jagannātha and Bhaṭṭoji", *COJ* 3: 41-51.
1936 "Some technical terms of Sanskrit grammar", *COJ* 3: 105-32. [Main discussion concerns the term *nadī*; pp. 108-32: text of the Mahā-bhāṣya, Kāśikā and their commentaries on the rules defining this term.]
1946 "Technical terms of Sanskrit grammar", *NIA* 8: 51-53. [Pāṇini's L-suffixes such as *laṭ*; terms used in other grammars.]
1952 "Pāṇini and Whitney", *CR* 125: 55-58.
1953 "Pāṇini and Whitney", *CR* 126: 49-52.
1953-61 (ed.) *Cāndravyākaraṇa of Candragomin*, 2 vol. (= *SIAL* 13) (Poona: Deccan College). [Part 1: chapters 1 - 3; part 2: chapters 4 - 6; Candragomin's varṇa-sūtras, 2: 394-95, paribhāṣā-sūtras, 2: 396-98; alphabetic index of rules, 2: 399-448.]
1954 "Samprasāraṇa", *Vāk* 4: 85-86.
1955 "On the interpretation of a rule of Pāṇini", *Festschrift S. K. Chatterji*, pp. 194-95. [Rule 1.1.36.]
1956-57 "How Patañjali has been misunderstood", *Festschrift Taraporewala*, pp. 100-02.
1957 (Tr.) *Patañjali's Mahābhāṣya; paspaśāhnika (introductory chapter)*[2] (= *UMS* 7) (Calcutta: A. Mukherjee). [Sanskrit text with English translation and notes; third edition (1964), unavailable to me.]
1964 *Technical terms and technique of Sanskrit grammar* (Calcutta: Calcutta University). [Enlarged version of *Technical terms and technique of Sanskrit grammar, part I* (= *UMS* 1) (Calcutta: Bhattacharjee 1948).]

Chaṭṭopādhyāya, Kshetresh Chandra (Kshetresachandra Chaṭṭopādhyāya)
1927 "Patañjali and his knowledge of science", *IHQ* 3: 181-82.
1937 "Pāṇini and the Ṛkprātiśākhya, II", *IHQ* 13: 343-49. [Companion article to Thieme (1937).]

1938 "Thieme and Pāṇini", *IC* 5: 95-98. [Rejoinder to B. Ghosh (1938).]

1974 "Did Pāṇini envisage 'A' as a close (saṁvṛta) vowel? ", *Festschrift Charudeva Shastri*, pp. 194-205.

Chaturvedi, Saraswati Prasad (Sarasvatī Prasāda Caturvedī).

1935a "Homogeneity of letters in the Pāṇinian system – a critical estimate of the views held by different commentators", *PAIOC* 7 (Baroda, 1933): 165-73.

1935b "Need for rewriting Pāṇini's grammar", *NUJ* 1: 5-10.

1937 "History of an important historical word in the Pāṇinian school of grammar", *PAIOC* 8 (Mysore, 1935): 739-44. [On the word devānāṃpriya.]

1938a "Pāṇini and the Ṛkprātiśākhya", *NIA* 1: 450-59.

1938b "On the original text of the Aṣṭādhyāyī", *NIA* 1: 562-69.

1940a "Dr. Ghosh on Pāṇini and the Ṛkprātiśākhya", *NIA* 2: 723-27. [Reply to B. Ghosh (1939).]

1940b "Technical terms of the Aṣṭādhyāyī", *PAIOC* 9 (Trivandrum, 1937): 1191-1208.

1940c "Scholastic disquisitions in the Pāṇinian system of grammar", *BhV* 2: 59-63.

1940d "Pāṇini's vocabulary – its bearing on his date", *Festschrift Woolner*, pp. 46-50.

1941a "Notes on a vārtika (?) and its misplaced occurrence in the Mahābhāṣya", *Festschrift P. V. Kane*, pp. 82-83.

1941b "On references to earlier grammarians in the Aṣṭādhyāyī and the forms sanctioned by them", *NUJ* 7: 46-53.

1942 "On Pāṇini's sūtra VII - 1 - 90 – wrong wording or corrupt reading? ", *ABORI* 23: 77-79.

1943 "Significance of Pāṇini's sūtra VI. 1. 92", *NUJ* 9: 68-69.

1944 "Gata dvisahasrābdi meṃ saṃskṛta vyākaraṇa kā vikāsa" [The development of Sanskrit grammar in the past two thousand years], *NPP* 49: 301-20. [In Hindi.]

1945 "On the arrangement of the taddhita sūtras in the Aṣṭādhyāyī", *Festschrift R. K. Mookerji*, pp. 209-14.

1950 "Pāṇini's vocabulary and his date", *Festschrift Siddheshwar Varma* 2, pp. 144-47. [Cf.: S. P. Chaturvedi (1940d).]

1951 "Some aspects of the technique of the anuvṛtti procedure in the Aṣṭādhyāyī", *PAIOC* 13 (Nagpur, 1946): 109-12.

1953 "A study into the principles of preference in the application of Pāṇinian sūtras and their working", *SPAIOC* 17 (Ahmedabad, 1953): 91-92.

Chintamani, T. R. (Ed.)
1933 *The Uṇādi sūtras in various recensions; part I: the Uṇādisūtras with the vṛtti of Śvetavanavāsin (Uṇādi-sūtrāṇi, prathamo bhāgaḥ: śvetavanavāsi-viracita-vṛtti-yutāni)* (= *MUSS* 7.1) (Madras: University of Madras). [Indices: works and authors referrred to, p. 1; quotations, pp. 2-8; sūtras, pp. 10-20; words derived, pp. 21-46; all separately paginated following the text.]
1939 *The Uṇādisūtras in various recensions; part IV: Auṇādikapadārṇava by Perusūri (Auṇādika-padârṇavaḥ perusūri-viracitaḥ)* (= *MUSS* 7. 4) (Madras: University of Madras). [Indices: works and authors referred to, pp. xix-xx; sūtras, pp. 1-9; words, 10-54; the first preceding, the others following the text and separately paginated. I have listed here only the recensions directly pertinent to the Pāṇinian school.]

Chitari, Saroja S.
1966 "Pāṇini and the Pāṇinīyas on the concept of guṇa", *PAIOC* 22 (Gauhati, 1965): 88 - 92.

Colebrooke, Henry T.
1803 "On the Sanskrit and Prākrit languages", *Asiatic Researches* 7: 199-231. [Reprint: *Miscellaneous Essays II:* 1-32, Staal (1972): 33-45.] *Miscellaneous Essays:* See Cowell.

Conference
1970 *Proceedings of the first all-India conference of linguists (Poona, December 1970)* Ed.: (A. M. Ghatge, M. M. Bhat, E. D. Kulkarni, P. B. Pandit) (Poona: Linguistic Society of India, 1971).
1972a *International Sanskrit conference (March 26th – 31st, 1972); summary of papers,* 5 vol. (Ed.: V. Raghavan) (New Delhi: Ministry of Education and Social Welfare, Government of India).
1972b *Proceedings of the second all-India conference of linguists (Delhi, March 1972)* (Ed.: Ashok R. Kelkar, H. S. Biligiri, H. S. Ananthanarayana, C. J. Daswani) (Poona: Linguistic Society of India, 1974).
1972c *The third all-India conference of linguists, December 29 – 30, 1972 (souvenir)* (Hyderabad: Osmania University). [Summaries of papers.]

Congres
1968 *Actes du Xe congrès international des linguistes,* 4 vol. (Bucarest: Edition de l'Académie de la République Socialiste de Roumanie, 1970).

Congress
1892 *Transactions of the ninth international congress of orientalists (held in London, 5th to 12th September 1892), volume I: Indian and Aryan sections* (Ed.: E. Delmar Morgan) (London: The Committee of the Congress 1893).
1960 *Logic, methodology and philosophy of science. Proceedings of the 1960 international congress* (Ed.: Ernest Nagel, Patrick Suppes, Alfred Tarski) (Stanford: Stanford University Press).
1962 *Proceedings of the ninth international congress of linguists, Cambridge, Mass., August 27 – 31, 1962.* (Ed.: Horace G. Lunt) (The Hague - Paris: Mouton, 1964).

1964 *Proceedings of the twenty-sixth international congress of orientalists, New Delhi, January 4 – 10, 1964,* 4 vol. (Ed.: R. N. Dandekar) (Poona: BORI, 1969).

1967 *Proceedings of the twenty-seventh international congress of orientalists, Ann Arbor, Michigan, 13th – 19th August, 1967.* (Ed.: Denis Sinor with the assistance of Tania Jaques, Ralph Larson, Mary-Elizabeth Meek) (Wiesbaden: Harrassowitz, 1971). [Only summaries are here published.]

Cowell, Edward Byles (ed.)
1868 *The Prākṛta-prakāśa or the Prākṛt grammar of Vararuchi, with the commentary (Manoramā) of Bhāmaha; with the text, notes, English translation, and index of Prākṛt words*[2] (London: Trübner). [Reprint: (Calcutta: Punthi Pustak, 1962).]
1873 *Miscellaneous essays of H. T. Colebrooke*[2], 2 vol. (London: Trübner).

Dadhi Rama Śarma, Sita Rama Śastri Shende, Madhava Śastri Bhaṇḍari
1914-25 (Ed.) *Vyākaraṇa Siddhānta Sudhānidhi by Viśveśvara Sūri (Vyākaraṇa-siddhânta-sudhā-nidhiḥ parvatīya-viśveśvara-sūri-viracitaḥ),* 15 fasc. (= *CSS* 193-95 (1914), 215-16 (1915), 218 (1916), 251-52 (1918), 275-76 (1920), 300 (1922), 306 (1923), 312 (1923), 321 (1924) 329 (1925)) (Benares: Chowkhamba). [Fasc. 1-5: (Ed.: Dadhi Rāma Śarmā); fasc. 6-8: (Ed.: Sītā Rāma Śastrī Shende); fasc. 9-15: (Ed.: Mādhava Śāstrī Bhāṇḍāri).]

Dandekar, Ramchandra Narayana
1946-73 *Vedic bibliography (an up-to-date, comprehensive, and analytically arranged register of all important work done since 1930 in the field of the Veda and allied antiquities including the Indus Valley civilisation),* 3 vol. [1: (Bombay: Karnatak Publishing

House, 1946), 2: (Poona: University of Poona, 1961), 3: (= *GovOS-B* 10) (Poona: BORI, 1973).] [The subtitle appears only in the first volume.]

Dange, Sadashiv Ambadas

1970a "The terms *gotra* and *yuvan* (their social significance)", *VSMV* 1970: 15-19.

1970b "Some peculiarities of the eastern dialect according to Pāṇini", *VSMV* 1970: 174-98.

Danielsson, O. A.

1885 "Die Einleitung des Mahābhāṣya, übersetzt", *ZDMG* 37: 20-53.

Das, Karunasindhu

1972 "On indicatory letters and symbols (*anubandhas*) in Pāṇinian pronouncements (*upadeśas*)", *SPAIOC* 26: 101-02. [Dandekar (1946-73) 3: 175, number 53.]

Das Gupta, Nalini Nath

1935 "Pāṇini and the Yavanas", *IC* 2: 356-58.

Dasgupta, Surendra Nath and Sushil Kumar De

1962 *A history of Sanskrit literature; classical period, volume 1* (Calcutta: Calcutta University).

Dasharatha Sharma

1950 "Devānāṃpriya", *IHQ* 26: 149-51.

Dave, T. N.

1966 "Shri Shankarācārya and sphoṭa", *ŚPP* 6: 19-27.

Dayānanda Sarasvatī, (Ed., tr.)

1927-61 *Aṣṭādhyāyī-bhāṣyam*[2], 2 vol. (Ajmer: Vaidika Pustakālaya, saṃvat 1984, 2018). [Sanskrit text with commentary in Sanskrit and Hindi paraphrases of adhyāyas 1-3; all that is available to me.]

1949/50 *Vedâṅga-prakāśaḥ; tatratyas trayo-daśo bhāgaḥ: uṇādi-koṣaḥ, pāṇini-muni-praṇītāyām aṣṭādhyāyyāṃ dvā-daśo bhāgaḥ, śrīmat-svāmi-dayānanda-sarasvatī-kṛta-vyākhyā-sahitaḥ*[5] [Vedâṅga-prakāśa; part 13: the Uṇādi-koṣa, the twelfth section in the Aṣṭādhyāyī of Pāṇini, with a commentary by Dayānanda Sarasvatī] (Ajmer: Vaidika Yantrālaya saṃvat 2006). [Uṇādi-sūtras with Sanskrit commentary by Dayānanda Sarasvatī; Hindi introduction, pp. 1-4; index of words derived, pp. 103 - 24. The introduction is dated saṃvat 1939 (1882 A. D.).]

1950/1 *Vedâṅga-prakāśaḥ; tatratyaḥ prathamo bhāgaḥ: varṇôccāraṇa-śikṣā pāṇini-muni-praṇītā, śrīmat-svāmi-dayānanda-sarasvatī-kṛta-vyākhyā-sahitā*[12] [Vedâṅga-prakāśa; part 1: Varṇôccāraṇa-śikṣā of Pāṇini, with a commentary by Dayānanda Sarasvatī] (Ajmer: Vaidika Yantrālaya saṃvat 2007). [The sūtra version of the

Paṇiniya-śikṣa with Hindi explanation by Dayananda Sarasvati; originally published in 1879; see Yudhiṣṭhira Mimaṃsaka (1967/8): introduction, p. 6.]

1969/70 *Vedâṅga-prakāśaḥ; tatratyaḥ tṛtīyo bhāgaḥ: nāmikaḥ, pāṇini-muni-praṇītāyām aṣṭādhyāyyāṃ dvitīyo bhāgaḥ, śrīmat-svāmi-dayānanda-sarasvatī-kṛta-vyākhyā-sahitaḥ (liṅgânuśāsana-sūtra-pāṭha-sahitaḥ)*[9] [Vedâṅga-prakāśa; part 3: nominal forms, the second part in the Aṣṭādhyāyī of Pāṇini, with a commentary by Dayānanda Sarasvatī (together with the text of the Liṅgânuśāsana)] (Ajmer: Vaidika Yantrālaya saṃvat 2026). [Rules pertinent to deriving nominal forms with case endings, with Hindi explanations; index of words, pp. 1-7; index of sūtras and vārttikas, pp. 1-5; text of the Liṅgânuśāsana, p. 1-6; all separately paginated after the main text.]

Dayananda, Svami

1969 "Varṇa-sphoṭa-nirūpaṇa" [Description of varṇa-sphoṭa, in Hindi], *Festschrift Satkari Mookerji*, pp. 590-93.

De, Sushil Kumar

1923 *Studies in the history of Sanskrit poetics, volume 1* (London: Luzac).

1960 *History of Sanskrit poetics*[2] (Calcutta: Mukhopadhyay).

de la Vallée Poussin, Louis

1930 *L'Inde au temps des Maurya et des Barbares, Grecs, Scythes, Parthes et Yue-Tchi* (= Histoire du monde, publiée sous la direction de M. E. Cavaignac, tome VI) (Paris: Boccard).

1936 "Patañjali and the Śakas", *IC* 2: 584.

Della Casa, Carlo

1951 "Uddhya e bhidya in Pāṇini e Kālidāsa" [*Uddhya* and *bhidya* in Pāṇini and Kālidāsa], *RSO* 26: 67-70. [In Italian.]

Deshpande, G. T.

1965 "Pāṇinian concept of pada", *NUJ* 16: 62-69.

1967a "On the accent of the vocative (āmantrita)", *NUJ* 18: 113-20.

1967b "Pāṇini: sūtras VII. 1. 9 and 10", *NUJ* 18: 192-200.

Deshpande, Madhav Murlidhar

1971 "Pāṇinīya-vyākaraṇa-paramparāyām upabhāṣā-tattvam" [The concept of dialect in the Pāṇinian grammatical tradition], *Festschrift Rajeshwar Shastri Dravid*, grammar section, pp. 17-25. [In Sanskrit. pp. 17-25. [In Sanskrit.]

1972a "Pāṇinian procedure of taparakaraṇa: a historical investigation", *KZ* 86: 207-54.

1972b *Kauṇḍabhaṭṭa on the philosophy of nominal meanings (the text of Kauṇḍabhaṭṭa's Nāmārthanirṇaya, with an English translation, explanation and an introductory essay).* [University of Pennsylvania dissertation, unpublished.]

1974 "A note on *kāka-peyā nadī* 'a crow-drinkable river' ", *JOIB* 23: 155-63.

forthcoming

a English version of M. M. Deshpande (1971), *JOR* golden jubilee volume.

b "The scope of homogeneous representation in Paṇini", *AOR* silver jubilee volume.

c Review of S. D. Joshi and J. A. F. Roodbergen (1971), *OLZ.*

d *Critical studies in Indian grammarians.* Michigan Series in South and Southeast Asian Languages and Linguistics, Ann Arbor, Michigan.

De Smet, Richard V.

1960 "Language and philosophy in India", in: *Proceedings of the xiith international congress of philosophy* (Venice, 12 – 18 September 1958), 10 (Eastern philosophies and western thought), pp. 47-54.

Devaprākaśa Pātañjala (Deo Prakash Patañjal): see Pātañjal, Deo Prakash Shastri.

Devasthali, Govind Vinayak

1942 "On the probable date of Śabara-svāmin", *ABORI* 23: 84-97.

1960-61 "The aim of the vārtikas of Kātyāyana", *Festschrift K. M. Munshi,* pp. 52-63. [Issued 1963]

1963 "Sāyaṇa utilising Pāṇini in his Ṛg-veda bhāṣya", *JBBRAS*[2] 38: 165-73.

1965 "Pāṇini as an aid to Ṛgvedic interpretation", in: *Festschrift H. D. Velankar,* pp. 20-26.

1967a (Ed., tr.) *Phiṭsūtras of Śāntanava; edited with introduction, translation, and critical and exegetical notes* (= *PCASS-C* 1) (Poona: University of Poona). [Introduction, pp. 1-45; critical and exegetical notes, pp. 61-150; index of sūtras, pp. 151-52; index of words, pp. 153-59.]

1967b *Anubandhas of Pāṇini* (= *PCASS-B* 2) (Poona: University of Poona). [Indices: A: affixes etc. together with their markers, pp. 166-92; B: affixes etc. without their markers, pp. 193-202; reverse index, pp. 203-24.]

1967c "Pāṇini and Ṛgvedic exegesis", *IA*[3] 2.3: 1-8. [See also Devasthali (1968b, c).]

1968a (ed., tr.) *Sārasiddhāntakaumudī of Varadarāja; edited with intro-*

duction, translation and critical and exegetical notes (= *PCASS-C* 4) (Poona: University of Poona). [Introduction, pp. xi-xiv; text and translation, pp. 1-225; index of sūtras and vārttikas, pp. 227-39; notes, pp. 1-259. Appendices: pratyāhāras, pp. 261-63; the Sanskrit alphabet arranged according to phonetic criteria, pp. 264-65; index of important words explained in notes, pp. 267-68; bibliography, pp. 269-71]

1968b "Pāṇini and Ṛgvedic exegesis", *ABORI* 48-49: 7. [See Devasthali (1967c, 1968c).]

1968c "Pāṇini and Ṛgvedic exegesis", *PCASS-A* 22. [Reprint of Devasthali (1968b).]

1969 "Paribhāṣā (introduction and general survey)", *Festschrift R. N. Dandekar,* pp. 1-13.

1974 "Vākya according to the munitraya of Sanskrit grammar", *Festschrift Charudeva Shastri,* pp. 206 - 15.

Devī, Prajñā: see Prajñā Devī.

Dīkṣita, T. V. Rāmacandra: see Rāmacandra Dīkṣita, T. V.

Dikshitar, V. R. Ramachandra: see Ramachandra Dikshitar, V. R.

Divanji, P. C.

1949 "Bhagavadgītā and Aṣṭādhyāyī", *ABORI* 30: 263-76.

Doshi, Bechardas Jivaraj (Ed.)

1967 *Ācārya Malayagiri's Śabdānuśāsana with autocommentary (Ācārya-śrī-malayagiri-viracitaṃ śabdânuśāsanaṃ svôpajña-vṛtti-yutam)* (= *LDS* 13 (Ahmedabad: Lalbhai Dalpatbhai Bhāratīya Saṃskṛti Vidyāmandira). [Pp. 419-63: concordance of Malayagiri's rules with those of Śākaṭāyana, Hemacandra, the Kātantra, Jainendra, Candragomin, and Pāṇini, in that order.]

Dviveda, Jānakīprasāda: see Jānakīprasāda Dviveda.

Dviveda, Maṅghārāma: see Maṅghārāma Dviveda.

Dvivedi, Kapila Deva

1951 *Arthavijñāna aur vyākaraṇadarśana* [Semantics and philosophy of grammar] (Allahabad: Hindusthani Academy) [In Hindi].

Dwarikadas Shastri (Ed.)

1964 *The Mādhavīyā Dhāturvṛtti (a treatise on Sanskrit roots based on the dhātupāṭha of Pāṇini) by Sāyaṇācārya (Śrī-sāyaṇâcārya-viracitā mādhavīyā dhātu-vṛttiḥ (pāṇinīya-dhātu-pāṭha-vyākhyānâtmikā))* (= *PBS* 1) (Varanasi: Prachya Bhāratī Prakāshana). [Sanskrit introduction, pp. 1-38. Indices: works and authors referred to, pp. 629-33; roots, pp. 634-68; roots contained in certain gaṇas, p. 669; denominative roots, pp. 670-75.]

1971 *Bhāṣāvṛtti (a commentary on Pāṇini's grammar) by Puruṣottamadeva (Śrīmat-puruṣottamadeva-viracitā bhāṣā-vṛttiḥ (pāṇinīyâṣṭādhyāyī-vyākhyā))* (= *PBS* 9) (Varanasi: Tara Publications). [Sanskrit introduction, pp. 7-10. Table of subjects treated in each section, pp. 11-14. Indices: works and authors referred to, p. 523; statements cited, pp. 524-36; verses cited, pp. 537-38.]

Dwarikadas Shastri and Kalika Prasad Shukla (Ed.)

1965-67 *Nyāsa or Pañcikā commentary of ācārya Jinendrabuddhipāda and Padamañjarī of Haradatta Miśra on the Kāśikāvṛtti (commentary on the Aṣṭādhyāyī of Pāṇini) of Vāmana – Jayāditya (Bodhisattvadeśiyâcārya-jinendrabuddhipāda-viracitayā nyāsâparaparyāya-kāśikā-vivaraṇa-pañcikayā vidvad-vara-haradattamiśra-viracitayā pada-mañjarī-vyākhyayā ca sahitā śrīmad-vāmana-jayāditya-viracitā kāśikā-vṛttiḥ (pāṇinīyâṣṭādhyāyī-vyākhyā)),* 6 vol. (= *PBS* 2-7) (1-2: Varanasi: Prāchya Bhāratī Prakāshana, 3-6: Varanasi: Tara Publications). [1: adhyāya 1; 2: adhyāyas 2.1 - 3.2; 3: adhyāyas 3.3 - 4; 4: adhyāyas 5.1 - 6.1; 5: adhyāyas 6.2 - 7.2; 6: adhyāyas 7.3 - 8; Sanskrit introduction, volume 1, pp. 9-12, repeated in subsequent volumes; each volume has an alphabetically arranged index of rules included therein, with page references.]

Dwivedi, S. S.

1974 *Bhartṛhari-kṛta Mahābhāṣya-dīpikā: eka adhyayana* [A study of Bhartṛhari's Mahābhāṣya-dīpikā]. [Gujarat University dissertation, unpublished] [In Gujarati]

Dyen, Isidore

1939 *The Sanskrit indeclinables of the Hindu grammarians and lexicographers* (= *LD* 31) (Philadelphia: Linguistic Society of America). [List of groups of items pertinent to the operations or classifications stated in particular rules: *pra* etc. (Pāṇini 1.4.58), pp. 30-31; *ūrī* etc. (1.3.61), pp. 35-37; *sākṣāt* etc. (1.4.74), pp. 38-39; *tiṣṭhad-gu* etc. (2.1.17), pp. 40-41; *svar* etc. (1.1.37), pp. 46-52; *ca* etc. (1.4.57), pp. 60-66. These tables include the lists of items as given in non-Pāṇinian as well as Pāṇinian treatises.]

Edgerton, Franklin

1941 "*Saṃprasāraṇa* 'emergence; emergent (vowel)' ", *JAOS* 61: 222-23.

1952 "*Karmadhāraya*", *JAOS* 72: 80-81.

Edgren, A. Hjalmar

1885 "On the verbal roots of the Sanskrit language and of the Sanskrit grammarians", *JAOS* 11: 1-55.

Eggeling, Julius (Ed.)
1879-81 *Vardhamāna's Gaṇaratnamahodadhi with the author's commentary; edited with critical notes and indices (Śrī-vardhamāna-viracitaḥ svakīya-vṛtti-sahito gaṇa-ratna-mahôdadhiḥ)* (London: Trübner). [Reprint: (Delhi: Motilal Banarsidass, 1963); the Sanskrit title appears in the reprint, alone available to me. To my knowledge, the indices and critical notes were not published.]

Emeneau, Murray Barnes
1955 "India and linguistics", *JAOS* 75: 145-53.

Faddegon, Barend
1929 "The mnemotechnics of Pāṇini's grammar", *AO* 7: 48-65. [Reprint: Staal (1972): 275-85]
1936 *Studies on Pāṇini's grammar* (= *VKAWA* 38.1)

Festschrift P. C. Bagchi
1957 *P. C. Bagchi memorial volume* (Ed.: Sukumar Sen) (= *IL* 18).

Festschrift S. K. Belvalkar
1957 *Felicitation vollume presented to Professor Sripad Krishna Belvalkar* (editorial board: S. Radhakrishnan, V. V. Mirashi, R. N. Dandekar, S. K. De, V. Raghavan, A. S. Altekar, managing editor) (Varanasi: Motilal Banarsi Dass).

Festschrift Bocheński
1965 *Contributions to logic and methodology in honor of J. M. Bocheński* (Ed.: Anna-Teresa Tymieniecka in collaboration with Charles Parsons) (Amsterdam: North-Holland Publishing Company).

Festschrift Bloch
1954 *Jules Bloch memorial volume* (– *IL* 14).

Festschrift Böhtlingk
1888 *Festgruss an Otto von Böhtlingk zum Doktor-Jubiläum. 3. Februar 1888 von seinen Freunden* (Stuttgart: Kohlhammer).

Festschrift Brown
1962 *Indological studies in honor of W. N. Brown* (Ed.: E. Bender) (= *AOS* 47) (New Haven: American Oriental Society).

Festschrift Charudeva Shastri
1973 *Śrī-cārudeva-śāstry-abhinandana-granthaḥ* [Charudeva Shastri felicitation volume] (Head of the editorial committee: Satyavrat Shastri) (Delhi: The Charudeva Shastri Felicitation Volume Committee).
1974 *Charudeva Shastri felicitation volume; presented to Prof. Charudeva Shastri on the occasion of his seventy-fifth anniversary by*

his friends and admirers (Editorial committee: S. K. Chatterji, V. Raghavan, R. N. Dandekar, Vishva Bandhu, A.D. Pusalkar, Satya Vrat Shastri, convener) (Delhi: Charudeva Shastri Felicitation Committee).

Festschrift S. K. Chatterji
1955 *S. K. Chatterji jubilee volume, presented on the occasion of his sixty-fifth birthday (26th November, 1955)* (= *IL* 16).

Festschrift K. C. Chaṭṭopādhyāya
1971-72 *K. C. Chaṭṭopādhyāya felicitation volume,* 2 vol. [continuous pagination] (Ed.: Babu Ram Saksena, S. P. Chaturvedi, A. P. Misra) (= *JGJKSV* 27. 3/4, 28. 1/2).

Festschrift R. N. Dandekar
1969 *Professor R. N. Dandekar felicitation volume* (Ed.: G. V. Devasthali) (= *IA*³ 3) (Bombay: Popular Prakashan).

Festschrift P. B. Desai
1971 *Studies in Indian history and culture; volume presented to Dr. P. B. Desai on the occasion of his completing sixty years* (Ed.: Shrinivas Ritti, B. R. Gopal) (Dharwar: Prof. B. P. Desai Felicitation Committee, Karnatak University).

Festschrift Emeneau
1968 *Studies in Indian linguistics (Professor M. B. Emeneau ṣaṣtipūrti volume)* (Ed.: Bhadriraju Krishnamurti) (Poona, Annamalainagar: Centres of Advanced Study in Linguistics, Deccan College, Annamalai University).

Festschrift Frauwallner
1968-69 *Beiträge zur Geschichte Indiens; Festschrift für Erich Frauwallner* (Ed.: G. Oberhammer) (= *WZKSOA* 12-13)

Festschrift Garbe
1927 *Aus Indiens Kultur; Festgabe für Richard von Garbe* (Ed.: J. Negelein) (= *VIGSUE* 3) (Erlangen: Palm und Enke).

Festschrift Grierson
1932-36 *George Abraham Grierson commemoration volume* 5 vol. (= *IL* 2 [1932], 3 [1933], 4 [1934], 5 [1935], 6 [1936]).

Festschrift A. N. Jha
1969 *Saṃskṛti; ḍākṭar Āditya Nātha Jhā abhinandana-grantha,* 3 vol. (Ed.: Gopinath Kaviraj) (Delhi: The Dr. A. N. Jha Felicitation Volume Committee).

Festschrift Gangānātha Jhā
1937 *Jha commemoration volume; essays on oriental subjects presented to Vidyāsāgara Mahāmahopādhyāya Paṇḍita Gangānātha Jhā on his completing the 60th year on 25th September, 1932*

by his pupils, friends and admirers (Editorial board: K. Chaṭṭopādhyāya, secretary, S. K. Belvalkar, S. N. Dasgupta, S. Kuppuswami Sastri, P. K. Acharya, A. Siddiqui, R. D. Ranade, A. C. Woolner) (= *POS* 39) (Poona: Oriental Book Agency).

Festschrift Kahane

1973 *Issues in linguistics; papers in honor of Henry and Renée Kahane* (Ed.: Braj B. Kachru, Robert B. Lees, Yakov Malkiel, Angelina Pietrangeli, Sol Saporta) (Urbana: University of Illinois Press).

Festschrift P. V. Kane

1941 *A volume of studies in Indology presented to Professor P. V. Kane on his 61st birthday, 7th May 1941* (Ed.: S. M. Katre, P. K. Gode) (Poona: Oriental Book Agency).

Festschrift S. M. Katre

1968-69 *S. M. Katre felicitation volume presented on the occasion of his sixty-sixth birthday (11 April 1971)*, 2 vol. (= *IL* 29-30).

Festschrift Gopinath Kaviraj

1967 *Kaviraj abhinandana grantha* (Editorial board: Baburam Saksena, convenor, S. M. Katre, Gaurinath Shastri, D. N. Shastri, V. V. Mirashi, V. Raghavan, K. A. Subramania Iyer, S. N. Tripathi, V. S. Agrawala, K. C. Chaṭṭopādhyāya, Jagannath Upadhyaya, Jayadamba P. Sinha, Gopal C. Sinha) (Lucknow: Akhil Bharatiya Sanskrit Parishad).

Festschrift Kirfel

1955 *Studia indologica; Festschrift für Willibald Kirfel zur Vollendung seines 70. Lebensjahres* (Ed.: O. Spies) (= *BOS* 3) (Bonn: Selbstverlag des Orientalischen Seminars der Universität).

Festschrift Krishnaswami Aiyangar

1936 *Dr. S. Krishnaswami Aiyangar commemoration volume* (Ed.: V. Rangacharya, C. S. Srinivasachari, V. R. R. Dikshitar) (Madras: The Dr. S. Krishnaswami Aiyangar Commemoration Volume Committee).

Festschrift Kuiper

1968 *Pratidānam; Indian, Iranian and Indo-European studies presented to Franciscus Bernardus Jacobus Kuiper on his sixtieth birthday* (Ed.: J. C. Heesterman, G. H. Schokker, V. I. Subramoniam) (The Hague: Mouton).

Festschrift B. C. Law

1945-46 *B. C. Law volume*, 2 vol. (Ed.: D. R. Bhandarkar, K. N. Nilakanta Sastri, B. M. Barua, B. K. Ghosh, P. K. Gode) (1: Calcutta: The Indian Research Institute, 2: Poona: BORI).

Festschrift Asutosh Mookerjee
1922-25 *Sir Asutosh Mookerjee silver jubilee volumes* 3, *(Orientalia)*. (Calcutta: University of Calcutta).

Festschrift R. K. Mookerji
1945-47 *Bhārata-kaumudī (studies in Indology in honour of Dr. Radha Kumud Mookerji)*, 2 vol. [continuous pagination] (Board of editors: N. K. Sidhantu, chairman, B. C. Law, C. D. Chatterjee, V. S. Agrawala, secretary) (Allahabad: The Indian Press).

Festschrift Satkari Mookerji
1969 *Dr. Satkari Mookerji felicitation volume* (Editorial board: B. P. Sinha, R. K. Choudhary, O. P. Jaiswal, S. Bhattacharya, S. Bagchi, M. L. Gosvami) (= *OSSt.* 69) (Varanasi: Chowkhamba).

Festschrift Morgenstierne
1964 *Indo-iranica; mélanges présentés à Georg Morgenstierne à l'occasion de son soixante-dixième anniversaire* (Ed.: G. Redard) (Wiesbaden: Harrassowitz).

Festschrift K. M. Munshi
1948 *Shri K. M. Munshi diamond jubilee volume, part 1* (= *BhV* 9).
1960-61 *Munshi indological felicitation volume* (= *BhV* 20-1). [Issued 1963]

Festschrift Nobel
1963 *Jñānamuktāvalī; commemoration volume in honour of Johannes Nobel on the occasion of his 70th birthday offered by pupils and colleagues* (Ed. C. Vogel) (= *SVS* 38) (New Delhi: International Academy of Indian Culture).

Festschrift Pokorny
1967 *Beiträge zur Indogermanistik und Keltologie Julius Pokorny zum 80. Geburtstag gewidmet* (Ed.: W. Meid) (= *IBKW* 13) (Innsbruck: Sprachwissenschaftliches Institut der Universität).

Festschrift V. Raghavan
1967-68 *Dr. V. Raghavan felicitation volume* (= *ALB* 31-32).

Festschrift Rajeshwar Shastri Dravid
1971 *Ṛṣikalpanyāsaḥ* (Ed.: Devadatta Śāstrī) (Prayāga (Allahabad): Bharati Parisad). [Reference is made to pages according to the separately paginated sections.]

Festschrift Renou
1968 *Mélanges d'indianisme à la mémoire de Louis Renou* (= *PICI* 28) (Paris: Boccard).

Festschrift Roth
1893 *Festgruss an Rudolf von Roth zum Doktor-Jubiläum* (Stuttgart: Kohlhammer).

Festschrift Baburam Saksena
1964 *Baburam Saksena felicitation volume presented on the occasion of his sixty-seventh birthday (12th May 1964)* (= *IL* 25).

Festschrift Sukumar Sen
1965 *Sukumar Sen felicitation volume presented on the occasion of his sixty-sixth birthday (1966)* (= *IL* 26).

Festschrift V. S. Sukthankar
1943-44 *V. S. Sukthankar memorial volume (21st January 1944)* (Ed.: V. M. Apte, H. D. Sankalia) (= *BDCRI* 5).

Festschrift Taraporewala
1956-57 *Irach Jehangir Sorabji Taraporewala memorial volume; completed on the occasion of the first anniversary of his death (15th January, 1957)* (= *IL* 17).

Festschrift Turner
1958-59 *Sir R. L. Turner jubilee volume presented on the occasion of his seventieth birthday (5th October, 1958)* (Ed.: Sukumar Sen) (= 19-20).

Festschrift Siddheshwar Varma
1950 *Siddha-bhāratī or the rosary of indology; presenting 108 original papers on indological subjects in honour of the 60th birthday of Dr. Siddheshwar Varma,* 2 vol. (Ed.: Vishva Bandhu Shastri) (= *VIS* 1-2) (Hoshiarpur: Vishveshwaranand Vedic Research Institute).

Festschrift H. D. Velankar
1965 *H. D. Velankar commemoration volume; a volume of Indological studies by his students presented to Professor H. D. Velankar on the occasion of his seventy-second birthday on 3rd October 1965* (Ed.: S. N. Gajendragadkar, S. A. Upadhyay) (Bombay: Professor H. D. Velankar Commemoration Volume Committee).

Festschrift Weber
1896 *Gurupūjākaumudī; Festgabe zum fünfzigjährigen Doctorjubiläum Albrecht Weber von seinen Freunden und Schülern dargebracht* (Leipzig: Harrassowitz).

Festschrift Weller
1954 *Asiatica; Festschrift Friedrich Weller* (Ed.: J. Schubert, U. Schneider) (Leipzig: Harrassowitz).

Festschrift Whatmough
1957 *Studies presented to Joshua Whatmough on his sixtieth birthday* (Ed.: E. Pulgram) ('s-Gravenhage: Mouton).

Festschrift Windisch
1914 *Festschrift für Ernst Windisch zum siebzigsten Geburtstag am 4. September 1914 dargebracht von Freunden und Schülern* (Leipzig: Harrassowitz).

Festschrift Woolner
1940 *Woolner commemoration volume (in memory of the late Dr. A. C. Woolner)* (Ed.: M. Shafi) (= *MSPS* 8) (Lahore: Mehar Chand Lachman Das).

Festschrift Yamaguchi
1955 *Studies in Indology and Buddhology presented in honour of Professor Susumu Yamaguchi* (Ed.: G. M. Nagao, J. Nozawa) (Kyoto: Hozokan).

Filliozat, Jean
1954 "A propos de la religion de Bhartṛhari", *Zenbunka-Kenkyu-Kai, Kyoto Silver Jubilee Volume* (Kyoto University), pp. 116-20.
1967 "Bibliographie des travaux de Louis Renou", *JAs* 255: 13-30. [Reprint: *Festschrift Renou,* pp. xiii-xxix]

Filliozat, Pierre Sylvain
1973 French introduction to M. S. Narasimhacharya (1973), pp. iii-xiii.

Fillmore, Charles J.
1968 "The case for case", *Universals in linguistic theory* (Ed.: E. Bach, R. T. Harms) (New York: Holt, Rinehart and Winston), pp. 1-88.

Foucher, A.
1900 "Pāṇini", *La grande encyclopédie* (Paris: Société Anonyme de la Grande Encyclopédie), pp. 945-46.

Fowler, Murray
1965 "How ordered are Pāṇini's rules? ", *JAOS* 85: 44-7.
1973 "Pāṇini's primary accent-rules", in: Konks - Numerkund - Mäll (1973), pp. 322-35.

Franke, R. Otto
1890a *Die indischen Genuslehren; mit dem Text der Liṅgānuçāsana's des Çākaṭāyana, Harṣavardhana, Vararuci, nebst Auszügen aus den Kommentaren des Yakṣavarman (zu Ç.) und des Çabarasvāmin (zu H.) und mit einem Anhang über die indischen Namen* (Kiel: Haeseler).
1890b "Die Kasuslehre des Pāṇini verglichen mit dem Gebrauch der Kasus im Pāli und in den Aśoka-inschriften", *BB* 16: 64-120.
1891a "Was ist Sanskrit? ", *BB* 17: 54-90.

1891b Review of Liebich (1891), *GGA* 1891: 951-83.

1892 "Pāli *maññe* (Skr. *manye*, Pāṇini I, 4, 106)", *ZDMG* 46: 311-12.

1894a "Einige Belege aus dem Pāli für unbelegte Wurzeln und Wurzelbedeutungen des Dhātupāṭha", *WZKM* 8: 321-31.

1894b "Miscellen; 1. *a-pacasi* etc., 2. Pāṇ. 6, 3, 57 (*uda* für *udaka*), 3. *pakṣa* = *rājakuñjara*, 4. *iti* = 'etc.' ", *ZDMG* 48: 84-88.

Frauwallner, Erich

1959 "Das Eindringen der Sprachtheorie in die indischen philosophischen Systeme", in: Waldschmidt (1959), pp. 239-43.

1960 "Sprachtheorie und Philosophie im Mahābhāṣya des Patañjali", *WZKSOA* 4: 92-118.

1961 "Landmarks in the history of Indian logic", *WZKSOA* 5: 125-48.

Gai, G. S.

1960 "Madhyamikā", *JOIB* 10: 180-81.

Gaṇapati Śāstrī, T. (Ed.)

1905 *The Daiva of Deva with the commentary* ***Purushakāra*** *of Krishṇalīlāśukamuni, edited with notes* (= *TSS* 1) (Trivandrum: Travancore Government Press). [English introduction, pp. i-vii; Sanskrit introduction, pp. 1-5. Indices: authors mentioned in the Puruṣakāra, pp. 1-4; works mentioned in the Puruṣakāra, p. 1; other grammatical works mentioned in the Puruṣakāra, pp. 1-3. All separately paginated, preceding text]

1909 *The Durghaṭavṛtti of Śaraṇadeva; edited with notes (Śrī-śaraṇadeva-viracitā durghaṭa-vṛttiḥ ..... saṃśodhitā laghu-ṭippaṇyā ca saṃyojitā)* (= *TSS* 6) (Trivandrum: Government Press). [English preface, pp. 1-2; Sanskrit preface, pp. 1-2. Indices: works mentioned, pp. 1-4; authors mentioned, pp. 1-3; rules interpreted, pp. 1-7; examples, pp. 1-19. All separately paginated and preceding the text.]

1913 *The Vāraruchasaṃgraha of Vararuchi with the commentary Dīpaprabhā of Nārāyaṇa (Vāraruca-saṃgrahaḥ śrī-vararuci-praṇītaḥ śrī-nārāyaṇa-kṛtayā dīpa-prabhâkhyayā vyākhyayôpêtaḥ)* (= *TSS* 33) (Trivandrum: Government Press).

1917 *The Sphoṭasiddhinyāyavichāra (Sphoṭa-siddhi-nyāya-vicāraḥ)* (= *TSS* 54) (Trivandrum: Government Press).

Gaṅgādatta Śāstrī (Commentator)

1950-62 *Pāṇinīyâṣṭakam; ..... paṇḍita-vara-śrīyuta-gaṅgādatta-śāstribhiḥ ..... nirmitayā tattva-prakāśikayā vyākhyayā sanāthīkṛtam* [Pāṇini's grammar with the commentary Tattva-prakāśikā by

Gaṅgādatta Śāstrī], (= *GSS* 8) (Gurukul Kangdi, Haridwar: Gurukul Kangdri University). [1[3] (1962): adhyāyas 1-4; 2[2] (1950): adhyāyas 5-8.]

Gaṅgādhara Śāstrī Bhāradvāja (Ed.)

1930 *The Vṛtti Dīpikā by Mauni Śrī Kṛṣṇa Bhaṭṭa; edited with introduction etc. (Vṛtti-dīpikā mauni-śrī-kṛṣṇa-bhaṭṭa viracitā)* (= *PWSBT* 29) (Benares: Sanskrit College). [Sanskrit introduction, pp. 1-8; index of authors mentioned, p. 53.]

Ganguli, Hemanta Kumar

1963 *Philosophy of logical construction; an examination of logical atomism and logical positivism in the light of the philosophies of Bhartṛhari, Dharmakīrti and Prajñākaragupta* (Calcutta: Sanskrit Pustak Bhandar).

Garge, Damodar Vishnu

1949 "Jaimini – Śabara and the science of grammar", *ABORI* 30: 254-62.

1952 *Citations in Śabara-bhāṣya (a study)* (= *DCDS* 8) (Poona: Deccan College). [Pp. 236-42: "Śabara and the science of grammar".]

Gaurinath Shastri

1939 "The doctrine of śabdabrahman -- a criticism by Jayantabhaṭṭa", *IHQ* 15: 441-53.

1956 "Philosophy of Bhartṛhari", *JASL* 22: 71-73.

1959 *The philosophy of word and meaning; some Indian approaches with special reference to the philosophy of Bhartṛhari* (= *CSCRS* 5) (Calcutta: Sanskrit College). [See also Gaurinath Bhattacharya (1937), which is by the same author.]

1968-69 "Monism of Bhartṛhari", *Festschrift Frauwallner*, pp. 319-22.

Gayācaraṇa Tripāṭhī (Ed.)

1961 *Kaumudī-kathā-kallolinī (Pāṇinīya-laukika-vyākaraṇa-samāpanīyā); racayitā Rāma-śaraṇa śāstrī, sampādakaḥ grantha-kartur ātmajaḥ ..... Gayācaraṇa Tripāṭhī* [The Kaumudī-kathā-kallolinī, illustrating Pāṇini's non-Vedic rules, by Rāma Śaraṇa Śāstrī, edited by his son Gayācaraṇa Tripāṭhī] (= *VBSGM* 54) (Varanasi: Chowkamba). [Modern composition illustrating Pāṇinian rules in the order of the Siddhānta-kaumudī.]

Gaydhani, M. G.

1953 "Patañjali's attitude towards Kātyāyana", *PAIOC* 16 (Lucknow, 1951): 95-104.

Geiger, Bernhard

1908 "Mahābhāṣya zu P. VI, 4, 22 und 132 nebst Kaiyaṭa's Kommentar, übersetzt, erläutert und mit einem Anhang", *SWAW* 160.8:

1-76. [Reprint: Staal (1972): 209-59.]

Ghatge, Amrit Madhav

1968 "Pāṇini 1.4.32", *Festschrift S. M. Katre* 2, pp. 150-54.

Ghosh, Amalananda

1935 "A study of the smṛti passages in the Mahābhāṣya", *IHQ* 11: 77-90.

Ghosh, Batakrishna

1927 "Max Müller's introduction to the Ṛgveda-Prātiśākhya", *IHQ* 3: 611-24, 757-68. [English translation of M. Müller (1869); introduction, pp. 3-32.]

1934 "Pāṇini and the Ṛkprātiśākhya", *IHQ* 10: 665-70.

1938 "Thieme and Pāṇini", *IC* 4: 387-99. [Reply to Thieme (1937).]

1939 "Mr. Chaturvedi on Pāṇini and the Ṛkprātiśākhya", *NIA* 2: 59-61. [Reply to S. P. Chaturvedi (1938a).]

1945 "Aspects of pre-Pāṇinean Sanskrit grammar", *Festschrift B. C. Law volume* 1, pp. 334-45.

Ghosh, Manomohan

1938 (Ed., tr.) *Pāṇinīya śikṣā or the śikṣā vedāṅga ascribed to Pāṇini (being the most ancient work on Indo-Aryan phonetics); critically edited in all its five recensions with an introduction, translation and notes together with two commentaries* (Calcutta: University of Calcutta). [Introduction, pp. ix-lxvi; reconstructed text, pp. 1-3; Agni-purāṇa recension, pp. 4-6; text with the Pañjikā commentary, pp. 7-22; text with the commentary Śikṣāprakāśa, pp. 23-34; the Yajus recension, pp. 35-38; the Ṛk recension, pp. 39-44; Candragomin's varṇa-sūtras, pp. 45-46; translation and notes, pp. 48-80. Indices: phonetic terms, pp. 81-82; general, pp. 82-83. Addenda and corrigenda, pp. 84-90.]

Giridhara Śarma Caturveda

1954 "Bhumikā" [introduction to Rudradhara Śarmā (1954), pp. 1-34]

1965 "Pāṇini ke pūrva vyākaraṇa kī sattā" [The existence of pre-Pāṇinian grammar, in Hindi], *Sarasvatī* (Allahabad) 66: 281-83. [*Prāci Jyoti* (1963-1972) 4: 135.]

Giridhara Śarmā Caturveda and Parameśvarānanda Śarmā Bhāskara (Ed.)

1958-61 *Śrī-bhaṭṭojī-dīkṣita-viracitā vaiyākaraṇa-siddhānta-kaumudī śrīmad-vāsudeva-dīkṣita-praṇītayā bālamanoramâkhya-vyākhyayā śrīmaj-jñānendra-sarasvatī-viracitayā tattva-bodhiny-ākhya-vyākhyayā ca sanāthitā* [Bhaṭṭojī Dīkṣita's Vaiyākaraṇa-siddhānta-kaumudī with the Bāla-manoramā of Vāsudeva Dīkṣita and Jñānendra Sarasvatī's Tattva-bodhinī], 4 vol. (Varanasi: Motilal Banarsidass). [1: 1958: 2 - 3: 1960; 4: 1961] [Sanskrit preface, l: 3 - 6; uṇādi-sūtras,

4: 120 - 265; phiṭ-sūtras, 4: 435 - 49; liṅgânuśāsana, 4: 554 - 66; pāṇinīya-śikṣā, 4: 567 - 70; gaṇa-pāṭha, 4: 571 - 600. Indices: sūtras, 1: 697 - 708, 2: 586 - 609, 3: 572 - 82, 4: 601 - 18; vārttikas, 1: 709 - 12, 2: 609 - 15, 3: 583 - 85, 4: 618 - 21; paribhāṣās, 1: 712, 2: 615, 3: 585, 4: 622; roots, 3: 585 - 617; uṇādi-sūtras, 4: 622 - 29; phiṭ-sūtras, 4: 629 - 30; liṅgânuśāsana rules, 4: 630 - 33.]

Gode, Parashuram Krishna

1939 "Date of the grammarian Bhīmasena", *NIA* 2: 108 - 10. [Reprint: Gode (1953 - 6.1: 105 - 08).]

1940 "A new approach to the date of Bhaṭṭojī Dīkshita", *ASVOI* 1.2: 117-27.

1941 "Varadarāja, a pupil of Bhaṭṭoji Dīkṣita, and his works – between 1600 and 1650", *Festschrift P. V. Kane*, pp. 188-99. [Reprint: Gode (1953 - 6.2: 316-29).]

1951 "Vidyāvilāsa, a commentary on the Siddhānta- kaumudī by Śivarāma Tripāthin (between A.D. 1700 and 1775)", *ALB* 15: 62-67. [Reprint: Gode (1953 - 6.2: 237-41).]

1954 "The chronology of the works of Koṇḍabhaṭṭa (a nephew of Bhaṭṭoji Dīkṣita), between A.D. 1610 and 1660", *ALB* 18: 210-16. [Reprint: Gode (1953-6.3: 207-11).]

1955 "The relative chronology of some works of Nāgojibhaṭṭa between c. A.D. 1670 and 1750", *OT* 1.2: 45-52. [Reprint: Gode (1953-6.3: 212-19).]

1953-56 *Studies in Indian literary history,* 3 vol. [1: (= *SJS* 37 = *BSSM* 4) (Bombay: Bhāratīya Vidyā Bhavan 1953), 2: (= *SJS* 38 = *BSSM* 5) (Bombay: Bhāratīya Vidyā Bhavan 1954), 3: (Poona: Prof. P. K. Gode Collected Works Publication Committee 1956).]

Godse, B. S.

1973 "Concept of vipratiṣedha in Pāṇinian grammar", *ABORI* 54: 250-56.

Gokhale, Gaṇeśa Śāstrī (Ed.)

1913 *Vaidyanātha-kṛta-gadā-ṭīkā-saṃvalitaḥ paribhāṣênduśekharaḥ,* [The Paribhāṣênduśekhara with the Gadā commentary of Vaidyanātha](= *ASS* 72) (Poona: Ānandāśrama).

Gokhale, V. D.

1956-57 "Unpāṇinian forms and usages in the critical edition of the Mahābhārata; 6. compounds", *Festschrift Taraporewala,* pp. 121-28. [Study 6 in the series begun by E. D. Kulkarni (1943a - 1950-51), according to Gokhale, p. 121, note 1]

Gokhale, V. N.

1939 "Studies in Pāṇini, part I: the taddhitaprakaraṇa and all other important matters relating to it", *PO* 4: 97-120.

1940 "Studies in Pāṇini, part II: some thoughts on Pānini's grammar" *PO* 5: 109-22.

Goldstücker, Theodor

1861 *Pāṇini, his place in Sanskrit literature; an investigation of some literary and chronological questions which may be settled by a study of his work (a separate impression of the preface to a fac-simile of ms. no. 17 in the library of her majesty's home government for India, which contains a portion of the Māṇava-kalpa-sūtra with the commentary of Kumārila-svāmin)* (London: Trübner). [Reprint: (Allahabad: The Pāṇini office, 1914); abridged reprint: (Ed.: Surendra Nath Shastri) (= *CSSt.* 48) (Varanasi: Chowkhamba 1965).]

Gonda, Jan

1954 *Aspects of early Viṣṇuism* (Utrecht: Oosthoek). [Reprint: (Delhi: Motilal Banarsidass, 1969).]

1973 "Pāṇini and modern linguistics", in: Konks – Numerkund – Mäll (1973), pp. 337-52.

1974 "Nimitta", *Festschrift Charudeva Shastri,* pp. 233-40.

Goonatilleke, W.

1882a *Pāṇini's eight books of grammatical sūtras* (Bombay: Education Society Press).

1882b "On the absence of the guṇa change of *bhū* in the preterite", *IA* 11: 123-24.

Gopal, Ram: see Ram Gopal

Gopāla Śāstrī

1966 "Veda aur Pāṇini" [The Veda and Pāṇini, in Hindi], *Vedavāṇī* (Sonipat, Haryana) 19.1: 63-64.

Gopāla Śāstrī Nene: see Nene, Gopāla Shastri

Gopinath Kaviraj: see Kaviraj, Gopinath.

Gourypathy Sastry, T. S.

1974 "Quotative nominals in Sanskrit", *IL* 35: 1-13.

Grantovskij, E. A.

1963 "Plemennoe ob edinenie paršu-paršava u Panini" [The tribal grouping Parçu-Parçava in Pāṇini's work], *Istorija i kul'tura drevnej Indii (k xxvi Meždunarodnomu kongressu vostokovedov)* (Ed.: W. Ruben, V. Struve, G. Bongard-Levin) (Moskva: Izdatel'stvo Vostočnoj Literatury), pp. 68-100.

Grierson, George Abraham

1893 Review of Liebich (1891), *IA* 22: 222-24.

1909 "Vāsudeva of Pāṇini IV, iii, 98", *JRAS* 1909: 1122.

Guleri, Chandradhar

1912 "On 'śiva-bhāgavata' in Patañjali's Mahābhāṣya", *IA* 41: 272.

Gune, Jayashree Achyut

1974 *Kauṇḍabhaṭṭa on the meaning of verbal endings (the text of Kauṇḍabhaṭṭa's Lakārārthanirṇaya, with English translation, explanatory notes, and introduction).* [University of Pennsylvania dissertation, unpublished.]

Gune, P. D.

1916 "Some notes on Yāska's Nirukta", *IA* 45: 157-60, 173-77.

Gupta, D. K.

1974 "Creative and critical writings of Prof. Charu Deva Shastri: a critique", *Festschrift Charudeva Shastri,* pp. xxv-lix.

Gupta, Sudhir Kumar

1951 "Authorship of the phonetic sūtras edited by Dayānand", *PO* 16: 66-69.

1968 "Pāṇinīya vyākaraṇa meṃ vaidika nirvacanoṃ kī prakriyā" [The procedure for deriving Vedic forms in Pāṇini's grammar, *Vedavāṇī* (Sonipat, Haryana) 20.6: 9-15. [in Hindi] [Dandekar (1946 - 73): 3: 177, number 77.]

Guruprasāda Śāstrī (Ed.)

1938 *Patañjali's Vyākaraṇa-Mahābhāṣya with Kaiyaṭa's Pradīpa and Nāgojībhaṭṭa's Uddyota,* 9 vol. (= *RSCG* 30) (Benares: Bhargava Pustakalaya). [Not available to me when I was compiling the present work.]

Hacker, Paul

1953 *Vivarta; Studien zur Geschichte der illusionistischen Kosmologie und Erkenntnistheorie der Inder* (= *AAWLM* 1953.5) (Mainz: Verlag der Akademie der Wissenschaften und der Literatur in Mainz).

Hara, Minoru

1969 "A note on the Sanskrit phrase *devānāṃpriya", Festschrift S. M. Katre* 2, pp. 13-26.

Haraprasāda Shāstrī

1931 *A descriptive catalogue of the Sanskrit manuscripts in the collections of the Asiatic Society of Bengal; volume 6: vyākaraṇa manuscripts* (Calcutta: Asiatic Society of Bengal). [Pp. vii-cxviii of the preface: a survey of grammars.]

Haridatta Śāstrī

1971 "Śabdâdvaita-vādaḥ" [The śabdâdvaita doctrine], *Festschrift Rajeshwar Shastri Dravid,* philosophy section, pp. 8-11. [In Sanskrit].

Hariścandramani Tripāṭhī
1970a "Nañ-artha-vicāraḥ" [On the meaning of the negative particle *na*, *VS* 7: 146-51. [In Sanskrit]. [See also Hariścandramaṇi Tripāṭhī (1971).]
1970b "Nipātârtha-nirṇaya" [The accepted conslusion regarding the meanings of particles], *SS* 24.4: 371-80. [In Sanskrit]
1971 "Nañ-artha-vicāraḥ", *Sāg.* 10.2: 219-23. [See also Hariścandramani Tripāṭhī (1970a).]

Hazra, Rajendra Chandra
1956 "Some observations on the repetition (*anuvṛtti*) of *'śeṣa'* from Pāṇini's rule *ṣaṣṭhī śeṣe", JASL* 22: 99-131.

Heimann, Betty
1941 "Sphoṭa and artha", *Festschrift P. V. Kane*, pp. 221-27.

Herman, A. L.
1962-63 "Sphoṭa", *JGJRI* 19: 1-21.

Hertel, Johannes
1908 "Von Pāṇini zu Phaedrus", *ZDMG* 62: 113-18.

Hillebrandt, Alfred
1918 "Zur Geschichte des indischen Dramas", *ZDMG* 72: 227-32.
1927 "Die Anschauungen über das Alter des Ṛgveda", *ZDMG* 81: 46-77.

Hiriyanna, M.
1938 "Vyāḍi and Vājapyāyana", *IHQ* 14: 261-66.

Hockett, Charles Francis (Ed.)
1970 *A Leonard Bloomfield anthology* (Bloomington: Indiana University Press).

Hoffmann, Karl
1974 "Pāṇini VII 2, 69 sanim̥ sasanivāṃsam", *MSS* 32: 73-80.
1975 "Pāṇini V 4, 61 ativyathane", *MSS* 33: 45-50.

Insler, Stanley
1963 *Verbal paradigms in Patañjali: 250 roots and their paradigmatic derivations as used and discussed by Patañjali in the Mahābhāṣya.* [Yale University dissertation, unpublished].

Īśvaran Namputiri, I.
1967 "Vyākaraṇa-darśanam" [Philosophy of grammar] *VS* 4: 339-45. [In Sanskrit]

Iyangar, V. Krishnaswami: see Krishnaswami Iyangar, V.
Iyengar, H. R. Rangaswami: see Rangaswami Iyengar, H. R.
Iyer, K. A. Subramania: see Subramania Iyer, K. A.
Iyer, P. S. Vedachala: see Vedachala Iyer, P. S.
Iyer, S. Venkitasubramonia: see Venkitasubramonia Iyer, S.

Jacobi, Hermann
1908 "*Mayūravyaṃsaka*", *ZDMG* 62: 358-60.
1911 "The dates of the philosophical sūtras of the Brahmans", *JAOS* 31: 1-29.
1913 "Was ist Sanskrit? ", *Scientia* 14: 251-74.
1931 "Über das Alter des Yogaśāstra", *ZII* 8: 80-88.

Jagannāthaswāmy Āryavaraguru, S. P. S. and Āchārya Bhaṭṭanāthaswāmy (Ed.)
1903-06 *Vyākaraṇamitāksharā, a gloss on Pāṇini's grammatical aphorisms by Śrī Annambhaṭṭa (Vyākaraṇa-mitâkṣarā sarva-tantra-svatantra-śrīmad-annaṃbhaṭṭa-praṇītā)* (= *BSS* 20: 76, 77, 82, 85, 93, 98, 115, 121, 122, 126) (Benares: Braj B. Das). [My copy does not show the dates of the individual fascicles.]

Jaini, Padmanabh S.
1959 "The Vaibhāṣika theory of words and meanings", *BSOAS* 22: 95-107.

Jambuvijaya, Muni
1951a "Ācārya Bhagavān Mallavādi-kṣamāśramaṇa ane Bhartṛhari-no samaya" [Ācārya Mallavādin and the date of Bhartṛhari], *JSP* 17.2: 26-30. [In Gujarati] [See also Jambuvijaya (1951b).]
1951b "Jainācārya Śrī Mallavādī ane Bhartṛhari-no samaya" [The Jaina teacher Mallavādin and the date of Bhartṛhari], *BP* 98.11: 332-35. [In Gujarati] [See also Jambuvijaya (1951a).]
1953 "On the date of Bhartṛhari, the author of the Vākyapadīya", *SPAIOC* 14: 50-51.
1954 "Bhartṛhari aur Diṅnāga kā samaya" [The date of Diṅnāga and Bhartṛhari], *NPP* 60.3/4: 227-33. [In Hindi]
1961 (Ed.) *Vaiśeṣikasūtra of Kaṇāda with the commentary of Candrānanda (Candrânanda-viracitayā prācīnayā vṛttyā samalaṅkṛtaṁ kaṇâda-praṇītaṃ vaiśeṣika-sūtram)* (= *GOS* 136) (Baroda: Oriental Institute). [Appendix 6: Vaiśeṣika works mentioned in Mallavādin's Naya-cakra and the commentary thereon, pp. 146-52.]
1966 (Ed.) *Dvādaśāraṃ Nayacakraṃ of Ācārya Śrī Mallavādi Kṣamāśramaṇa with the commentary Nyāyāgamānusāriṇī of Śrī Siṃhasūri Gaṇi Vādi Kṣamāśramaṇa; edited with critical notes; part I (1-4 aras) (Tārkika-śiromaṇi-jina-śāsana-vādi-prabhāvakâcārya-pravara-śrī-mallavādi-kṣamāśramaṇa-praṇītaṃ dvādaśâraṃ naya-cakram ācārya-śrī-siṃhasūri-gaṇi-vādi kṣamāśramaṇa-viracitayā nyāyâgamânusāriṇyā vṛttyā samalaṅkṛtam; tippaṇâdibhiḥ pariṣkṛtaḥ; prathamo vibhāgaḥ (1 - 4 arāḥ))* (= *AJGM* 92) (Bhavnagar: Sri Jain Atmanand Sabha). [English introduction by

E. Frauwallner, pp. 1-6; Sanskrit preface and Gujarati introduction by Jambuvijaya, pp. 7-43, 44-89, separately paginated preceding the text.]

Janáček, Adolf

1958 "Two texts of Patañjali and a statistical comparison of their vocabularies", *Arch. Or.* 26: 88-100.

Jānakīprasāda Dviveda

1967 *Pāṇinīya-vyākaraṇe śāstrīya-saṃjñānāṃ tātparya-vimarśaḥ* [A study on the import of technical terms in Pāṇini's grammar]. [Vārāṇaseya Saṃskṛta Viśvavidyālaya dissertation, unpublished.] [In Sanskrit.]

1969 "Vyākaraṇe lokasya prāmāṇyam" [The authority of usage in grammar], *SS* 24.1: 31-55. [In Sanskrit.]

1971 "Pāṇini-prayuktā icchârthakāḥ kecana śabdāḥ" [Some words meaning 'desire' as used by Pāṇini], *Sag.* 10.1: 105-12. [In Sanskrit.]

Jani, A. N.

1963 "An emendation of a sūtra of Pāṇini", *JMSUB* 12: 71-73. [Rule 7.1.90]

1966 "The śivasūtras and music", *JOIB* 15: 400-02.

1971 "Fresh light on Pāṇini's sūtra 'tasyādita udāttam ardhahrasvam' (I. 2. 32)", *Festschrift K. C. Chaṭṭopādhyāya,* pp. 261-64. [See also A. N. Jani (1972).]

1972 "Fresh light on Pāṇini's sūtra 'tasyādita udāttam ardhahrasvam'", *PAIOC* 24 (Varanasi, 1968): 257-59. [See also A. N. Jani (1971).]

1974 "On the mātrā and the mode of recitation of an independent svarita", *Festschrift Charudeva Shastri,* pp. 77-81.

Jayadatta Śāstrī

1965 "Pāṇinīyâṣṭaka-stha-pratyāhāra-sūtrāṇāṃ racayitā" [The author of the pratyāhāra-sūtras of Pāṇini's grammar, *GKP* 18. 4: 237-41. [In Sanskrit.] [Dandekar (1946 - 73): 3: 177, number 80.]

Jayapāla Vidyālaṅkāra

1972 "Kātyāyana ke kāla-nirdhāraṇa meṃ devānāṃpriya śabda kā mahattva" [The importance of the word *devānāṃpriya* in determining Kātyāyana's date], *JDSDU* 1.2: 106-21. [In Hindi.]

Jayaswal, Kashi Prasad

1918 "Dates of Pāṇini and Kātyāyana", *IA* 47: 138.

1919 "Kātyāyana and Pārthiva", *IA* 48: 12.

1943 *Hindu polity; a constitutional history of India in Hindu times*[2] (Bangalore: The Bangalore Printing and Publishing Company).

Jhā, Madhukānta Śarmā: see Madhukānta Śarmā Jhā.

Jha, Subhadra (Tr.)

1967 *History of Indian literature by M. Winternitz; vol. III, part II (scientific literature); translated from the German into English with additions* (Delhi: Motilal Banarsidass). [Translation of the second part of Winternitz (1920a).]

Jhā, Vedānanda: see Vedānanda Jhā.

Jhalakīkar, Bhīmācarya and Vāsudev Shāstrī Abhyankar

1928 *Nyāyakośa or dictionary of technical terms of Indian philosophy, by Mahāmahopādhyāya Bhīmācārya Jhalakīkar; revised and re-edited by Mahāmahopādhyāya Vāsudev Shāstrī Abhyankar (Nyāya-kośaḥ (sakala-śāstrôpakāraka-nyāyâdi-śāstrīya-padârtha-prakāśakaḥ) ......)*[3] (= *BSPS* 49) (Poona: BORI).

Jijñāsu, Brahmadatta: see Brahmadatta Jijñāsu.

Joshi (Jośī), Bhārgavaśāstrī Bhikājī (Ed.)

1942 *Patañjali's Vyākaraṇa Mahābhāṣya with Kaiyaṭa's Pradīpa and Nāgeśa's Uddyota; vol. IV* [adhyayas 4 - 5], *edited with foot-notes etc. (Śrīmad-bhagavat-patañjali-muni-viracitaṃ pāṇinīya-vyākaraṇa-mahā-bhāṣyam, etad-vyākhyāna-bhūta upādhyāya-kaiyaṭa-praṇīto bhāṣya-pradīpas tad-vyākhyāna-bhūto nāgeśabhaṭṭa-viracito bhāṣya-pradīpôddyotaḥ; tatra caturtha-pañcamâdhyāya-vyākhyāna-bhūtaṃ caturtha-khaṇḍam; .... viṣama-sthala-ṭippaṇībhiḥ pāṭha-bhedâdi-saṃdarśanena ca saṃbhūṣya saṃskṛtam)* (Bombay: Nirnaya-Sagar Press). [Sanskrit introduction, pp. 1-6; list of vārttikas in the order of rules, pp. 425-50.]

1945 *Patañjali's Vyākaraṇa Mahābhāṣya with Kaiyaṭa's Pradīpa and Nāgeśa's Uddyota; vol. V* [adhyāya 6], *edited with foot-notes etc. (Śrīmad-bhagavat-patañjali-maharṣi-praṇītasya pāṇinīya-vyākaraṇa-mahā-bhāṣyasya ṣaṣṭho'dhyāyaḥ, sa ca ṛṣikalpôpādhyāya-kaiyaṭa-praṇītena mahā-bhāṣya-vyākhyānena pradīpena parivṛtaḥ sarva-tantra-svatantra-nāgojībhaṭṭa-kṛtena bhāṣya-pradīpa-vyākhyānenôddyotêty-anvartha-nāmadheyena samullāsitaś ca, prathamataḥ sthāne-vidhi-rūpaṃ pañcamaṃ khaṇḍam; .... viṣama-sthala-ṭippaṇyā pāṭha-bhedâdi-rūpeṇa ca saṃbhūṣya saṃskṛtam)* (Bombay: Nirnaya-Sagar Press). [Sanskrit introduction, pp. 1-18; list of vārttikas in the order of rules, pp. 373-92; list of śloka-vārttikas for the entire Mahā-bhāṣya, pp. 393-400; alphabetic list of sūtras discussed in this section, pp. 401-04.]

1951 *Śrīmad-bhagavat-patañjali-maharṣi-praṇīte vyākaraṇa-mahābhāṣye navâhnikam, aṣṭādhyāyī-prathamâdhyāya-prathama-pāda-vyākhyānam, śrīmad-upādhyāya-kaiyaṭa-nirmita-pradīpa-prakāśitam, sarva-tantra-svatantra-śrīman-nāgeśabhaṭṭa-viracitôddyotôdbhāsitam; .... ṭippaṇa-pāṭha-bhedâdi-pradarśana-puraskāreṇa pariṣkṛtam)*[5] [Patañjali's Vyākaraṇa Mahā-bhāṣya with Kaiyaṭa's Pradīpa and Nāgeśa's Uddyota; vol. 1: navāhnikam, first pāda of the first adhyāya, edited with foot-notes etc.[5]] (Bombay: Nirnaya-Sagar Press). [Map of Āryāvarta, facing p. 1 of introduction. Sanskrit introduction, pp. 1-24. Indices: sūtras, pp. 587-88; vārttikas, pp. 589-99, particular words, pp. 601-08.]

Joshi, Dayashankar Madhusudan

1969 *Pāṇini's taddhita affixation rules.* [University of Pennsylvania dissertation, unpublished.]

1971 "On expressing kārakas, a propos of Pāṇini 2.3.1", *IL* 32: 107-12.

1972 Review of Scharfe (1971a), *IL* 33: 94-97.

Joshi, Sadāśiva Śāstrī, (Ed.)

1939 *The Vaiyākaraṇa Bhūṣaṇasāra by M. M. Śrī Kauṇḍa Bhaṭṭa with the Darpaṇa commentary by Śrī Harivallabha, the Parīkṣā commentary by Bhairava Miśra and a short commentary by Śrī Kṛṣṇa Mitra with Tiṅ-artha-vāda-sāra by Śrī Khuddī Jhā Śarmā; edited with notes, introduction etc. (Mahāmahôpādhyāya-kauṇḍa-bhaṭṭa-viracitaḥ vaiyākaraṇa-bhūṣaṇa-sāraḥ śrī-harivallabha-viracita-darpaṇa-ṭīkayā mahāmahôpādhyāya-paṇḍita-śrī-bhairava-miśra-kṛtayā parīkṣā-ṭīkayā śrī-kṛṣṇa-mitra-kṛta-bhūṣana-vyākhyayā paṇḍita-śrī-khuddī-jhā-śarma-kṛta-tiṅ-artha-vāda-sāreṇa ca sahitaḥ)* (= *KSS* 133) (Benares: Chowkhamba). [Sanskrit introduction, pp. 1-6. Kṛṣṇa Mitra's commentary and the Tiṅ-artha-vāda-sāra printed separately, following the text with other commentaries, pp. 443-57, 548-68. Indices: authors and works referred to, facing p. 468; verses of the text, pp. 1-2, separately paginated.]

1946 *The Parama Laghu Mañjūṣā of Nāgeśa Bhaṭṭa with notes by M. M. Pt. Śrī Nityānanda Pant Parvatīya; edited with the Arthadīpikā commentary by Pandit Śrī Sadāśiva Śarmā Śāstrī*[2] *(Mahāmahôpādhyāya-p[aṇḍita]-śrī-nāgeśabhaṭṭa-kṛta-parama-laghu-mañjūṣā, mahāmahôpādhyāya-paṇḍita-śrī-nityânanda-panta-parvatīya-kṛta-ṭippaṇī-sahitā; sā ca jośīty-upāhva-paṇḍita-śrī-sadāśiva-śāstriṇā saṃśodhitā sva-kṛtârtha-dīpikâkhya-vyākhyayā ca saṃyojitā*[2]*)* (= *HSS* 43) (Benares: Chowkhamba).

Sadāśiva Śāstrī Joshi and Rāma Candra Jhā (Ed., commentators)

1960 *Śrī-varadarājâcārya-viracitā madhya-siddhānta-kaumudī "sudhā"-"indumatī"-saṃskṛta-hindī-vyākhyôpêtā* [Varadarāja's Madhya-siddhānta-kaumudī with the Sanskrit commentary Sudhā of

Sadāśiva Śāstrī Joshi and the Hindi commentary Indumatī of Rāma Candra Jhā] (= *HSS* 213) (Varanasi: Chowkhamba). [Sanskrit introduction by Sadāśiva Śāstrī Joshi, pp. 1-6. Indices: works and schools mentioned, p. 1; verses cited, pp. 1-2; following the main text.]

Joshi, Shivaram Dattatray

1960 *Kauṇḍabhaṭṭa on the meaning of Sanskrit verbs.* [Harvard University dissertation, unpublished.]

1962 "Verbs and nouns in Sanskrit", *IL* 23: 60-63.

1965 "Two methods of interpreting Pāṇini", *PCASS-A* 5. [Also in *JUP* 23 (1966): 53-61]

1966a "Patañjali's definition of a word – an interpretation", *BDCRI* 25: 65-70. [Reprint: S. D. Joshi (1969b).]

1966b "Adjectives and substantives as a single class in the 'parts of speech' ", *PCASS-A* 9. [Also in *JUP* 25 (1967): 19-30.]

1967 (Ed., tr.) *The Sphoṭanirṇaya (chapter xiv of the Vaiyākaraṇabhūṣaṇasāra) of Kauṇḍabhaṭṭa; edited with introduction, translation and critical and exegetical notes* (= *PCASS-C 2)* (Poona: University of Poona). [Introduction, pp. 1-91; translation and notes, pp. 113-230; bibliography, pp. 231-35; Sanskrit index, pp. 237-43.]

1968a (Ed., tr.) *Patañjali's Vyākaraṇa-mahābhāṣya samarthāhnika (P. 2.1.1.); edited with translation and explanatory notes* (= *PCASS-C* 3) (Poona: University of Poona). [Introduction, pp. i-xix. Translation and notes, pp. 1-208. Indices: Sanskrit words, pp. 211-19; English terms, pp. 220-23]

1968b "Word-integrity and syntactic analysis", *PCASS-A* 20. [Also in *JUP* 27 (1968): 165-73]

1969a (Ed., tr.) *Patañjali's Vyākaraṇa-mahābhāṣya avyayībhāvatatpuruṣāhnika (P. 2.1.2 - 2.1.49); edited with translation and explanatory notes by S. D. Joshi in collaboration with J. A. F. Roodbergen* (= *PCASS-C* 5) (Poona: University of Poona). [Introduction, pp. i-xxvii. Translation and notes, pp. 1-238. Indices: Sanskrit words, pp. 241-49; English terms, pp. 250-51. In addition to the text of the Mahā-bhāṣya, the Pradīpa and Uddyota are also printed and translated.]

1969b "Patañjali's definition of a word: an interpretation", *PICO* 27: 3: 94-95. [See also S. D. Joshi (1966a).]

1969c "Sentence structure according to Pāṇini", *Festschrift R. N. Dandekar,* pp. 14-26.

1971 "Dhātusambandhe pratyayāḥ (Pā. 3.4.1)" [Pāṇini's rule 3.4.1], *Festschrift Rajeshwar Shastri Dravid,* grammar section, pp. 48-50. [In Sanskrit.]

1974 "Pāṇini's treatment of kāraka-relations", *Festschrift Charudeva Shastri,* pp. 258-70.

Joshi, Shivram Dattatray, and J. A. F. Roodbergen (Ed., tr.)

1969 see S. D. Joshi (1969a)

1971 *Patañjali's Vyākaraṇa-mahābhāṣya karmadhārayāhnika (P. 2.1.51 - 2.1.72); edited with translation and explanatory notes* (= *PCASS-C* 6) (Poona: University of Poona). [Introduction, pp. i-xxviii. Translation and notes, pp. 1-258. Indices: Sanskrit words, pp. 259-71; English terms, p. 272. In addition to the text of the Mahā-bhāṣya, the Pradīpa is also printed and translated.]

1973 *Patañjali's Vyākaraṇa-mahābhāṣya tatpuruṣāhnika (P. 2.2.2 - 2.2.23); edited with translation and explanatory notes* (= *PCASS-C* 7) (Poona: University of Poona). [Introduction, pp. i-xxiv. Translation and notes, pp. 1-251. Indices: Sanskrit words, pp. 253-66, English terms, pp. 267-69. In addition to the text of the Mahā-bhāṣya, the Pradīpa is also printed and translated.]

forthcoming *Patañjali's Vyākaraṇa-mahābhāṣya kārakāhnika.* [Mentioned as forthcoming in S. D. Joshi (1974): 259, note 1.]

Joshi, Venkatesh Laxman

1957 "Does the root 'niñj' belong to the seventh conjugation? " *BDCRI* 18: 265-66. [Title and footnotes in English, text in Sanskrit.]

1964 *Prauḍha Manoramā with commentary Śabdaratna; appendices 1 - 3* (= *DCMS* 31-A) (Poona: Deccan College). [Separate issue of appendices 1 - 3 of V. L. Joshi (1966), with the pagination as given therein.]

1965 "Pāṇini and the Pāṇinīyas on saṃhitā", *Festschrift Sukumar Sen,* pp. 66-71. [Reprint: V. L. Joshi (1969).]

1966 (Ed.) *Prauḍha Manoramā with commentary Śabdaratna critically edited; volume 1* (= *DCMS* 31) (Poona: Deccan College). [Sanskrit introduction, pp. 3-110. Appendices: 1: citations in Vaidyanātha's Bhāvaprakāśa of noteworthy passages from Haridīkṣita, pp. 273-93; 2: other works of his own mentioned by the author of the Laghuśabdaratna, pp. 295-306; 3: refutations of the Śabdaratna in the Laghuśabdaratna, pp. 307-28; 4: technical terms, pp. 329-52 (part 1: Sanskrit explanations of Sanskrit terms, pp. 330-45; part 2: Sanskrit glosses of English terms, pp. 346-50); 5. 1: unavailable works and their authors mentioned in the Śabdaratna, pp. 355-56; 5. 2: works and authors mentioned in the Prauḍha-manoramā and Śabdaratna, pp. 356-61; 5. 3: principles mentioned in the Śabdaratna, pp. 362-64; 5. 4: graceful phrases used in the Śabdaratna, pp. 365-70; 5. 5: some particular final views, introductions, and technical terms in the Śabdaratna, pp. 371-72; 5. 6: alphabetic index of sūtras commented on, pp. 373-76. Appendices 1 - 3 were issued separately; see V. L. Joshi (1964).]

1969 "Pāṇini and the Pāṇinīyas on saṃhitā", *PICO* 26: 3: 96-98. [See also V. L. Joshi (1965).]

1971 "Treatment of loanwords in Sanskrit grammar", *IL* 32: 113-22.

Joshi, Vināyak Nārāyaṇ Shāstrī, and Wāsudev Laxmaṇ Paṇśikar (Ed.)

1928 *The Bhaṭṭikāvya of Bhaṭṭi with the commentary (Jayamaṅgalā) of Jayamaṅgala (Mahā-kavi-śrī-bhaṭṭi-viracitaṃ bhaṭṭi-kāvyam, jayamaṅgala-kṛta-ṭīkayā jayamaṅgalayā samêtam)*[7] (Bombay: Nirnaya-Sagar Press).

Kali Charan Shastri

1947 "Maitreya-rakṣita (a Bengali grammarian of the Pāṇinian system)", *Festschrift R. K. Mookerji*, pp. 887-903.

1956 "Maitreyarakṣita", *OH* 4: 89-98.

1957 "Sīradeva", *OH* 5: 103-17.

1972 *Bengal's contribution to Sanskrit grammar in the Pāṇinian and Cāndra systems; part one: general introduction* (= *CSCRS* 53) (Calcutta: Calcutta Sanskrit College).

Kalipada Mitra

1922 "About Buddhist nuns", *IA* 51: 225-27.

Kane, Pandurang Vaman

1909-14 "Bhāmaha, the Nyāsa and Māgha", *JBBRAS* 23: 91-95.

1930 *History of Dharmaśāstra (ancient and mediaeval religious and civil law in India), volume 1* (= *GovOS-B* 6) (Poona: BORI).

1941 *History of Dharmaśāstra (ancient and mediaeval religious and civil law in India), volume 2* (= *GovOS-B* 6) (Poona: BORI).

1942 "The meaning of *ācāryāḥ*", *ABORI* 23: 206-13.

1945 "The Mahābhāṣya and the bhāṣya of Śabara", *BhV* 6: 43-45.

1951 "Ancient cities and towns mentioned in the Mahābhāṣya", *JBBRAS*[2] 27: 38-42.

1961 *History of Indian poetics*[3] (Delhi: Motilal Banarsidass).

1962 *History of Dharmaśāstra (ancient and mediaeval religious and civil law in India), volume 5, part 2* (= *GovOS-B* 6) (Poona: BORI).

Kanitkar, Shrikrishna Shastri (Śrīkṛṣṇa Śāstrī)

1961-62 "Pāṇinīya-pluta-vimarśaḥ" [On Pāṇini's rules for extra-long vowels], *Medhā* 1.1/2: 90-104. [In Sanskrit] [Dandekar (1946-73): 3: 179, number 95.]

1962-63 "Pāṇinīyôpasarga-gatiḥ" [Pāṇini's rules concerning preverbs], *Medhā* 2.1/2: 85-118. [In Sanskrit] [*Prāci Jyoti* (1963-72) 2: 135.]

1963-65 "Pāṇinīyāḥ kāla-vācaka-śabdāḥ" [Pāṇinian terms denoting time], *Medhā* 3: 17-38. [In Sanskrit].

Kanjilal, Dileep Kumar

1955 "The picture of ancient India as revealed in Patañjali's Mahābhāṣya", *IHQ* 31: 375-82.

Kānta, Sūrya: see Sūrya Kānta.

Kapil Deva (Kapiladeva, Kapila Deo) Shastri

1961/2 *Saṃskṛta vyākaraṇa meṃ gaṇapāṭha kī paramparā aur ācārya Pāṇini (gaṇapāṭha meṃ eka tulanātmaka-adhyayana)* [The gaṇa-pāṭha tradition in Sanskrit grammar and Pāṇini (a comparative study concerning the gaṇa-pāṭha)] (Ajmer: Bhāratīya-Prācyavidyā-Pratiṣṭhāna saṃvat 2018). [Hindi version of the first chapter of Kapil Deva Shastri (1959) (see (1967a) with notes by Yudhiṣṭhira Mīmāṃsaka. Indices: pre-Pāṇinian gaṇas, pp. 169-71; Pāṇinian gaṇas, pp. 172-78; gaṇas referred to by Kātyāyana, pp. 179-80; post-Pāṇinian gaṇas, pp. 181-83; gaṇas the term for referring to which was changed by post-Pāṇinian grammarians, pp. 184-85; works referred to, pp. 186-88.]

1963 "Significance of the word *prakāra* in the sūtras of the Aṣṭādhyāyī", *VIJ* 1: 239-46.

1964a "Bhartṛhari kī dṛṣṭi meṃ aṣṭādhyāyī kā prakāra śabda" [The word *prakāra* in the Aṣṭādhyāyī according to Bhartṛhari], *NPP* 69: 302-15. [In Hindi] [*Prāci Jyoti* (1963-72) 4: 146-47.]

1964b "Bhartṛhari's discussion on sāmānādhikaraṇya", *ALB* 28: 41-54.

1964c "Bhartṛhari's discussion on the relation between upamāna and upameya in his Vākyapadīya", *Festschrift Baburam Saksena,* pp. 229-33.

1964d "Bhartṛhari on the relation between *upamāna* and *upameya*", *VIJ* 2: 87-92.

1965 "Upamāna, upameya and sāmānyavacana according to the Vākyapadīya of Bhartṛhari", *VIJ* 3: 19-28.

1966 " 'Catvāri vākparimitā padāni' ity atra bhartṛhariḥ" [Bhartṛhari on the verse *catvāri vāk-parimitā padāni*], *VS* 3: 144 - [In Sanskrit.]

1967a *The gaṇapāṭha ascribed to Pāṇini* (Kurukshetra: Kurukshetra

University). [Text of the gaṇas, with references to Pāṇinian and non-Pāṇinian texts, pp. 77-216. Appendix: words considered interpolations in gaṇas, pp. 217-60. Notes, pp. 261-390. Indices: 1: gaṇas, pp. 391-93; 2: gaṇa-sūtras (text), pp. 394-96; 3: gaṇa-sūtras (appendix), p. 397; 4: gaṇa-sūtras (notes), p. 398; 5: word index (text), pp. 399-444; 6: word index (appendices), pp. 445-74; 7: word index (notes), pp. 475-76. Originally a Banaras Hindu University dissertation, 1959, entitled *A critical edition of the gaṇapāṭha of Pāṇini;* see Kapil Deva Shastri (1961/2).]

1967b "Vaiyākaraṇānāṃ sphoṭa-vādaḥ" [The sphoṭa doctrine of the grammarians], *VS* 4: 40-51, 68. [In Sanskrit.]

1974 "On the authenticity of *Parama-laghu-mañjūṣā*", *Festschrift Charudeva Shastri,* pp. 299-304.

forthcoming A critical study of the Parama-laghu-mañjūṣā. [Announced as in the press by Kapil Deva Shastri (1974): 299, note 1]

Katre, Sadashiv Lakshmidhar

1938 "Kautsavyākaraṇa: a detailed notice", *NIA* 1: 383-96.

1948 "Harisvāmin the commentator of the Śatapatha-brāhmaṇa: a protégé of Vikramāditya the great of tradition, his date – c. 54 B. C.", *Festschrift K. M. Munshi,* pp. 325-40.

Katre, Sumitra Mangesh

1938-39 "Materials for a dhātupāṭha of Indo-Aryan, I - II", *IC* 4: 485-93, 5: 239-44.

1944 *Some problems of historical linguistics in Indo-Aryan* (= The Wilson Philological Lectures of 1941) (Bombay: University of Bombay). [Reprint: (= *DCBCSJS* 21) (Poona: Deccan College 1965).]

1967 *Pāṇinian studies I* (= *DCBCSJS* 52) (Poona: Deccan College). [Alphabetically arranged sūtras in transliteration, pp. 1-55; dhātu-pāṭha in transliteration, pp. 57-74; alphabetic list of roots in the dhātu-pāṭha, pp. 75-107.]

1968-69 *Pāṇinian studies II - IV: dictionary of Pāṇini,* 3 vol. (= *DCBCSJS* 53, 62, 63) (Poona: Deccan College).

1971 *Pāṇinian studies V - VII: dictionary of Pāṇini, gaṇapāṭha* (= *DCBCSJS* 72-74) (Poona: Deccan College).

Kaushi Ram

1971 *A study of Sanskrit uṇādi-sūtras.* [Delhi University dissertation, unpublished].

Kavi, Ramakrishna, M.: see Ramakrishna Kavi, M.

Kaviraj, Gopinath

1924 "The doctrine of pratibhā in Indian philosophy", *ABORI* 5: 1-18, 113-32. [Reprint: Gopinath Kaviraj (1966): 1-44].

1966 *Aspects of Indian thought* (Burdwan: University of Burdwan). [Collection of papers.]

Keith, A. Berriedale

1908 "Bhagavat and Kṛṣṇa", *JRAS* 1908: 847-48.

1914 (Tr.) *The Veda of the black yajus school entitled Taittirīya Saṃhitā, translated from the original Sanskrit prose and verse*, 2 vol. (= *HOS* 18-19) (Cambridge, Mass.: Harvard University Press). [Reprint: (Delhi: Motilal Banarsidass, 1967).]

1920a *A history of Sanskrit literature* (London: Oxford University Press). [Reprint: 1948].

1920b "The śaubhikas and the Indian drama", *BSOS* 1.4: 27-32.

1924 *The Sanskrit drama in its origin, development, theory and practice* (Oxford: Oxford University Press).

1936 "Pāṇini and the Veda", *IC* 2: 735-48.

1945 "Pāṇini's vocabulary", *Festschrift R. K. Mookerji*, pp. 343-45.

Kevalānandasaraswatī (Ed.)

1952-66 *Mīmāṃsākoṣaḥ*, 7 vol. (= *PPMGM* 357, 336, 272, 257, 162, 110, 132) (Wai: Prajna Pathasala Mandal).

Kharbas, Datta S. and Rama Nath Sharma

1974 *Sanskrit grammar: a bibliography of selected western language materials* (Rochester: Center for Asian Studies, University of Rochester).

Kharwandikar, D. K.

1973 *Haradatta: a critical study (with special reference to his Padamañjarī).* [University of Poona dissertation, unpublished.]

Kielhorn, Lorenz Franz

1866 (Ed., tr.) *Phiṭsūtrāṇi; Çāntanava's Phiṭsūtra, mit verschiedenen indischen Commentaren, Einleitung, Uebersetzung und Anmerkungen herausgegeben* (= *AKM* 4. 2) (Leipzig: Brockhaus). [Introduction, pp. 1-18. Translation and comments, pp. 19-54. Indices: of sūtras, pp. 55-56, of terms used in the sūtras, pp. 56-60. All after the text with commentaries.]

1868 (Ed.) *The Paribhāṣenduśekhara of Nāgojībhaṭṭa, edited and explained by F. Kielhorn; part I: the Sanskrit text and various readings* (= *BSPS* 2, 7) (Bombay: The Indu Prakash Press). [Revised edition: see K. V. Abhyankar (1962).]

1874a (Tr.) *The Paribhāṣenduśekhara of Nāgojībhaṭṭa, edited and explained by F. Kielhorn; part II: translation and notes*

(= *BSPS* 9, 12) (Bombay: Government Central Book Depot). [New edition: see K. V. Abhyankar (1960).]

1874b "The concluding verses of the second or Vākya-kāṇḍa of Bhartṛhari's Vākyapadīya", *IA* 3: 285-87. [Reprint: Rau (1969: 156-57).]

1875 "Note on Rājataranginī I 176", *IA* 4: 107-08. [Reprint: Rau (1969: 15057).]

1876a *Kātyāyana and Patañjali: their relation to each-other and to Pāṇini* (Bombay: The Educational Society). [Reprint: (Varanasi: Indological Book House 1963), (Osnabrück: Zeller 1965), Rau (1969: 1 - 64).]

1876b "Remarks on the śikshās", *IA* 5: 141-44, 193-200. [Reprint: Rau (1969: 158-69).]

1876c "On the Mahābhāshya", *IA* 5: 241-51. [Reprint: Rau (1969: 169-79).]

1878 "Aruṇad yavano madhyamikām", *IA* 7: 266-67. [Reprint: Rau (1969: 179).]

1880-85 (Ed.) *The Vyākaraṇa-mahābhāshya of Patañjali,* 3 vol. (= *BSPS* 18-22, 28-30) (Bombay, Government Central Press). [1: 1880, 2: 1883, 3: 1885; reprint: (Osnabrück: Zeller 1970).
2nd edition: 1: 1892, 2: 1906, 3: 1909. 3rd edition: see K. V. Abhyankar (1962-72). Preface to 1st edition: 1: 7-10, 2: 7-23, 3: 7-10. Variant readings: 1^1: 503-47, 2^1: 445-93, 3^1: 469-539. References are given to volumes, pages, and lines of the first edition; implicit reference is thereby made also to the third edition, the pagination of which is the same.]

1881 "On the Jainendra-vyākaraṇa", *IA* 10: 75-79. [Reprint: Rau (1969: 180-84).]

1883 "On the grammarian Bhartṛhari", *IA* 12: 226-27. [Reprint: Rau (1969: 185-86).]

1885a "Quotations in the Mahābhāshya and the Kāśikā-vritti", *IA* 14: 326-27. [Reprint: Rau (1969: 187-88).]

1885b "Der Grammatiker Pāṇini", *NGGW* 1885: 185-99. [Reprint: Rau (1969: 188-202): partial reprint: Staal (1972: 103-05).]

1885c "Prākṛtworte im Mahābhāshya", *ZDMG* 39: 327.

1886a "Indragomin and other grammarians", *IA* 15: 181-83. [Reprint: Rau (1969: 242-44).]

1886b "The Chāndra-vyākaraṇa and the Kāśikā-vritti", *IA* 15: 183-85. [Reprint: Rau (1969: 244-46).]

1886c "Notes on the Mahābhāshya; 1. āchāryadeśīya", *IA* 15: 80-81. [Reprint: Rau (1969: 202-03).]

1886d "Notes on the Mahābhāshya; 2. goṇikaputra and gonardīya", *IA* 15: 81-84. [Reprint: Rau (1969: 203-06).]

1886e "Notes on the Mahābhāshya; 3. on some doubtful vārttikas", *IA* 15: 203-11. [Reprint: Rau (1969: 206-14).]

1886f "Notes on the Mahābhāshya; 4. some suggestions regarding the verses (kārikās) in the Mahābhāshya", *IA* 15: 228-33. [Reprint: Rau (1969: 214-19).]

1886g Review of W. D. Whitney, *The roots, verb-forms, and primary derivatives of the Sanskrit language* (= *BIG* 2, Anhang 2) (Leipzig: Breitkopf und Härtel 1885), *IA* 15: 86-87. [Reprint: Rau (1969: 1042-43), Staal (1972: 150-51).]

1887a "The Maurya-passage in the Mahābhāshya (P. V, 3. 99)", *WZKM* 1: 8-12. [Reprint: Rau (1969: 251-55).]

1887b "On the grammar of Śākaṭāyana", *IA* 16: 24-28. [Reprint: Rau (1969: 246-50).]

1887c "Notes on the Mahābhāshya; 5. the authorities on grammar quoted in the Mahābhāshya", *IA* 16: 101-06. [Reprint: Rau (1969: 220-25), Staal (1972: 107-14).]

1887d "Notes on the Mahābhāshya; 6. the text of Pānini's sūtras, as given in the Kāśika-vritti, compared with the text as known to Kātyāyana and Patañjali", *IA* 16: 178-84. [Reprint: Rau (1969: 226-32), Staal (1972: 115-23).]

1887e "Notes on the Mahābhāshya; 7. some devices of Indian grammarians", *IA* 16: 244-52. [Reprint: Rau (1969: 233-41), Staal (1972: 123-34).]

1888 "Scheinbare Citate von Autoritäten in grammatischen Werken", *Festschrift Böhtlingk,* pp. 52-53. [Reprint: Rau (1969: 256-57).]

1891 "Die Colebrooke'schen Pāṇini-Handschriften der Kgl. Bibliothek zu Göttingen", *NGGW* 1891: 101-12. [Reprint: Rau (1969: 921-31).]

1894 "Die Śākaṭāyana-Grammatik", *NGGW* 1894: 1-14. [Reprint: Rau (1969: 276-89). Pp. 2-9: concordance of Śākaṭāyana 2. 4. 128-239 with Pāṇini's and Hemacandra's rules; see Birwé (1971).]

1896 "Pāṇini i, 3, 11 *svaritenādhikāraḥ*", *Festschrift Weber,* pp. 29-32. [Reprint: Rau (1969): 290-93).]

1898 "The Jātakas and Sanskrit grammarians", *JRAS* 1898: 17-21. [Reprint: Rau (1969: 294-98).]

1903 "Epigraphic notes; 10. The Jarta conquered the Hūṇas", *NGGW* 1903: 305-07. [Reprint: Rau (1969: 421-23).]

1906 "Epigraphic notes; 19. Vasantagaḍh inscription of Varmalāta of the [Vikrama] year 682; and the age of the poet Māgha", *NGGW* 1906: 143-46. [Reprint: Rau (1969: 428-31).]

1908a "On Śiśupālavadha II 112", *JRAS* 1908: 499-502. [Reprint: Rau (1969: 1017-20).]

1908b "Bhagavat, tatrabhagavat, and devānāṃpriya", *JRAS* 1908: 502-05. [Reprint: Rau (1969: 1020-23).]

Kleine Schriften: see Rau (1969).

Kiparsky, Paul and J. F. Staal

1969 "Syntactic and semantic relations in Pāṇini", *FL* 5: 83-117.

Kittel, Ferdinand

1893 "Dravidische Elemente in den Sanskrit-Dhātupāṭhas", *Festschrift Roth,* pp. 21-24.

1895 "On some Sanskrit verbs", *IA* 24: 81-82.

Knauer, Friedrich

1888 "Zu *iti* und *ca*", *Festschrift Böhtlingk,* pp. 62-67.

Kongress

1957 *Akten des vierundzwanzigsten internationalen Orientalisten-Kongresses* (28. August bis 4. September 1957) (Ed.: H. Franke) (Wiesbaden: Steiner).

1968 *Verhandlungen des zweiten internationalen Dialektologenkongresses* (Ed.: L. E. Schmitt) (= *ZMF,* Beihefte, NF. 4) (Wiesbaden: Steiner).

Konks, I., P. Numerkund, L. Mäll (Ed.)

1973 *Oriental studies II. 2* (= *ACUT*) (Tartu: Tartu University).

Konow, Sten

1923 "Some problems raised by the Kharavela inscription", *AO* 1: 12-42.

1935 "Notes on the Sakas", *IC* 2: 189-98.

1936 "Professor Poussin on śakayavanam", *IC* 3: 1-7. [See de la Vallée Poussin (1936).]

1937-38 "Future forms denoting past time in Sanskrit and Prakrit", *NTS* 9: 231-39.

1943 "The authorship of the Śivasūtras", *AO* 19: 291-328.

Koparkar, D. G. (Ed.)

1952 *Liṅgānuśāsana of Durgasiṃha, critically edited* (= *SIAL* 10) (Poona: Deccan College).

Kotulkar, Mahadeva Vinayaka (Mahādeva Vināyaka Kotuḷkara)

1967 "Arthavad adhātur apratyayaḥ prātipadikam" [Pāṇini's rule 1.2.45], *SBh* 5: 56-58. [In Sanskrit.]

Krishnamacharya, V.

1946 (Ed., commentator) *Sphoṭavāda by Nāgeśa Bhaṭṭa; edited by*

Vyākaraṇaśiromaṇi V. Krishnamacharya with his own commentary Subodhinī (Sphoṭa-vādaḥ nāgeśabhaṭṭa-kṛtaḥ) (= *ALS* 55) (Madras: The Adyar Library). [Sanskrit introduction, pp. 1-31. Indices: 1: citations, pp. 105-12, 2: sources, pp. 113-14.]

1962 (Ed.) *Laghûpasarga-vṛttiḥ, ALB* 26: 81-90.

1973 "Ghisaṃjñāvicāre navaprācīnamatabhedaḥ" [Differences of opinion among ancient and later commentators concerning the technical term *ghi*], *Festschrift Charudeva Shastri,* pp. 102-03. [In Sanskrit.]

Krishnamurti Sarma, B. N.

1932 "Indra and Pāṇini", *IHQ* 8: 380.

Krishnaswami Ayyangar

1971 "Pāṇinīya vyākaraṇa kā vivecana: viṣayapraveśa" [A study of Pāṇini's grammar: introduction to the subject], *Gaveṣaṇā* (Agra) 9.18, part 2: 1-49. [In Hindi.]

Krishnaswami Iyangar, V.

1972 "Kathaṃ vyutpattir vaktavyā" [How is the derivation of nouns to be stated?], *SVUOJ* 15, Sanskrit section, pp. 7-18. [In Sanskrit.]

Kudāla, Śivadatta D. (Ed.)

1912 *Patañjali's Vyākaraṇa Mahābhāshya with Kaiyaṭa's Pradīpa and Nāgeśa's Uddyota; edited with foot-notes, collected from Padamañjarī and Prātiśākhyas as well as supplied by the editor's own originality; vol. 2 (vidhiśesharūpam)* [adhyāyas 1. 2 - 2] *(Śrīmad-bhagavat-patañjali-muni-nirmitaṃ pāṇinīya-vyākaraṇa-mahā-bhāṣyam, etad-vyākhyāna-bhūta upādhyāya-kaiyaṭa-praṇīto bhāṣya-pradīpaḥ, etad-vyākhyāna-bhūto nāgeśabhaṭṭa-viracito bhāṣya-pradīpôddyotaḥ; tatra prathamâdhyāya-dvitīya-pādâdi-dvitīyâdhyāya-paryantaṃ vidhi-śeṣa-rūpaṃ dvitīya-khaṇḍam; ...... pada-mañjarī-prātiśākhyâdikaṃ prātibhaṃ saṃdarbhaṃ ca samavalambya ṭippaṇyā pāṭha-bheda-yojanena ca pariṣkṛtam)* (Bombay: Nirnaya-Sagar Press).

Kuiper, F. B. J.

1965 Review of Bhawe (1957-62), *IIJ* 8: 245-47.

Kulkarni, E. D.

1943a "Unpāṇinian forms and usages in the critical edition of the Mahābhārata; 1. indiscriminate use of *mā* and *na*", *ABORI* 24: 83-93.

1943b "Unpāṇinian forms and usages in the critical edition of the Mahābhārata; 2. participles", *BDCRI* 4: 227-45.

1943c "Unpāṇinian forms and usages in the critical edition of the Mahābhārata; 3. non-finite forms", *NIA* 6: 130-39.

1943-44 "Unpāṇinian forms and usages in the critical edition of the Mahābhārata; 4. sandhi", *Festschrift Sukthankar*, pp. 13-33.

1950-51 "Unpāṇinian forms and usages in the critical edition of the Mahābhārata; 5. the use of *sma*", *BDCRI* 11: 361-78. [Study 6: see V. D. Gokhale (1956-57).]

Kunhan Raja, C.

1936 "I-Tsing and Bhartṛhari's Vākyapadīya", *Festschrift Krishnaswami Aiyangar*, pp. 285-98.

1947 *Descriptive catalogue of Sanskrit manuscripts in the Adyar Library; volume VI: grammar, prosody and lexicography* (= *ALS* 60) (Madras: The Adyar Library).

1957 "The śiva sūtras of Pāṇini (an analysis)", *AOR* 13: 65-81.

Kunjunni Raja (Rajah), K.

1950 "Prabhāvali (a rare work dealing with Sanskrit roots)", *JOR* 19: 289-90.

1951 "The date of Nārāyaṇa Bhaṭṭa", *PAIOC* 13 (Nagpur, 1946): 183-86.

1954 "The theory of meaning according to the Buddhist logicians", *ALB* 18: 178-95.

1955a "The theory of suggestion in Indian semantics", *ALB* 19: 20-26.

1955b "Indian theories on homophones and homonyms", *ALB* 19: 193-222.

1956a (Ed.) *Uṇādikośa of Mahādeva Vedāntin, edited with the uṇādi sūtras and full glossarial index (Uṇādikośaḥ vedānti-mahādeva-viracitaḥ)* (= *MUSS* 21) (Madras: University of Madras). [Glossarial index of words with their derivations and meanings, pp. 121 - 260.]

1956b "Sphoṭa: The theory of linguistic symbols", *ALB* 20: 84-116.

1956c "Transfer of meaning – a Buddhist view", *ALB* 20: 345-48.

1957a "Ākāṅkṣā: the main basis of syntactic unity", *ALB* 21: 282-95.

1957b "Yāska's definition of the 'verb' and the 'noun' in the light of Bhartṛhari's explanation", *AOR* 13: 86-88.

1957c "Diachronic linguistics in ancient India", *JMU* 29: 127-30.

1958a "The elliptic sentence – Indian theories", *ALB* 22: 25-31.

1958b "The Indian influence on linguistics", *JMU* 30: 93-111.

1961 "Tātparya as a separate vṛtti", *PAIOC* 20 (Bhubaneshwar, 1959): 319-32.

1962 "Prārthayanti – a ghost word discussed by the grammarians", *ALB* 26: 26-28.

1964 "Bhartṛhari's list of sentence definitions", *ALB* 28: 206-10.

1965 "Pāṇini's attitude towards lakṣaṇā", *ALB* 29: 177-87.

1969 *Indian theories of meaning*² (= *ALS* 91) (Madras: The Adyar Library). [First edition: (Madras: The Adyar Library 1963). Bibliography, pp. 317-46; additional bibliography (added to the second edition), pp. 347-54.]

1972 (Ed.) *Uṇādimaṇidīpikā of Rāmabhadra Dīkṣita* (Madras: University of Madras). [Text through the second pāda. Variant readings and corrections, pp. 115-20. Indices: words, pp. 121-30; names of persons and places, p. 131; works, p. 132. Originally published serially, 1966-71: *AOR* 21: 1-24, 22.1: 25-48, 22.2: 49-64, 23.1: 65-80, 23.2: 81-88].

Laddu, Sureshachandra Dnyaneshwar

1964 "Pāṇini and the 'akālakaṁ vyākaraṇam' ", *Festschrift Baburam Saksena,* pp. 187-99. [Reprint: S. D. Laddu (1969b).]

1966 "Kātyāyana's vārttika on Pāṇini 3.1.133 and its bearing on the text of the Mahābhāṣya", *VIJ* 4: 14-18.

1967a "A possible light on the relative age of Yāska and Patañjali", *VIJ* 5: 58-62.

1967b "A pre-Patañjalian grammatical observation", *IA*³ 2.4: 40-41.

1967c *Evolution of the Sanskrit language from Pāṇini to Patañjali with reference to the primary formations.* [University of Poona dissertation, unpublished.]

1968 "The sphere of reference of the technical term *tṛjādi* according to Kātyāyana and Patañjali", *PCASS-A* 23. [Also in *JUP* 29 (1969): 1-10.]

1969a "The laukika, vaidika and yājñika accentuation with the munitraya of Sanskrit grammar", *Festschrift R. N. Dandekar,* pp. 93-111.

1969b "Pāṇini and the 'akālakaṁ vyākaraṇam' ", *PICO* 26: 3: 99-104. [See S. D. Laddu (1964).]

1970 "Authorship of a vārttika from the Mahābhāṣya", *PCASS-A* 38. [Also in *JUP* 33 (1971): 13-22.]

1971a "Ancient Sanskrit grammarians and the literary records", *VIJ* 9: 315-22.

1971b "Vedic forms and Pāṇini – a glance", *Festschrift Rajeshwar Shastri Dravid,* English section, pp. 54-68.

1972 "The device of contiguity as a key to interpreting Pāṇini's rules", *CASS-St.* 1: 157-71.

Lahiri, Prabodh Chandra

1935 *Concordance Pāṇini – Patañjali (Mahābhāṣya)* (= *IndF* 10) (Breslau: Marcus). [See Birwé (1966).]

Lakshman Rao, K. V.
1921 "Did Pāṇini know Buddhist nuns? ", *IA* 50: 82-84.

Lévi, Sylvain
1890 "Notes sur l'Inde à l'époque d'Alexandre; I. Le roi Taxile", *JAs* 1890: 234-36.
1891 "Notes de chronologie indienne; *devānāṃpriya;* Aśoka et Katyayana", *JAs* 1891: 549-53.
1903 "Notes chinoises sur l'Inde; III. La date de Candragomin", *BEFEO* 3: 38-53.
1906-08 "Des préverbes chez Pāṇini (sūtra I, 4, 80-82)", *MSL* 14: 276-78.
1925 "Gonarda, le berceau du Gonardīya", *Festschrift Asutosh Mukherjee,* 3. 2, pp. 197-205.

Liebich, Bruno
1886-87 "Die Kasuslehre der indischen Grammatiker verglichen mit dem Gebrauch der Kasus im Aitareya-Brāhmaṇa (ein Beitrag zur Syntax der Sanskrit-Sprache)", *BB* 10: 205-34, 11: 274-315. [I have modernised the spelling.]
1891 *Pāṇini; ein Beitrag zur Kenntnis der indischen Literatur und Grammatik* (Leipzig: Haessel). [Reprint of chapter 5: Staal (1972: 159-65).]
1892 *Zwei Kapitel der Kāśikā, übersetzt und mit Einleitung versehen* (Breslau: Preuss und Jünger). [Translation of the Kāśikā on rules of adhyāyas 2.1 - 2.2; introduction, pp. i-xxxx.]
1899 "Das Datum des Candragomin", *WZKM* 13: 308-15.
1902 *Cāndra-vyākaraṇa; die Grammatik des Candragomin; Sūtra, Uṇādi, Dhātupāṭha* (= *AKM* 11.4) (Leipzig: Brockhaus).
1919a *Zur Einführung in die indische einheimische Sprachwissenschaft: 1: Das Kātantra* (= *SHAW* 1919.4) (Heidelberg: Winter).
1919b *Zur Einführung in die indische einheimische Sprachwissenschaft: 2: Historische Einführung und Dhātuṗāṭha* (= *SHAW* 1919.15) (Heidelberg: Winter).
1920a *Zur Einführung in die indische einheimische Sprachwissenschaft: 3: Der Dhātupāṭha* (= *SHAW* 1920.10) (Heidelberg: Winter). [Edition of the dhātu-pāṭha, pp. 5-26; survey of markers used with roots, with lists of roots with particular markers, pp. 29-56; index of roots, pp. 63-86.]
1920b *Zur Einführung in die indische einheimische Sprachwissenschaft: 4: Analyse der Candra-Vṛtti* (= *SHAW* 1920.13) (Heidelberg: Winter).
1921 *Materialien zum Dhātupāṭha* (= *SHAW* 1921.7) (Heidelberg:

Winter). [I: verb roots which are given together with their meanings in the Nighaṇṭus and Nirukta, compared with the teachings of grammarians, pp. 4-14; II: roots of the dhātu-pāṭha arranged according to their meanings, pp. 15-30; III: roots which take parasmaipada endings, ātmanepada endings, and both sets, according to Pāṇini and Candra, pp. 30-56.]

1923 "Über den sphoṭa (ein Kapitel über die Sprachphilosophie der Inder)", *ZDMG* 77: 208-19.

1928 *Konkordanz Pāṇini – Candra* (= *IndF* 6) (Breslau: Marcus). [Introduction, pp. 1-8; also includes Candra's paribhāṣās, pp. 49-52.]

1930 *Kṣīrataraṅgiṇī, Kṣīrasvāmin's Kommentar zu Pāṇini's Dhātupāṭha, zum ersten Mal herausgegeben; mit fünf Anhängen* (= *IndF* Doppelheft 8/9) (Breslau: Marcus). [Text, pp. 1-201. Introduction: Kṣīrasvāmin's date, pp. 201-04. Appendix I: (a) authors and works cited, pp. 205-07, (b) undetermined citations, pp. 207-10; introduction to appendix I: Kṣīrasvāmin's dhātu-pāṭha, pp. 210-15. Appendix II: Śarvavarman's dhātu-pāṭha, Tibetan text, pp. 216-32; introduction to appendix II: Kṣīrasvāmin's dhātu-pāṭha, continuation, pp. 232-47. Appendix III: Śākaṭāyana's dhātu-pāṭha, pp. 248-64; introduction to appendix III: evidence for dating the Mahābhāṣya, I-Tsing's evidence on Bhartṛhari's date, pp. 264-89. Appendix IV: synopsis of the seven oldest dhātu-pāṭhas, pp. 290-359; introduction to appendix IV: Maitreya-rakṣita's date, pp. 360-65. Appendix V: alphabetic index of roots, pp. 366-79.]

Limaye, S. K.

1966 "On the meaning of *sukeśī rathyā*", *NUJ* 17.1: 18-20. [*Prācī Jyoti* (1963-1972) 5: 144-45.]

Limaye, V. P.

1964-65 "Additions and corrections to Sarup's edition of the commentaries on Yāska's Nirukta", *VIJ* 2: 221-38; 3: 29-56, 205-38.

1966a "Necessity for new vārttikas to Pāṇini 1.1.27 and 5.2.39", *VIJ* 4: 5-13.

1966b "Dhyānagraha-kāra or Dhyāna-kāra: a pre-Bhartṛhari grammarian", *VIJ* 4: 228-29.

1967a "Pāṇini 6.1.121: *avapathāsi ca* or *apavathāsi ca*? ", *VIJ* 5: 193-95.

1967b "The basis of Pāṇini (8.1.59 and 65) in *Ṛgveda*", *Festschrift Gopinath Kaviraj*, pp. 282-88.

1974 *Critical studies on the Mahābhāṣya* (= *VIS* 49) (Hoshiarpur: Vishveshvaranand Vedic Research Institute). [Treatment of Mahā-bhāṣya passages, distributed among three sections (pp. 1-146, 147-425, 456-778, supplement, pp. 779-98), following the order of Kielhorn's edition (Kielhorn [1880 - 85]); index of Mahā-bhāṣya lines discussed or referred to: pp. xi-xxxii, preceding text. Indices and appendices: I: author index, pp. 801-06; II: text index, pp. 807-901; III: word index, pp. 902-20; IV: untraced quotations, pp. 921-32; V: subject index: A. textuo-linguistic criticism, pp. 933-37; B. linguistics, pp. 937-39; C. literature, pp. 939-41; D. Society and culture, pp. 941-42; E. history, pp. 942-43; F. Geography, p. 943. Indices compiled by S. D. Laddu.]

Lüders, Heinrich

1894 *Die Vyāsa-śikshā besonders in ihrem Verhältnis zum Taittirīya-Prātiśākhya* (Göttingen: Dieterich).

1916 "Die Śaubhikas, ein Beitrag zur Geschichte des indischen Dramas", *SBAW* 1916: 698-373. [Reprint: Lüders (1940: 391-428).]

1919 "Die śākischen Mūra", *SBAW* 1919: 734-66. [Reprint: Lüders (1940: 463-93).]

1940 *Philologica indica; ausgewählte kleine Schriften von Heinrich Lüders; Festgabe zum siebzigsten Geburtstag am 25. Juni dargebracht von Kollegen, Freunden und Schülern* (Göttingen: Vandenhoeck und Ruprecht).

Ludwig, Alfred

1893 "Jīvikārthe cāpaṇye (Pāṇ. 5, 3, 99)", *Festschrift Roth*, pp. 57-60.

Madhava Krishna Sarma, K.

1940a "Bhartṛhari not a Buddhist: evidence from nearer home", *PO* 5: 1-5.

1940b "Śabdadhātusamīkṣā: a lost work of Bhartṛhari", *ASVOI* 1.3: 65-70.

1940c "Bhartṛhari: a great post-Upanishadic intuitionist", *AP* 11: 538-39.

1940d "Patañjali a lakṣyaika-cakṣus: his lofty realism", *JOR* 14: 204-09. [Included in K. Madhava Krishna Sarma (1968): 113-18.]

1940e "Technical terms in the Aṣṭādhyāyī", *JOR* 14: 259-67. [Included in K. Madhava Krishna Sarma (1968): 15-23.]

1940f " 'Pacati bhavati' and 'bhaved api bhavet' in the Mahābhāṣya" *IC* 7: 83-91.

1940-41 "Kātyāyana", *PO* 5: 126-32, 6: 74-92. [Included in K. Madhava Krishna Sarma (1968): 46-77.]

1941a "Authorship of the uṇādi sūtras", *Festschrift P. V. Kane,* pp. 395-404.

1941b "Some problems in Pāṇini", *JMU* 13: 203-25. [Included in K. Madhava Krishna Sarma (1968), as follows: *"Its (anubandhas)"*, pp. 203-11 = 1968: 24-31; "The authorship of the *akṣarasamāmnāya*", pp. 211-21 = 1968: 32-41; "The general scheme of the Aṣṭādhyāyī", pp. 222-25 = 1968: 42-45.]

1941-42 "The Pāṇinian school and the prātiśākhyas: post-Pāṇinian reciprocity of influence", *BhV* 2: 230-38, 4: 85-94.

1942 "Gleanings from the commentaries on the Vākyapadīya", *ABORI* 23: 405-12.

1943a "Helārāja, not a disciple of Bhartṛhari", *IHQ* 19: 79-82.

1943b "Vāk before Bhartṛhari", *PO* 8: 21-36.

1944-45 "Patañjali and his relation to some authors and works", *IC* 11: 75-83.

1945-59 "Patañjali and linguistic change", *QJMS* 35: 135-42, 49: 263-70

1968 *Pāṇini, Kātyāyana and Patañjali* (= *SVPM* 4) (Delhi: Shri Lal Bahadur Shastri Rashtriya Sanskrit Vidyapeeth). [Originally a master's degree thesis, Madras University, the precise date of which I cannot verify; see K. Madhava Krishna Sarma (1940d), (1940e), 1941b).]

Madhukānta Śarmā Jhā

1950 *Mahābhāṣya-prakāśaḥ* (= *HSS* 199) (Varanasi: Chowkhamba).

Madhusūdana Prasāda Mishra (Ed., commentator)

1967 *Vyākaraṇa-mahābhāṣya of maharṣi-Patañjali with the 'Pradīpa' Sanskrit commentary by Kaiyaṭa upādhyāya edited with the 'Prakāśa' Hindi commentary by Ācharya Madhusūdana Prasāda Mishra (Śrīmad-bhagavat-patañjali-muni-viracitaṃ vyākaraṇa-mahā-bhāṣyam śrīmad-upādhyāya-kaiyaṭa-nirmita-'pradīpa'-prakāśitam ācārya-madhusūdana-prakāśa-miśra praṇītayā 'prakāśa'-hindī-vyākhyayôpêtam)* (= *VBSGM* 138) (Varanasi: Chowkhamba). [Foreword by Yudhiṣṭhira Mīmāṃsaka, pp. 1-27; text and commentary through the fifth āhnika.]

Mahā-bhāṣya of Patañjali

1967 *Śrīmad-bhagavat-patañjali-maharṣi-praṇīte vyākaraṇa-mahābhāṣye prathamaḥ khaṇḍaḥ, ... dvitīyaḥ khaṇḍaḥ, ... tṛtīyaḥ khaṇḍaḥ* [Patañjali's Vyākaraṇa-mahā-bhāṣya, volume 1, 2, 3] (Delhi: Motilal Banarsidass). [Anonymous edition; volumes 1.1, 1.2, 2 are reprints of the Nirnaya-Sagar Press edition (see Bhārgavaśāstrī Joshi (1942), (1945), (1951), Raghunātha Śarmā – Śivadatta Kudāla (1937), Śivadatta Kudāla (1912)), excluding the introductions, footnotes, and indices; volume 3 is a reprint of the fifth volume of the Rohatak edition (see Vedavrata [1962-63]) without the index.]

Mahādeva Śāstrī and K. Rangācarya (ed.)

1894-1903 *The Dhātu Vṛtti of Mādhavāchārya,* 2 vol. in 4 parts (= *GovOS* Bibliotheca Sanskritica 23, 24, 3, 31) (Mysore: Government Branch Press). [vol. 1.1: 1900, 1.2: 1901, 2.1: (Ed.: Mahādeva Śāstrī) 1894, 2.2: 1903]

Mahesh Dutt Sharma (Maheśadatta Śarmā)

1969/70 "Kāśikāyāṃ pāṇinīyêtara-vyākaraṇānāṃ prabhāvaḥ" [Influence of non-Pāṇinian grammars on the Kāśikā, *Sāg.* 8.3: 1-21 (saṃvat 2026) [In Sanskrit.]

1971a "Kāśikā-siddhānta-kaumudyor vedavacanāni" [Vedic rules in the Kāśikā and the Siddhānta-kaumudī, *Sāg.* 10.2: 135-43 (saṃvat 2028) [In Sanskrit.]

1971b "A note on the Siddhāntakaumudī 2882 and 2940 (Pāṇ. vii. 3. 66, iii. 2. 26)", *MO* 4: 35-37. [Reprint: Mahesh Dutt Sharma (1972).]

1971c "Mahābhāṣyôttara-varti-vyākaraṇa-grantheṣu laukikôdāharaṇānāṃ sthitiḥ" [The position of examples from normal usage in post-Mahābhāṣya grammatical works], *Festschrift Rajeshwar Shastri Dravid,* grammar section, pp. 51-64. [In Sanskrit.]

1972 "A note on the Siddhāntakaumudī (Pāṇ. vii 3. 66 and Pāṇ. iii. 2. 26)", *PAIOC* 25 (Calcutta, 1969): 317-19. [See Mahesh Dutt Sharma (1971b).]

Mānavallī, Rāmaśāstrī – Nārāyaṇa Śāstrī Bhāradvāja (Ed.)

1887 *Laghu-śabdêndu-śekharaḥ, nānā-vidha-grantha-nirmāṇa-dhurīṇa-mahāmahôpādhyāya-śrīman-nāgeśabhaṭṭa-viracitaḥ* [Nāgeśabhaṭṭa's Laghu-śabdêndu-śekhara] (Benares: Medical Hall Press).

Mangala (Mangal) Deva Shastri

1927 "The relation of Paṇini's technical devices to his predecessors", *PAIOC* 4 (Allahabad, 1926): 465-74.

1937 (tr.) *The Ṛgveda-prātiśākhya with the commentary of Uvaṭa, edited from original manuscripts, with introduction, critical and additional notes, English translation of the text, and several appendices; volume 3: English translation of the text, additional notes, several appendices and indices* (Lahore: Motilal Banarsidass). [Appendix III: a comparison of the Ṛgveda-prātiśākhya with the Pāṇinian grammar, pp. 329-44.]

1947 "The traditional basis of the udāharaṇas in the Kāśikā and the Mahābhāṣya and the mutual relation of the two works regarding the same", *PAIOC* 12 (Banaras, 1943 - 4): 333-39.

Maṅghārāma Dviveda

1971 "Pāṇinīya-vyākaraṇasya viśeṣatvam" [The particularity of Pāṇini's grammar], *Festschrift Rajeshwar Shastri Dravid,* grammar section, pp. 8-16. [In Sanskrit.]

Mārulkara, Śaṅkara Śāstrī (Ed., commentator)

1938 *Vyākaraṇa-mahā-bhāṣyam; (tatrâṅgâdhikāraḥ) nāgojībhaṭṭa-viracitôddyota-samalaṅkṛta-kaiyaṭôpādhyāya-kṛta-pradīpa-samudbhāsitam; ṣaṣṭhâdhyāya-stha-caturtha-pādam ārabhya saptamâdhyāya-gata-dvitīya-pāda-stha-prathamâhnikântaḥ prathamo bhāgaḥ; ...... saptamâdhyāya-gata-dvitīya-pāda-stha-dvitīyâhnikam ārabhya saptamâdhyāyânto dvitīyo bhāgaḥ* [Vyākaraṇa-mahā-bhāṣya (Aṅga section), with Kaiyaṭa's Pradīpa and Nāgojībhaṭṭa's Uddyota; part 1: from the fourth pāda of the sixth adhyāya to the first āhnika of the seventh adhyāya, second pāda (6.4.1 - 7.2.35); part 2: from the second āhnika of the seventh adhyāya, second pāda, to the end of the seventh adhyāya (7.2.36 - 7.4.93)], 2 vol. (= *ASS* 108) (Poona: Ānandāśrama).

1957 *Mārulkarôpāhva-śaṅkara-śāstri-praṇīta-śāṅkarī-vyākhyā-saṃvalitaḥ śrīmad-bhaṭṭojī-dīkṣita-viracita-vaiyākaraṇa-siddhānta-kārikā-vyākhyāna-bhūtaḥ śrī-kauṇḍabhaṭṭa-viracitaḥ vaiyākaraṇa-bhūṣaṇa-sāraḥ* [Kauṇḍabhaṭṭa's Vaiyākaraṇa-bhūṣaṇa-sāra, a commentary on Bhaṭṭoji Dīkṣita's Vaiyākaraṇa-siddhānta-kārikās, with the commentary Śāṅkarī of Śaṅkara Śāstrī Mārulkara] (= *ASS* 135) (Poona: Ānandāśrama). [Sanskrit introduction by K. V. Abhyankar, pp. 1-13.]

Matilal, Bimal Krishna

1960 "The doctrine of *karaṇa* in grammar and logic", *JGJRI* 17: 63-69. [See also Matilal (1961).]

1961 "The doctrine of *karaṇa* in grammar and logic", *PAIOC* 20 (Bhubaneshwar, 1959): 303-08. [See Matilal (1960).]

1966 "Indian theorists on the nature of the sentence *(vākya)*", *FL* 2: 377-93.

1971 *Epistemology, logic and grammar in Indian philosophical analysis* (The Hague - Paris: Mouton).

1973 "The notion of substance and quality in ancient Indian grammar", in: Konks - Numerkund - Mäll (1973), pp. 384-405.

Mazumdar, B. C.
1910 "Vāsudeva of Pāṇini", *JRAS* 1910: 170-71.
1925 "Some observations on Puṣyamitra and his empire", *IHQ* 1: 91-94, 214-19. [Incomplete; the remainder unavailable to me].

Mehendale, Madhukar Anant
1957 "Nirukta notes, I: *tṛca*", *Festschrift P. C. Bagchi*, pp. 46-50. [Reprint: Mehendale (1965a: 1-7).]
1960 "Nirukta notes, IV: Yāska's etymology of *daṇḍa*", *JAOS* 80: 112-15. [Reprint: Mehendale (1965a: 22-30).]
1965a *Nirukta notes, series I* (= *DCBCSJS* 24) (Poona: Deccan College)
1965b "Nirukta notes, XI: *ardhanāma*", *Festschrift Sukumar Sen*, pp. 203-06.
1967 "Nirukta notes, XII: *vibhakti*", *Festschrift Gopinath Kaviraj*, pp. 17-19.
1968 *Some aspects of Indo-Aryan linguistics* (= The Wilson Philological Lectures for 1963-64) (Bombay: University of Bombay).

Millonig, Harald
1969 *Stumme Laute: Untersuchung einer Beschreibungstechnik altindischer Linguistik.* [Dissertation, Würzburg, unpublished].
1973 Review of Cardona (1969), *ZDMG* 123: 424-27.

Mīmāṃsaka, Yudhiṣṭhira: see Yudhiṣṭhira Mīmāṃsaka.

Mirashi, V. V.
1928 *Laghu-Siddhāntakaumudī, part I (comprising sections on saṃjñās, sandhis, kṛit affixes, senses of case-affixes and compounds; edited with an original Sanskrit commentary, English translation, copious critical and explanatory notes and appendices* [Reprint: (Delhi: Motilal Banarsidass 1967); notes, pp. 105-77; glossary of select technical terms, pp. 180-90.]

Mishra, Avadh Bihari: see Avadh Bihari Mishra.

Mishra, Madhusūdana Prakāśa: see Madhusūdana Prakāśa Mishra.

Mishra, Vedpati: see Vedpati Mishra.

Mishra, Vidhata: see Vidhata Mishra.

Miśra, Ādyā Prasāda: see Ādyā Prasāda Miśra.

Misra, H.
1961 *A critical study of some aspects of Sanskrit grammar with special reference to the Mahābhāṣya of Patañjali.* [University of Poona dissertation, unpublished.]

Miśra, Muralīdhara: see Muralīdhara Miśra.

Miśra Nandi Nātha: see Nandi Nātha Miśra.

Miśra, Rādhāśyāma: see Rādhāśyāma Miśra.

Miśra, Ramākānta: see Ramākānta Miśra.

Miśra, Satī Prasāda: see Satī Prasāda Miśra.
Miśra, Śobhita: see Śobhita Miśra.
Miśra, Suśīla Candra: see Suśīla Candra Miśra.
Miśra, Vāma Deva: see Vāma Deva Miśra.
Misra, Vidya Niwas: see Vidya Niwas Misra.
Mitra, Kalipada: see Kalipada Mitra.
Mitra, Rājendralāl: see Rājendralāl Mitra.

Moghe, S. G.
1971 "Paribhāṣās of vyākaraṇa and the Mīmāṃsā rules of interpretation", *Festschrift Rajeshwar Shastri Dravid,* English section, pp. 90-100.

Mokāṭe, Kṛṣṇa Śāstrī
1969 "Liṅga-vimarśaḥ" [On gender], *Festschrift Aditya Nath Jha* 1, pp. 263-67. [In Sanskrit.]

Mookerji, Radha Kumud (Radhakumud)
1923 "History of Sanskrit literature from the works of Pāṇini, Kātyāyana and Patañjali", *IA* 52: 21-24.
1935 "Further historical data from Patañjali's Mahābhāṣya", *IC* 2: 362-63.
1969 *Ancient Indian education (Brahmanical and Buddhist)*[4] (Delhi: Motilal Banarsidass).

Mukhopadhyaya, Sujit Kumar
1944 "Tibetan translations of Prakriyā-kaumudī and the mention of Siddhānta-kaumudī therein", *IHQ* 20: 63-69.

Müller, Friedrich Max(imilian)
1853 "Das Mahābhāshya", *ZDMG* 7: 162-71.
1859 *A history of ancient Sanskrit literature so far as it illustrates the primitive religion of the Brahmans* (London: Williams and Newgate).
1869 (Ed., tr.) *Rig-veda-prātiśākhya, das älteste Buch der vedischen Phonetik; Sanskrittext mit Übersetzung und Anmerkungen* (Leipzig: Brockhaus).
1880 "The Kāśikā", *IA* 9: 305-08.
1887 "On the dhātupāṭha", *IZAS* 3: 1-26.

Muralīdhara Miśra
1963 "La-kārârtha-vicāraḥ" [On the meanings of L-suffixes], *SS* 18: 4-16. [In Sanskrit.] [*Prāci Jyoti* (1963-1972) 2: 140-41.]
1971 "Mukhaṃ vyākaraṇaṃ smṛtam" [Grammar, known from tradition as the mouth of the Vedas], *Festschrift Rajeshwar Shastri Dravid,* grammar section, pp. 1-7. [In Sanskrit.]

Nāganātha Śāstrī, P. V. (= Naganatha Sastry, P. V.)

1963 *Vaiyākaraṇa Siddhānta Kaumudī (the standard Sanskrit grammar): an analysis in English.* [Reprint: 1974. Original edition without date or place of publication. The first of two volumes, covering major sandhi rules and rules relative to nominal inflection.]

1974 *Vaiyākaraṇa-Siddhānta-Kaumudī of Bhaṭṭojī Dīkshita: an English analysis, volume I* (Delhi: Motilal Banarsidass).

Nakamura, Hajime

1955 "Tibetan citations of Bhartṛhari's verses and the problem of his date", *Festschrift Yamaguchi,* pp. 122-36.

1960 "Bhartṛhari the scholar", *IIJ* 4: 282-305.

1972 "Bhartṛhari and Buddhism", *Festschrift K. C. Chaṭṭopādhyāya,* pp. 395-405.

Nandi Nātha Miśra (Ed.)

1960 *Gokulanāthôpādhyāya-viracitaḥ pada-vākya-ratnâkaraḥ yadunātha-miśra-viracita-gūḍhârtha-dīpikā-saṃvalitaḥ* [Gokulanātha's Pada-vākya-ratnâkara with the commentary Gūḍhârtha-dīpikā of Yadunātha] (= *SBGM* 88) (Varanasi: Vārāṇaseya Saṃskṛta Viśvavidyālaya). [Sanskrit introduction, pp. 1-22.]

Nandkishore Shastri (Ed.)

1936 *Laghu Shabdendu Shekhar of M. M. Nagesh Bhatt with rare commentaries: (1) Abhinava Chandrika, (2) Chidasthimala, (3) Sadashiva Bhatti, (4) Visamapadavivriti, (5) Jyotsna, (6) Vijaya, (7) Varavarnini; explanatory note by Pt. Guru Prasad Shastri (Mahā-mahôpādhyāya-nāgeśabhaṭṭa-viracitaḥ laghu-śabdêndu-śekharaḥ śrī-viśvanātha-daṇḍibhaṭṭa-viracitayâbhinava-candrikā-ṭīkayā śrī-vaidyanātha-pāyaguṇḍe-viracitayā cidasthimālā-ṭīkayā śrī-sadāśiva-bhaṭṭa-viracitena tilakena śrīmad-bhaṭṭodayaṅkara-pāṭhaka-viracitayā jyotsnā-ṭīkayā śrī--rāghavendrācārya-kṛtayā viṣamapadavivṛtyā kāraka-prakaraṇe śrī-śivanārāyaṇa-śāstri-viracitayā vijayā-ṭīkayā śrī-guruprasāda-śāstri-viracitayā nyāsa-pariṣkāra-pūrṇayā varavarṇinyā kiñca ṭippaṇyā ca virājitaḥ)* (= *RSCG* 14) (Benares: Bhargava Pustakalaya). [2 parts, separately paginated, in one volume; through the avyayībhāva compound section.]

Naradeva Śāstrī

1968a "Pāṇiniyaṃ śabdasvarūpam" [Speech unit according to Pāṇini], *VS* 6: 91-99. [In Sanskrit.]

1968b *Śabdârtha-saṃbandhe pāṇinīya-siddhāntaḥ* [The accepted Pāninian view regarding the relation between word and meaning, in Sanskrit] [Vārāṇaseya Saṃskṛta Viśvavidyālaya dissertation, unpublished.]

Narang, Satya Pal
1967 *A study of śāstra-kāvyas in Sanskrit literature.* [Delhi University dissertation, unpublished.]
1969 *Bhaṭṭi-kāvya: a study* (Delhi: Motilal Banarsidass).

Narasimhacharya, M. S. (Ed.)
1973 *Mahābhāṣya Pradīpa vyākhyānāni; commentaires sur le Mahābhāṣya de Patañjali et le Pradīpa de Kaiyaṭa; présentation par Pierre-Sylvain Filliozat* (= *PIFI* 51.1) (Pondichéry: Institut français d'Indologie). [French introduction by P.-S. Filliozat, pp. iii-xiii; Sanskrit introduction by M. S. Narasimhacharya, pp. xiv-xxii.]

Narasimhia, A. N. (Ed.)
1952 *Kāśakṛtsna-śabdakalāpa-dhātupāṭha of Cannavīrakavi* (= *SIAL* 5) (Poona: Deccan College). [Dhātu-pāṭha with Kannada commentary, in Kannada script; for Roman transliteration see A. N. Narasimhia (1958-59); for Sanskrit translation see Yudhiṣṭhira Mīmāṃsaka (1965/6a)].
1958-59 "Kāśakṛtsna-śabdakalāpa-dhātupāṭhaḥ", *BDCRI* 19: 154-235, 330-414. [Roman transliteration of A. N. Narasimhia (1952).]

Nārāyaṇa Miśra (Ed., commentator)
1969-72 *Pāṇinīyavyākaraṇasūtravṛtti Kāśikā of Pt. Vāmana and Jayāditya; edited with the 'Prakāśa' Hindi commentary and introduction by Śrī Nārāyaṇa Miśra; preface by Pt. Brahmadatta Jijñāsu (Śrīmad-vidvad-vara-vāmana-jayāditya-viracitā pāṇinīya-vyākaraṇa-sūtra-vṛttiḥ kāśikā saṭippaṇa-'prakāśa'-hindī-vyākhyôpêtā; vyākhyā-kāraḥ śrī-nārāyaṇa-miśraḥ, upôdghāta-lekhakaḥ p[aṇḍita-] brahmadatta-jijñāsuḥ)* (= *KSS* 37) 2 vol., (Varanasi: Chowkhamba). [Sanskrit preface by Brahmadatta Jijñāsu, 1: 7-21, Hindi introduction by Nārāyaṇa Miśra, 1: 23-93. Sanskrit text of Pāṇini's rules with the Kāśikā and brief Hindi glosses of the rules; indices of sūtras: 1: 413-38, 2: 479-507; see Śobhita Miśra (1952).]

Narayana Murti, M. S.
1967 "Ekasaṃjñādhikāra in the Aṣṭādhyāyī", *SVUOJ* 10: 11-22.
1969 "Two versions of the ekasaṃjñādhikāra", *SVUOJ* 12: 75-83.
1971a "A note on the iva-samāsa", *SVUOJ* 14: 47-52.
1971b "A note on ekaśeṣa", *SVUOJ* 14: 83-98.
1972a "Bhartṛhari on 'viśeṣaṇānāṃ cājāteḥ' of Pāṇini", *SVUOJ* 15: 49-62.
1972b "Bhaṭṭoji Dīkṣita and Koṇḍabhaṭṭa on the primary denotation", *SVUOJ* 15: 87-97.

1973a *Sanskrit compounds, a philosophical study* (= *CSSt.* 93) (Varanasi: Chowkhamba).

1973b "Philosophy of grammar", *SVUOJ* 16 (= Proceedings of the Seminar on Andhra's contribution to Indian culture): 37-54.

Nārāyaṇa Rām Ācārya (Ed.)

1948 *Śrī-varadarāja-paṇḍita-viracitā laghu-siddhānta-kaumudī anuvṛtty-ādi-nirdeśaka-ṭippaṇa-dvi-catvāriṃśat-pratyāhāra-varṇa-vyavahāra-jñāpaka-koṣṭhaka-pāṇinīya-śikṣā-sutrâṇukrama-sūcy-ādi-vividha-viṣayair alaṅkṛtā*[14] [Varadarāja's Laghu-siddhānta-kaumudī, with notes indicating anuvṛtti etc., charts showing the 42 pratyāhāras, sounds and how they are articulated, the Pāṇinīya-śikṣā, and index of sūtras[14]] (Bombay: Nirnaya-Sagar Press). [Charts of pratyāhāras, showing what sounds they denote, pp. 5-7; charts relative to the phonetics of sounds, pp. 7-8; śikṣā, pp. 1-3; alphabetic index of sūtras, pp. 4-20; the last two following the text.]

1950 *Varadarāja-praṇītā madhya-siddhānta-kaumudī viṣama-sthala-ṭippaṇy-ādi-samullāsitā*[7] [Varadarāja's Madhya-siddhānta-kaumudī, with notes on difficult passages, etc.[7]] (Bombay: Nirnaya-Sagar Press). [Charts of pratyāhāras, pp. 1-3; charts relative to the phonetics of sounds, pp. 3-4; liṅgânuśāsana, pp. 235-38; alphabetic index of sūtras, pp. 1-27 following the text.]

Narendra Chandra Nath

1969 *Pāṇinian interpretation of the Sanskrit language* (= *BHUSS* 2) (Varanasi: Banaras Hindu University). [Originally a Banaras Hindu University dissertation, 1967.]

1970 "Are feminine bases prātipadikas according to Pāṇini? ", *VIJ* 8: 82-85.

Nawathe, P. D.

1966 "Some un-Pāṇinian forms in the śrauta-sūtras", *PAIOC* 21 (Srinagar, 1961): 2.1: 210-12.

1971 "Pāṇini-vihitāḥ yajña-karma-gatāḥ plutayaḥ" [Prolation of vowels in the ritual, as provided for by Pāṇini], *Festschrift Rajeshwar Shastri Dravid,* Vedic section, pp. 74-76. [In Sanskrit.] [See also P. D. Nawathe (1972).]

1972 "Ritualistic prolation and its treatment in Pāṇini's grammar", *CASS-St.* 1: 55-64. [Revised version of P. D. Nawathe (1971).]

Nene, Gopāla Shastri (Ed.)

1925 *Laghuśabdendu Śekhara, avyayībhāvānta, by Śrī Nāgeśa Bhaṭṭa, with a commentary called Dīpaka by M. M. P. Śrī Nityananda Pant Parvatīya (Laghu-śabdêndu-śekharaḥ mahāmahôpādhyāya-*

śri-nageśabhaṭṭa-viracitaḥ (avyayibhavânto bhagaḥ) nityânanda-panta-parvatiya-viracitena śekhara-dipakâkhyena ṭippaṇena samujjvalitaḥ) (= *KSS* 27) (Benares: Chowkhamba). [2nd edition: 1954.]

1929 *The Śabda Kaustubha by Pandit Bhattoji Dīkshit, vol. II – fas. 5 to 10, from the second pāda of the 1st adhyāya to second pāda of 3rd adhyāya; and Sphoṭa Chandrikā by Pandit Srikrisna Mauni (Śabda-kaustubhaḥ śrīmad-bhaṭṭojī-dīkṣita-viracitaḥ, tasya prathamâdhyāya-dvitīya-pādam ārabhya tṛtīyâdhyāya-dvitīya-pādânto dvitīyo bhāgaḥ tathā sphoṭa-candrikā paṇḍita śrī-kṛṣṇa-mauni-kṛtā)* (= Reprint from the *CSS* 7-10, 13, 14.) (Benares: Chowkhamba).

1939 *The Prauḍhamanoramā of M. M. Bhaṭṭoji Dīkṣita (a commentary upon his Siddhānta Kaumudī) with its gloss called Laghuśabda-ratna by M. M. Haridīkṣita with three commentaries, the Bhairavī, Bhāvaprakāśa and Saralā by M. M. Pandit Śrī Bhairava Miśra, Vaidyanātha Pāyagunde and Gopāl Śastrī Nene (Prauḍha-manoramā mahāmahôpādhyāya-śrīmad-bhaṭṭojī-dīkṣita-viracitā mahāmahôpādhyāya-bhaṭṭojī-dīkṣita-pautra-śrī-hari-dīkṣita-kṛto laghu-śabda-ratnaś ca mahāmahôpādhyāya-bhairava-miśra-viracita-ratna-prakāśikā-pāyaguṇḍôpāhva-vaidyanātha-paṇḍita-kṛta-bhāva-prakāśa-vyākaraṇâcārya-p[aṇḍita-] gopāla-śāstri-nene-kṛta-saralā-ṭīkā-traya-vibhūṣitaḥ)* (= *KSS* 125) (Benares: Chowkhamba).

1958-61 *M. M. śrīmad-bhaṭṭojī-dīkṣita-viracitā vaiyākaraṇa-siddhānta-kaumudī śrī-vāsudeva-dīkṣita-kṛta-'bālamanoramā'-vyākhyā-sahitā* [Bhaṭṭojī Dīkṣita's Vaiyākaraṇa-siddhānta-kaumudī with Vāsudeva Dīkṣita's Bāla-manoramā], 2 vol. in 4 parts [parts 1-2, 3-4 continuously paginated] (= *KSS* 136) (Varanasi: Chowkhamba). [Uṇādi-sūtras, 2: 527-611; phiṭ-sūtras, 2: 735-43; liṅgânuśāsana, 2: 811-24; śikṣā, 2: 825-27; gaṇa-pāṭha, 2: 827-50. Indices: sūtras, I.1.1-8, I.2.1-15 (following text), 2: 291-94, 851-61; vārttikas: I.1.8-10, I.2.16-20, 2: 294, 861-64; paribhāṣās, I.1.10, I.2.20, 2: 864; roots: 2: 295-306, uṇādi-sūtras, 2: 865-71; phiṭ-sūtras, 2: 871.]

Nene, Gopāla Śāstrī and Mukund Śāstrī Puṇtamkar (Ed.)

1933 *The Śabda Kaustubha by Śrī Bhaṭṭoji Dīkshita, vol. I, fas. I to IV, first pāda of the first adhyāya complete (Śabda-kaustubhaḥ śrīmad-bhaṭṭojī-dīkṣita-viracitaḥ, prathamâdhyāyasya prathama-pādo navâhnika-paryantaḥ)* (= Reprint from the *CSS* 3-6) (Benares: Chowkhamba).

Nilakantha Sastri, K. A.

1934 "A note on the Rūpāvatāra", *JOR* 8: 277-80.

Nitti-Dolci, Luigia (Ed., tr.)

1938a *Les grammairiens prakrits* (Paris: Adrien-Maisonneuve). [Translation: *The Prakrita grammarians by Luigia Nitti-Dolci, translated from the French into English by Prabhākara Jhā* (Delhi: Motilal Banarsidass, 1972).]

1938b *Le prākṛtānuśāsana de Puruṣottama* (= *CSA* 6) (Paris: Société Asiatique).

Ojihara, Yutaka

1956 "Quelques remarques sur ḷ voyelle dans l'Aṣṭādhyāyī", *JIBS* 4: 591-97.

1957 "Paṇin – Pāṇina – Pāṇini – Pāṇinīya", *JIBS* 5: 328-18. [In Japanese, with French summary.]

1958-60 "Causerie vyākaranique (I): 1. 1. 62 vis-à-vis de 1. 1. 56", *JIBS* 6: 302-05 [= (7) - (10)], 8: 369-70 [= (39) - (40)].

1959 "Causerie vyākaraṇique (II): antériorité du gaṇapāṭha par rapport au sūtrapāṭha", *JIBS* 7: 785-97 [= (36) - (48)]. [See Ojihara (1963a).]

1961 "Le Mahābhāṣya, adhyāya I, āhnika 8: un essai de traduction", *MIK* 2: 9-22.

1961-62 "Causerie vyākaraṇique (III^1 - III^2): incohérence interne chez la Kāśikā", *JIBS* 9: 749-53 [= (11) - (15)], 10: 766-76 [= (7) - (17)]. [See Ojihara (1964).]

1963a "Causerie vyākaraṇique (II): addenda et corrigenda: la nécessité ultime des sū. 1. 1. 34 - 36", *JIBS* 11: 846-52 [= (25) - (31)]. [See Ojihara (1959).]

1963b "Mahābhāṣya ad Pāṇini 1. 1. 56; un essai de traduction", *AA* 4: 43-69.

1964 "Causerie vyākaraṇique (III^3): incohérence interne chez la Kaśika (III)", *JIBS* 12: 847-55.

1965a "À la recherche de la motivation ultérieure du Pāṇini-sūtra 1. 1. 62", *MIK* 6-7: 69-85.

1965b Review of Birwé (1961), *IIJ* 8: 285-93.

1967a (Tr.) *La Kāśikā-vṛtti (adhyāya I, pāda 1) traduite et commentée par Yutaka Ojihara et Louis Renou; 3e partie par Y. Ojihara* (= *PEFEO* 48) (Paris: École Française d'Extrême-Orient). [Rules 1.1.60-75; index of Sanskrit forms, pp. 127-76; see Ojihara - Renou (1960-62).]

1967b "Causerie vyākaraṇique (IV): *jāti* 'genus' et deux définitions pré-patañjaliennes", *JIBS* 16: 451-59 [= (16) - (24)]. [Reprint: with author's corrections: Staal (1972: 425-31).]

1967-68 "Sur l'énoncé pāṇinéen *astrīviṣaya* (IV. 1. 63): deux interprétations et leur rapport avec le gaṇapāṭha", *Festschrift V. Raghavan,* pp. 125-43.

1968a "Les discussions patañjaliennes afférentes au remaniement du gaṇapāṭha", *Festschrift Renou,* pp. 565-76.

1968b "Read 'parṇaṃ ná véḥ': Kāśikā ad P. 1. 1. 4: a notice", *ABORI* 43-45: 403-09.

1970 "Les discussions patañjaliennes afférentes au remaniement du gaṇapāṭha", *IIJ* 12: 81-115.

1971 "Un chapitre de la Saddanīti comparé aux données pāninéennes", *JAs* 259: 83-97.

Ojihara, Yutaka and Louis Renou (Tr.)

1960-62 *La Kāśikā-vṛtti (adhyāya I, pāda 1) traduite et commentée,* 2 vol. (= *PEFEO* 48) (Paris: École Française d'Extrême-Orient). [1: 1.1.1-44, 2: 1.1.45-59; see Ojihara (1967a).]

Oppert, Gustav (Ed.)

1894 *The grammar of Śākaṭāyana with the Prakriyāsaṃgraha commentary of Abhayacandrasūri, published for the first time* (Madras: Printed at the S. P. C. K. Press, Vopery).

Orara, E. de Guzman

1967 "An account of ancient Indian grammatical studies down to Patañjali's Mahābhāṣya", *AS* 5: 369-76.

Pade, Jagannath Shridhar

1958 *Tāmbūlamañjarī* (= *MSUOS* 1) (Baroda: Oriental Institute). [pp. viii-xix: "The authorship of the uṇādisūtras"; originally published in installments as supplements to *JOIBS* 1-7 (1951-58).]

Paik, T. S.

1973 *Pāṇini's treatment of the augment i in Sanskrit.* [Dissertation, University of California, Berkeley.]

1974 Review of Staal (1972), *Lg.* 50: 591-98.

Palsule, Gajanan Balakrishna

1949 "An interpolated passage in the Aṣṭādhyāyī", *ABORI* 30: 135-44.

1952 "A new explanation of the term *karmadhāraya*", *ABORI* 33: 245-50.

1953a "A concordance of the Sanskrit dhātupāṭhas", *BDCRI* 15: 1/2: 1-203. [See also Palsule (1955).]

1953b "A glimpse into the Kāśakṛtsna school of Sanskrit grammar", *PAIOC* 17 (Ahmedabad, 1953): 349-55.

1954 (Ed.) *Kavikalpadruma of Vopadeva, critically edited* (= *SIAL* 15) (Poona: Deccan College).

1955 *A concordance of Sanskrit dhātupāṭhas (with index of meanings)* (= *DCDS* 14) (Poona: Deccan College). [Concordance of the dhātu-pāṭhas of Pāṇini (as in Böhtlingk (1887a)), Kṣīrā-taraṅgiṇī, Dhātu-pradīpa, Mādhavīyā dhātu-vṛtti, Candra, Jainendra, Kāśakṛtsna, Kātantra, Śakaṭāyana, Hemacandra, Vopadeva, pp. 1-164; index of meanings (roots followed by Sanskrit glosses), pp. 165-202; see also Palsule (1953a).]

1957a "A survey of pre-Pāṇinian grammatical thought in the matter of the verbal root", *Festschrift P. C. Bagchi,* pp. 116-39. [Included in Palsule (1961): 1-24 (chapter 1).]

1957b "Tṛph-tṛmph-ādīnāṃ vimarśaḥ" [On the roots *tṛph, tṛmph* etc.], *BDCRI* 18: 267-70. [In Sanskrit.]

1958a "Groupings, anubandhas and other technical devices used in the dhātupāṭhas", *BDCRI* 19.1/2: 1-30. [Included in Palsule (1961): 59-88 (chapter 3).]

1958b "A brief account of the different dhātupāṭhas", *Festschrift Turner,* pp. 103-33. [Included in Palsule (1961): 27-56 (chapter 2).]

1961 *The Sanskrit dhātupāṭhas, a critical study* (Poona: University of Poona). [Originally a University of Poona dissertation, 1957; see Palsule (1957a), (1958a), (1958b).]

1966 " '*Saṃjñāyām*' in Pāṇini", *PCASS-A* 10. [Also in *JUP* 25 (1967): 31-75.]

1968a "Some primary nominal formations missing in Pāṇini", *PCASS-A* 18. [Also in *JUP* 27 (1968): 145-51.]

1968b "The role of √*kṛ-* in the Sanskrit grammatical terms", *PCASS-A* 24. [Also in *JUP* 29 (1969): 11-29.]

1969a "*Devānāṃpriyaḥ*", *Festschrift S. M. Katre* 2, pp. 134-61.

1969b "Patañjali's interpretation of RV 10. 71. 2", *Festschrift R. N. Dandekar,* pp. 27-29.

1970 "Some views of Pāṇini and his followers on object-language and meta-language", *PCASS-A* 36. [Also in *JUP* 33 (1971): 1-7; reprint: Palsule (1973).]

1972a "Pāṇini 3. 4. 87 - 8 vis-à-vis Vedic imperatives in *-si*", *Festschrift K. C. Chaṭṭopādhyāya,* pp. 443-53.

1972b "Pāṇini's treatment of tense and mood formations", *CASS-St.* 1: 173-83.

1973 "Some views of Pāṇini and his followers on object-language and meta-language", in: Konks - Numerkund - Mäll (1973), pp. 310-20. [See Palsule (1970).]

Pancholi, Bala Krishna (Bāla Kṛṣṇa Pañcoli) (Ed.)

1966 *Śrī-bhaṭṭoji-dīkṣita-viracitā vaiyākaraṇa-siddhānta-kaumudī paṇḍita-śrī-sabhāpati-śarmôpādhyāya-viracitayā 'lakṣmī'-vyākhyayôpêtā, śrī-bāla-kṛṣṇa-pañcolinā sampāditā* [Bhaṭṭojī Dīkṣita's Vaiyākaraṇa-siddhānta-kaumudī with the commentary Lakṣmī of Sabhāpati Śarma Upādhyāya], 2 vol. (Delhi: Motilal Banarsidass). [Through the kāraka section.]

Pandey, Kanti Chandra

1963 *Abhinavagupta, an historical and philosophical study*[2] (= *CSSt.* 1) (Varanasi: Chowkhamba). [Revised and enlarged from the first edition of 1936.]

Pandey, Ram Awadh

1963 *A comparative study of uṇādi-sūtras.* [Banaras Hindu University dissertation, unpublished.]

Pandey, Ram Chandra Sharma

1963 *The problem of meaning in Indian philosophy* (Delhi: Motilal Banarsidass). [Originally a Banaras Hindu University dissertation, 1957.]

Pāṇḍeya, Gaṅgārāma

1971 "Varṇa-viṣayiṇī vyākaraṇa-śāstrīyā mānyatā" [The merit of Sanskrit grammarians' observations regarding sounds], *Sāg.* 10.1: 79-84 (saṃvat 2028). [In Sanskrit.]

Pandeya, Kalika Charan

1960-61 "The theory of śabdabrahma and sphoṭa", *JGJRI* 17: 235-55.

Pāṇḍeya, Keśava Deva (Ed.)

1973 *Vimalasūri-viracitā Rūpa-mālā,* 4 vol. (Delhi: Motilal Banarsidass). [Text with Hindi paraphrase].

Pāṇḍeya, Rādhāramaṇa

1966 *Siddhānta-Kaumudī-arthaprakāśikā (arthāt siddhānta-kaumudī gata udāharaṇoṃ ke artha evaṃ viśiṣṭa śabdoṃ kā paricaya* [Siddhānta-kaumudī-arthaprakāśikā: dictionary of the examples given in the Siddhânta-kaumudī and of particular words used therein] (Delhi: Motilal Banarsidass). [Hindi translation of examples, Sanskrit word index; area names, pp. 1-59; terms for coins and measures, pp. 61-62; dictionary of examples (in the order of the Siddhânta-kaumudī), pp. 1-332; alphabetic index pp. 1-106.]

Pandeya, Rajmani

1971 "Saṃskṛta-sandhi-samīkṣā" [A study of Sanskrit sandhi], *KURJ* 1: 37-72. [In Sanskrit.]

Pandeya, Ramajna

1954 *An introduction to the philosophy of Sanskrit grammar* –

(Vyākaraṇa-darśana-bhūmikā) (= *PWSBS* 11) (Varanasi: Government Sanskrit Library). [In Sanskrit.]

Pandit, M. D.

1962 "Zero in Pāṇini", *JMSUB* 11.1: 53-66.

1963a "Some linguistic principles in Pāṇini's grammar", *IL* 24: 50-69.

1963b "Pāṇini – a study in non-compounded word structures", *VIJ* 1: 224-38.

1963c "Pāṇini – a study in compound word-structures", *JMSUB* 12.1: 81-98.

1966a "Mathematical representation of some Pāṇinian sūtras", *PCASS-A* 7. [Also in *JUP* 23 (1966): 139-52.]

1966b "Pāṇinian *IT-saṃjñā* – a symbolic zero", *BDCRI* 25: 77-94.

1969 "Pāṇini: a statistical picture of Sanskrit sounds", *Festschrift R. N. Dandekar,* pp. 128-38.

1971a "Pāṇini and the Vedic interpretation", *Festschrift Rajeshwar Shastri Dravid,* English section, pp. 49-53.

1971b "Pāṇini: statistical study of Sanskrit formations", *ABORI* 52: 175-209.

1971c "Pāṇini: a statistical picture of Sanskrit sounds – II", *IA*[3] 5: 154-71. [See M. D. Pandit (1969).]

1972a "Pāṇini – a study in abbreviations", *Vimarśa* (Delhi) 1 (English section): 21-30.

1972b *A comparative study of all Sanskrit grammars with special reference to past passive participle formations.* [University of Poona dissertation, unpublished.]

1973 "Formal and non-formal in Pāṇini", *ABORI* 54: 179-92.

Paṇsīkar, Wāsudev Laxman Shāstrī (Ed.)

1913 *Siddhānta Kaumudī or Bhaṭṭojī Dīkshit's vṛtti on Pāṇini's vyākaraṇa-sūtras; containing Pāṇini's shikshā, sūtrapāṭha, gaṇapāṭha, dhātupāṭha and lingānushāsana with alphabetical list of sūtras and of all roots with pages*[8] *(Vaiyākaraṇa-siddhânta-kaumudī nāma bhaṭṭojī-dīkṣita-viracitā pāṇinīya-sūtra-vṛttiḥ, bhagavat-pāṇinīya-śikṣā-sūtrapāṭha-gaṇapāṭha-dhātupāṭha-liṅgânuśāsana-samêtā, akārâdy-anukrameṇa sarva-sūtrānāṃ sūtrâṅka-pṛṣṭhâṅka-sūcī-sahitā, sarva-dhātūnāṃ pṛṣṭhâṅka-sūcī-saṃyutā ca*[8]*)* (Bombay: Nirnaya-Sagar Press). [Liṅgânuśāsana, pp. 379-85, 482-84; śikṣā, pp. 386-87; Aṣṭādhyāyī-sūtra-pāṭha, pp. 388-432; gaṇa-pāṭha, pp. 433-62; dhātu-pāṭha, pp. 463-82. Indices: sūtras, pp. 1-34; roots, pp. 35-44.]

Pant, Mohanvallabh

1962 *Kāraka-dīpikā (Siddhānta-kaumudī ke kāraka-prakaraṇa kī 'saralā' hindī vyākhyā)* [Kāraka-dīpikā: the 'Saralā' Hindi commentary on the kāraka section of the Siddhānta-kaumudī] (Allahabad: Ram Narayan Lal Venimadhav).

Panthi, Tika Rama

1967 *Pāṇinīya-vyākaraṇāt prāktana-vyākaraṇānāṃ paryālocanam* [Critical survey of pre-Pāṇinian grammars]. [In Sanskrit.] [Vārāṇaseya Saṃskṛta Viśvavidyālaya dissertation, unpublished.]

Paranjpe, Vāsudeva Gopāla

1922 *Le vārtika de Kātyāyana; une étude du style, du vocabulaire et des postulats philosophiques* (Heidelberg: Weiss).

Paranjpe, Vinayak W.

1957 "Analysis of case suffixes with special reference to Pāṇini's grammar", *AIOK* 24: 574-77.

forthcoming

a "Discrepancy in Kāśikā", *BDCRI*.

b "Pragṛhya rules in Ṛk-prātiśākhya and Pāṇini", *PAIOC* 26 (Ujjain, 1972).

Patañjal, Deo Prakash Shastri (Devaprakāśa Pātañjala)

1963 *A critical study of Ṛgveda (1. 137-163), particularly from the point of view of Pāṇinian grammar* (New Delhi: Patañjal Publications).

1965 *Aṣṭādhyāyī-prakāśikā* (New Delhi: Patañjal Publications, distributed by Motilal Banarsidass). [Sanskrit text of most of the Aṣṭādhyāyī, with Sanskrit paraphrases and Hindi explanations; preface by Yudhiṣṭhira Mīmāṃsaka, pp. 1-11; introduction, pp. 12-19; explanation of topics for Hindi speakers, pp. 20-99; text of sūtras reordered with Sanskrit paraphrase and Hindi explanation, pp. 1-509. Summaries: nominal forms, pp. 510-13; verb forms, pp. 514-49.]

Paṭavardhana, Rāmakrishṇa Śāstrī (alias Tātyā Śāstrī) (Ed.)

1900 *(Bṛhad)Vaiyākaraṇa-bhūṣaṇa, a treatise on Sanskrit grammar by Pt. Kauṇḍabhaṭṭa; also Padārtha-dīpikā by the same author ((Bṛhad)vaiyākaraṇa-bhūṣaṇaṃ padārtha-dīpikā ca* [sic] *sahitam, sarva-tantra-svatantra-śrīmat-kauṇḍabhaṭṭa-viracitam* (= *BSS* 51-54) (Benares: Braj B. Das).

Paṭavardhana, Rāmakrishṇa Śāstrī (alias Tātyā Śāstrī), Gaṅgādhara Śāstrī Mānavallī, Rāmachandra Śāstrī Koṭibhāskara, Gosvāmī Dāmodara Śāstrī (Eds.)

1884-1937 *Vākyapadīya, a treatise on the philosophy of Sanskrit grammar by Bhartṛhari, with a commentary by Puṇyarāja* [kāṇḍas 1 - 2]; *...... with a commentary by Helārāja* [kāṇḍa 3] *(Vākya-padīyam, sâṅga-vaiyākaraṇa-siddhānta-nirūpaṇaṃ śrī-bhartṛhari-(mahā-*

vaiyākaraṇa-)viracitaṃ, śrī-puṇyarāja-kṛta-prakāśâkhya-ṭīkā-yutam; ...... śrī-helārāja-kṛta-prakāśâkhya-ṭīkā-yutam), 2 vol. in 11 fascicles (= *BSS* 6) (Benares: Braj B. Das). [Volume 1: fasc. 1 (= *BSS* 11): (Ed.: Rāmakrishṇa Śāstrī Paṭavardhana 1884), fasc. 2-3 (= *BSS* 19, 24): (Ed.: Gaṅgādhara Śāstrī Mānavallī 1886-87); volume 2: fasc. 1, 2, 3 (= *BSS* 95, 102, 103): (Ed.: Rāmachandra Śāstrī Koṭibhāskara 1905, 1905, 1907); fasc. 4, 5, 6, 7-8 (= *BSS* 160, 161, 162, 163-4): (Ed.: Gosvāmī Dāmodara Śāstrī 1928, 1930, 1933, 1937).]

Pathak, Kashinath Bapuji

1890-94a "Bhartṛhari and Kumārila", *JBBRAS* 18: 213-28.

1890-94b "Was Bhartṛhari a Buddhist? ", *JBBRAS* 18: 341-49.

1897-1900 "On the date of the poet Māgha", *JBBRAS* 20: 303-06.

1909-14a "Bhāmaha's attack on the Buddhist grammarian Jinendrabuddhi", *JBBRAS* 23: 18-31.

1909-14b "The divine Vāsudeva different from the kshatriya Vāsudeva in Patañjali's opinion", *JBBRAS* 23: 96-103.

1912 "Daṇḍin, Nyāsakāra and Bhāmaha", *IA* 41: 232-36.

1915-16 "The Nyāsakāra and the Jaina Śākaṭāyana", *IA* 44: 275-79.

1921-22 "Pāṇini and the authorship of the uṇādi sūtras", *ABORI* 4: 111-36.

1930a "The age of Pāṇini and Sanskrit as a spoken language", *ABORI* 11: 59-83.

1930b "Were the Vājasaneyi Saṃhitā and the Śatapatha Brāhmaṇa unknown to Pāṇini? ", *ABORI* 11: 84-89.

1930c "Further remarks on the uṇādi sūtras of Pāṇini", *ABORI* 11: 90-93.

1931 "Jinendrabuddhi, Kaiyaṭa and Haradatta", *ABORI* 12: 246-51.

1932 "On the text and interpretation of some passages in the Mahābhāṣya of Patañjali", *ABORI* 13: 17-24.

Pathak, Shridhar Shastri and Siddheshvar Shastri Chitrao

1927 *Word index to Patañjali's Vyākaraṇa-mahābhāṣya (Mahābhāṣya-śabda-kośaḥ)* (= *GovOS-C* 1) (Poona: BORI).

1935 *Word index to Pāṇini-sūtra-pāṭha and pariśiṣṭas (Pāṇinīya-sūtra-pāṭhasya tat-pariśiṣṭa-granthānāṃ ca śabda-kośaḥ)* (= *GovOS-C* 2) (Poona: BORI). [Word indices: vārttikas, pp. 1-203; Aṣṭādhyāyī sūtras, pp. 205-329; dhātu-pāṭha, pp. 331-59; roots mentioned only in rules, pp. 359, 747; gaṇa-pāṭha, pp. 360-428; gaṇa-pāṭha words given in vārttikas, pp. 428-31; liṅgânuśāsana, pp. 431-42; words derived by uṇādi-sūtras, pp. 442-56; phiṭ-sūtras; pp. 457-60 Texts: the sūtras of the Aṣṭādhyāyī with vārttikas, variant readings and notes, pp. 461-648; other vārttikas mentioned by commentators, pp. 648-49; dhātu-pāṭha, pp. 649-70, gaṇa-pāṭha with variants, pp. 670-711; gaṇas given in vārttikas, pp. 711-14; sūtras included in gaṇas, pp. 715-18; liṅgânuśāsana, pp. 719-23; uṇādi-sūtras with variants, pp. 724-42; gaṇas in the uṇādi-sūtras, pp. 742-44; phiṭ-sūtras, pp. 744-46.]

Pathak, Yugalakiśora (Ed.)

1889 *A collection of śikshās by Yājñavalkya and others with commentaries on some of them; edited and annotated (Śrīmad-yājñavalkyâdi-maharṣi-praṇītaḥ śikṣā-saṃgrahaḥ kvacid vyākhyāna-yutaḥ)* (= *BSS* 35) (Benares: Braj B. Das). [Pāṇinīya-śikṣā, pp. 378-84; the commentary Prakāśa on the former, pp. 385-93.]

Pavolini, P. E.

1938 "La grammatica di Pāṇini" (Pāṇini's grammar), *Asiatica* (Roma) 3.1: 1-9. [In Italian].

Pawte, I. S.

1935 *The structure of the Aṣṭādhyāyī* (Hubli: the Author).

Periveṅkaṭeśvara Śāstrī

1971 "Pāṇinīya-śabdânuśāsane sphoṭa-brahma-nirūpaṇam" [Description of sphoṭa-brahman in Pāṇinian grammar], *Festschrift Rajeshwar Shastri Dravid*, grammar section, pp. 34-39. [In Sanskrit.]

Peterson, Peter

1883-85 "Note on the date of Patañjali", *JBBRAS* 16: 181-89. [Reprinted in *The Auchityâlaṃkâra of Kshemendra, with a note on the date of Patañjali, and an inscription from Kotah. Two papers read before the Bombay Branch of the Royal Asiatic Society; with a preface in reply to Professor Bhandarkar* (Bombay: Education Society's Press, 1885).]

Peterson, Peter – Durgāprasād (Ed.)

1886 *The Subhāṣitāvali of Vallabhadeva* (= *BoSS* 21) (Bombay: Educational Society). [Unrevised second edition: (Ed.: Raghunath Damodar Karmarkar) (Poona: BORI 1961).]

Phadake, Ananta Śāstrī – Sadā Śiva Śarmā Śāstrī Joshi (Ed.)

1934 *The Mādhavīyadhātuvṛtti of Sāyaṇāchārya, edited with introduction, index, etc. (Mādhavīya-dhātu-vṛttiḥ śrī-sāyaṇâcārya-kṛtā ...... bṛhad-bhūmikayâkārâdi-dhātu-sūcikayā ca saṃyojya susampāditā* (= *KSS* 103) (Benares: Chowkhamba). [Sanskrit introduction by Sadāśiva Śāstrī Joshi, pp. 1-10; alphabetic index of roots, pp. 1-26 after the text. There are also two lists of authors and works mentioned in the work (pp. 1-6 after the text and before the root index), but these give no page references.]

Phaḍake, Śrīhara Ananta Śāstrī

1966-67 "Uṇādi-sūtrāṇi pāṇiniś ca" [The uṇādi-sūtras and Pāṇini, in Sanskrit], *Saṃvid* 3.2-4: 196-209. [See also Phaḍake (1967).]

1967 "Uṇādi-sūtrāṇi pāṇiniś ca", *Festschrift Gopinath Kaviraj*, pp. 289-92. [See also Phaḍake (1966-67).]

Phatak, Madhukar

1969 *Pāṇinīya-śikṣāyāḥ śikṣântaraiḥ saha samīkṣâtamakam adhyayanam* [A critical study of the Pāṇinīya-śikṣā in comparison with other śikṣās, in Sanskrit]. [Vārāṇaseya Saṃskṛta Viśvavidyālaya dissertation, unpublished.]

Pillai, K. Raghavan: see Raghavan Pillai, K.

Pisani, Vittore

1934 "Pāṇini 1, 2, 23", *RSO* 14: 84.

1956 "A note on Āpiśali", *JOIB* 5: 272.

Pischel, Richard

1885 "Der Dichter Pāṇini", *ZDMG* 39: 95-98, 313-16. [Pp. 313-16 contain additions to the article.]

1900 *Grammatik der Prakrit-Sprachen* (= Grundriss der indo-arischen Philologie und Altertumskunde I.8) (Strassburg: Trübner). [Translation: *Comparative grammar of the Prākṛt languages by R. Pischel; translated from the German by Subhadra Jhā*[2] (Delhi: Motilal Banarsidass, 1965).]

Prabhudayāla Agnihotrī

1963 *Patañjali-kālīna Bhārata* [India at the time of Patañjali] (Patna: Bihar Rāṣṭrabhāṣā Pariṣad). [In Hindi.]

Prācī Jyoti

1963-72 *Prācī Jyoti: digest of Indological studies* (Kurukshetra: Institute of Indian Studies, Kurukshetra University). [1: (Ed.: D. N. Shastri and Buddha Prakash 1963), 2: (Ed.: D. N. Shastri and Buddha Prakash 1964), 3: (Ed.: Buddha Prakash 1965), 4: (Ed.: Buddha Prakash 1966), 5. 1: (Ed. Buddha Prakash 1967), 5. 2: (Ed.: Buddha Prakash and V. C. Pandey 1967), 6: (Ed.: Sūrya Kānta 1968), 7: (Ed.: Gopikamohan Bhattacharya 1971), 8: (Ed.: Gopikamohan Bhattacharya 1972).]

Prajñā Devī

1969 *Kāśikāyāḥ samīkṣâtmakam adhyayanam* [A critical study of the Kāśikā]. [In Sanskrit.] [Vārāṇaseya Saṃskṛta Viśvavidyālaya dissertation, unpublished.]

Prakash, Buddha: see Buddha Prakash.

Puri, Baij Nath

1957 *India in the time of Patañjali* (Bombay: Bhāratīya Vidyā Bhavan). [Reprint: 1968; originally an Oxford University dissertation.]

Rādhāśyāma Miśra

1967 *Vyākaraṇa-śāstra-dṛṣṭyā jāti-svarūpa-vimarśaḥ* [On the character of jāti ["generic property"] from the point of view of grammar]. [In Sanskrit.] [Vārāṇaseya Saṃskṛta Viśvavidyālaya dissertation, unpublished.]

Raghavan, V.

1945 "Indu, the author of the Anunyasa", *JOR* 15: 78.

1950 "Chronological notes: Kaiyaṭa and Dhanañjaya", *JOR* 19: 223-24.

1974 "How many grammars? ", *Festschrift Charudeva Shastri,* pp. 271-78.

Raghavan Pillai, K. (Ed., tr.)

1971 *Studies in the Vākyapadīya, volume I: the Vākyapadīya, critical text of cantos I and II (with English translation, summary of ideas and notes)* (Delhi: Motilal Banarsidass). [Introduction, pp. xi-xxii; summary of cantos 1-2, pp. xxiii-xxxvi; notes, pp. 147-89. Indices: general, pp. 191-95, words, pp. 196-222, verses, pp. 223-32. Originally a University of London dissertation, 1951.]

Raghunātha Śarmā (Sharmā)

1963 (Ed.) *Vākyapadīya with the commentary Ambākartrī by Raghunātha Sharmā, part I (brahma-kāṇḍa) (Vākya-padīyam, prathamo bhāgaḥ (brahma-kāṇḍam), śrī-raghunātha-śarmaṇā viracitayā ambākartrī-samākhyayā vyākhyayā sahitam)* (= *SBGM* 91) (Varanasi: Vārāṇaseya Saṃskṛta Viśvavidyālaya). [Sanskrit preface by K. A. Subramania Iyer, pp. *a-ṭa;* index of verses, pp. 270-72.]

1964 *Citra-nibandhâvaliḥ (Vividha-śāstrīya-nibandhānāṃ saṃgrahaḥ* [Citranibandhâvali: a collection of various learned papers] (Delhi: Motilal Banarsidass). [In Sanskrit.] [For the next four entries, the original journal issues were not available to me.]

1964a "Vyākaraṇe śabdârtha-saṃbandha-vicāraḥ" [On the relation between word and meaning in grammar], in: Raghunātha Śarmā (1964: 1-10). [Originally: *SS* 13: 205-24.]

1964b "Śabda-saṃjñā-vimarśaḥ" [On technical terms], in: Raghunātha Śarmā (1964: 11-26).

1964c "Sabdâdvaita-vimarśaḥ" [On the śabdādvaita doctrine], in: Raghunātha Śarmā (1964: 27-42). [Originally: *SS* 17.1/2: 81-96.]

1964d "Pratibhā-vimarśaḥ" [On pratibhā], in: Raghunātha Śarmā (1964: 193-215). [Originally: *SS* 16.3/4: 103-23.]

1968 (Ed.) *Vākyapadīyam, part II (vākya-kāṇḍam), with the commentary Ambākartrī by Raghunātha Sharmā (Vākya-padīyam (dvitīyo bhāgaḥ) (vākya-kāṇḍam) śrī-raghunātha-śarmaṇā viracitayā ambākartrī-vyākhyayā samalaṅkṛtam)* (= *SBGM* 91) (Varanasi: Vārāṇaseya Saṃskṛta Viśvavidyālaya). [Includes excerpts from the Vṛtti; index of verses, pp. 583-91.]

1971 *Vyākaraṇa-darśana-binduḥ* [Abstract of the philosophy of grammar] (= *GJPM* 8) (Varanasi: Vārāṇaseya Saṃskṛta Viśvavidyālaya). [In Sanskrit.]

1974 (Ed.) *Vākyapadīyam part III (pada kāṇḍa, jāti, dravya and sambandha samuddeśa) with the commentary Prakāśa by Helārāja and Ambākartrī by Pt. Raghunātha Śarmā (Vākya-padīyam (tṛtīyo bhāgaḥ, pada-kāṇḍam, jāti-dravya-saṃbandha-samuddeśa-trayâtmakam) śrī-helārāja-viracitayā prakāśa-vyākhyayā śrī-raghunātha-śarmaṇā viracitayā ambākartrī-vyākhyayā ..... ca samalaṅkṛtam)* (= *SBGM* 91) (Varanasi: Vārāṇaseya Saṃskṛta Viśvavidyālaya). [Sanskrit introduction by K. A. Subramania Iyer, pp. *ka-ca;* index of verses, pp. 339-42.]

Raghunātha (Kāśinātha) Śāstrī and Śivadatta D. Kudāla (Ed.)

1937 *Patañjali's Vyākaraṇa Māhābhaṣya with Kaiyaṭa's Pradīpa and Nāgeśa's Uddyota; edited with foot notes collected from Chhāyā, Padamañjarī and Śabdakaustubha as well as supplied by the editors' own originality, vol. III* [3rd adhyāya] *(Śrīmad-bhagavat-patañjali-muni-nirmitaṃ pāṇinīya-vyākaraṇa-mahā-bhāṣyam, etad-vyākhyāna-bhūta upādhyāya-kaiyaṭa-praṇīto bhāṣya-pradīpas tad-vyākhyāna-bhūto nāgeśabhaṭṭa-viracito bhāṣya-pradīpôddyotaḥ, tatra tṛtīyâdhyāyâtmakaṃ vidhi-prakaraṇa-rūpaṃ tṛtīya-khaṇḍam ..... śivadatta-śarmaṇā ..... kāśīnātha-śāstri-tanu-janmanā ..... raghunātha-śāstriṇā ca vaidyanātha-praṇīta-bhāṣya-pradīpôddyota-chāyā-sāraṃ pada-mañjarī-śabda-kaustubhau samavalambya viṣama-sthala-ṭippaṇyā pāṭha-bhedâdi-rūpeṇa ca saṃbhūṣya saṃśodhitam)* [The first editor's name is given on the English title page as Raghunāth Kāśīnāth Śāstrī, on the Sanskrit title page as Raghunātha Śāstrī son of Kāśinātha; this is the same author as Raghunātha Śarmā, listed above.]

Raghu Vira

1930 "The authorship of the śiva-sūtras", *JRAS* 1930: 400-2.

1931 "Discovery of the lost phonetic sūtras of Pāṇini", *JRAS* 1931: 653-70. [Includes an edition and translation of the śikṣā.]

1934 "Āpiśaliśikṣā", *JVS* 1: 225-48.

Raja, C. Kunhan: see Kunhan Raja, C.

Raja, K. Kunjunni: see Kunjunni Raja, K.

Rājanārāyaṇa Śāstrī (Ed.)

1943 *The Paribhāṣenduśekhara of M. M. Śrī Nāgeśa Bhaṭṭa with the Śāstrārthakalā commentary by Paṇḍitarāja Śukla Śrī Veṇīmādhava Śāstrī; edited with notes, introduction etc. (Mahā-mahôpādhyāya-śrī-nāgeśabhaṭṭa-viracitaḥ paribhāṣêndu-śekharaḥ ..... paṇḍita-rāja-śrī-veṇīmādhava-śāstri-praṇīta-"bṛhacchāstrârtha-kalā"-ṭīkā-sahitaḥ tad-ātmajena ..... ācārya-śrī-rāja-nārāyaṇa-śāstriṇā ..... ṭippaṇy-ādibhiḥ pariṣkṛtya ..... sampāditaḥ .....)* (= *KSS* 137) (Benares: Chowkhamba).

Rajavade, V. K.

1940 *Yāska's Nirukta, volume I. Introduction, full texts of Nighaṇṭu and Nirukta, cursory examination of Nighaṇṭu, notes on chapters I - III of Nirukta, 25 indices (Yāskâcārya-praṇītaṃ niruktam, prathamo bhāgaḥ, upôdghātaḥ, nighaṇṭu-mūlaṃ ca, nighaṇṭu-parīkṣaṇam, naighaṇṭuka-kāṇḍa-vivaraṇam, pañca-viṃśatiḥ sūcyaḥ)* (= *GovOS*-A 7) (Poona: BORI). [Index xxiii: grammatical terms in the first 3 chapters of Nirukta, pp. 690-91.]

Rājendralāl Mitra

1874 "On the supposed identity of the Greeks with the Yavanas of the Sanskrit writers", *JASB* 43: 246-79.

1883 "On *Goṇikaputra* and *Gonardīya* as names of Patañjali", *JASB* 52: 261-69.

Ram Gopal

1968 "Vedic quotations in the Kāśikā and Siddhānta-kaumudī", *ABORI* 48-49: 227-30.

Ram, Sadhu: see Sadhu Ram.

Rāmacandra Dīkṣita, T. V.

1971 "Śabdârtha-sambandha-mīmāṃsā" [Concerning the relation between word and meaning], *Festschrift Rajeshwar Shastri Dravid*, grammar section, pp. 84-88. [In Sanskrit.]

Ramachandra Dikshitar, V. R.

1935 "Kātyāyana – the grammarian", *IHQ* 11: 316-20.

Ramachandra Rao, S. K.

1959 "Specimens of Pāṇini's poetry", *QJMS* 50: 115-27.

Ramachari, C.
1968 "Takṣan and similar artisans in the Aṣṭādhyāyī", *MO* 1: 105-14.
Ramākānta Miśra
1966 *Vyākaraṇa-śāstra kā saṃkṣipta itihāsa* [A short history of Sanskrit grammar] (= *VRGM* 106) (Varanasi: Chowkhamba). [In Hindi.]
Ramakrishna Kavi, M.
1930 "The discovery of the author's vṛtti on the Vākyapadīya", *JAHRS* 4: 235-41.
Rāmalāl
1970 "Vaiyākaraṇa pāṇini kā śabda-saṃskāra" [The grammarian Pāṇini's purification of speech], *Bhāṣā* 9.4: 122-32. [In Hindi.]
Ramamurti, K. S.
1973 "Vyākaraṇa", *SVUOJ* 16 (= Proceedings of the Seminar on Andhra's contribution to Indian culture): 25-35.
Rāmanārāyaṇa Tripāṭhī
1970 "Vyākaraṇa-darśanam" [Philosophy of grammar], *VS* 7: 157-68, 219-26. [In Sanskrit.]
1971 "Vyākaraṇasya darśanatvam" [On grammar as a philosophy], *Festschrift Rajeshwar Shastri Dravid*, grammar section, pp. 67-77. [In Sanskrit.]
Rāmanātha Śāstrī (Ed.)
1931 *The Sphoṭasiddhi of Ācārya Maṇḍanamiśra with the Gopālikā of Ṛṣiputra Parameśvara (Ācārya-maṇḍana-miśra-viracitā sphoṭa-siddhiḥ ṛṣi-putra-paramêśvara-kṛta-gopālikôpêtā)* (= *MUSS* 6) (Madras: University of Madras).
Rama Nath Sharma
1971 *Padavidhi in Pāṇini.* [University of Rochester doctoral dissertation, unpublished.]
1972 "Referential indices in Pāṇini", *AICL* 3: 19-20.
forthcoming "Referential indices in Pāṇini", *IIJ*. [See Rama Nath Sharma (1972).]
Ramanujacharya, N. S.
1966 "Kriyā-viśeṣaṇānāṃ karmatvam" [Adverbs as objects], *SVUOJ* 9 (Sanskrit section): 9-14. [In Sanskrit.]
Ramanuja Tatacharya, N. S.
1972 (Ed., comm.) *Jñāpakasaṃgraha of Nāgeśa Bhaṭṭa with Vivṛti of N. S. Ramanuja Tatacharya (Nāgeśa-bhaṭṭa-kṛtaḥ jñāpaka-saṃgrahaḥ śrī en. es. Rāmānuja-tātācārya-kṛta-vivṛti-samêtaḥ)* (= *KSVS* 18) (Tirupati: Kendriya Sanskrit Vidyapeetha). (Sanskrit introduction, pp. vi-ix. Appendices: 1: Mahā-bhāṣya

passages in which jñāpakas are invoked but which are not included in Nāgeśa's collection, pp. 133-201; 2: Siddhânta-kaumudī jñāpakas, pp. 202-24. Index, pp. 225-31.

1972b "Uṇādiprakaraṇaṃ pāṇinīyavyākaraṇaṃ ca" [The Uṇādi text and Pāṇini's grammar], *SVUOJ* 15, (Sanskrit section) pp. 19-30. [In Sanskrit.]

Rāma Prasāda Tripāṭhī

1952 (Ed.) *Śrīmat-kauṇḍabhaṭṭa-viracito vaiyākaraṇa-bhūṣaṇa-sāraḥ nene-ity-upāhva-gopāla-śāstriṇā abhinava-'saralā'-vyākhyayā pariṣkṛtaḥ paṇḍita-rāma-prasāda-tripāṭhinā 'subodhinī'-ṭippaṇyā samalaṅkṛtya saṃśodhitaḥ* [Kauṇḍabhaṭṭa's Vaiyākaraṇa-bhūṣaṇa-sāra with the modern commentary Saralā by Gopāla Śāstrī Nene, edited with his own notes called Subodhinī by Rāma Prasāda Tripāṭhī] (= *HKNMM* 7) (Varanasi: Chowkhamba).

1969 "Caturdaśa-sūtrī-vimarśaḥ" [On the 14 śiva-sūtras], *Festschrift Aditya Nath Jha* 1, pp. 248-62. [In Sanskrit.]

1971 "Vyākaraṇa-darśane sṛṣṭi-prakriyā" [Creation according the philosophy of grammar], *Festschrift Rajeshwar Shastri Dravid*, philosophy section, pp. 131-40. [In Sanskrit.]

1972 *Pāṇinīya-vyākaraṇe pramāṇa-samīkṣā* [A critical study of means of knowledge in the Pāṇinian grammatical system, in Sanskrit] (= *SBAM* 20) (Varanasi: Vārāṇaseya Saṃskṛta Viśvavidyālaya). [Dissertation for the vidyā-vācaspati degree, Vārāṇaseya Saṃskṛta Viśvavidyālaya, 1970.]

Rāmaśaraṇa Dāsa Vaiṣṇava

1969 *Vyākaraṇa-śāstre vaiśeṣika-tattvānāṃ vimarśaḥ* [On Vaiśeṣika elements in Sanskrit grammar, in Sanskrit] [Vārāṇaseya Saṃskṛta Viśvavidyālaya doctoral dissertation, unpublished.]

Ramasubba Sastri, S., V. Srivatsankaracharya and T. K. Pranatartiharan

1965-71 (Ed.) *Kṛdantarūpamala, a concordance of verbal derivatives*, 5 vol. (Madras: The Sanskrit Education Society). [1-2: (Ed.: S. V. Ramasubba Sastri 1965, 1966), 3-5: (begun by the late Pt. S. Ramasubba Sastri and completed by his students V. Srivatsankaracharya and T. K. Pranatartiharan 1967, 1968, 1971).]

Rāma Sureśa Tripāṭhī

1960 *Mahābhāṣya ke antargata vārtikoṃ kā ālocanātmaka adhyayana* [A critical study of the vārttikas included in the Mahā-bhāṣya, in Hindi]. [D. Litt. thesis, Agra University, unpublished.]

1972 *Saṃskṛta vyākaraṇa-darśana* (Delhi: Rajkamal). [Originally a D. Phil. dissertation, Agra University, 1956, entitled *Vākyapadīya viśeṣataḥ ākhyātārtha kā adhyayana* (A study of the Vākyapadīya, with special emphasis on the meaning of verbal forms).]

Ram Sharma

1971 "Pāṇini's *chatvarimsa Brāhmaṇa*", *Festschrift B. P. Desai*, pp. 436-40.

Ramaswami Sastri, V. A.

1932-33 "The doctrine of sphoṭa", *AUJ* 1: 231-40, 2: 109-20.

1936-37 "Bhartṛhari a bauddha? ", *AUJ* 6: 65-69. [Reprint: V. A. Ramaswami Sastri (1937).]

1937 "Bhartṛhari a bauddha? ", *PAIOC* 8 (Mysore, 1935): 254-57. [See V. A. Ramaswami Sastri (1936-37).]

1938 "Bhartṛhari a pre-Śaṅkara advaitin", *AUJ* 8: 42-53.

1952a "Bhartṛhari as a Mīmāṃsaka", *BDCRI* 14: 1-15.

1952b "Mukhya and gauṇa words in language", *BDCRI* 14: 183-94.

1955-56 "Bhartṛhari's interpretation of *'grahaṃ saṃmārṣṭi'* and *'paśunā yajeta'* ", *JOR* 25: 74-78. [Reprint: V. A. Ramaswami Sastri (1958).]

1958 "Bhartṛhari's interpretation of *'grahaṃ saṃmārṣṭi'* and *'paśunā yajeta'* ", *PAIOC* 18 (Annamalainagar, 1955): 185-88.

Rangacharya, M. and M. B. Varadarajiengar (Ed.)

1916-17 *The Rūpāvatāra of Dharmakīrti with additions and emendations for the use of college students*, 2 vol. [1: (Madras: Natesan 1916), 2: (Bangalore: The Bangalore Press 1927).]
[M. B. Varadarajiengar is given as editor of the second volume on the title page of this volume; but in the preface to this he states he merely saw through the press that part of this volume which M. Rangacharya did not live to see through the press. English preface, 1: v-vii. Sanskrit introduction, 1: i-xix. Indices (following text): sūtras, 1: 1-37, 2: 29-76; vārttikas and paribhāṣās, 1: 38-55, 2: 3-13; examples, 1: 56-141, 2: 77-226; roots, 2: 14-28; verses cited, 2: 1-2.]

Rangaswami, O. P.

1937 "Bhartṛhari and the Bhāgavṛtti", *JOR* 11: 45-50.

Rangaswami Iyengar, H. R.

1951 "Bhartṛhari and Diṅnāga", *JBBRAS*[2] 26: 147-49.

Rao, S. K. Ramachandra: see Ramachandra Rao, S. K.

Rau, Wilhelm

1962 "Über sechs Handschriften des Vākyapadīya", *Oriens* 15: 374-98.

1964 "Handschriften des Vākyapadīya, zweiter Teil: Mss. 7 - 10 (G - K)", *Oriens* 17: 182-98.

1969 (Ed.) *Franz Kielhorn, Kleine Schriften, mit einer Auswahl der epigraphischen Aufsätze,* 2 vol. [continuous pagination] (= Glasenapp-Stiftung 3,1 - 3,2) (Wiesbaden: Steiner). [Pp. viii-xxiii, bibliography of Kielhorn's writings, compiled by J. Wackernagel and enlarged by W. Rau.]

1971 *Die handschriftliche Überlieferung des Vākyapadīya und seiner Kommentare* (= *AMGG* 1971.1) (München: Fink). [Pp. 44-50, published editions and translations of the Vākyapadīya; pp. 50-54, bibliography of major articles on Bhartṛhari.]

forthcoming A critical edition of the Vākya-padīya kārikā text.

Ravi Varma, L. A. (Ed.)

1942 *The Vākyapadīya (3rd kāṇḍa) with the commentary Prakīrṇa-prakāśa of Helārjāja son of Bhūtirāja, part II* (= *UTSS* 148) (Trivandrum: Government Press) [English introduction, pp. 1-6; index of quotations, pp. 1-14 (following text).]

Renou, Louis

1931 *Bibliographie védique* (Paris: Adrien-Maisonneuve).

1932 "L'oeuvre de M. Bruno Liebich", *JAs* 202: 149-64.

1937 *Monographies sanskrites; I: la décadence et la disparition du subjonctif* (Paris: Adrien-Maisonneuve). [Appendix; three indices: of Bhaṭṭikāvya, pp. 48-53, of Paribhāṣêndu-śekhara, pp. 53-55, of Gaṇa-ratna-mahôdadhi, pp. 55-56.]

1940a *La Durghaṭavṛtti de Śaraṇadeva, traité grammatical en sanskrit du xiie siècle, édité et traduit; tome 1, fascicule I: Introduction* (Paris: Les Belles Lettres [Collection Emile Senart]). [Aperçu de la littérature grammaticale en sanskrit, pp. 5-44].

1940b "On the identity of the two Patañjali's", *IHQ* 16: 586-91.

1941 "The valid forms in 'bhāṣā' ", *IHQ* 17: 245-50. [Translated from the French by N. Chandra.]

1941-42 "Les connexions entre le rituel et la grammaire en Sanskrit", *JAs* 233: 105-65. [Reprint: Staal (1972: 435-69).]

1941-56 (Ed., tr.) *La Durghaṭavṛtti de Śaraṇadeva, traité grammatical en sanskrit du xiie siècle, édité et traduit,* 2 vol. in 5 fascicles. (Paris: Les Belles Lettres [Collection Emile Senart]). [Volumes I.2, I.3, II.1, II.2, II.3; for I.1 see Renou (1940a). Indices: paribhāṣās, II.3: 53-54; authors and works referred to, II.3: 55-60; words, II.3: 61-79.]

1942 *Terminologie grammaticale du sanskrit,* 3 vol. (= *BEPHE* 280-2) (Paris: Champion). [Reprint in one volume: (Paris: Champion 1957).]

1948-54 (Tr.) *La grammaire de Pāṇini traduite du sanskrit avec des extraits des commentaires indigènes,* 3 fasc. (Paris: Klincksieck). [Revised edition, in two volumes, with the Sanskrit text of rules: (Paris: École Française d'Extrême-Orient 1966).]

1951 "Index of remarkable words and forms in the Durghaṭavṛtti of Śaraṇadeva (edition by Louis Renou, Paris 1940 and following years)", *Vāk* 1: 19-37.

1952 "List of remarkable words (or meanings) from (1) Paribhāṣenduśekhara of Nāgojībhaṭṭa (ed. F. Kielhorn, Bombay, 1868) (quoted by pages and lines, without any other mention), (2) Paribhāṣāvṛtti of Puruṣottamadeva (ed. D. Ch. Bhattacharya, Rajshahi, 1946 (quoted by the current number of the paribhāṣā's, with the mention PurPV), (3) Paribhāṣāvṛtti of Sīradeva (ed. Harinātha Dube, Benares, 1887) (quoted by pages, with the mention SirPV)", *Vāk* 2: 117-29.

1953a "Études pāṇinéennes, I: les transitions dans la grammaire de Pāṇini", *JAs* 241: 412-27.

1953b "Études pāṇinéennes, II: le véda chez Patañjali", *JAs* 241: 427-64.

1953c "Les spéculations sur le langage", in: Renou - Filliozat (1953: 79-84 [§§ 1508-16]).

1953d "Les grammairiens sanskrits", in: Renou - Filliozat (1953: 86-94 [§§ 1519-32]).

1953e "Words from the Bhāṣāvṛtti of Puruṣottamadeva (which are missing in previous grammatical works)", *Vāk* 3: 1-36.

1955 "Les nipātana-sūtra de Pāṇini et questions diverses", *EVP* 1 (= *PICI* 1) (Paris: Boccard), pp. 103-30. [Annexe A: "Les sūtra *bhāṣāyām*", pp. 114-15; Annexe B: "La reconduction du terme 'chandasi' ", pp. 115-17; Annexe C: "L'emploi de *iti*", pp. 117-20; Annexe D: "L'ordre des mots", pp. 120-22; Annexe E: "Les formes verbales", pp. 122-24; Annexe F: "Les *adhikāra*", pp. 124-26; Annexe G: "La mention *nityam*", pp. 126-27; Annexe H: "La mention *striyām*", pp. 128-30.]

1956a *Histoire de la langue sanskrite* (Paris: IAC [Collection "Les langues du monde"]).

1956b "Études pāṇinéennes, III: les uṇādisūtra", *JAs* 244: 155-65.

1956c "Études pāṇinéennes", *EVP* 2 (= *PICI* 2) (Paris: Boccard), pp. 129-49. [A: "La grammaire prākrite de Trivikramadeva", pp. 129-32; B: "Le Paribhāṣenduśekhara", pp. 132-49, a: "La liste des paribhāṣā chez Sīradeva", pp. 132-36, b: "L'arrangement des paribhāṣā chez Nāgojībhaṭṭa", pp. 137-49.]

1957a *Jakob Wackernagel, Altindische Grammatik; Introduction générale, nouvelle édition du texte paru en 1896* (Göttingen: Vandenhoeck und Ruprecht). [See Wackernagel (1896).]
1957b "Grammaire et védanta", *JAs* 245: 121-33. [Reprint: Staal (1972: 470-78).]
1960a "La forme et l'arrangement interne des Prātiśākhya", *JAs* 248: 1-40.
1960b "La théorie des temps du verbe d'après les grammairiens sanskrits", *JAs* 248: 305-37. [Reprint: Staal (1972: 500-25).]
1961 "Grammaire et poétique en sanskrit", *EVP* 8 (= *PICI* 14) (Paris: Boccard), pp. 105-31. [Reprint: Staal (1972: 478-99).]
1963 "Sur le genre du sūtra dans la littérature sanskrite", *JAs* 251: 165-216.
1969 "Pāṇini", *Current trends in linguistics, volume 5: Linguistics in South Asia* (Ed.: T. A. Sebeok; associate editors: M. B. Emeneau and C. A. Ferguson; assistant editors: G. B. Kelley and N. H. Zide) (The Hague - Paris: Mouton), pp. 481-98.

Renou, Louis and Jean Filliozat
1953 *L'Inde classique; manuel des études indiennes; tome 2, avec le concours de Paul Demiéville, Olivier Lacombe, Pierre Meile* (= *BEFEO*) (Paris: École Française d'Extrême-Orient).

Rocher, Ludo
1961 "Geschiedenis en achtergrond van de Pāṇini-interpretatie" [History and background of Pāṇinian interpretation], *Handelingen van het xxive Vlaams Filologencongres* (Leuven, 6 - 8 april 1961), pp. 112-19. [In Dutch.]

Rocher, Ludo and Rosane Debels
1960 "La valeur des termes et formules techniques dans la grammaire indienne, d'après Nāgeśabhaṭṭa", *AIPHOS* 15: 129-51.

Rocher, Rosane
1962 "The Hindu grammarians and linguistic change", *JOIB* 11: 260-68.
1964a " 'Agent' et 'objet' chez Pāṇini", *JAOS* 84: 44-54.
1964b "The technical term *hetu* in Pāṇini's Aṣṭādhyāyī", *VIJ* 2: 31-40.
1965a "La formation du futur périphrastique sanskrit selon Pāṇini: un exemple de description linguistique", *AIONSL* 6: 15-22.
1965b Review of reprint of Böhtlingk (1887a), *Kratylos* 10: 67-70.
1965-66 "Les grammairiens indiens, leurs buts et leurs méthodes", *RUB* 18: 77-88.

1966 "*Bhāva* 'état' et *kriyā* 'action' chez Pāṇini", *Recherches linguistiques en Belgique* (Ed.· Yvan Lebrun) (Wetteren: Universa), pp. 113-20.

1967 Review of Birwé (1966), *JAOS* 87: 582-88.

1968a *La théorie des voix du verbe dans l'école pāṇinéenne (le 14e āhnika)* (= *ULBTFPL* 35) (Bruxelles: Presses Universitaires de Bruxelles).

1968b "Dhāṭupātha et dialectologie indienne", *VIDK* 2,II: 699-707.

1969 "The concept of verbal root in Indian grammar (a propos of Pāṇini 1. 3. 1)", *FL* 5: 73-82. [Summary: *PICO* 27: 312-13.]

forthcoming

a "Studies in the Indian grammarians", *Semiotica.* [review-article of Staal (1972).]

b "India", *Current trends in linguistics, volume 13: historiography of linguistics.*

Rogers, David Ellis

1969 *A study on the context of Pāṇini's kārakas.* [University of Michigan doctoral dissertation, unpublished.]

forthcoming "Pāṇinian characteristics in Bloomfield's description of word-formation", *Proceedings of the 9th southeastern conference on linguistics* (University of Virginia, April 20-21, 1973).

Roodbergen, J. A. F. and S. D. Joshi (Ed., tr.)

1974 *Patañjali's Vyākaraṇa-mahābhāṣya bahuvrīhidvandvāhnika (P. 2. 2. 23 - 2. 2. 38); text, translation and notes by J. A. F. Roodbergen; edited by S. D. Joshi* (= *PCASS-C* 9) (Poona: University of Poona). [Introduction, pp. i-lxix. Translation and notes, pp. 1-229. Indices: Sanskrit terms, pp. 233-43; English terms, pp. 244-48.]

Roth, Rudolf (Ed.)

1848-49 *Yāska's Nirukta sammt den Nighaṇṭavas,* 2 parts (Göttingen: Dieterich).

Rudradhara Jhā Śarmā (Ed., commentator)

1954 *Śrīmad-bhagavat-patañjali-muni-nirmitaṃ vyākaraṇa-mahā-bhāṣyam (navâhnikam), aṣṭādhyāyī-prathamâdhyāya-prathama-pāda-vyākhyānam, śrīmad-upādhyāya-kaiyaṭa-nirmita-'pradīpa'-prakāśitam, sarva-tantra-svatantra-śrīman-nāgeśabhaṭṭa-viracitôddyotôdbhāsitam, paṇḍita-śrī-rudradhara-jhā-śarma-praṇītayā 'tattvâloka'-ṭīkayā samullasitam; bhūmikā-lekhakaḥ mahā-mahôpādhyāya-śrī-giridhara-śarmā caturvedaḥ* [Patañjali's Vyākaraṇa-mahā-bhāṣya (navâhnika): 1st pādā of the 1st adhyāya, with Kaiyaṭa's Pradīpa, Nāgeśa's Uddyota and the commentary Tattvâloka of Rudradhara Jhā Śarmā; introduction by Giridhara Śarmā Caturveda] (= *KSS* 153) (Varanasi: Chowkhamba). [Sanskrit introduction by Giridhara Sarmā Caturveda, pp. 1-34. Indices: sūtras, pp. 557-58; vārttikas, pp. 559-67.]

Rudra Prasāda Śarmā (Ed., commentator)

1947/8 *The Pāṇinīya Śikṣā with Pradīpa commentary* [of Rudra Prasāda Śarmā] *and Svaravaidikapanktivivaraṇa*[3] *(Pāṇinīya-śikṣā paṇḍita-śrī-rudra-prasāda-śarma-kṛtayā pradīpa-vyākhyayā svara-vaidika-paṅkti-vivaraṇena ca sahitā*[3]*)* (= *HSS* 59) (Varanasi: Chowkhamba, saṃvat 2004). [The name of the editor - commentator is given as it appears in the Sanskrit title; the colophon to the commentary (p. 18) gives his name as Rudra Pratāpa Śarmā Avasthi.]

Ruegg, David Seyfort

1958 "On the term *buddhivipariṇāma* and the problem of illusory change", *IIJ* 2: 271-83.

1959 *Contributions à l'histoire de la philosophie linguistique indienne* (= *PICI* 7) (Paris: Boccard).

Sabhāpati Śarmā Upādhyāya (Ed., commentator)

1963 *Vaiyākaraṇa-siddhānta-laghu-mañjūṣā of Nāgeśabhaṭṭa up to the end of tātparya nirūpaṇa with the commentary Ratnaprabhā and notes by Pt. Sabhāpati Śarmā Upādhyāya (Pada-vākya-pramāṇa-pāravārīṇa-śrī-nāgeśabhaṭṭa-viracitā vaiyākaraṇa-siddhānta-laghu-mañjūṣā saṭippaṇā 'ratnaprabhā'-vyākhyôpêtā (tātparya-nirūpaṇântā))* (= *KSS* 163) (Varanasi: Chowkhamba).

Sadhu Ram

1952 "Bartṛhari's date", *JGJRI* 9: 135-51.

1956 "Authorship of some kārikās and fragments ascribed to Bhartṛhari", *JGJRI* 13: 51-79.

1972 "Hāthīgumphā cave inscriptions of king Khāravela of Orissa – a study", *JGJKSV* 28.3/4: 11-66.

Sag, Ivan A.

1974 "The Grassmann's Law ordering paradox", *Linguistic Inquiry* 5: 591-607.

Salus, Peter

1971 *Pāṇini to Postal; a bibliography in the history of linguistics* (= *LBS* 2) (Edmonton - Champaign: Linguistic Researches, Inc.).

Sāmaśramī, Satyavrat

1890 *The Niruktalochanum (a guide to Jaska's Nirukta)* (Calcutta). [Title as given in Renou (1931): 93, number 16.]

Sāmbaśiva Sastri, K. (Ed.)

1927 *The Sphoṭasiddhi of Bharatamiśra (Sphoṭa-siddhiḥ bharatamiśra-praṇītā)* (= *TSS* 89 = *ŚSLPM* 1) (Trivandrum: Government Press).

1935 *The Vākyapadīya (3rd kāṇḍa) with the commentary Prakīrṇakaprakāśa of Helārāja son of Bhūtirāja (Vākya-padīyam (tṛtīyakāṇḍam) (bhūtirāja-tanaya-helārāja-kṛta-prakīrṇaka-prakāśâkhyavyākhyôpêtam)* (= *TSS* 116 = *ŚCOM* 5) (Trivandrum: Government Press). [English preface, pp. 1-5; Sanskrit preface, pp. 1-5; index of citations (after text), pp. 1-9.]

Sankara Rama Sastri (Ed.)

1937 *Aṣṭādhyāyī-sūtra-pāṭha of Pāṇini with vārtikas, gaṇas, dhātupāṭha, pāṇinīya-śikshā and paribhāṣā-pāṭha*[2] *(Bhagavat-pāṇini-munipraṇītaḥ aṣṭādhyāyī-sūtra-pāṭhaḥ, vārtika-gaṇa-pāṭha-dhātu-pāṭhapāṇinīya-śikṣā-paribhāṣā-pāṭha-sahitaḥ*[2]*)* (= *SBMS* 2) (Madras: The Sri Balamanorama Press). [Select vārttikas and gaṇas are given under individual rules; dhātu-pāṭha, pp. 235-69; pāṇinīyaśikṣā, pp. 269-72; paribhāṣās, pp. 273-76.]

Sankaran, C. R.

1934-35 "Five stages of pre-Vedic determinative-compound-accentuation as surmised by the historical survivals of their representatives in Sanskrit", *JOR* 8: 335-51, 9: 119-33.

Śānti Bhikṣu Śāstrī (Shanti Bhikshu Shastri)

1954 "An incorrect reading existing from a long time in the Siddhāntakaumudī", *Festschrift Bloch,* pp. 553-56.

1963 "Āgamasamuccaya alias Vākyapadīya-brahmakāṇḍa of Bhartṛhari, translated and annotated", *WZKMUL* 12.1: 191-228.

Sarma, B. N. Krishnamurti: see Krishnamurti Sarma, B. N.

Sarma, K. Madhava Krishna: see Madhava Krishna Sarma, K.

Śarmā, Raghunātha: see Raghunātha Śarmā.

Śarmā, Rudradhara Jhā: see Rudradhara Jhā Śarmā.

Śarmā, Rudra Prasāda: see Rudra Prasāda Śarmā.

Śarmā, Umeśa Miśra: see Umeśa Miśra Śarmā.

Sarma, V. Anjaneya: see Anjaneya Sarma, V.

Sarma, V. Venkatarama: see Venkatarama Sarma, V.

Sarup, Lakshman

1927a (Ed.) *The Nighaṇṭu and the Nirukta, the oldest Indian treatise on etymology, philology and semantics; critically edited from original manuscripts and translated for the first time into English, with introduction, exegetical and critical notes, three indexes and eight appendices; Sanskrit text, with an appendix showing the relation of the Nirukta with other Sanskrit works (Nighaṇṭu-samanvitaṃ niruktam (śabda-vyutpatti-bhāṣā-vijñānârtha-vijñāna-viṣayako bhāratīyaḥ prācīnatamaḥ prabandhaḥ); mūla-mātram, saṃhitā-brāhmaṇa-prātiśākhyâṣṭādhyāyī-mahā-bhāṣyâdi-granthântaraiḥ sākaṃ nirukta-sambandha-pradarśinā pariśiṣṭena sahitam)* (Lahore: University of the Panjab). [Reprint: (Delhi: Motilal Banarsidass 1967); appendix I-21: relation of the Nirukta to the Aṣṭādhyāyī, p. 274; I-22: relation of the Nirukta to the uṇādi-sūtras, pp. 274-75; I-23: relation of the Nirukta to the Mahābhāṣya, pp. 275-79.]

1927b (Ed.) *Fragments from the commentaries of Skandasvāmin and Maheśvara on the Nirukta; edited for the first time from the original palm leaf and paper manuscripts written in Malayalam and Devanāgarī characters with an introduction and critical notes (Śrī-skandasvāmi-maheśvara-viracitā nirukta-bhāṣya-ṭīkā nighaṇṭu-ṭīkāyāṃ devarāja-yajvôddhṛtasya skandasvāmi-praṇīta-bhāṣyasya saṃdarbhaiḥ sahitā; malaya-devanāgarī-lipi-likhitāni prācīna-tāla-patrâdarśa-pustakāni paryālocya ..... upôdghātena samālocanâtmikayā ṭippaṇyā supariṣkṛtā)* (Lahore: University of the Panjab).

1934 (Ed.) *Commentary of Skandasvāmin and Maheśvara on the Nirukta; vols. III and IV: chapters VII - XIII; critically edited for the first time from original manuscripts with an introduction, indices and appendices (Śrī-skandasvāmi-maheśvara-viracitā nirukta-bhāṣya-ṭīkā (tṛtīya-caturtha-bhāgau – adhyāyāḥ 7 - 13); malaya-devanāgarī-lipi-likhitāni prācīna-jīrṇa-tāla-patrâdarśa-pustakāni paryyālocya ...... upôdghātena, pariśiṣṭair anukramaṇībhiś ca supariṣkṛtya saṃpāditā)* (Lahore: University of the Panjab.) [Appendix IV: a list of quotations cited by Skandasvāmin and Maheśvara in the commentary on the Nirukta, pp. 372-496.]

1937 "Date of Skandasvāmin", *Festschrift Gangānātha Jhā*, pp. 399-410.

Sarveswara Sharma, Peri (Ed., tr.)

1970 *The Kālasamuddeśa of Bhartrhari's Vākyapadīya (together with Helārāja's commentary translated from the Sanskrit for the first time)* (Delhi: Motilal Banarsidass). [Inaugural-Dissertation, Philipps-Universität Marburg/Lahn 1970; English introduction, pp. 1-39; corrections to Sāmbaśiva Sastri (1935), pp. 143-45. Indices: verses, pp. 146-48; authors and works, pp. 149-50; Sanskrit terms with varying meanings, p. 151.]

Śāstrī, Bhīmasena: see Bhīmasena Śāstrī.
Śāstrī, Gaṅgādatta: see Gaṅgādatta Śāstrī.
Śāstrī, Gopāla: see Gopāla Śāstrī.
Śāstrī, Guruprasāda: see Guruprasāda Śāstrī.
Śāstrī, Haradatta: see Haradatta Śāstrī.
Sastri, K. A. Nilakantha: see Nilakantha Sastri, K. A.
Sastri, K. Sāmbaśiva: see Sāmbaśiva Sastri, K.
Sastri, P. P. S. and A. Sankaran (Ed.)
1948 *The Vyākaraṇa-mahābhāṣya by bhagavat-Patañjali with Pradīpa by Kaiyaṭa and Mahābhāṣya-pradīpoddyotana by Annambhaṭṭa; part I (āhnikas 1st to 4th)* (= *MGOMS* 7) (Madras: Government Press).
Sastri, P. S. Subrahmanya: see Subrahmanya Sastri, P. S.
Śāstrī, P. V. Nāganātha: see Nāganātha Śāstrī, P. V.
Śāstrī, Rājanārāyaṇa: see Rājanārāyaṇa Śāstrī.
Śāstrī, Rāmanātha: see Rāmanātha Śāstrī.
Sastri, S. S. Suryanarayana: see Suryanarayana Sastri, S. S.
Sastri, S. V. Ramasubba: see Ramasubba Sastri, S. V.
Sastri, Sankara Rama: see Sankara Rama Sastri.
Śāstrī, Śānti Bhikṣu: see Śānti Bhikṣu Śāstrī.
Sastri, T. Gaṇapati: see Gaṇapati Sastri, T.
Sastri, V. A. Ramaswami: see Ramaswami Sastri, V. A.
Śāstrī, V. Subrahmanya: see Subrahmanya Śāstrī, V.
Satī Prasāda Miśra
1965 *Saṃskṛta vyākaraṇa meṃ kātyāyana kā samīkṣātmaka adhyayana* [A study of Kātyāyana's position in Sanskrit grammar]. [Vārāṇaseya Saṃskṛta Viśvavidyālaya doctoral dissertation, unpublished.] [In Hindi.]
Satyavrat (Satya Vrat)
1955 *Some important aspects of the philosophy of Bhartṛhari.* [Banaras Hindu University doctoral dissertation, unpublished.]
1957 "Conception of space (*dik*) in the Vākyapadīya", *JASL* 23: 21-26. [Revised version: Satyavrat (1966: 205-15).]
1958 "The conception of time according to Bhartṛhari", *ABORI* 39: 68-78. [Revised version: Satyavrat (1966: 165-90).]
1963 "Un-Pāṇinian forms in the Yogavāsiṣṭha", *VIJ* 1: 247-66.
1964 *The Rāmāyaṇa – a linguistic study* (Delhi: Munshi Ram Manohar Lal). [Chapter 9, pp. 172-241: The un-Pāṇinian forms and other anomalies.]
1966 *Essays in Indology* (Delhi: Meharchand Lachmandass).

1967-68 "Conception of time in the Mahābhāṣya", *MO* 1: 19-21, 88-91. [Reprint: Satyavrat (1969).]

1969 "Conception of time in the Mahābhāṣya", *PAIOC* 23 (Aligarh, 1966): 361-67.

Scharfe, Hartmut

1954 "Kleine Nachlese zu Kielhorns Übersetzung von Nāgojībhaṭṭas Paribhāṣenduśekhara", *Festschrift Weller*, pp. 570-74.

1961a *Die Logik im Mahābhāṣya* (= *DAWIOF* 50) (Berlin: Akademie-Verlag).

1961b "Pāṇini's Kunstsprache", *WZMLUH* 10. 6: 1396. [Summary.]

1965 "*Vacana* 'Numerus' bei Pāṇini? ", *KZ* 79: 239-46.

1971a *Pāṇini's metalanguage* (= *MAPS* 89) (Philadelphia: American Philosophical Society).

1971b "The Maurya dynasty and the Seleucids", *KZ* 85: 211-25.

forthcoming "A second 'Leitfossil' of Sanskrit grammarians", *JAOS.*

Schmidt, Richard

1908 *"Mayūravyaṃsakaḥ", ZDMG* 62: 119.

Schroeder, Leopold von

1879 "Ueber die Maitrāyaṇī Saṃhitā", *ZDMG* 33: 177-207. [194-201: Verhältnis zu Pāṇini und anderen Grammatikern sowie zu den Lexicographen]

1895 "Das Kaṭhaka, seine Handschriften, seine Accentuation und seine Beziehung zu den indischen Lexicographen und Grammatikern", *ZDMG* 45: 145-71.

Schröpfer, Johann

1937 "Ein Werk über die Philosophie der Sanskrit-Grammatik", *Arch. Or.* 9: 417-29. [Discussion of P. C. Chakravarti (1930).]

Sen, Malati

1934 "The Kāśikā and the Kāvyālaṅkārasūtravṛtti", *COJ* 1: 229-40, 258-61.

Sen, Nilmadhav

1950 "Un-Pāṇinian sandhi in the Rāmāyaṇa", *JASL* 16: 13-39.

1951 "Un-Pāṇinian perfect forms in the Rāmāyaṇa", *Vāk* 1: 11-18.

1952-53 "Un-Pāṇinian infinitives in the Rāmāyaṇa", *IL* 12: 201-04.

1955 "Un-Pāṇinian nominal declension in the Rāmāyaṇa", *JOIB* 4: 169-86.

1956 "Un-Pāṇinian pronouns and numerals in the Rāmāyaṇa", *JOIB* 5: 266-71.

Sen, Sukumar

1952-53 "The story of Devadatta in the Mahābhāṣya", *IL* 12: 189-96. [Reprint: Sukumar Sen (1953).]

1953 "The story of Devadatta in the Mahābhāṣya", *PAIOC* 16 (Lucknow, 1951): 268-75. [See Sukumar Sen (1952-53).]

1962 "The names of the samāsas in Pāṇini's grammar", *BPSC* 3: 90-92.

1970 *Paninica* (= *CSCRS* 74) (Calcutta: Calcutta Sanskrit College). [Three lectures: 1: "The language style described by Pāṇini", pp. 1-16; 2: "On some words from Pāṇini", pp. 17-26; 3: "The tenses in Pāṇini", pp. 27-34.]

Sengupta, Sailendranath

1961 "Contributions towards a critical edition of the gaṇapāṭha", *JASC* 3: 89-186.

1964 "Uṇādi suffixes and words derived with such suffixes (a concordance based on the works of Śākaṭāyana, Bhoja and Hemacandra)", *JASC* 6: 123-206.

1966 "Contribution towards a critical edition of the dhātupāṭha", *JASC* 8: 191-217.

Shah, Umakant Premanand (Ed.)

1960 *Girvāṇapadamañjarī and Girvāṇavāṅmañjarī, edited with an introduction* (= *MSUOS* 4) (Baroda: Oriental Institute).

Sharma, Aryendra: see Aryendra Sharma.

Sharma, Dasarath: see Dasarath Sharma.

Sharma, E. R. Sreekrishna: see Sreekrishna Sharma, E. R.

Sharma, Mahesh Dutt: see Mahesh Dutt Sharma.

Sharma, Peri Sarveswara: see Sarveswara Sharma, Peri.

Sharma, Rama Nath: see Rama Nath Sharma.

Shastri, Charudeva: see Charudeva Shastri.

Shastri, D. N.

1967 "A reappraisal of Pāṇini", *Festschrift Gopinath Kaviraj*, pp. 296-301.

1974 "Vedic conjugational system", *Festschrift Charudeva Shastri*, pp. 294-98.

Shastri, Deo Prakash Patanjal: see Patanjal, Deo Prakash Shastri.

Shastri, Dwarikadas: see Dwarikadas Shastri.

Shāstrī, Haraprasāda: see Haraprasāda Shāstrī.

Shastri, Kali Charan: see Kali Charan Shastri.

Shastri, Mangala Deva: see Mangala Deva Shastri.

Shastri, Naradeva: see Naradeva Shastri.

Shastri, Shiva Narayana: see Shiva Narayana Shastri.

Shastri, Sitaram: see Sitaram Shastri.

Shefts, Betty

1961 *Grammatical method in Pāṇini: his treatment of Sanskrit present stems* (= *AOSE* 1) (New Haven: American Oriental Society). [Doctoral dissertation, Yale University, 1955, originally entitled *Pāṇini 3, 1, 68-85: A study in the procedure of the Indian grammarians.*]

Shembavnekar, K. M.

1944 "Sanghas in Pāṇini", *ABORI* 25: 137-40.

Shivaganesha Murthy (Śivagaṇeśmūrti), R. S.

1968 "Māheśvarāṇāṃ sūtrāṇāṃ vyavasthā" [The arrangement of the māhêśvara-sūtras], *MO* 1: 102-04. [In Sanskrit.]

Shiva Narayana (Śivanārāyaṇa) Shastri

1968a "Asti kṛñir bhauvādiko na vā" [Is there a first-class verb *kṛ*?], *VS* 5: 183-86. [In Sanskrit.]

1968b "Kṛpo ro laḥ sūtre repha-śruti-vicāraḥ" [On the sound *r* in Pāṇini's rule 8. 2. 18], *VS* 5: 362-67. [In Sanskrit.]

1969a *Nirukta-mīmāṃsā* [A study of the Nirukta] (Varanasi: Indological Book House). [In Hindi.]

1969b "Yāskâcāryasya kaḥ kālaḥ" [What is the date of Yāska?], *VS* 6: 301-16. [In Sanskrit.]

1972a *Vaidika vāṅmaya meṃ bhāṣā-cintana* [Thought about language in Vedic literature] (Varanasi: Indological House). [In Hindi.]

1972b *Nirukta ke pāṃca adhyāya (1 - 4 tathā 7 adhyāya), ṛju-vivṛti nāmaka vyākhyā sameta* [Five chapters of the Nirukta (chapters 1 - 4 and 7), with the commentary Rju-vivṛti] (Varanasi: Indological Book House). [Commentary and translation by Shiva Narayana Shastri.] [In Hindi.]

Shivaramaiah, B. K.

1969 "A note on 'bahulaṃ chandasi' ", *MO* 2: 7-11.

Shukla, Jayadev Mohanlal

1953 "The concept of time according to Bhartṛhari", *PAIOC* 17 (Ahmedabad, 1953): 379-84.

1954 *Bhartṛhari's contribution to the philosophy of Sanskrit grammar.* [Doctoral dissertation, University of Bombay, unpublished.]

1966 "Vākyapadīya-kāra Bhartṛhari" [Bhartṛhari, author of the Vākyapadīya], *Svādhyāya* 3: 185-212, 277-300. [In Gujarati.]

Shukla, Kālikāprasād (Ed., commentator)

1961 *Paramalaghumañjūṣā of Śrī Nāgeśa Bhaṭṭa with the commentary Jyotsnā by Pt. Kālikāprasād Shukla (Mahā-mahôpādhyāya-śrī-nāgeśabhaṭṭa-viracitā parama-laghu-mañjūṣā ..... p*[*aṇḍita*]*-śrī-kālikā-prasāda-śukla-viracitayā jyotsnâkhya-ṭīkayā samalaṅkṛtā*

(= *MSURS* 7) (Baroda: M. S. University of Baroda). [English introduction, pp. i-xiii; Sanskrit introduction, pp. 1-28.]

Sil, Harendra Chandra

1960-61 "A study of un-Pāṇinian verb-forms in the critical edition of the ādiparvan of the Mahābhārata; the present system", *IHQ* 36: 35-57, 37: 38-47.

1966 "The un-Pāṇinian causative verb forms in the ādi-parvan of the Mahābhārata", *BPSC* 6: 28-39.

Silverstein, Michael (Ed.)

1971 *Whitney on language; selected writings of William Dwight Whitney* (Cambridge, Mass.: The MIT Press).

Simenschy, Th.

1957 "Grammatical lui Pāṇini. Syntaxa cazurilor" [Pāṇini's grammar; case syntax], *Analele Ştiinţifice ale Universităţii "Al. I. Cuza" din Yaşi*, new series, section 3,3: 189-248. [In Rumanian.]

Siṃha, Baladeva

1969 *Padapadārthasamīkṣā: prācīna bhāratīya vaiyākaraṇa tatha anya dārśanikoṃ ke saṃskṛtapadaracanā evaṃ uske avayavoṃ ke arthasambandhī vicāroṃ kā ālocanātmaka adhyayana* [A study of word and meaning: a critical study of discussions concerning Sanskrit word formation and the meanings of components of words among grammarians and other philosophers of ancient India, in Hindi] (Kurukshetra: Kurukshetra University). [Originally a Kurukshetra University doctoral dissertation.]

1973 "Pāṇineḥ prathamācintā" [On Pāṇini's rule introducing nominative endings, in Sanskrit], in: *Charudeva Shastri Volume*, pp. 79-83.

Simonsson, Nils

1961 "Audumbarāyaṇa's theory of sound", *OS* 10: 22-30.

Singh, Jag Dev

1968 "The bases of Sanskrit phonology", *KURJ* 2: 107-15. [See also J. D. Singh (1970).]

1970 "The bases of Sanskrit phonology", *ACIL* 10.4: 145-53. [See J. D. Singh (1968).]

1971a "Pāṇini's theory of language", *KURJ* 5: 73-86. [See also J. D. Singh (1971b), (1972).]

1971b "Pāṇini's theory of language", *PAICL* 1: 257-70. [See also J. D. Singh (1971a), (1972).]

1972 "Pāṇini's theory of language", *IJDL* 1: 80-96. [See also J. D. Singh (1971a, b).]

1974a "Pāṇini's technique of description", *Festschrift Charudeva Shastri,* pp. 279-93.

1974b "Phonologic component in Pāṇini", *PAICL* 2: 7-46.

1974c "Pāṇini's theory of kārakas", *IJDL* 3: 287-320.

Singh, Jag Dev and K. Doraswamy

1972 "The case: Tolkāppiyam and Pāṇini, a comparative study", *KURJ* 4: 119-29.

Sinha, Anil C.

1973 "Generative semantics and Pāṇini's kārakas", *JOIB* 23: 27-39.

Sircar, Dinesh Chandra

1939 "Date of Patañjali's Mahābhāṣya", *IHQ* 15: 633-38.

1969 (Ed.) *Select inscriptions bearing on Indian history and civilization; volume I: from the sixth century B. C. to the sixth century A. D.*[2] (Calcutta: University of Calcutta).

Sitaram Shastri (Ed.)

1960 *Bṛhat-śabdenduśekhara by Nāgeśa Bhaṭṭa (Nāgeśabhaṭṭa-viracitaḥ bṛhac-chabdêndu-śekharaḥ),* 3 vol. [continuous pagination] (= *SBGM* 87) (Varanasi: Vārāṇaseya Saṃskṛta Viśvavidyālaya). [Sanskrit introduction, pp. 1-62. Indices (volume 3, following text): authors and works mentioned, pp. 1-4; Pāṇinian sūtras, pp. 5-66; uṇādi-sūtras, pp. 67-75; phiṭ-sūtras, pp. 76-77.]

1964 *Prauḍhamanoramā of Śrī Bhaṭṭoji Dīkshita together with Bṛihachchhabdaratna, an unpublished commentary of Śrī Hari Dīkṣita, and Laghuśabdaratna of Śrī Nāgeśa Bhaṭṭa* [and attributed to his teacher Hari Dīkṣita], *first volume* [through the avyayī-bhāva section] *(Mahā-mahôpādhyāya-śrī-bhaṭṭojī-dīkṣita-viracitā vaiyākaraṇa-siddhānta-kaumudī-vyākhyāna-bhūtā prauḍha-manoramā mahāmahôpādhyāya-śrī-hari-dīkṣita-viracito bṛhac-chabda-ratnaḥ mahā-mahôpādhyāya-śrī-nāgeśabhaṭṭena svayaṃ viracya ātma-guror hari-dīkṣitasya nāmnā prakāśam ānīto laghu-śabda-ratnaḥ iti ṭīkā-dvayâlaṅkṛtā, tasyā ayam avyayī-bhāva-samāsântaḥ prathamo bhāgaḥ* (= *HVNRSS* 8) (Varanasi: Banaras Hindu University). [Sanskrit introduction, pp. 1-56. Variant readings from two manuscripts in the India Office Library, pp. 757-59; additional variant readings, pp. 777-826. Indices: works and authors mentioned in the Prauḍha-mano-ramā, pp. 762-63; works and authors mentioned in the Bṛhac-chabda-ratna, pp. 764-65; works and authors mentioned in the Laghu-śabda-ratna, p. 766; Pāṇinian rules commented on, pp. 767-73; vārttikas commented on, pp. 774-75; paribhāṣās commented on, p. 776.]

Sītārāmācārī Śāstrī (Ed.)
1926/7 *Vākya-padīya-brahma-kāṇḍaḥ yogi-rāja-mahā-vaiyākaraṇa-śrī-bhartṛhari-viracitaḥ ...... śrī-dravyeśa-jhā-śāstri-pratyekârtha-prakāśikā-ṭīkā-parigumphitaḥ ..... śrī-sītārāmācāri-śāstriṇā saṃśodhitaḥ* [Bhartrhari's Vākya-padīya, brahma-kāṇḍa, with the commentary Pratyekârtha-prakāśikā of Dravyeśa Jhā Śarmā] (Vrindavan: Brajendra Press saṃvat 1983).

Śivaprasāda Bhāradvāja
1968 "Kecit kālidāsīyā apāṇinīyāḥ prayogāḥ" [Some un-Pāṇinian usages in Kālidāsa], *VS* 5: 255-62, 264. [In Sanskrit.]

Sköld, Hannes
1926a *Papers on Pāṇini and Indian grammar in general* (= *LUÅS* 21.8) (Lund: Gleerup). [1: "Pāṇini's last sūtra", pp. 1-8; 2: "Facts and conjectures about the śivasūtras", pp. 8-22; 3: "Bhāṣye na vyākhyātam", pp. 22-24; 4: "Pāṇini and the Grecians", pp. 24-27; 5: "Does Pāṇini quote the Rik Prātiśākhya? ", pp. 27-33; 6: "Does Pāṇini quote the Nirukta? ", pp. 34-35; 7: "Pāṇini and the Nirukta", pp. 36-40; 8: "Was the Rik Prātiśākhya a work of the Śākalas? ", pp. 42-46.]
1926b *The Nirukta, its place in Old Indian literature and its etymologies* (= *ARSHLL* 7) (Lund: Gleerup).
1926c "The relative chronology of Pāṇini and the Prātiśākhyas", *IA* 55: 181-85.

Smith, Vincent A.
1954 *The early history of India from 600 B. C. to the Muhammedan conquest, including the invasion of Alexander the Great*[4] (Oxford: Clarendon Press).

Śobhita Miśra (Ed.)
1952 *Pāṇinīya-vyākaraṇa-sūtra-vṛttiḥ kāśikā vidvad-vara-vāmana-jayāditya-viracitā; upôdghāta-lekhakaḥ paṇḍita-śrī-brahmadatta jijñāsuḥ*[3] [The Kāśikā-vṛtti of Vāmana and Jayāditya on Pāṇini's grammatical rules, with a preface by Brahmadatta Jijñāsu], 2 parts [continuous pagination] (= *KSS* 37) (Benares: Chowkhamba). [1st edition: (Ed.: Gaṅgādhara Śāstrī Mānavallī and Ratna Gopāla Bhaṭṭa) (Benares: Chowkhamba 1908); 2nd edition: (Ed.: Ananta Śāstrī Phadake) (Benares: Chowkhamba 1931); see also Nārāyaṇa Miśra (1969). Sanskrit introduction by Brahmadatta Jijñāsu, pp. 1-18; alphabetic index of sūtras, pp. 773-835.]

Speijer, J. S.
1886 *Sanskrit syntax* (Leyden: Brill). [Reprint: (Kyoto: The Rinsen-Shoton Bookstore 1968).]

Sreekrishna Sharma (Srikrishna Sarma), E. R.

1954 *Die Theorien der alten indischen Philosophen über Wort und Bedeutung, ihre Wechselbeziehung, sowie über syntaktische Verbindung.* [Doctoral dissertation, Philipps-Universität Marburg/Lahn, unpublished. Dissertation in English, with English title *The theories of the ancient Indian philosophers about word, meaning, their mutual relationship and syntactical connection.*]

1957 "The words *ākṛti* and *jāti* in the Mahābhāṣya", *ALB* 21: 54-65.

1959 "Syntactic meaning – two theories", *ALB* 23: 41-61.

1962 "Some aspects of Bhartṛhari's philosophy", *SVUOJ* 5: 37-42.

1963 "Controversies over śabda", *Festschrift Nobel,* pp. 182-93.

1965 "Apāṇinīya-prāmāṇya-sādhanam of Nārāyaṇabhaṭṭa", *SVUOJ* 8, supplement. [Introduction, pp. i-iii; textual note, p. iv; Sanskrit text, pp. 1-12; English translation: "Proving the authority of non-Pāṇinian grammars", pp. 1-33.]

Śrīkṛṣṇamācārya, Veṅkaṭādyahara

1971 "Yathôttaraṃ munīnāṃ prāmānyam" [The view that subsequent teachers are more authoritative than previous ones, in Sanskrit], *Festschrift Rajeshwar Shastri Dravid,* grammar section, pp. 65-66.

Staal, Johan Frederik

1960 Review of Ruegg (1959), *PEW* 10: 53-57.

1961 "The theory of definition in Indian logic", *JAOS* 81: 122-26.

1962a "A method of linguistic description: the order of consonants according to Pāṇini", *Lg.* 38: 1-10.

1962b "Negation and the law of contradiction in Indian thought: a comparative study", *BSOAS* 25: 52-71.

1962c "Contraposition in Indian logic", *PICLMP* 634-49.

1963 Review of Scharfe (1961a), *JAOS* 83: 252-56.

1965a "Context-sensitive rules in Pāṇini", *FL* 1: 63-72. [Reprint: *Festschrift Emeneau,* pp. 332-9.]

1965b "Euclid and Pāṇini", *PEW* 15: 99-116. [Revised and abridged version of Amsterdam University inaugural lecture, "Euclides en Pāṇini: twee methodische richtlijnen voor de filosofie", 1963.]

1965c "Reification, quotation and nominalization", *Festschrift Bocheński,* pp. 151-87.

1966a "Room at the top in Sanskrit: ancient and modern descriptions of nominal composition", *IIJ* 9: 165-98.

1966b "Pāṇini tested by Fowler's automaton", *JAOS* 86: 206-09. [Against Fowler (1965).]

1966c "Indian semantics, I", *JAOS* 86: 304-11. [Review-article of K. Kunjunni Raja (1963) (see K. Kunjunni Raja (1969) and R. C. Pandey (1963).]

1966d "Analyticity", *FL* 2: 67-93.

1967 *Word order in Sanskrit and universal grammar* (= *FLSS* 5) (Dordrecht: Reidel).

1969 "Sanskrit philosophy of language", *Current trends in linguistics, volume 5: Linguistics in South Asia* (Ed.: T. A. Sebeok; associate editors: M. B. Emeneau - C. A. Ferguson; assistant editors: G. B. Kelly - N. H. Zide) (The Hague - Paris: Mouton), pp. 449-531.

1970 Review of Cardona (1969), *Lg.* 46: 502-07.

1972 (Ed.) *A reader on the Sanskrit grammarians* (= *SIL* 1) (Cambridge, Mass.: The MIT Press).

1974 "The origin and development of linguistics in India", *Studies in the history of linguistics; traditions and paradigms* (Ed.: Dell Hymes) (Bloomington: Indiana University Press), pp. 63-74.

forthcoming Revised version of Staal (1969), *History of linguistic thought and contemporary linguistics* (Ed.: H. Parret) (Berlin: de Gruyter).

Strauss, Otto

1927a "Altindische Spekulationen über die Sprache und ihre Probleme", *ZDMG* 81: 99-151.

1927b "Mahābhāṣya ad Pāṇini 4, 1, 3 und seine Bedeutung für die Geschichte der indischen Logik", *Festschrift Garbe,* pp. 84-94.

Subba Rao, Veluri

1969 *The philosophy of a sentence and its parts (Śābda-bodha-dhātu-nāma-pratyayâdy-artha-bodha-viṣayakaḥ prabandhaḥ)* (New Delhi: Munshi Ram Manohar Lal). [Only the subtitle is in Sanskrit, the rest of the work in English.]

Subrahmanya Sastri, P. S.

1934 *History of grammatical theories in Tamil and their relations to the grammatical literature in Sanskrit* (Madras: University of Madras). [Originally in parts: *JOR* 5 (1931): 183-95, 271-95; 6 (1932): 30-53, 130-48, 236-46, 371-94; 7 (1933): 113-59, 255-76, 376-97].

1951-62 *Lectures on the Mahābhāṣya,* 6 vol. [2: (= *AUSS* 11) (Annamalainagar: Annamalai University, 1951); 1^2, 6: (Thiruvaiyaru: The author, 1960, 1962); 3, 4, 5: (Tiruchirapalli: The author, 1955, 1956, 1957); 1: āhnikas 1-3; 2: āhnikas 4-6; 3: āhnikas 7-9; 4: āhnikas 10-14; 5: āhnikas 15-22; 6: āhnikas 23-28;

English preface to 1st edition, 1: viii-lvii; chart showing number of sūtras in each quarter-chapter of Aṣṭādhyāyī and the number of sūtras discussed in the Mahābhāṣya, 1: iv. Indices: sūtras: 1: 184, 2: 272, 3: 282, 4: 325-26, 5: 343, 6: 220-21; vārttikas: 1: 184-85, 2: 273-77, 3: 283-86, 4: 326-31, 5: 344, 6: 221-25; paribhāṣās etc.: 1: 186, 2: 278-79, 3: 287, 4: 331-32, 5: 350, 6: 225; Sanskrit words: 1: 186-92, 2: 280-93, 3: 288-310, 4: 332-38, 5: 350, 6: 226-28; English terms: 1: 193, 2: 294, 3: 311, 4: 338, 5: 359.]

1969 "Yasya ca bhāvena bhāva-lakṣaṇam (2/3/37), ṣaṣṭhī cânādare (2/3/38)" [Pāṇini 2.3.37-38], *Festschrift Aditya Nath Jha* 1, p. 247. [In Sanskrit.]

Subrahmanya Śāstrī, V.

1973 "Nyāyanibandheṣu śābdikaprakriyābhedaḥ" [Differences in the interpretation of the meanings of grammatical elements in Nyāya works], *Festschrift Charudeva Shastri,* pp. 104-12. [In Sanskrit.]

Subrahmanyam, K. G.

1924 "Patañjali and kāvya literature presumed by him", *PAIOC* 3 (Madras, 1924): 96-99.

1926a "A note on the evidence of Pāṇinian Vāsudeva-worship", *IHQ* 2: 186-88. [Against Bhattacharjee (1925).]

1926b "Evidence of Pāṇini on Vāsudeva-worship", *IHQ* 2: 864-65. [Against Bhattacharjee (1926a).]

1926c "A short note on Mr. Jayaswal's interpretation of a Mahābhāṣya passage in his 'Hindu Polity' (p. 122)", *IHQ* 2: 416-18.

Subrahmanyam, P. S.

1972 "Deep structure and surface structure in Pāṇini", *AICL* 3: 20-21.

Subramania Iyer, K. A. (K. A. Subrahmaṇya Ayyar)

1927 "On the fourteen māheśvara sūtras", *PAIOC* 4 (Allahabad, 1926): 133-43.

1937 "Who are the anityasphoṭavādinaḥ? ", *PAIOC* 8 (Mysore, 1935): 258-63.

1941 "Pratibhā as the meaning of a sentence", *PAIOC* 10 (Tirupati, 1940): 326-32.

1942 "The conception of guṇa among the vaiyākaraṇas", *NIA* 5: 121-30.

1945 "The vaiyākaraṇa conception of 'gender' ", *Festschrift R. K. Mookerji,* pp. 291-307. [See K. A. Subramania Iyer (1971b).]

1947 "The doctrine of sphoṭa", *JGJRI* 5: 121-47.

1948 "The point of view of the vaiyākaraṇas", *JOR* 18: 84-96. [Reprint: Staal (1972: 393-400).]

1950 - 51 "The conception of action among the vaiyākaraṇas", *JGJRI* 8: 165-88.

1953 - 54 "On the concept of upagraha among the vaiyākaraṇas", *JOR* 23: 79-88.

1963a (Ed.) *Vākyapadīya of Bhartṛhari with the commentary of Helārāja; kāṇḍa III, part 1* (= *DCMS* 21) (Poona: Deccan College). [English introduction, pp. vii-xvi. Indices: verses, pp. 371-82; citations in Helārāja's commentary, pp. 383-98; authors, works and doctrines mentioned in text and commentary, pp. 399-402.]

1963b "Upôdghātaḥ" [Preface to Raghunātha Śarmā (1963), pp. *a-ṭa.*]

1964a "Bhartṛhari on vyākaraṇa as a means of attaining mokṣa", *ALB* 28: 112-31.

1964b "Bhartṛhari on apabhraṃśa", *VIJ* 2: 242-46.

1965a *The Vākyapadīya of Bhartṛhari with the Vṛtti, chapter I; translation* (= *DCBCSJS* 26) (Poona: Deccan College). [Introduction, pp. ix-xxxviii.]

1965b "Bhartṛhari on dhvani", *ABORI* 46: 49-65.

1966a (Ed.) *Vākyapadīya of Bhartṛhari with the commentaries Vṛtti and Paddhati of Vṛṣabhadeva* (= *DCMS* 32) (Poona: Deccan College). [English introduction, pp. vii-xviii. Indices: verses, pp. 236-41; quotations in the Vṛtti, pp. 242-55; quotations in the Paddhati, pp. 255-60; authors, works and doctrines mentioned in the Vṛtti, p. 261; in the Paddhati, pp. 262-63.]

1966b *Sphoṭasiddhi of Maṇḍana Miśra (English translation)* (= *DCBCS* 25) (Poona: Deccan College). [Also contains the Sanskrit text.]

1967 "Bhartṛharer abhipretaḥ śabdârtha-saṃbandhaḥ" [The relation between word and meaning as intended by Bhartṛhari] *VS* 4: 207-19. [In Sanskrit.]

1968 "Bhartṛhari on the primary and secondary meanings of words", *Festschrift S. M. Katre* 1, pp. 97-112.

1969 *Bhartṛhari; a study of the Vākyapadīya in the light of ancient commentaries* (= *DCBCSJS* 68) (Poona: Deccan College). [Bibliography, pp. 565-74.]

1971a *The Vākyapadīya of Bhartṛhari, chapter III, part 1; English translation* (= *DCBCSJS* 71) (Poona: Deccan College).

1971b "Liṅga-tattva-vimarśaḥ" [On gender], *Festschrift Rajeshwar Shastri Dravid*, grammar section, pp. 78-83. [In Sanskrit.] [An article with the same title appeared in *SS* 2: 41-47; see also K. A. Subramania Iyer (1945).]

1973 (Ed.) *Vākyapadīya of Bhartṛhari with the Prakīrṇaprakāśa of Helārāja; kāṇḍa III, part II.* (Poona· Deccan College). [Introduction, pp. iii-vi. Appendices: 1. index of verses, pp. 433-56, index of quotations in Helārāja's commentary, pp. 457-82, 3. index of authors, works, doctrines and upholders of doctrines mentioned in the Vākya-padīya and Prakīrṇa-prakāśa, pp. 483-85.]

1974 "Bhartṛhari on taddhita formations involving comparison", *Festschrift Charudeva Shastri,* pp. 241-57.

Sudāmā Miśra Śāstrī and Sadāśiva Śāstrī Joshi (Ed.)

1938 *The Laghuśabdenduśekhara of M. M. Pt. Śrī Nāgeśa Bhaṭṭa with the Nāgeśoktiprakāśa commentary by Paṇḍit Śrī Khuddījhā Śarmā (Laghu-śabdêndu-śekharaḥ mahā-mahôpādhyāya-śrī-nāgeśabhaṭṭa-viracitaḥ (na-padânta-sūtrânto bhāgaḥ) ..... śrī-khuddī-jhā-śarmaṇā .... viracitayā nāgeśôkti-prakāśa-vyākhyayā saṃvalitaḥ ...... paṇḍita-śrī-sudāmā-miśra-śāstriṇā pariśodhitaḥ paṇḍita-jośīty-upāhva-sadāśiva-śāstriṇā ca pariṣkṛtaḥ)* (= *KSS* 128) (Benares: Chowkhamba). [Through the vowel sandhi section.]

Śukla, P. S.

1969 "In-han-pūṣâryamṇāṃ śau, sau ca ity etayoḥ niyamârthatva-vicāraḥ" [On rules 6.4.12-13 as restrictions], *SBh* 7: 67-68. [In Sanskrit.]

Śukla, Sītārāma

1966 *Pāṇinīya vyākaraṇa meṃ avyaya prakaraṇa* [The section on indeclinables in Pāṇini's grammar]. [In Hindi.] [Vārāṇaseya Saṃskṛta Viśvavidyālaya doctoral dissertation, unpublished.]

Śukla, Sūryanārāyaṇa and Rāmagovinda Śukla

1961 *The Vākyapadīya, a treatise on the philosophy of Sanskrit grammar by Bhartṛhari (brahma kāṇḍa), with the Bhāvapradīpa Sanskrit commentary and notes by ...... Sūryanārāyaṇa Śukla; edited with Hindi commentary etc. by* [his son] ...... *Rāmagovinda Śukla*[2] *(Mahā-vaiyākaraṇa-śrī-bhartṛhari-viracitaṃ vākya-padīyam (brahma-kāṇḍam) paṇḍita-śrī-sūryanārāyaṇa-śuklena sva-praṇītena bhāva-pradīpâkhya-vyākhyānena ṭippaṇena ca samalaṅkṛtam, tat-putreṇa śrī-rāmagovinda-śukleṇa hindī-vyākhyayā viśiṣṭayā bhūmikayā ca samalaṅkṛtya sampāditam*[2]*)* (= *KSS* 124) (Varanasi: Chowkhamba). [First edition: 1937. Hindi introduction, pp. 1-20; verse index, pp. 161-63. The English title page gives the Vākya-padīya's author's name as "Bhartrī Hari", which I have corrected.]

Sūrya Kānta (Ed.)

1933 *Ṛktantram, a Prātiśākhya of the Sāmaveda; critically edited with an introduction, appendices, exhaustive notes, a commentary called Ṛktantravivṛti and Sāmavedsarvānukramaṇī* (Lahore: Mehar Chand Lachhman Dass). [Reprint: (Delhi: Meharchand Lachhmandas, 1970).]

1939 *Atharva Prātiśākhya; edited with an introduction, English translation, notes and indices* (Lahore: Meher Chand Lachhmi Dass). [Reprint: (Delhi: Mehar Chand Lachhman Das, 1968).]

Suryanarayana Sastri, S. S.

1932 "Vācaspati's criticism of the sphoṭa theory", *JOR* 6: 311-21.

Suśīla Candra Miśra

1968 *Vākya-padīyânusāraṃ darśanântarīya-tattvānāṃ tulanâtmakaṃ samīkṣaṇam* [A comparative study of the principles of other philosophical systems from the point of view of the Vākyapadīya]. [In Sanskrit.] [Vārāṇaseya Saṃskṛta Viśvavidyālaya doctoral dissertation, unpublished.]

Swaminathan, V.

1961 "Bhartṛhari and Mīmāṃsā", *PAIOC* 20 (Bhubaneshwar, 1959): 309-17.

1963 "Bhartṛhari's authorship of the commentary on the Mahābhāṣya", *ALB* 27: 59-70.

1965 (Ed.) *Mahābhāṣya Ṭīkā by Bhartṛhari* 1 [through the fourth āhnika] *(Śrī-bhartṛhari-viracitā-mahābhāṣya-ṭīkā (caturthâhnika-paryantā) bhāgaḥ 1)* (= *HVNRSS* 11) (Varanasi: Banaras Hindu University). [Part of an M.Litt. thesis, University of Madras, 1956.]

1966 "The Nirukta and Patañjali", *PAIOC* 21 (Srinagar, 1961): 1: 185-209.

1967 "On the date of Helārāja", *SVUOJ* 10: 23-35.

1971 "Pāṇinīya-mata-darpaṇa – a forgotten work", *SVUOJ* 14: 61-76.

Takakusu, Junjiro (Tr.)

1896 *A record of the Buddhist religion as practised in India and the Malay archipelago (A.D. 671-695) by I-Tsing* (Oxford: Clarendon Press). [Reprint: (Delhi: Munshi Ram Manoharlal, 1966).]

Tārakeśvara Śāstrī Caturvedī (Tarkeshwar Chaturvedi Shastri) (Ed.)

1947 *Vaiyākaraṇ[a] Bhūṣaṇ[a] sār[a] of Kauṇḍ[a] Bhaṭṭa with Prabhā and Darpaṇ[a] commentaries by Pt. Bal Krishna Pancholi and Pt. Hari Vallabha Shastri (Śrī-kauṇḍa-bhaṭṭa-viracito vaiyākaraṇa-bhūṣaṇa-sāraḥ ...... śrī bāla-kṛṣṇa-pañcoli-nirmitayā 'prabhā'-vyākhyayā darpaṇena ca samullasitaḥ* (= *AGM* 2) (Varanasi: Tarkeshwar Chaturvedi Shastri).

Tata Subbaraya Sastri (Ed.)

1932 *Chitraprabhā, a commentary on Haridīkshita's Laghuśabdaratna by Bhāgavata Hari Śāstrī, edited with notes (Citra-prabhā, śrī-hari-dīkṣitasya laghu-śabda-ratnasya vyākhyā, bhāgavatôpanāmaka-paṇḍita-vara-śrī-hari-śāstri-viracitā ...... tātôpanāmaka-subrahmaṇya-śāstriṇā saṃśodhya svakṛta-laghu-ṭippaṇyā samyojitā)* (= *AUS* 6) (Waltair: Andhra University).

Telang, Kashinath Trimbak

1874 "The Rāmāyaṇa older than Patañjali", *IA* 3: 124.

Thieme, Paul

1930 Review of Sköld (1926a), *OLZ* 33: 549-51.

1931 "Grammatik und Sprache, ein Problem der altindischen Sprachwissenschaft", *ZII* 8: 23-32. [Reprint: Budruss (1971: 514-23).]

1932 "Zur Geschichte der einheimischen indischen Grammatik", *OLZ* 35: 236-42. [Reprint: Budruss (1971: 524-27).]

1935a *Pāṇini and the Veda; studies in the early history of linguistic science in India* (Allahabad: Globe Press).

1935b "Bhāṣya zu vārttika 5 zu Pāṇini 1. 1. 9 und seine einheimischen Erklärer; ein Beitrag zur Geschichte und Würdigung der indischen grammatischen Scholastik", *NGGW* 1935: 171-216. [Reprint: Staal (1972: 299-32).]

1935c "Zur Datierung des Pāṇini", *ZDMG* 89: *21*-*24*. [Reprint: Budruss (1971: 528-31).]

1935d "*Hemantaśiśirau* and *ahorātre* (Paṇ. II. 4. 28)", *Festschrift Gangānātha Jhā*, pp. 415-19. [Reprint: Budruss (1971: 532-36).]

1937 "Pāṇini and the Ṛkprātiśākhya, I", *IHQ* 13: 329-43. [Reprint: Budruss (1971: 537-51); companion article to K. C. Chaṭṭopādhyāya (1937).]

1937-38 "On the identity of the vārttikakāra", *IC* 4: 189-209. [Reprint: Budruss (1971: 552-72), Staal (1972: 333-56).]

1939 "A few remarks on Indian Culture IV (pp. 387 ff.)", *IC* 5: 363-66. [Reply to B. Ghosh (1938).]

1955a Review of Jacob Wackernagel, *Altindische Grammatik II, 2:* Albert Debrunner, *Die Nominalsuffixe, GGA* 1955: 195-210. [Reprint: Budruss (1971: 661-95).]

1955b Review of T. Burrow (1955) *Lg.* 31: 428-48. [Reprint: Budruss (1971: 696-716).]

1956 "Pāṇini and the Pāṇinīyas", *JAOS* 76: 1-23. [Review-article of Renou (1948-54); reprint: Budruss (1971: 573-95).]

1957a "The interpretation of the learned", *Festschrift S. K. Belvalkar*, pp. 47-62. [Reprint: Budruss (1971: 596-611).]

1957b "Pāṇini and the pronunciation of Sanskrit", *Festschrift Whatmough*, pp. 263-70. [Reprint: Budruss (1971: 612-18).]

1957c Review of W. S. Allen (1963), *ZDMG* 107: 664-66.

1958 Review of Renou (1957 [see Renou (1942)]), *GGA* 212: 19-49. [Reprint: Budruss (1971: 727-57).]

1961 Introduction to Shefts (1961), pp. ix-x.

1962 "Chess and backgammon (tric-trac) in Sanskrit literature", *Festschrift Brown*, pp. 204-16. [Reprint: Budruss (1971: 413-25).]

1963 "Zu o. S. 94" [On the use of participial forms for finite perfect forms], *KZ* 78: 95. [Reprint: Budruss (1971: 619).]

1964a "Linguistic sciences", *India, Pakistan, Ceylon*² (Ed.: W. N. Brown) (Philadelphia: University of Pennsylvania Press), pp. 72-74.

1964b "Patañjali über Varuṇa und die sieben Ströme", *Festschrift Morgenstierne*, pp. 168-73. [Reprint: Budruss (1971: 620-25).]

1965 "Die Kobra bei Pāṇini", *KZ* 79: 55-68. [Reprint: Budruss (1971: 626-39).]

1967 "Vedisch *manīṣā*", *Festschrift Pokorny*, pp. 99-106. [Reprint: Budruss (1971: 239-46).]

1968 *"Ādeśa", Festschrift Renou*, pp. 715-23. [Reprint: Budruss (1971: 259-67).]

Kleine Schriften: see Budruss (1971).

Tiwari, Lakshmi Narayan (Ed., tr.)

1962 *Bhadanta Ācārya Kaccāyana Mahāthera's Kaccāyana Vyākaraṇa (Pāli grammar), critically edited, translated and annotated with notes and indices (Bhadanta ācārya kaccāyana-mahā-sthavira praṇīta kaccāyana vyākaraṇa (pāli-vyākaraṇa), sampādaka anuvādaka tathā pariṣkāraka lakṣmīnārāyaṇa tivārī)* (Varanasi: Tara Publications). [Appendix 10: concordance of rules, Kaccāyana - Pāṇini, pp. 448-51.]

Tiwari, Udai Narain

1971 "Pāṇini, Kātyāyana tathā Patañjali" [Pāṇini, Kātyāyana and Patañjali], *Pāṇini ke uttarādhikārī* [Pāṇini's successors] (Allahabad: Lokabhāratī Prakāśan), pp. 8-15. [In Hindi.]

Tiwary, Kapil Muni

1968 *Pāṇini's description of nominal compounds.* [University of Pennsylvania doctoral dissertation, unpublished.]

1971 "Asiddhaṃ bahiraṅgam antaraṅge: a metarule of rule-ordering in Pāṇini", *IL* 32: 241-57.

Toporov, V. N.
1961 "O nekotoryx analogijax k problemam i metodam sovremennogo jazykoznanija v trudax drevneindijskix grammatikov" [On some analogies with the problems and methods of contemporary linguistics in the works of ancient Indian grammarians], *KSINA* 57: 123-33. [In Russian.]

Trapp, Valentin (Tr.)
1933 *Die ersten fünf Āhnikas des Mahābhāṣyam ins Deutsche übersetzt und erklärt* (Leipzig: Harrassowitz). [Inaugural-Dissertation zur Erlangung der Doktorwürde der Philosophischen Fakultät (1. Sektion) der Ludwig-Maximilians-Universität zu München.] [Introduction, pp. i-iv; remarks, pp. 352-80.]

Tripāṭhī, Gayācaraṇa: see Gayācaraṇa Tripāṭhī.

Tripāṭhī, Hariścandramaṇi: see Hariścandramaṇi Tripāṭhī.

Tripāṭhī, Rāma Prasāda: see Rāma Prasāda Tripāṭhī.

Tripāṭhī, Rāma Sureśa: see Rāma Sureśa Tripāṭhī.

Tripathi, Shambu Nath (Ed.)
1956 *Jainendra Vyākaraṇam by Pūjyapāda Devanandi with Jainendra Mahāvṛtti by Shri Abhayanandi (Pūjyapāda-devanandi-viracitam jainêndra-vyākaraṇam, tasya ṭīkā ācārya-abhayanandi-praṇītā jainêndra-mahā-vṛttiḥ)* (= *JPMJG* 17) (Varanasi: Bhāratīya Jñānapīṭha). [Assistant to the editor: Mahadeo Chaturvedi. Index of paribhāsās. pp. 455-56. Concordances Pāṇini - Jainendra: technical terms, pp. 459-60; sūtras, pp. 461-88.]
1971 *Śākaṭāyana-vyākararaṇam of Ācārya Śākaṭāyana (with the svopajña commentary, Amoghavṛtti) (Ācārya-śākaṭāyana-viracitam śākaṭāyana-vyākaraṇam (svôpajña-amogha-vṛtti-samalaṃkṛtam))* (= *JPMGM* 37) (Varanasi: Bhāratīya Jñānapīṭha). [English introduction by R. Birwé (1971).]

Trivedi, Harihar
1938 "A note on *śakayavanam*", *IC* 5: 115-20.

Trivedī, Kamalāśaṅkara Prāṇaśaṅkara (Ed.)
1915 *The Vaiyākaraṇabhūshaṇa of Koṇḍabhaṭṭa with the Vaiyākaraṇabhūshaṇasāra and the commentary Kāśikā of Harirāma surnamed Kāla and with a critical notice of manuscripts, introduction, and critical and explanatory notes (Śrī-koṇḍabhaṭṭa-viracitaṃ vaiyākaraṇa-bhūṣaṇaṃ kālôpanāmaka-harirāma-praṇīta-kāśikâkhya-ṭīkā-samêta-vaiyākaraṇa-bhūṣaṇa-sāra-sahitaṃ trivedy-upapada-dhāriṇā prāṇaśaṅkarâtmajena kamalāśaṅkareṇa saṃśodhitaṃ svanirmitângla-bhāṣā- bhūmikā-ṭippaṇībhyāṃ ca sanāthī-kṛtam)* (= *BSPS* 70) (Bombay: Department of Public Instruction).

[English introduction, pp. 17-20. Vaiyākaraṇa-bhūṣaṇa, pp. 1-259; Vaiyākaraṇa-bhūṣaṇa-sāra with Kāśikā, pp. 261-608; notes, pp. 609-727. Indices: verses, pp. 728-29; authors and works mentioned, pp. 730-33; variant readings, pp. 734-65.]

1925-31 *The Prakriyākaumudī of Rāmachandra (in two parts) with the commentary Prasāda of Viṭṭhala and with a critical notice of manuscripts and an exhaustive and critical introduction (Śrī-rāmacandrâcārya-praṇītā prakriyā-kaumudī, pūrvârdham [..... uttarârdham], śrī-viṭṭhalâcārya-kṛtayā prasādâkhyayā ṭīkayā samêtaṃ trivedy-upapada-dhāriṇā prāṇaśaṅkara-sūnunā kamalāśaṅkareṇa saṃśodhitaṃ svanirmitâṅgla-bhāṣā-bhūmikayā sanāthī-kṛtam)* (= *BSPS* 78, 82) (Poona: BORI).

Umarji, Varadaraj

1954-55 "The Aindra school of Sanskrit grammar", *PO* 19: 47-54, 20: 31-40.

1958 "Aindra school of Sanskrit grammar (its history and geographical extent)", *SVUOJ* 1: 5-11.

Umeśa Miśra Śarmā (Umesh Mishra)

1926 "Physical theory of sound and its origin in Indian thought", *AUSt.* 2: 239-90.

1968 (Ed.) *Nāgeśabhaṭṭa-kṛtaḥ paribhāṣêndu-śekharaḥ mahā-mahôpādhyāya-śrī-jayadeva-śarma-miśra-viracitayā vijayâkhyâkhyayā samalaṅkṛtaḥ, tad-ātmajena ...... śrīmad-umeśa-miśra-śarmaṇā saṃśodhitam*[4] [Nāgeśabhaṭṭa's Paribhāṣêndu-śekhara, with the commentary Jayā of Jayadeva Śarmā Miśra, edited by his son ......[4]] (Allahabad: Tīrabhukti-Prakāśana).

Upadhyaya, Basudev

1936 "Geographical data in Pāṇini", *IHQ* 12: 511-17.

Upadhyaya, Krishnadeva

1937 "New verses of Pāṇini", *IHQ* 13: 167-71.

Upādhyāya, Sabhāpati Śarmā: see Sabhāpati Śarmā Upādhyāya.

Utgikar, Narayana Bapuji – Vasudev Gopal Paranjpe (Ed.): see: R. G. Bhandarkar (1927 - 33).

Vaidya, C. V.

1930 *History of Sanskrit literature, volume 1 – śruti (Vedic) period (c. 4000 to 800 B. C.) in four sections; I. Sanhitās (c. 4000 to 3000 B. C.), II. Brāhmaṇas (c. 3000 to 2000 B. C.), III. Vedāngas (c. 2000 to 800 B. C.), IV. the Bhagavadgītā (c. 1200 B. C.)* (Bombay: Ramchandra Govind and sons). [References to pages of section III.]

Vaiṣṇava, Rāmaśaraṇa Dāsa: see Rāmaśaraṇa Dāsa Vaiṣṇava.

Vāma Deva Miśra (Vama Deo Mishra)
1968 *Pāṇinīya svaraprakriyā: a critical study.* [Banaras Hindu University doctoral dissertation, unpublished.]

van Nooten, Barend A.
1967 "Pāṇini's replacement technique and the active finite verb", *Lg.* 43: 883-902.
1968 "The grammarian Kātyāyana and the White Yajur Veda school", *Festschrift S. M. Katre* 1, pp. 43-46.
1969 "Pāṇini's theory of verbal meaning", *FL* 5: 242-55.
1970a "The vocalic declensions in Pāṇini's grammar", *Lg.* 46: 13-32.
1970b "Sanskrit *gaṃsyate,* an aniṭ future", *JAOS* 90: 159.
1973 "The structure of a Sanskrit phonetic treatise", in: Konks – Numerkund – Mäll (1973), pp. 408-36. [Pp. 422-34: text and translation of Āpiśali-śikṣā.]

Varma, L. A. Ravi: see Ravi Varma, L. A.

Varmā, Satyakāma
1963 "Śabda kā svarūpa" [The character of a word], *BIES,* Hindi section, pp. 35-42. [In Hindi.] [*Prāci Jyoti* (1963-1972) 2: 145-6.]
1964 *Bhāṣātattva aur Vākyapadīya (Linguistics and Vākyapadīya), with a summary in English* (New Delhi: Bhāratīya Prakāshan). [Hindi text; English summary, pp. 228-38.]
1970 *Vākyapadīyam (Brahmakāṇḍa) of Shrī Bhartṛhari, the great linguist and grammarian, with trilingual commentary (Vākyapadīyam (brahmakāṇḍam) saṃskṛta-āṅgla-hindī-bhāṣā-ṭīkôpetam pada-vākya-pramāṇa-jñena mahā-vaiyākaraṇena bhartṛhariṇā nibaddham)* (New Delhi: Munshiram Manorharál). [Text of the kārikās with comments in Sanskrit, English, and Hindi and Hindi notes. Appendices: 1: index of verses, pp. 153-55; 2: maxims of Bhartṛhari in Vākya-padīya's first canto, pp. 156-60; 2a: Hindi paraphrases of verses, pp. 161-64; 3: notes on particular topics treated in the verses, pp. 165-76.]
1971a *Saṃskṛta vyākaraṇa kā udbhava aur vikāsa* [Origin and development of Sanskrit grammar] (Delhi: Motilal Banarsidass). [In Hindi.]
1971b *Vyākaraṇa kī dārśanika bhūmikā (Bhartṛhari par mukhyataḥ ādhārita); The philosophy of grammar according to Bhartṛhari* (New Delhi: Munshi Ram Manohar Lal). [In Hindi.]
1973 "Śabdapūrvako yogaḥ" [Śabdapūrvaka yoga], *Festschrift Charudeva Shastri,* pp. 124-29. [In Sanskrit.]

Varma, Siddeshwar
1925 "Analysis of meaning in the Indian philosophy of language", *JRAS* 1925: 21-35.

1926 "An analysis of meaning in Indian semantics", *JDLCU* 13. 2: 1-38.

1929 *Critical studies in the phonetic observations of Indian grammarians* (= *James G. Forlong Fund* 7) (London: Royal Asiatic Society). [Reprint: New Delhi: Munshi Ram Manohar Lal, 1961.]

1950-51 "The Vedic accent and the interpreters of Pāṇini", *JBBRAS*[2] 26: 1-9.

1953 *The etymologies of Yāska* (= *VIS* 5) (Hoshiarpur: Vishveshvaranand Vedic Research Institute). [With the assistance of Bhim Dev.]

1963 "Scientific and technical presentation of Patañjali as reflected in the Mahābhāṣya", *VIJ* 1: 1-36.

1968 "Plurality – philosophical and grammatical – in Sanskrit tradition", *SVUOJ* 11: 1-4.

1969 "Object – philosophical and grammatical – in Sanskrit", *SVUOJ* 12: 39-44.

1971 " 'Kartṛtvam' – darśana-dṛṣṭyā ca vyākaraṇa-dṛṣṭyā ca" [The concept of 'agent' from the point of view of philosophy and grammar], *Festschrift Rajeshwar Shastri Dravid,* philosophy section, pp. 1-3. [In Sanskrit.] [See also Siddheshwar Varma (1972).]

1972 "The concept of 'agent' – philosophical and grammatical – in Sanskrit, *Festschrift K. C. Chaṭṭopādhyāya,* pp. 713-21. [See Siddheshwar Varma (1971).]

Vasu, Śrisa Chandra (Ed., tr.)

1891 *The Aṣṭādhyāyī of Pāṇini, edited and translated into English,* 2 vol. (Allahabad: The Pāṇini Office). [Reprint: (Delhi: Motilal Banarsidass, 1962). Indices (volume 2, after text): sūtras (with additional numbering according to the Siddhânta-kaumudī order), pp. 1*-53*; roots, pp. 54*-62*; uṇādi-sūtras (numbered according to the Siddhânta-kaumudī), pp. 63*-69*; phiṭ-sūtras, p. 69*. Text of Pāṇini's sūtras, pp. 70*-106*.]

1905-07 *The Siddhānta Kaumudī of Bhaṭṭoji Dīkṣita, edited and translated into English,* vol. I, II. 1, II. 2, III, IV (Allahabad: The Pāṇini Office). [Reprint: (Delhi: Motilal Banarsidass, 1962) in two volumes; indices etc. (after text): identical in form and pagination with those of Vasu (1891).]

Vedachala Iyer, P. S.

1933 "The sources of Tolkāppiyam", *JOR* 7: 53-58.

Vedānanda Vedavāgīśa (Ed.)

1968/9 *Phiṭ-sūtra-pradīpaḥ (ācārya-śāntanu-praṇīta-phiṭ-sūtrāṇāṃ vyākhyānam); vyākhā-kāraḥ śrī-sudarśana-deva ācāryaḥ, sampādakaḥ svāmī vedânando vedavāgīśaḥ* [Phiṭ-sūtra-pradīpa, [Sanskrit] commentary on the phiṭ-sūtras by Sudarśana Deva] (Gurukula Jhajjar (Rohatak): Haryāṇā Sāhitya Saṃsthāna, saṃvat 2025). [Index of words derived, pp. 55-58.]

Vedavatī, Vyākaraṇopādhyāyā (Ed.)

1964/5 *Vāmanīyaṃ liṅgânuśāsanam, svôpajña-vṛtti-sahitam* [Vāmana's liṅgânuśāsana, with his autocommentary] (Ajmer: Bhāratīya-Prācyavidyā-Pratiṣṭhāna, saṃvat 2021). [Text and introduction (pp. 1-6) in Sanskrit.]

Vedavrata (Ed.)

1962-63 *Śrī-bhagavat-patañjali-viracitaṃ vyākaraṇa-mahā-bhāṣyam (śrī-kaiyaṭa-kṛta-pradīpena nāgojībhaṭṭa-kṛtena bhāṣya-pradīpôddyotena ca vibhūṣitam), ... bhāgaḥ, vedavratena sampāditaḥ ṭippaṇitaś ca* [Patañjali's Vyākaraṇa-mahābhāṣya with Kaiyaṭa's Pradīpa and Nāgojībhaṭṭa's Uddyota, part ....., edited and annotated by Vedavrata], 5 vol. (Gurukula Jhajjar (Rohatak): Haryāṇā Sāhitya Saṃsthāna). [1, 5: 1962; 2-4: 1963. Sanskrit introduction, 1: 1-5. Indices: sūtras and vārttikas, 1: 569-82; śloka-vārttikas, 2: 912-14. (for first two adhyāyas), 3: 755-62, 4: 811-16, 5: 513-18.]

Vedpati Mishra (Vedapati Miśra)

1970 *Vyākaraṇa vārttika – eka samīkshātmaka adhyayana (A critical study on Vyākaraṇa-vārttika)* (Varanasi: Prithivi Prakashan). [Part of a doctoral dissertation, Banaras Hindu University.]

Venkatacharya, T.

1946 "Tatpuruṣâdi-samāsīyāḥ saṃjñā anvarthāḥ" [The terms *tatpuruṣa* etc., which name compounds, are etymological], *JSVOI* 7.2: 1-8. [In Sanskrit.] [Continued in *JSVOI* 7.3, unavailable to me; independent pagination for the paper.]

1947 "Anvarthāḥ pāṇinīyāḥ saṃjñāḥ [Pāṇinian technical terms which have their etymological values] *JSVOI* 8.1 - 8.2: 1-23. [In Sanskrit.] [Independent pagination for the paper.]

1959 "A critique of Dr. Agrawala's 'India as known to Pāṇini' ", *JUG* 10: 85-112. [Review-article of V. S. Agrawala (1953) (see V. S. Agrawala [1963a]).]

Venkatarama Sarma, V.

1935 *Critical studies on Kātyāyana's Śuklayajurvedaprātiśākhya* (Madras: University of Madras).

1966-67 "Paspaśâśaya-prākaśaḥ" [Light on the introductory chapter of the Mahā-bhāṣya], *VS* 4: 3-11, 124-30, 135. [In Sanskrit.]

Venkatasubbia, A.

1936 "On the date of Skandasvāmin, Maheśvara and Mādhava", *JOR* 10: 201-30.

Venkitasubramonia Iyer, S.

1947 English introduction to *Prakriyāsarvasva of Nārāyaṇabhaṭṭa, part III* (Ed.: V. A. Ramaswami Sastri) (= *TSS* 153) (Trivandrum: University of Travancore), pp. vii-lvi.

1970a (Ed.) *Dhātukāvya of Nārāyaṇabhaṭṭa with the commentaries Kṛṣṇārpaṇa and Rāmapāṇivāda's Vivaraṇa* (= *KUDSP* 6) (Trivandrum: University of Kerala).

1970b "The difference between Bhaṭṭoji Dīkṣita and Nārāyaṇa Bhaṭṭa with regard to certain phonetic observations", *VIJ* 8: 86-102.

1972 *Nārāyaṇabhaṭṭa's Prakriyāsarvasva; a critical study* (= *KUDSP* 7) (Trivandrum: University of Kerala). [Bibliography, pp. 320-32.]

Vidhata Mishra

1972 *A critical study of Sanskrit phonetics* (= *CSSt.* 83) (Varanasi: Chowkhamba).

Vidyadhar, Dharmadhikari

1966 *Nāgeśa's life, works and contributions to Sanskrit grammar.* [Doctoral dissertation, Department of Sanskrit, University of Allahabad, unpublished.]

Vidyālaṅkāra, Jayapāla: see Jayapāla Vidyālaṅkāra.

Vidya Niwas Misra

1964a "Pāṇini's grammar as a mathematical model", *Festschrift Baburam Saksena,* pp. 157-78. [Included in Vidya Niwas Misra (1966): 110-29 (chapter 4).]

1964b "The structural framework of Pāṇini's linguistic analysis", *PICL* 9: 743-47.

1966 *The descriptive technique of Pāṇini, an introduction* (= *JLSP* 18) (The Hague - Paris: Mouton).

1970 "Structural meaning: an Indian standpoint", *ACIL* 10.2: 555-59.

Vidyasagara, Jibananda (Ed.)

1873 *Ujjaladatta's commentary on the uṇādisūtras (Uṇādi-sūtra-vṛttiḥ, mahā-mahôpādhyāya-śrīmad-ujjaladatta-viracitā)* (Calcutta: Ganesha Press). [The commentator's name Ujjvaladatta is given as shown.]

Vindhyeśvarī Prasāda Dvivedī – Gaṇapati Śāstrī Mokate (Ed.)

1917 *Śabdakaustubha by Paṇḍit Bhaṭṭoji Dīkshita, vol. III (Śabdakaustubhaḥ sarva-tantra svatantra-śrīmad-bhaṭṭoji-dīkṣita-viracitaḥ)* (= *CSS* 234, 235) (Benares: Chowkhamba). [Fourth adhyāya.]

Vira, Raghu: see Raghu Vira.
Virendra
1969 "Mātrā-vṛtti-kālayoḥ saṃbandhaḥ" [The relation between length and speed of articulation], *VS* 6: 237-48. [In Sanskrit.]
Vishva Bandhu Vidyārthī Śāstrī (ed.)
1923 *The Atharva-prāstiśākhyam or the phonetico-grammatical aphorisms of the Atharva-veda critically edited for the first time from original mss. with an introduction and appendices,* part I *(Atharva-prātiśākhyam, tac câprakāśita-caram, atharva-saṃhitāyā lakṣaṇa-granthānām anyatamaṃ sūtra-ratnaṃ vividha-viṣayayā bhūmikayánvitaṃ naika-pariśiṣṭa-cakreṇa côpaskṛtam ...... saṭippanaṃ sampāditam, prathamo'yaṃ bhāgaḥ* (Lahore: The Panjab University). [English introduction, pp. 1-38.]
Viśvanātha (Miśra)
1965 "Pāṇini-vyākaraṇa meṃ niyamasūtroṃ kī paramparā", [The tradition of restrictive rules in Pāṇini's grammar], *Viśvambharā* (Bikaner) 3.1: 43-46. [In Hindi.]
1967 "Viśeṣaṇa-vibhakty-artha-vicāraḥ" [On the meanings of endings which occur after qualifiers], *VS* 4: 373-78. [In Sanskrit.]
1971a "Vaiyākaraṇa-sampradāye sphoṭa-paramparā" [Sphoṭa in the grammatical tradition], *Festschrift Ṛajeshwar Shastri Dravid,* grammar section, pp. 40-47. [In Sanskrit.]
1971b "Vyapekṣā ekârthībhāvaś ca" [Semantic-syntactic relatedness and meaning unification], *Saṃgamanī* 6.1: 10-17. [In Sanskrit.]
Vohrā, Amarajīta
1971 "Mahābhāṣya-kāra Patañjali" [Patañjali the author of the Mahābhāṣya], *Bhāṣā* 10.4: 144-49. [In Hindi.]
Wackernagel, Jakob
1896 *Altindische Grammatik; erster Band: Lautlehre* (Göttingen: Vandenhoeck und Ruprecht). [Reprint: 1957, with new version of the introduction by Louis Renou (1957a).]
1914 "Indo-Iranica, 15. Zur Bildung des 7. Aorists im Altindischen", *KZ* 46: 273-75. [Reprint: Wackernagel (1953: 291-93).]
1938 "Eine Wortstellungsregel des Pāṇini und Winklers Aleph-Beth-Regel", *IF* 56: 161-70. [Reprint: Wackernagel (1953: 434-43).]
1942 "Indo-Iranica, 54. Vedische Zitate bei Patañjali (aus dem Nachlass von Jakob Wackernagel, herausgegeben von Albert Debrunner) *KZ* 67: 178-82. [Reprint: Wackernagel (1953: 394-98).]
1953 *Kleine Schriften von Jakob Wackernagel, herausgegeben von der Akademie der Wissenschaften zu Göttingen,* 2 vol. [continuous pagination] (Göttingen: Vandenhoeck und Ruprecht).

Wackernagel, Jakob und Albert Debrunner

1930 *Altindische Grammatik; III. Band: Nominalflexion - Zahlwort - Pronomen* (Göttingen: Vandenhoeck und Ruprecht).

1942 see Wackernagel (1942).

Wadegaongkar, Narayana Dadaji (Vāḍegaoṃkara, Nārāyaṇa Dādājī) (Tr.)

1945-64 *Bhaṭṭojī-dīkṣita-kṛta prauḍha-manoramā va tya granthāvarīla śabdaratna nāmak ṭīkā ...... marāṭhīṃt vistṛta vivaraṇa saha va prakriye saha subodha bhāṣāntara* [Bhaṭṭojī Dīkṣita's Prauḍhamanoramā with the commentary Śabdaratna; Marathi translation with explanations and derivations], 7 vol. (Nagpur: The author). [No dates are given on the title pages; the dates here given are those of the translator's prefaces to the first and seventh volumes.]

Waldschmidt, Ernst (Ed.)

1959 *Indologen-Tagung 1959; Verhandlungen der indologischen Arbeitstagung in Essen-Bredeney, Villa Hügel 13. - 15. Juli 1959* (Göttingen: Vandenhoeck und Ruprecht).

Weber, Albrecht

1850 "Skizzen aus Pāṇini's Zeit, I. Ueber den damals bestehenden Literaturkreis", *IS* 1: 141-57.

1858a "Das Vājasaneyi-Prātiśākhyam", *IS* 4: 65-160, 177-331. [Text, translation, comments.]

1858b "Die Pāṇinīya śikṣā", *IS* 4: 345-71. [Text, translation, comments; '*śikṣā*' is here written '*çixâ*'.]

1862 "Zur Frage über das Zeitalter Pāṇinis, mit specieller Beziehung auf Th. Goldstückers 'preface' zum 'Mānavakalpasūtra' ", *IS* 5: 1-176. [Review-article of Goldstücker (1861).]

1873a "Remarks on parts X and XI", *IA* 2: 57-59. [Reaction to R. G. Bhandarkar (1872b).]

1873b "Weber on the date of Patañjali", *IA* 2: 61-64. [English translation by D. D. Boyd of a portion of Weber (1862), appended to R. G. Bhandarkar (1873a).]

1873c "Professor Weber on Patañjali, etc.", *IA* 2: 206-10. [Reply to R. G. Bhandarkar (1873a).]

1873d "Das Mahābhāsya des Patañjali, Benares 1872", *IS* 13: 293-496. [Additions: 497-502.]

1875 "Professor Weber on the Yavanas, Mahābhāshya, Rāmāyaṇa, and Krishṇajanmāṣṭamī", *IA* 4: 244-51.

1876 *Akademische Vorlesungen über indische Literaturgeschichte*[2] [With a separately paginated supplement] (Berlin: Dümmler).

[English translation: *The history of Indian literature by Albrecht Weber; translated from the second German edition by John Mann and Theodor Zachariae* (London: Kegan Paul, Trench, Trübner 1878); reprint of the translation: (= *CSSt.* 8) (Varanasi: Chowkhamba 1961).]

1877 "Professor Weber on the Mahābhāshya", *IA* 6: 301-07.
[Pp. 303b-307a are a translation of Weber (1873d): 319-30.]

Wecker, Otto

1906 "Der Gebrauch der Kasus in der älteren Upaniṣad-literatur verglichen mit der Kasuslehre der indischen Grammatiker", *BB* 30: 1-61, 177-207.

Westergaard, N. L.

1841 *Radices linguae sanscritae ad decreta grammaticorum definivit atque copia exemplorum exquisitorum illustravit N. L. Westergaard* [Sanskrit roots, according to the statements of the grammarians, illustrated with numerous select examples] (Bonn: König). [Preface, pp. i-xiii; roots listed alphabetically with Latin glosses and references, pp. 1-341; dhātu-pāṭha, pp. 342-79.]

Wezler, Albrecht

1969 *Paribhāṣā IV, V und XV; Untersuchungen zur Geschichte der einheimischen indischen grammatischen Scholastik* (Berlin - Zürich: Gehlen).

1972 "Marginalien zu Pāṇini's Aṣṭadhyayi, I: *sthanin*", *KZ* 86: 7-20.

1974 "Ein bisher missverstandener Vers in der Vākyapadīyavṛtti", *MSS* 32: 159-64.

forthcoming

a "Some observations on the grammatical terminology of Pāṇini (= Marginalien zu Pāṇini's Aṣṭādhyāyī, II)", *German scholars in India* 2 (Delhi: Max Müller Bhavan).

b *Bestimmung und Angabe der Funktion von Sekundär-Suffixen durch Pāṇini* (Wiesbaden: Steiner).

Whitney, William Dwight

1862 "The Atharva-veda prātiśākhya, or Śaunakīya Caturādhyāyikā: text, translation and notes", *JAOS* 7: 333-615. [Reprint: (= *CSSt.* 20) (Varanasi: Chowkhamba, 1962).]

1869-70 "On the nature and designation of the accent in Sanskrit", *TAPA* 1869-70: 20-45. [Reprint: Silverstein (1971: 261-86).]

1884 "The study of Hindu grammar and the study of Sanskrit", *AJP* 5: 279-97. [Reprint: *IA* 14 (1885): 33-43, Silverstein (1971: 287-305), Staal (1972: 142-54).]

1889 *Sanskrit grammar, including both the classical language, and the older dialects, of Veda and Brahmana*[2] [Eighth issue: (Cambridge, Mass.: Harvard University Press 1955).]

1893a "On recent studies in Hindu grammar", *AJP* 14: 171-97. [Reprint: Staal (1972: 165-84).]

1893b "The Veda in Pāṇini", *GSAI* 7: 243-54.

Winternitz, Moritz

1920a *Geschichte der indischen Litteratur; dritter Band: Die Kunstdichtung, die wissenschaftliche Litteratur, neuindische Litteratur, Nachträge zu allen drei Bände* (Leipzig: Amelang). [Translation: see S. Jha (1967).]

1920b "Kṛṣṇa-Dramen", *ZDMG* 74: 118-44.

Woods, J. H.

1927 *The Yoga-system of Patañjali*[2] (= *HOS* 17) (Cambridge, Mass.: Harvard University Press). [First edition: 1914.]

Yaśapāla

1966 " 'Sthānivad ādeśo'nal-vidhau' iti sūtrasya pariśīlanam" [A study of Pāṇini 1.1.56], *VS* 3: 162-74. [In Sanskrit.]

Yudhiṣṭhira Mīmāṃsaka

1943 (Ed.) *Daśapādyuṇādivṛtti; edited with critical notes, introduction and several appendices (Daśa-pādy-uṇādi-vṛttiḥ)* (= *PWSBTS* 81) (Benares: Government Sanskrit College). [Sanskrit introduction, pp. 1-53. Indices (following text): authors mentioned, p. 1; sūtras, pp. 2-16; affixes, pp. 17-24; examples, pp. 25-59.]

1957/8 (Ed.) *Kṣīra-taraṅgiṇī, kṣīrasvāmi-viracitā pāṇinīya-dhātu-pāṭhasya paścimôttara-śākhāyā vyākhyā* [Kṣīra-taraṅgiṇī, Kṣīrasvāmin's commentary on the north-western recension of Pāṇini's dhātupāṭha] (= *RLKTS* 25) (Amritsar: Rāma Lāl Kapūr Trust, saṃvat 2014). [Sanskrit introduction, pp. 1-48. Indices: roots pp. 325-52; works and authors cited, pp. 353-56.]

1962/3 (Ed.) *Deva-kṛtaṃ daivam, śrī-kṛṣṇalīlaśuka-muni-viracita-puruṣakārâkhya-vārtikôpêtam, paṇḍita-yudhiṣṭhira-mīmāṃsakena saṃśodhitaṃ ṭippaṇībhir alaṃkṛtam ca* [Deva's Daiva with the commentary Puruṣakāra of Kṛṣṇalīlaśuka, edited with notes] (Ajmer: Bhāratīya-Pracyavidyā-Pratiṣṭhāna, saṃvat 2019). [Sanskrit introduction, pp. 1-10. Indices: citations in Puruṣakāra, pp. 140-42; authors mentioned therein, pp. 143-45; works mentioned therein, pp. 146-47; roots, pp. 148-56.]

1964/5 *Bhāgavṛtti-saṃkalanam, bhartṛhary-upanāmakena vimalamatinā viracitāyā aprāpyamāṇāyā bhāgavṛtty-ākhyāyā aṣṭādhyāyī-vṛttyā uddharaṇānāṃ saṃkalanam* [Bhāgavṛtti-saṃkalanam, collection of citations from the Bhāgavṛtti, an inextant commentary on the Aṣṭādhyāyī by Vimalamati alias Bhartṛhari] (Ajmer: Bhāratīya-Prācyavidyā Pratiṣṭhāna, saṃvat 2021) [Sanskrit introduction, pp. 1-7. – This is the third such collection published by Yudhiṣṭhira Mīmāṃsaka; the second appeared in 1953/4: "Bhāgavṛtti-saṃkalanam", *SS* 8.1: 1-16, 8.2: 83-106, "Bhāgavṛtti-saṃkalana-pariśiṣṭam" [supplement to the preceding], *SS* 8.4: 227-33; the first appeared in the Panjab University Oriental magazine, unavailable to me; see Yudhiṣṭhira Mīmāṃsaka (1964/5); Introduction, p. 4.]

1965/6a *Kāśakṛtsna-dhātu-vyākhyānam, śrī-cannavīra-kavi-kṛta-karnāṭaka-ṭīkāyāḥ saṃskṛta-rūpântaram* [Kāśakṛtsna-dhātu-vyākhyāna, Sanskrit translation of the Kannada commentary by Cannavīrakavi] (Ajmer: Bhāratīya-Prācyavidyā-Pratiṣṭhāna, saṃvat 2022). [Sanskrit translation of the commentary edited by A. N. Narasimhia (1952).]

1965/6b *Kāśakṛtsna-vyākaraṇam, yudhiṣṭhira-mīmāṃsaka-viracitayā vyākhyayā sahitam* [Kāśakṛtsna's grammar, with a commentary by Yudhiṣṭhira Mīmāṃsaka] (Ajmer: Bhāratīya-Prācyavidyā-Pratisthāna, saṃvat 2022). [Collection of rules cited and attributed to Kāśakṛtsna in various texts, with Sanskrit commentary. The title given above appears on p. 31; the title page reads simply *Kāśakṛtsna-vyākaraṇam.* Sanskrit introduction, pp. 1-30; index of sūtras, pp. 84-86.]

1965/6c *Nirukta-samuccayaḥ ācārya-vararuci-praṇītaḥ*[2] [Vararuci's Nirukta-samuccaya] (Ajmer: Bhāratīya-Prācyavidyā-Pratiṣṭhāna, saṃvat 2022).

1967/8 *Śikṣā-sūtrāṇi āpiśali-pāṇini-candragomi-viracitāni*[2] [The śikṣā-sūtras of Āpiśali, Pāṇini, Candragomin] (Ajmer: Bhāratīya-Prācyavidyā-Pratiṣṭhāna, saṃvat 2024). [Hindi introduction, pp. 1-12; Āpiśali-śikṣā, pp. 1-8; Pāṇinīya-śikṣā, pp. 9-23; Candras's varṇa-sūtras, pp. 24-26.]

1973 *Saṃskṛta vyākaraṇa-śāstra kā itihāsa (tīn bhāgoṃ meṃ pūrṇa)* [History of Sanskrit grammar, complete in 3 volumes] (Sonipat: Rāma Lāl Kapūr Trust, saṃvat 2030). [In Hindi.] [Vol. 1: 3rd edition, volume 2: 2nd edition, volume 3: 1st edition; 1^1: (Ajmer: Bhāratīya-Prācyavidyā-Pratiṣṭhāna, 1950 [saṃvat 2007]), 1^2: (Ajmer: Bhāratīya-Prācyavidyā-Pratiṣṭhāna, 1963 [saṃvat 2020]), 2^1: (Ajmer: Bhāratīya-Prācyavidyā-Pratiṣṭhāna, 1966 [saṃvat 2019]). Volume 3 consists of 11 appendices: Appendix 9: person and place names, pp. 111-50; appendix 10: names of works, pp. 151-92; appendix 11: bibliography, pp. 193-98. (lacking full details).]

Zgusta, Ladislav
1969 "Pāṇini – descriptivist or transformationalist? (in margine of two recent publications)" *Arch. Or.* 37: 404-15. [Review-article of Vidya Niwas Misra (1966) and Staal (1967).]

PART 2:

THE SURVEY

I: INTRODUCTION

I treat in this volume research done on the major school of Indian grammarians, Pāṇini's, the fundamental work of which is Pāṇini's grammatical treatise called the Aṣṭādhyāyī. Second in antiquity among works fully preserved in this school are the scholia, called vārttikas, on Pāṇinian rules by Kātyāyana. Patañjali's Mahā-bhāṣya, the work of the third of the three sages (*muni-traya*) of the most ancient period, deals both with Kātyāyana's vārttikas and also independently with Pāṇinian statements. Subsequently, Pāṇini's work was the object of two types of commentaries. Some commentators followed the order of rules as they appear in the Aṣṭādhyāyī, others reordered these and dealt with them in major sections concerning definitions, metarules, rules of sandhi, etc.

The Mahā-bhāṣya itself contains discussions of topics of more general linguistic and philosophical interest than the interpretation and application of rules. These discussions foreshadow later, more extensive treatments of such subjects in semantic treatises, of which the three major ones are Bhartṛhari's Vākya-padīya, Kauṇḍabhaṭṭa's Vaiyākaraṇa-bhūṣaṇa and Nāgeśabhaṭṭa's Vaiyākaraṇa-siddhânta-(laghu-)mañjūṣā.

In accord with this brief outline, I divide this work into the following parts: Pāṇini, Kātyāyana and Patañjali (section III), later commentaries on the Aṣṭādhyāyī (section IV), evaluations of commentaries (section V), semantic treatises (section VI), literary works composed to illustrate Pāṇini's grammatical rules (section VII). These are preceded by a survey of more general works (section II) and followed by a summary of trends in research (section VIII).

II: HISTORIES OF SANSKRIT GRAMMAR, SURVEYS OF RESEARCH, BIBLIOGRAPHIES.

1. HISTORIES OF SANSKRIT GRAMMAR.

The most complete history of Sanskrit grammarians written to date is that of Yudhiṣṭhira Mīmāṃsaka (1973), in which are treated all important questions of chronology and text attribution, with very full documentation.

This is a mine of useful and well organized information.[1] Another history of Sanskrit grammar in Hindi is Satyakāma Varmā's (1971), not as fully documented as the work of Yudhiṣṭhira Mīmāṃsaka. Varmā frequently disagrees with views propounded by Yudhiṣṭhira Mīmāṃsaka in the earlier edition of his history, and the latter has devoted some effort to answering these objections in the latest edition of his work. Two early works in English (S. K. Belvalker [1915], Haraprasāda Shāstrī [1935]),[2] though not as complete in documentation as Yudhiṣṭhira Mīmāṃsaka's, provide good surveys of major works and their relations. The most recent history of the subject in English is by Kali Charan Shastri (1972), who, while providing extensive textual references, does not add new perspectives or conclusions. A survey of major works, with extensive bibliographic references, was supplied by Renou (1940a). In addition, K. V. Abhyankar's introductory volume to his father's translation of the Mahā-bhāṣya (see Vasudev Shastri Abhyankar - K. V. Abhyankar [1938-54]) also contains a survey of Sanskrit grammarians.[3] Ramākānta Miśra's brief history of Sanskrit grammar (1969) is essentially a student's handbook, but it does sketch major points usefully. Two more limited surveys are those by V. S. Agrawala (1945), in which the author provides a sketch of Pāṇini and his work, and D. C. Bhattacharya (1922), which the author characterizes (1922: 206) as " .... a brief sketch of the Bengal development of the school of Pāṇini." There is, in addition, a brief sketch of pre-Pāṇinian grammarians and Pāṇiniyas by Mādhava Śāstrī Bhāṇḍāri (1940). A more recent, very summary, survey of early Indian grammar was written by Orara (1967). The most recent short sketch, by Staal (1974), differs from the above in aim. Staal emphasizes the methodological contrast between the prātiśākhyas (see section III.3.2.2) and Pāṇini.[4]

P. C. Chakravarti (1933) presented a great deal of material relative to Indian linguistic thinking in general. Later, a sketch of early Indian thought on the subject was supplied by Ruegg (1959: 15-21). And recently an entire work (Shiva Narayana Shastri [1972a]) has been devoted to Vedic thinking concerning language. In a more restricted domain, Liebich (1919b) dealt with pre-Pāṇinian thought concerning the verb root and also with questions of chronology in connection with the Vājasaneyi-prātiśākhya and the Aṣṭādhyāyī (see section III.3.2.2).[5] A more recent study of early Indian thinking concerning verb roots appears in Palsule (1957a).

2. SURVEYS OF RESEARCH.

Renou's introduction to his edition of the Durghaṭa-vṛtti (1940a) is at once a brief history of the major works of Indian grammarians and an extensive bibliographic survey of research in this field. The same is true of the pertinent part of Renou 1957a (pp. 34-42, 112-25). The usefulness of both these contributions, however, is small to any but an expert in the area since the author assumes familiarity with the questions at issue, the problems dealt with by commentators, and the terminology they use and also because Renou's bibliographic information is not full and is presented in an extremely abbreviated manner. More recently, two more surveys of research have appeared, by Renou (1969) and Staal (1969), both quite summary. Staal's has the merit of setting forth clearly some of the issues of dispute and saying why they are so. The last survey of the field is by R. Rocher (forthcoming b). This also is a broad treatment of work done, in broad strokes, and not limited to Pāṇini and his school. In all three of the last-mentioned surveys, the attention paid to work published by Indian scholars in languages other than English is minimal.

3. BIBLIOGRAPHIES.

There are, in addition to the works already mentioned (section II. 2), two works devoted exclusively to bibliography, in which Pāṇinian studies are included. These are by Renou (1931: 97-99, section 92) and Dandekar (1946-73: I: 62-66, section 75; II: 94-106, section 25; III: 168-94, section 25).[6] Dandekar's is the more extensive bibliography. However, it is of uneven quality; some titles are accompanied by scanty bibliographic information, dates or page references being omitted. Nevertheless, this work is useful for the summaries which accompany some of the entries.[7] The section on Indian grammar in Salus' bibliography (1971: 4-9) is both extremely small and undependable.[8] The most recent bibliographic work on this subject is by Datta S. Kharbas and Rama Nath Sharma (1974), in which are included only works in western languages. Bibliographies of the writings of three major European scholars in the field, Kielhorn, Renou and Thieme, have been published by Rau (1969), J. Filliozat (1967) and Budruss (1971). Further, Renou (1932) gave some bibliographic details concerning Liebich's work and D. K. Gupta (1974) has compiled a bibliography of the works of Charudeva Shastri, upon which he has commented. Other extensive bibliographies appear in some of the works included in the present survey; see the bibliography for details.

III: PĀṆINI, KĀTYĀYANA AND PATAÑJALI.

1. PĀṆINI: THE AṢṬĀDHYĀYĪ.

1.1. *Introduction.*

The Aṣṭādhyāyī, also called Aṣṭaka (see Yudhiṣṭhira Mīmāṃsaka 1973: I: 222), is a grammar of Sanskrit.[9] It consists of eight (*aṣṭa-*) chapters (*adhyāya*), further subdivided into quarter-chapters (*pāda*), and contains about 4,000 rules,[10] called sūtra,[11] preceded by a catalog of sounds itself subdivided into 14 groups and variously called the pratyāhāra-sūtras ("abbreviation sūtras"), śiva-sūtras, and māhêśvara-sūtras.[12] In these rules Pāṇini refers to groups of verb and nominal bases in various ways.[13] These bases appear in two ancillaries to the corpus of rules, a catalog of roots called the dhātu-pāṭha and a catalog of nominal bases called the gana-pāṭha.[14]

There has been considerable discussion concerning whether the text of the sūtras (the sūtra-pāṭha), the gaṇa-pāṭha and the dhātu-pāṭha were all compiled by one person, Pāṇini, or resulted from the conflation of various texts. In the following I shall use the term 'Aṣṭādhyāyī' to refer to all of these together with the śiva-sūtras and the term 'sūtra-pāṭha' to refer to the corpus of sūtras alone.

1.2. *Editions, translations, indices and lexica of the Aṣṭādhyāyī.*

1.2.1. *Editions and translations of the sūtra-pāṭha.*

There is available a good number of editions of the Aṣṭādhyāyī sūtra-pāṭha of which some merit special mention. The edition included in Pathak - Chitrao 1935 clearly separates modifications to the rules introduced in the Kāśikā (see section III.1.3.3c) and adds vārttikas of Kātyāyana after sūtras. Sankara Rama Sastri's edition (1937) also includes vārttikas, printed after rules, and shows the groups (*gaṇa*) of nominals referred to in rules under the rules themselves, in the fashion which was probably original (see Birwé [1961: 21-23], Scharfe [1971a: 50]). Böhtlingk published first (1839-40) a text of the sūtra-pāṭha with a modern Sanskrit commentary, both from an earlier Calcutta edition, and ancillaries. Later (Böhtlingk 1887a), he published what in Europe is considered (Renou 1969: 483) the standard edition of the text, with a German translation.

R. Rocher (1965b) has noted some corrections to be made in this work. Renou (1969: 483-84) remarked that Böhtlingk's translation contains "certain deficiencies". In fact, Böhtlingk's version of Pāṇini's grammar, though it merits praise as a pioneer work, hardly serves to give a student insight into the way in which the rules apply and are related to each other. It fails to give anywhere near the cross-referencing necessary to show this. For example, Böhtlingk translates rule 7.2.115 (*aco ñ-ṇ-iti* [*vṛddhiḥ* 114]): "Vṛddhi wird auch für den Endvokal eines Stammes substituirt vor einem Suffix mit stummen *ñ* oder *ṇ*." No reference is given to any other rule. Yet a good number of rules has to be considered in order to interpret this one rule correctly.[15] Böhtlingk's translation gives the impression that rules such as 7.2.115 can stand by themselves as independently interpretable statements, thus obscuring the extraordinary degree to which metarules, definitions and headings (see section III.1.5.2) must be considered constantly in order to interpret any given rule. A translation, "The final (1.1.52) vowel (*ac:* 1.1.71, 69) of a presuffixal base (1.4.13, 6.4.1) which ends in (1.1.72) a vowel is replaced by (1.1.49) vṛddhi (1.1.1, 50) when it is followed by (1.1.66) an item marked with *ñ* or *ṇ*" is admittedly cumbersome. However, it may be necessary to resort to precisely such renditions in order to bring out clearly how Pāṇini's rules operate. Especially since translations of the Aṣṭādhyāyī are apt to be used not by those familiar with Pāṇini's system but by linguists and others who wish merely to become acquainted with what Pāṇini did.[16] Renou's translation (1948-54, 1966), based on the Bhāṣā-vṛtti (see section IV.2.2.1), suffers, though to a lesser degree, from the same fault. Thieme (1956) wrote a critique of this translation, which, though harsh at times, brings out an important point: it is exceedingly dangerous to dismiss as overly scholastic argumentation certain points made by commentators such as Kātyāyana and Patañjali and to follow instead the apparently – but only apparently – straightforward and simple paraphrases of rules given in texts such as the Bhāṣā-vṛtti or one's own opinion of what was Pāṇini's intent.

There are two English translations of the complete sūtra-pāṭha by Goonetilleke (1882a) and Vasu (1891). Vasu closely follows the Kāśikā, hence is trustworthy, provided one recognizes that the Kāśikā makes certain assumptions of the reader (see note 16). Colebrooke (see Kielhorn [1891]) translated a small part of the sūtra-pāṭha (rules 1.1.1-75) beautifully; it is regrettable that he did no more or that no more is available. Another small section of rules (3.1.68 - 85) has been translated into English by Shefts (1961: 4-6).[17]

There are, in addition, various translations in Indian languages. Those of Brahmadatta Jijñāsu - Prajñā Devī (1964-68) and Deo Prakash Patañjal (1965) are quite useful because, in addition to giving the analysis of each rule, they provide details concerning derivational procedures (*prakriyā*).[18]

1.2.2. *Editions of the dhātu-pāṭha and gaṇa-pāṭha.*

Since Böhtlingk's edition (1887a) of the dhātu-pāṭha, based on the work of Westergaard (1841), this text has been published numerous times; for example, by Paṇsīkar (1913), S. C. Chakravarti (1918), Liebich (1920a), Pathak - Chitrao (1935), Sankara Rama Sastri (1937), S. M. Katre (1967).[19] The gaṇa-pāṭha too has been repeatedly published; see, for example, Böhtlingk (1887a), Paṇsīkar (1913), S. C. Chakravarti (1918), Pathak - Chitrao (1935), Gopāla Shastri Nene (1958-61), Giridhara Śarmā Caturveda Parameśvara Śarmā Bhāskara (1958-61).

However, there has not yet been produced an edition of either of these texts which scholars could universally consider a finally settled critical edition. Liebich (1920a: 5) modestly noted that his edition of the dhātu-pāṭha could not be called critical and should be considered only a basis for further work. Since that time additional steps have been taken towards the goal. Palsule (1953a, 1955) has tabulated the roots of different dhātu-pāṭha versions, both Pāṇinian and non-Pāṇinian, and discussed (1961: 27-56) these versions. Sengupta (1966) has also taken up the variations in different versions of the dhātu-pāṭha.

Considerable work has been done toward arriving at a critical text of the gaṇa-pāṭha.[20] Dyen (1939) made a comparative study of versions of lists of indeclinables (*avyaya*) as given in texts of both Pāṇinian and non-Pāṇinian commentators. Birwé (1961) made a similar study of a larger group of items, those referred to in rules of chapter three of the Aṣṭādhyāyī. And Agrawala (1963a, b) has attempted to reconstruct a critical version of the groups of nominals involved in the derivation of patronymics and geographic names. The most comprehensive studies, encompassing the gaṇas of the entire grammar, are those by Sengupta (1961) and Kapil Deva Shastri (1967). The latter is especially useful for its details and annotations.

1.2.3. *Lexica and indices.*

Böhtlingk's edition and translation (1887a) is accompanied by extensive indices and a glossary of technical terms which are, in general, trustworthy.[21] The most complete set of indices for the Aṣṭādhyāyī is that of Pathak - Chitrao (1935), in which the authors attempt consistently to distinguish among homophonous items, but not always succesfully.[22] The more recent lexicon by S. M. Katre (1968-69) is more successful in distinguishing among such homophones. This lexicon includes not only Pāṇini's terms, including affixes and augments, but also items derived by the rules and examples given in the Kāśikā (section IV.2.1).[23] More general than Böhtlingk's or

Katre's work are the lexica by Renou (1942), K. V. Abhyankar (1961) and K. C. Chatterji (1964). Renou excludes items such as affixes and augments, pertinent strictly to derivations, and concentrates on the terminology of Pāṇini, Kātyāyana and Patañjali, giving glosses and select references to texts. In addition, he treats separately, in a third section, the vocabulary of the śikṣās (see section III.1.4.4), prātiśākhyas (section III.3.2.), and etymologists. Thieme (1958) has discussed the organization of Renou's work and argued that this is theoretically unsatisfactory, since it obscures the relations among the usages in various texts.[24] K. C. Chatterji treats the major terms of both Pāṇinian and non-Pāṇinian treatises, with extensive references to the texts. The treatment is somewhat diffuse but enormously rich and informative. K. V. Abhyankar compresses possibly too much into a short span. He treats not only technical terms and grammatical units such as affixes, but also includes authors' names – ancient and modern, Indian and western – and titles of works, with brief references. A very brief but useful list of major Pāṇinian technical terms with their definitions was provided by S. P. Chaturvedi (1940a: 1199-1208).

Several alphabetic indices of Pāṇini's sūtras have been compiled; see for example, Böhtlingk (1887a), Vasu (1891), Śobhita Miśra (1952),[25] S. M. Katre (1967), Nārāyaṇa Miśra (1969-72). Indices and concordances of the dhātu-pāṭha appear in Böhtlingk (1887a), Paṇsīkar (1913), Liebich (1920a, 1930), Palsule (1955), Yudhiṣṭhira Mīmāṃsaka (1957/8), Gopāla Shastri Nene (1958-61), Giridhara Śarmā Caturveda - Parameśvara Śarmā Bhāskara (1958-61), Dwarikadas Shastri (1964), S. M. Katre (1967). For the gaṇa-pāṭha there are indices by Böhtlingk (1887a), Pathak - Chitrao (1935), Birwé (1961) and, most recently, the very useful index of Kapil Deva Shastri (1967). In addition, S. M. Katre (1971) has recently produced a lexicon of the gaṇa-pāṭha based on Böhtlingk's edition (1887a).

There are also indices and lexica useful for comparing Pāṇini's grammar with other systems. Two of these (Renou [1942], K. C. Chatterji [1964]) I have already noted. Liebich (1928) supplied a concordance of Pāṇini's rules with Candragomin's grammar. Shambhunath Tripathi's edition of the Jainendra grammar (1956) contains concordances of technical terms and rules of this grammar and Pāṇini's. Kielhorn (1894) compiled a brief concordance of some rules of the Aṣṭādhyāyī and the comparable rules from the grammars of Śākaṭāyana and Hemacandra,[26] and this has been enlarged by Birwé (1971). An extensive concordance of rules has been compiled by B. J. Doshi (1967), but the usefulness of this work is diminished by the fact that Malayagiri's grammar is used as the point of reference. L. M. Tiwari (1962) includes in his edition of Kaccāyana's Pāli grammar a concordance of rules from this grammar and Pāṇini's.

As I mentioned above, the third section of Renou's dictionary (1942) includes terminology from the prātiśākhyas. More specifically intended for a comparison of prātiśākhya statements and Pāṇinian rules is the index by Mangala Deva Shastri (1937). In addition, the index of grammatical terms in Rajavade (1940) is useful for comparing Pāṇinian terminology with terminology in the Nirukta (see section III.3.2.1).

For comparing major terms as they are used by Pāṇini and Pāṇinīyas and by logicians of the Nyāya school the dictionary by Jhalakīkar and Abhyankar (1928) is the major work available. Though excellent, this work is in need of updating, since the editions and manuscripts referred to are not always available now. Finally, the Mīmāṃsā dictionary edited by Kevalānandasaraswatī (1952-66) is extremely useful for comparing Pāṇinian and ritual usage. One must, however, be fairly familiar with the major theoretical text on ritual exegesis, the Jaimini sūtras, since a great part of this dictionary is organized according to sections (*adhikaraṇa*) in this text.

1.3. *Concerning the original text of the Aṣṭādhyāyī.*

1.3.1. *Evidence of pre-Pāṇinian grammarians.*

In the Aṣṭādhyāyī Pāṇini mentions by name ten other persons, all presumably grammarians:[27] Āpiśali, Kāśyapa, Gārgya, Gālava, Cakravarman, Bhāradvāja, Śākaṭāyana, Śākalya, Senaka, Sphoṭāyana. The most complete survey of information on these appears in Yudhiṣṭhira Mimaṃsaka (1973: I: 134-77); see also S. K. Belvalkar (1915: 9-10), S. P. Chaturvedi (1941b: 49-53), V. S. Agrawala (1963a: 343-49), Birwé (1966: 1-4), Kali Charan Shastri (1972: 55-102), Vidhata Mishra (1972: 30-35). According to commentators, Pāṇini's mentioning such other grammarians indicates that the operations in question are optional; and later grammarians indeed substituted *vā* 'or' for names (Kielhorn [1881: 87], [1887b: 27]). When, however, a rule contains both the name of a grammarian and an item such as *vā* indicating that the operation in question is optional, commentators then say that this name is stated honoris causa (*pūrjârtha*). However, most modern scholars have recognized that Pāṇini's mention of other grammarians serves to convey differences in usage; and when the name of another grammarian is coupled with a term such as *vā*, the rule in question states an optional operation recognized by that grammarian. In effect, these are mentions of dialectal usages; see C. V. Vaidya (1930: 130), Thieme (1937: 335-36), S. P. Chaturvedi (1941b: 46-48; 1943), R. S. Bhattacharya (1952), S. A. Dange (1970), M. M. Deshpande (1971). The view of commentators is based on the position that Sanskrit is eternal, perennial, fixed,[28] so that the mention of a particular view concerning given forms can be reconciled only with an option; see Thieme (1937: 336), R. S. Bhattacharya (1952: 168). Pāṇini also mentions easterners and northerners, and commentators consider that the terms *udīcām* "of northerners" and *prācām* "of easterners" refer both to areas in which certain usages obtain and to schools of grammarians. Many modern scholars have also accepted that Pāṇini thereby refers to schools of grammar; for example, Goldstücker (1861: 90 n. 97), R. G. Bhandarkar (1873b [= 1927-33 1: 123-24]), Böhtlingk (1887a: ix), Franke (1891b: 957, 975), S. K. Belvalkar (1915: 10-11), Renou (1940a: 6 n. 2), R. S. Bhattacharya (1952: 178-79), K. V. Abhyankar (1954: 124, 148-49; 1961: 255, *sv. prācya-vaiyākaraṇa*), P. S. Subrahmanya Sastri (1960: x), S. M. Katre (1968-69: 397, *sv. prāñc-*), and, most recently, Gonda (1973: 338). Bahulikar (1972: 131-49) discusses the views of earlier scholars and the rules in question and concludes that in all cases the rules refer not to schools of grammarians but to dialectal usages; see also M. M. Deshpande (1971: 24 n. 3). I think this view is acceptable, although there remains more to be done concerning the details of what commentators say.

From the above information it is proper to conclude that other grammarians, predecessors or contemporaries of Pāṇini, had, like him, noted particular usages, of which Pāṇini took notice in his own work. Moreover, evidence in the Mahā-bhāṣya of Patañjali makes it licit to assert that, at the time of Kātyāyana and Patañjali, grammars by Āpiśali and Śākaṭāyana were known. In vārttika 3 on 4.1.14 (Kielhorn [1880-85: II: 205.20], see also Kielhorn [1887c: 102]), Kātyāyana cites the utterance *āpiśalam adhīte* "studies the grammar of Āpiśali".[29] In addition, Patañjali refers to a rule (*vidhi*) of Āpiśali[30] according to which the item *dhenu* "cow" is followed by the affix *ka* to form the derivate *dhainuka* "group of cows" unless it is preceded by the negative particle. Moreover, Patañjali refers to grammars promulgated (*prôkta*) by Pāṇini, Āpiśali and Kāśakṛtsna: *pāṇininā prôktaṃ pāṇinīyam, āpiśalam, kāśakṛtsnam* (Kielhorn [1880-85: I: 12.5-6]). And a verse cited in the Mahā-bhāṣya on 3.3.1 (Kielhorn [1880-85: II: 138.16], see also Kielhorn [1887c: 102]) refers to Śākaṭāyana as the grammarian who held that all nouns were derived from verbs.[31] Kātyāyana and Patañjali also use the term *pūrva-sūtra* to refer to earlier (*pūrva*) grammars; see Kielhorn (1887c: 101), Yudhiṣṭhira Mīmāṃsaka (1973: I: 241)

In addition, Pāṇini himself occasionally uses terms which he has not introduced in his own rules. For example, he himself introduces the accusative dual ending *au* with the appended marker *ṭ* (*auṭ*). But in rule 7.1.18 (*auṅa āpaḥ*) he uses the term *auṅ* to refer to the nominative and accusative dual endings *au*, thus making use of a marker *ṅ* attached to *au*. Patañjali (Kielhorn 1880-85: III: 247.12) considers this a term from a *pūrva-sūtra.*[32]

Finally, there is good evidence to show that considerable thought had been devoted before Pāṇini to phonologic and grammatical statements; see Liebich (1919b: 1-17), Palsule (1957a), Cardona (1969: 8, 30).[33]

The evidence noted and referred to lends itself to one conclusion only: Pāṇini indeed had predecessors in the field of grammar. Two questions now arise. First, is the text of any of these predecessors' works extant either in the original form or in a recast? Second, whether or not such a work be extant, is Pāṇini's grammar to be considered a recast of such earlier treatises?

1.3.2. *Extant works which have been attributed to pre-Pāṇinians.*

1.3.2a. *Āpiśali.*

As I have noted (section III.1.3.1), sūtras ascribed to Āpiśali are referred to in texts as early as the Mahā-bhāṣya. However, a full grammatical treatise ascribed to Āpiśali is not available. Nevertheless, there is a phonetic treatise, the Āpiśala-sikṣā,[34] attributed to Āpiśali. Yudhiṣṭhira Mīmāṃsaka (1967/8: introduction, pp. 2-4, 1973: I: 144-45) argues that this text is by Āpiśali, the early grammarian mentioned by Pāṇini. As far as I can see, there is no solid evidence which would definitively prove otherwise.[35]

Yudhiṣṭhira Mīmāṃsaka (1967/8: introduction, p. 8; 1973: III: 194-95) has suggested that the pañca-pādī version of the uṇ-ādi-sūtras (see section III.1.4.1) also was composed by Āpiśali. He reasons as follows. In the Āpiśala-śikṣā, nasals appear in the order: (1) *ñ, m, ṅ, ṇ, n* (see section III. 1.4.4b with note 145). This is the order of nasals also in Pāṇini's śiva-sūtras (section III.1.1). In the sūtra version of the Pāṇinīya-śikṣā, however, these sounds appear in the order: (2) *ṅ, ñ, ṇ, n, m* (see section III.1.4.4b with note 146). This follows the usual order of stops: velar (*k* etc.), palatal (*c* etc.), retroflex (*ṭ* etc.), dental (*t* etc.), labial (*p* etc.). Order (2) must have been replaced by (1) to allow forming an abbreviation (*pratyāhāra*, see section III.1.1 with note 12) *ñam.* Such an abbreviation is used in the uṇ-ādi-sūtras (pañca-pādī 1.113, Aufrecht 1859: 27). Accepting that the sūtra version of the Pāṇinīya-śikṣā was composed by Pāṇini, then, Yudhiṣṭhira Mīmāṃsaka concludes that order (1) found in the śiva-sūtras was originally Āpiśali's, from whom Pāṇini then took it. Moreover, since the abbreviation *ñam* is used in the uṇ-ādi-sūtras and the only reason for replacing (2) with (1) was to allow forming this abbreviation, the uṇ-ādi rule in question must be Āpiśali's. In addition, the daśa-pādī version of the uṇ-ādi-sūtras is based on the pañca-pādī, which is older (see section III.1.4.1). Hence, the pañca-pādī must be attributed to Āpiśali. Yudhiṣṭhira Mīmāṃsaka (1973: III: 195) admits, "This is only an inference on my part" (*yah hamārā anumānamātra hai*). And indeed the evidence on which this conclusion is based is small. In fact, I do not think the evidence proves the conclusion. Given that order (1) appears in the śiva-sūtras, but (2) in a work the authorship of which is disputed, it is of doubtful propriety to accept immediately that the former must be a borrowing despite the fact that it appears in a series of sūtras which are clearly attributable to Pāṇini (see section III.1.3.4). Moreover, the basic assumption underlying the above argument is that (2) was replaced by (1) only to form the abbreviation *ñam*. However, it is not obvious that this is the only reason for adopting order (1). Given (2), Pāṇini had to change this arrangement in order to allow (by rule 8.3.32: *ṅamo hrasvād aci ṅamuṇ nityam*) sequences such as *pratyaṅṅāste* 'is seated facing west' (< *pratyaṅ āste*), *kurvannāste* 'is seated while working' (< *kurvan āste*) and prevent the same kind of augmenting in sequences such as *tvam āse* 'you are seated', where *-m* is followed by a vowel (see Cardona [1969: 9 n. 12; 15-16; 30-31]). To allow an initial augment for a vowel preceded by *ṅ, ṇ, n,* themselves preceded by short vowels, and preclude this when the nasal was *ñ* or *m*, Pāṇini had to rearrange the nasals to refer to *ṅ, ṇ, n* by means of the abbreviation *ṅam*. Once the basic assumption noted is thus shown to be unnecessary, then, the argument noted above loses cogency.

1.3.2b. *Śākaṭāyana.*

Oppert (1894: vi-vii) tacitly assumed that the treatise he published was ancient, although several years earlier Burnell (1875: 97) had explicitly said that the available Śākaṭāyana grammar was post-Pāṇinian. Still earlier, however, Bühler (1864: 703), in the course of describing the text of the Śākaṭāyana grammar, had assumed it was pre-Pāṇinian and claimed that Pāṇini's Aṣṭādhyāyī was a reworking of this treatise. Kielhorn (1894, see also 1887b) reacted to Oppert and vigorously argued that the extant Śākaṭāyana grammar was post-Pāṇinian. Later, Liebich (1930: 236) characterized Bühler's view as outdated. The view generally held by scholars now, even by traditional Indian scholars (see Yudhiṣṭhira Mīmāṃsaka [1973: I: 164]), is that this treatise is not by the Śākaṭāyana mentioned in the Aṣṭādhyāyī. A full statement of the question, with literature, has recently been supplied by Birwe (1971: 1-13).

Another extant work attributed by some to Śākaṭāyana is the Ṛk-tantra. But this has also been ascribed to Audavraji. Sūrya Kānta (1933: 33-41) discussed the evidence and advanced the hypothesis that Śākaṭāyana the pre-Pāṇinian grammarian reworked an original treatise by Audavraji.

1.3.2c. *Indra.*

There are statements in various treatises which have been attributed to an Aindra grammar; see K. C. Chatterji (1932: 224-25), Yudhiṣṭhira Mīmāṃsaka (1973: I: 86-87).[36] Moreover, there is a legend told in the Taittirīya Saṃhitā according to which speech (*vāk*) was at one time undiscriminated (*avyākṛtā*); the gods asked Indra to discriminate it (*vyākṛ*), which he did. Further, in the introductory section of the Mahā-bhāṣya, Patañjali (Kielhorn 1880-85: I: 5.23 - 6.2), in the course of saying that correct usage cannot be taught by means of a word-for-word (*pratipada*) enumeration of correct forms, says: "Thus is it handed down: Bṛhaspati proclaimed to Indra for a thousand heaven years a complete text of words listed individually and yet he did not get to the end" (*evaṃ hi śrūyate: bṛhaspatir indrāya divyaṃ varṣa-sahasraṃ prati-padôktānāṃ śabdānāṃ śabda-pārāyaṇaṃ prôvāca nântaṃ jagāma*). On the bases of such passages, it has been supposed that there was a grammar (*vyākaraṇa*) by Indra (hence called Aindra), the pupil of Bṛhaspati.

Burnell (1875) propounded the theory that a series of grammars, among them the Kātantra grammar of Sanskrit and Tolkāppiyar's Tamil grammar, which he termed "Aindra treatises" (1875: 31), "represent a school of grammar older than that of Pāṇini" (1875: 31). After discussing evidence, Burnell (1875: 31-32) stated his position in the following terms: "It follows from the preceding enquiry that by Aindra grammar one must understand a school of grammar, and not a specific work by an individual; and if the passages in which the Aindra Grammar is mentioned and which I have collected above be examined closely, it will be seen that they really bear out this meaning and do not attribute an actual grammatical treatise to the god Indra." If I understand Burnell correctly, he proposed that there was an early, pre-Pāṇinian, system of grammar, which he chose to call Aindra, obviously in accord with the terminology of the legends noted above. But he did not attribute to the god Indra a single treatise. Other scholars have believed otherwise. Peterson (apud Kielhorn [1886a: 181]) claimed to have discovered the beginning of "the Indra grammar". Kielhorn (1886a) argued against this, saying that there was an Indragomin, whose work Hemacandra used and who was post-Pāṇinian. Kielhorn's position was accepted by S. K. Belvalkar (1915: 11-12), who suggested that the Aindra school might be none other than the Kātantra school, itself definitely post-Pāṇinian. Böhtlingk (1887d: 659) noted that the Kātantra is a recast of Pāṇini's grammar (see also Liebich [1919a: 5]) and Liebich (1930: 236) therefore rejected the view that the Kātantra might represent a resurrection of the Aindra system. However, several scholars have more recently maintained not only that there was an Aindra system but also that there was a single treatise by Indra. V. R. Ramachandra Dikshitar (1935: 319) argued against Burnell, claiming that the Aindra grammar was indeed a single work by Indra. Varadaraj Umarji (1954-55) claimed to have reconstructed the structure of the Aindra grammar, and Prabhudayāla Agnihotrī (1966: 7-9, 66-67) also has accepted that there was an Aindra grammar on which was based the Kātantra. Vidya Niwas Misra (1966: 14) also speaks of the Aindra school "founded by Indra". Yudhiṣṭhira Mīmāṃsaka (1973: I: 80-88) discusses Indra's date,[37] his grammar, and its influence on Tamil grammar.[38] Western scholars, on the other hand, generally reject not only the position that there was a single Aindra treatise but also Burnell's thesis. Renou's (1969: 482, cf. 1940a: 6 n. 2) strong rejection of Burnell is representative: "In any case, the restoration of a complete tradition preceding Pāṇini, which A. C. Burnell . . . . had at one time attempted to set forth, must certainly be rejected."

It is unfortunate that Burnell accepted the name Aindra, obviously in keeping with the legends I have referred to. For his thesis, with some modification, is, I think, not so outlandish as its opponents claim. Clearly there is evidence to show that Pāṇini had some grammatical antecedents, that he was not the first grammarian of India (see section III.1.3.1). If, instead of "Aindra grammar", one used "older method", the thesis might be more palatable. For the similarities in system between the prātiśākhyas and works such as the Kātantra are indeed striking and at least some of the method and terminology in question is plausibly pre-Pāṇinian (see Cardona [1969: 6-9, 32-33]). One need not posit a single treatise by the god Indra; one need posit no more than a pre-Pāṇinian methodology. As for treatises such as the Kātantra, it is obvious that they do not represent a direct continuation of a pre-Pāṇinian tradition. However, it is equally patent that the Kātantra, in recasting Pāṇini's grammar, fell back on a methodology which is identical with one which we have a right to consider pre-Pāṇinian.

1.3.2d. *Kāśakṛtsna.*

Kāśakṛtsna is frequently referred to in the commentatorial literature, as early as the Mahā-bhāṣya (see section III.1.3.1). Yudhiṣṭhira Mīmāṃsaka (1965/6b) has ably collected the fragments attributed to Kāśakṛtsna and composed a commentary on them. There is also a dhātu-pāṭha ascribed to Kāśakṛtsna, the Kāśakṛtsna-śabda-kalāpa-dhātu-pāṭha. This has been edited, with Cannavīra's Kannada commentary, by A. N. Narasimhia (1952, 1958-59), and Yudhiṣṭhira Mīmāṃsaka (1965/6a) has translated the commentary into Sanskrit. This scholar has also (1965/6b: introduction, pp. 8-11, 1973: I: 111-14) set down eleven reasons for considering this Kāśakṛtsna to be pre-Pāṇinian. I consider here a few of these, the ones I think strongest.

In the list (*gaṇa*) accompanying Pāṇini's rule 2.4.69, the name Kaśakṛtsna appears (see Kapil Deva Shastri 1967: 97 with n. 13), and the name Kāśakṛtsna appears in the list to 4.2.80 (see Kapil Deva Shastri [1967: 136 with n. 18]), so that Kāśakṛtsna was known to Pāṇini. Kāśakṛtsna is mentioned in the Vedānta-sūtras, which are pre-Pāṇinian. Patañjali mentions the grammars propounded by Pāṇini, Āpiśali and Kāśakṛtsna, in that order (see section III.1.3.1). Since Patañjali mentions Āpiśali's work after Pāṇini's and the former is pre-Pāṇinian, so must Kāśakṛtsna's grammar be pre-Pāṇinian, since it is mentioned after Apiśali's. The number of roots given in the Kāśakṛtsna-śabda-kalāpa-dhātu-pāṭha is greater than the number of roots in Pāṇini's dhātu-pāṭha. The general trend in later dhātu-pāṭhas is towards condensation. Therefore, Pāṇini's is later than Kāśakṛtsna's. I do not think such arguments are sufficient to prove the point. The appearance of *kăśakṛtsna* in the gaṇa-pāṭha no more proves Pāṇini knew Kāśakṛtsna's grammar than does the appearance of *yaska* therein prove that Pāṇini knew Yāska's Nirukta (see section III.3.2.1). As for the Vedānta-sūtras, granting for the sake of argument that in their present form they are pre-Pāṇinian – an assumption not all scholars would make – it does not follow that the Kāśakṛtsna mentioned therein is the same as the grammarian who composed the works in question. And as for Patañjali's statement, this shows that Patañjali knew of a grammar propounded by Kāśakṛtsna, an early teacher, but it does not demonstrate that the texts we have are pre-Pāṇinian. Finally, the argument concerning the dhātu-pāṭha is general and vague. Indeed, Palsule (1953b; 1961: 44-48) has shown that Kāśakṛtsna's dhātu-pāṭha uses markers (*anubandha*) with functions identical to those of Pāṇini's markers and pointed out affinity with the definitely post-Pāṇinian Daurga-dhātu-pāṭha of the Kātantra school.[39] Earlier, K. C. Chatterji (1932: 225-27) had concluded, after considering evidence, that Kāśakṛtsna was posterior to Pāṇini but earlier than Kātyāyana. Birwé (1966: 10) also is of the opinion that the evidence does not warrant considering Kāśakṛtsna definitely a predecessor of Pāṇini. More recently, S. D. Joshi and J. A. F. Roodbergen (1971: iii) have concluded, on the basis of the discussion on vārttika 1 to 2.1.51 concerning a formulation which Kaiyaṭa (see section III.2.2.1) attributes to Kāśakṛtsna, that Kāśakṛtsna was "probably a pre-Pāṇinian grammarian". They also argue (1971: iii n. 2) for accepting that Āpiśali and Kāśakṛtsna were closely connected. M. M. Deshpande (forthcoming c) discusses these claims and argues that Joshi and Roodbergen have reached unwarranted conclusions.

1.3.2e. *Conclusion*

There is, then, no single complete grammatical work extant which is universally accepted by competent scholars to be a pre-Pāṇinian work. Hence, it is not possible to single out a specific rule of a pre-Pāṇinian grammar and show definitively that a given rule of the Aṣṭādhyāyī is that very statement, borrowed by Pāṇini.[40] Nevertheless, given the evidence noted in section III.1.3.1. it is licit to say that Pāṇini not only had predecessors in the field of grammar but also that he built upon such previous work. The degree of Pāṇini's indebtedness to his antecedents, however, has been the source of much dispute.[41]

1.3.3. *Interpolations in and modifications of the Aṣṭādhyāyī sūtra-pāṭha.*

1.3.3a. *Introduction.*

Kielhorn (1887c: 106) adopted a cautious stance, saying of Kātyāyana and Patañjali that "like Pāṇini himself, both have based their own works on, and have preserved in them all that was valuable in, the writings of their predecessors." A similarly cautious attitude was expressed by Renou (1940a: 6-7). Others, on the other hand, have held views similar to Bühler's (see section III.1.3.2b). Wackernagel (1896: lxxiii)[42] maintained that Pāṇini's grammar was essentially a reworking of previous work and that it showed this in its organization and terminology.[43] Thieme (1935a: 71-72) refuted Wackernagel's opinion on the use of terms such as *chandas* (see note 43) and showed that Pāṇini was quite precise in employing these (see section III.1.5.6a). Faddegon (1936: 68) also spoke strongly against Wackernagel's view, which Renou (1957a: 116 n. 543) later characterized as hardly probable. The opinion that Pāṇini's grammar was the work of one person has been most emphatically stated by Bloomfield (1929: 274), who maintained that "although Pāṇini's work has a history behind it, it is the achievement of one man." More recently, a similar position has been taken by P. S. Subrahmanya Sastri (1960: xiv) and V. S. Agrawala (1963a: xi).

1.3.3b. *Kinds of and evidence for interpolations.*

Many scholars have attempted to show not merely that Pāṇini owed a debt to his predecessors but also that the Aṣṭādhyāyī shows evidence of this in that certain rules do not fit properly in the grammar and certain terms also do not fit well, so that these have to be assumed borrowed bodily from antecedents. Some of these scholars see in the Aṣṭādhyāyī's corpus of rules massive interpolation.

Now, it is known that there are variant readings in the text of rules, some of which variants are discussed by even Kātyāyana and Patañjali; see R. S. Bhattacharya (1954 - 55; 1966f), Birwé (1958), V. S. Agrawala (1963a: 25 with n. 2), Narayana Murti (1969), Yudhiṣṭhira Mīmāṃsaka

(1973: I: 215-16).[44] It is also known that the text suffered some interpolation.[45] Indeed, commentators such as Kaiyaṭa (see section III.2.2.1) directly state that certain rules or parts of rules as read in the Kāśikā (section IV.2.1) are interpolated (*prakṣipta*). Two kinds of interpolations have to be considered separately: those for which there is clear and incontrovertible evidence and others.

1.3.3c. *Modifications made by the authors of the Kāśikā.*

The first kind of interpolation mentioned above (section III.1.3.3b end) has been treated by Kielhorn (1885b: 191-99; 1887d), who showed how the Kāśikā incorporated into its text of rules modifications suggested in the Mahā-bhāṣya; see also Nārāyaṇa Miśra (1969-72: introduction, pp. 44-58). These changes involve splitting what was originally a single rule into two (*yoga-vighāga,* see section III.2.6.2), modifying words, adding words, and adding whole rules. Many of these modifications were accepted also in Candragomin's grammar, which influences the Kāśikā (Kielhorn 1886b). Most scholars have accepted Kielhorn's conclusions; see, for example, S. K. Belvalkar (1915: 37-38), Renou (1940a: 25), Kapil Deva Shastri (1961: 82-83; 1967a: 34-35). However, Yudhiṣṭhira Mīmāṃsaka (1973: I: 216-20) disagrees, arguing that these modifications cannot be attributed to the authors of the Kāśikā but must go back to much earlier grammarians. He gives (1973: I: 216-18) four pieces of evidence to demonstrate that the authors of the Kāśikā did not themselves introduce such modifications on the basis of statements in the Mahā-bhāṣya. Consider the first of these. Rule 3.3.122 as given in the Kāśikā reads: *adhyāya-nyāyôdyāva-saṃhārâdhārâvāyāś ca.*[46] The original rule, however, must have been: *adhyāya-nyāyôdyāva-saṃhārāś ca,*[47] excluding the items *ādhāra* and *āvāya.* Now, in his vārttika on 3.3.121 (Kielhorn [1889-85: I: 155.19]), Kātyāyana suggests that, in the rule which introduces the affix *ghañ* (= *a*), an addition should be made to include the items *avahāra, ādhāra, āvāya.* As can be seen, the Kāśikā does not include *avahāra* in its rule. Instead, it is said (Aryendra Sharma - K. R. Deshpande - D. G. Padhye [1969-70: I: 278]), *ca* 'and' of the rule is intended to include an item not actually stated,[48] so that *avahāra* is accounted for. Kielhorn (1887d: 181, see also 1885b: 192) simply said, "P[āṇini] III. 3, 122 .... originally did not contain the words *ādhāra* and *āvāya,* which have been inserted from Kātyāyana's Vārttika on the preceding rule ...." Yudhiṣṭhira Mīmāṃsaka (1973: I: 216-17), on the other hand, argues that the Kāśikā could not have made an interpolation on the basis of Kātyāyana's vārttika, since the addition made is not exactly the one suggested in the vārttika. This argument loses its force if one accepts that the Kāśikā was influenced by Candragomin's grammar. In the commentary on Candragomin's rule 1.3.101 (K. C. Chatterji [1953-61: I: 112]), are given the items *adhyāya, nyāya, udyāva, saṃhāra, ādhāra, āvāya,* exactly those that appear in the Kāśikā rule.[49] Yudhiṣṭhira Mīmāṃsaka (1973: I: 218-20) argues that the Kāśikā was not influenced by Candra's grammar. Concerning the Pāṇinian rule in question, he says (1973: I: 218) that a comparable rule does not appear in Candra's grammar, although some of the items given in Kātyāyana's vārttika on 3.3.121 appear in the commentary. This argument loses force if one accepts that the commentary on Candra's grammar was composed by Candra himself (see note 49). Yudhiṣṭhira Mīmāṃsaka (1973: I: 576-77) does accept this. Although space does not allow a full discussion of all of Yudhiṣṭhira Mīmāṃsaka's arguments, I think it justified to say that Kielhorn's conclusions have not been shown to be unacceptable.

In these cases the evidence is clear. The text of rules known to Kātyāyana and Patañjali differs from the text adopted in the Kāśikā and one can trace the sources of modifications. Other, less clearly substantiated, interpolations have been suggested.

1.3.3d. *Principles for discovering rules to be interpolations which Kātyāyana and Patañjali knew as parts of the Aṣṭādhyāyī.*

R. S. Bhattacharya (1951, 1966c) has set forth some principles for determining when a rule included in the text of the Aṣṭādhyāyī is to be considered borrowed from earlier grammarians. For example, the use of terms such as *auṅ* (7.1.18, see section III.1.3.1) is an indication of borrowing (R. S. Bhattacharya [1966c: 65-66]). Some of Bhattacharya's principles have to do with style and method: a conflict in style or method indicates that given rules were taken by Pāṇini from predecessors. For example, Pāṇini normally uses a genitive form to refer to a substituend.[50] Therefore, if a nominative is so used, the rule which contains this form has been borrowed.[51] Again, Pāṇini usually uses an ablative form to refer to a base after which an affix is introduced,[52] but he also occasionally uses genitive forms; rules which contain such forms are borrowings.[53] Bhattacharya also argues (1966c: 86-88) that a rule or series of rules which fits into a metrical scheme is pre-Pāṇinian.[54]

Bhattacharya's principles were for the most part rejected by Birwé (1966: viii-ix), with whom S. Bahulikar (1972: 15; 1973: 82) agrees on this point.[55] However, Birwé himself operates with the principle that a conflict in the way of stating operations indicates that Pāṇini has taken over statements from predecessors. Birwé's approach is essentially a continuation of the method used by I. S. Pawte (1935). For example, Pawte (1935: 46-49) argued as follows. Rules 1.1.66-67 (see section III.1.5.3d with note 217) provide for the interpretation of locative and ablative forms in certain rules: a locative denotes a unit the item preceding which undergoes an operation – a right context – and an ablative denotes a left context. However, there are exceptions, rules where locative and ablative forms should be interpreted by 1.1.66, 67 but cannot be interpreted thus without providing undesirable results.[56] Pawte concluded (1935: 109): "The Astd. [Aṣṭādhyāyī] contains sūtras from various earlier grammatical works."[57]

As I noted above, Birwé continues in the same vein as Pawte. Now, commentaries such as the Bāla-manoramā on the Siddhânta-kaumudī (see section IV.3.2) frequently note that certain rules contain genitive, locative or nominative forms used in the sense of an ablative. These are interpretive devices used to make the particular rules in question conform to the usual way in which rules are formulated: an affixation rule normally states in the ablative a unit after which an affix is introduced. Birwé (1966: 31-36) studies such usages[58] and concludes, as did Pawte, that the Aṣṭādhyāyī contains many rules not original to Pāṇini. He gives (1966: 93-140) a systematic analysis of the third chapter of the grammar and reconstructs (1966: 141-46) what he considers the basic original text and additions to it: 376 and 255 rules respectively. That is, over forty percent of the rules in the third chapter are interpolations, according to Birwé.

The attitude and method of these scholars have led to some controversy. P. S. Subrahmanya Sastri (1960: xii-xiii) criticized Pawte but was in turn criticized by Birwé (1966: 21), whose own work has met with sharp criticism from R. Rocher (1967) and Scharfe (1971a: 16 with notes 25, 26).[59] More recently, S. Bahulikar (1972, 1973) has criticized Pawte and Birwé (Bahulikar [1972: 11-12], [1973: 80]) for not being historical because they depended on commentators' statements and not on the Aṣṭādhyāyī by itself. She has taken a slightly different theoretical stand from these two authors by insisting on an analysis of the statements in the Aṣṭādhyāyī independent of commentatorial views. However, her approach is compatible with that of Pawte, Bhattacharya and Birwé: Bahulikar seeks to find in the grammar anomalies which indicate that given rules do not fit in the whole. For example, she argues (1972: 10-11, 1973: 79) that rules 4.1.1 and 4.1.66-72[60] are incompatible, so that one must suspect that they were composed by different authors. This although these rules were known to Kātyāyana and Patañjali as parts of the Aṣṭādhyāyī. Bahulikar argues as follows. 4.1.1 is a heading (see section III.1.5.2c) whereby affixes introduced by subsequent rules are introduced after nominal bases (*prātipadika*) and items ending in the feminine affixes denoted by *ṅī* and *āp*. Rule 4.1.2[61] then states the nominal endings introduced after such units. 4.1.66-72, on the other hand, introduce the feminine affix *ūṅ* (= *ū*). Now, since 4.1.1 mentions *ṅī* and *āp* (differently accented affixes *ī*, *ā*) but not *ūṅ*, the endings given in 4.1.2 cannot be introduced after an item which ends in *ūṅ*. This means one cannot now derive a form such as the nominative singular *kurūḥ*, with the ending *s* (nom. sg.) after *kurū* "female descendant of a Kuru king" (⟨ *kuru-ū*). On the basis of such arguments and stylistic observations, Bahulikar concludes also that nipātana rules (see section III.1.5.2c) "may be later additions to the original scheme of the Aṣṭādhyāyī"[62] by different authors (1972: 115),[63] that the Vedic rules (see section III.1.5.5e.1) and and the rules referring to usages of easterners and northerners (see section III.1.3.1) also possibly are works of different authors and not part of the original Aṣṭādhyāyī (Bahulikar [1972: 129, 131, 148-49]).

I find one major problem in the work of those who see such massive interpolation in the Aṣṭādhyāyī: these authors have not segregated pseudo-problems from real ones. Consider one of the cases dealt with by Birwé under the rubric of improper genitives.[64] Rule 3.1.80[65] provides that the affix *u* is introduced after the roots *dhiv* 'nourish' and *kṛv* 'make'; in addition (*ca* "also"), the final sound of these roots is simultaneously replaced by *a*: *dhinv-ti* → *dhina-u-ti* (. . . → *dhinoti*, 3rd sg. pres.). Now, says Birwé (1966: 32), since this is an affixation rule, the genitive *dhinvi-kṛṇvyoḥ* is out of order; by rule 1.1.67 the ablative should have been used here (see note 64). This argument has no force. The rule simultaneously provides for a substitution, so that the genitive form used to denote a substituend is perfectly in order. Moreover, since the rule states *ca* 'also', one understands that this replacement is additional to the affixation of *u*, so that one understands also an ablative form.[66] Similarly, Bahulikar's problem concerning 4.1.1 and 4.1.66-72 is also a pseudo-problem. After *ūṅ* has been affixed to a base such as *kuru* – and this affix is added only to bases which end in *u* – the final vowel of the base and the affix itself are both replaced by a single sound *ū*. Moreover, this single replacement is treated as the final of the base.[67] Hence, *kurū-* is indeed treated as a nominal base (*prātipadika*), so that an ending such as *s* is properly introduced after it by 4.1.1-2.

Some of the conclusions reached by such arguments as those noted also lead to what I consider absurdity. For example, Birwé (1966: 96) considers 3.1.43 a possible interpolation. At the same time, he considers 3.1.44 part of the original text. The former rule introduces the affix *cli* and the latter provides that *cli* is replaced by *sic* (sigmatic aorist affix *s*); see note 259. What Birwé does not note is this: how can a unit which has not been introduced by some rule in the original text be given as a substituend in another rule?

Finally, some of the views propounded by scholars mentioned fail to take into consideration reasonable arguments supplied by Pāṇiniyas, arguments which solve their problems. In her argument concerning 4.1.1 and 4.1.66-72, Bahulikar ignores that the solution I have noted above was set forth with perfect clarity in the Mahā-bhāṣya (Kielhorn [1880-85: II: 191. 11-12]).

I do not mean to say that all the problems brought up by the authors mentioned above are simply to be set aside. There are recalcitrant cases for which I now see no immediate solution. However, I think it justified to say that the researcher should be intent not on finding an interpolation in every case where there is an apparent conflict but on studying carefully all such apparent anomalies and trying to reconcile them with the whole of the Aṣṭādhyāyī, this while taking into consideration what is said in the commentatorial literature. Once the pseudo-problems are segregated from the real ones, at least there will be a solid basis for further consideration.

1.3.3e. *Rules supposed to be interpolations because they were not discussed in the Mahā-bhāṣya.*

Another approach to the question of interpolation was suggested by Weber (1873d: 299): a rule which is neither discussed nor mentioned in the Mahā-bhāṣya is to be considered a possible interpolation. Straightforward as this criterion might seem, the fact is that at the time Weber enunciated it there was no complete edition of the Mahā-bhāṣya available to scholars, so that the criterion was liable to misuse. Sköld (1926a: 22-24, 33, 37) went even further than Weber, whose principle he accepted, and was willing to consider an interpolation not only such a rule but also one actually discussed in the Mahā-bhāṣya (see section III.3.2.2). He was roundly criticized by Liebich (1928: 3-7), who pointed out that superficial arguments were now rendered useless by Kielhorn's edition (1880-85), which made research into the Mahā-bhāṣya possible in a way it was not at Weber's time. Sköld's views were also criticized by B. Ghosh (1934: 665 n. 1) and K. Madhava Krishna Sarma (1968: 9). Nevertheless, his opinions have not been totally forgotten. Mehendale (1968: 1-2) accepted Sköld's contention that rule 2.4.63 is a possible interpolation because it is not discussed in the Mahā-bhāṣya. Cardona (1972b: 172 n. 1) pointed out that this is inappropriate.

1.3.3f. *Other suggested interpolations.*

Several rules other than those noted have been treated as interpolated.[68] A full discussion of each suggestion is beyond the scope of this survey, so that I merely give opinions and counteropinions. The set of rules 1.2.53-57 (see section III.1.5.3a with note 192) or part of it has been considered interpolated by many scholars: Böhtlingk (1887a: 18), Wackernagel (1896: lxvii n. 3),[69] Pawte (1935: 110-14),[70] Faddegon (1936: 57), Renou (1941 - 2: 115 n. 3; 1957a: 120 n. 582), Palsule (1949),[71] P. S. Subrahmanya Sastri (1960: xiv).[72] V. G. Paranjpe (1922: 51-52) defended the authenticity of these rules, and others also have assumed they were Pāṇini's.[73] Bloomfield (1929: 274-75) considered 1.1.6 a possible interpolation, but gave no arguments for his view. K. Madhava Krishna Sarma (1968: 5-6) argued that 1.4.106 did not belong in the original text. Della Casa (1951) argued, on lexicographic grounds, that 3.1.115 and 6.1.65 are not original, but Birwé (1966: 181-86) discussed his reasons and found them insufficient. Böhtlingk (1887a: 96) considered that 3.2.30 was interpolated, a view against which K. Madhava Krishna Sarma (1968: 6-7) presented arguments. The last rule of the grammar (8.4.68) was viewed as interpolated by Sköld (1926a: 1-8) for reasons which were later shown to be insufficient (Thieme 1930a; K. Madhava Krishna Sarma 1968: 11-12), although Vidya Niwas Misra (1966: 20) still espoused Sköld's position. Vidya Niwas Misra (1966: 63-64) has also suggested that a series of rules has been transmitted poorly and should be reconstructed differently for the original text. M. M. Deshpande (1972: 245 n. 65) has shown that this position is untenable. Recently, Scharfe (1971a: 26, 48) has claimed that rule 6.1.67 (*ver apṛktasya*) was originally formulated without the term *apṛktasya,* which was added at some time between Kātyāyana and Patañjali. Cardona (forthcoming d) argues that this view rests on a misunderstanding of the Mahā-bhāṣya discussion of the rule. Most recently, Joshi and Roodbergen (1973: ii-iv) have claimed that rules 2.2.1-5, which provide for particular tatpuruṣa compounds, are to be considered interpolations. They say (1973: iv): 'There is every appearance that these rules have been interpolated in the text of the *Aṣṭādhyāyī,* not just because the cps [compounds] prescribed here can be derived in other ways, but also because the *tp.*- [*tatpuruṣa*] analysis assumed here is clumsy.' The arguments given by Joshi and Roodbergen are not all cogent. Consider rule 2.2.1 (*pūrvâparâdharôttaram ekadeśinaikâdhikaraṇe*). This provides that nominal forms of *pūrva* 'front', *apara* 'back', *adhara* 'lower', *uttara* 'upper' combine with semantically and syntactically related nominal forms which denote a whole (*ekadeśin* 'which has parts') to form a tatpuruṣa compound, provided the whole in question is a single entity (*ekâdhikaraṇa*). The rule thus provides for a compound such as *pūrva-kāya* 'front of the body', equivalent to *pūrvaṃ kāyasya* 'front of the body'. Both the compound and the related string derive from a structure containing a genitive form of *kāya: pūrva-s kāya-as.* Now rule 2.2.8 (*ṣaṣṭhī*) states that a genitive form combines with a related nominal to form a tatpuruṣa compound; e.g., *rāja-puruṣa* (see section III.1.5.1a). Rule 2.2.1 is an exception to 2.2.8. It thus prevents the derivation of a compound **kāya-pūrva* 'front of the body.' Now, commentators note that *pūrva-kāya* can also be analysed differently. Assume that the term *kāya* 'body' is used to refer to a part of the whole body. Then *pūrva* 'front' and *kāya* 'part of the body' can be coreferential (*samānâdhikaraṇa*): *pūrvaś ca kāyaś ca* 'that which is both the front and part of the body.' This analysis allows deriving *pūrva-kāya* as a karmadhāraya compound of the type *nīlôtpala* 'blue lotus'. One might, then, think that rule 2.2.1 is thereby rendered useless. But this is not true. The use of *kāya* to refer to part of the body is metaphoric (*lākṣaṇika*). Such usage does not preclude the use of *kāya* to refer to a whole. Hence, in the absence of 2.2.1, two compounds would now be allowed: (a) if *kāya* is used to refer to a part of the body, *pūrva-kāya* is derived; (b) if *kāya* is used to refer to the whole body, **kāya-pūrva* is derived. Obviously, something is needed to preclude the derivation of an unused compound here. The correct results are provided by 2.2.1. It is hardly warranted to say that the analysis of *pūrva-kāya* etc. as tatpuruṣa compounds is clumsy.[74]

1.3.3g. *Conclusion.*

In the present state of our knowledge I think it wise to accept as a working hypothesis Kielhorn's view (1887d: 232) that the Aṣṭādhyāyī has, at least from the time of the Mahā-bhāṣya, been well preserved.[75] Moreover, I think it reasonable to say that attempts to demonstrate massive interpolation or borrowing in the text received by Kātyāyana and Patañjali cannot be deemed successful. There remain many details to be studied concerning the precise formulations of given rules.

1.3.4. *Authorship of the śiva-sūtras.*

Some scholars (for example, Sköld [1926b: 22], Mangala Deva Shastri [1927: 469], Faddegon [1929: 56], Konow [1943]) have claimed that the śiva-sūtras were not set up by Pāṇini but by a predecessor. However, research into the relation between this set of sounds and the rules of the Aṣṭādhyāyī has brought out their intimate relation with eachother and no serious student of Pāṇini, as far as I know, any longer holds the above view; see K. A. Subramania Iyer (1927: 142), Thieme (1935a: 109-10), K. Madhava Krishna Sarma (1941: 211-15; 1968: 32-36),[76] Jayadatta Sastri (1965), Cardona (1969: 3), Yudhiṣṭhira Mīmāṃsaka (1973: I: 211-15).

Although he accepts that Pāṇini composed the śiva-sūtras, Yudhiṣṭhira Mīmāṃsaka (1973: II: 195) also suggests that one of these sūtras, namely the seventh (*ñ, m, ṅ, ṇ, n, m*), was taken from Āpiśali (see section III.1.3.2a). This opinion is based on Yudhiṣṭhira Mīmāṃsaka's assumption that the sūtra version of the Pāṇinīya-śikṣā was composed by Pāṇini. However, this is open to doubt; see section III.1.4.4b.

1.3.5 *The dhātu-pāṭha.*

1.3.5a. *Interpolations.*

The dhātu-pāṭha is preserved only as it was known to commentators such as Maitreya-rakṣita (see section IV.4). It is known that this text suffered additions (see section III.1.5.8c). Moreover commentators themselves recognize that some roots given in known versions of the dhātu-pāṭha were not contained in the version of this text received by Kātyāyana. For example, included in the tenth section of the dhātu-pāṭha are the items *sūtra, mūtra*[77] and several sūtras. One of these sūtras (*prātipadikād dhātv-arthe bahulam iṣṭhavac ca*) provides that *ṇic* (= *i*) is frequently (*bahulam*) affixed to a nominal base (*prātipadika*) to derive an item denoting an action (*dhātv-artha* 'root meaning'); the nominal base is then treated as though it were followed by the superlative suffix *iṣṭha,* that is, it is subject to those operations which apply before *iṣṭha.* Two other sūtras give particular meanings for which such derivatives are formed: "make ..." (*tat karoti*), "explain ..." (*tad ācaṣṭe*).[78] Now, in his fifth vārttika on 3.1.26, Kātyāyana states that a supplement is to be made to the grammar in order to include the introduction of *ṇic* to form derivatives meaning "make ...". This is to cover cases such as *sūtrayati* 'makes ... a sūtra'.[79] In his Uddyota on this rule, Nāgeśa notes the following (Vedavrata [1962-3: III: 91]). Kātyāyana's vārttika shows that the pseudo-roots *sūtra* and *mūtra* and the sūtras given above are interpolations in the tenth section of the dhātu-pāṭha. For, if these had been included in the text as known to Kātyāyana, vārttika 5 on 3.1.26 would have been useless.[80]

A good deal of attention has been paid to considering the number of "false roots" in the dhātu-pāṭha; this question will be considered in section III.1.5.8c. In the present section I shall consider two associated questions. First, did the original dhātu-pāṭha contain meaning entries? And is this text properly considered a work of Pāṇini or did he take it over from predecessors?

1.3.5b. *Meaning entries: were they included in the original dhātu-pāṭha?*

The dhātu-pāṭha known to and commented on by Maitreya-rakṣita etc. (section IV.4) lists roots accompanied by meaning entries. For example, the first root entry is: *bhū sattāyām.*[81] Pāṇinian commentators are themselves not in accord concerning whether such meaning entries were originally included in the dhātu-pāṭha. The major evidence concerning this point is well summarized by Yudhiṣṭhira Mīmāṃsaka (1973: II: 51-58).[82]

There is evidence in the Mahā-bhāṣya to show that at the time of Kātyāyana the root entries of the dhātu-pāṭha were recited continuously, without the intervention of glosses. Thus the first two roots, *bhū* "be" and *edh* "thrive" were recited *bhv-edh*... In his second vārttika on rule 1.3.1[83] Kātyāyana argues as follows (Kielhorn [1880-85: I: 254.10-12]). If an item is assigned the name *dhātu* – that is, is classed as a root (*dhātu*) – by virtue merely of being recited in the dhātu-pāṭha, one has to make a provision that a particular stretch of sound in this text constitutes a separate root. Otherwise, instead of considering *bhū* and *edh* as two roots, one might consider the sequence *bhvedh* a single root. Commenting on this vārttika, Kaiyaṭa notes (Vedavrata [1962-63: II: 178]) that the meaning entries do not serve to show the limits of roots, since they are non-Pāṇinian. And, commenting on this, Nāgeśa states (Vedavrata [1962-63: II: 178]) that it was Bhīmasena who, according to tradition, entered the glosses in the dhātu-pāṭha. This was also the view of commentators such as Kauṇḍabhaṭṭa (see K. P. Trivedi [1915: 48]) and Bhaṭṭoji Dīkṣita (see S. C. Chakravarti [1919: 1 n. 2]). Liebich (1919b: 49-50; 1930: 243-44) accepted that these glosses were post-Pāṇinian additions and pointed out also (1930: 244-46) that Patañjali's way of referrring to root meanings was different from the way which is known from later dhātu-pāṭha versions. For example, Patañjali does not say *rautiḥ śabde* ('The root *ru* in the meaning "bellow" ', see note 81) but *rautiḥ śabda-karmā* ('The root *ru* has the meaning "bellow" '). Palsule (1961: 91-95) has summarized the evidence from the Mahā-bhāṣya and agreed with Liebich that the meaning entries were not part of the original dhātu-pāṭha.[84]

However, Yudhiṣṭhira Mīmāṃsaka (1973: II: 54-58) has argued that a version of the dhātu-pāṭha with glosses should be attributed to Pāṇini. Most of the reasons he gives are, to me, not convincing. Consider one of them. Yudhiṣṭhira Mīmāṃsaka cites Patanjali's statement, "The root *vap* is seen (to occur) in (the meaning) 'strew', (but) it also occurs in (the meaning) 'cut'."[85] Yudhiṣṭhira Mīmāṃsaka (1973: II: 54) notes that *dṛṣṭa* "seen" is not equivalent to *vartate* "occurs" and says: "Therefore, the intent of this statement is this: those root meanings of which [Patañjali] says *'dṛṣṭa'* are [meaning entries] recited in the dhātu-pāṭha, which were seen in the dhātu-pāṭha, and those for which [Patañjali] used *'vartate'* are [meanings] which occur in normal usage."[86] This is not a conclusion necessarily warranted by the passage in question. The context (Kielhorn [1880-85: I: 256.10-16]) is a discussion concerning whether preverbs (*upasarga*) are to be assigned independent meanings or rather considered cosignifiers[87] of meanings assigned to roots, which are polysemic (*bahv-artha*). A series of roots is brought up to illustrate the latter alternative. For example, *kṛ* means not only 'make, do', but also 'shampoo' (*nirmalī-karaṇa*) and 'set down' (*nikṣepaṇa*). Hence, the term *dṛṣṭa* used in this context can be considered used merely with reference to roots seen to occur in certain meanings, not necessarily with reference to meaning entries in the *dhātu-pāṭha.* There is, however, one piece of evidence cited by Yudhiṣṭhira Mīmāṃsaka (1973: II: 54) which is not easily dismissed. In his discussion of rule 1.3.7, Patañjali says (Kielhorn [1880-85: I: 264.8-9]) that the teacher Pāṇini recites some roots with infixed *n.* Patañjali gives the following examples: *ubundir niśāmane* (*bund* 'perceive'), *skandir gati-śoṣaṇayoḥ* (*skand* 'jump, dry'). In his Uddyota on the passage, Nāgeśa directly notes (Vedavrata [1962-63: II: 211]) that this Mahā-bhāṣya passage indicates some roots were indeed recited in the early dhātu-pāṭha accompanied by meaning entries. And Patañjali's citations is in accord with the way of listing roots and their meanings in the later versions of the dhātu-pāṭha. Liebich (1930: 246-47) had noticed this and suggested, on the basis of a manuscript reading (see Kielhorn [1880-85: I: 525]), that the locative forms *niśāmane, gati-śoṣaṇayoḥ* were later glosses which made their way into the text of the Mahā-bhāṣya.

1.3.5c. *Authorship of the dhātu-pāṭha.*

S. K. Belvalkar (1915: 25) accepted that the dhātu-pāṭha is correctly attributed to Pāṇini because he refers to roots and classes of roots in his rules and because the functions of markers (section III.1.5.3c) in rules and the dhātu-pāṭha are in accord with each other. On the other hand, I. S. Pawte (1935: 10) argued that the dhātu-pāṭha was a work of the etymological school of grammarians such as Śākaṭāyana (see section III.1.3.1), which work Pāṇini took over from his predecessors. Pawte's reasons for his view are as follows. The dhātu-pāṭha contains many more roots than are necessary for the rules of the grammar proper (1935: 7, 9). In addition, Pāṇini uses the term *upadesa* ('instruction') to refer to the dhātu pāṭha,[88] which "... shows that the author of the Astd. [Aṣṭādhyāyī] had the Dhātupāṭha handed down to him as *upadeśa* from his Acharyas [teachers]" (1935: 13). Moreover, there are sūtras of the grammar which conflict with what is taught in the dhātu-pāṭha.[89] Palsule (1961: 16-24) effectively refuted Pawte's arguments. And indeed some of these are very weak. Rule 1.3.1 (see note 83) introduces the term *dhātu* as referring to items of the list beginning with *bhū.* It is difficult to see how such a list contains more than is necessary for the rules of the grammar. For a rule which introduces an affix after a root (*dhātu*) applies to all items of this list (cf. Palsule [1961: 17]). Pawte's second argument rests on the assumption that Pāṇini used the term *upadeśa* to refer directly to the dhātu-pāṭha. This is unacceptable. Pāṇini uses *upadeśa* (loc. sg. *upadeśe*) to refer to a stage of derivation at which items have been introduced (taught) but have not yet undergone true grammatical operations (see Cardona 1972a, forthcoming a). Pawte's third argument is also less strong than he makes it out to be; see Palsule 1961: 17-19 for a discussion. Liebich (1919b: 51, 1920a: 57) also thought that Pāṇini received his dhātu-pāṭha from predecessors. According to him, this would explain the peculiar order in which roots are arranged in the dhātu-pāṭha.[90] For roots are here subdivided into ten groups: *bhū* etc. (roots whose present forms contain unaccented *-a-: bháv-a-ti*). *ad* etc. (athematic unreduplicated presents: *at-ti* 'eats'), *hu* etc. (athematic reduplicated presents: *juhoti* 'pours an oblation'), *div* etc. (presents in *-ya-: dīv-ya-ti* 'gambles'), *su* etc. (presents in *-nu-: su-no-ti* 'presses'), *tud* etc. (presents in *-á-: tud-á-ti* 'shoves'), *rudh* etc. (presents with infixed *-na-: ru-ṇa-d-dhi* 'holds down'), *tan* etc. (presents in *-u-: tan-o-ti* 'stretches'), *krī* etc. (presents in *-nā-: krī-ṇā-ti* 'buys'), *cur* etc. (derived with *-i-: cor-ay-a-ti* 'steals'). However, such an argument is one of ignorance: one cannot perceive why Pāṇini should have arranged roots in this particular order, hence one attributes the text to a predecessor. Of course the question still remains why a predecessor should have chosen this order. Moreover, Shefts (1961: 2-3) has suggested a rationale for the order of roots, part of which at least I consider convincing. It is, for example, eminently sensible to place the group *ad* etc. after *bhū* etc.: present forms of the former are derived by deleting the *-a-* which occurs after the latter.

It is not only modern scholars who have suggested that the dhātu-pāṭha was not composed by Pāṇini. The commentator Jinendrabuddhi (see section IV.2.1) also says this on occasion. Yudhiṣṭhira Mīmāṃsaka (1973: II: 43-51) has given the pertinent passages and supplied counterarguments.

1.3.6. *The gaṇa-pāṭha.*

1.3.6a. *Interpolations.*

Like the dhātu-pāṭha (section III.1.3.5a), the gaṇa-pāṭha also underwent accretions. R. G. Bhandarkar (1872a [= 1927-33 I: 103]) was so cautious as to say, "The groups or Gaṇas, therefore, seem to have been tampered with by his [Pāṇini's] successors, but we think we are safe in ascribing the first three names at least, in each, to him." In addition, commentators, as early as in the Mahā-bhāṣya distinguish between exhaustive listings (*parigaṇana*) and type listings (*ākṛti-gaṇa*); see Birwé (1961: 4-14), Kapil Deva Shastri (1967a: 25-29). The latter are open-ended in that they contain only typical items subject to given operations; all items which share these features are allowed to be considered referred to thereby.[91]

Research on the gaṇa-pāṭha has included efforts to arrive at a critical version of exhaustive lists (see section III.1.2) and to discriminate such lists from type listings. One area basic to such researches is a careful study of what can be known about the gaṇa-pāṭha as it existed at the time of Kātyāyana and Patañjali, as reflected by discussions in the Mahā-bhāṣya. Work in this area has been done by Ojihara (1967-68; 1968a; 1970), who has taken up some of the Mahā-bhāṣya discussions where it is proposed to include certain items in gaṇas.

1.3.6b. *Authorship of the gaṇa-pāṭha.*

It is plausible to posit that lists comparable to Pāṇinian gaṇas had been compiled before Pāṇini's time, and there is some evidence in the discussions of the Mahā-bhāṣya to support this. For example, in vārttika 4 on 4.1.79 Kātyāyana mentions a gaṇa *rauḍhi* etc., not known in the Pāṇinian gaṇa-pāṭha and which, says Patañjali (Kielhorn [1880-85: II: 233.17-18]), corresponds to the Pāṇinian *krauḍi* etc. Kaiyaṭa directly attributes the list *rauḍhi* etc. to early teachers (*pūrvâcārya*); see Vedavrata (1962-63: III: 540), Birwé (1961: 2-3), Kapil Deva Shastri (1967a: 15-17). In addition, there are found in the gaṇa-pāṭha terms such as *sa,* equivalent to Pāṇini's *samāsa* 'compound', which are possibly to be considered pre-Pāṇinian; see Birwé (1961: 26-27), Yudhiṣṭhira Mīmāṃsaka (1973: II: 139-40).

Pawte (1935: 86-92) argued that, like the dhātu-pāṭha (see section III. 1.3.5c), the gaṇa-pāṭha also was received by Pāṇini as a teaching of predecessors. I find Pawte's arguments here too unconvincing. For example, he reasons (1935: 86-87) as follows. Rule 1.3.2 (see section III.1.5.3c) provides that a nasalized (*anunāsika*) vowel (*ac*) in *upadeśa* is a marker (*it*). According to Pawte, the term *upadeśa* refers to the gaṇa-pāṭha as well as the dhātu-pāṭha, from which he concludes that Pāṇini received the former too as a teaching (*upadeśa*). I consider this unacceptable. In rules which define what sounds are markers, the term *upadeśa* is used to refer to items at a stage before they have entered into grammatical operations, and there is no question of Pāṇini's here stating *upadeśe* showing that he refers to the teaching of predecessors (see Cardona forthcoming a). Ayachit (1961: 55) has also supposed that the gaṇa-pāṭha was not originally Pāṇini's. However, he also says that Pāṇini received and settled a text which he made an integral part of his system. Yudhiṣṭhira Mīmāṃsaka (1973: II: 141-46) has taken up arguments for and against attributing the gaṇa-pāṭha to Pāṇini and concluded that it should be ascribed to him.[92] I agree with this conclusion.

1.3.6c. *The relation between the gaṇa-pāṭha and the sūtra-pāṭha.*

One thing is obvious about the relation between the gaṇa-pāṭha and the rules of the grammar. These rules refer to groups of items (see section III.1.1

with note 13), so that they presuppose these lists. For example, 1.1.27[93] assigns the items *sarva* ('whole, all') etc. to the class of pronominals (*sarvanāman*); the rule presupposes the set *sarva* etc. Moreover, the list in question must have a particular order. For there are other rules which provide operations for subgroups of this set. For example, 7.2.102 states that the final sound of *tyad* ('that') etc. is replaced by *a*, and there is a series of rules which apply to pronominals other than *dvi* ('two') etc.[94] It is clear that such rules require that lists have been set up and in particular orders. It is equally obvious, however, that these lists were set up in the first place in view of operations stated in rules. However, some scholars have drawn more far reaching conclusions on the basis of such facts and a discussion in the Mahā-bhāṣya.

The Mahā-bhāṣya's discussion concerning rule 1.1.34 has been the object of consideration by several scholars: Bloomfield (1927), Pawte (1935: 88-91), P. S. Subrahmanya Sastri (1960: xvii-xviii), Birwé (1961: 24-26, 1966: 163-64), Ojihara (1959; 1963a; 1965b; 290; see also Ojihara - Renou 1960: 97-98), Kapil Deva Shastri (1967a: 266-67), Scharfe (1971a: 49-50). The question at issue is as follows. The gaṇa accompanying rule 1.1.27 (see note 93) contains not only the items *sarva* etc. but also three sūtras. These sūtras are, moreover, identical with three rules of the sūtra-pāṭha, 1.1.34-36 For example, the gaṇa-sūtra *pūrva-parâvara-dakṣiṇôttarâparâdharāṇi vyavasthāyām asaṃjñāyām* provides that certain items are pronominal (*sarvanāman*) if they are used with reference to a relative position (*vyavasthāyām*) but are not used to name particulars (see note 96). The items are: *pūrva* 'prior, eastern', *para* 'which is beyond, farther', *avara* 'lower, more recent', *dakṣiṇa* 'right, southern', *uttara* 'upper, northern', *apara* 'which is in back, western', *adhara* 'lower'. This sūtra included in the gaṇa is identical with rule 1.1.34, which, in the traditional interpretation, provides that these same items, under the same conditions, are optionally pronominal with respect to the nominative plural ending *jas* (= *as*).[95] That is, after these items under the conditions stated, *jas* is optionally replaced by *sī* (= *ī*) by rule 7.1.17; this substitution applies to *jas* after pronominals. Now, if both the gaṇa-sūtra noted and rule 1.1.34 are considered part of the grammar, one derives from an item such as *pūrva* forms such as the following: *pūrvasmai* (dat. sg. masc. - nt.), with replacement of the ending *ṅe* (= *e*) by *smai* after a pronominal in *-a* (7.1.14), *pūrve* or *pūrvāḥ* (nom. pl. masc.), with optional replacement of *jas*.[96] In his first vārttika on 1.1.34, Kātyāyana claims that this rule (and by implication also 1.1.35-36) is useless, since the gaṇa-sūtra to 1.1.27 has already been stated. After a fairly long discussion (summarized by Pawte [1935: 88-90] and translated most recently by Scharfe [1971a: 49-50]), Patañjali concludes that the rules are still necessary in order to provide for the optional replacement of *jas* by *śī*.

From Kātyāyana's first vārttika Pawte (1935: 88) concluded that, for Kātyāyana, the gaṇa clearly preceded the sūtra-pāṭha and further (Pawte [1935: 91]) that rules 1.1.34-36 were borrowed by Pāṇini from the gaṇa-pāṭha and incorporated into his grammar. Birwé (1961: 26; 1966: 163) reached similar conclusions.[97] Bloomfield (1927) interpreted rules 1.1.34-36 differently from the usual way,[98] and claimed that the gaṇa-sūtras of 1.1.27 were taken from the sūtra-pāṭha. Scharfe (1971a: 49) has claimed that Birwé's opinion[99] is based on a misinterpretation of the Mahā-bhāṣya passage in question. He has accepted Bloomfield's opinion, though not in full, since he also accepts that *vibhāṣā jasi* is valid in 1.1.34-36 (see notes 95, 98).

A full treatment of the arguments in question is not possible here. However, my opinion is that most of the scholars noted have not appreciated the problem correctly.[100] I think P. S. Subrahmanya Sastri (1960: xvii) is correct in considering both the gaṇa-sūtras to 1.1.27 and rules 1.1.34-36 original and part of Pāṇini's grammar. The only problem remaining is the one noted by Kapil Deva Shastri (1967a: 267): Pāṇini could as well have inserted a rule *vibhāṣā jasi* (see note 95) after the gaṇa-sūtras.

1.3.7. *Metarules.*

Pāṇini states metarules in the Aṣṭādhyāyī (see section III.1.5.2c); a list of these rules, called *paribhāṣā,* is given by K. V. Abhyankar (1967a: 4n. 3).[101] There are additional metarules which, though not given in the Aṣṭādhyāyī, are either directly stated or implied in the Mahā-bhāṣya.[102] Various collections of these paribhāṣās were made by commentators, both Pāṇinian and others; see K. V. Abhyankar (1955; 1967a: 1-64) for a survey. The major collections of these metarules have been edited recently by K. V. Abhyankar (1967a).[103] The most widely known such collection in the Pāṇinian school is the Paribhāṣêndu-śekhara of Nāgeśabhaṭṭa (early 18th century), edited and translated by Kielhorn (1868; 1874a). Scharfe (1954) suggested some minor improvements in Kielhorn's translation and Rocher - Debels (1960) retranslated one section (on paribhāṣās 2-3, see section III.1.5.2c below), suggesting improvements in Kielhorn's rendition. Kielhorn's work has also been re-edited (K. V. Abhyankar [1960, 1962]) together with a commentary by Vasudev Shastri Abhyankar. The Paribhāṣêndu-śekhara has been the object of a great many other commentaries,[104] of which one was composed by Nāgeśa's own student, Vaidyanātha Pāyaguṇḍa (G. S. Gokhale [1913]).[105]

Some of these metarules not found in the Aṣṭādhyāyī are called *nyāya-siddha* ('established by nyāya'), that is, they are assumed valid simply because the procedure stated in them is axiomatic and one would not think of proceding otherwise. Others are termed *jñāpaka-siddha* ('established by an indicator'): a certain way of formulating a given rule in the Aṣṭādhyāyī indicates (*jñāpayati* 'makes known') that Pāṇini accepted, albeit tacitly, the validity of a certain metarule. This type has been studied by Boudon (1938). Still others are termed *vācanikī*, that is, they require a direct statement (*vacana*). These classifications of such metarules as were not given in the Aṣṭādhyāyī were discussed in detail by Kielhorn (1874a: iv-xvi); more recently they have been treated again by Devasthali (1969). More recently still, Ramanuja Tatacharya (1972a) has edited a collection, attributed to Nāgeśa, of Mahā-bhāṣya passages in which appeal is made to jñāpaka.

Concerning these metarules the question arises, were they tacitly accepted by Pāṇini, so that they do in fact constitute part of his grammatical system, or were they suggested first by commentators? And, if such metarules antedate Kātyāyana, are they also pre-Pāṇinian? Kielhorn (1874a: xxi-xxii) believed that most of these paribhāṣās were tacitly accepted by Pāṇini, a view to which several other scholars subscribed: Belvalkar (1915: 25), P. C. Chakravarti (1930: 71), Devasthali (1969: 6). Renou also accepted this at one time (1940a: 12-13), but later (Renou [1956c: 147]) doubted it. On the other hand, Goldstücker (1861: 109-18) claimed that, though each paribhāṣā had to be treated individually, most were invented after Pāṇini but before Kātyāyana. Buiskool (1939: 39, cf. 1934: 53-80) believed, on the contrary, that all such metarules, in so far as they do not occur in the prātiśākhyas,[106] originated in the time between Kātyāyana and Patañjali. K. V. Abhyankar thinks the Paribhāṣā-sūcana of Vyāḍi (in K. V. Abhyankar [1967a]) antedates Patañjali: "The style and contents of the Paribhāṣāsūcana show that the work was written some time before the Mahābhāṣya of Patañjali" (1962: introduction, p. 4). Wezler, who has given a summary of opinions on this issue (1969: 23-26), disagrees with Abhyankar (Wezler [1969: 20-23]) and concludes, I think correctly, that general considerations are not sufficient to permit reaching conclusions; one has to study each paribhāṣā individually, in the context of the commentatorial arguments associated with it.

Wezler's own work (1969) is a study of a group of such paribhāṣās with a translation of the pertinent commentatorial passages. In my opinion, Wezler has not considered all the necessary materials and points at issue. Consider the first two metarules treated by Wezler and to which he devotes considerable space (1969: 27-120). These paribhāṣās have to do with markers (*it, anubandha,* see section III.1.5.3c). Now, Pāṇini uses terms such as *daip*. This is used to refer to the root *dai* 'clean', which is marked with *p*.

This marker *p* can be considered either to constitute a part of the item in question (*ekânta*) or not to be a part (*anekânta*) of this item: *daip* or *dai-p*. Similarly, all markers can be considered to constitute parts of the items to which they are attached or not.[107] The *-ai* of *dai* (*daip*), like the *-ai* of *gai* 'sing', should be replaced by *-ā* to derive forms such as the third singular aorist *adāsīt* (cf. *agāsīt*). This is provided by rule 6.1.45 (*ād eca upadeśe'ś-iti*). But this rule states that *-e, -o, -ai, -au* of a root is replaced by *-ā* if the root ends in one of these vowels at the stage when it is taught (*upadeśe*). If, then, the *-p* of *daip* is considered part of the item as taught, 6.1.45 cannot apply to it: *daip* ends in *p*, not *ai*. If, on the other hand, the *p* is not treated as part of the item as taught, 6.1.45 can apply to *daip*. However, another problem arises. Pāṇini uses terms such as *k-it* 'marked with *k*' with reference to items such as *kta* (= *ta*). The term *k-it* is properly understood only as a bahuvrīhi compound meaning 'which has an *it k*' (in Sanskrit: *ka id yasya*). Yet this is not possible if the marker is not considered part of the item. One way around this dilemma is to posit additional metarules, one of which states that an item's having a marker does not preclude its being treated as ending in *-e, -o, -ai, -au*.[108] Another question needs answering, however: what does Pāṇini mean by *upadeśa* ('instruction') in a rule such as 6.1.45? The objection noted above is valid only if by *upadeśa* Pāṇini means the stage at which an item is first introduced. But if this term refers to the stage encompassing the moment at which an item is first introduced and also the stage at which markers have been unconditionally deleted (see section III.1.5.3c) but the item has not yet entered into grammatical operations, all is in order: after the deletion of the marker *p*, *daip* ends in *ai*. Wezler (1969: 94-96) argues that Kātyāyana considered markers not to constitute parts of items. As for the objection that a term such as *k-it* is then not properly interpreted in terms of the semantics of Sanskrit compounds, Wezler (1969: 119) argues that Pāṇini's grammar is couched in an artificial technical language which need not always accord with normal Sanskrit. He has, however, nowhere discussed in any detail the import of the term *upadeśa* in Pāṇini's rules, a very important question. Cardona (1972a: forthcoming a) has argued that there is good evidence to show that Kātyāyana too adopted the view that markers constitute parts of items as they are introduced in the grammar, has discussed all the rules in which Pāṇini uses the term *upadeśa*, and has concluded that, in terms of Pāṇini's metalanguage, which is not radically different from normal Sanskrit (see section III.1.5.3d below), only the *ekânta* view is justifiable. Nevertheless, it is not necessary to set up the additional metarules which appear as paribhāṣās 6-8 in the Paribhāṣêndu-śekhara (see note 108). Karunasindhu Das (1972) has also concluded that these additional metarules are not needed.

Narendra Chandra Nath (1970) has discussed the paribhāṣā[109] according to which, when a nominal base (*prātipadika*) is stated, one is to understand a reference also to that base as qualified by a feminine gender suffix (*liṅga-viśiṣṭa*), that is, the base followed by such a suffix. He correctly points out that this metarule cannot be attributed to Pāṇini, who mentions separately[110] nominal bases (*prātipadika*) and items ending in feminine affixes referred to by the terms *ṅī* and *āp*. Nath also suggests (1970: 83) that this metarule antedates Kātyāyana. However, his argument for this does not seem cogent to me. It is as follows. Kātyāyana states[111] that the mention of *ṅī* and *āp* (*ṅy-āb-grahaṇam*) in 4.1.1 (see note 110) is useless (*anarthakam*) because, when a nominal base is mentioned, that base as qualified by a feminine affix is also mentioned. Nath argues that, because Kātyāyana uses the ablative *grahaṇāt* (see note 111) when giving a reason for his contention, this is "a known principle in the above vārttika. Had it been a new principle initiated by Kātyāyana, we should have *grahaṇam* [nominative] (not *grahaṇāt*)." However, whether or not Kātyāyana knew of this metarule from a predecessor, the syntax of his statement – ". . . . is useless because . . . ." – requires an ablative, not a nominative, form.

1.4. *Other texts usually associated with the Aṣṭādhyāyī.*

There is a series of treatises, the authorship and dates of which have been disputed, which are usually considered together with the Aṣṭādhyāyī. These are: the uṇ-ādi-sūtras (section III.1.4.1), the phiṭ-sūtras (section III.1.4.2), the liṅgânuśāsana (section III.1.4.3) and the texts called Pāṇinīya-śikṣā (section III.1.4.4).

1.4.1. *The uṇ-ādi-sūtras.*

1.4.1a. *The texts.*

The uṇ-ādi-sūtras are rules which provide for introducing certain affixes after verb roots to derive nominal bases. These rules are called *uṇ-ādi* ('*uṇ* etc.') because the first rule[112] provides for affixing *uṇ* (= *u*) to a series of roots to derive nominals such as *kāru* 'artisan' (< *kṛ* 'make'), *vāyu* 'wind' (< *vā* 'blow'). The rules are contained in two versions of treatises, one divided into five sections and called the *pañca-pādī*, the other divided into ten sections and called *daśa-pādī*.

Yudhiṣṭhira Mīmāṃsaka (1943: introduction, p. 29; 1973: II: 229-31) has set forth evidence to show that the daśa-pādī version is later than and in fact based on the pañca-pādī version. I think this evidence is convincing.

For example, the daśa-pādī has two consecutive rules (9.1-2, Yudhiṣṭhira Mīmāṃsaka [1943: 376]) providing for affixes to follow the root *kliś* 'torment, distress, be distressed'. Both rules contain the ablative form *kliśeḥ* 'after *kliś*'. Yet this is out of keeping with the sūtra style. One would expect *kliśeḥ* to be stated only in the first rule, whence it would be considered to recur (*anuvṛtti,* see sections III.1.5.2c, III.1.5.3g) in the immediately following rule. In the pañca-pādī, on the other hand, the same rules are not consecutive; they appear as rules 5.56 and 5.33 respectively. Here it is necessary to state *kliśeḥ* twice. The redundancy in the daśa-pādī is immediately explained once one posits that its author has taken bodily rules of the pañca-pādī and rearranged them. This rearrangement was made according to the final sounds of the derivatives formed. First come rules which derive items in *-i,* then those which derive items in *-ī, -u, -ū,* etc. And within each such group, the rules which appear in the first chapter of the pañca-pādī are given first, then those of the second chapter, etc.

The pañca-pādī is the version usually commented on by Pāṇinīyas. It has been edited several times. Aufrecht's edition (1859), with the commentary of Ujjvaladatta, is the standard edition of this version. Jibananda Vidyasagara's edition (1873) also contains Ujjvaladatta's commentary but lacks indices. Other commentaries have been edited by T. R. Chintamani (1933, 1939), and K. Kunjunni Raja (1972), who has also (1956a) edited Mahādeva Vedântin's Uṇ-ādi-kośa, wherein are given synonyms of the items derived by the uṇ-ādi-sūtras. In addition, Dayānanda Sarasvatī (1949/50) edited the text with his own comments. The pañca-pādī was also commented on by Bhaṭṭojī Dīkṣita in his Siddhânta-kaumudī (section IV.3.2), in turn commented on in the Bāla-manoramā and Tattva-bodhinī supercommentaries (see Paṇsīkar [1913], Gopāla Shastri Nene [1958-61], Giridhara Śarmā Catruveda - Parameśvarānanda Śarmā Bhāskara [1958-61]) as well as in Nāgeśa's Laghu-śabdêndu-śekhara (Rāmaśāstrī Mānavalli - Nārāyaṇa Śāstrī Bhāradvāja [1887: 475-80]). The text alone has been published also by Pathak - Chitrao (1935).[113]

The daśa-pādī version has been edited, with a commentary, by Yudhiṣṭhira Mīmāṃsaka (1943). It is this version which Viṭṭhala followed in his commentary on the Prakriyā-kaumudī (section IV.3.1.2); see K. P. Trivedi (1925-31: II: 601-47).

Indices of sūtras, items derived by them, etc. appear in editions noted above; see the bibliography for details.

1.4.1b. *Questions of authorship and dates.*

Several questions regarding the uṇ-ādi-sūtras have been the objects of research and disagreement. First, are these rules as we know them attributable to Pāṇini? Or do they predate or postdate him? And if they cannot be attributed to Pāṇini, did he nevertheless compile a comparable set of affixes?

Commentators do not themselves agree regarding the authorship of these rules. Some attribute them to Śākaṭāyana (see section III.1.3.1 with note 31), others to Kātyāyana, still others to Pāṇini, and some merely refer to them as the work of another school; see Aufrecht (1859: ix), Belvalkar (1915: 27), Chintamani (1933: introduction, p. ix; text pp. 1-2), J. S. Pade (1958: x-xvi),[114] Vedavrata (1962;63: III: 311), Yudhiṣṭhira Mīmāṃsaka (1973: II: 196-97). Pāṇini himself uses the term *uṇ-ādi* in two rules[115] and refers in several sūtras to affixes which he does not introduce by rules of his own grammar but which are introduced by uṇ-ādi-sūtras. For example, Pāṇini 7.3.85 (*jāgro'vi-ciṇ-ṇal-ṅitsu*) teaches that the *-ṛ* of *jāgṛ* 'wake' undergoes replacement by guṇa (that is, ultimately, by *ar*) in certain contexts. The rule also states exceptions. This replacement does not apply before certain affixes, among them *vi*; thus *jāgṛvi* '(wakeful one,) king'. Pāṇini does not provide for introducing *vi* after *jāgṛ*, but the uṇ-ādi-sūtras do (pañca-pādī 4.56, daśa-pādī 1.24). It is thereby patent that Pāṇini knew of a set of affixes beginning with *uṇ* and that he accepted some of the derivations involving these.

Aufrecht (1859: viii-ix) argued that the text edited by him was, in its core, pre-Pāṇinian. The basis for his view is as follows. Pāṇini refers to the uṇ-ādi affixes. The uṇ-ādi-sūtras provide for deriving *kārṣaka* 'farmer' and *kāri* 'artisan' and "this distinction refers to a period of the language, of which no mention is made by any grammarian after *Pāṇini.*" Further, the uṇ-ādi-sūtras refer to Śākravarmaṇa, "an old grammarian, who is only once more quoted, namely in *Pāṇini* VI, 1, 130," and treat some words as Vedic which Pāṇini treats as belonging to everyday speech. Goldstücker (1861: 158-62) reviewed Aufrecht's arguments and rightly noted that they do not prove the conclusion reached. Goldstücker's own position was somewhat subtler. He argued (1861: 170-71) that the uṇ-ādi-sūtras used terms defined by Pāṇini and in the same senses which they have in the Aṣṭādhyāyī, so that these terms show the treatise to be post-Pāṇinian. On the other hand, Goldstücker (1861: 171-81) maintained that Pāṇini himself also composed a list of uṇ-ādi affixes. His two principal arguments for this view are as follows. Kātyāyana frequently objects to the formulation of a Pāṇinian rule by pointing out problems which arise in its application with respect to items derived with uṇ-ādi affixes.[116] Therefore, Kātyāyana must have assumed there was a set of uṇ-ādi affixes compiled by Pāṇini. In addition, the uṇ-ādi affixes bear markers (see section III.1.5.3c) which have the same functions as do markers in Pāṇini's system. Belvalkar (1915: 25-27) argued in a similar fashion, although he also noted (1915: 26 with note 2) that the uṇ-ādi sūtras and the Aṣṭādhyāyī conflict in some cases; see below on this point. A more extreme position was taken by K. B. Pathak (1921-22; 1930c), who not only maintained that Pāṇini composed the uṇ-ādi-sūtras but also (1921-22: 126) that he originally inserted them after rule 3.3.1 (see my note 115). Pathak's arguments need not detain us, since his opinion is so extreme and has been combatted effectively by J. S. Pade (1958: xvii-xix).[117] Nevertheless, Pathak's arguments temporarily won at least one adherent to his position. Renou (1940a: 17) cautiously accepted, on account of Pathak's articles, that Pāṇini not only composed a list of uṇ-ādi affixes but also sūtras which were either very close to or identical with the ones known to us. Renou later gave up this view; see below. In his early work Yudhiṣṭhira Mīmāṃsaka (1943: introduction, pp. 11, 26) simply admitted he could not decide who was the author of either version of the uṇ-ādi-sūtra treatises. Later, however, he expressed the opinion (1973: I: 144, II: 201) that the pañca-pādī version was propounded by Āpiśali (see section III.1.3.2a), the daśa-pādī by Pāṇini himself. But Yudhiṣṭhira Mīmāṃsaka admits this is only an opinion.

In the 1940s and 1950s two important papers were written, by K. Madhava Krishna Sarma (1941a) and Renou (1956b), which went a long way toward eliminating any possibility that the presently known uṇ-ādi treatises could be attributed correctly to Pāṇini. Both pointed out conflicts between Pāṇinian rules and uṇ-ādi sūtras, adding considerable evidence to what Belvalkar had earlier pointed out (see above).[118] Renou (1956b: 159) noted that Pāṇini did know a set of uṇ-ādi affixes but that he did not accept all possible derivations with these, only derivations involving items which he considered clearly analyzable.[119] In his last writing on the subject Renou (1969: 485) expressed the opinion that the extant uṇ-ādi treatises are not Pāṇini's, "which means that they are partly pre- and partly post-Pāṇinean." Meanwhile, J. S. Pade (1958: viii-xix) also discussed the question thoroughly, concluding that the presently known texts are post-Pāṇinian. More recently, Śrīhara Ananta Śāstrī Phaḍake (1966;67; 1967) again took up the question, discussed previous views, and suggested (1967: 291-92) a novel solution, namely that these were two Śākaṭāyanas, one who preceded Pāṇini and another who came between Pāṇini and Kātyāyana. According to Phaḍake, it is the latter who composed the uṇ-ādi-sūtras and linked them to Pāṇini's grammar. Still more recently, Staal (1972: 62) has categorically stated that no derivation involving uṇ-ādi affixes was accepted by Pāṇini. Cardona (1973g: 46) has argued against this extreme position.

The most acceptable view in accord with the evidence appears to me to be the following. Not all the rules which appear in the uṇ-ādi treatises we have can be Pāṇini's, as is clear from conflicts between the works. Further, Pāṇini's referring to uṇ-ādi affixes (see note 115) does not mean he himself compiled a list of such affixes. He could simply have accepted as proper some but not all of the derivations with such affixes as posited by predecessors or contemporaries. Moreover, Goldstücker's arguments (see above) are by no means probative. His argument concerning technical terms rests on his view regarding Pāṇini's technical terminology, a view which has been shown to be untenable (see section III.1.5.3a). And the use of markers is not conclusive evidence, since such markers in all probability were used before Pāṇini (see K. V. Abhyankar 1970: 331), as they were after him. In sum, the only certainty is that Pāṇini knew of uṇ-ādi affixes and accepted some of the derivations involving them.

1.4.2. *The phiṭ-sūtras.*

1.4.2a. *The text.*

The phiṭ-sūtras, attributed to Śāntanava (or Śantanu) state rules for the accentuation of nominal bases according to their phonologic shapes and meanings. For example, the first rule (*phiṣo'nta udāttaḥ*) states that the final (*anta*) vowel of a nominal base (*phiṣ*) is high pitched (*udātta*). The third rule (*gehârthānām astriyām*) provides that nominal bases meaning 'house' (*gehârtha*) are thus accented provided they are not feminine (*astriyām*); e.g., *gehá* but *śā́lā*. The sixth rule (*khântasyâś-m-ādeḥ*) provides that a nominal base which ends in *khă* (*khânta*) has a high-pitched final vowel provided it does not also begin with *ś* or *m* (*aś-m-ādi*); e.g., *sukhá* 'happiness' but *múkha* 'mouth, face'.

This set of rules is known as the *phiṭ-sūtras* by virtue of its using the term *phiṣ*[120] to refer to nominal bases instead of the Pāṇinian term *prātipadika*. The text alone was edited by Pathak - Chitrao (1935). Kielhorn (1866) edited the text together with Bhaṭṭoji Dīkṣita's commentary, Nāgeśa's supercommentary and the Phiṭ-sūtra-vṛtti, along with a German translation and indices. The text with Bhaṭṭojī's comments and Jayakṛṣṇa's supercommentary Subodhinī has been published in editions of the Siddhânta-kaumudī; see Gopāla Shastri Nene (1958 - 61), Giridhara Śarmā Caturveda - Parameśvarānanda Śarmā Bhāskara (1958 - 61); the latter edition also includes Nāgeśa's supercommentary. The text without Sanskrit commentary but with an English translation and notes was later reedited by Devasthali (1967). In addition, Sudarśanadeva recently composed a simple modern commentary in Sanskrit, which has been edited by Vedānanda Vedavāgīśa (1968/9). For indices see the editions mentioned.

1.4.2b. *Authorship and date.*

The purposes of the phiṭ-sūtra accentual rules and Pāṇini's rules on accentuation are radically different. The former attempt to state the accentuation patterns of nominal bases per se. Pāṇini's rules, on the other hand, regulate accentuation in a derivational system. At each stage of a derivation an accentual adjustment is made such that each element terminating in a verbal or nominal ending contains only one high-pitched vowel.[121] Affixes normally have high pitch on their first vowel, but affixes marked with *p* and nominal endings normally have no high-pitched vowel.[122] In the course of a derivation, then, the accent of an item introduced cancels whatever accent there was before.[123] For example, given the base *rā́jan* 'king', the instrumental singular and plural forms derived are *rā́jñā, rā́jabhiḥ;* the nominal endings *ā, bhis* do not have high pitch. But given the base *vā́c* 'speech, voice', the instrumental forms should be *vācā́, vāgbhíḥ.* To provide for this Pāṇini states a special rule: endings of the third and subsequent triplets of nominal endings (instrumental etc.) are high-pitched if they occur after a base which is monosyllabic (*ekâc*) before the locative plural ending *su* (6.1.168: *sāv ekâcas tṛtīyâdir vibhaktiḥ*). The endings *ā, bhis* thereby have high pitch after *vā́c,* whose locative plural is *vāk-ṣú.* Moreover, the erasure procedure noted precludes deriving **vā́cā́.* Similar adjustments are made in verb forms, compounds and other derivatives. All this presupposes that one is given the accentual features of primitive bases such as *rā́jan* etc. Pāṇini has no rules for providing the accents of such primitive bases.

Given this, it is clear that the phiṭ-sūtras cannot be attributed to Pāṇini. Commentators ascribe them to Śantanu or Sāntanava (see Yudhiṣṭhira Mīmāṃsaka 1973: II: 314-5). However, there has been some discussion concerning whether such rules should be considered pre- or post-Pāṇinian. Max Müller (1859: 152) expressed the early view, that the phiṭ-sūtras antedate Pāṇini. However, as Goldstücker (1861: 214) already pointed out, Müller did not present solid evidence to buttress this opinion. His only two arguments were that the technical terms used in the phiṭ-sūtras differ from Pāṇini's and that, since the former rules deal with accent and accent was Vedic, they must predate Pāṇini. The first is no argument at all. The second argument is unacceptable. The phiṭ-sūtras do not deal with Vedic matters alone, nor was the accentual system seen to operate in Vedic dead at Pāṇini's time, as is clear from the detailed accentual rules of the Aṣṭādhyāyī. Goldstücker (1861: 216-20) gave evidence to show that the phiṭ-sūtras are, in fact, later than Pāṇini. Kielhorn (1866: introduction, pp. 5-11) even more definitively showed this by demonstrating that the phiṭ-sūtras presuppose Pāṇini's rules.[124] For example, phiṭ-sūtra 2.16 (*lub-antasyôpameya-nāmadheyasya*)[125] provides that a base has a high-pitched first vowel if it names a person (*nāmadheya*) who is the object of a comparison (*upameya*) and ends in a zero replacement (*lub-anta*); e.g., *cáñcā* 'straw man'. This presupposes Pāṇini's rule 5.3.98 (*lub manuṣye*), whereby an affix is deleted in deriving an item like *cáñcā.* The view that the phiṭ-sūtras are post-Pāṇinian is generally accepted (see recently Devasthali [1967: 42], earlier Belvalkar [1915: 27]), and this is also the view of Nāgeśa (see Devasthali [1967: 41-42]). However, Kapil Deva Shastri (1961: 29) and Yudhiṣṭhira Mīmāṃsaka (1973: II: 317) have brought forth one piece of evidence which they believe establishes that the phiṭ-sūtras are pre-Pāṇinian. It is this. Pāṇini has a pratyāhāra-sūtra (see section III.1.1) *ai au c*, wherein the sounds *ai* and *au* are followed by the marker *c.* The commentary on the 13th pratyāhāra-sūtra of Candragomin's grammar (K. C. Chatterji [1953-61: I: 9-10]) states that previous grammars (*pūrva-vyākaraṇa*) contained instead *ai au ṣ,* with a marker *ṣ.* To illustrate the use of terms formed with this marker *ṣ* are cited phiṭ-sūtras 2.4 and 2.19, where the terms *dvy-aṣ* "disyllabic" and *bahv-aṣ* "polysyllabic" occur; Pāṇini's equivalent terms are *dvy-ac, bahv-ac.* Kapil Deva notes (1961: 29, see also Yudhiṣṭhira Mīmāṃsaka [1973: II: 317]) that this example eliminates any doubt concerning whether the phiṭ-sūtras are pre-Pāṇinian. However, neither he nor Yudhiṣṭhira Mīmāṃsaka has reconciled this with the evidence given by Kielhorn. Moreover, this only shows that Candragomin considered *ṣ* a marker used in early grammar; it does not prove the point claimed. Liebich (1930: 215) cited the evidence from the commentary on Candra's grammar and cautiously concluded only that the phiṭ-sūtras are definitely prior to Candra and the Kāśikā (see section IV.2.1).

There remains another question. Accepting that the phiṭ-sūtras are indeed post-Pāṇinian, are they also later than Patañjali? Kielhorn (1866: introduction, pp. 10-1) believed that the phiṭ-sūtras as we have them were as yet unknown to Patañjali. He discussed one passage from the Mahā-bhāṣya pertinent to the question and noted that neither the term *phiṣ* nor the rule *phiṣo'nta udāttaḥ* (see section III.1.4.2a) was actually cited by Patañjali. Yudhiṣṭhira Mīmāṃsaka (1973: II: 315-16), on the other hand, cites passages from the Mahābhāṣya which, in his opinion, establish that Patañjali indeed knew the phiṭ-sūtras. Here I think the evidence is stronger than Kielhorn believed. In the Mahā-bhāṣya passage treated by Kielhorn Patañjali says:[126] "But there is no rule, 'The first vowel of a nominal base is high-pitched;' there is, however, a rule, 'The last vowel of a nominal base is high-pitched.' " Patañjali uses the term *lakṣaṇa* 'rule', which he uses also to refer to Pāṇinian rules (see section III.1.5.1a). Now, Kielhorn (1866: introduction, p. 11) simply says that a rule such as that cited by Patañjali might have existed prior to Śāntanava. But if such a rule existed and Patañjali refers to it as a rule (*lakṣaṇa*), we must, I think, take this at its face value. A rule is not an isolated observation, in the Indian context, but part of a set of rules. Thus, for example, Patañjali refers to a rule of Āpiśali (see section III.1.3.1 with note 30), and this is not merely an isolated statement but part of a set of rules. Indeed, Patañjali knew of a grammar by Āpiśali (see section III. 1.3.1). It is plausible, then, to conclude that Patañjali was also citing an accentual rule which formed part of an accentual treatise. And only one such treatise of relative antiquity is known, the phiṭ-sūtras themselves.

In my opinion, then, the state of the question is best put as follows. The phiṭ-sūtras are almost certainly post-Pāṇinian. But Patañjali knew of such accentual rules. Though there is no direct evidence to show that he knew a treatise which began with the rule now found at the beginning of the phiṭ-sūtras, the fact remains that this is indeed the only such accentual treatise of antiquity – dating from before Candragomin – which has come down to us in association with Pāṇini's grammar. It is at least plausible, then, to say that Patañjali probably knew this treatise or one very similar to it.

1.4.3. *The liṅgânuśāsana.*

1.4.3a. *The text.*

As the phiṭ-sūtras (section III.1.4.2) attempt to formulate general rules for the accentual features of nominal bases, so the liṅgânuśāsana ("treatise on instruction concerning gender") attempts to state rules, based on the structure and meaning of items, to describe their genders (*liṅga*). For example, the third rule (*ṛkārântā mātṛ-duhitṛ-svasṛ-yātṛ-nanāndaraḥ* [*striyām*]) states that five bases in *-ṛ* are feminine: *mātṛ* 'mother', *duhitṛ* 'daughter', *svasṛ* 'sister', *yātṛ* 'husband's brother's wife', *nanāndṛ* 'husband's sister'. Another rule (6: *mi-ny-antaḥ*) provides that items derived with the suffixes *mi, ni* are feminine; e.g., *bhūmi* 'earth', *glāni* 'fatigue'. And still another (36: *ghañ-ab-antaḥ*) teaches that derivatives ending in *ghañ* or *ap* (= *a*) are masculine; e.g., *pāka* 'cooking'.

The text alone of the *liṅgânuśāsana* associated with the Aṣṭādhyāyī appears in Panṣīkar (1913), S. C. Chakravarti (1918), Pathak - Chitrao (1935), Dayānanda Sarasvatī (1969/70). The text with Bhaṭṭojī Dīkṣita's comments and the supercommentary of Bhairava Miśra appears in the editions of the Siddhânta-kaumudī by Gopāla Shastri Nene (1958-61) and Giridhara Śarmā Caturveda - Parameśvarānanda Śarmā Bhāskara (1958-61).

1.4.3b. *Authorship and date.*

Pāṇini's grammar contains rules regulating gender. For example, there is a rule (2.4.26: *paraval liṅgam dvandva-tatpuruṣayoḥ*) which provides that the gender of a dvandva or tatpuruṣa compound is that of the subsequent member; e.g., *kukkuṭa-mayūrī* 'cock (*kukkuṭa,* masc.) and pea-hen (*mayūrī,* fem.)', *rāja-bhāryā* 'wife (*bhāryā,* fem.) of a king (*rājan,* masc.)', both feminine. Such rules assume as given the genders of single bases. Pāṇini has no rules comparable to those noted in section III.1.4.3a. In addition, Franke (1890: 17) pointed out a conflict between the liṅgânuśāsana and the Aṣṭādhyāyī: the noun *śiśira* 'cool season' was normally neuter for Pāṇini, but the liṅgânuśāsana lets it be both masculine and neuter.[127] Liebich (1930: 233) also noted that at the time of Candragomin (see note 524 below) a liṅgânuśāsana was not yet considered a necessary part of a grammatical treatise, as shown by Candra's paribhāṣā stating that gender is not to be taught (*aśiṣya*) explicitly, since it is assumed as known from normal usage (*lokâśrayatvāt*).[128] Precisely this statement appears already in the Mahā-bhāṣya (Kielhorn [1880-85: I: 477.3]). From all the above, one can conclude properly that Pāṇini did not compose the liṅgânuśāsana usually associated with the Aṣṭādhyāyī. And this is the opinion of most scholars; see, in addition to the above, Belvalkar (1915: 27), Renou (1940a: 18), Ramākānta Miśra (1966: 32).

However, Yudhiṣṭhira Mīmāṃsaka (1973: II: 256-57) and Vedavatī (1964/5: introduction, pp. 2-3)[129] have maintained that the text was propounded by Pāṇini.[130] Yudhiṣṭhira Mīmāṃsaka gives two kinds of evidence to support his view. First, commentators accept this.[131] Secondly, he cites a passage from the Mahā-bhāṣya which, in his opinion, shows that Kātyāyana and Patañjali knew the liṅgânuśāsana ascribed to Pāṇini. In vārttika 5 on 7.1.33 (Kielhorn [1880-85: III: 253.8]) Kātyāyana notes that a certain procedure is not necessary because the pronouns *yuṣmad* (2nd person) and *asmad* (1st person) have no fixed gender. Patañjali states (Kielhorn [1880-85: III: 253.9]): *aliṅge yuṣmad-asmadī* '*Yuṣmad* and *asmad* are genderless.' Yudhiṣṭhira Mīmāṃsaka argues that this shows Kātyāyana and Patañjali knew the liṅgânuśāsana rule (184: *avyayaṃ kati-yuṣmad-asmadaḥ* [*aviśiṣṭa-liṅgam* 183]) according to which certain items, among them *yuṣmad* and *asmad*, do not have a fixed gender (*aviśiṣṭa-liṅga*). He says:[132] "If one compares Kātyāyana's vārttika and Patañjali's explanation of it with the liṅgânuśāsana sūtras . . . , it is clear that Kātyāyana and Patañjali were acquainted with this Pāṇinīya liṅgânuśāsana." I do not think these arguments are cogent. Haradatta's statement (see note 131) of course shows that he considered the liṅgânuśāsana to form an ancillary part of Pāṇini's grammatical treatise. It does not, however, show that Pāṇini himself actually composed this treatise on gender. As for the passage from the Mahā-bhāṣya, this only demonstrates that Kātyāyana and Patañjali knew the obvious fact that the pronouns *yuṣmad* and *asmad* do not have fixed genders.

Their statements in no way show either that they are quoting from a liṅgânuśāsana or are acquainted with the particular liṅgânuśāsana associated with Pāṇini's grammar.

1.4.4. *Śikṣā.*

There are various texts on phonetics which are called *śikṣā*. Of these, most have to do with particular aspects of phonetics in connection with branches of Vedic texts. However, there are also treatises which deal with general aspects of Sanskrit phonetics. Among these are two texts for which considerable antiquity has been claimed, one attributed to Āpiśali (see section III. 1.3.2a), the other to Pāṇini.[133] For general surveys of śikṣās and their contents see Kielhorn (1876b), Siddheshwar Varma (1929: 28-52), Vidhata Mishra (1972: 8-18).

1.4.4a. *The Pāṇiniya-śikṣā texts.*

There are two texts which have been called Pāṇinīya-śikṣā, one in verse, the other in sūtra form. It is the former which is usually referred to as the Pāṇinīya-śikṣā by commentators. This text has various recensions differing in the number of verses included. Two versions were published by Weber (1858b). Some years later Yugalakiśora Pathak (1889) edited a version together with the commentary called Prakāśa. Manomohan Ghosh (1938) edited five recensions together with two commentaries – the Prakāśa and Pañjikā – and also reconstructed what he considered to be the original text of 18 verses. Rudraprasāda Śarmā (1947) later edited a version of the verse text together with his commentary, the Pradīpa. In addition, the bare text of the versified Pāṇinīya-śiksā appears in some editions of the Aṣṭādhyāyī (e.g., Sankara Rama Sastri 1937) and in editions of the Siddhânta-kaumudī (Panṣīkar [1913], Gopāla Shastri Nene [1958-61], Giridhara Śarmā Caturveda - Parameśvarānanda Śarmā Bhāskara [1958-61]). The sūtra form of the text called Pāṇinīya-śikṣā was discovered by Dayānanda Sarasvatī in 1879 and published by him (see Dayānanda Sarasvatī [1950/1]) and, later, by Yudhiṣṭhira Mīmāṃsaka (1967/8). Raghu Vira (1931) published the text of this work with an English translation.

1.4.4b. *Authorship and date.*

The usual version of the versified Pāṇinīya-śikṣā begins with a verse stating that the author will set forth the śikṣā according to the Pāṇinian doctrine (*atha śikṣāṃ pravakṣyāmi pāṇinīyaṃ mataṃ yathā*). And the Prakāśa commentary notes that the work was composed by Piṅgala (see M. M. Ghosh [1938: 23]). Thieme (1935a: 86 n.) argued that this verse "hardly can prove that Pāṇini himself composed a similar work."

The opinion that Pāṇini did not himself compose the versified śikṣā usually associated with the Aṣṭādhyāyī is shared by most modern scholars. Renou (1940a: 18) called this a phonetic treatise of rather doubtful authenticity; see also Belvalkar (1915: 27), Ramākānta Miśra (1966: 32), Yudhiṣṭhira Mīmāṃsaka (1967/8: introduction, pp. 5-6).[134] However, Manomohan Ghosh has attempted to demonstrate that the text reconstructed by him[135] is correctly attributable to Pāṇini. Ghosh's major arguments (1938: L) are as follows. This Pāṇinīya-śikṣā uses abbreviatory terms such as *ac* "vowels", *ku* "velar stops", in accord with Pāṇini's conventions. In addition, "The P[āṇinīya] Ś[ikṣā] (17) includes the Anunāsika into [sic] speech-sounds while its definition has been given in the Aṣṭādhyāyī (I. 1. 8) *mukha-nāsikā-vacano'nunāsikaḥ.*"[136] Moreover, terms such as *hrasva* 'short vowel', *dīrgha* 'long vowel', which are defined in the Aṣṭādhyāyī, are used in the śikṣā. Finally, Pāṇini provides that *n*, when it is preceded by *ṛ* or *ṣ*, is replaced by *ṇ*, which shows that *ṛ* was a retroflex sound; the śikṣā agrees in classing *ṛ* as a retroflex sound. According to Ghosh (1938: L), "All these fairly settle the question of the authorship of the P[āṇinīya] Ś[ikṣā]." I do not think Ghosh's evidence is as substantial or cogent as he believed. The use of terms such as *ac, ku* cannot prove identity of authors, since a later author could as well have used these terms, especially if he was composing a treatise in accord with Pāṇinian doctrine. Similarly, Ghosh's second and third points prove only that the author of the śikṣā knew terms for nasal sounds, short vowels, etc., as did also Pāṇini and later grammarians. Again, I do not see how Pāṇini's letting *n* be replaced by *ṇ* after *ṛ*[137] can prove that the śikṣā author who classed *ṛ* as a cerebral sound is indeed Pāṇini. In fact, as far as I can see, Ghosh omitted mentioning one piece of evidence which speaks against his thesis. Even the text reconstructed by Ghosh contains verses (16-17, Ghosh [1938: 3]) which state that vowels are articulated with no contact (*aspṛṣṭa*) of an articulator with a point of articulation, semivowels with slight contact (*īṣat* [*-spṛṣṭa*]), spirants (*ś, ṣ, s, h*) with half contact (*nema-spṛṣṭa*), and other consonants with full contact (*spṛṣṭa*).[138] Ghosh (1938: xli, 74) gives a chart showing this and translates the passage in question. He does not, however, note that in fact this conflicts with what Pāṇini says. For Pāṇini does not distinguish spirants and vowels by their internal efforts (*ābhyantara-prayatna*) stoppedness (*spṛṣṭatā*) and half-stoppedness (*nema-spṛṣṭatā*); see section III.1.5.4a. This strongly indicates that even the expurgated version of the versified Pāṇinīya-śikṣā reconstructed by Manomohan Ghosh is not correctly attributable to Pāṇini. Nevertheless, Ghosh's arguments have impressed some more recent scholars. M. D. Pandit (1969: 129 n. 4) speaks of Ghosh's "substantial evidence", though he does not categorically accept the attribution of this śikṣā to Pāṇini. J. D. Singh (1970: 148) speaks of "his [Pāṇini's] treatises, i.e., *śikṣā* and *aṣṭādhyāyī*", thus apparently accepting Ghosh's conclusions.[139] However, Singh appears to be somewhat confused. For he says (1970: 150), "Pāṇini has listed four such manners of articulation . . . " and goes on to list *spṛṣṭa, īṣat-spṛṣṭa, īṣad-vivṛta* ("slightly open") and *vivṛta* ("open"). In fact, Pāṇini does not list any of these in his Aṣṭādhyāyī. Nor does the Pāṇinīya-śikṣa in question mention *īṣad-vivṛta* (see above with note 138).[140]

In 1879 Dayānanda discovered a manuscript of, and published a work he called, the Pāṇinīya-śikṣā. This is the sūtra form of the text; see Yudhiṣṭhira Mīmāṃsaka (1967/8: introduction, p. 6; 1973: I: 237, II: 63). Dayānanda's text was not complete. Moreover, according to Yudhiṣṭhira Mīmāṃsaka, this was only the textus simplicior (*laghu-pāṭha*); there is, according to him, also a textus amplior (*vṛddha-pāṭha*). Yudhiṣṭhira Mīmāṃsaka has (1967/8: introduction, pp. 5, 11-12; 1973: III: 71-81) edited, published and compared the two.[141] Raghu Vira (1931) accepted the authenticity of the śikṣā discovered by Dayānanda, although he admitted (1931: 654) that he did not know the real basis of Dayānanda's attribution, since the single manuscript was not found after his death. Thieme (1935a: 86-7 n.) argued, against Raghu Vira, that there was nothing in his text which in any way showed it to be archaic. Manomohan Ghosh (1938: xlvi-xlvii) was more harsh. According to Ghosh, Dayānanda himself composed the work he attributed to Pāṇini and did this on the basis of such sources as the Mahā-bhāṣya and Candragomin's phonetic sūtras.[142] S. K. Gupta (1951) defended Dayānanda against this accusation, but he gave no detailed rebuttal. Yudhiṣṭhira Mīmāṃsaka (1967/8: introduction, p. 7) also argued against Ghosh's accusation. However, he did not here give any detailed arguments of his own. Instead, he referred to an article, inaccessible to me, in which, he said, he had demonstrated the falseness of Ghosh's claims.[143] Leaving aside such accusations of fraud and defenses against them, the fact remains, however, that there are differences in doctrine and detail between Pāṇini's Aṣṭādhyāyī and the sūtra version of the Pāṇiniya-śikṣā. The latter says of spirants (*ūṣman*) that they are pronounced either with partial opening or complete opening between an articulator and points of articulation.[144] But Pāṇini's statements show that he considered spirants to be articulated with full opening and this alone; see section III.1.5.4a. As for details: The nasals appear in the śiva-sūtras (see section III.1.3.4) in the order *ñ, m, ṅ, ṇ, n.*[145] In the sūtra version of the Pāṇinīya-śikṣā, however, they appear in the order *ṅ, ñ, ṇ, n, m.*[146] If one accepts that the śiva-sūtras were compiled by Pāṇini, one must also ask why there is this discrepancy. One possible explanation would be the following. In his phonetic treatise Pāṇini reverted to the usual order, abandoning the order required in the śiva-sūtras for the statement of a morphophonemic operation (see section III.1.3.2a). Such an explanation, however, would be in order only if one had already established that the Pāṇinīya-śikṣā had, on other grounds, to be attributed to Pāṇini. Alternatively, one could argue that only the second order of nasals shown above is truly Pāṇini's and that he took the other one from Āpiśali (see sections III.1.3.2a, III.1.3.4). But this argument rests on the assumption that Āpiśali changed the regular order of the nasals to form an abbreviation which he used in the uṇ-ādi-sūtras (see section III.1.3.2a), which remains doubtful.

In sum, I think the evidence available precludes one's considering with confidence, that Pāṇini composed either of the śikṣā texts which have been attributed to him.[147]

1.5. *The system of the Aṣṭādhyāyī.*

1.5.1. *General introduction.*

1.5.1a. *Pāṇini's derivational system: generalities.*

Pāṇini's grammar is descriptive, not prescriptive (Staal [1965b: 109]). The rules of the grammar serve to derive forms which accord with correct usage.[148] These rules (*sūtra,* see note 10) are also called *lakṣaṇa* 'characteristic, that by which ... is characterized' in that they serve as means to characterize, that is, to explain by derivation, the forms of correct usage. These correct forms are, accordingly, called *lakṣya* 'that which is to be characterized'.[149] Basic to this derivational system is the distinction between bases (*prakṛti*) and affixes (*pratyaya*). The grammar provides for introducing affixes after bases[150] under given conditions to derive items terminating in verbal or nominal endings. These are called *pada.*[151] The bases themselves are of two general types: verb roots (*dhātu*) and nominal bases (*prātipadika*). In addition, bases are either primitive or derived. Primitive verb roots appear in the dhātu-pāṭha (see sections III.1.1, III.1.3.5 and note 83). Primitive nominal bases would appear in a lexicon; the gaṇa-pāṭha (see sections III.1.1, III.1.3.6) represents a partial lexicon of items which undergo particular operations. Derived bases are gotten by applying rules of the grammar. Derived verb roots are formed from both primitive roots and nominal forms. Examples of the first are causatives such as *kār-i* 'make do, have do' (⟨ *kṛ* 'do, make'), desideratives such as *cikīr-ṣa-* 'wish to do'; examples of the latter are denominatives such as *putrīya-* 'desire a son (*putra*) for oneself', *putrakāmya-* 'idem'. Derived nominal bases too are gotten from both verb roots and nominal forms. Bases such as *pāk-a* 'cooking', *pāc-aka* 'cook' are derived from the root *pac* by introducing the primary affixes (called *kṛt*) *ghañ* (= *a*) and *ṇvul* (= *aka*) respectively. From nominal forms are derived compounds such as *rāja-puruṣa* 'king's man' and items such as *aupagava* 'descendant of Upagu', *tatra* 'there', which contain affixes called *taddhita.*

The conditions under which affixes are introduced are of the following types. Some rules state meanings as conditions: affix A is introduced after item I when meaning M is to be denoted.[152] Some rules state cooccurrence conditions: affix A is introduced after item I if item J occurs.[153] Some rules state a combination of these conditions: A is introduced after I if M is to be denoted and J occurs.[154] In addition, some rule introduce affixes without giving any condition. Such affixes are said to be introduced redundantly;[155] the meaning denoted by the derivative is the same as that denoted by the item to which the affix is added. For example, *tatra* 'there' is derived by affixing *tra* to a form (*tad-i*) which contains a locative ending denoting a locus; *tatra* too denotes a locus.

The meanings which serve as conditions for affixation are themselves of two general kinds. In most rules which introduce affixes under such conditions Pāṇini uses terms such as *bhūta* 'past', *bhaviṣyat* 'future', *vartamāna* 'current, present', *vidhi* 'command', which are not introduced in the grammar by definition. Such rules involve purely semantic notions. Other notions are not purely semantic and the terms used for them require definition. These are the terms denoting kārakas, on which see section III.1.5.5c.[156]

The padas (see above with note 151) which result from affixation are subject to morphophonemic rules[157] whereby are gotten items as they occur in actual usage. For example, the strings

(1) *rājñaḥ puruṣo grāmaṃ gacchati* 'The king's man is going to the village.'
(2) *upagor apatyaṃ grāmaṃ gacchati* 'A descendant of Upagu is going to the village.'

derive from

(1a) *rājan-as puruṣa-s grāma-am gam-a-ti*
(2a) *upagu-as apatya-s grāma-am gam-a-ti*

which contain the padas *rājan-as* (gen. sg. of *rājan* 'king'), *puruṣa-s* (nom. sg. of *puruṣa* 'man'), *grāma-am* (acc. sg. of *grāma* 'village'), *gam-a-ti* (3rd sg. pres. of *gam* 'go'), *upagu-as* (gen. sg. of the name *upagu*), *apatya-s* (nom. sg. of *apatya* 'descendant'), themselves consisting of bases and affixes introduced to denote a relation (genitive *-as*), an object (accusative *-am*) and an agent (verb ending *-ti*).

On the other hand, related padas such as *rājan-as* and *puruṣa-s* are subject to other rules, whereby are formed compounds. Given these padas, then, one can also form the compound *rājan-as-puruṣa-s,* whence derives *rāja-puruṣa.* Similarly, to the pada *upagu-as* can be introduced the taddhita affix *a* to form *upagu-as-a*, whence derives *aupagava.* The pertinent rules are optional, so that *rāja-puruṣa, aupagava* and the sequences *rājñaḥ puruṣaḥ, upagor apatyam* are derived as alternates.[158]

Also derived as alternates are active and passive sentences such as

(3) *devadatta odanaṃ pacati* 'Devadatta is cooking rice.'
(4) *odanaḥ pacyate devadattena* 'Rice is being cooked by Devadatta.'

In introducing affixes to denote kārakas (see section III.1.5.5c), primacy is granted to verb affixes.[159] For deriving (3), then, the L-suffix *laṭ* is introduced (by 3.4.69, see note 152) to denote an agent; the accusative ending *am* is introduced after *odana* to denote an object. But in deriving (4) the L-suffix *laṭ* is introduced to denote an object; here the instrumental ending is introduced after *devadatta* to denote an agent. This is not done in (3), since an agent is denoted by the post-verbal affix *laṭ*. There is no other hierarchical relation between (3) and (4), however, and one sentence is not derived from the other. They are alternative derivations.

In any given derivation such as illustrated above substitution rules can be involved. In Pāṇini's system a unit Y is allowed to occur in place of another unit X, respectively termed *ādeśa* 'substitute' and *sthānin* 'substituend'.[160] The substituends and replacements can be bases, affixes or sounds alone.[161] For example, the derivation of (1) and (2) involves stages still earlier than (1a) and (2a), at which the root *gam* is followed by the L-suffix *laṭ*. This is then replaced by the ending *ti* (see section III.1.5.5b.1). In deriving (1) the *-s* of *rājan-as* is replaced by *-r*, in turn replaced by *-ḥ*; the *-s* of *puruṣa-s* is replaced by *-r*, which is then replaced by *-u*; *-o* then substitutes for the sequence *au*; and the two sounds *-a-*$_1$ and *a-*$_2$ in *grāma-am* are both replaced by *a*$_1$. Moreover, there are zero replacements. The *-a-* of *rājan* in *rājan-as* is deleted, as is the *-n* of *rājan* in the compound *rāja-puruṣa.* Similarly, the endings contained in this compound (*rājan-as-puruṣa-s*) and in the taddhita derivative *aupagava* (*upagu-as-a*) are also replaced by zero.[162] In all such cases Pāṇinīyas consider that the substitute occurs instead of the substituend, which is said tentatively to occur in the given context. That is, on the level of grammatical operations one can speak of Y replacing X, but what this accounts for is that, in the given context, X does not occur, Y being used instead.[163] It has been recognized that Pāṇini's substitution procedure is different from and probably later than another procedure wherein an element

X is said to become Y, see Thieme (1958: 45), Cardona (1969: 32), and below, section III.3.2b.

1.5.1b. *Pāṇini's system: studies of general aspects.*

There has not been published to date in a European language a single work in which Pāṇini's total system is set forth clearly and with insight. The most comprehensive work of this sort to have appeared is Charudeva Shastri's (1969-73), an excellent survey of Pāṇinian grammar, in which are incorporated the thoughts of major Pāṇiniyas and copious examples are given to illustrate grammatical statements. The most ambitious work attempting to give a full picture of Pāṇini's system in a European language is by Vidya Niwas Misra (1966). However, this suffers from two drawbacks. The author is so intent on presenting parallels between Pāṇini's system and various western approaches to linguistics (see section III.1.5.6b below) and the book is organized in such a manner that the work suffers and one who is not already well acquainted with Pāṇini cannot easily gain an understanding; see Cardona (1968b) for a discussion of these points. There is, nevertheless, a considerable number of articles in which are considered particular aspects of Pāṇini's general system and attitudes.[164]

As I noted earlier (section III.1.5.1a) Pāṇini accepts that verb roots are basic units to which are added affixes. The question has arisen whether, like Śākaṭāyana (see section III.1.3.1), Pāṇini viewed all nouns as derivable from such verb roots. Several scholars have maintained that this was Pāṇini's position: Keith (1920: 424), Emeneau (1955: 148), Staal (1969: 508). However, this is not a correct appreciation, as others have recognized; see section III.1.4.1b with note 119.

Pāṇiniyas such as Patañjali refer to Pāṇini's grammar as a *śabdânuśāsana* '(treatise on) instruction (concerning the formation of correct) words'. Earlier scholars such as Wackernagel (1896: lxii) and, more recently, Thieme (1956: 4) considered, therefore, that the grammar dealt exclusively with word formation, to the exclusion of syntax. In fact, however, Pāṇini operates with a syntactic system, as has been recognized more recently; see for example, Cardona (1965b: 306; 1967a: 35 n. 3; 1967b: 213 n. 19), S. D. Joshi (1969: 16, 20, 26). Al-George (1958: 44) agrees with Wackernagel that Pāṇini's principal aim was to provide a word analysis, but he also notes that Pāṇini's kāraka system (see section III.1.5.5c) implies a sentence analysis. I think some subtlety is required here. It cannot be denied that Pāṇini does deal with syntactic relations and relations among certain kinds of sentences. On the other hand, it is also patent that his basic derivational procedure consists in introducing affixes to bases (see section III.1.5.1a), so that he also deals essentially with the relations among padas which constitute sentences. This is important for appreciating the limits of his syntactic and semantic interests; see section III.1.5.7b. In a recent work, Narendra Chandra Nath (1969: 209) has reverted to the earlier claim. He insists that Pāṇini's grammar deals with phonology and morphology "but has not a word on syntax." However, this claim is based on Nath's own rather narrow conception of syntax as being "strictly, order of words in sentences."

In recent years several papers have appeared in which is treated Pāṇini's derivational system in general, including syntax. S. D. Joshi (1969) deals with Pāṇini's syntactic system and illustrates the complete derivation of a sentence by Pāṇinian rules.[165] Complete derivations are also illustrated by Cardona (1970c), who has also written an elementary introduction to Pāṇini's system of derivation (forthcoming c). In addition, M. D. Pandit (1963b) has discussed in general terms Pāṇini's method of affixing to bases,[166] and van Nooten (1967) has dealt with Pāṇini's derivation of finite forms such as *pacati* 'is cooking'.

Concerning meaning conditions for the introduction of affixes (see section III.1.5.1a), van Nooten (1969) has devoted a paper to demonstrating that Pāṇini's statements "... are not of the type 'element *a* means *x*', but rather 'to express notion *x*, use element *a*'" (van Nooten [1969: 244]). What van Nooten has tried to prove was well known before; see Thieme (1958: 25), Cardona (1974b: 283 n. 14).

Pāṇini's substitution procedure has received renewed attention in recent years. Particularly interesting are attempts to formalize Pāṇini's morphophonemic substitution rules. To my knowledge, this was initiated by Staal (1965a), whose notation has been adopted and refined by Cardona (1969). Staal's initial effort is praiseworthy for its attempt to clarify. However, his paper also contains elementary errors and misrepresentations of what Pāṇini said; see Cardona (1965b) for a critique. Van Nooten (1967; 1970a) has also recently dealt with aspects of Pāṇinian substitutions. In the latter article (1970a: 25-26), he suggests a formulaic statement of replacements such as *au* → *o* (see section III.1.5.1a above). He proposes to write "x + y → z / C", which is to be read, "In the context *C*, a succession of elements *x* and *y* is replaced by one element, *z*." He does not, however, note the important fact that Pāṇini accounts for such replacements by the interesting stratagem of making the substituends their own left and right contexts; see Cardona (1965b: 309-10).

One particular replacement, zero, has attracted special attention. This has been discussed by W. S. Allen (1955), who proposed that the linguistic zero was known before the mathematical zero (cf. Toporov [1961: 127-8], Staal [1974: 69]). M. D. Pandit's discussion (1962) is, I think, also worthwhile. On the other hand, I personally find Al-George's treatment of zero (1967) confusing, in no small part because the author insists on drawing broad metaphysical and speculative conclusions. Typical is the following statement (Al-George [1967: 117]): "In the archaic mentality the symbolic substitute is an incomplete mirror of the original, and the analogy is a means of approaching a reality inaccessible in a direct way."

1.5.2. *The composition of the grammar: general organization, rule order, types of rules.*

1.5.2a. *General organization.*

As I noted earlier (section III.1.1), the Aṣṭādhyāyī consists of eight chapters subdivided into quarter chapters. The major divisions in these chapters are evident from the major headings (*adhikāra*, see section III.1.5.2c) included therein. For example, rules 2.1.3 and following, to the end of the second quarter chapter of the second chapter, apply to form compounds.[167] Rules of chapter 2.3 introduce post-nominal endings.[168] Rules of the section beginning with 3.1.1, through the fifth chapter, introduce units classed as affixes.[169] This large section of rules has subsections: rules which introduce post-verbal affixes, those which introduce affixes after nominal bases and elements terminating in the affixes denoted by *ṅī* and *āp*, taddhita affixation rules.[170] 6.1.1 and following provide for doubling certain elements in given contexts.[171] Rules under the heading of 6.1.84 let a single replacement substitute for two sounds in contiguity.[172] Rules of the section beginning with 6.4.1 state operations for presuffixal bases and those of the section beginning with 8.1.16 operations for padas.[173] The final three quarter chapters – called the *tripādī* – constitute a separate section, the rules of which do not generally supply operands for rules of the preceding seven and one-quarter chapters.[174]

Such general features of the Aṣṭādhyāyī's organization are well known. Nevertheless, there has been some debate concerning the degree of organization exhibited in the grammar and the principles underlying this. Faddegon (1936: 49-66) gave a general sketch of what is covered in different sections of the grammar and also analyzed subsections. He perceived in the arrangement of the Aṣṭādhyāyī a "tendency towards dichotomy" (1936: 51) and divided the rules into two main sections (chapters 1-5 and 6-8) which he called respectively the analytic and synthetic parts of the Aṣṭādhyāyī. As Faddegon himself admitted (1936: 67), however, his analysis is not wholly satisfactory. Bahulikar (1972: 6-8; 1973: 77-78) has objected to this analysis, especially to Faddegon's putting the tripādī together with chapters 6-8.1. She has also objected to Faddegon's resorting to a mnemotechnical principle: "Finally, I fail to find any enlightenment in the term 'mnemotechnical principle' so frequently resorted to by Faddegon" (Bahulikar [1972: 8]; [1973: 78]). I think Bahulikar's dissatisfaction is well founded. Nevertheless, Faddegon is to be praised for his strong reaction (1936: 67-68) against Wackernagel (1896: lxii), who saw confusion in the Aṣṭādhyāyī despite an inkling of a rational plan. Faddegon's student Buiskool also (1939: 17-21) analyzed the grammar into analytic and synthetic sections. And again like Faddegon before him, Buiskool (1939: 26, 155) considered that the principles of organization, "All of them have a mainly mnemotechnical scope, inasmuch as they tend to simplify memorizing . . ." (1939: 26).[175] This extreme emphasis on the technique of memorizing in explaining how the grammar was organized is objectionable at least in that it could lull one into believing one had explained something when one had merely made an appeal to a general technique assumed to have been in use (see note 175). And Bahulikar (1972: 8; 1973: 78) has also reacted unfavorably to Buiskool's claim. As to her own study of the organization of the Aṣṭādhyāyī, Bahulikar's principal aim is to discover different layers of composition (see section III.1.3.3d), so that it cannot be said truly to clarify how Pāṇini organized his work. Renou's analysis (1953a) is extremely general. He did not discuss in detail how different sections of the grammar are related and why certain rules appear where they do. Instead, he remained satisfied with finding divergent principles of organization, including pedagogy (1953a: 427), saying: "[Ces exemples] . . . suffisent, croyons-nous, pour montrer que le plan de l'Aṣṭādhyāyī ne se laisse ramener à un principe unique, et qu'en particulier les transitions sont de types divers, subordonnées à des intentions diverses: économie d'abord, sans doute, mais aussi souci pédagogique, esthétique." Less imaginative but by the same token more satisfactory than the above is R. S. Bhattacharya's (1966a) description of the structure of the Aṣṭādhyāyī. Bhattacharya (1956a, b) has also nicely shown how some arrangements of rules which might seem objectionable are to be explained. For example, rules 1.3.12 and following use the terms *ātmanepada* and *parasmaipada* to refer to sets of verb affixes, but these terms themselves are defined in 1.4.99-100. This is necessary in order that the rules defining the terms be included in the section headed by 1.4.1 (see section III.1.5.2b) so that the particular rule 1.4.100 block the general rule 1.4.99; see also Cardona (1970a: 44-45). In addition, S. P. Chaturvedi (1945) gave an excellent exposition of the organization of the section of rules introducing taddhita affixes (see note 170), a complex section in which headings stating meanings and affixes are juxtaposed. Less clear than the above is Vidya Niwas Misra's (1966: 39-82) outline of the groupings of rules in the Aṣṭādhyāyī. Instead of detailed exposition, the reader finds brief statements accompanied by charts which are not always lucid.[176]

1.5.2b. *Rule order and the application of rules.*

Some rules of the Aṣṭādhyāyī are extrinsically ordered. The rules of the tripādī (see section III.1.5.2a with note 174) are so ordered. Not only do these rules not supply operands for rules of the preceding sections, but within the tripādī itself a rule R + 1 is treated as nonexistent (*asiddha*) with respect to a preceding (*pūrvatra*) rule R; it does not supply operands for the latter. This section of rules has been studied excellently by Buiskool (1934, 1939).

Another section where the external order of rules is pertinent is the group of sūtras 1.4.3 - 2.2.38. This section is headed by 1.4.1 (*ā kaḍārād ekā saṃjñā*): only one (*ekā*) name (*saṃjñā*)[177] introduced by rules which follow, up to 2.2.38, applies at once to a given entity. That is, something is not allowed simultaneously to be assigned to two or more of the classes in question. Pāṇini further provides[178] that if two rules of this section come into conflict (*vipratiṣedha*) the subsequently stated (*para*) operation (*kārya*)[179] takes effect preferentially. For example, by 1.4.10 (*hrasvaṃ laghu*) a short vowel (*hrasva*) is termed *laghu* 'light'; 1.4.11 (*saṃyoge guru*) provides that a short vowel, if it is followed by a consonant cluster (*saṃyoga*), is called *guru* 'heavy'; and 1.4.12 (*dīrghaṃ ca*) states that a long vowel (*dīrgha*) is also (*ca*) called *guru*. Now, a short vowel not followed by a cluster is *laghu* by 1.4.10 and a long vowel is *guru* by 1.4.12. But a short vowel followed by a cluster can be both *laghu* by 1.4.10 and *guru* by 1.4.11. If it were classed as both, rules could apply which would produce wrong results. 1.4.1-2 provide that a short vowel followed by a consonant cluster is uniquely classed as *guru*; see Cardona (1970a: 45).

In other cases the external order of rules is not pertinent to their application: the order of application is not the same as the external order of the rules. Here Pāṇini makes use of other decision procedures to allow one to select proper rules and apply them correctly at any given stage of derivation. For example, in deriving the utterance *ayaja indram* 'I sacrificed to Indra' there is a stage *ayajä-i indra-am*. Here two operations can apply: *a-i* → *e* or *i-i* → *ī*. Only if the former applies can the correct utterance be derived: *ayaja-i indra-m* → *ayaje indram* → *ayaja indram*. Bracketing is recognized: an operation the cause of which is internal relative to a condition which causes another operation applies prior to the latter. In the present instance one starts with ((*ayaja-*)*i*) *indra-am* and works outwardly from internal brackets; see Cardona (1970a: 52). Another principle has to do with the relation of rules with each other. Given the root *dah* 'burn' followed by the participial affix *ta*, one should derive *dag-dha* (‹ *dah-ta*). Two rules can apply. By one (8.2.31: *ho ḍhaḥ*), *-h* is replaced by *ḍh* when there follows a consonant such as *t*. The other rule (8.2.32: *dâder dhātor ghaḥ*) provides that *-h* which is part of a root (*dhātu*) beginning with *d* (*dâdi*) is replaced by *gh*. Only the latter should apply here: *dah-ta* → *dagh-ta* → *dagh-dha* → *dag-dha*. A general principle allows one to chose 8.2.32. 8.2.31 is a general rule (*utsarga*) applicable to any *-h*. But 8.2.32 is a particular rule (*apavāda*) related to 8.2.31: its domain of application is included in that of the latter. If 8.2.32 is not to lack a proper domain of application, it must block 8.2.31. In all such cases a principle of vacuity is used: a particular rule applies instead of a related general rule, from the domain of which it extracts its own domain of application. These and other principles are discussed in Cardona (1970a); bracketing has also been treated by K. M. Tiwary (1971).

Pāṇinīyas beginning with Kātyāyana attempted to let rule 1.4.2 (see above with note 178) apply throughout the grammar, thus providing a mechanical decision procedure based on the external order of rules. This use of 1.4.2 has also been accepted by several modern scholars: Pawte (1935: 33-35), Staal (1965a: 70-71; 1966: 208; 1974: 68), Ananthanarayana (1969: 1), J. D. Singh (1974: 282-83).[180] However, this leads to serious difficulties (discussed recently by Cardona [1970a: 60-61]), and other scholars have accepted that 1.4.2 applies only in the section headed by 1.4.1; thus Faddegon (1936: 26-27), Scharfe (1961a: 50), Shefts (1961: 28-29 n. 33), Vidya Niwas Misra (1966: 105), Cardona (1970a: 41). Birwé (1966: 51-63) is among those who have accepted that 1.4.2 applies throughout the grammar. Moreover, he has also attempted (1966: 60-63) to refute the arguments of those who held the contrary opinion, although he admitted there remained room for discussion. However, Birwé's own argument in support of his position is weak. He argues as follows. Rule 8.3.32 (see section III.1.3.2a) should provide that an initial augment is added to a vowel (*ac*) which occurs after *ṅ, ṇ, n* (*ṅam*). The rule contains an ablative form *ṅamaḥ* and a locative form *aci*, to be interpreted respectively by 1.1.67 and 1.1.66 (see section III.1.5.3d with note 217) as denoting left and right contexts. Therefore, 1.4.2 must apply to allow only 1.1.67 to apply. For only thus can correct sequences such as *pratyaṅṅāste* 'is seated facing west' (⟨ *pratyaṅ āste*) be obtained: by 1.1.67, *ṅamaḥ* denotes a left context for an operation, so that *aci* here now denotes the vowels subject to augmenting. This shows that 1.4.2 applies throughout the grammar.[181] This is a poor choice of example to show Birwé's agreement with Pāṇinıyas, since even Kātyāyana and Patañjali, who would like to have 1.4.2 apply generally, do not let it apply here. Indeed, in his thirteenth vārttika on 1.1.66-67 (Kielhorn [1880-85: I: 174.3]), Kātyāyana shows that there is no conflict here at all. A general principle of vacuity such as lets a particular rule block a general rule (see above) is invoked here. The locative *aci* is to recur in the next rule (8.3.33), where it denotes a right context. But the ablative *ṅamaḥ* plays a role in rule 8.3.32. If, now, *aci* were interpreted as denoting a right context in this rule also, the ablative *ṅamaḥ* would serve no purpose. Therefore, the ablative *ṅamaḥ* is interpreted in 8.3.32 as denoting a left context.

Birwé's disagreement with one scholar, Scharfe, is, nevertheless, well founded in one respect. For Scharfe (1961a: 11, 50-51) has claimed that Pāṇini neither needed nor provided any formal decision principles in his grammar except in the case of rules which define technical terms. Instead, argues Scharfe, the speaker's knowledge of Sanskrit was allowed to play the decisive role. Since the user of the grammar was a speaker of Sanskrit, he would know how to apply the rules to obtain only correct results. However, I think such a procedure would weaken the grammar. In effect, one is now saying that where rules conflict the desired results determine the choice of a rule, which itself is to account for the correct forms. To be sure, Patañjali himself considered a similar procedure. He would interpret the term *para* of the generalized metarule 1.4.2 as meaning 'desired' (*iṣṭa*). The rule would then provide that in case of conflict that operation prevails which is desired (see Kielhorn [1887e: 248], Cardona [1970a: 61]). However, I think this should and can be avoided. Cardona (1970a) has discussed how this can be done in the context of principles seen to operate in the Aṣṭādhyāyī.[182]

One of the aspects of rule order in the Aṣṭādhyāyī which has disconcerted some is that a given rule can require for its interpretation information available only from rules stated later. For example, rule 1.1.1 requires that one consult 1.1.70-71 to interpret the terms *āt* and *aic* (see note 15) and 1.3.12 and following require that one consult 1.4.99-100 (see section III. 1.5.2a). Fowler (1965) objected to Pāṇini's rule order on such grounds and suggested that the order adopted in the Siddhânta-kaumudī (section IV.3.2) was better. Fowler's objections are easily set aside once one considers general principles governing how rules are related to each other. For example, definitions and metarules do not stand alone; they apply with all rules which they serve to interpret (see section III.1.5.2c).[183] Staal (1966b) has refuted the more theoretical arguments given by Fowler.

1.5.2c. *Types of rules.*

The major types of rules are: definitions (*saṃjñā-sūtra*), metarules (*paribhāṣā*), headings (*adhikāra-sūtra*), operational rules (*vidhi-sūtra*), restrictions (*niyama-sūtra*), extension rules (*atideśa-sūtra*), negation rules (*niṣedha-sūtra*).

Definitions and metarules have this in common that they do not function independently.[184] They have to be considered together with rules they serve to interpret. In Pāṇinīya parlance, a definition or metarule forms a single utterance (*eka-vākya*) with the rules it serves to interpret. Two views are held concerning this. First, definitions and metarules are considered to take effect at the place in the grammar where they are stated. Alternatively, they are considered to take effect at the time rules requiring them come into play. These views have been discussed by S. D. Joshi (1965) and Rocher - Debels (1958-60).

The usual relation between associated operational rules such as 8.2.31-32 (see section III.1.5.2b) is that one is a general rule, the other a particular rule which applies in part of the domain of the former, blockings its application. On the other hand, the norm for classifications, whether this is effected by headings such as 2.1.3, 3.1.1 (see notes 167, 169) or definition rules is that a given entity may belong to more than one class at once. Where, however, a unique classification is required, rules are stated in the section headed by 1.4.1-2 (see section III.1.5.2b). This has been discussed recently by Cardona (1970a: 41-43).

As I have noted, metarules and definitions are applied together with the rules they serve to interpret. Similarly, related general and particular rules have to be considered together. So also have negations to be considered in conjunction with their neganda. In such cases, the rules to be treated together can be spatially separated in the grammar. It is their relation which brings them together. These points have been treated by Cardona (1965a: 35-36; 1967a: 35-39; 1970a: 40-43).

The grammar contains major headings which divide it into major sections (see section III.1.5.2a). In addition, parts of rules are considered to recur (*anuvartate*) in subsequent rules.[185] Both major headings of the type 3.1.1 (see note 169) and the parts of rules which are to recur in subsequent sūtras are metalinguistically marked, with a svarita vowel.[186] This accentual feature was originally recited but lost early in the tradition. These aspects of the grammar have been discussed by Kielhorn (1896), Böhtlingk (1897), S. P. Chaturvedi (1951), Cardona (1968a); see also section III.1.5.3g.[187]

A restriction serves to exclude an item or operation which would otherwise occur. For example, in deriving sentence (1) of section III.1.5.1a the L-suffix *laṭ* is introduced to denote an agent (see note 152). This affix is then replaced (3.1.67-68) tentatively by a series of endings. To select the particular ending *ti* restriction rules apply which allow only certain endings in particular contexts and exclude others; see Cardona (1970c: 210-12) for a brief exposition.

An extension rule extends to a given item a property or operation or other feature which it would of itself not otherwise have. Consider, for example, the dative singular form *puruṣāya* (< *puruṣa* 'man'). Rule 7.3.102 (*supi ca*) applies to replace the *-a* of *puruṣa* with *-ā*. The right context for this substitution is one of the nominal endings denoted by the term *sup*. The dative ending *ṅe* is one of the affixes denoted by *sup*. But it is replaced by *ya* after a base in *-a* (7.1.13: *ṅer yaḥ*). In order to let 7.3.102 apply to *puruṣa-ya*, then, some provision has to be made. Pāṇini states[188] that a replacement (*ādeśa*) is treated lik· the original (*sthānivat*) except with respect to operations which would thereby be conditioned by a sound per se (*anal-vidhau*). Another example of an extension rule in 6.1.85 (see note 67). There are different kinds of extension rules, for a brief discussion of which see Ojihara - Renou (1962: 44).

There is another kind of rule which calls for some comment. It is known that Pāṇini generalized as much as possible (see recently Cardona 1969: 26-28, 41). A point is reached, however, where the derivation of a particular item might require one or more separate rules for that item alone. Pāṇini generally avoids this. Instead of stating distinct operations for deriving such forms, he lists the items as ready made. The rules in which this is done are called *nipātana-sūtras*. As I have noted (section III.1.3.3d), some scholars have claimed that some or all of the nipātana-sūtras are later additions to the grammar. R. S. Bhattacharya (1966f) has discussed such rules and pointed out (1966f: 109) the essential feature I noted above.[189] And it is this point, I think, which seriously weakens the arguments for considering nipātana rules later additions. The procedure followed in giving such rules fits neatly into Pāṇini's general procedure of generalization. We may compare, for example, the procedure followed in setting up the śiva-sūtras (section III.1.3.4). Pāṇini set apart groups of consonants pertinent to particular operations and closed these sets of sounds with markers. But he did not separate into separate sets couples such as *t*, *th* (see Cardona [1969: 30]).

1.5.3. *Metalanguage: technical terminology, metarules, stylistics.*

1.5.3a. *Pāṇini's technical terminology: generalities.*[190]

Goldstücker (1861: 162-69) discussed some possible principles governing Pāṇini's technical terminology. His conclusions are as follows (1861: 166). Pāṇini did not treat "of those saṁjñās or conventional names which are known and settled otherwise." Further, the term *saṃjñā* in rule 1.2.53 (see note 192) must be understood "to concern only such conventional names as have an etymology." However, this term " . . . applies also to grammatical terms which admit of an etymology but not to those which are merely grammatical symbols." Finally, Goldstücker claims "That such terms as *ṭi*, *ghu*, and *bha*[191] were known and settled before Pāṇini's grammar, but that nevertheless they are defined by Pāṇini, because they are not etymological terms." Goldstücker's basis for these conclusions was the Mahā-bhāṣya discussion concerning rule 1.2.53, as well as rules 1.2.54-57, all of which he called (1861: 163 n. 194) "the keystone of his [Pāṇini's] work."[192] However, Goldstücker's theory was based on a near total misunderstanding of what Patañjali said, as was pointed out by R. G. Bhandarkar (1877) and later by K. A. Subramania Iyer (1927: 140-42).[193] Nevertheless, Goldstücker's views have been revived in recent times by B. Bhattacharya (1958: 3-5) in order to draw conclusions regarding the relative chronology of Pāṇini and Yāska (see section III.3.2). But Goldstücker's opinions have also been refuted anew by K. Madhava Krishna Sarma (1968: 16-20). In fact, there is nothing to commend Goldstücker's views. For example, he claimed (1861: 166-67) that Pāṇini used the term *pratyaya* 'affix' without defining it because this was used before him and had an etymology. On the other hand, he said, Pāṇini did define the term *karmadhāraya*,[194] so that one knows he was the first to use this term. But of course the term *pratyaya* is stated in a heading (3.1.1, see note 169), so that the precise denotata of this term are indeed specified in the grammar, as R. G. Bhandarkar pointed out (1887 [= 1927-33 I: 496/7]).

Although so sweeping a theory as Goldstücker's is out of the question, it is nevertheless possible to make some reasonable conjectures concerning Pāṇini's technical vocabulary as contrasted with that of other Indian grammarians. Patañjali remarks that compounds can be assigned to four classes according as to whether the principal meaning of a compound is that of the first or second member, both members, or neither (see Liebich [1892: vii], Cardona [1969: 29-30]). Moreover, it is evident that such a semantic classification was not used by Pāṇini because it was not sufficient to account for all compounds.[195] In addition, it is known that Pāṇini did not include in his grammar rules defining such terms as *adya* 'today'.[196] This much is certain. Now, the Kāśikā on 1.2.56 (see note 192) notes that early teachers (*pūrvâcārya*) stated metarules providing that a principal and subsidiary item together denote the meaning of the former and that a base and an affix together denote the meaning of the latter.[197] And the Kāśikā on 1.2.57 (see note 192) remarks that other grammarians (*anye vaiyākaraṇāḥ*) did define what was meant by *adya*, etc.[198] It is true that these rules have been considered interpolations (see section III.1.3.3f). Nevertheless, the rules themselves, whether interpolated or not, show that at some time some grammarians held the views noted by the Kāśikā. And of course it is highly improbable that Patañjali should himself have invented the quadripartite classification of compounds he alludes to. I think it reasonable, therefore, to draw the following conclusions. Some grammarians thought it necessary to define terms of time reference (*adya*, etc.). For Pāṇini this was unnecessary. Presumably, he assumed this known from normal usage. Some grammarians used the terms *avyayībhāva, tatpuruṣa, dvandva* and *bahuvrīhi* to refer to classes of compounds defined in terms of their meanings. Pāṇini, on the other hand, did not follow this procedure.[199]

There are other general features which are definitely known about Pāṇini's technical vocabulary. One salient feature of this vocabulary is that much of it is based on forms of the verb *kṛ* 'do, make'. Palsule (1968b) has discussed this in detail. Earlier, Liebich (1919b: 13-14) also dealt with this point, with particular emphasis on terminology in the Brāhmaṇas. In addition, Pāṇini uses certain terms in different values. A given term may have a value assigned to it by definition in the grammar and yet also be used in a nontechnical value. For example, *vṛddhi* denotes (by 1.1.1, see note 15) vowels *ā, ai, au.* Yet Pāṇini also uses this term in the meaning 'interest charged on a loan' (5.1.47). Similarly, *adhikaraṇa* denotes (by 1.4.45) a locus relative to an action but Pāṇini also uses this term to mean 'thing (denoted)' e.g., (2.4.13). A term used in its technical value as defined in the grammar is called by Pāṇinīyas a *kṛtrimā saṃjñā* 'artificial term'. The same term used in values it has in normal Sanskrit and which are not assigned to it by rules of the grammar is called an *akṛtrimā saṃjñā* 'nonartificial term'. These usages have recently been discussed by Cardona (1970b: 196-98); see also S. P. Chaturvedi (1940: 1193). Technical terms defined in the grammar are at times also considered to retain their etymological values. Pāṇinīyas refer to these as *anvartha-saṃjñā* 'terms (used) in accord with the meanings (of their constituent elements)'. For example, Pāṇini defines the term *sarvanāman* 'pronominal' (1.1.27, see section III.1.3.6c with note 93). Yet this term is also considered to retain its etymological meaning: an item (*nāman*, lit. 'name') which names all (*sarva*) things. It is not always easy to discern which particular terms Pāṇini intended to be understood in their etymological meanings. Venkatacharya (1946, 1947) and Raghunātha Śarmā (1964b) have made suggestions regarding which terms they believe should be considered *anvartha-saṃjñās*; see also Cardona (1969: 29-30).

The fact that Pāṇini used some terms in different values has caused some confusion to some modern scholars. Pawte (1935: 100) concluded that Pāṇini's use of *adhikaraṇa* 'thing' indicated he took some of his rules from grammarians who were also logicians and conceived of a substance as the substrate (*adhikaraṇa*) of properties. This suggestion does not commend itself. Patañjali himself notes that *adhikaraṇa* meaning 'thing' is a nonartificial term, so that the reasonable conclusion to be drawn is that in Patañjali's speech this was a normal meaning of the term. In the absence of any evidence stronger than Pawte's, there is nothing to show this was not also so at Pāṇini's time. More recently, Scharfe (1971a: 34-35) has involved himself in problems of interpretation because he did not see that the term *upapada*, used as a technical term by Pāṇini, has also the meaning 'cooccurring item'; it is this meaning that the term has in the rules considered by Scharfe (see Cardona [1973c: 219-21]).

1.5.3b. *Pāṇini's technical terminology: particular terms.*[200]

1.5.3b.1. *General.* Pāṇini's terms *ādeśa* 'substitute' and *sthānin* 'substituend' (see section III.1.5.1b) have recently been dealt with by Thieme (1968) and Wezler (1972) respectively. These scholars are concerned more with how the terms are used in Sanskrit in general and the relations of various meanings they have than with the detailed analysis of how the terms are used by Pāṇini. Wezler especially stresses the ritual uses of *sthānin.*[201]

The nominative singular of *rājan* 'king' is *rājā.* The derivation of this form involves deleting the *-n* of the base. This deletion applies to a pada (see note 151). The same deletion should apply in deriving forms such as *rājasu* (loc. pl.). Therefore, Pāṇini defines a pada also as a base when followed by certain affixes, among them the ending *su.* G. T. Deshpande (1965) has discussed these two definitions (1.4.14, 17) and concluded that Pāṇini was indebted for his analysis to the analyzed texts (*pada-pāṭha*) of Vedic texts. This should probably be put less categorically. Pāṇini did know the pada-pāṭha of the Ṛg-veda (see section III.3.2.2), wherein endings such as *su* were separated from bases and the fact was recognized that before such endings bases such as *rājan* behaved as though they were padas.

In a discussion of rule 2.3.46 Speijer (1886: 26 n. 1) attempted to show that Pāṇini did not here use the term *vacana* in the meaning 'number' (see section III.1.5.6b). Scharfe (1965) has tried to show that *vacana* in 1.2.51 (see note 192) also does not mean 'number' and that *vyakti* in the same rule does not mean 'gender'.[202] He suggests that *vyakti-vacane* in this rule is not a nominative dual of a dvandva compound ('gender and number') but the locative singular of a tatpuruṣa compound meaning 'expression (*vacana*) of an individual (*vyakti*)', so that the rule provides that a derivative behaves like an original base when there is to be expressed an individual (Scharfe [1965: 241]). In my opinion, Scharfe has not proved his point. He takes up the crucial examples brought up in the Mahā-bhāṣya, but he avoids the issue by saying (1965: 243) that Patañjali's argumentation involves "eine logische Delikatesse".[203]

1.5.3b.2. *Phonologic terminology.*[204] Thieme (1935a: 94 n. 1) claimed that Pāṇini's use of the terms *āsya-prayatna* ('effort in the mouth') and *mukha-nāsikā-vacana* ('pronounced through the mouth together with the nose') "... seem to betray that he [Pāṇini] did not know the doctrine of *sthāna* [point of articulation] and *karaṇa* [articulator] ..." Later (1958: 42-44),

Thieme repeated that Pāṇini's terminology reflects a less accurate analysis than the one known from the phonologic texts known as *prātiśākhya* (see section III.3.2). However, this is predicated on Thieme's opinion (1935c: *22*) that the term *āsya* in *āsya-prayatna* means merely 'mouth' whereas *prayatna* means not merely 'effort' but 'effort at a point of articulation'. The burden of proof would appear to be on Thieme. For *āsya-prayatna* can mean 'effort at a point in the mouth (that is, point of articulation)', since *āsya* can be a derivative meaning '(point) located in the mouth'. And Thieme has not given evidence to support his own interpretation of the term *prayatna.*[205]

Cardona (1968a: 455-57) has discussed Pāṇini's use of the terms *udātta, anudātta, svarita,* which refer respectively to vowels that are high-pitched, low-pitched and pronounced with a combination of these two pitches.

Pāṇini uses the term *saṃprasāraṇa* to denote vowels *i, u, ṛ, ḷ,* which replace *y, v, r, l.*[206] Edgerton (1941) dealt with this term, claiming that it originally meant 'emergence', whence 'emergent vowel', and not 'extension', as had been thought before. However, Edgerton's suggestion has little support to buttress it, and has not met with approval; see Renou (1942: 325), Allen (1953: 13), K. V. Abhyankar (1961: 377).[207]

1.5.3b.3. *Terms pertinent to the verbal system.* Two important terms of general import, *kriyā* 'action' and *bhāva* (lit. 'becoming, being'), have been treated by R. Rocher (1966), who has attempted to distinguish between them consistently. She translates them respectively 'action' and 'state'. However, Rocher also admits (1968a: 13) that "le terme *bhāva* est une notion assez floue", difficult always to distinguish from *kriyā.* Cardona (1970e: 213 - 19) has given evidence to show that Pāṇini indeed uses *kriyā* and *bhāva* both to refer to actions in certain rules, and attempted to show how this came about. According to him, *bhāva*, originally meaning 'becoming, being', was proper to a subject-predicate analysis: all predications are considered aspects of becoming, a view noted explicitly by Yāska in his Nirukta. This term was kept by Pāṇini in his system, which, however, did not involve a subject-predicate analysis.[208] Pāṇini also uses *bhāva* with reference to an action in the abstract (e.g., *pāka* 'cooking'), not viewed in process (e.g., *pacati* '... is cooking'), and with reference to abstract properties (e.g., *aśvatva* 'horseness'). A good discussion of these usages was provided by S. D. Joshi (1960: xxvi-xlvi); see also S. D. Joshi (1962).

R. Rocher (1969) has also treated the term *dhātu* 'verbal base, root' and the concepts associated with it, with special emphasis on the Mahā-bhāṣya discussion concerning how an action is to be defined. A fuller treatment of this subject was earlier supplied by K. A. Subramania Iyer (1950: 169-75).

Pāṇini introduces L-suffixes such as *laṭ* on condition that an agent, an object, or an action is to be denoted. Different L-suffixes are introduced according to time references and modalities (see section III.1.5.5a with note 152). K. C. Chatterji (1946) dealt with these L-suffixes, but his study is little more than an enumeration of the affixes.[209]

The affixes which replace L-suffixes and also post-verbal affixes marked with *ś* are called *sārvadhātuka* ('having to do with a whole root'); other post-verbal affixes are called *ārdhadhātuka* ('having to do with a half root').[210] Shefts (1961: 13-16) translated the rules in which these terms are defined and also sought to give a rationale for the use of these terms. Her suggestion, though unprovable in my opinion, is quite attractive. Shefts considers (1961: 16) that the terms originally referred to two sets of affixes which were in complementary distribution, as follows. An ārdhadhātuka affix was originally one which occurred directly after a root, without the intervention of another suffix; for example, in the infinitive *pak-tum*, the suffix *tum* occurs immediately after *pac* 'cook'. A sārvadhātuka suffix originally was one which occurred after a root itself followed by an affix; for example, in the third singular present form *pac-a-ti, ti* occurs after *pac-a.* Shefts sets up a pre-Pāṇinian stage at which this was the distribution and in which there were terms **ardhadhātu* ('half root') and **sarvadhātu*, equivalent respectively to Pāṇini's *dhātu* and *dhātu* plus *pratyaya* ('affix').

In the derivation of a perfect form such as *bibheda* '. . . split' (3rd sg.), the root is doubled (*bhid-bhed-*). Pāṇini uses the term *abhyasta* to refer to such a sequence resulting from doubling and *abhyāsa* to refer to the first element of the sequence. Bhāgīratha Prasāda Tripāṭhī (1972) has discussed the rules in which Pāṇini uses these terms.[211]

1.5.3b.4. *Terms pertinent to the nominal system.* Pāṇini uses the term *nadī* ('river') to refer to a class of feminine nouns. This was treated by K. C. Chatterji (1936).

Mehendale (1965b; 1968: 10-11) has briefly taken up Pāṇini's term *sarvanāman* 'pronominal', contrasting it with Yāska's term *ardhanāman* (lit. 'half-noun'). Mehendale's chief aim in doing so is to suggest evidence of Pāṇini's priority to Yāska (see section III.3.2).

Faddegon (1936: 14-17) discussed several technical terms proper to the nominal system. Among these is *karmadhāraya*, which denotes a particular kind of compound (see section III.1.5.5b.3). Faddegon (1936: 17) considered that this term originally meant 'owing a *karman* to a creditor'. The same term was the subject of three studies which appeared in the same year (1952) by K. V. Abhyankar, Edgerton, and Palsule. Edgerton (1952: 81) suggested that *karmadhāraya* meant "a *tatpuruṣa* compound which maintains . . . . the construction or case meaning of its parts." He also claimed that this was a reasonable paraphrase of Pāṇini's rule concerning this compound.[212] K. V. Abhyankar (1952) discussed Edgerton's proposal and the views of commentators. He himself proposed (1952: 244) to interpret the term as meaning "a tatpuruṣa compound bearing [*dhāraya*] the action [*karman*] of conveying the idea of the same thing by means of its components." Palsule, on the other hand, came closer to Faddegon's view. He suggested (1952: 247) that *karmadhāraya* was originally an agricultural term meaning 'one who owes labor.' More recently, Sukumar Sen (1962: 91) suggested that, like *tatpuruṣa* ('his man') and *bahuvrīhi* ('one who has much rice'), *karmadhāraya* is also a member of the class it names, so that it originally meant 'act of possessing or holding.' The technical meaning of the term is patent in Pāṇini's grammar, since he defines it (see note 212). As for all these suggestions concerning the original meaning of the term, they remain interesting conjectures. The one proposal I consider impossible to countenance is Edgerton's. For neither *karman* in *karmadhāraya* nor *adhikaraṇa* of *samānâdhikaraṇa* in rule 1.2.42 (note 212) means 'case relation', 'case meaning', or 'construction' in Pāṇini's grammar.

1.5.3c. *Markers.*[213]

Paṇini uses markers appended to items. He calls them *it* and Pāṇinīyas refer to them also using the term *anubandha.* Originally the grammar was not transmitted in writing but recited. Therefore, the markers used to appear as parts of the items which they characterize (see section III.1.3.7 with note 107). In order, then, to show which sounds are markers, Pāṇini states a series of rules (1.3.2-8). For example, 1.3.2 (*upadeśe'j anunāsika it*) states that a nasalized (*anunāsika*) vowel (*ac*) in an item when it has been introduced but has not yet entered into grammatical operations (*upadeśe*, see sections III.1.3.5c, III. 1.3.7) is an *it*; and 1.3.3 (*hal antyam*) provides that the final consonant (*hal*) of an item at the same stage is an *it.* Markers are obviously not part of linguistic items as they are actually used. They appear with items only in the grammar. Hence, they are unconditionally deleted before items enter into operations. Rule 1.3.9 (*tasya lopaḥ*) provides that a marker (*tasya* '[in place] of that') is replaced by zero (*lopa*).

Markers serve various purposes: to indicate that an item conditions or undergoes certain operations or belongs to a certain class, to distinguish homophonous units, to allow reference to a group of items by means of a common referend (see Cardona [1973c: 208-09]). Moreover, markers are used in forming abbreviations. A unit X followed by a marker M denotes not only itself but also all items which are listed between X and M.[214] For example, *ac* is an abbreviation denoting *a* and the following sounds of the śiva-sūtras (see section III.1.1 with note 12) through *au*, which is itself followed by the marker *c*; *tiṅ* denotes all the verb endings beginning with *tip* (= *ti*) and ending with *mahiṅ* (= *mahi*); *sup* denotes all the nominal endings beginning with *su* (= *s*) and ending with *sup* (= *su*).

The functions which markers serve have been treated by Liebich (1920a: 29-56), K. Madhava Krishna Sarma (1941b: 203-11; 1968: 24-31), Palsule (1961: 62-88), Dwarikadas Shastri (1964: introduction, pp. 29-33), Vidya Niwas Misra (1966: 39-67), Devasthali (1967b), Scharfe (1971a: 31), Cardona (1973c: 208-10). The most useful general treatment is Devasthali's, an unpretentious presentation of the materials. For markers appended to verbal bases the expositions by Liebich, Palsule and Dwarikadas Shastri are clear and accurate. Misra's presentation is not very useful to one who is not already familiar with the facts; materials are put in charts with exceedingly brief notations. Scharfe's treatment is admittedly sketchy. Another study of markers is by M. D. Pandit (1966b). This is a reasonable presentation of the facts. However, there is some naiveté behind Pandit's remark (1966b: 78) that it is "... a rather strange technique – to assume something merely to negate it as soon as it makes its appearance!" For obviously Pāṇini's use of sounds as metalinguistic markers is comparable to the use of super- and subscripts in written grammars. The abbreviations used to denote sets of sounds (*ac* etc.) have most recently been studied by Cardona (1969: 9-22).

Pāṇini also uses the sound *t* after vowels to form terms which denote vowels of particular time durations.[215] For example, *at* denotes varieties of short *a*, *āt* varieties of long *ā*.

In some cases commentators cannot discern any good reason for Pāṇini's having used *t* after a vowel. Similarly, there are instances where commentators cannot see a reason for the use of certain markers. They then say that these sounds have been used either to facilitate pronunciation (*mukhasukhârtha, uccāraṇârtha*) or to avoid an ambiguity (*asandehârtha*) which could arise through morphophonemic alterations, by separating contiguous units. The uses of *t* after vowels have been studied thoroughly by M. M. Deshpande (1972), who, however, does not reach definitive conclusions in all cases. Scharfe (1971a: 7-9) has discussed vowels which commentators consider inserted to ease pronunciation and which some treat as markers, others not. Scharfe reaches the conclusion that Pāṇini's metalanguage, unlike Sanskrit, contained "a very short vowel of an unspecified character" (1971a: 7), which he transcribes ə. According to Scharfe, Pāṇini himself was possibly not aware of pronouncing this vowel, which in the later tradition was written variously as *i, u, a.* Although Scharfe's suggestion is interesting, I think the arguments for it involves some contradiction (see Cardona [1973c: 213-14]).

1.5.3d. *The grammar of Pāṇini's metalanguage.*

Details of the grammar of Pāṇini's metalanguage were not studied in depth until quite recently. The major study in this area is by Scharfe (1971a); Palsule (1970: 4-7; 1973: 313-17) also has dealt with some aspects of morphology. The single most pressing question in this area of inquiry is: does Pāṇini' Sanskrit as used in the grammar to describe Sanskrit differ in essential ways from the Sanskrit which is described?

It is known that the rules of the Aṣṭādhyāyī do not always observe the morphophonemic conventions of Sanskrit. For example, the *-c* of a base such as *vāc* 'speech, voice' is replaced by *k* in forms such as the nominative singular (*vāk*). But the very first rule of the grammar (1.1.1: *vṛddhir ād aic*) contains the nominative *aic*, with *-c*.[216] It can be argued that such deviations were necessary to make clear that markers such as *c* were being used. The question posed above remains to be answered with respect to the syntax of Pāṇinian rules.

Pāṇini uses three case forms for particular purposes. A locative form is used to denote a right context for an operation, an ablative to denote a left context, and a genitive to denote a substituend.[217] Scharfe (1971a: 33) has maintained that Pāṇini redefined the uses of these three case forms. He speaks of "the new value of the ablative". The view implicit here was made explicit by Scharfe earlier (1961b), when he said that Pāṇini's metalanguage differed from Sanskrit "so strongly that one must speak of a particular, artificial language" ("so stark, dass man von einer eigenen Sprache, einer Kunstsprache, sprechen muss").[218] Though Scharfe thus maintains that Pāṇini in effect invented special syntactic uses proper to his grammatical statements, he also has to admit (1971a: 34) that Pāṇini committed " . . . slips, violating the style and system of the metalanguage." It is noteworthy that Pāṇinīyas, from Kātyāyana on, do not view rules 1.1.49, 1.1.66-67 (see note 217) as stating any syntactic uses different from those of the object language Sanskrit. Instead, according to them, the metarules in question apply to provide single unambiguous interpretations of rules which, otherwise, the user of the grammar, a speaker of Sanskrit, could not interpret uniquely. Consider one example. Rule 8.1.28 (*tiṅ atiṅaḥ*) should provide that an item terminating in a verb ending (*tiṅ*) has no high-pitched vowel. The rule contains an ablative form *atiṅaḥ*, which should denote the left context for this provision: after an item which terminates in an ending other than a verb ending (*atiṅ*). However, this cannot be known directly from the rule as stated. Let us assume that, since the grammar deals with the derivation of items as parts of utterances, the ablative *atiṅaḥ* is a directional ablative; a form containing a verb ending occurs followed and preceded by other items. Pāṇini does, in fact, provide for introducing fifth-triplet endings (ablative endings) after nominals construed with words denoting directions.[219] This is necessary to account for normal Sanskrit utterances. For example, the ablative *grāmāt* (*grāma* 'village') occurs in construction with items such as *pūrva* 'eastern', *uttara* 'northern' in sentences such as *grāmāt pūrvaḥ parvataḥ* 'The mountain is east of the village', *grāmād uttaraḥ parvataḥ* 'The mountain is north of the village'. This does not, however, help in arriving at a unique interpretation of rule 8.1.28. The user of the grammar may assume that *atiṅaḥ* is a directional ablative, but he is not in a position to know precisely what is intended. Left to his own devices as a speaker of Sanskrit, he could supply various directional words such as *pūrva, uttara* to complete the sentence. It is here that 1.1.67 comes into play. In such cases, one is to understand an ablative form as denoting a left context. In conjunction with 1.1.67, then, rule 8.1 28 is uniquely interpretable as stating *atiṅa uttaras tiṅ* 'an item terminating in a verb ending and which occurs after . . . '. This of course involves no departure from the Sanskrit described in the grammar. What Pāṇini has done is simply this. Instead of repeating *uttara* ('following'), *pūrva* ('preceding'), *sthāne* ('in place of') in hundreds of rules, he has provided metarules for interpreting rules without these. Cardona (1973c: 215-21; 1974a) has argued that the Pāṇinīya interpretation of rules 1.1.49, 1.1.66-67 (see note 217) is alone acceptable.

1.5.3e. *The domains of metarules.*

It has to be accepted that Pāṇinīyas extended the domains of some metarules formulated by Pāṇini; see section III.1.5.2b regarding rule 1.4.2. The domain of rule 1.1.67 (see note 217) has been the source of some disagreement among western scholars.[220] Birwé (1966: 31) assumed that this rule should apply together with rules which introduce affixes. This opinion is shared by other western scholars: Shefts (1961: 4 n. 8), van Nooten (1967: 883-85). Cardona (1970a: 65 n. 5) argued that this is improper; see also D. M. Joshi (1972: 96). Affixation rules are stated in the section headed by rule 3.1.1 (see section III.1.5.2a with note 169). Within this section, another heading is valid. Rule 3.1.2 (*paraś ca*) states that items introduced by subsequent rules and classed as affixes (*pratyaya*) also occur following (*para*) the units to which they are introduced. If the general metarule 1.1.67 were to apply in such affixation rules, 3.1.2 would be vacuous. Moreover, 1.1.67 states that an ablative form denotes a left context for an operation on a following item. But in affixation rules there is no operand to undergo an operation in such a context; the affixes are themselves introduced by these rules. Scharfe (1961a: 36 n. 24, 38 n. 40) has disagreed with this position and maintained that 1.1.67 does indeed apply in affixation rules: these introduce affixes as replacements of zero, which is the operand in the left context of other items. However, Scharfe did not perceive that this view leads to intolerable results. Not only is the heading 3.1.2 now vacuous but one now has to allow deriving forms such as **de-ya-ti* in addition to *dīv-ya-ti* 'gambles'. Cardona (1973c: 221) has pointed this out and argued that the Pāṇinīya position (see note 220) is alone acceptable. The ablative forms which occur in affixation rules are construed with *para* of 3.1.2, according to the syntactic construction provided for by 2.3.29 (see note 219).

1.5.3f. *Quotation.*

In Sanskrit an item is of course used to denote its meaning. To refer to a linguistic item itself, one uses the Sanskrit equivalent of quotation marks, the particle *iti: agniḥ* 'fire' but *agnir iti "agni"*. However, Pāṇini reverses this convention. He provides (1.1.68: *svaṃ rūpaṃ śabdasyâśabda-saṃjñā*) that an item (*śabda*) serves to denote itself (*svaṃ rūpam* 'own form') unless it is a technical term (*aśabda-saṃjñā*). This new convention is understandable. The grammar states rules which generally concern items themselves. For example, rule 4.3.23 (*agner ḍhak*) introduces the affix *ḍhak* (= *eya*) after a nominative form of the item *agni*, not after fire. The convention established in 1.1.68 has been treated by Brough (1951: 28-29), Staal (1965c: 164-67; 1969: 505), Palsule (1970: 3; 1973: 312-13).[221] A corollary of this convention is that a form followed by *iti* now denotes the meaning of that form. For example, *navêti* (*na vā iti*)[222] does not refer to the sequence *navā* itself but to its meaning 'or not', that is, 'optionally'. This was recognized by Pāṇinian commentators; see Ojihara - Renou (1960: 120-21), Staal (1965c: 166-67, 1969: 505), Palsule (1970: 3).

Some modern scholars have evinced some confusion concerning these conventions. Renou (1955: 117-18) considered that *navêti* was an instance of normal quotation. He also considered 4.2.57[223] and 1.1.66 (see note 217) instances of normal quotation. On the other hand, Scharfe (1961a: 28, 1971a: 45) saw in *tasminn iti* of 1.1.66 something akin to quasi-quotation in modern logic. What neither Renou nor Scharfe has noted is that *tasminn iti* is properly interpretable as denoting the meaning of a locative form, that is, a locus.[224] In addition, the claim that a rule such as 4.2.57 contains an instance of normal citation obscures the fact that such rules cannot be treated as normal examples of taddhita affixation rules. Renou (1955: 118) did in fact note, "Il suffira de relever que, dans les cas nombreux où la définition du sens d'un dérivé nominal ne se conforme pas au schéma précité, '*iti*' fait défaut." Indeed, *iti* is lacking in most rules which introduce taddhita affixes. More typical of such rules are 4.1.92 (*tasyâpatyam* 'descendant of . . .'), which serves to derive patronymics such as *aupagava* (see sections III.1.5.1a, III.1.5.5b.3), or 4.2.69 (see note 192). Commentators have at least been aware of this and consistent in assigning a special function to the *iti* in rules such as 4.2.57. For example, it is claimed that *iti* is used therein to indicate that a derivative is formed if it is found in actual usage.[225] Further investigation of such rules is needed.

1.5.3g. *Stylistics.*

Parts of rules are considered to recur in subsequent rules (see section III.1.5.2c). That is, Pāṇini makes use of ellipsis. Pāṇinīyas, beginning with Patañjali, make use also of a slightly different kind of recurrence. For example, they invoke the frog's gait (*maṇḍūka-gati,* also *maṇḍūka-pluti* 'frog's jump'), whereby an item is considered to skip over intervening rules to recur in later rules. This was discussed by Kielhorn (1887e: 247-48) and, more recently and exhaustively, by Bahulikar (1972: 79-94). Kielhorn considered the frog's gait technique a mere device of commentators. This view was shared by S. P. Chaturvedi (1946: 110) and is now generally accepted as valid. Bahulikar also rejected the use of maṇḍūka-gati in the Aṣṭādhyāyī. However, she did so on more general grounds. She considers that recurrence (*anuvṛtti*) itself is an invention of commentators (1972: 30; 1973: 89).

Most scholars would not accept Bahulikar's view. They consider that Pāṇini himself used anuvṛtti. Many of these scholars also view anuvṛtti as a technique used to achieve economy. Staal (1970: 503) has spoken of anuvṛtti as a "non-functional abbreviation". The context of this statement[226] leads me to believe that Staal viewed anuvṛtti as a grammatical technique comparable to using abbreviations like *ac* 'vowels'. Staal has also stated (1967: 19, similarly 1965: 65) that Pāṇini's adoption of "the economy criterion" " . . . led him to adopt numerous special devices, including *anuvṛtti* . . .". Other scholars have also stressed that anuvṛtti was an economy technique. For example, R. Rocher (1968a: 27; cf. 1965-66: 79-81) says, "Tout l'enseignement pāṇinéen vise à la concision" and goes on to discuss anuvṛtti in a part of the grammar.[227] Bahulikar (1972: 28-29; 1973: 88) has objected vigorously to the opinion of such scholars. She assumes (Bahulikar 1972: 18; 1973: 82-83) that allowing an item of one rule to be understood in a subsequent rule is not normal, so that the use of anuvṛtti somehow implies that Pāṇini invented a new syntax. She concludes that the technique was invented by later commentators, who split the original continuous text into separate rules, " . . . and who found, when they wished to use any particular sūtra, they must supply the context.[228] This supplying of the context they called *anuvṛtti.* When we read the sūtra without the anuvṛtti, it appears to be written in an abnormally elliptical style. But the same would be true of any fragment of any man's speech." (Bahulikar [1973: 83])

I think there is some misunderstanding here. Let us consider first Bahulikar's arguments. Granted that the Aṣṭādhyāyī was originally recited in continuous form, the fact remains that Pāṇini himself considered separate statements therein to constitute individual rules. For he does provide in one section that, in case of conflict, a subsequently stated operation takes precedence (see section III.1.5.2b). Moreover, it is difficult to accept the assertion that anuvṛtti was an invention of post-Pāṇinian commentators. For what purpose would then be served by rule 1.3.11 (see note 186)? [229] In addition, I do not think it acceptable to claim that allowing such recurrence is somehow abnormal. Elliptical sentences in which one is to understand something said in a previous sentence of the same context are certainly nothing strange. And Kātyāyana and Patañjali, to whom Sanskrit was certainly known as a normal means of educated communication, recognized explicitly that the type of recurrence in question was part of normal Sanskrit speech (see Cardona [1968a: 449-50]). Further, Pāṇini does indeed make use of extremely elliptical formulations, to be interpreted by means of metarules (see section III.1.5.3d). Bahulikar's arguments do not, therefore, seem cogent to me.

On the other hand, if the statements of other scholars mentioned above are meant to imply, as they appear to, that anuvṛtti is in some way a special economy technique used in the grammar, especially to facilitate memorizing (Buiskool [1939: 24], R. Rocher [1965-66: 79]), this too I find unacceptable as such. For I think it patent that, in using anuvṛtti, Pāṇini has not invented any special technique. He has made use of real language ellipsis.[230]

I have already noted (see note 11) that most sūtras are verbless statements. There are, however, several groups of rules which do contain verb forms. Renou (1955: 122-24) has discussed these. But his treatment is less than satisfactory. In the case of one type, I think Renou is in error. He remarks (1955: 123) that a great many verb forms occur in rules which serve to introduce taddhita affixes.[231] For example, rule 5.1.63 states *tad arhati* 'merits that'. Renou (1955: 123) attributed the use of verb forms in such rules to the requirements of oral instruction.[232] This speculation overlooks the obvious. The verb form *arhati* is used to give the meaning of the taddhita affix; see section III.1.5.5b.3.

Renou (155: 120-22) has also briefly discussed word order in Pāṇini's rules. This study too is, I think, unsatisfactory. For example, Renou does not mention that in the taddhita affixation rules the order of words is, unlike word order in normal Sanskrit, fixed: the affix introduced by a rule occurs after the first item stated therein (see section III.1.5.5b.3).

There have been other studies of details which may be considered under the general rubric of stylistics. R. S. Bhattacharya has discussed Pāṇini's uses of the particle *ca* 'and' (1953a) and the plural (1954c); on the former topic there is a more recent and detailed study by Bahulikar (1974). Bhagavat (1966) surveyed the various ways in which Pāṇini refers to groups of items (*gaṇa*, see section III.1.1).

1.5.4. *Pāṇini's system of phonology and morphophonemics.*

1.5.4a. *Phonetics.*

Pāṇini generally dispenses with details of phonetic description, though he presupposes knowledge of such details (see below). M. D. Pandit (1963: 53) claimed that "Pāṇini dismisses the phonetic studies in only eleven sūtras . . ." I think this is unacceptable as stated, since all but one of the rules mentioned by Pandit are definitely not phonetic descriptions (see Cardona [1969: 11]). Thieme (1957b: 265) expressed the opinion that two of Pāṇini's rules are best interpreted as teaching phonetic details: 1.1.8 (see section III.1.4.4b with note 136) and 1.2.32.[233] However, Cardona (1968a: 460) pointed out that the first rule is not a phonetic description but a definition of the term *anunāsika.* There remains one rule which, it is agreed upon, deals directly with phonetic details. The very uniqueness of such a rule requires an explanation. Thieme (1957b: 266) suggested that Pāṇini describes the pronunciation of svarita vowels for two reasons: such vowels are composite (see note 233) and they substitute for other sounds. Cardona (1968a: 458-59) has disagreed with this explanation, pointing out that other sounds, to the phonetic description of which Pāṇini does not devote special rules, are equally composite and also replace other sounds. Cardona suggests instead that Pāṇini had to describe svarita vowels for metalinguistic reasons: in order to specify which of the possible pronunciations he used for the svarita marking of headings (see section III.1.5.2c with note 186).

Although Pāṇini does not provide other detailed phonetic statements, it is possible to extrapolate his views from his rules. It is clear that Pāṇini made use of classifications involving points of articulation (*sthāna*) and kinds of articulation at these points (*āsya-prayatna*, see section III.1.5.3b.1). Rule 1.1.9[234] provides that two or more sounds are homogeneous (*savarṇa*) with each other if their articulation involves the same (*tulya*) kind of effort at a point in the oral cavity (*āsya-prayatna*). It is also clear that Pāṇini considered spirants such as *h, ś* articulated with the same internal effort as vowels *a, i.* For rule 1.1.9 has an exception (see note 234). This exception requires that some vowels and consonants could have been eligible for being classed as savarṇa with each other by 1.1.9; for example, *a* and *h*, both pharyngeal (*kaṇṭhya* 'articulated in the throat'), *i* and *ś*, both palatal. These pairs could be tentatively classed as homogeneous only if they had the same kind of articulation within the oral cavity, namely open (*vivṛta*).[235] Pāṇini also makes use of extra-buccal features of articulation.[236] He states a rule (1.1.50:

sthāne'ntaratamaḥ) according to which, when there is a choice of various substitutes for a given unit, that one is selected which is closest (*antaratama*) to the original. Now, rule 7.4.62 (*ku-hoś cuḥ*) provides that a velar stop (*ku*) or *h* which occurs in a reduplicated syllable (*abhyāsa*, see section III.1.5.3b.3) is replaced by a palatal stop. Given a root which begins with *h* (e.g., *han* 'kill'), one has to select a replacement among the palatal stops *c, ch, j, jh, ñ*. By 1.1.50, only *jh* is chosen: like the original *h*, this is voiced and aspirated.

In addition to Allen's general work (1953) and to the papers already mentioned in this section, there have been several studies of Pāṇini's views on phonetics. J. D. Singh (1968, 1970) has given a very sweeping and, in my opinion, unsatisfactory survey of Pāṇini's phonetic views. For example, Singh (1968: 12; 1970: 150) assumes that Pāṇini distinguished between vowels and spirants by articulatory effort (see section III.1.4.4b), although Thieme (1935b [Staal 1972: 299 n. 1]) had, years earlier, correctly given the kinds of articulation accepted by Pāṇini. M. D. Pandit's paper (1969) is a general survey of Sanskrit sounds intended "to find out the original phones" (1969: 129). Although Pandit's purpose is not clear to me, his presentation of facts is reasonable.

Pāṇinīyas, starting with Kātyāyana, generally accept that rules 1.1.9-10 (see above with note 234) apply within the context of a series of rules, as follows. First sounds are taught as given in the śiva-sūtras (see section III.1.1); then the markers contained in the śiva-sūtras are identified (by 1.3.2 etc., see section III.1.5.3c); then abbreviations are formed by 1.1.71 (see section III.1.5.3c with note 214); then 1.1.9 applies with its exception; finally, 1.1.69 (see section III.1.5.4b with note 240) applies, whereby a sound such as *a* is made a term denoting all sounds homogeneous with it; see Cardona (1965a: 227-28). S. P. Chaturvedi (1933: 167-68; 1935: 8) objected to this interpretation, but he did not present substantial evidence to support his objection.[237]

One particular point has been the topic of several discussions, namely whether *ṛ* and *ḷ* should be treated as though they were homogeneous, a suggestion made by Kātyāyana. This subject has been taken up by K. C. Chatterji (1934c),[238] Thieme (1935b [Staal 1972: 300-04]), Ojihara (1956), K. V. Abhyankar (1965).

Pāṇini himself must have considered two other sounds homogeneous with each other in the context of grammatical operations, although they were not naturally homogeneous. He treats *a*, a close (*saṃvṛta*) vowel, as though it were open (*vivṛta*) like *ā*. This is done to let *a* and *ā* undergo the same morphophonemic operations. The last rule of the grammar (8.4.68: *a a*) then restores *a* to its normal value. But this rule has no effect on any preceding rules, since it comes under the heading of 8.2.1 (see sections III.1.5.2a, b). K. C. Chaṭṭopādhyāya (1974), while admitting (1974: 196) that "according to the text of the Aṣṭādhyāyī as preserved to us and the comments on it by Kātyāyana and Patañjali, '*a*' is a close vowel," nevertheless has attempted to show that "A proper scrutiny of Pāṇini's grammar and history of the Sanskrit language through the stages of Indo-European and Indo-Iranian show [sic] that '*a*' and '*ā*' were *savarṇas* in actual usage and not in *prakriyā* [grammatical procedure] only" (1974: 203). However, a proof of this would have to show either that Pāṇini's rule 8.4.68 had a purpose other than the one noted above or that it is in fact a later interpolation (see section III.1.3.3f). As far as I can see, Chaṭṭopādhyāya has demonstrated neither, so that it seems best to accept that for Pāṇini *a* was indeed a close vowel.

R. S. Bhattacharya (1966s) has discussed details regarding the point of articulation of velar stops. Different phonetic treatises speak of the kaṇṭha (lit. 'throat') or the jihvā-mūla ('root of the tongue') as the point of articulation for these sounds, and Pāṇinīyas generally speak of them as *kaṇṭhya.* Battacharya has attempted to show that, though different terms are used, the point of articulation envisaged is one and the same.

1.5.4b. *Morphophonemics.*

Pāṇini's statements allow one to see also the principles he observed in stating morphophonemic alterations. As I noted above (section III.1.5.4a), he provides that *h* in a reduplicated syllable is replaced by *jh* (7.4.62, 1.1.50). That is, a voiced pharyngeal spirant is replaced by a voiced aspirated palatal stop. This *jh* is subsequently (8.4.54) replaced by *j*, a voiced unaspirated palatal stop. As opposed to other descriptions, wherein *h* is directly replaced by *j*, then, Pāṇini's description does not here treat of an atomic sound *h* being replaced by *j*. Instead, his rules provide for replacing features which make up sounds.[239] In his rules dealing with vowel replacements also Pāṇini extracts, where proper, features of length, accentuation, and nasalization – that is, the external efforts (*bāhya-prayatna,* see section III.1.5.4a) – and formulates replacements in terms of vowels and their points of articulation. Short vowels *a, i, u, ṛ, ḷ* alone are given in the śiva-sūtras, not also long vowels *ā* etc. Rule 1.1.69[240] serves to make such short vowels terms denoting all sounds homogeneous with them; for example, *a* now denotes eighteen sounds: *a, ā, ā*3 (extra long), nasalized and unnasalized, with three accentual varieties.[241] In his semivowel replacement rule, then, Pāṇini (6.1.77: *iko yaṇ aci*) uses the terms *ik* and *yaṇ* to denote, respectively, the vowels *i, u, ṛ, ḷ* and the semivowels *y, v, r, l.* The vowels themselves also denote all sounds homogeneous with them. The rule thus accounts for replacements such as *ǐ* → *y,* where length is not pertinent to the operation.

K. C. Chatterji (1935a) dealt with Pāṇini's morphophonemic rules (sandhi rules) and comparable rules of other descriptions. Cardona (1965a, 1969) has also studied Pāṇini's morphophonemic rules in comparison with those of other treatises, seeking to extract Pāṇini's principles.[242] V. N. Jha (1972) has considered how Pāṇini and others treated the sandhi alterations of *ḥ*.[243]

1.5.4c. *The śiva-sūtras.*

As I have noted (section III.1.5.4b), Pāṇini's sound catalog, the śiva-sūtras, reflects his system of morphophonemics. These sūtras themselves have been studied frequently from different points of view: Sköld (1926a: 8-22), K. A. Subramania Iyer (1927), Breloer (1929, 1935-36), Faddegon (1929), K. C. Chatterji (1934a),[244] Thieme (1935a: 100-10), K. Madhava Krishna Sarma (1941b: 211-19; 1968: 32-41), Konow (1943), C. Kunhan Raja (1957), Staal (1962), Vidya Niwas Misra (1966: 40-61), Shivaganesha Murthy (1968), Cardona (1969; 1973c: 214-15), Rāma Prasāda Tripāṭhī (1969), Scharfe (1971a: 20, 28-30).[245] In addition to the question of authorship (see section III.1.3.4), three principal points have been topics of discussion: the purposes of the śiva-sūtras, their relation to other sound lists, and the way the latter were modified to arrive at the śiva-sūtras.

Faddegon (1929: 50) claimed the śiva-sūtras had two purposes: to give a phonetic classification and "to afford the means of formulating concisely euphonic and morphologic rules." K. C. Chatterji (1934a: 3-4) correctly rejected the first of Faddegon's proposed aims and later scholars have generally accepted only the second as valid. The majority of these scholars has, like Faddegon, stressed economy.[246] Scholars who have dealt with the śiva-sūtras have also overwhelmingly concentrated on the reorganization of a traditional consonant list which was modified to produce Pāṇini's list.[247] Cardona (1969: 32-36) has argued that, on the contrary, the modification carried out in the consonant order is theoretically minor and consequent on a change made in the set of vowels, whose order, paradoxically, was changed little. The major change occurred, according to Cardona, in the vowel listing: instead of listing both long and short vowels (*a ā, i ī* etc.), as do other treatises, Pāṇini listed only short vowels. These were then made terms denoting whole sets of vowels (by 1.1.69, see section III.1.5.4b with note 240). This reduction in the vowel inventory reflects Pāṇini's morphophonemic principles (see section III.1.5.4b). The semivowels *y, v, r, l* were then placed immediately after the vowels – not after stops, as in earlier lists – because, with the exception of *r*, they share with vowels the property of having nasalized and unnasalized pairs.[248] From this point on other changes were required in the consonant list. Scharfe (1971a: 20) has preferred to return to the older view. In my opinion, however, he has not presented evidence to support this position (see Cardona [1973c: 215]).

Another point which has attracted attention is the rationale behind the use of certain sounds as markers to close off sets of sounds in the śiva-sūtras.

For example, *ṇ* closes off the first set (*a i u ṇ*), *k* the second (*ṛ ḷ k*), *ṅ* the third (*e o ṅ*), and *l* the fourteenth (*h l*).[249] Some scholars have claimed that Pāṇini could not use certain sounds as markers here either because of the morphophonemic behavior of these sounds in certain contexts or because certain sounds served other purposes in Pāṇini's system.[250] Cardona (1969: 39-40; 1973c: 215) has given evidence to show that the arguments for these opinions are not cogent. Other suggestions have been made by Faddegon (1929: 52) and Cardona (1969: 40-41).

1.5.5. *Pāṇini's system of grammar.*

1.5.5a. *Introduction.*

As I have already noted (section III.1.5.1a), Pāṇini's is a derivational system whereby sentences and their components are derived by introducing affixes. It is evident that in this system no sharp distinction is made between morphology and syntax (see Vidya Niwas Misra [1966: 113], Cardona [1969: 4, first note]). Once affixes are introduced to yield what we may call initial strings,[251] rules apply to lead to final strings such as (1) - (2) of section III.1.5.1a. It is equally evident that compounds such as *rāja-puruṣa* and taddhita derivatives such as *aupagava* (see section III.1.5.1a) are not necessarily derived from padas which occur in what one would call a full sentence. The sources of these derivatives are simply the sequences *rājan-as-puruṣa-s* and *upagu-as-a.* I therefore consider separately in this section studies concerned with verbal and nominal derivatives (section III.1.5.5b) and studies of a more generally syntactic nature (section III.1.5.5c). If I further consider verb and noun morphology separately, it is because some authors (e.g., van Nooten [1967: 883]) explicitly call their studies work on Pāṇini's morphology.[252]

1.5.5b. *Studies on verbal and nominal derivatives.*

1.5.5b.1. *Verb morphology.* A form such as *pacati* in sentence (3) of section III.1.5.1a is derived as follows. The L-suffix *laṭ* is introduced after *pac.* Two conditions apply for this affixation. One is common to all L-suffixes: that an agent is to be denoted (see note 152). The other condition is particular to *laṭ*: this is introduced if the action is referred to the present (*vartamāna*).[253] All L-suffixes are replaced by verb endings or participial affixes,[254] divided into two major groups called *parasmaipada* and *ātmanepada.* Each of the groups of endings consists of nine endings distributed among three triplets of endings called *prathama, madhyama* and *uttama*, third, second and first person endings, respectively, in western terminology. The first, second and third ending of each such triplet is further called *ekavacana, dvivacana* and *bahuvacana* (singular, dual, plural). Restrictive rules (*niyama-*

sūtra, see section III.1.5.2c) apply to narrow the choice of ending to replace an L-suffix. Once these have applied, one gets *pac-ti*, which contains the third person (*prathama*) singular (*ekavacana*) parasmaipada ending *ti*. The affix *śap* (= *a*) is then introduced after the root: *pac-a-ti*.[255] Other forms are derived by a similar procedure. The particular operations to be performed depend on the L-suffix introduced. For example, the L-suffix *laṅ* is introduced[256] if an action is referred to the past (*bhūta*) excluding the day on which one is speaking (*anadyatana* 'excluding today'). After restrictive rules have applied to provide a particular ending *ti*, the *-i* of this ending is deleted, since it derives from *laṅ*:[257] *apac-a-t* (3rd sg. imperfect). The L-suffix *luṅ* is introduced on condition that an action is referred to the past (*bhūta*).[258] Since this affix is marked with *ṅ*, the *-i* of an ending such as *-ti* is deleted (see note 257). Further, the affix *cli* is introduced after a root followed by an ending which derives from *luṅ*; this is, in turn, replaced by other affixes, in this case the sigmatic affix *sic* (= *s*): *apāk-ṣ-īt* (3rd sg. aor.).[259]

Renou (1960b) treated rules pertinent to the derivation of finite verb forms with time references and some modal forms. This is a useful survey, though not at all theoretical. A more detailed exposition of rules for deriving forms with the L-suffixes *liṭ* (perfect forms) and *luṅ* (aorist forms), together with Hindi paraphrases, is provided by Bāṃsīlāl (1969). The derivation of some temporal forms has also been treated by Shefts (1961: 4-6) and M. D. Pandit (1963: 227-30). A fairly detailed exposition of the derivation of finite forms was also provided by van Nooten (1967).[260] Muralidhar Mishra (1969) has discussed verbal derivations with particular emphasis on the semantics involved, expecially with regard to optative forms. R. Rocher (1965a) set forth the way in which Pāṇini derives future forms of the type *kartā* 'will do' (3rd sg.), and pointed out that Pāṇini does not treat these as periphrastic forms. S. P. Chaturvedi (1935a: 6-7) had earlier considered this a fault in Pāṇini's grammar, though he did not deal with the details of how such forms fit in Pāṇini's system.[261] The restrictive rules which allow a choice between parasmaipada and ātmanepada affixes were treated briefly by Liebich (1891: 82-101) and have more recently been the subject of a monograph by R. Rocher (1968a). The method and organization involved in these rules was summarized by Cardona (1970e: 210-12), who has (1973b) also dealt with details concerning the restrictive rules which provide for the use of the first, second and third person sets of endings.

1.5.5b.2. *Nominal morphology*. V. W. Paranjpe (1957) has given a good summary of Pāṇini's rules for introducing case endings in deriving forms such as *odanam* in sentences such as (3) of section III.1.5.1a. This was also treated briefly by M. D. Pandit (1963b: 226-30), and van Nooten (1970a) more recently dealt in greater detail with rules for deriving forms of nominal bases. Pāṇini's rules for deriving feminine stems such as *devī* 'goddess' (⟨ *deva*, with the affix *ī*) were treated by Liebich (1891: 102-45) and have more recently been studied by Ananthanarayana (1969). There is little to comment on with regard to these, since the topic is a straightforward one, with few complications.[262]

1.5.5b.3. *Compounds and taddhita derivatives.*[263] Compounds are generally derived from two or more padas (see section III.1.5.1a with note 151). Like all operations relative to padas, composition applies only to such padas as are syntactically and semantically related (*samartha*).[264] For example, the compound *rāja-puruṣa* derives from a sequence *rājan-as puruṣa-s.* Now, given

(1) *bhāryā-s rājan-as* (→ *bhāryā rājñaḥ* 'the king's wife')
(2) *puruṣa-s devadatta-as* (→ *puruṣo devadattasya* 'Devadatta's man')

a compound *rāja-puruṣa* should not be derived by combining the padas *rājan-as* of (1) and *puruṣa-s* of (2). For, such a compound is optionally formed, so that it alternates with a string. And clearly, a compound *rāja-puruṣa* 'king's man' should not be an alternate expression to *rājñaḥ puruṣaḥ* in which the padas and their meanings are not related. In the present instance, the king in question is spoken of as related to his wife, the man in question as related to Devadatta. Rule 2.1.1 (note 264) precludes such a derivation. This aspect of composition, together with rule 2.1.1, has been discussed by S. D. Joshi (1968: v-ix), Viśvanātha (1971b), Cardona (1973f: 229-31); see also K. Kunjunni Raja (1957a: 285-86). Full details on rules of composition were treated by K. M. Tiwary (1968). M. S. Narayana Murti (1974) has more recently treated Pāṇini's system of composition in a broader scope, including problems dealt with by later Pāṇinīyas and thinkers of other schools. The discussion in Staal (1966a) is more summary. The accentuation of compounds was treated by Aufrecht (1847), but this area of the grammar, and accentual rules in general, have not attracted much attention recently except with respect to Vedic rules (see sections III.1.5.6a, b).

The order of items in compounds has, of course, to be accounted for in a derivational system like Pāṇini's. The order of items in most compounds is taken care of by two rules. One of these is a classificatory rule whereby items referred to by terms stated in the nominative in compositional rules are called *upasarjana* (1.2.43: *prathamā-nirdiṣṭaṃ samāsa upasarjanam*). The other rule (2.2.30: *upasarjanaṃ pūrvam*) provides than an upasarjana occurs as the prior (*pūrva*) element of a compound. For example, the rule which applies to derive the compound *rāja-puruṣa* (2.2.8: *ṣaṣṭhī*) contains the nominative form *ṣaṣṭhī* referring to a pada which terminates in an ending of the sixth-triplet (*ṣaṣṭhī*). A genitive such as *rājan-as* is thus classed as upasarjana and thereby is the prior element of the compound. In addition, special rules are required for particular compounds. For example, rule 2.2.34 (*alpâctaram*) states that, in a dvandva compound, the item which contains the lesser number of syllables is the prior member; e.g., *kārya-kāraṇa* 'cause (*kāraṇa*) and effect (*kārya*)'. Again in the case of dvandva compounds, rule 2.2.33 (*aj-ādy-ad-antam*) provides that an item which begins with a vowel and ends with *a* is the prior member; e.g., *uṣṭra-khara* 'camel and donkey'. The provisions made in these two particular rules have been discussed respectively by Caland (1931) and Wackernagel (1938).

There has been some controversy concerning Pāṇini's classification of compounds. He recognizes four general types, called *tatpuruṣa, bahuvrīhi, dvandva* and *avyayībhāva.* The first type has two subtypes called *karmadhāraya* (see section III.1.5.3b.4 with note 212) and *dvigu.* Commentators note a classification of compounds on the basis of meaning: compounds are avyayīybhāva, tatpuruṣa, dvandva and bahuvrīhi according to whether the principal meaning is that of the prior member, subsequent member, both members or neither; e.g., *upâgni* 'near the fire', *rāja-puruṣa* 'king's man', *mātā-pitarau* 'mother and father', *bahu-vrīhi* 'who has much rice' (see section III.1.5.3a with notes 192, 195, 197). Pāṇini does not follow this procedure. Liebich (1892: vi-xii) considered this general classification a good one. He admitted that Pāṇini did not make use of it, but noted (1892: ix) that Pāṇini had here sacrificed scientific method on the altar of practical necessity, perhaps with a heavy heart.[265] Whitney (1893a: 188-91) severely chided Liebich, and through him also Pāṇini, for not recognizing the obvious and for sacrificing "every other desirable truth" in the name of brevity. However, Whitney was here guilty of his characteristic fault. Though he could see what Pāṇini did, he could not conceive of a well-composed grammar written except as he or a contemporary would, hence arrogantly rejected Pāṇini's procedure as ill-conceived. On the other hand, Liebich himself was mistaken. For Pāṇini did not give up a four-fold classification of compounds on the basis of their meanings simply for the sake of convenience. The fact is that this scheme is insufficient. Pāṇini classed compounds according to the operations proper to them. For example, the compound *śāka-prati* 'a little bit of vegetables' would, in the general classification scheme noted, have to be classed as a tatpuruṣa compound, since its principal meaning is that of the subsequent member *prati* 'little bit'. Pāṇini, on the other hand, classes this as an avyayībhāva compound.[266] There is a reason for this. An avyayīybhāva compound is further classed as an indeclinable (*avyaya*), after which nominal endings are deleted.[267] This has to apply to *śāka-prati.*

Several studies have dealt with particular compound types and individual compounds. Hariścandra-maṇi Tripāṭhī (1970, 1971) treated negative compounds of the type *abrāhmaṇa* 'non-Brāhmaṇa (that is, a member of other castes)'.[268] One particular compound, *mayūra-vyaṃsaka*, has been the subject of considerable discussion. Hertel (1908) dealt with this compound, which he translated 'one who deceives a peacock (*mayūra*)', in order to show that the story of the crow who adorned himself with peacock feathers was old in India. Hertel's view received support from Schmidt (1908) but was rejected by Jacobi (1908), who (1908: 359) interpreted the compound to mean 'a hunter's peacock who deceives others', hence 'deceiver'.[269] The subject was taken up anew by Thieme (1965), who concluded that *mayūra-vyaṃsaka* originally meant 'peacock-cobra'.

Nominal bases such as *aupagava* (see section III.1.5.1a), containing taddhita affixes, are also derived from padas. In the case of items of the type *aupagava*,[270] the rules for their derivation make a metalinguistic use of word order. Affixes are introduced optionally (*vā*) after the first (*prathama*) of syntactically and semantically related (*samartha*) padas referred to in the affixation rules.[271] For example, the rule which applies to derive *aupagava* is 4.1.92 (with 4.1.83): *tasyâpatyam* (*tasya apatyam*). Here the pronoun *tad* 'that' is used as a variable; the genitive form *tasya* refers to any pada terminating in a genitive ending. The affix (in this case *aṇ* [= *a*]) is introduced after an item which is a value of *tasya*, for example, *upagu-as*. The term *apatyam* 'descendant' in 4.1.92 gives the meaning of the affix, and 4.1.92 in its entirety gives a string with which the derivative alternates: *aupagavaḥ* = *upagor apatyam*. Similarly, rule 5.1.63 (*tad arhati*, see section III.1.5.3g) contains the accusative *tad*, so that it applies to form derivatives in which an affix meaning 'merits' (*arhati*) is introduced after an accusative form. The system of taddhita derivation has been studied in detail by D. M. Joshi.[272]

In a rule such as 5.1.63, a variable such as *tad* is used to refer to an accusative form of a nominal. Similarly, *tad* in 5.2.94 (*tad asyâsty asminn iti matup*) refers to a nominative form. This rule provides for introducing *matup* (= *mat*) after such a nominative form to form a derivative meaning '. . . is located in' (*asty asmin*), '. . . pertains to' (*asyâsti*); e.g., *vṛkṣavān* (< *vṛkṣa-mat-*) *parvataḥ* 'a mountain on which there are trees', *gomān* 'who has (many) cows'. Here the nominal forms which are values of the variable *tad* denote objects. Now, rule 5.2.59 (*matau cchaḥ sūkta-sāmnoḥ*) introduces the affix *cha* (= *īya*) to form derivatives with the meanings ascribed to *matup*, but on condition that what is to be denoted by such derivatives are hymns (*sūkta*) and sāman (hymns with particular chants); e.g., *yajñā-yajñīya* refers to a hymn which begins with *yajñā yajñā*. Here the nominal forms which are values of *tad* are citations, parts of Vedic hymns. Gourypathy Sastry (1974) has studied such derivatives and other formations involving what he calls quotative nominals.

1.5.5c. *Syntax.*

In this section I shall concentrate on the following: kārakas and kāraka rules, levels assumed to have been recognized by Pāṇini, concord and parts of speech. For additional studies on Pāṇini's syntax see section III.1.5.7.

1.5.5c.1. *Kārakas and kāraka rules.* Some affixes are introduced on condition that kārakas are to be denoted (see notes 152, 159). The notion of kāraka is basic to Pāṇini's derivational system. A kāraka is a thing viewed in relation to an action, in the accomplishment of which it plays a given role. There are six such kārakas: *apādāna, saṃpradāna,*[273] *karaṇa* 'instrument', *adhikaraṇa* 'locus', *karman* 'object', *kartṛ* 'agent'. In addition, there is a subtype of agents, namely a causal agent (*hetu*).

The terms noted above are introduced in a series of definition rules (*saṃjñā-sūtra*, see section III.1.5.2c) which come under the heading of 1.4.1-2 (see section III.1.5.2b with note 179). Pāṇini's rules reflect that a participant in an action (a kāraka) is assigned to a particular kāraka class for the purpose of deriving particular sentences: a thing may be classed in one way if it plays a certain role with respect to any action at all; or it may belong to a certain kāraka class if it plays a particular role with respect to particular actions denoted by sets of verbs; and a given kāraka classification may apply only if a given action is denoted by particular items. For example, 1.4.54 (*svatantraḥ kartā*) provides that the kāraka which functions independently (*svatantra* 'independent') with respect to other participants in a given action is called (that is, is classed as) kartṛ 'agent'; 1.4.49 (*kartur īpsitatamaṃ karma*) classes as karman 'object' that participant in an action which the agent (*kartṛ*) most wishes to reach (*īpsitatama*) through the action in question; 1.4.42 (*sādhakatamaṃ karaṇam*) assigns to the instrument (*karaṇa*) category that kāraka which, more than any other participants in a given action, serves as means (*sādhakatama*) for its accomplishment; 1.4.45 (*ādhāro'dhikaraṇam*) provides that the kāraka which functions as substrate (*ādhāra*) relative to an action is called *adhikaraṇa* 'locus'; 1.4.32 (*karmaṇā yam abhipraiti sa saṃpradānam*) classes as *saṃpradāna* that kāraka which the agent intends (*abhipraiti*) as goal through the object (*karman*) of the action in which he participates. Rule 1.4.24 (*dhruvam apāye'pādānam*) assigns to the category of apādāna that kāraka which functions as a point of departure (*dhruvam apāye* 'stable point relative to departure'). By 1.4.37 (*krudha-druhêrṣyâsūyârthānāṃ yaṃ prati kopaḥ*) a participant in the actions denoted by *krudh* 'be angry', *druh* 'wish harm to', *īrṣya* 'not tolerate', *asūya* 'find fault with' and their synonyms is classed as saṃpradāna if he is the one towards whom anger is felt (*yaṃ prati kopaḥ*). 1.4.38 (*krudha-druhor upasṛṣṭayoḥ karma* [*yaṃ prati kopaḥ* 37]), on the contrary, assigns the person towards whom anger is felt to the object (*karman*) category if the verb used is *krudh* or *druh* with a preverb (*upasṛṣṭa*). Similarly, by 1.4.46 (*adhiśīṅ-sthâsāṃ karma* [*ādhāraḥ* 45]) provides that a kāraka which functions as substrate of an action is a karman if the action in question is lying, being in a place or being seated as denoted by the particular verbs *adhiśī, adhiṣṭhā, adhyās* respectively. It is obvious that the rules noted serve, like 1.4.10-12 (see section III.1.5.2b), to classify and that, in cases of conflict, the order of rules serves to provide unique classifications. For example, rules 2.3.13 (*caturthī saṃpradāne*) and 2.3.36 (*saptamy adhikaraṇe ca*) respectively provide that a fourth-triplet nominal ending (dative ending) is introduced when a saṃpradāna is to be denoted, a seventh-triplet ending (locative ending) when an adhikaraṇa is to be denoted; but 2.3.2 (see note 159) states that a second-triplet ending (accusative ending) is introduced when an object (*karman*) is to be denoted. Since rules 1.4.37-38 and 1.4.45-46 are stated under the heading of 1.4.1-2, then, the participant towards whom anger is felt and the substrate of an action are uniquely classed as object (*karman*) instead of saṃpradāna and locus. Therefore, only 2.3.2, not also 2.3.13, 36 apply, to derive

(1) *devadattaṃ abhikrudhyati* '... is angry at Devadatta.'
(2) *parvatam adhyāste* '... is seated on the mountain.'

Sentences

(*3) **devadattāya abhikrudhyati*
(*4) **parvate adhyāste*

with a dative and locative form respectively, as in

(5) *devadattāya krudhyati* '... is angry at Devadatta.'
(6) *parvate āste* '... is seated on the mountain.'

are thereby precluded.

There has been considerable discussion regarding the precise status of these kāraka categories.[274] In 1893, Whitney (1893a: 171-72), reacting to Liebich's dissertation (1886-87) in a typically acerbic manner, nevertheless made an important comment. Though Whitney could not fathom why Pāṇini proceded as he did,[275] still he noted appositely that the kāraka categories "are not an independent product of his [Pāṇini's] logical faculty, but simply a reflection of case forms" (1893a: 171). Some later scholars have emphasized instead the extra-linguistic, logical, ideational[276] aspects of Pāṇini's kāraka categories. According to Faddegon (1936: 18), "By *kārakas* Pāṇini understands the logica or ideational relations between a noun and a verb, or more precisely between an object and an action or anything conceived after the analogy of an action. It is clear that Faddegon considered this rather vague and unsophisticated. For later on in the same work he spoke (1936: 49) of "Hindu grammar" as being "rather undeveloped" in respect of grammatical notions, lacking, for example, the notion of subject, and cited as an example of this lack of development the kāraka categories. M. D. Pandit (1963b: 22) referred to the kārakas as being "more extra-linguistic or psychological, rather than linguistic or formal in nature." R. Rocher has expressed a similar opinion on various occasions. According to her (1964a: 51), "Les définitions données du *kartṛ* et du *karman* – et le même jugement vaudrait pour les autres *kāraka* – n'ont rien de grammatical." In the same vein, Rocher (1964b: 40) says, concerning the rule which defines *hetu* (see below), that, like other kāraka rules, it too "has a purely extra-linguistic bearing and is not at all concerned with the way or ways in which the *hetu* is expressed."[277] Al-George (1957, especially p. 40; 1968; 1970: 238) has also maintained that Pāṇini's kāraka categories are extra-linguistic in nature. However, he maintains that they are notions taken over from the categories established in the ritual.[278] Most recently, A. C. Sinha (1973) has gone even further than Rocher. Indeed, Sinha (1973: 28) ascribes to Rocher the view that Pāṇini's grammar had a semantic component. His own view is that the position held by some modern theorists, that grammatical relations are universal, is Pāṇini's position too: "The Sanskrit grammarians, by and large, were proponents of this latter view [that is, that grammatical relations are universal]. One of their main contributions to grammatical philosophy has been the kāraka theory which treats these relations." (A. C. Sinha 1973: 27): "All grammatical relations are semantic relations in Pāṇini" (1973: 34); "In short, the kārakas are well-defined semantic concepts independent of Sanskrit noun morphology in so far as the vibhaktis [endings] are concerned and thus must, therefore, be viewed as semantic categories in Pāṇini's grammar" (1973: 35); "The real advantage of considering the kārakas as semantic rather than syntactic categories lies in the fact that as semantic categories the kārakas can be deemed to have been established independent[ly] of all grammatical devices that may express them in Sanskrit – the nominal affixes, the verbal affixes, and the nominal compounds. Once the kāraka categories are established, it is comparatively simple to state the distributions of the affixes that depend on the kāraka conditions. This appears to be the scheme of Pāṇini's kāraka theory . . ." (1973: 35).

Cardona (1967b) argued that the points of view held by R. Rocher and Al-George were misrepresentations, and presented evidence to show that Pāṇini set up his kāraka categories in order to set up conditions under which affixes – both post-verbal and post-nominal – would be introduced, so that, far from having nothing to do with syntax or the derivation of correct Sanskrit utterances derived by Pāṇinian rules, the kāraka rules are intimately related to Pāṇini's syntactic rules.[279] He noted (Cardona [1967b: 214]) that "It is possible, though not completely exact, to say that Pāṇini's definitions of *kārakas* are *set up* on the semantic level . . . " but rejected the proposition that these categories have nothing to do with grammar. Al-George (1968) reacted by reiterating his view that the kāraka categories are calques of the categories established in the ritual and suggesting some evidence to buttress this opinion. Cardona (1970b) then took up the question anew, giving evidence to demonstrate that, though Pāṇini was of course intimately acquainted with the sacrifice, there is no precise correlation between the two systems of categories such as could establish that Pāṇini simply took over a sacrificial categorization for his set of rules. In sum, argued Cardona, the parallels drawn by Al-George rest on vague comparisons not substantiated by evidence. Kiparsky and Staal (1969) maintained, like Cardona, that Pāṇini's kāraka categories were not purely semantic categories divorced from syntax. After noting (Kiparsky - Staal [1969: 84]) that Cardona had brought the questions regarding kārakas "tantalizingly close to what we believe to be their solution," they gave what they considered to be the correct appreciation of the status of Pāṇini's kārakas. This differs from Cardona's scheme essentially as follows. Cardona recognized that Pāṇini operates with: semantic characterizations, kāraka categorization rules, grammatical rules in which the denotations of kāraka as categorized in the former serve as conditions for introducing affixes. Kiparsky and Staal set up a fourth level by recognizing semantic representation, deep structure, surface structure and phonologic representation.[280] They also noted (1969: 109) that "there is no justification for supposing that the semantic level, let alone the level of *kārakas*, has any kind of ontological significance, as Rocher (1964a, b) has come close to suggesting." Other scholars too have stressed the intimate connection between Pāṇini's kāraka categories and syntactic features; see D. M. Joshi (1972: 94), S. D. Joshi (1974: 261).[281]

I think the scholars who maintain that Pāṇini's kāraka categories are purely semantic in nature hold this view in no small part because of a lack of subtlety. It is obvious, for example, that R. Rocher, while considering only a small number of rules – some of the rules in which no set of verbs or particular verb is mentioned – drew extremely far-reaching conclusions.[282] A. C. Sinha is equally guilty not only of a lack of subtlety but also of a rather naive acceptance of the proposition that any one who does not hold that Pāṇini was a generative semanticist or ascribe to Pāṇini views in accord with this position is, automatically, a "structuralist" who dismisses meaning.[28] Of course, Cardona, Kiparsky and Staal, and others have done no such thing. A careful study of all of Pāṇini's kāraka categorization rules shows this position with clarity.

Now, it is obvious that the notion of a kāraka – a participant in an actior – is semantic. It is equally obvious that, had he wished to, Pāṇini could have defined his kāraka categories in purely semantic terms. For example, instead of stating rules such as 1.4.38 and 1.4.46 (see above), he could have stated 1.4.37, 45 alone in the section of kāraka rules. To prevent sentences such as (*3) and (*4) from being derived by his rules, Pāṇini could then have stated particular syntactic cooccurrence rules such as, for example, exclude the introduction of locative endings in deriving (2). Such rules do occur in the grammar.[284] Instead, he included in rules 1.4.38, 46 syntactic cooccurrence features. Such rules can hardly be said to assign a particular kāraka to a category under purely semantic conditions. Consequently, it is not possible to maintain that the category object (*karman*) is defined in purely semantic terms. By 1.4.46 a kāraka which functions as substrate of an action is assigned to the karman category. If we speak, as Indian commentators do, in terms of properties, this then provides that a locus is qualified by the property of being an object (*karmatva* 'objectness'). This is certainly not properly a semantic property of a locus. It is, however, proper if the category object is not purely semantic. Consider also a sentence such as

(7) *paraśur vṛkṣaṃ chinatti* 'The axe is cutting the tree.'

To derive this sentence in terms of Pāṇini's rules requires that the axe (*paraśu*) be classed as an agent (*kartṛ*) of cutting (*chid*). Now, obviously an axe does not of itself cut a tree; it is an instrument (*karaṇa*) for cutting. Pāṇini recognizes this by the order of the kāraka rules. The axe in question must simultaneously be considered to function as an instrument. It thereby can be assigned to two kāraka categories at once. But, by 1.4.1-2, it is unique classed as an agent (1.4.54) and not also as an instrument (1.4.42).[285] The fact remains, however, that, in Pāṇini's categorization, the axe is assigned uniquely to the class of agents. The property of agency (*kartṛtva*) can therefore hardly be considered purely a semantic notion. In assigning the axe of (7) to the class of agents, Pāṇini's purpose is clear: this allows introducing the L-suffix *laṭ* on condition that an agent is to be denoted. Again, consider sentence

(8) *devadattāya rocate vidyā* 'Devadatta likes knowledge.'

The derivation of this sentence requires that Devadatta be assigned to the category saṃpradāna and that knowledge (*vidyā*) be an agent. The former is provided by 1.4.33 (*rucy-arthānāṃ prīyamāṇaḥ*), which states that the kāraka which plays the role of one being pleased (*prīyamāṇa*) is saṃpradāna relative to actions denoted by *ruc* 'please' and its synonyms. But now how does one reasonably consider knowledge a semantic agent and being pleasing (*ruc*) an action? Pāṇinian commentators do, in fact, make several suggestions concerning the semantics of (8). One of these is as follows. The semantics of (8) are such as conveyed by

(9) *devadattaṃ vidyā prīṇayati* 'Knowledge pleases Devadatta.'

Semantically, Devadatta is here an object (*karman*), which the grammar classes as a saṃpradāna, and knowledge is the agent of pleasing.[286]

From such facts and many others,[287] I think it improper to say that Pāṇini's kāraka categories are defined in purely semantic terms. This categorization serves as an intermediary between semantics and grammatical expressions derived by rules of the grammar.

There has been some debate concerning one particular kāraka rule. Pāṇini states a rule[288] which provides that the kāraka which instigates (*prayojaka*) a kāraka classed as agent is both agent (*kartṛ*) and (*ca*) *hetu*. Pāṇinīyas distinguish between the term *hetu* used to refer to such a causal agent (*prayojaka-kartṛ*) and *hetu* meaning 'cause'.[289] A causative sentence related to sentence (3) of section III.1.5.1a (*devadatta odanaṃ pacati*) is

(10) *yajñadatta odanaṃ devadattena* ***pācayati*** 'Yajñadatta has Devadatta cook some rice.'

The form ***pācay-a-ti*** (3rd sg. pres.) is derived from the root ***pāci*** itself a derived root. This consists of the primitive root *pac* 'cook' and the affix *ṇic* (= *i*). For Pāṇinīyas, ***pāci*** denotes two activities: cooking and causing. To these are related two agents: the agent of cooking and the agent of causing. In deriving (10), then, the L-suffix *laṭ*, replaced by *ti*, is introduced to denote an agent of causation, while the instrumental ending (in *devadattena*) is introduced to denote an agent of cooking. Pāṇinīyas distinguish between such a cause (*hetu*) which is simultaneously an agent (*kartṛ*) – a causal agent – and a mere cause (*hetu*) such as 'knowledge' (*vidyā*) in

(11) *vidyayā yaśaḥ bhavati* 'There is fame through knowledge.'

R. Rocher (1964b) has attempted to show that this distinction is not properly attributed to Pāṇini. According to Rocher (1964b: 33), "there is only one *hetu* 'cause', a technical term indicating as basic an element of the action as any other *kāraka*, without any difference whether the action is expressed by a causative or a non-causative verb form." Cardona (1971), on the other hand, has argued that the distinction made by Pāṇinīyas is both necessary for a correct description of Sanskrit and properly attributed to Pāṇini.[290] Rocher did not consider examples such as the following. Sentence (11) can have a passive counterpart, where the L-suffix *laṭ* is introduced on condition that an action is to be denoted (see note 152). The instrumental ending *-ā* is then introduced after *yaśas* 'frame' to denote an agent:

(12) *vidyayā yaśasā bhūyate*

In addition, the following sentence is correctly derived:

(13) *vidyā yaśo bhāvayati* 'Knowledge causes fame to come about.'

The passive counterpart of this is

(14) *vidyayā yaśo bhāvyate* 'Fame is made to come about by knowledge.'

Here the instrumental ending *-ā* is introduced after *vidyā* to denote an agent of causation. The correct derivation of (11) - (12) as distinct from (13) - (14) requires that knowledge be merely a cause in one case and a causal agent in the other.

In my opinion Rocher has also interpreted wrongly rule 1.4.55 (see above with note 288). Of this rule, Rocher (1964b: 40) says, "The sūtra simply says that the *hetu*, like the *kartṛ*, is a *kāraka* which operates independently." However, the rule contains the word *ca* 'also'. This is necessary because 1.4.55 is stated under the heading of 1.4.1-2. Had Pāṇini not stated *ca* in this rule, the instigator of an agent would have been classed uniquely as a hetu, not simultaneously also as an agent (*kartṛ*). Rule 1.4.55 thus provides that the kāraka in question is both an agent and a cause. Pāṇini then uses the term *hetu* to refer to such a causal agent.

1.5.5c.2. *Levels assumed to have been recognized by Pāṇini.* Another aspect of Pāṇini's general syntactic system which has received attention recently is the question of levels. Cardona (1967b: 212) noted that Pāṇini's kāraka classifications (see section III.1.5.5c.1) serve as intermediaries between grammatical expressions and their semantics. Kiparsky - Staal (1969: 84) operate with what they call four levels: semantic representation, deep structure, surface structure, and phonologic representation. Of these, the second corresponds to Pāṇini's kāraka categorization. The third is "represented in terms of morphologic categories, e.g., by nominal cases . . ." According to Kiparsky and Staal, a context-free rule then introduces endings such as *am* (acc. sg.): "Thus, the basic affix for the Accusative is first introduced by the context-free rule: *dvitīyā* → *am* . . . (corresponding to part of 4.1.2)" (Kiparsky - Staal 1969: 88-89). Cardona (1970d: 237; 1974b: 285-86 n. 34) has pointed out that such a replacement rule has no basis in Pāṇini's grammar. Terms such as *dvitīyā* 'second' refer to endings of triplets of nominal endings (in this case *am, auṭ, śas*) and not to morphologic categories such as Accusative. In the derivation of verbal forms, to be sure, Pāṇini does use abstract symbols replaced by endings – the L-suffixes (see note 152) – but there are no comparable abstract symbols in the derivation of nominal forms like *odanam* 'rice' (acc. sg.).[291]

As opposed to Cardona and Kiparsky - Staal, A. C. Sinha (1973: 36) insists that the kāraka categorizations do not constitute a separate level: "These terms [*kartṛ* etc.] do not appear to constitute a separate level in the kāraka theory . . ." This is in accord with Sinha's view (see section III. 1.5.5c.1) that Pāṇini's kāraka categories are purely semantic. For now terms such as *kartṛ* are mere labels for semantic notions. However, if the kāraka rules are categorization rules which assign to categories such as *karman* 'object' etc. participants in actions that would semantically be eligible for different classifications, then these rules indeed constitute a distinct classificatory level which mediates between semantics and grammatical expressions. I say this although I am aware that, since kāraka classification rules take into consideration particular morphologic features (1.4.53 and 54 refer to the causative affix *ṇic*), they are not, strictly speaking, a separate level in the sense of a totally self-contained subsystem not having reference to features of any other subsystem.

1.5.5c.3. *Concord and parts of speech.* In accord with Pāṇini's derivational system (see section III.1.5.1a), there are two basic kinds of items involved: those to which are introduced verbal affixes and those to which are introduced nominal affixes. At a stage in all derivations, then, items terminate in either verb endings (*tiṅ*) or nominal endings (*sup*). The operations stated in the grammar of course require that Pāṇini recognize such classes of items as particles (*nipāta*) and preverbs (*upasarga*), but the above is the broadest dichotomy; for particles and preverbs are, in Pāṇini's derivation, also followed by nominal endings at an early stage, endings which are then deleted.[292]

A particular nominal base (*prātipadika*) can, in a given derivation, function as a qualifier; it is what western grammar calls an adjective. Pāṇini makes no essential distinction between adjectives and nouns; this point has been discussed by S. D. Joshi (1966b).[293] Moreover, there are no rules in Pāṇini's grammar devoted specifically to providing concord between nouns and adjectives. For example, there is no rule to provide that in the sentence

(1) *kaṭaṃ darśanīyaṃ karoti* '. . . is making a handsome mat.'

the adjective *darśanīya* 'handsome' and the noun *kaṭa* 'mat' are followed by the same ending, *am* (acc. sg.). Cardona (1970d: 234-35) has recently discussed such derivations and pointed out that Pāṇini here makes use of a concept of coreference (*sāmānâdhikaraṇya*): the items *kaṭa* and *darśanīya*, though lexically distinct, refer in (1) to the same object, a mat which is handsome. Hence, there is only one object (*karman*) to be denoted in deriving (1), by iterating the affix *am* (*kaṭa-am darśanīya-am*).[294]

As Pāṇini has no special rules for describing adjective - noun concord, so also does he not state particular rules for providing the forms of adverbs in sentences such as

(2) *suṣṭhu pacati* '. . . cooks well.'

The various ways suggested by commentators to derive such sentences have been treated by N. S. Ramanujacharya (1966) and Cardona (1973a). Bahulikar (1966) also treated the commentatorial discussions regarding constructions of the types

(3) *stokaṃ pākaḥ* 'cooking a little'

and

(4) *stokaḥ pākaḥ* 'a little cooking'

where *stokam* in (3) is an adverb and *stokaḥ* in (4) is an adjective in concord with the action noun *pākaḥ*.

One major omission in Pāṇini's grammar is worthy of note: nowhere does Pāṇini define a sentence.[295] He uses the term *vākya*, usually translated 'sentence', but there is no definition in the Aṣṭādhyāyī. Later Indian thinkers of various schools did attempt to define a vākya.[296] Kātyāyana suggests two definitions,[297] both for technical purposes: to allow stating that certain operations apply within a vākya. Consider one problem this is intended to overcome.[298] In the sequence

(5) *ayaṃ daṇḍo harânena* 'Here is a stick, fetch with it.'

the imperative form *hara* 'fetch' should have high pitch on its first vowel. However, this occurs here preceded by a nominal form, the nominative *daṇḍaḥ* 'stick'. Rule 8.1.28 (*tiṅ atiṅaḥ*, see section III.1.5.3d) provides that a finite verb form preceded by such a form has no high-pitched vowel. To avoid letting this apply to *hara* in (5), then, one can define a sentence (*vākya*) and let 8.1.28 apply only when the left context and the verb form in question occur in the same sentence. Now (5) would consist of two sentences – *ayaṃ daṇḍaḥ* and *harânena* – so that all is in order. It is, nevertheless, possible to make another suggestion. Paṇini's rules serve to derive sentences, not to analyze them. Presumably, (5) would, in this system, result from two distinct derivations.

1.5.5d. *Semantics.*

It is obvious that semantics played a role in the formulation of Pāṇinian rules.[299] Meanings serve as conditions for the introduction of affixes (see section III.1.5.1a) and Pāṇini's kāraka classification rules (see section III.1.5.5c.1) serve to bridge the gap between semantic relations and grammatical expressions. Now, as I have noted, a sentence such as (7) of section III.1.5.5c.1 involves classing an axe as an agent of cutting, although such an inanimate object does not function as a true agent in this activity. Pāṇinīyas stress that the grammarian is not concerned with ontology but with what people say, how they speak of things and events. And people do indeed use sentences in which axes are said to cut trees, knowledge pleases (see section III.1.5.5c.1 (8)) and knowledge is viewed as a causal agent (see section III.1.5.5c.1 (13)-(14)). K. A. Subramania Iyer (1948) has given a good exposition of this view, which is not only held by Pāṇinīyas but also attributable to Pāṇini; see also Cardona (1974b: 238-43, 245-46, 270-73; forthcoming e).

In the same vein, it is noteworthy that Pāṇini nowhere makes a provision to the effect that an utterance derived by his rules must be semantically appropriate. Now, for followers of certain schools, a correct sentence[300] had to meet certain conditions. Among these is that the denotata of elements in the sentence be semantically compatible (*yogya*).[301] A sentence such as

(1) *agninā siñcati puṣpāṇi devadattaḥ* 'Devadatta is sprinkling the flowers with fire.'

is, by this criterion, not proper, since one cannot irrigate with fire, which is not a liquid. However, the sentence is grammatically correct (see Matilal 1966: 383]) even if it is not acceptable as a proposition conveying a knowledge (see note 300). And Pāṇini's concern is precisely with rules which account for grammatically correct utterances. The semantic compatibility of denotata or the truth or falsehood of such utterances is not a criterion for judging them as proper results of derivation. This has been emphasized recently by Vidya Niwas Misra (1970).

The fact that meaning conditions are used for introducing affixes of course requires that certain meanings were assigned to these units (see note 152). Pāṇinīyas such as Bhartṛhari (see section VI.2.4) consider all such assignments of meanings to subsentential units such as affixes to be merely a fiction useful in formulating grammatical rules. Bhartṛhari also points out that different grammarians made different meaning assignments. Some cases of such meaning assignments prompted considerable discussion. For example, Pāṇini states (3.3.161: *vidhi-nimantraṇâmantraṇâdhīṣṭa-saṃpraśna-prārthaneṣu liṅ*) that the L-suffix *liṅ* (introduced to derive what western grammars call optative forms) is introduced when the following are to be expressed: injunction (*vidhi*), a summoning to do something which one must do (*nimantraṇa*), an invitation to do something (*āmantraṇa*), respectful command (*adhīṣṭa*), deliberation (*saṃpraśna*), request (*prārthana*). The question arises whether it would be as well to consider four of these as mere varieties of one meaning, namely, prompting someone to action (*pravartanā*). Further, the question arises, what precisely is meant by *vidhi*. Aspects of these questions are treated by Muralidhar Miśra (1963) and J. A. Gune (1974). Another object of discussion is the status of preverbs such as *pra* in sequences such as *pravasati* 'is away on a trip' (cf. *vasati* 'is staying'): should particular meanings be assigned to such preverbs, which meanings they then denote, or should the preverbs be considered cosignifiers (*dyotaka*, see note 152) of meanings assigned to the verbs in question? This issue has been taken up recently by Charudeva Shastri (1972).

As I noted earlier (section III.1.5.5c.1), Pāṇini provides that a locative ending is introduced when a locus is to be denoted, thus accounting for sentences like (6) of section III.1.5.5c.1. Now, there are different kinds of loci. For example, sesame seeds (*tila*) totally contain the oil (*taila*) which is in them. But a person seated on a mountain is merely in contact with it. Consider now a sentence such as *gaṅgāyāṃ ghoṣaḥ* 'The cowherd colony is on the Ganges'. The locative form *gaṅgāyām* should be derived by introducing a locative ending to denote a locus. However, it is obvious that a group of people cannot actually be living in a flow of water. What this sentence conveys is that they are living on the banks of the Ganges. Some Indian thinkers therefore considered that in this sentence the word *gaṅgā* does not have its primary meaning but a secondary meaning, namely, the banks of the river. Pāṇini himself makes no such statement. And Pāṇinīyas agree that the notion of locus includes a locus of proximity: that near which an action occurs. Kunjunni Raja (1965) has dealt with this question.

1.5.6. *Studies of particular rules.*

1.5.6a. *Vedic rules.*

Pāṇini includes in his grammar particular rules valid only for Vedic Sanskrit. Two major questions have engaged scholars concerning Pāṇini's Vedic rules: what Vedic texts did Pāṇini exploit in formulating these rules, and how correct is his description of these Vedic facts?

Goldstücker (1861: 139-43) maintained that Pāṇini did not know the Atharva-veda or the Vājasaneyi-saṃhitā. He also held that the latter text had not yet been composed at Pāṇini's time. Weber (1862: 50-53, 57-59, 77-78) showed that Goldstücker's argument concerning the Atharva-veda was not acceptable. He also attempted to demonstrate that Pāṇini actually had made use of the Vājasaneyi-saṃhitā. Weber's evidence for the second point, however, was not probative, as Thieme (1935a: 73-74) later demonstrated. Nevertheless, Weber did note that the White Yajur-veda was studied in the East, whereas Pāṇini was from the North-west of the subcontinent, which explains Pāṇini's not describing usages particular to the Vājasaneyi-saṃhitā (Thieme [1935a: 74-75]). K. B. Pathak (1930) tried to show that Pāṇini used not only the Vājasaneyi-saṃhitā but also the brāhmaṇa text associated with it, the Śata-patha-brāhmaṇa. However, the weakness of Pathak's evidence was pointed out by Thieme (1935a: 75 n. 1).[302] Thieme himself (1935a: 39, 41, 66) gave evidence to show that Pāṇini made use of the Atharva-veda in the Paippalāda recension. In addition, he concluded (1935a: 63) that Pāṇini also exploited the Kāṭhaka-saṃhitā, Maitrāyaṇi-saṃhitā, Taittirīya-saṃhitā and also possibly the Sāma-veda. These conclusions are now generally accepted.[303] In the most recent paper on this subject, K. Hoffmann (1974: 75) has presented evidence to show that Pāṇini made use of the Mānava-śrauta-sūtra and the Vārāha-śrauta-sūtra. Pāṇini's rule 7.2.69 (*saniṃ sasanivāṃsam*) gives the ready-made form *sasanivāṃsam*, accusative singular masculine of the perfect participle of *san* 'gain', in construction with *sanim* (acc. sg. of *sani* 'gain'). This sequence appears in verses which appear in the śrauta-sūtra texts noted.

The most important single work concerned with Pāṇini's Vedic rules and their validity with respect to the Vedic facts as known is by Thieme (1935a). Nearly half a century earlier, Whitney (1893b) had discussed Pāṇini's Vedic rules and concluded (1893b: 254) that "no discoverable principle seems to underlie his selections [of Vedic facts described]." Whitney also claimed (1893b: 254) that Pāṇini's use of "an unexplained variety of designations" for Vedic texts[304] showed that his Vedic materials "were raked together from a variety of sources, perhaps from this and that and another grammarian, his predecessors, and combined without being properly arranged or unified." This view was held by others also, for example, Wackernagel

(1896: lxxv) and Keith (1920: 424, see section III.1.3.3a). That this position was not proper was later demonstrated by Thieme (1935a), who showed in some detail how Pāṇini's observations on Vedic were precise and his terminology for referring to different aspects of Vedic usage accurate. Earlier, Hillebrandt (1927: 67-68) had defended the accuracy of Pāṇini's Vedic observations. In later years, K. Madhava Krishna Sarma (1941b: 222; 1968: 42) again said that "Pāṇini's treatment of the Vedic language is not satisfactory." However, this claim is not buttressed with detailed arguments. More recently still, D. N. Shastri (1974: 295, cf. 296) has claimed that "Pāṇini's presentation of the conjugational system is unrealistic." One of his arguments concerns the form labelled injunctive by western grammarians, regarding which D. N. Shastri (1974: 296) says, "He [Pāṇini] does not take it as a separate *lakāra* [L-suffix], as he does the other three moods called *loṭ, vidhi-liṅ* and *leṭ.*" There appears to be some confusion here. It is of dubious propriety to speak of *loṭ, leṭ* and *vidhi-liṅ* as moods. The elements in question are affixes introduced under given meaning conditions and, like all L-suffixes, replaced by endings; after replacements and other operations have applied, roots with these affixes appear in what western grammar calls respectively imperative, subjunctive and optative forms. Moreover, Pāṇini does not have a separate name *vidhi-liṅ.* This term is used by Pāṇinīyas to refer to the *liṅ* which has been introduced when an injunction is to be expressed (see section III.1.5.5d) as opposed to *liṅ* introduced when a wish (*āśis*) is to be expressed (the precative affix in western terminology). Finally, Pāṇini does, in fact, provide for the derivation, in the domain of Vedic usage, of what westerners have called injunctive forms. Rule 6.4.75 (*bahulaṃ chandasy amāṅ-yoge'pi*) provides that, in forms of sacred literature (*chandas*), the augment *aṭ* (= *a*) or *āṭ* (= *ā*), which in normal Sanskrit does not appear in aorist and imperfect forms when these are construed with the negative particle *mā*, does not appear in these forms even if *mā* is not used.

There has appeared in recent years a series of studies concerning Pāṇini's Vedic rules, the usages accounted for by these rules, and how the rules fit the known facts: Balasubrahmanyam (1961-62, 1962-63; 1965; 1966; 1966-67; 1969; 1971; 1972; 1974), M. S. Bhat (1966-67), V. P. Limaye (1967a, b),[305] Bhavānīprasāda Bhattacharya (1969), Laddu (1969, 1971b), Shivaramaiah (1969), P. D. Nawathe (1971).[306] In a very recent paper Palsule (1972) has suggested an interpretation of a Pāṇinian rule different from the one usually accepted by Pāṇinīyas.[307] The purpose of this reinterpretation is to have the rule account for Vedic imperatives such as *yakṣi* 'sacrifice' (2nd sg.). Nawathe (1966) has also dealt with un-Pāṇinian forms in the śrauta-sūtras, a valid area of study in view of the relative antiquity of these texts.[308]

The use of Pāṇini's rules to interpret Vedic texts is of course the norm for commentators such as Sāyaṇa. Among modern scholars also there are several who have defended this procedure as fruitful and given examples of how, in their opinion, Pāṇini's rules help to solve problems of Vedic interpretation. S. S. Bhawe (1953; 1955) set forth his view that the Aṣṭādhyāyī should be used to interpret Vedic hymns and put this procedure to use in translating the Soma hymns of the Ṛg-veda (1957-62). Devasthali (1963; 1965; 1967c; 1968b) also defended this position in a series of papers.[309] In addition, Deo Prakash Patanjal (1963) used Pāṇinian rules for interpreting Ṛg-vedic hymns in the conviction that " . . . there is no word, whether Vedic or Classical, which cannot be derived or explained by Pāṇini's system" (1963: 23). On this point there is a near absolute difference of opinion between Indian and western scholars. For the latter, this is not a fruitful pursuit, and Kuiper's (1965) negative reaction to Bhawe's method is probably typical.

1.5.6b. *Other rules.*

Related sets of rules have been studied. Some of these studies deal with general features common to these rules, others concentrate more on certain terms used in several rules.

C. R. Sankaran (1934-35) treated accentual rules in the context of the historical development of tatpuruṣa compounds and their accentuation as he envisioned it. More recently, Pāṇini's accentual rules (see section III.1.4.2b with notes 121-23) have been treated by Fowler (1973).[310]

Kanitkar has treated Pāṇinian rules which account for the use of extra-long vowels (1961-62), rules involving preverbs (*upasarga*) (1962-63) and those rules in which terms are used referring to time (1963-65).

Cardona (1967a) has treated rules which contain negative compounds in order to make clear the distinction to be observed between sentence negation (*prasajya-pratiṣedha*) and nominal negation (*paryudāsa*) and how the adoption of one or the other affects the way in which rules apply.

Hazra (1956) took up the section of rules beginning with 2.3.50 and discussed details concerning the carry-over (*anuvṛtti*) of the term *śeṣe* from 2.3.50 into subsequent rules.

Renou (1955: 126-27, 128-30) discussed briefly rules which contain the term *nityam* 'necessarily' and those in which the locative singular of the term *strī* 'feminine, femininity' is used.[311]

Kapil Deva Shastri (1963) studied rules in which the term *prakāra* 'kind, sort, manner' is used, discussed commentatorial views, and concluded that the sense 'likeness' is predominant, so that the view of Bhartṛhari appears more acceptable than that of other grammarians who understood this term in the sense 'differentiation'; see also Kapil Deva Shastri (1964a).

R. S. Bhattacharya has taken up rules of derivation involving the meanings 'praise' and 'censure' (1966i, j) and also rules which contain forms of verbs whose meanings are in the sphere of knowing, cognizing (1966y).

Palsule (1966) has given an exhaustive survey of sūtras in which the form *saṃjñāyām* (loc. sg. of *saṃjñā*, lit. 'name') occurs and concluded (1966: 68) that the term *saṃjñā* in these rules refers to "a word whose etymological meaning is restricted by convention." This topic was also treated, though not as exhaustively, by R. S. Bhattacharya (1966g).

Individual rules have been the objects of separate studies, many of which have been noted in the course of previous discussions. Other such treatments are noted below, with brief comments where I think this is in order. Some of the references are short notes, others detailed discussions. References are given in the order of rules.

1.1.36: K. C. Chatterji (1955).

1.2.6: Goonetilleke (1882b).

1.2.23: Pisani (1934).

1.2.45: Kotulkar (1967).

1.3.3: K. C. Chatterji (1935c); see section V.

1.4.7: V. Krishnamacharya (1973).

1.4.32: Ghatge (1968). Ghatge discusses an addition to the rule suggested by Patañjali and the question of rule ordering in connection with the application of what the new statements provide.

2.1.33: M. M. Deshpande (1974). Deshpande discusses the meaning of the term *kāka-peyā* (*nadī*), a compound derived by this rule. According to the usual interpretation, this refers to a river (*nadī*) which is so full that a crow (*kāka*) can drink from it while standing on its bank.

2.3.46: Speijer (1886: 26 n. 1), Böhtlingk (1887e: 179-80), Thieme (1956: 2-10), Baladeva Siṃha (1973), Cardona (1974b: 287-88 n. 42). Speijer claimed that the usual interpretation given this rule by Pāṇinīyas beginning at least with Patañjali was not proper. Böhtlingk disagreed. Thieme not only accepted Speijer' view but also suggested that Speijer's own interpretation was the one given to the rule by Kātyāyana. Cardona points out that Kātyāyana appears to share the view of later Pāṇinīyas. The point of contention is the word *vacana*. The rule states: *prātipadikârtha-liṅga-parimāṇa-vacana-mātre prathamā*. In the usual interpretation, the rule serves to introduce endings of the first triplet (*prathamā*), that is, nominative endings, when the following are to be denoted: the meaning of a nominal base (*prātipadikârtha*), gender (*liṅga*), a measure (*parimāṇa*), number (*vacana*). According to Speijer and Thieme, *vacana* does not here mean 'number'.[312] The rule is to be interpreted, they say, as providing that nominative endings are introduced when only the gender and number of a meaning of a nominal base is to be expressed (*-vacana*).

3.2.112-13: Konow (1938: 234-36).

3.4.1: S. D. Joshi 1971. According to Joshi the rule is, contrary to the usual interpretation, a heading.

4.1.54: S. K. Limaye (1966). Limaye suggests that the example *sukeśī rathyā* is to be interpreted as meaning a soft or fine haired seat of a chariot or the owner.

4.2.66: R. S. Bhattacharya (1966hh).

4.3.87: R. S. Bhattacharya (1966o).

5.2.28-29: M. D. Balasubrahmanyam (1972).

6.4.12-13: P. S. Śukla (1969).

7.2.57-58: van Nooten (1970).

7.3.73: Wackernagel (1914), Cardona (1964; 1969: 23 n. 70).

8.2.18: Shiva Narayana Shastri (1968b).[313]

1.5.7. *Comparisons of Pāṇini's system with other systems.*

1.5.7a. *Comparisons with other Indian systems.*

Pāṇini's grammar has been compared with other Indian treatises for various purposes. Liebich and Thieme compared some of Pāṇini's sūtras with statements of prātiśākhyas and the Nirukta in order to establish the relative chronology of these texts (see section III.3.2). More recently, Cardona (1965a, 1969) has compared Pāṇinian rules with those of prātiśākhyas and other grammars in order to emphasize the principles governing Pāṇini's formulations or morphophonemic rule (see section III.1.5.4b).[314] Nevertheless, it must be said that detailed comparativ studies of different Indian grammars from the point of view of their theoretical assumptions remain desiderata. Much work has been done to compare various versions of gaṇa-pāṭhas (see section III.1.2.2) and various lexica and indices have been compiled which facilitate comparative studies (see section III.1.2.3). However, no fully documented studies have been made of the systems of non-Pāṇinian grammar which bring out the reasons for following certain procedures instead of others.[315]

Several short discussions have dealt with the relations between Pāṇinian grammar and the Indian logical system called *Nyāya*. Matilal (1959; 1960-61) compared the Nyāya concept of *karaṇa* 'cause' with the Pāṇinian concept of *karaṇa* 'instrument, means' and concluded (1959: 307; 1960-61: 67) that Nyāya took its concept from grammarians, who in turn simply followed real language usage. Matilal (1966) has also discussed the Nyāya analysis of sentences, which deals in terms of subjects and predications, in contrast with the Pāṇinian analysis, which considers an action (*kriyā*) the principal qualificand (*mukhya-viśeṣya*) in any sentence meaning. Cardona (1974b: 245-46, 251-54) has also compared the Nyāya and Pāṇinian approaches, with special emphasis on agency and animation: Nyāya insists that an agent is necessarily a sentient being (*cetana*), Pāṇini does not (see section III.1.5.5c.1). Barlingay (1964: 97-100) has also treated briefly the Nyāya and grammarians' views concerning what is considered the basic unit of meaning, whether a sentence or subsentential elements (see section VI.2.4), and V. Subrahmanya Śāstrī (1973) has discussed some differences between grammarians and Naiyāyikas concerning the concept of object (*karman*).

There have been other, more general studies in which Pāṇini's system is compared with others. In two such studies, Renou (1957b; 1961) dealt with the Vedānta philosopher Śaṅkara's reasoning in so far as it reflects an indebtedness to grammatical methods and with the poetician Mammaṭa's discussions of grammatical points. Of more direct interest in the present context, because it attempts to establish some direct historical relation of indebtedness, is Renou's study (1941-42) of the connection between the ritual and the major school of ritual exegesis and theory (Mīmāṃsā) on the one hand and Pāṇini's system on the other.[316] Garge (1949; 1952: 235-42) approached a similar topic differently; he investigated the indebtedness of the Mīmāṃsā thinkers Jaimini and Śabara to Pāṇini and the Mahā-bhāṣya by studying direct citations.[317] Moghe (1971) dealt with the metarules and techniques common to Mīmāṃsā and grammar.

Renou, on the other hand, attempted to demonstrate that much of the method and terminology of Pāṇinian grammar had its origin in the ritual. For example, he remarked (1941-42: 156), "*Karman* 'action' (en tant qu'objet direct, objet du verbe transitif)[318] appartient aux milieux rituels où le mot, depuis le RV [Ṛg-veda], désignait l'acte par excellence, c'est-à-dire le rite." Nevertheless, Renou (1941-42: 156-57) cautiously admitted that the kāraka category names (see section III.1.5.5c.1) were particular to grammar and could not be equated directly with homophonous terms of the ritual. Despite this, Al-George (1957; 1968) assumed, on the basis of Renou's study, that these kāraka category names were direct calques on the ritual; see section III.1.5.5c.1. I think it worth noting, in view of the sweeping generalization that Renou's rather cautious study led to, that some of Renou's comparisons are themselves not very precise. For example, he says (Renou 1941-42: 127), "Quant à *niyama*, le mot est aussi du rituel . . ." and later on the same page refers to the definition of a niyama given in the late Mīmāṃsā handbook Mīmāṃsā-nyāya-prakāśa, a definition which he calls "conforme à l'esprit des grammairiens." This is imprecise. Consider the sentences

(1) *vrīhīn avahanti* 'One thrashes (that is, one is to thrash) the rice.'
(2) *pañca pañca-nakhā bhakṣyāḥ* 'Five five-nailed animals are to be eaten (that is, one may eat only five five-nailed animals).'

Now, husked rice has to be used in the offering at a sacrifice. But one can remove the husk from rice in ways other than by thrashing; for example, one could use ones nails to do this. Moreover, the two methods cannot be used at once. Given that one might remove the husk from rice in a way other than through thrashing, (1) states that one must thrash the rice. The sentence serves to enjoin an act which, in given circumstances, might not obtain. The case is different with (2). This is what in Mīmāṃsā terminology is called a *parisaṃkhyā* (' **exclusion** '). If one is hungry, one might eat different animals at once. Sentence (2) serves to exclude other animals than the ones mentioned by enumerating these. However, to grammarians (2) is a niyama, a restriction which serves to exclude something which could tentatively apply (see section III.1.5.2c), and commentators recognize that what the Mīmāṃsakas call a *parisaṃkhyā* is treated as a niyama by them (see Vedavrata [1962-63: I: 23]).[319]

1.5.7b. *Comparisons with modern systems and techniques.*

The most sweeping comparison of Pāṇini's grammatical system with modern western linguistic approaches[320] is by Vidya Niwas Misra (1966). He sees in Pāṇini's system a synthesis of item-and-arrangement and item-and-process (1966: 66), transformational grammar (1966: 34. 36. 120), and stratificational grammar (1966: 94, 103). He also calls Pāṇini's syntax "a combination of transformational and stratificational techniques" (1966: 113). Vidya Niwas Misra does not justify these comparisons in detail, so that they remain mere claims, with some justification, to be sure, but certainly subject to much more study.

Staal (1967) has also attempted to find in Pāṇini's system an array of transformational techniques (1967: 37-38) and speaks (1967: 39) of "transformationally derived sentences" in the context of Pāṇini's grammar. Moreover, Staal (1967: 46) has brought into the Indian scene the distinction between competence and performance, drawing a sharp line between Mīmāṃsā, which, he suggests, " . . . is interested in language from the point of view of performance, but not of competence . . .", and Pāṇinian grammar, interested in competence and performance: "in fact Mīmāṃsā pays no attention to the deep structure which represents competence and which was studied so intensively by the grammarians." Cardona (1970d) has argued that this is too sweeping a claim and represents an importation of ideas – themselves of arguable validity – onto the Indian scene which are not supported by the statements found in the Indian texts.[321]

Kiparsky and Staal (1969), in addition to treating Pāṇini's kāraka categories as deep structure (see sections III.1.5.5c.1, 2), claim that, unlike a typical transformational grammar, Pāṇini's grammar does not include syntactic rules

rules which operate on what has been derived by other syntactic rules. Cardona (forthcoming c, section 19) presents evidence to show that Pāṇini does indeed state such rules. A sentence such as

(1) *devadattam grāmaṃ gacchantaṃ paśyāmi* 'I see Devadatta (who is) going to the village.'

derives from an earlier string

(2) *devadatta-am grāma-am gam-laṭ dṛś-laṭ*

in which the L-suffix *laṭ* has been introduced twice to denote an agent (see note 152); there are two agents involved, one an agent of going (*gam*), the other an agent of seeing (*dṛś*, in suppletive relations with *paś*). Similarly, there are two objects, one relative to going, the other relative to seeing, so that the affix *am* is introduced twice. Now, the agent of going, specifically the person named Devadatta, is also the object of seeing. The L-suffix *laṭ* introduced after *gam* is thus coreferential (*samānâdhikaraṇa*) with the form *devadatta-am*, which terminates in a second-triplet ending. Pāṇini provides (3.2.124: *laṭaḥ śatṛ-śānacāv aprathamā-samānâdhikaraṇe*) that *laṭ* is replaced by the participial affixes *śatṛ* (= *at*), *śānac* (= *āna*) if it is coreferential (*samānâdhikaraṇa*) with a form which terminates in an affix belonging to a triplet of endings other than the first (*aprathamā-*). In (2), then, the non-nominative form *devadatta-am* is coreferential with the *laṭ* which follows *gam*, so that the latter is replaced by *at: gam-laṭ* → *gam-at* → *gacchat*. After iteration of the rule which introduces a second-triplet ending when an object is to be denoted, one derives *gacchat-am* (→ *gacchantam*).

Ananthanarayana (1970) compared Pāṇini's grammar with case grammar. However, this is not a true comparison, since Ananthanarayana has simply carried into Pāṇini's grammar the apparatus of case grammar as formulated by Fillmore (1968), thereby omitting to note that, though case grammar is indeed possibly the closest modern analog to Pāṇini's system, there are nevertheless important differences between the two. Cardona (1974b: 244-45) has briefly sketched one difference: the notion of subject is absent from Pāṇini's system. In my opinion, Pāṇini's approach differs in an essential way from case grammar. In the latter, one is forced to posit surface categories such as subject or others, depending on the "surface phenomena" of individual languages. This is motivated, I think, in the first instance because the deep syntactico-semantic categories such as Agent, Object, have, in this system, to be defined in purely semantic terms. This requirement is, in turn, motivated by another attitude, namely that the grammarian is seeking to posit universal categories of language. It is, I think, clear that Pāṇini did not define his kāraka categories in purely semantic terms (see section III.1.5.5c.1). Nor is there a scintilla of evidence anywhere in the writings of Pāṇinīyas or in Pāṇini's Aṣṭādhyāyī to suggest that they were seeking to posit universal categories of language. There aim was straightforward: to give a set of rules which account for correct Sanskrit usage.

The same considerations I think serve to indicate that A. C. Sinha's (1973) recent attempt to find in Pāṇini's system a system of generative semantics is at best misguided.

In view of these recent attempts to read several modern theories into Pāṇini's grammar, I think it worthwhile to consider possible reasons for this phenomenon. For I think most of the scholars who have propounded such views have done so in the honest belief that Pāṇini indeed held the positions they attribute to him. Consider now the following features of Pāṇini's system.

(a) Pāṇini states rules of the type, "When meaning M is to be denoted, introduce affix A" (see section III.1.5.1a).

(b) Among such rules are such as state, "When an agent (object, etc.) is to be denoted, introduce affix A", so that Pāṇini operates with categories such as agent, object – the kāraka categories (see section III.1.5.5c.1).

(c) The sentences

(3) *kaṭaṃ karoti* 'He is making a mat.'
(4) *kāṣṭhaṃ bhasma karoti* 'He is turning the log to ashes.'
(5) *grāmaṃ gacchati* 'He is going to the village.'

are all derived in precisely the same way, with the affix *-am* introduced to denote an object, and given the same analysis: there is an object - action relation. This although the mat is an effected object (*kārya* 'faciendum'), the log an affected object (*vikārya*), and the village an object which is reached (*prāpya*).

(d) Pāṇini relates utterances to each other (see section III.1.5.1a). Moreover, he distinguishes between items which, in an utterance actually used, have the same form. For example,

(6) *rājñaḥ puruṣaḥ* 'king's man'

and

(7) *odanasya paktā* 'cooker of rice'

both contain genitive forms. But in (6) the genitive affix is introduced to denote a relation (*saṃbandha*), whereas in (7) it is introduced to denote an object (*karman*, see Cardona [1970c: 229-30 n. 11]).

(e) Pāṇini posits basic bases and affixes which are replaced. For example, *paś* replaces *dṛś* 'see' and *ina* replaces the instrumental singular ending *ā* in given contexts.

Taken separately, these can lead to certain conclusions. From (a) one could conclude that, since Pāṇini states meaning conditions as the first conditions for derivations, he is indeed a generative semanticist. And this conclusion could appear to be supported by (b). However, once one considers all of Pāṇini's kāraka categorization rules, it becomes clear that the kāraka categories are not defined in purely semantic terms, so that this conclusion is attenuated. Moreover, had Pāṇini's principal emphasis been on semantics, one should expect him to make some explicit statement about the differences among sentences (3) - (5) of (c), differences well known to and discussed by Pāṇinīyas (see Cardona [1974b: 28 n. 7a and below, section III. 2.6.2]). In addition, Pāṇini classes as agent (*kartṛ*) such things as an axe, so that sentences such as III.1.5.1a (4) (*devadatta odanaṃ pacati*) and III. 1.5.5c.1 (7) (*paraśur vṛkṣaṃ chinatti*) receive the same analysis and derivation. On the other hand, Pāṇini does recognize a distinction between agents which are sentient beings (*cittavat*) and those which are not. He has a special rule (1.3.88) which provides that only active endings occur after a causative verb if the agent of the action denoted by the primitive verb is a sentient being (see Cardona [1974b: 285 n. 28]). These facts are best accomodated as follows. Pāṇini does indeed derive sentences and account for relations among sentences. However, his is truly a *śabdânuśāsana* (see section III.1.5.1b) For Pāṇini is principally concerned with accounting for forms which occur within sentences and the relations among such forms. In this context, the distinction between a sentient agent and one who is not is pertinent in that it is associated with a rule of the grammar which provides for the use of affixes. But a distinction among effected, affected, and reached objects is not pertinent to the affixation rules which serve to derive (c) (3) - (5) above. Of course, this distinction is not merely semantically pertinent but also syntactically pertinent, since (4) can answer to the question *kāṣṭhasya kiṃ karoti* 'What is he doing to the log? ', but (3) and (5) do not answer similar questions. However, this distinction is not grammatically pertinent in the context of Pāṇini's system. For here a grammatically pertinent distinction is one which requires a particular rule of affixation, affix replacement, suppletion, or augmenting. And this gets to the core of Pāṇini's system, the grammar provides derivations in terms of bases and affixes (see section III.1.5.1a).[322] From this one might conclude that Pāṇini's grammar deals essentially with morphology, in an item-and-process way at that, as shown by (e). But this is an untenable view, since Pāṇini does deal with syntactic relations and relations among certain sentences. Again, since Pāṇini does indeed relate sentences such as III.1.5.1a (3) - (4), one might conclude that he was a transformationalist (cf. Staal [1967: 39]). But this too is an untenable view. Pāṇini does not derive one sentence from another, nor does he operate with actual embedding to derive a sentence such as (1) derived from (2) given above.

My point is this. As one blind man, touching the trunk of an elephant, might say he is touching a snake, whereas another, touching the elephant's legs, might say he is among trees, yet the elephant remains what he is, so have the modern authors whose views I have noted looked only at parts of Paṇini's system in isolation, concluding therefrom that Pāṇini was this or that. None of these views is without some foundation, yet none of them is fully acceptable either. The fault lies in taking some small part of the system, comparing it with a modern system, and concluding that the two are indeed the same.

1.5.7c. *A note regarding methodology.*

There has arisen recently a controversy based, in the first instance, on a misunderstanding. Thieme (1961: x) warned against a temptation on the part of modern linguists "to be more interested in our own theories concerning the Sanskrit grammarians than their actual teachings." This sentiment was echoed by R. Rocher (1968a: 339) who noted – though without referring to Thieme – that scholars often too quickly make comparisons of Indian grammarians' statements with other systems before the former are themselves sufficiently well understood. Cardona (1969: 3) reiterated Thieme's warning in Thieme's own words and said that "the comparisons of this kind that have been made (e.g. Misra [1966], Staal [1967]) risk both being superficial and committing the error alluded to by Thieme . . ." Staal unfortunately understood such statements – Cardona's in particular – in a manner different from the one in which they were intended. He believes that two claims were being made: "The first is that the Sanskrit grammarians have in the past been studied by philologists but neglected by linguists. The second, turning the previous supposition into a principle of research, is that the materials have first to be made available and interpreted by philologists before they can be evaluated by linguists" (Staal [1972: xi, cf. 1970: 507]). As has subsequently been noted (Cardona [1973e: 46-47], R. Rocher [forthcoming a]), this is not what was claimed by Thieme, Rocher, or Cardona. None of them has claimed that the grammarians were earlier not studied by linguists such as Whitney or Bloomfield. Nor have they made this a principle of research. What they have warned against is simply a hasty superimposition of modern systems onto Indian grammarians such as Pāṇini. That some theories have been read into Pāṇini without sufficient justification is, I think, patent (see section III.1.5.7b). I agree on this point with R. Rocher, who speaks (forthcoming a) of "a genuine concern that hurried comparisons between familiar Western methods and partly understood Indian methods may distort – and in fact have distorted – the interpretation of Pāṇinian grammar."

A historical note is in order in this context. In the last quarter of the nineteenth century there were scholars like Bhandarkar, Kielhorn and his student Liebich, who truly understood Pāṇini's grammar and communicated their ideas. Of the scholars of that epoch who dealt with Pāṇini, however, only Whitney can, I think, be said to have had an interest in purely linguistic questions and an insight into them. And in the early twentieth century only Bloomfield among scholars working in Pāṇini can be considered to have had a particular attitude towards linguistic questions.[323] But Whitney, though I think he had a deeper insight into the methodological aspects of Pāṇini's grammar than his contemporaries, was totally unsympathetic and arrogant: he did not like what he saw in Pāṇini because it did not agree with his concept of grammar or Sanskrit, hence he rejected it outright. And Bloomfield devoted almost none of his scholarly energies to questions concerning Pāṇini's system per se. This is tragic. For, at the time Whitney was addressing his polemics against scholars like Böhtlingk and Liebich (see section III.1.5.8), great insight might have resulted from a scholarly exchange if Whitney's opponents had been able to answer his more theoretical objections – such as his dismissal of the kāraka theory (see section III.1.5.5c.1) – with equal insight. The result has been that there has indeed developed a chasm between those who know Pāṇini well but have little interest in questions of a purely linguistic and theoretical nature and those who, though interested in these questions, know little Sanskrit and less Pāṇini. These scholars, if they show any interest in Pāṇini's work at all, have to depend on translations, which are themselves inadequate (see section III.1.2.1). Moreover, of the great mass of commentatorial literature of the Pāṇinīyas, in which all major questions are discussed thoroughly and in which are also treated many questions of contemporary interest, only recently has there begun to appear a small number of trustworthy translations.

It is perhaps impossible for a student of Pāṇini who also has some familiarity with some modern theories completely to avoid seeking parallels or to interpret what he studies in the light of what he knows. And the situation I have outlined above makes this all the more probable. Yet an effort can and should be made, I think, to make broad comparisons only after one has considered Pāṇini in toto.

1.5.8. *Evaluations of Pāṇini's grammar and its purpose.*

In evaluating Pāṇini's grammar as a description of a language – and not from the point of view of theoretical models – one has to accept that he indeed describes a real language. In connection with this three major questions have been the objects of discussion: With what known specimens of Sanskrit does the grammar most closely accord? What is meant by the term *bhāṣā* in Pāṇini's rules? And is one justified in speaking of a "grammarians' Sanskrit"?

1.5.8a. *The language described by Pāṇini.*

The basic work in comparing Pāṇini's rules and what they provide with the language represented in literary texts was done by Liebich (1886-87; 1891), who was followed by Franke (1890b) and Wecker (1906).[324] Liebich's principal conclusion (1891: 47) was that the language described by Pāṇini was syntactically as good as identical with the language of the brāhmaṇas and sūtra texts.[325] That Pāṇini's description of how the aorist was used tallied closely with the use of the aorist in the Aitareya-brāhmaṇa had earlier been pointed out by R. G. Bhandarkar (1864 [= 1927-33 2: 416-19]; see also 1885 [= 1927-33 1: 159-61]).

In his grammar Pāṇini uses the term *bhāṣā* (*bhāṣāyām* "in the bhāṣā"). Franke (1891: 55-78; cf. 1890b: 117-20) took up the rules in which Pāṇini uses this and came to an interesting conclusion. According to Franke, *bhāṣā* refers to a real language. But it is a spoken language, Sanskrit, of a type which Pāṇini himself would not consider exemplary. As for Pāṇini's Sanskrit, says Franke, it is really neither bhāṣā nor a living language. For the Aṣṭādhyāyī does not teach a single organic language; Pāṇini has taken from both a living language and secondary sources.[326] Franke's view was rejected I think correctly, by Liebich (1892: xxv), although Whitney (1893a: 175) accepted it as "reasonable and safe". Liebich (1891: 48) held what is now probably the most generally accepted view, namely that Pāṇini's bhāṣā was a spoken language – though perhaps not a common vernacular – and a model for his rules. V. S. Agrawala (1963a: 319, 354) was also of this opinion: *bhāṣā* refers to the Sanskrit spoken by the cultured (*śiṣṭa*) model speakers. Renou (1941; 1955: 114-15) again studied Pāṇini's use of this term, but without reaching any definite conclusions (cf. Renou [1969: 492-93]). Most recently, S. Sen (1970: 10-12) has denied that Pāṇini referred to a specific language at all, claiming instead that " . . . it is evident that *Bhāṣā* in the sūtras of Pāṇini indicates the 'style' of discourse." I do not think this is incompatible with the communis opinio, which I consider acceptable, namely that *bhāṣā* in the Aṣṭādhyāyī refers to the spoken Sanskrit of model speakers. There remains some work to be done concerning the contexts of rules in which this term is used.[327]

1.5.8b. *"Grammarians' Sanskrit"*.

The major proponent of the view that there was a "grammarians' Sanskrit" was Whitney. Before him, Benfey (1874: 3-4) had spoken of two legacies of India: Vedic, a language without a grammar, and a most wonderful grammar without the language on which it was based.[328] Whitney himself (1884: 282 [= Silverstein 1972: 290]) spoke of "the subject of Hindu grammatical science, a peculiar dialect of Sanskrit, different both from the pre-classical dialects and from the classical, and standing either between them or beside them in the general history of Indian language." This is not to say that Whitney believed Pāṇini had somehow invented a fictional language. On the contrary. Whitney's attitude, as far as I can discern from his writings, is as follows. Pāṇini described a real language.[329] However, this language was not a vernacular in the normal stream of Indic development; it was a learned dialect,[330] which suffered from pedantry at the hands of grammarians: "Moreover, as soon as it took on the character of a learned dialect, it began to be stiffened into something a little unnatural; no dialect ever fell into the hands of grammarians without suffering from their pedantry" (1893a: 176). It is on account of this, I surmise, that Whitney (1893a: 181) distinguished "between the purely hypothetical 'grammarians' Sanskrit' and the Sanskrit of the literature".

As opposed to Whitney, most other scholars have maintained that Pāṇini described not only a real language but one that was in current use at his time among certain strata, not necessarily just among grammarians; see Goldstücker (1861: 198, 216), Burnell (1875: 109), Böhtlingk (1887a: xviii), K. B. Pathak (1930: 77-78), Thieme (1935a: 81), Renou (1940a: 9; 1941: 248 n. 1). In fact, Whitney's thesis is hardly tenable in the terms he put it. For he claimed that Pāṇini sanctioned forms which were either "barbaric" or simply not part of Sanskrit, and these claims are not proper (see section III.1.5.8c).

1.5.8c. *Deficiencies seen in the grammar.*

Whitney attacked Pāṇini's grammar from two points of view. He asserted (1893a: 176) that Pāṇini left his grammar "abounding in errors, both of omission and commission" and that he couched his description in a form "which is one that no sensible man should ever have chosen . . ."

In judging the correctness of Pāṇini's description, Whitney exhibited both his linguistic prejudices and more than a little arrogance. He had his own ideas about what should be considered correct Sanskrit. For example, he branded a "barbarism" the use of forms such as *prabhavatitarām* 'is quite powerful', in which a finite form (*prabhavati*) is followed by the comparative suffix *tara* (Whitney 1889: 471). Speijer (1886: 189 n. 1) and Liebich (1891: 61) chided Whitney for this and pointed out that such forms were provided for by Pāṇini and used by authors such as Kālidāsa, to which Whitney retorted (1893a: 192): "Now I maintain, and without any fear of successful contradiction, that such formations, no matter who authorizes them, are horrible barbarisms, offenses against the proprieties of the universal Indo-European speech." Such assertions of Whitney's were later properly criticized by K. C. Chatterji (1952; 1953). On the other hand, there are areas which require additional research. Recently Palsule (1968) and Laddu (1971a) have discussed the question of possible omissions in Pāṇini's grammar. Palsule (1968: 151) judiciously notes that it is difficult to determine precisely where Pāṇini drew the line between items he would derive by his rules and those which, either because he treated them as derived with uṇādi affixes (see section III.1.4.1b) or because he considered them obscure with respect to derivation, he left unmentioned. Laddu is less cautious and concludes (1971a: 322) that there are two pairs of forms concerning which "the early grammarians appear to be severely diverging from the recorded literary usages extant before us."

Whitney's principal target in accusing Pāṇini and Pāṇinīyas of unreliability was the dhātu-pāṭha (see sections III.1.2.2, III.1.3.5). He set forth his views in 1884 (282-84 [= Silverstein 1972: 290-92]), but had arrived at them some years before, since by 1879 his student Edgren had written his dissertation (Edgren 1882, see Whitney [1884: 283] [= Silverstein 1972: 291]) separating the "real" from the "fictitious" roots of Sanskrit. The main points of Whitney's – and Edgren's – are as follows. Of the nearly two thousand roots of the dhātu-pāṭha as published by Westergaard (1841) and Böhtlingk (1887a) more than half are not attested in literature. Some might occur in texts not yet found (in Whitney's day), but certainly not the entire remainder. Others may have been posited as bases for derivatives, but such instances are not too numerous. Liebich (1891: 51-52) and Böhtlingk (1893) answered Whitney, but their arguments were not strong. For example, Liebich pointed out that an attack on Pāṇini should not be concentrated on the dhātu-pāṭha, since this is not the strongest or most trustworthy part of the Aṣṭādhyāyī, liable to interpolation. Whitney retorted scathingly, speaking of "this free and easy way of disposing of the subject" (1893a: 183). Whitney was cautious and anticipated avenues of escape from his objections. He envisaged, as I noted, that some roots were posited not because finite forms derived from them were used but because they served as bases for deriving nominal forms (see already Westergaard [1841: viii]). He also anticipated that some of the roots in question might appear in texts yet to be edited. Von Schroeder (1879, 1895) did indeed make known such forms in a Vedic text.

Another approach was yet to be explored fully: roots given in the dhātu-pāṭha might appear in their Middle Indic shapes and be attested in Middle and even Modern Indic. This approach was used by Bühler (1894) and, following him, Franke (1894a).[331] In addition, Kittel (1893; cf. 1895: 81-82) proposed to show that the dhātu-pāṭha contained Dravidian roots. Two of these approaches – the positing of roots to account for nominal derivatives and the occurrence of later Indic forms – have been investigated more fully by Palsule (1961: 208-13); and S. M. Katre (1944: 65-72; cf. 1938-39: 485-86) considered Middle Indicisms. However, Palsule (1961: 213) admits that questions remain unanswered and that one has ultimately to resort to the hypothesis of lost literary texts. He nevertheless concludes (1961: 215-16) that it is unproductive simply to speak of fictitious roots. The most ambitious work in the direction noted is by Bhāgīratha Prasāda Tripāṭhī (1965), wherein the author gives an alphabetically arranged catalog of roots found in different dhātu-pāṭhas together with attestations – verbal and nominal forms – in Sanskrit, Pāli, Aprabhraṃśa, other Prākṛts, and also Hindi and Bundeli (see 1965: *cha*). Bhāgīratha Prasāda Tripāṭhī's professed aim (1965: *ca*) is to refute Whitney's claims. More recently, R. Rocher (1968b) has reconsidered the approach adopted by Bühler and others. After pointing out some factual errors in Edgren's and Bühler's studies, she notes (1968b: 705) that it is wrong to think that Pāṇini or a successor of his should have included in the dhātu-pāṭha large numbers of non-Sanskrit roots.[332] However, she does admit that middle-Indicisms which had been adopted in Sanskrit could be admitted by the grammarians. Rocher ends with a worthwhile appeal: more detailed work has to be done on the commentaries to the dhātu-pāṭha.

In my opinion the present state of this particular issue is as follows. It is admitted that the dhātu-pāṭha as now known contains roots forms of which do not occur in literary Sanskrit texts. However, it is also accepted that some Middle Indic can account for some roots. Moreover, the dhātu-paṭha suffered interpolations. Before one can come close to a final answer, more studies are required on the commentaries through which we know the dhātu-pāṭha, aimed at reaching, if possible, a critical edition of this text. In any case, no knowledgeable scholar would now hold the view that the dhātu-pāṭha reflects wholesale and willful fabrication by grammarians bent on propagating their pedantically ossified "grammarians' Sanskrit".

Very few scholars followed Whitney in his extreme criticisms, although others did remark on the alleged strangeness of Pāṇini's system (Foucher [1900: 946]) or even the lack of system (Jacobi [1913: 265-66]). However, a recent work by Narendra Chandra Nath (1969) is very Whitneyesque in its approach. The author's main thesis is that Pāṇini's description is unsatisfactory, and he goes to great lengths to prove this for all aspects of the grammar. However, Nath's work is characterized by a naiveté concerning grammatical method and an unwillingness to accept basic presuppositions of Pāṇini's system which severely attenuate all his conclusions. Two examples will illustrate this. Nath claims (1969: 29) that the items *avara* etc., which Pāṇini classes as pronominals (*sarvanāman*, see section III.1.3.6c), should not be so classed, so that Pāṇini's definition of *sarvanāman* 'pronoun' is too broad. Although Nath recognizes the obvious, namely that *avara* behaves like other pronominals such as *tad* with respect to grammatical operations, still he says, "But outward appearance need not be the testing ground for deciding parts of speech," as though it were not proper to place items in a class on the basis of shared operations. Again, Nath (1969: 33) argues that Pāṇini's definition of a pada (see note 151) as an item which terminates in a nominal or verbal ending is improper because there are forms such as *pitā* 'father' (nom. sg.) which contain no ending. Nath of course admits, as he must, that here an ending has indeed been introduced and then deleted. He insists nevertheless that this is improper because, if such deletion is admitted, "then anything can be admitted anywhere." However, Nath does not, indeed he cannot, demonstrate that Pāṇini indulged in such unprincipled procedures.[333]

1.5.8d. *On the origins and purposes of grammar.*

In recent years there has arisen a controversy concerning the origins and purposes of Indian grammars, Pāṇini's in particular. In the introductory section of the Mahā-bhāṣya, Kātyāyana and Patañjali note that one of the purposes of grammar is merit (*dharma*) obtained through the knowledge and use of correct speech (see Thieme [1931: 29-32], Biardeau [1964a: 35-36]). Indeed, Pāṇinīyas consider grammar not only a means whereby correct usage is taught and discriminated from incorrect usage but also a means of attaining ultimate release (*mokṣa*).[334] This is obviously connected with a general Indian attitude towards knowledge and speech. Scharfe (1961a: 10) stressed the magical purpose of grammar, basing his claim on a passage from the Mahā-bhāṣya where Pāṇini is said to have sat in a pure place facing east, with a ring of Kuśa grass around his fourth finger,[335] when he composed his grammar. Staal (1963: 256) reacted strongly against this and objected to the "trend to discern 'magico-religious' backgrounds in everything Indian," to which Scharfe (1971a: 5 n. 42) responded by saying that he had merely been setting down Patañjali's view.[336] I agree that Staal has missed the point to an extent. His contention (1963: 256) that Pāṇini's assuming this attitude is comparable "with the fact that some Western professors put on their gown before they teach" is not to the point. There is clearly more in the Indian's attitude towards grammar. Yet I also think a bit of subtlety is required in considering this question. Though it is true that an Indian grammarian attached a deeper purpose to grammar, this does not mean he had to seek all his ideas in his ritual background. The degree of influence on grammar of this ritual is a possible area of research. But I do not think it proper or profitable simply to assume or insist that every aspect of grammar has a religio-ritual origin (see section III.1.5.5c.1).

1.5.8e. *Conclusion.*

Pāṇini's grammar has been evaluated from various points of view. After all these different evaluations, I think the grammar merits asserting, with Bloomfield (1933: 11), that it is "one of the greatest monuments of human intelligence."

2. THE MAHĀ-BHĀṢYA.

2.1. *General introduction: early commentaries.*

It is common in India that an author composes an autocommentary on his work. In the case of a grammar, an explanation (*vyākhyāna*) of rules consisted, according to Patañjali (Kielhorn [1880-85: I: 11. 22-23, 12. 24-26]), of the following: an analysis of a rule into its components;[337] suppletion of items necessary to the understanding of the rule;[338] citation of examples (*udāharaṇa*) and counterexamples (*pratyudāharaṇa*) illustrating how the rule operates. It is possible that Patañjali himself knew of such commentaries on the Aṣṭādhyāyī.[339] And there is some support for supposing this. For example, in his discussion of rule 3.3.131, Patañjali says (Kielhorn [1880-85: I: 158. 7]), "Only the L-suffix *laṭ* (that is, a form containing this) is given as an example (of the rule)" (*laḍ evôdāhriyate*). Now, the preceding discussion does not contain such a citation. Yet Patañjali directly uses the form *udāhriyate* "is given as an example". Kaiyaṭa comments on this and notes that Patañjali assumes such an example to have been given in running commentaries (*vṛtti*) on the rules (Vedavrata [1962-63: III: 347]: *vṛttiṣv iti bhāvaḥ*). Renou (1940a: 11, 1969: 486) unequivocally assumed that such a commentary contemporary with Pāṇini did at one time exist; see also Yudhiṣṭhira Mīmāṃsaka (1973: I: 437). R. S. Bhattacharya (1955a) devoted a study to a consideration of such ancient vṛttis, including the ones which, he assumed, were cited in the Mahā-bhāṣya. Bhattacharya proposed (1955a: 174) some ways of determining when Patañjali cites such an old vṛtti. For example, when Patañjali says *kim ihôdāharaṇam* "What is an example for this rule? " and goes on to give an example, this is supposed to belong to an old vṛtti. Mangala Deva Shastri (1947) noted that the Siddhânta-kaumudī (see section IV.3.2) replaces traditional examples for rules with sectarian examples, while the Kāśikā (see section IV.2.1) generally agrees in its examples with the Mahā-bhāṣya. He proposed (1947: 336) that this is satisfactorily explained "only by assuming the pre-existence of a common stock of traditional *udāharaṇas* . . ."[340] On the other hand, Thieme (1932: 241-42) believed that at Patañjali's time there were no such vṛttis. However, his emphasis is on the fact that Patañjali does not directly refer to such commentaries using the term *vṛtti.*

Whether or not one accepts the existence of an autocommentary by Pāṇini or of vṛttis either contemporary with him or earlier than Patañjali, the fact remains that the earliest extensive discussion of Pāṇini's rules preserved to us now are contained in the vārttikas of Kātyāyana, which themselves are known as cited and discussed in Patañjali's Mahā-bhāṣya. This text[341] is not, however, a true commentary on the grammar. Kātyāyana and Patañjali do not explain all rules, with examples to show how they operate. They discuss the validity of rules, how they are stated, their relations to other rules, and whether some rules or parts of them can be eliminated without harm and additional rules need to be stated.

2.2. *Editions, translations, and indices of the Mahā-bhāṣya and its commentaries.*

2.2.1. *Editions.*

The standard edition of the text alone of the Mahā-bhāṣya is Kielhorn's (1880-85). This has been reedited by K. V. Abhyankar (1962-72), who has added some notes, entered accents where these are pertinent to the discussions, and cited the text of rules where Kielhorn had earlier given only the number of each rule referred to but not directly cited in the course of a discussion.

The earliest extant commentary on the Mahā-bhāṣya is by Bhartṛhari (see section V.2.3), a commentary to which Kaiyaṭa was indebted (see Vedavrata 1962-63: I: 1). Only one, poor, manuscript of this work is available. The text has been edited recently by Abhyankar and Limaye (1967b, 1969) and, in part, by Swaminathan (1965); see also Kielhorn (1880-85: II: introduction, pp. 12-20). A dissertation (S. S. Dwivedi 1974) has recently been devoted to this text. The question has arisen whether Bhartṛhari's was a commentary on the entire Mahā-bhāṣya or only on the first three quarter-chapters (*pāda*).[342]

Renou (1940a: 24) held the former view, but Aklujkar (1971: 168-9) has presented evidence in support of the second view, arguing that the text is correctly to be called the Tripādī "collection of three pādas".[343]

The two major commentaries on the Mahā-bhāṣya preserved in full are the Mahā-bhāṣya-pradīpa – or simply the Pradīpa – by Kaiyaṭa (early eleventh century)[344] and the Mahā-bhāṣya-pradīpôddyota – or simply Uddyota – by Nāgeśabhaṭṭa.[345] The latter is in the first instance a commentary on the Pradīpa, but Nāgeśa often differs from Kaiyaṭa and offers what he considers the proper interpretation of a Mahā-bhāṣya passage. An excellent though incomplete edition of the Mahā-bhāṣya with the Pradīpa and the Uddyota and also excerpts from the Chāyā commentary by Nāgeśa's student Vaidyanātha was produced by Bhārgavaśāstrī Joshi (1942, 1945, 1951), Śivadatta Kudāla (1912), and Raghunātha Śarmā - Śivadatta Kudāla (1937). Part of the Mahā-bhāṣya with the Pradīpa and Uddyota was also edited by Śaṅkar Śāstrī Mārulkara (1938). A complete edition of the Mahā-bhāṣya with the two major commentaries noted was produced by Guruprasāda Śāstrī (1938) and, more recently, by Vedavrata (1962-63).[346] Kaiyaṭa's Pradīpa was also commented on by the polymath Annambhaṭṭa (17th century, see Bodas [1918: liii-lv]) in his Mahā-bhāṣya-pradīpôddyotana (Uddyotana). The first nine āhnikas of this were edited by P. P. S. Sastri (1948) and T. Chandrasekharan (1952). A new edition of this commentary has been started by M. S. Narasimhacharya (1973), who is also editing other commentaries on the Pradīpa – the Vivaraṇa, Bṛhad-vivaraṇa and Nārāyaṇīya – in addition to the Ratna-prakāśa, another commentary on the Mahā-bhāṣya.[347] Rudradhara Jhā (1954) edited the first nine āhnikas of the Mahā-bhāṣya with the Pradīpa, the Uddyota and his own comments on all three called Tattvâloka.

2.2.2. *Translations.*

There is only one complete translation of the Mahā-bhāṣya, the Marathi translation by V. S. Abhyankar edited by his son (see Abhyankar - Abhyankar [1938-54]). This includes also the text of the Mahā-bhāṣya and notes. P. S. Subrahmanya Sastri (1951-62) undertook what was intended as a full English translation of the text, but finished only 28 āhnikas (to rule 2.4.85). This translation is not very useful to one who is not already familiar with the Aṣṭādhyāyī and the complexities of the argumentation which is portrayed in the Mahā-bhāṣya. For it is a literal translation with almost no annotations, however necessary, and Sanskrit terms are often left untranslated. At the other end of the spectrum is the English translation begun by S. D. Joshi (1968, 1969a) and continued in collaboration with J. A. F. Roodbergen (1971; 1973; Roodbergen - Joshi [1974]). Literal translations are here accompanied by extensive notes clarifying the arguments involved. Charudeva Shastri (1968) has translated into Hindi, with annotations, the first nine āhnikas, and the first five āhnikas have been translated into Hindi by Madhusūdana Prasāda Mishra (1967). The first five āhnikas were translated into German by Trapp (1933), an unsatisfactory work which Thieme criticized (1935b: 173 n. 2 et passim, see Thieme [1956: 20 n. 50]). K. V. Abhyankar and J. M. Shukla (1968) have begun an English translation of which the first fascicle (containing the first āhnika) has appeared and in which extensive references are given to Bhartṛhari's commentary on the Mahā-bhāṣya (section III.2.2.1). The introductory chapter of the Mahā-bhāṣya – the Pasaśā – has also been translated by Danielssohn (1883) and K. C. Chatterji (1957). The latter is to be singled out for its extensive notes. The collaborative effort of Renou and Ojihara (1960-62; Ojihara [1967a]), though ostensibly only a translation of the Kāśikā (see section IV.2.1), contains useful and extensive summaries of the materials in the Mahā-bhāṣya which form the background of the Kāśikā's statements. Ojihara (1958-60; 1961; 1963; 1965a) has also devoted several papers to detailed translations of some Mahā-bhāṣya discussions. Two such discussions were also translated and studied by Geiger (1908) and Thieme (1935b). Shefts (1961: 18-38) has translated extracts from the Mahā-bhāṣya on rules (3.1.67-83) which deal with the introduction of post-verbal affixes such as the *-a-* of *pac-a-ti* 'is cooking'. More recently, R. Rocher (1968a) has paraphrased the Mahā-bhāṣya arguments on restrictive rules concerning the distribution of parasmaipada and ātmanepada affixes (see section III.1.5.5b.1). Wezler (1969) also cites and translates passages relative to the metarules he has studied. And Cardona (1973b: 11-32; 1974b: 254-79) has given paraphrases with explanations of the Mahā-bhāṣya discussions on rules 1.4.105-08, 1.4.23, vārttikas 12-15 on 3.1.7, vārttikas 5, 8-10 on 3.1.87, and vārttikas 7-9 on 2.3.1. Two short but important passages were translated by Renou (1956a: 76-80): the Mahā-bhāṣya on 6.3.109, in which Patañjali takes up what is meant by *śiṣṭa* ('élite, educated', that is, speakers of correct Sanskrit) and on 2.4.56, a famous passage in which is presented a short dialogue between a charioteer and a grammarian, the latter being one who knows what the grammar provides but not necessarily what is required (*iṣṭa* 'desired') by correct usage.

Of special interest have been passages from the Mahā-bhāṣya wherein are discussed questions of general linguistic and philosophical import (see section III.2.6.3). Such passages have been translated and studied by V. G. Paranjpe (1922), Strauss (1927b), Frauwallner (1960), Scharfe (1961), and Biardeau (1964a: 35-63).

2.2.3. *Indices.*

There is a complete word-index to the Mahā-bhāṣya, with references to pages and lines of Kielhorn's edition (1880-85), compiled by Pathak and Chitrao (1928). The same authors compiled (1935) a word-index to Kātyāyana's vārttikas.[348] Lahiri (1935) composed a concordance showing the rules of the Aṣṭādhyāyī to which Patañjali refers in the course of discussions without citing them directly. Necessary modifications to Lahiri's work are supplied in Birwé (1966).

2.3. *On criteria for distinguishing Kātyāyana's and Patañjali's statements; śloka-vārttikas.*

As I have noted (section III.2.1), Kātyāyana's vārttikas are known only as incorporated in the Mahā-bhāṣya. The essential work in arriving at criteria for separating Kātyāyana's and Patañjali's statements was done by Kielhorn (1876a;[349] 1880-85: II: introduction, p. 8 n. 2; 1886e): Patañjali normally repeats or paraphrases a vārttika, which he then goes on to discuss. This topic has been restudied recently by Vedpati Mishra (1970: 75-113) and Laddu (1970), both of whom differ from Kielhorn concerning the attribution of some statements to Kātyāyana.[350]

The Mahā-bhāṣya contains also vārttika-like statements in verse form called *śloka-vārttikas.*[351] Goldstücker (1861: 93-99) studied some of these and concluded that they were the work of different authors.[352] Kielhorn (1886f) also discussed these śloka-vārttikas and concluded similarly that many of the verses which state arguments cannot be attributed to Kātyāyana or Patañjali. Later Bhārgavaśāstrī Joshi (1945: introduction, pp. 2-9) discussed a selection of these vārttikas. The most recent treatment of śloka-vārttikas is by Vedpati Mishra (1970: 166-75), who also attributes these to various authors, and includes among the authors also Kātyāyana and Patañjali. No full study has yet been made of all the śloka-vārttikas and how they relate in detail to the statements of Kātyāyana and Patañjali.[353]

2.4. *On the history of the Mahā-bhāṣya text.*

The history of the text of the Mahā-bhāṣya has involved scholars in considerable controversy over a long time, and views which were once refuted have been restated, again refuted, only to be repeated once more. Two principal views have been held. Some scholars, above all R. G. Bhandarkar and Kielhorn, maintained that the text of the Mahā-bhāṣya preserved in manuscripts represents quite faithfully the text as composed by Patañjali. Other, principal among them Weber, held that the text was at one time destroyed – or nearly destroyed – and then reconstituted, so that what is now available is not Patañjali's own work.

The controversy centered about the interpretation of two sets of verses, by Bhartṛhari in his Vākya-padīya (see section VI.2) and by the Kashmiri chronicler Kalhaṇa in his Rāja-taraṅgiṇī. At the end of the second book of the Vākya-padīya,[354] Bhartṛhari briefly recounts the earlier history of the grammatical tradition before him. He says that the Saṃgraha of Vyāḍi[355] fell into disuse and practically perished because students at one time liked only summary works, hence neglected this massive treatise. Then Patañjali composed the Mahā-bhāṣya, a work which contained all the germs of reasoning to be followed in grammatical interpretations and of such depth as to be unfathomable but also of such excellent style as to appear shallow. But those whose intellects had not attained a stage of sufficient expertise through proper study could not reach decisions about the final views contained in this work. Hence, the work of the ṛṣi Patañjali (see note 357) was reduced to a mere semblance of itself by those who, in dealing with it, followed their own dry reasoning, without a tradition to support it. In time that grammatical tradition which had fallen from the students of Patañjali came to exist in the south and there only in books, not as a living tradition. Then Candra and others obtained that traditional knowledge from the Trikūṭa mountain and, following the germs of reasoning found in the Mahā-bhāṣya, they made of this many branches of grammatical thought. In his Rāja-taraṅgiṇī Kalhaṇa speaks of Candra and others as having set into active use in the Kashmir the Mahā-bhāṣya, which is characterized as having been *vicchinna* 'interrupted (that is, which had ceased to be studied traditionally)'.[356]

The sources of mischief and controversy are the phrases *ārṣe viplāvite granthe* 'when the work of the ṛsi[357] had been reduced to a mere semblance of itself', *bhraṣṭo vyākaraṇâgamaḥ* 'the grammatical tradition which had fallen from . . . ', *grantha-mātre vyavasthitaḥ* 'which came to exist in books only', and *vicchinnaṃ mahābhāṣyam* 'the Mahābhāṣya, whose study had been interrupted'. Weber (1862: 159-61) considered the Vākya-padīya verses.[358] He translated *viplāvite* 'devastated' (verwüstet) and *grantha-mātre* 'remained in only one manuscript' (in einer Handschrift nur bestand) instead of "only in books'. Further, Weber (1862: 167) rendered Kalhaṇa's *vicchinna* 'cut up" (zerspalten). He later (1873a: 58; 1873c) emphasized that the Mahā-bhāṣya had undergone much remodeling and asked (1873d: 319-20) what guarantee one had that the text available was not a recast of the original.

R. G. Bhandarkar (1873d [= 1927-33 1: 134-35]), on the other hand, said he saw no evidence in the Vākya-padīya or Rāja-taraṅgiṇī passages indicating any such reconstruction of the text. Kielhorn was of the same opinion and protested (1875: 108) "against the statement ... that at some time or other the *text* of the Mahābhāṣya had been lost, that it had been reconstituted, etc." Weber (1876: 242 n. 38) reiterated his view, upon which Kielhorn (1876c) pointed out[359] the correct interpretation of the words *viplāvita* 'reduced to a semblance' and *grantha-mātre* 'only in books' (thus already Stenzler [1862]). Weber (1877) retorted, but with no new arguments. Later, Bühler (1878) upheld Kielhorn's view and (1882) rejected Weber. Kielhorn himself later (1880-85: I: introduction, p. 8) remained content to emphasize that the manuscripts offer no evidence of various recensions of the text.

Another point which Weber maintained pertinaciously in defending his thesis is that the word *ācārya* 'teacher' in the Mahā-bhāṣya regularly referred to Patañjali, spoken of in the third person (Weber [1862: 155]). From this Weber concluded (1862: 168) that the Mahā-bhāṣya was composed by others than Patañjali.[360] R. G. Bhandarkar (1873c [= 1927-33 1: 126-28]) rebutted Weber and pointed out that *ācārya* in the Mahā-bhāṣya normally refers to Pāṇini. Weber (1873d: 322-23) then retrenched a bit, but refused to give up his view completely. Kielhorn (1876c: 248-50) and R. G. Bhandarkar (1876 [= 1927-33 1: 136-40]) then showed definitively that Weber's view was untenable.

Some of the earlier views, though they had been refuted, were nevertheless repeated by later scholars. Belvalkar (1915: 33) repeated the claim that the Mahā-bhāṣya was spoken of in the Vākya-padīya as existing in only one manuscript. Sköld (1926a: 31-32) too spoke, amid a mass of unsubstantiated generalizations, of "only one authentic manuscript" and doubted that the Mahā-bhāṣya and Pāṇini's grammar "have been so well preserved through thousands of years, as Kielhorn believes." Liebich (1928: 2-3) rightly opposed this revival of an antiquated view: neither Belvalkar nor Sköld gave substantive evidence to support his assertion. Later, Sūrya Kānta (1939: 27) said that his study of the Atharva-veda Prātiśākhya "revealing as it does, at every step, the great role additions and abbreviations have played in Sanskrit literature, have made me feel skeptical about Kielhorn's well-argued plea for the genuineness of the MBh. [Mahā-bhāṣya] text, and I feel to-day more inclined towards the opposite [view] held by Weber, although not in that form, to that extent ... " But Sūrya Kānta did not support his feeling with evidence from the Mahā-bhāṣya itself. More recently, Vidya Niwas Misra (1966: 26) reiterated what was said by Belvalkar, without further consideration.

I think the view held by R. G. Bhandarkar and Kielhorn stands. There are, to be sure, some differences in readings between the text established by Kielhorn on the basis of manuscripts and the text known to Bhartṛhari as reflected in his Tripādī (section III.2.2.1), and some unoriginal remarks may have been incorporated into the text after Bhartṛhari's time (see Kielhorn [1880-85: II: introduction, pp. 18-21]; Liebich [1930: 246-47]; above, section III.1.3.5b). Moreover, some evidence has been suggested of interpolations and minor "corruptions" in the Mahā-bhāṣya.[361] But none of the evidence proposed supports the supposition that the Mahā-bhāṣya was at any time lost and reconstituted.

2.5. *The relation between Kātyāyana and Patañjali and their attitudes towards Pāṇini.*

2.5.1. *Was Kātyāyana an antagonist of Pāṇini and Patañjali his defender?*

Goldstücker (1861: 119-21) maintained that Patañjali was a critic of Kātyāyana, who criticized Pāṇini, but also independently subjected Pāṇini's rules to scrutiny. Weber (1873d: 297-98, 321, 399, 502) carried Goldstücker's position farther, saying that Patañjali's aim was to defend Pāṇini against Kātyāyana (see Kielhorn [1876a: 3-4]). Weber was followed by Burnell (1875: 91) and Böhtlingk (1875a: 188, 1875b: 483), who assumed that Patañjali, as a defender of Pāṇini against Kātyāyana, could not have been the author of the paraphrases of some vārttikas. R. G. Bhandarkar (1876 [= 1927-33 1: 140-48]) and Kielhorn (1876a: 46-56), but especially the latter, demonstrated that this was an improper view: both Kātyāyana and Patañjali had as their aim to discuss the rules and test their validity and consistency. This view has been accepted by most later scholars; see, for example, K. Madhava Krishna Sarma (1940-41: 127; 1968: 48), Gaydhani (1951),[362] Thieme (1956: 12 n. 26), Vedpati Mishra (1970: 60-69).[363] However, the antiquated position has also been set forth as correct even after Kielhorn's definitive study. Belvalkar (1915: 29) still said of Kātyāyana that "... his object was not to explain Pāṇini but to find fault in his grammar." More recently, Vidya Niwas Misra (1966: 25-26) has again accepted the view that one of Kātyāyana's purpose was "... to doubt the validity of the rules of Pāṇini with reference to the language in use in his time and area" and cited Goldstücker as a reference (see Cardona [1968b: 647]).

2.5.2. *Were Kātyāyana and Patañjali adherents of different systems?*.

Another view which has gained some currency is that Kātyāyana somehow belonged to a different school of grammar than did Pāṇini or Patañjali.

Belvalkar (1915: 30-31) believed that, because Kātyāyana used terms such as *svara* 'vowel' in addition to Pāṇinian terms such as *ac* 'vowel' and because a story in the Kathā-sarit-sāgara (12th century) makes Kātyāyana a follower of an earlier school of grammar, it is "probable that he belonged to a school of grammar different from Pāṇini's."[364] Vidya Niwas Misra (1966: 25) not only accepted this, he also claimed that "... Kātyāyana could not understand properly the real significance of the definitional terms in Pāṇini." I think this claim remains unsubstantiated (see Cardona [1968b: 647]).

More recently, S. D. Joshi (1968: i) has again claimed that Kātyāyana was an adherent of a school other than Pāṇini's. Joshi also claims (1968: iii) that Patañjali's discussions were meant to bridge the gap between these schools. According to Joshi (1968: xvi), Pāṇini and Patañjali were descriptive grammarians, as opposed to Kātyāyana, whose views were more philosophical.[365] Cardona (1973d: 235-38) has argued that Joshi's contention rests to a large extent on an argument of silence and that there is no substantive evidence sufficient to demonstrate that Patañjali or Pāṇini was an adherent of a system different from Kātyāyana's.

2.5.3. *Historical change as a motivation for some of Kātyāyana's vārttikas.*

Goldstücker (1861: 122-28) presented evidence to support the thesis that Pāṇini and Kātyāyana were separated by an interval of time sufficient to permit: grammatical forms current at Pāṇini's time to become obsolete by Kātyāyana's time; words to develop different meanings; words and meanings to become obsolete. R. G. Bhandarkar (1883-85 [= 1927-33 4: 267-70]) later translated and discussed a passage from the Mahā-bhāṣya (Kielhorn [1880-85: I: 8.23 - 10.3]) concerning forms such as *ūṣa* (2nd pl. perfect of *vas* 'stay, dwell') which, according to Patañjali, were not used in his time; instead, one used participial forms such as *uṣitāḥ*. Bhandarkar noted that in the time of Kātyāyana and Patañjali such verbal forms as *ūṣa* had become obsolete, gave more examples of this phenomenon, and concluded (1883-85 [= 1927-33 4: 273])[366] – in agreement with Goldstücker – that a considerable time had elapsed between Pāṇini and Kātyāyana and Patañjali. He assigned Pāṇini to the middle period of Sanskrit, towards the end of the Vedic period, Kātyāyana to the classical period. Other scholars have also noted that changes occurred in Sanskrit between the time of Pāṇini and Kātyāyana's time such that the latter introduced additional statements to account for the derivation of new forms. One example is the following.[367] Pāṇini directly provides (3.1.40) for the use of *kṛ* 'do, make' in periphrastic perfect forms of the type *īhāṃcakre* 'desired, strove' (*īh*). However, the verbs *as, bhū* 'be' also occur in this formation; for example, *āmantrayāmāsa* 'invited'. Kātyāyana declares (3.1.40 vārttika 3) that the use of all three verbs is to be accounted for in the periphrastic derivation, and Patañjali shows how Pāṇini's rule can be interpreted to provide this: *kṛ* is considered an abbreviation (see Kielhorn [1887e: 248]).

C. Kunhan Raja (1947: xvii-xviii), after noting that changes occurred in Sanskrit which required the reinterpretation of some rules, stated: "Thus the grammar holds more or less the same relation to a language which a statute bears to a situation in civic life." The same view was expressed later by Thieme (1956: 22): "Both Kātyāyana and Patañjali look upon Pāṇini's grammar as a code containing the laws of correct word formation and make the assumption that this code must be valid for all times." Thieme went on to note (1956: 23), however, that the instances where reinterpretation was made necessary by linguistic change "are few and far between."

The degree to which historical changes in Sanskrit are to be made to account for Kātyāyana's comments has caused controversy. K. Madhava Krishna Sarma (1940-41; 1945-59; 1968: 8, 9, 49, 54, 55, 79, 119) argued that such changes in Sanskrit were the major cause for Kātyāyana's vārttikas. According to him (1940-41: 128), " . . . Kātyāyana's duty as a commentator was not to justify or defend Pāṇini, but to introduce the necessary modifications in order to make Pāṇini keep abreast of later developments in the language."[368] K. Madhava Krishna Sarma did distinguish (1968: 54) between what he called historical vārttikas and others, which he called academic vārttikas. But from the copious number of passages he cited as evidence for historical vārttikas, it is, I think, fair to say that he considered language change the principal motivation for Kātyāyana's statements. One of Madhava Krishna Sarma's papers (1945-59) met with strong opposition from R. Rocher (1962), who examined three rules with Kātyāyana's comments on them and concluded (1962: 268) by expressing the hope that the evidence submitted was sufficient " . . . to make the case of linguistic change a highly improbable one." She also noted (1962: 268) in a programmatic fashion, "In our opinion, it is a most dangerous procedure, to introduce into ancient Hindu grammar a concept which is a purely Western creation, and, even more so, a Western creation of a very recent date." Devasthali (1960-61 [1963]) reacted to Rocher's article, defending the position espoused by K. Madhava Krishna Sarma and citing Bhandarkar in support of this position. According to Devasthali (1960-61 [1963]: 57-58), " . . . the aim of Kātyāyana (and even of Patañjali) in composing their works must have been not to correct him [Pāṇini]. . . , but to supplement him . . . " in view of the changes that had occurred in Sanskrit.[369]

The opposing opinions have been judiciously discussed by S. D. Joshi (1969a: viii-x), who concludes (1969a: x) that " . . . on purely theoretical grounds, the question, whether we can infer an evolution of Sanskrit from the examples [in the Mahā-bhāṣya], must be answered in the negative." Rocher (forthcoming a) returns briefly to this question. She dismisses it in what, in my opinion, is a rather cavalier fashion, sweeping aside Bhandarkar's discussion by saying that, divested of their style, his arguments are flimsy. I do not think this is proper. It is undeniable that there are some instances – few, to be sure – where Kātyāyana's suggested additions to the grammar indeed account for newer forms, as Rocher herself accepts (see note 367). It is equally clear, however, that such linguistic changes cannot be made to account for all or even most of Kātyāyana's vārttikas. The controversy arose, I think, because of extremes adopted by the adherent of the opposing positions. One side claimed that historical changes were the major reason for Kātyāyana's vārttikas. Rocher, on the other hand, has to an extent misunderstood the arguments of others. For, as far as I can see, the adherents of the view she opposes have not made Kātyāyana guilty of the anachronism she perceived. They have merely claimed that Kātyāyana was aware of the need to account for forms which were, historically, posterior to Pāṇini. The fault of the adherents of this view is not that they have superimposed on Kātyāyana a modern western principle of historical linguistics but that they have exaggerated the degree to which changes in Sanskrit are to be considered the basis for Kātyāyana's remarks.

2.6. *Methods and ideas found in the Mahā-bhāṣya.*

2.6.1. *Generalities.*

The Mahā-bhāṣya is composed in the form of dialogues in which take part a student (*śiṣya*) who questions the purpose (*prayojana*) of rules and their formulations, an unaccomplished teacher (*ācāryadeśīya*) who suggests solutions which are not fully acceptable, and a teacher (*ācārya*) who states what is the finally acceptable view (*siddhânta*). Commentators also refer to an *ekadeśin* 'one who knows only part (*ekadeśa*) of the final answer' and a *siddhântin* 'one who establishes the final view'.[370] In keeping with the purpose of the Mahā-bhāṣya (see section III.2.5.1), not all of Pāṇini's rules are subjected to independent discussions. The argumentation involved in these discussions includes the citation of examples (*udāharaṇa*) and counter-examples (*pratyudāharaṇa*) for rules and also illustrations (*dṛṣṭânta*) showing how things procede in grammar in some ways parallel to real life.

R. S. Bhattacharya (1952-53) has discussed the purposes of the examples cited: essentially to indicate the import of rules and the terms contained in them.[371]

Although I spoke above of a *siddhânta* 'finally accepted view', it is not always easy to determine what, in Kātyāyana or Patañjali's opinion, this *siddhânta* is. For Patañjali commonly presents arguments to support or reject several views (see Geiger [1908: 3 - 9], Thieme [1956: 3]). One is left to infer what is the true *siddhânta*. In doing this, commentators make use of a principle of brevity (*lāghava*). That solution of competing solutions is acceptable which avoids prolixity (*gaurava*). For example, if two solutions which provide identically correct results are under consideration and one of them involves splitting a rule into two rules (*yoga-vibhāga*), the one which does not require this is preferred. In addition, prolixity involved in understanding a rule (*pratipatti-gaurava*) is avoided. If, given two competing solutions, one requires more assumptions and metarules for the proper interpretation of a rule than the other, the latter is preferred (see Cardona [1967a: 43-44]).

2.6.2. *Techniques of interpretation.*

In the course of their discussion, Kātyāyana and Patañjali make use not only of metarules which were not directly stated by Pāṇini (see section III. 1.3.7) but also of general techniques of interpretation. These were discussed summarily by Kielhorn (1887e), and were later treated in extenso by Renou (1940a: 76-139).[372]

Some of these techniques and principles have been the objects of more recent discussions also. Kātyāyana and Patañjali frequently argue that a certain item will not be derived "because (it is) not (used to) denote (the meaning to be conveyed)" (*anabhidhānāt*). For example, rule 3.2.1 (*karmaṇy aṇ*) serves to introduce the affix *aṇ* (= *a*) after a root to form derivatives of the type *-kāra*, which then combine with syntactically related items to form compounds of the type *kumbha-kāra* 'pot maker' (⟨ *kumbha-as kāra-s*, see note 158). Now, the compound *kumbha-kāra* is related to a sentence such as *kumbhān karoti* 'makes pots': in both the pots in questions function as objects (*karman*) of making. Similarly, if the sun (*āditya*) functions as objects of seeing, one can say *ādityaṃ paśyati*. However, there was, at least according to Kātyāyana and Patañjali, no compound *āditya-darśa* related to this sentence as *kumbha-kāra* is related to *kumbhān karoti*. To avoid deriving *-darśa* by 3.2.1 to form a compound *āditya-darśa*, then, the suggestion is made (Kielhorn [1880-85: II.94.2]) that rule 3.2.1 be made more specific. It should not merely state that *aṇ* is affixed to a root which is construed with an item denoting an object (*karman*) of the action denoted by the root. Instead, 3.2.1 should specify that the object in question is something brought into being (*nirvartya*) or modified (*vikriyamāṇa*). The rule thus modified now allows for deriving items such as *kumbha-kāra* and *kāṇḍa-lāva* 'branch cutter' but prevents the derivation of a compound such as *āditya-darśa*. However, this is not sufficient. It is accepted as given that the Veda is neither created nor modified by anyone. Yet a compound *vedâdhyāya* 'who studies the Veda' is to be derived. Under the new formulation of the rule this is not possible. Therefore, Kātyāyana and Patañjali end up by invoking the principle of *anabhidhāna*:[373] a compound such as *āditya-darśa* is simply not used to convey the meaning conveyed by *ādityaṃ paśyati*.

This principle has been discussed by Kielhorn (1887e: 245-46), Renou (1940a: 129-31), R. S. Bhattacharya (1966t) Charudeva Shastri (1967: 107), S. D. Joshi (1969a: vii), Cardona (1972c: 228-32). Kielhorn (1887e: 246) considered " . . . that the device of *anabhidhāna*, beyond acquainting us with the views of the commentators who happened to make use of it, is really of no value whatever." This is a harsh judgment indeed. Moreover, I think that, in so quickly rejecting this, Kielhorn failed to make one aware of a point which is of some interest. It is obvious that Kātyāyana, like later Pāṇinīyas (see section III.1.5.7b), recognized that there were different kinds of objects (*karman*). It is equally obvious that this distinction was not considered pertinent by Pāṇini in stating rule 3.2.1.[374] Indeed, as the discussion in the Mahā-bhāṣya shows, Pāṇini would have been hard put to state a single rule of any generality once he brought such a distinction into play here. There would have to be a series of rules relative to particular compounds. Instead of proceding in such a way, Pāṇini[375] formulated a very general rule. Theoretically, this rule allows deriving items such as *āditya-darśa*. Moreover, such a compound is grammatically well-formed in that it conforms to the formal pattern of compounds like *kumbha-kāra*. It happens, however, that *āditya-darśa* is not used. Not because there is something particularly strange about it; for the relation (object - action) involved is the same as in *kumbha-kāra*, and compounds such as *vedâdhyāya*, where the object is neither effected nor affected, are used. One may, then, consider that the absence of a compound such as *āditya-darśa* is an accidental gap. Pāṇini's rules allows for its formation according to the rules of Sanskrit, but it happens not to be used.

Another principle which Kielhorn (1887e: 246, cf. Renou [1940a: 131-32]) considered of no value is *vivakṣā* (lit. 'the wish to say').[376] This rejection fails to recognize an important fact. The concept of *vivakṣā* is invoked in connection with sentences such as III.1.5.5c (7) (*paraśur vṛkṣaṃ chinatti*). In this context, invoking *vivakṣā* amounts simply to this: the grammar is not concerned with things as they are but as they are spoken about, that is, with sentences of the language. If a speaker uses a sentence such as this, so that he wishes to speak of an axe as an agent of cutting, the grammar has to account for it. In this connection, then, *vivakṣā* is simply part of a basic outlook of Pāṇinian grammar: the grammarian deals with language, not with ontology. Moreover, one should distinguish carefully between *vivakṣā* as it is employed by early Pāṇinīyas such as Kātyāyana and Patañjali and the use of this principle by later commentators.[377]

In all such cases, another aspect of the question which Kielhorn and others have neglected to consider in detail is whether what are involved can be considered unprincipled inventions of commentators or, on the contrary, extensions of tenets already valid for Pāṇini. It is clear, for example, that the use of rule order as a decision procedure in the grammar is not an invention of Kātyāyana or Patañjali, who merely extended the domain of rule 1.4.2 already stated by Pāṇini (see section III.1.5.2b and Cardona [1970a: 48, 56]). In sum, I think there remains a great deal of work to be done on the techniques of interpretation and the principles used in the Mahā-bhāṣya.

2.6.3. *Discussions of philosophical import.*

The Mahā-bhāṣya contains discussions of subjects on the threshold of grammar and philosophy, many of them concentrated in the introductory section (*paspaśā*).[378] These discussions have been the objects of a number of studies.

A basic premise of grammar is, according to Pāṇinīyas, that the relation (*sambandha*) between linguistic items (*śabda*) and their meanings (*artha*) is fixed and permanent (*nitya*), not the invention of someone. A question discussed at the beginning of the Mahā-bhāṣya is this. What is it precisely that one calls *śabda*? Two answers are given. A śabda is that which, when articulated, serves to convey an understanding of a meaning. Alternatively, one can understand a śabda to be merely sound. That is, any item can be viewed either qua signifier or qua sound complex. S. D. Joshi (1966a) has taken up in detail the discussion of these views; see also Brough (1951: 31-32), Biardeau (1964a: 371), Naradeva (1968).[379]

A related question taken up in the Mahā-bhāṣya is whether these linguistic items (*śabda*) are perennial, eternal (*nitya*) or susceptible of production (*kārya*). Moreover, a distinction is made between absolute eternality (*kūṭastha-nityatā*) such that an item is susceptible to no modification whatever, and what is called *pravāha-nityatā*, the perennity of linguistic items as used through generations of speakers.[380] On these questions see Ruegg (1958: 273-77; 1959: 39, 43-45), Biardeau (1964a: 35-43).

Concerning what items signify (*artha*), one important question discussed is: does a noun such as *go* 'cow, bullock' designate an individual thing (*dravya*) or a type?[381] The Mahā-bhāṣya discussions concerning this question have been dealt with by quite a few scholars: Strauss (1927a: 137-50), Hiriyanna (1938), Gaurinath Shastri (1959: 143-55), Ruegg (1959: 38-40), Frauwallner (1960), Biardeau (1964a: 43-61), K. Kunjunni Raja (1969: 75-78), Matilal (1971: 106-09; 1973: 386-87), Narayana Murti (1971). The meaning of the term *ākṛti* (see note 381) has itself been the subject of some discussion. Commentators consider that this term was used in two values by Patañjali: as an equivalent of *jāti* 'generic property' and to denote a form, a particular arrangement of parts (*avayava-saṃniveśa-viśeṣa*, see Cardona [1967-68: 326], Aklujkar [1970: 22]). Sreekrishna Sharma (1957: 61) concluded that Patañjali used *ākṛti* to mean 'structural form' viewed in two ways: common form (= universal) and particular form. He distinguished (1957: 65) between *ākṛti* 'structural pattern' and *jāti* 'kind or class', which, he noted, is an abstract concept. Some modern scholars (e.g., Strauss [1927a: 135 n. 2]) have considered *ākṛti* synonymous with *jāti*, others have consistently distinguished between *ākṛti* 'form' and *jāti* (see Frauwallner [1960: 93], Scharfe [1961a: 129-41], Biardeau [1964a: 43-49]). M. M. Deshpande (1972b: 26-40) has given a survey of different opinions.

The Mahā-bhāṣya on rule 4.1.3 takes up the question of gender. The term *liṅga*, used in the meaning 'gender', denotes, in normal Sanskrit, a mark or characteristic. If the term is understood in this sense in grammar, then a liṅga is a characteristic of males, females, and things which are neither. A female (*strī*) would then be characterized by breasts and hair, a male (*puruṣa*) by his body hair, others by neither. This conception of liṅga does not work in grammar, it is noted, so that another concept is introduced. Any thing is characterized by different states of constituent elements or properties (*guṇa*) and these states constitute the genders of things.[382] On this see Strauss (1927b), K. A. Subramania Iyer (1945: 294-96, 298-301; 1971: 80), Ruegg (1959: 40), Scharfe (1961a: 147), Sabhāpati Upādhyāya (1963), Kṛṣṇa Śāstri Mokāṭe (1969), Matilal (1971: 104). This question is related to another topic discussed in the Mahā-bhāṣya, namely whether one is justified in recognizing a substance (*dravya*) as something distinct from its constitutent parts and properties. On this question see Ruegg (1959: 41), Matilal (1971: 101-03; 1973: 388-91).[383]

The concept of time (*kāla*) and its divisions are also discussed in the Mahā-bhāṣya (especially on rule 3.2.123, see section III.3.1.4(c)). Two of the questions treated are the following. One speaks of actions as taking place currently (*vartamāna*), in the past (*bhūta*), and in the future (*bhaviṣyat*). Now, one can properly say *ihâdhīmahe* 'We are studying (*adhīmahe*) here (*iha*)', using the present form of a verb, and the grammar accounts for this by introducing the L-suffix *laṭ* on condition that an action is characterized as current (3.2.123: *vartamāne laṭ*). But the sentence *ihâdhīmahe* can be proper even if, at the moment, one is not actually studying. Therefore, current time (*vartamāna-kāla*) is characterized more specifically: once an action has begun and has not ended, the entire stretch of time included therein is referred to as current. The other question is this. One can say of mountains "The mountains are standing" (*tiṣṭhanti parvatāḥ*), as one also says of rivers "The rivers are flowing" (*sravanti nadyaḥ*). Such sentences are derived on condition that an action is referred to current time (*vartamāna*). Yet, the mountains are always there and the rivers always are flowing, so that it is difficult to see how one can speak of current actions here, as opposed to past and future ones. Kātyāyana answers that there are indeed time divisions (*kāla-vibhāga*) here too. And Patañjali explains as follows. There are individuals such as kings, who existed in the past, exist now, and will exist. These different individuals perform activities. And it is with respect to these activities that one can speak of mountains as having stood at the time of past kings, standing at the time of present kings, etc.[384] Aspects of the Mahā-bhāṣya discussions on time have been treated by J. M. Shukla (1953: 380-81) and Satyavrat (1967-68).

One recent work (Scharfe [1961a]) has been devoted to an investigation of logical concepts, terms, and techniques found in the Mahā-bhāṣya. The work is a loose assemblage of translations of passages with brief comments on their import. This is a useful collection of materials. Nevertheless, Scharfe's work suffers from two faults. First, the author procedes rather mechanically, equating terms used in other Indian systems in particular values with homophonous terms which occur in the Mahā-bhāṣya, and he does not always note important differences. For example, Scharfe (1961a: 93-96) says that the terms *anvaya* and *vyatireka* are used in the Mahā-bhāṣya with the meanings they have in the context of contraposition (see Staal [1960]), that is: $a \rightarrow b$ (*anvaya*) and $\bar{b} \rightarrow \bar{a}$ (*vyatireka*). However, these terms are used in other values in the context of showing that a is the cause of b: $a \rightarrow b$ (*anvaya*) and $\bar{a} \rightarrow \bar{b}$ (*vyatireka*). And it is this value which the terms have in the Mahā-bhāṣya discussions considered by Scharfe (see Cardona [1967-68: 314] and note 152 above). Moreover, Scharfe appears not to have full command of the modern logical apparatus he has used; this was pointed out by Staal (1963: 254-55). Less ambitious than Scharfe's work, yet by the same token more trustworthy, is the recent work by Rāma Prasāda Tripāṭhī (1972), who discusses the views found in the Mahābhāṣya and other Pāṇinīya texts concerning the means of obtaining and conveying correct knowledge, what are called *pramāṇa*. This is a very useful work, rich in information. It is also written from a traditional point of view and in Sanskrit, which will doubtless limit its audience.[385]

Frauwallner (1959: 243; 1960: 92) and Scharfe (1961a) have agreed in chiding Patañjali for what they considered his lack of philosophical acumen. Frauwallner (1960: 92) declared that Patañjali had neither an interest in nor a head for philosophical questions and claimed (1960: 106-07) that Patañjali took a topic of discussion from an earlier source and mangled it. Scharfe (1961a: 23, 83-84) asserted that, in the passage considered, Patañjali did not recognize the essential feature of citation, that he argued instead from primitive analogy. Frauwallner has been answered by Biardeau (1964a: 31 n. 1) and Staal (1967: 48 n. 19), and Scharfe was rebutted by Staal (1963: 253-55), both I think quite justly. Scharfe simply misunderstood the discussion in question. Frauwallner either misunderstood or refused to understand the context of Patañjali's discussion. Patañjali's aim, after all, was not to set forth in the Mahā-bhāṣya a fully elaborated philosophical system. We do not know whether he had in fact arrived at such a consistent system. But even if he had, his aim in the Mahā-bhāṣya was to discuss Pāṇini's grammatical rules, not to set down his own philosophical views in full array.

2.7. *Other studies of the Mahā-bhāṣya.*

There is a large number of passages in the Mahā-bhāṣya where etymologies are given. Swaminathan (1966) has discussed the etymologies given there and their relation to the etymologies which appear in Yāska's Nirukta (section III.3.2.1).

In the Mahā-bhāṣya (Kielhorn [1880-85: I: 22.21-23, 117. 21-23]), Patañjali notes that, according to certain chanters of the Sāma-veda, there are short (*ardha* 'half') vowels *e* and *o*. K. V. Abhyankar (1957) has discussed details concerning this question.

In the introductory section of the Mahā-bhāṣya, Patañjali cites a verse (Kielhorn [1880-85: I: 2.19-20]) which he calls a *bhrāja-śloka*.[386] R. S. Bhattacharya (1953b) has suggested that another verse, cited by Kaiyaṭa in his commentary on 3.1.1 (Vedavrata [1962-63: III: 4]), is also a Bhrāja verse. R. S. Bhattacharya (1963) has also dealt with the term *pada-kāra*, used to refer to the authors of analyzed texts (*pada-pāṭha*) of Vedic texts.

Vedic quotations in the Mahā-bhāṣya have been compiled, though not exhaustively, by Kielhorn (see 1880-85: II: introduction, p. 22), Wackernagel (1942), and Renou (1953b). V. P. Limaye (1964-65: 222 n. 3) remarks that he has compiled a complete list of Vedic citations in the Mahā-bhāṣya.

This has been incorporated in Limaye (1974). Thieme (1964b, 1967) has studied Patañjali's interpretation of two important Ṛg-vedic verses (8.58.12, 1.164.5) in the context of grammar, and Palsule (1969b) has studied Patañjali's interpretation of another Vedic verse.[387]

3. CHRONOLOGY AND REALIA.

3.1. *The dates of Pāṇini, Kātyāyana and Patañjali.*

3.1.1. *Introduction.*

Pāṇini, Kātyāyana and Patañjali have been assigned widely divergent dates.[388] Renou gave the fourth century B. C., as Pāṇini's date on two occasions (1940a: 9; 1956a: 62), but later (1957a: 34 with note 515) said that Pāṇini's date was either the fourth century or possibly the fifth. In 1953 he remarked (1953d: 87) that Pāṇini's mention of Greek writing (see section III.3.1.2) indicated he could not be dated earlier than the fifth or fourth century B. C. And in his last treatment of the subject (1969: 483) Renou remarked, "Generally, I have decided, without absolute certainty, on the 4th or 5th centuries B. C." Thieme, on the other hand, has steadily maintained that Pāṇini's date certainly was earlier than the fourth century (1935a: 80; 1955b: 429), probably not later than 500 B. C. (1964: 72). Similarly, V. S. Agrawala (1949; 1951; 1963a: 478) placed Pāṇini at about 500 B. C., and S. Bhattacharya (1963) also put him at no later than the sixth century. Similarly, Charpentier (1923: 150) argued that Pāṇini's rule 4.1.175 shows he must have known of a Kamboja king, so that he could not be dated later than the second half of the sixth century. Some scholars have claimed earlier dates: seventh century B. C. (K. B. Pathak [1930]), 700 - 600 B. C. (S. K. Belvalkar [1915: 15]), five hundred to six hundred years before the Buddha (V. N. Gokhale [1940: 109]). Certainly, most competent scholars have favored placing Pāṇini at a time earlier than the fourth century B. C.[389]

Despite these divergent views, in none of the surveys of Pāṇinian scholarship written to date (Renou [1940a; 1957a; 1969], R. Rocher [forthcoming b]) is the evidence cited in support of these views summarized or evaluated, so that a reader could get the impression that opinions are not well founded or even whimsical. I think it worthwhile, therefore, briefly to set down the major arguments in favor of the opinions given above and others. Although the conclusion reached is not surprising (see section III.3.1.7), I believe a sifting of evidence is worthwhile.

There are two major kinds of evidence for determining Pāṇini's date:

internal evidence: what Pāṇini says in his own rules; and external evidence: stories, Pāṇini's possible identity with another author of the same name, the gap one thinks has to be assumed between Pāṇini and Kātyāyana. Similar evidence is to be considered for determining the dates of Kātyāyana and Patañjali.

3.1.2. *Possible internal evidence for Pāṇini's date.*

The ideal internal evidence for setting Pāṇini's date would be his mentioning persons whose dates were definitely known. Pāṇini does mention grammarians such as Āpiśali (see section III.1.3.1), but nothing definite is known about the dates of these. Some scholars have claimed, however, that Pāṇini's rules do contain references which allow one to date him. There are two major pieces of such evidence, both used to place Pāṇini at a relatively late date.

Rule 4.1.49 (*indra-varuṇa-bhava-śarva-rudra-mṛḍa-himâraṇya-yava-yavana-mātulâcāryāṇām ānuk*) provides for deriving certain feminine items by affixing *ī* to nominal bases given in the rule; concurrently, the bases receive a final augment *ān*. Two types of feminine nouns are thus derived. Some denote a female associated with a male; for example, *indrāṇī* 'wife of Indra', *mātulānī* 'maternal uncle's wife'. Others do not; for example, *yavānī* 'a kind of barley'.[390] The rule serves to derive *yavanānī* from *yavana*. Two questions arise. First, is *yavanānī* of the type *indrāṇī* or of the type *yavānī*? And, in either case, to what does *yavana* refer? According to Kātyāyana (4.1.49 vārttika 3: *yavanāl lipyām*), *yavanānī* should be derived as a noun referring to a writing (*lipi*). Goldstücker (1861: 16-17) considered that *yavanānī* referred to cuneiform writing. Weber (1862: 2, 16-18) disagreed. According to him, *yavana* referred to Greeks, so that *yavanānī* referred to Greek writing. Therefore, he assigned Pāṇini a date after Alexander the Great (Weber [1875: 244; 1876: 237-38]).[391] This argument is not acceptable. To begin with, it was Kātyāyana, not Pāṇini, who specified that *yavanānī* should refer to a writing. Hence, for Pāṇini this noun could simply have referred to a Yavana woman (see Liebich [1891: 7], C. V. Vaidya [1930: 150], R. S. Bhattacharya [1966m]). Moreover, it is known that Indians were associated with Greeks (Ionians) before Alexander (see Keith [1914: clxix], Belvalkar [1915: 15-16], V. Smith [1924: 40], V. S. Agrawala [1963a: 469]). Therefore, the derivative *yavanānī* cannot serve to demonstrate that Pāṇini post-dated Alexander.[392]

Pāṇini's rule 2.1.70 (*kumāraḥ śramaṇādibhiḥ*) serves to derive the compound *kumāra-śramaṇā* '(virgin) girl who is a Śramaṇā'. Weber (1862: 141-42, see also Lakshman Rao [1921]) considered that this referred to Buddhist nuns, so that Pāṇini had to post-date the Buddha. On the other hand,

K. B. Pathak (1930, see also Kalipad Mitra [1922]) argued that this term could refer also to Jaina nuns, so that Pāṇini need not be placed after the Buddha.[393]

The internal evidence suggested to demonstrate that Pāṇini post-dated Alexander the Great or the Buddha or to show that he came before the Buddha (see note 393) is thus not probative.

3.1.3. *External evidence for Pāṇini's date.*

According to a story told in the Kathā-sarit-sāgara, Pāṇini and Kātyāyana were contemporaries. One of the few scholars who accepted this story as evidence on which to base arguments regarding Pāṇini's dates was Böhtlingk (1839-40: xv-xviii). However, by a series of calculations, Böhtlingk still placed the Mahā-bhāṣya at about 150 B. C. and Pāṇini in the fourth century. But Böhtlingk's arguments were hardly cogent, as was noted by Goldstücker (1861: 85-86).[394]

There is a poet Pāṇini, to whom verses are attributed in anthologies; see Aufrecht (1860, 1882, 1891b), Pischel (1885), Peterson - Durgāprasāda (1886: 54-58), K. C. Chatterji (1933a, b), Krishnadeva Upadhyaya (1937), Ramachandra Rao (1959), Dasgupta - De (1962: 610 with note 1), Yudhiṣṭhira Mīmāṃsaka (1973: I: 239-40; III.82 - 92).[395] Pischel identified Pāṇini the poet with Pāṇini the grammarian and proposed to place the latter in the fifth or sixth century A. D. for this reason. However, Pischel's arguments for this chronology could not stand, and he was rebutted by Kielhorn (1885b, see also R. G. Bhandarkar [1883-85a] [= 1927-33 1: 164]). Indeed, Dasgupta and De assumed that, if the two authors were identical, Pāṇini the poet had to be placed in the fourth or fifth century B. C. K. C. Chatterji argued vigorously against identifying the poet and the grammarian because the former used ungrammatical forms, because relatively early commentators such as the authors of the Kāśikā (section IV.2.1) did not invoke verses attributed to Pāṇini in support of particular usages, and because the poem Jāmbavatī-vijaya is not mentioned in the Mahā-bhāṣya. Several other scholars have nevertheless accepted the identification: Krishnadeva Upadhyaya, Ramachandra Rao, Yudhiṣṭhira Mīmāṃsaka, and also P. S. Subrahmanya Sastri (1960: xxvii). P. V. Kane (1961: 332 n. 3) was noncommittal.

I have no definite opinion on this problem. However, whatever one's view, this cannot serve as solid evidence for the date of Pāṇini. One must, then, depend on relative chronology: if the dates of Patañjali and Kātyāyana can be determined, Pāṇini's date can be approximated.

3.1.4. *The date of Patañjali.*

Three major pieces of evidence from the Mahā-bhāṣya have been used to determine Patañjali's date.

(a) Rule 5.3.99 (*jīvikârthe câpaṇye*) provides that an affix (*ka*) is deleted in deriving nominals such as *śiva* 'image of Śiva', provided the object denoted by the derivative is used to earn a livelyhood (*jīvikârtha*) and is not sold (*apaṇya*). The derivative *śiva* thus refers to an image which mendicants carry as they beg. In the Mahā-bhāṣya (Kielhorn [1880-85: II: 429.2-4]) the following discussion is held concerning this rule. The rule states *apaṇye*, so that the deletion applies only if a derivative refers to an object which is not sold. Hence, it does not apply properly to provide *śiva*, etc. For the Mauryas, who were greedy for gold, arranged to sell such images. This objection is met as follows. Let the rule not apply to delete *ka* in the case of derivatives referring to these statues. But it does apply in the case of derivates which refer to images that nowadays are intended for worship and not for sale.

Goldstücker (1861: 228-29) used this passage to establish that Patañjali post-dated the Maurya king Candragupta Maurya, hence came later than 315 B. C.[396]

(b) Rule 3.2.111 (*anadyatane laṅ*) provides that the L-suffix *laṅ* is introduced after a root when the action signified by the root is referred to the past exclusive of the day on which one is speaking (*anadyatana* 'excluding today'). In his second vārttika on this rule Kātyāyana states that a provision is to be made that *laṅ* is also introduced if a root denotes an action which the speaker has not actually observed (*parokṣe*), which is famous (*loka-vijñāte*), and which the speaker could possibly witness, it being in the realm of his seeing (*prayoktur darśana-viṣaye*). Patañjali illustrates this use of imperfect forms with two examples:

(1) *aruṇad yavanaḥ sāketam* 'The Yavana besieged Sāketa.'
(2) *aruṇad yavano madhyamikām* 'The Yavana besieged Madhyamikā.'

Goldstücker (1861: 229-30, 234) considered this passage,[397] and concluded that the Yavana was Menander.[398] From this he concluded that Patañjali wrote his comments on rule 3.2.111 between 140 and 120 B. C.[399] For the events in question had to be such as were famous, Patañjali had not seen, but could have seen.

(c) Rule 3.2.123 (*vartamāne laṭ*) introduces the L-suffix *laṭ* if an action is referred to the present. Now, *vārtamāna* in the rule means 'current'. In his first vārttika on this rule, Kātyāyana states that the present endings (*bhavantī*) are to be taught (*śiṣyā*) as introduced after a root when there is reference to to an action which has begun (*pravṛttasya*) but not ended (*avirāme*). Such an action is not necessarily always in process (*avartamānatvāt*). One can, for example, correctly say *ihâdhīmahe* 'We are studying here' even if, at the moment, one is not studying (see section III.2.6.3). Another example given by Patañjali to illustrate this use of the present is

(3) *iha puṣyamitraṃ yājayāmaḥ* 'We are officiating here at Puṣyamitra's sacrifice.'

R. G. Bhandarkar (1872b) used this example to argue as follows.[400] As an example for Kātyāyana's vārttika this shows that Puṣyamitra, the beginner of the Śuṅga dynasty, was having a sacrifice performed at the time of Patañjali. Therefore, Patañjali's date is set at between 178 and 142 B. C.

The evidence noted above was the source of much debate. Weber (1862: 151-55) read *mādhyamikān* in (2) (see note 397) and identified the Mādhyamikas in question with followers of the Buddhist school founded by Nāgārjuna (ca. 150 A. D.). He interpreted (2) as saying that a Yavana had suppressed the Mādhyamikas. On the basis of the reading noted, Weber concluded that the Yavana (1) and (2) could not be Menander. He considered him to be the Indo-Scythian Kaniṣka. But Kaniṣka was a Buddhist, so that Weber had further to suppose that he had suppressed the Mādhyamikas before becoming a Buddhist. In terms of his chronology, Weber put the event referred to in (2) at between five and forty-five A. D. After Bhandarkar's paper (1872b) appeared, Weber (1873a) replied, placing Patañjali at 25 A. D. Bhandarkar (1873a) then answered, pointing out that both Goldstücker and Weber were mistaken: *madhyamikā* was the name of a city.[401] Weber (1873b) repreated what he had said in 1862 and then (1873c) answered to Bhandarkar's paper (Bhandarkar [1873a]). He admitted that *mādhyamikā* (see note 401) need not refer to a Buddhist school, but he insisted that example (3) did not prove Patañjali was a contemporary of Puṣyamitra. After Bhandarkar (1873d) answered, Weber admitted (1873d: 305) that example (2) involved a city. He still insisted, however, that the Yavana was not Menander (1873d: 305-06).[402] Finally, Weber (1873d: 319-20, 498; 1876: 240 n. 237), with his back to the wall, resorted to a counsel of despair: examples such as (1) and (2) are not necessarily Patañjali's, he claimed; they could be consecrated examples (*mūrdhâbhiṣikta udāharaṇa*). For the Mahā-bhāṣya was once reconstructed (see section III. 2.4 and Weber [1875: 244]).

Earlier, Böhtlingk (1875a: 188) had argued that example (3) was not Patañjali's. But his argument was based on a false assumption: that Patañjali was Kātyāyana's adversary, so that the paraphrase of this vārttika, with examples, could not be Patañjali's (see section III.2.5.1). Arguments concerning whether such examples were really Patañjali's continued until fairly recently. Liebich (1899: 312; 1930: 264-67) cited parallels from Candragomin's and other grammars, showing that examples comparable to (1) and (2) given in these grammars referred to contemporary events; the commentaries did not simply take over old examples like (1) and (2). For example, the commentary on Candra's rule 1.2.81 (K. C. Chatterji [1953-61: I: 76]) cites vārttika 1 on Pāṇini 3.2.111 and then gives the example *ajayaj jarto hūṇān* 'The Jarta conquered the Hūṇa.'[403] The Jainendra-mahā-vṛtti also cites the vārttika noted and gives the example *aruṇan mahêndro mathurām* 'Mahendra besieged Mathurā.'[404] Liebich (1930: 264-65) accepted that examples (1) and (2) were indeed Patañjali's own, so that his date could be set at ca. 150 B. C.; so also V. Smith (1924: 227-29), Ramaprasad Chandra (1929), Haraprasāda Shāstrī (1931: xxii), V. S. Agrawala (1956-57), and, most recently, Yudhiṣṭhira Mīmāṃsaka (1973: I: 337-38).[405] Nevertheless, C. Kunhan Raja (1947: xvi) again expressed doubts: "We have yet to ascertain whether he [Patañjali] gave the examples *aruṇad yavanaḥ sāketam* ... as a contemporary event, as his own sentence, or whether he took it from any record that was contemporaneous with the event." And more recently Frauwallner (1960: 108) again said that Patañjali could have taken example (2) from some source.

It is true that Patañjali might have taken such examples from earlier sources. The fact remains that these events could have been contemporaneous with Patañjali, in accord with the provisions of the vārttikas in question. And commentaries on the Cāndra and Jainendra grammars do indeed give different examples, although, to be sure, the Kāśikā on 3.2.111 repeats the Mahā-bhāṣya examples. What one wishes to conclude depends, then, on how skeptical one wishes to be. I personally accept that these were Patañjali's examples, and I think the resultant dating is buttressed by the results of research concerning Kātyāyana's date (section III.3.1.5).

Other arguments have been made against placing Patañjali in the middle of the second century B. C. Peterson (1883-85: 183-88) argued against Goldstücker's claim regarding the Maurya kings (see (a) above). He accepted (1883-85: 189) that Patañjali was a contemporary of Puṣyamitra, but argued that, since there were several Puṣyamitras in Indian history, this particular Puṣyamitra could be a later one. He chose Puṣyamitra from the fourth to fifth centuries A. D. Peterson's arguments were countered, effectively in my opinion, by R. G. Bhandarkar (1883-85a, 1885).

De La Vallée Poussin (1930: 199-202) argued from a different point of view. Pāṇini's rule 2.4.10 (*śūdrāṇām aniravasitānām*) provides that a dvandva compound formed with terms denoting śūdras (those who are not members of the three twice-born castes) who are not excluded (*aniravasita*) is treated as singular; for example, *rajaka-tantuvāyam* 'washerman and weaver'. In his discussion of this rule, Patañjali (Kielhorn [1880-85: I: 475.2-10]) asks what the exclusion refers to: excluded from what or where? The first suggestion made is that the rule refers to exclusion from the country of the Ārya (*āryâvarta*, see section III.3.3.2). This meets with an objection. The rule will now not provide for letting certain compounds be treated as singular which should be so treated. Among the examples given is *śaka-yavanam* 'Śakas and Yavanas'. The Śakas (Scythians) and the Yavanas dwell beyond the bounds of Āryâvarta. De La Vallée Poussin argued that the Brāhmaṇas of India could not have considered the Śakas so important by 150 B. C. as to couple them with Yavanas. He suggested, therefore, that Patañjali be assigned to ca. 50 B. C.[406] Patañjali's example *śaka-yavanam* engaged the attention of other scholars also. D. R. Bhandarkar (1934: 276, 279-80) considered that by the time of Patañjali the Śakas had been Aryanized, like the Yavanas, and established their power in the north-west of the subcontinent. According to him, the Śakas had to be dated earlier than usual. Harihar Trivedi (1938) agreed with Bhandarkar. On the other hand, Konow (1935: 191) concluded that the Śakas mentioned by Patañjali were known only as a foreign tribe connected with the Yavanas. Both scholars agreed, however, in assigning Patañjali to the second century B. C. De La Vallée Poussin later (1936) disagreed with both and reiterated his view. I am not sufficiently versed in details of early Indian history to make a sound judgement on this controversy. However, it is accepted generally that there was a Śaka kingdom in India by the middle of the first century B. C. And it remains possible that north-western Indians knew them better than has been assumed before. I do not think the evidence from the Mahā-bhāṣya permits a definite decision for dating here.

Still another kind of argument was advanced by D. C. Sircar (1939). One of his major arguments against positing an early date for the Mahābhāṣya is that in this text are cited verses in various meters and that Patañjali knew of many kinds of literary productions: the Mahā-bhārata, Hari-vaṃśa and ornate poetry (*kāvya*). This led Sircar (1939: 634) to place Patañjali somewhere in the second century A. D. However, this argument is not telling. It is equally licit to say that such literary production had developed by the second century B. C. (see section III.3.3.2).

The evidence is thus not absolutely probative but sufficient to warrant considering seriously that Patañjali lived in the second century B. C.[407]

3.1.5. *Kātyāyana's date.*

There is little evidence for determing Kātyāyana's date. Lévi (1891) argued for considering him a contemporary of Alexander the Great. The basis for Lévi's view is the term *devānāṃ-priya*, which he considered a chancellery title.[408] This term and others have recently been studied anew for their implications regarding Kātyāyana's dates in papers by Scharfe (1971b) and Jayapāla Vidyālaṃkāra (1972). Scharfe (1971b: 215) suggests that *devānāṃ-priya* "is a translation of the hellenistic court title *phílos tôn basiléōn* 'friend of the kings'." [My transliteration] He also suggests (1971b: 224) that the term *śāka-pārthiva* "king who eats vegetables"[409] was used by Kātyāyana to refer to king Aśoka, so that Kātyāyana is to be placed in the middle of the third century B. C. Jayapāla Vidyālaṃkāra (1972: 121) also puts Kātyāyana at about 250 B. C.

K. P. Jayaswal (1918; 1919) arrived at a similar date (248 - 180 B. C.) in a different manner. He interpreted the compound *śāka-pārthiva* as meaning "Pārthivas who are Śākas" and characterized Patañjali's interpretation of the compound (see note 409) as absurd.[410] Jayapāla Vidyālaṃkāra (1972: 109-10) has argued, correctly in my opinion, that Jayaswal's interpretation is not appropriate to Kātyāyana's vārttika.[411]

3.1.6. *The intervals to be assumed between Pāṇini and Kātyāyana and Kātyāyana and Patañjali.*

Patañjali does not always give a single interpretation of a vārttika. He has to arrive at an interpretation through reasoning (S. P. Chaturvedi 1950: 144-45], Thieme [1955b: 429]). It is also known that between Kātyāyana and Patañjali there intervened authors who composed vārttikas and interpreted Kātyāyana's statements (Kielhorn [1887c: 104-06]). Moreover, Kātyāyana did not himself receive the grammar directly from Pāṇini. He too had to interpret the meaning and intention of rules (Thieme [1935a: 130]). In addition, Kātyāyana knew of predecessors who had subjected Pāṇini's rules to the same kind of scrutiny as his (Kielhorn [1887c: 103-04]). Finally, the language of Kātyāyana's time and place shows differences from Pāṇini's which are best interpreted as historical and not merely dialectal, which therefore warrant assuming an interval of some time between the two (see section III.2.5.3).[412]

All these factors require that Pāṇini have preceded Kātyayana by some time. Now subjectivism enters in that one must suggest what would be a sufficient time to allow for these factors. If one accepts that Patañjali is to be dated at about 150 B. C. (see section III.3.1.4) and one assumes a gap of two hundred years between him and Kātyāyana (see S. P. Chaturvedi [1950: 145]) and a similar gap between Kātyāyana and Patañjali, these authors are then assigned respectively to the mid fourth and sixth centuries B. C. If, on the other hand, one accept the arguments proposed for placing Kātyāyana in the middle of the third century B. C. (see section III.3.1.5) and a similar gap of one hundred years is allowed between Kātyāyana and Pāṇini, then the latter is assigned to the early to mid fourth century B. C.

3.1.7. *Conclusion.*

The evidence for dating Pāṇini, Kātyāyana and Patañjali is not absolutely probative and depends on interpretation. However, I think there is one certainty, namely that the evidence available hardly allows one to date Pāṇini later than the early to mid fourth century B. C.

3.1.8. *Excursus: The places of origin of Pāṇini, Kātyāyana and Patañjali.*

3.1.8a. *Pāṇini.*

According to tradition, Pāṇini came from Śalātura in the north-west of the subcontinent. This is reasonable and, to my knowledge, only one scholar has seriously argued that Pāṇini was not a north-westerner pure and simple. Franke (1891a: 76, 1891b: 957, 975) claimed that, because Pāṇini referred to easterners more commonly than others, he was to be considered an eastern grammarian. But even Franke assumed that Pāṇini had migrated from the north-west. Franke's view was shared by de La Vallée Poussin (1930: 37). However, Thieme showed that the evidence does not support this thesis.[413]

3.1.8b. *Kātyāyana.*

Goldstücker (1861: 217, 236) and Weber (1862: 44) considered Kātyāyana an eastern grammarian. However, R. G. Bhandarkar (1873b [= 1927-33 1: 123-24]) noted, "But it is a question whether the distinction between Northern or Eastern grammarians, which Pāṇini mentions [but see note 413], really existed in the time of Kātyāyana" and gave evidence to show that, at least according to Patañjali, Kātyāyana was a southerner. In the first vārttika in the introductory section of the Mahā-bhāṣya, the phrase *yathā laukika-vaidikeṣu* is used, for which Patañjali (Kielhorn [1880-85 I: 8.8-10]) suggests two possible interpretations. Since the term *laukika-vaidika* is composed of items containing taddhita affixes, the phrase can mean 'as in (utterance of) worldly (usage and) Vedic (utterances, which convey) established norms (of behavior) (*yathā laukikeṣu vaidikeṣu ca kṛtânteṣu*).'

However, Patañjali also suggests that Kātyāyana has here used *laukika-vaidika* as equivalent to *loke vede ca* 'in worldly usage and in the Veda.' Regarding this, Patañjali says: southerners are fond of items containing taddhita affixes (*priya-taddhitā dākṣiṇātyāḥ*); where one should say *yathā loke vede ca*, they use *yathā laukika-vaidikeṣu* (*yathā loke vede câti prayoktavye yathā laukika-vaidikeṣv iti prayuñjate*). From this Bhandarkar concluded that Kātyāyana was a southerner, and this view has not been refuted.[414] It has been accepted explicitly by modern scholars (Renou [1957a: 17, 38], Yudhiṣṭhira Mīmāṃsaka [1973: I: 304-06]).

3.1.8c. *Patañjali.*

Goldstücker and Weber tried to show that Patañjali was an easterner. Goldstücker (1861: 235-37) advanced two arguments. First, Patañjali calls himself *gonardīya* and Gonarda is an eastern area according to the Kāśikā. Secondly, Kaiyaṭa refers to Patañjali as *ācāryadeśīya*, which must mean 'who belongs to the country of the *ācārya*', that is, who comes from the same area as the teacher Kātyāyana, who is an easterner (see section III.3.1.8c). These arguments are unacceptable. To begin with, it is at least doubtful that *gonardīya* refers in the Mahā-bhāṣya to Patañjali.[415] In addition, *ācāryadeśīya* refers simply to a participant in the dialogue who holds a particular position (see section III.2.6.1).

Weber (1862: 157) used a statement from the Mahā-bhāṣya on 1.1.57 (Kielhorn [1880-85: I: 144.10-11]) to show that Patañjali was an easterner. In the course of an argument, it is noted that the term *pūrva* 'prior, eastern' can be used even if an object A which is said to occur before or east of B is separated from the latter by another object. An example of this is cited:

(1) *pūrvaṃ mathurāyāḥ pāṭaliputram* 'Pāṭaliputra is east of Mathurā.'

Weber (1862: 157; reiterated 1873b) interpreted this sentence differently. He considered that it meant 'Pāṭaliputra comes before Mathurā.' From this he concluded that Patañjali's example shows he came from an area east of Pāṭaliputra, modern Patna.

R. G. Bhandarkar (1873b [= 1927-33 1: 122-23]) reached a different conclusion on the basis of another passage. He concluded that Patañjali came from an area north by north-west of Oudh (Ayodhya). In the course of the discussion on rule 3.3.136, the following examples are cited (Kielhorn [1880-85: II: 162.6-7, 11]):[416]

(2) *yo'yam adhvā gata ā pāṭaliputrāt tasya yad avaram sāketāt*

'(Something was done on that part of) the path traversed going from Pāṭaliputra (and which lies) this side of Sāketa.'

(3) *yo'yam adhvâ pāṭaliputrād gantavyas tasya yat paraṃ sāketāt*

'(Something will be done on that part of) the path which is to be traversed going to Pāṭaliputra and which lies beyond Sāketa.' Here Sāketa (Ayodhya) is between Pāṭaliputra and the place where the speaker is situated. If this is Patañjali's place, concluded Bhandarkar, then Patañjali came from an area north by north-west of Ayodhya. Bhandarkar (1873c [= 1927-33 1:128]) also answered to Weber's suggestion, pointing out that example (1) means "... is east of ..." and not "... is before ..." Weber (1873d: 314-15) attempted to answer Bhandarkar, but could not do so convincingly. To reconcile his interpretation of (1) with examples (2) and (3), Weber fell back on the supposition that the Mahābhāṣya had at one time been reconstituted (see section III.2.4), so that these examples could belong to different authors. This is obviously a desperate attempt to salvage an unwarranted conclusion. Weber's position has nothing to recommend it and has been rightly rejected in recent works.[417]

3.2. *Relative chronology: Pāṇini and Yāska, Pāṇini and the prātiśākhyas.*

3.2.1. *Pāṇini and Yāska.*

Yāska, the author of the Nirukta, a treatise dealing with Vedic words and their etymological explanations, has frequently been considered to antedate Pāṇini. The early arguments advanced in favor of this view were usually vague generalities. Roth (1848: xv) considered it implausible that Pāṇini should have antedated Yāska because the latter's grammatical views are less advanced than Pāṇini's. Max Müller (1869: introduction, p. 5) considered Yāska the earlier author,[418] but admitted he had no definite basis for this opinion.[419]

Goldstücker (1861: 222-25), on the other hand, advanced two pieces of evidence to support the view that Yāska was prior to Pāṇini. They are as follows. Pāṇini knew the name *yāska.* Since there is no other Yāska in ancient literature, this must be the author of the Nirukta. Secondly, Pāṇini does not define the term *upasarga* 'preverb'. Yāska enters into a discussion concerning preverbs and mentions various views concerning them, but he does not mention Pāṇini, whose treatment of these is more scientific and complete. The first argument is unacceptable, as was noted by Müller (1869: introduction, p. 4) and Liebich (1891: 19). Pāṇini's rule 2.4.63 (*yaskâdibhyo gotre*) serves to derive the name *yāska* 'descendant of Yāska', but there is no indication whatever that this is anything but a patronymic.[420] Goldstücker's second point is also unacceptable, on two counts. First, the Nirukta and the Aṣṭādhyāyī are works of very different aims involving different areas of concern, so that one cannot immediately draw firm chronological conclusions on the basis of such methodological differences as mentioned by Goldstücker (see Liebich [1891: 19]). Moreover, it is wrong to claim that Pāṇini did not define the term *upasarga.* Rules 1.4.58 (*prâdayaḥ*) and 1.4.59 (*upasargāḥ kriyā-yoge*) together provide that the items *pra* etc., when they are connected with items denoting actions, are called *upasarga.* And of course Goldstücker's general theory regarding technical terminology has been shown to be unacceptable (see section III.1.5.3a).

Liebich (1891: 19) said in an early work that he would not be surprised if a precise study of Yāska's work showed it to be later than Pāṇini, of an epoch with Patañjali.[421] Later, however, Liebich (1919b: 22-29) cautiously suspected that Yāska preceded Pāṇini. His evidence for this is terminological and stylistic: the development of technical terminology and the use of certain elements in compounds. However, none of the evidence is precise enough to warrant the assumption (Liebich [1919b: 25]) that Pāṇini took over a paraphrase from Yāska.[422]

S. K. Belvalkar (1915: 6-8) also considered that Yāska antedated Pāṇini, and his argument too was based on stages of theoretical development and terminology. However, Belvalkar (1915: 7-8) also noted a negative argument which might be used to show that Yāska was later than Pāṇini. If Yāska gives a certain explanation for a given word and this is not provided by Pāṇini, one assumes that the word in that meaning was unknown to Pāṇini. For, in a grammar of the caliber of Pāṇini's, such an omission is not to be countenanced. Hence, Yāska's knowledge of such a word in a particular meaning indicates he came after Pāṇini, when that word gained currency. Belvalkar rightly noted that this method leads to contradictory results. I have mentioned it, and other early discussions, because, as we shall see, the same arguments have again been propounded more recently.

Those who have argued for Pāṇini's priority have proposed two kinds of evidence: negative evidence of the kind mentioned by Belvalkar and positive evidence which is supposed to indicate that Yāska knew Pāṇini's grammar.

Thieme (1935c: *23*-*24*, summarized in Mehendale [1968: 4-7]) argued that Yāska knew Pāṇini's grammar. Thieme's main points are as follows. In the introduction to the second chapter of the Nirukta (Sarup [1927a: 44]), Yāska presupposes that at his time an exhaustive analysis of regular formations had already been carried out. Yāska is also familiar with the concept of a verb root (*dhātu*). Moreover, Yāska's etymological explanations show that he knew Pāṇini's sūtras. For example, he explains (Nirukta 2.2, Sarup [1927a: 45]) *daṇḍyaḥ* 'punishable' as *daṇḍam arhati* 'merits punishment', in accord with

Pāṇini's rules 5.1.63, 66 (see note 422).[423] In a later paper, Thieme (1958: 46-48) added evidence to buttress his view. In connection with forms such as *santi* 'they are', *rājā* 'king' (nom. sg.), Yāska (Nirukta 1.1, Sarup [1927a: 44]) speaks of the deletion of the initial sound (*ādi-lopa*) of *as* 'be' before nivṛtti-sthāna (lit. 'place of turning back') and the modification (*vikāra*) of the penultimate sound (*upadhā*) of the base *rājan*. Thieme argued that this shows Yāska knew Pāṇini's system. He must have known that endings such as *-anti* were treated in Pāṇini's system as marked with *ṅ* and that before such endings the *a-* of *as* was deleted; Yāska used the term *nivṛtti-sthāna* to refer to such endings. Yaska must have been familiar also with Pāṇini's concept of a presuffixal base (*aṅga*) such as *rājan*, which underwent operations.

Thieme does not say this explicitly, and I may be reading more into his statements than he intended, in which case I apologize in advance; however, I cannot help but feel that the only presupposition which makes his argument hold together is that before Pāṇini composed his grammar no comparable analysis of Sanskrit had ever been carried out. This was explicitly assumed by Satyavrat Sāmaśramī (1890), according to the summary given by Giridhara Śarmā Caturveda (1954: 1-6). Satyavrat Sāmaśramī argued that Pāṇini's predecessors (see section III.1.3.1) were concerned only with sandhi rules, not with grammar. Giridhara Śarmā Caturveda (1954: 6-8) correctly pointed out that this position is untenable. Though it is true that Pāṇini's is the first full grammar of Sanskrit we have, it does not follow that no grammarian before him had made any comparable analysis; on the contrary (see section III.1.3.1). Now, the Ṛg-veda pada-pāṭha (analyzed text), to which Pāṇini refers (see section III.3.2.2) analyzes compounds into component members (e.g., *soma-pāḥ* 'soma-drinker'), separates taddhita affixes (*soma-vat* 'soma-ful'), and also separates bases from the so-called pada endings (*rajaḥ-bhiḥ* [*rajobhiḥ*] 'through the space'), thus evincing more than a mere rudimentary analysis of sandhi phenomena (see Siddheshwar Varma [1953: 150-52]). Moreover, the uṇ-ādi affixes can plausibly be considered at least in part pre-Pāṇinian (see section III.1.4.1), and these presuppose the abstraction of roots. It is, therefore, not licit immediately to assume that Yāska's knowledge of the verb root or of presuffixal bases requires that he have known Pāṇini's rules in particular. As for the claim that Yāska's explanation of an item like *daṇḍya* shows he knew Pāṇini's rules, this is hardly acceptable. For all that such an explanation shows is that Yāska, like Pāṇini, knew what such a word meant.

B. Bhattacharya (1958: 3-6) revived Goldstücker's views concerning technical terminology (see section III.1.5.3a) and reasoned as follows. Yāska uses terms such as *upadhā* 'penultimate sound', which Pāṇini defines. "Thus, if Prof. Goldstücker's deductions be accepted, these evidences [sic] form to make a strong presumption in favour of the view that Yāska might have come after Pāṇini."

However, Goldstücker's theory is not acceptable (see section III.1.5.3a).

Mehendale (1968: 7-12; see also 1957, 1960, 1965a: 47-49, 1965b) has reintroduced negative arguments of the kind noted and rejected by Belvalkar (see above).[424] His arguments are, in my opinion, open to serious doubts (see Cardona [1972b: 172-74, forthcoming b]). Laddu (1967) also argued that Pāṇini antedated Yāska, whom he considered a near contemporary of Kātyāyana and Patañjali. The basis for Laddu's conclusion is that Kātyāyana and Patañjali derive items not derived by Pāṇini and that their derivations agree with Yāska's. This is the same negative argumentation noted already, and I agree with S. Bhate (1968: 130) that the evidence adduced is not probative.

In the most recent treatments of this issue, Shiva Narayana Shastri (1969a: 68-79; 1969b; 1972b: 66-70) has argued in favor of Yāska's priority. Interestingly, the same evidence that led Thieme, whom Shiva Narayana does not mention, to conclude that Pāṇini antedated Yāska has led Shiva Narayana to the opposite conclusion. He notes (1969a: 72) that Yāska used the term *nivṛtti-sthāna*, while Pāṇini marked affixes with *k* or *ṅ*. According to him the former terminology is older. Shiva Narayana's arguments concern both comparisons of terminology and meanings attributed to words.[425]

After all the arguments and evidence adduced in support of both views, I think the only reasonable conclusion that can be reached at present is, as Giridhara Śarmā Caturveda remarked (1954: 23), that the question of priority remains open.[426]

3.2.2. *Pāṇini and the prātiśākhyas.*

The relative chronology of Pāṇini and the prātiśākhyas[427] is a vexed question which has not yet been answered satisfactorily. Indeed, scholars do not agree concerning the chronology of the prātiśākhya texts themselves.[428] The issue is complicated by the fact, accepted generally, that the texts of the prātiśākhyas as we have them now contain accretions to older core texts.

The arguments of early scholars in the 19th century concerning the relation between Pāṇini and the prātiśākhyas were for the most part vague generalities. For example, Weber (1858a: 90) stated epigrammatically: the older a sūtra, the more easily understood it is, the later a sūtra, the less easily understood it is; and he concluded that the Vājasaneyi-prātiśākhya was pre-Pāṇinian. Roth (1848: xliii) and Müller (1859: 120) considered that the prātiśākhyas, qua Vedic texts, had to be earlier than Pāṇini. Goldstücker, who, to my knowledge, was the first to say that the prātiśākhyas were post-Pāṇinian, also argued partly in a vague and subjective manner: "In Pāṇini there is organism and life. In the Prātiśākhyas there is mechanism and death."[429]

Somewhat more particular evidence was later given by Liebich (1919b: 35-45) to show that the Vājasaneyi-prātiśākhya was pre-Pāṇinian. The two works contain rules which are identical or nearly so. Hence, one may have borrowed from the other. According to Liebich, the rules of the Vājasaneyi-prātiśākhya are stylistically less sharp and evolved than Pāṇini's, so that they must be earlier. Venkatarama Sarma (1935: 109-17) argued in similar fashion and agreed with Liebich. But such stylistic arguments can cut both ways. Thieme (1935a: 81-98; see also 1958: 41-45) argued that, on the contrary, the Vājasaneyi-prātiśākhya rules in question represent attempts by Kātyāyana to make clearer Pāṇinian statements.[430]

Another approach involves the mention of names. Goldstücker (1861: 209-12) argued as follows. The Ṛk-prātiśākhya mentions Vyāḍi, and this must be the same author mentioned by Kātyāyana and Patañjali (see note 355). The Ṛk-prātiśākhya must therefore be posterior to Pāṇini. K. C. Chaṭṭopādhyāya (1937: 349) noted, however, that this is not probative evidence: the passage where Vyāḍi is mentioned could be an addition to the original text. Max Müller (1869: 10-17) argued that where Pāṇini attributes a view to Śākalya this is a reference to the Śākalya whose work was the basis of the Ṛk-prātiśākhya, actually composed by Śaunaka. Sköld (1926a: 27-29) attempted to refute Müller. However, his arguments lose force because of his assumption that, since all but one of the rules in question are not the objects of independent discussions in the Mahā-bhāṣya, they probably did not exist at the time of Patañjali (see section III.1.3.3e). A view similar to Müller's was later espoused by B. Ghosh (1934), who claimed that Pāṇini took rules 1.1.16-19 and 8.4.67 from the Ṛk-prātiśākhya. Ghosh assumed that a reference to Śākalya in the Aṣṭādhyāyī showed dependence on the Ṛk-prātiśākhya.[431] Keith (1936: 742-44) agreed with Ghosh. However, Thieme (1937) and K. C. Chaṭṭopādhyāya (1937) pointed out that Ghosh was in error: 1.1.16 refers to the view of Śākalya, the author of the pada-pāṭha of the Ṛg-veda, while the Ṛk-prātiśākhya was composed by Śaunaka (see also Sköld 1926a: 42-46). This exchange of arguments led to a series of articles. Ghosh (1938) maintained his view against Thieme and was rebutted by K. C. Chaṭṭopādhyāya (1938) and Thieme (1939). Then S. P. Chaturvedi (1938a) entered the controversy, speaking against Ghosh, who answered (1939), upon which Chaturvedi (1940a) again rebutted him. In my opinion, Ghosh's view is not supported by the evidence.

There is, nevertheless, definite evidence to show that some prātiśākhya rules were borrowed from Pāṇini's system. As I have noted (section III.1.5.1a), Pāṇini uses a substitution procedure whereby an element Y is said to occur instead of an element X, the latter denoted by a genitive (see section III. 1.5.3d with note 217). There is another method: an element X is considered to change to Y, denoted respectively by a nominative and an accusative forr (see Thieme [1935c: *22*; 1958: 45], Cardona [1965a: 230; 1969: 32], Staal [1974: 64]). The second method is the norm in the prātiśākhyas. Moreover, it is licit to say that this technique is earlier than Pāṇini's substitution procedure (Thieme [1958: 45]). For the modification procedure is immediately reconcilable with the morphophonemic statements of the prātiśākhyas, whereby elements of the pada-pāṭha are converted to forms of the continuous text (*saṃhitā*). But this procedure is not immediately reconcilable with grammatical operations such as letting *bhū* occur in certain environments instead of *as* 'be' (see Cardona [1969: 32-33]). If, then, one finds in a text such as the Vājasaneyi-prātiśākhya a rule identical with Pāṇini's 1.1.49 (see note 217), it is correctly to be treated as a borrowing from Pāṇini.[432]

Thieme (1935c: *22*-*23*) attempted to demonstrate that there is also evidence to prove that the Ṛk-prātiśākhya is posterior to Pāṇini. He argued as follows. Pāṇini did not use the term *sthāna* in the meaning 'point of articulation' (but see section III.1.5.3b.2). To him this term meant simply 'place', as in rule 1.1.49 (see note 217). The author of the Vājasaneyi-prātiśākhya wished to avoid using *sthāna* in this nontechnical value. Hence, he replaced Pāṇini's substitution procedure with a system of modification.[433] The Ṛk-prātiśākhya is also to be considered post-Pāṇinian if this reasoning is correct, since it too replaced Pāṇini's substitution procedure with a modification technique. I do not think this is acceptable. To begin with, Thieme predicates a major methodological shift on a rather tenuous terminological feature, a dubious one at that. Moreover, there is no evidence to show that the modification procedure of the prātiśākhyas was resorted to as a replacement for Pāṇini's substitution procedure. Indeed, as Thieme himself later noted (1958: 45), it is more correctly considered older that Pāṇini's method.

The present state of the question, in my opinion, is this. It can be demonstrated that some prātiśākhya rules imitate Pāṇinian rules. However, it can also be shown with considerable conviction that the morphophonemic technique of letting a unit change into another, a procedure used in the prātiśākhyas, is older that Pāṇini's substitution method. But none of the evidence adduced is sufficient to show that all the prātiśākhyas are earlier than or posterior to Pāṇini.[434]

3.3. *Realia.*

3.3.1. *The Aṣṭādhyāyī.*

The most complete treatment of realia reflected in Pāṇini's Aṣṭādhyāyī is by V. S. Agrawala (1963a), a study which was preceded by a series of articles on particular subjects.[435] There are, in addition, quite a few other studies devoted to particular topics.

A large number of Pāṇinian rules is devoted to the derivation of patronymics of the type *aupagava* (see sections III.1.5.1a, 1.5.5b.3). The patronymic system reflected in these rules was studied in detail by Agrawala (1963a: 522-35; 1963b). This subject was also treated briefly by Brough (1946: 41-45), who stressed (1953: 51) the importance of Pāṇini's lists (*gaṇa*) for the editing of texts dealing with ancestral names.[436]

Geographic data reflected in Pāṇini's grammar were studied by Basudev Upadhyaya (1936) and then in greater detail by Agrawala (1953a: 1963a: 35-76); see also R. G. Bhandarkar 1871-74 (= 1927-33 1: 104-07). Pāṇini's reference to the Parśu, which scholars have identified with Persians (see V. S. Agrawala [1963a: 447, 470]), has beeṇ taken up anew in some detail by Grantovsky (1963), who not only discusses many details concerning Afghanistan in the time of Pāṇini but also relates the term *parśu* with "Pashto" (1963: 89-90).

One detail having to do with governmental organization has been the source of a dispute, namely whether the term *saṃgha* used by Pāṇini refers to a republic. Jayaswal (1943: 30-41) claimed it did, but Shembavnekar (1944) argued that this was false. According to him (1944: 139), a saṃgha was a confederacy or league of tribes or states. More recently, Agrawala (1963a: 400) again spoke of saṃghas as republics.

Some work has been done on the literary materials reflected in the Aṣṭādhyāyī.[437] V. N. Gokhale (1939: 6-9) treated taddhita rules in so far as they showed evidence of such literary works. Other studies have concentrated on particular works mentioned in the Aṣṭādhyāyī. R. S. Bhattacharya (1966k, l) has discussed two such works. He argued, in agreement with P. V. Kane (1941: 422, cf. P. V. Kane [1962: 1168-69]), that the bhikṣu-sūtras were a work concerning mendicants, not a Vedānta text, as Agrawala (1963a: 393) had claimed.[438] Bhattacharya also argued that the Śiśu-krandīya was not a poem (Weber 1876: 210, note, Agrawala 1963a: 341) or a nursery book for naughty children (Goldstücker 1861: 28-29) but a medical work. P. C. Divanji (1949) proposed that Pāṇini knew the original Bhārata-saṃhitā 'composed by the same sage who arranged the Vedic *saṃhitās*' (1949: 276).

3.3.2. *The Mahā-bhāṣya.*

Considerable effort has been devoted to the realia reflected in the Mahā-bhāṣya, a topic on which two books have appeared in the last twenty years (Puri [1957 Prabhudayāla Agnihotrī [1966]). Many of the materials were already dealt with by Weber (1873d); see also Kanjilal (1955). Information about realia reflected in the Mahā-bhāṣya is also found throughout V. P. Limaye's recent work (1974).

According to Patañjali, the śiṣtas of Āryâvarta are the model speakers of Sanskrit (see section III.2.2.2). Patañjali also specifies the bounds of Āryâvarta. This has been discussed by S. B. Chaudhuri (1949, especially p. 115), Puri (1957: 202-04), Prabhudayāla Agnihotrī (1966: 71-73). D. G. Bhave (1940) devoted a short note to Patañjali's mention of the Ābhīras, and P. V. Kane (1951) discussed the Mahā-bhāṣya's mention of cities.

One of the major questions discussed is the extent of the literature known in Patañjali's time. Most scholars agree that this literature was extensive and included epic and other poetry; see R. G. Bhandarkar (1871-74; 1874), Telang (1874), Kielhorn (1885a), R. K. Mookerji (1923; 1969: 234-35), K. G. Subrahmanyam (1924), P. C. Chakravarti (1926: 275-88, 464-70), V. S. Agrawala (1943; 1963a: 23-24), P. V. Kane (1961: 333).[439] One topic which has been the source of considerable debate is the question whether Patañjali knew theatrical representations and if so of what kind. The debate centers about a passage in the Mahā-bhāṣya (on rule 3.1.26, Kielhorn [1880-85: II: 34.14-24, 36.13-21]) concerning how the grammar accounts for sentences such as *kaṃsaṃ ghātayati* (lit. '. . . has Kaṃsa killed'), equivalent to *kaṃsa-vadham ācaṣṭe* '. . . relates the killing of Kaṃsa.' This topic has been dealt with by Weber (1873d: 353-54, 488-91), Lüders (1906), Hillebrandt (1918), Keith (1917-20; 1924: 32-36), Winternitz (1920), P. V. Kane (1961: 333-35) and, most recently, K. V. Abhyankar (1967: 257-59). The views proposed regarding the Mahā-bhāṣya passage are that it concerns a shadow play (Lüders, Winternitz, but see Dasgupta - De [1962: 47]), a pantomime (Keith), and an actual full theatrical representation (Kane). Puri (1957: 217-20) discussed earlier views and concluded that the Mahā-bhāṣya shows evidence of full theatrical representations. K. V. Abhyankar (1967: 260-61) similarly concluded that "There were prevalent in the days of Patañjali all three representations of past events – the dramatical, the pictorial, and the verbal . . ."

Several studies have been devoted to religious matters reflected in the Mahā-bhāṣya. Guleri (1912) noted that the Mahā-bhāṣya contains evidence for the existence of a Śiva cult (Śiva-bhāgavata) at the time of Patañjali; see also R. G. Bhandarkar (1913: 115), Puri (1957: 188-89). One particular topic which has attracted a great deal of attention and led to considerable debate is the Mahā-bhāṣya comments on rule 4.3.98 (*vāsudevârjunābhyāṃ vun*) and its use as evidence for the existence of Vāsudeva worship at the time of Patañjali and also Pāṇini's time. On this topic see Grierson (1908), Keith (1908), K. B. Pathak (1910-14b), R. G. Bhandarkar (1910; 1913: 3), Mazumdar (1910), U. C. Bhattacharjee (1925; 1926a; 1926b), K. G. Subrahmanyam (1926a; 1926b), Gonda (1954: 160), Buddha Prakash (1967) and, most recently, Hazra (1970), who has taken up the question again in full.[440]

In his comments on 5.2.9 Patañjali discusses what is meant by terms which refer to the movement of pieces in a board game. Thieme (1962) took up this passage, presented other evidence, and concluded that the game in question is chess.

IV. LATER COMMENTARIES.

1. INTRODUCTION.

As I have noted (section III.2.1), the Mahā-bhāṣya is not a true commentary on Pāṇini's grammar. Full commentaries in which all the rules are paraphrased, with examples and counterexamples given to illustrate their application, are all later by at least about seven hundred years.[441] These commentaries are of two general kinds: what I shall call running commentaries, which take up rules in the order in which they appear in the Aṣṭādhyāyī, and reordered commentaries. In the latter, rules concerning particular topics are brought together in sections although they might not occur together in the Aṣṭādhyāyī. For example, the Siddhânta-kaumudī (see section IV.3.2) starts with a section of definition rules introducing terms (*saṃjñā-prakaraṇa*), then treats major meta-rules (*paribhāṣā*) and goes on to deal with: sandhi, operations which apply to or are conditioned by nominal endings, feminine affixes, kāraka rules together with nominal affixation rules, compounds, taddhita affixation, finite verb forms, derived verb roots, rules restricting the occurrence of verb endings (ātmanepada and parasmaipada), the meanings of L-suffixes, primary verbal affixes (kṛt affixes, including uṇ-ādi affixes), Vedic rules, accentual rules. This organization results in one's having to reiterate parts of rules which, by anuvṛtti (see section III.1.5.3g), did not have to be repeated explicitly in Pāṇini's corpus. However, this new organization does not do violence to the organization of the grammar in terms of major headings (see section III.1.5.2c).

2. RUNNING COMMENTARIES.

2.1. *The Kāśikā-vṛtti and its commentaries.*

The Kāśikā-vṛtti – usually referred to simply as the Kāśikā – is the oldest extant complete running commentary on Pāṇini's grammar. It is the work of two authors, Jayāditya and Vāmana (Kielhorn [1876a: 12, note], Belvalkar

[1915: 35-36], S. C. Chakravarti [1919-25: I: introduction, pp. 15-17]), who commented respectively on the first five and the last three chapters of rules.[442] As a vṛtti (see section III.2.1 with note 339), the Kāśikā comments on rules by giving paraphrases which include what is to be supplied for the understanding of the rules through the application of definitions and metarules as well as through anuvṛtti and giving examples to illustrate how the rules apply. For example, it comments as follows on rule 6.1.78 (*eco'y-av-āy-āvaḥ* [*aci* 77]): *ecaḥ sthāne'ci parato'y av āy āv ity ete ādeśā yathā-saṃkhyaṃ bhavanti; cayanam, lavanam, cāyakaḥ, lāvakaḥ* ... "In place of [the sounds *e, o, ai, au* denoted by the abbreviation] *ec* there occur respectively *ay, av, āy, āv* when a vowel follows; [for example,] *cayanam* ['heaping, gathering' ⟨ *ce-ana*], *lavanam* ['cutting' ⟨ *lo-ana*], *cāyakaḥ* ['who gathers' ⟨ *cai-aka*], *lāvaka* ['who cuts' ⟨ *lau-aka*] ...". Like all comparable later vṛttis, the Kāśikā appears at first sight straightforward and simple. However, its comments presuppose conclusions based on arguments which cannot be known fully unless one returns to the Mahā-bhāṣya, where these arguments appear. This question has been well discussed by Thieme (1956: 7-8).

The Kāśikā often cites vārttikas in the course of its comments.[443] It has also incorporated some vārttikas as separate rules in the grammar and otherwise modified rules (see section III.1.3.3c). These changes were studied by Kielhorn (1885b: 190-97; 1887d), and more recently Mahesh Dutt Sharma (1969) has again taken up the influences on the Kāśikā of other grammarians.

The Kaśika has two major commentaries: the Kāśikā-vivaraṇa-pañjikā – alias Nyāsa, by which name it is commonly called – of Jinendrabuddhi and the Pada-mañjarī of Haradatta. The important characteristic of the Nyāsa is that it regularly tries to show how what is achieved through an addition to the grammar as stated in a vārttika can equally well be achieved by the original rule interpreted in a given way, so that no step is taken beyond the sūtras themselves (see S. C. Chakravarti [1919-25: I: introduction, pp. 22-23], Renou [1940a: 27]). The Pada-mañjarī is a long commentary in which arguments carried out earlier are commonly restated and rediscussed, with extensive citations and criticism of predecessors.[444]

There have been several editions of the Kāśikā.[445] Recently, a new edition of the text was produced by Aryendra Sharma, Khanderao Deshpande and D. G. Padhye (1969-70). Though not truly critical (see Birwé [1973]), this is an improvement over earlier editions (see notes 397, 459). A good edition of the Nyāsa alone was made by S. C. Chakravarti (1919-25). More recently, the Kāśikā together with the Nyāsa and the Pada-mañjarī was edited by Dwarikas Shastri and Kalika Prasad Shukla (1965-67).[446]

The earliest translation of a sizeable part of the Kāśikā into a European language appears to have been made by Liebich (1892),[447] who translated, with brief notes, chapters 2.1 - 2.2 concerning compounds. Vasu's translation of the Aṣṭādhyāyī (1891) is also a fairly close paraphrase of the Kāśikā. A translation of the first chapter of the Kaśika, with extensive summaries of arguments from the Mahā-bhāṣya and commentaries on the Kāśikā, was produced by Ojihara and Renou (Ojihara - Renou [1960-62], Ojihara [1967a]).

The upper limit for the time of composition of the Kāśikā can be set with fair certainty. In his commentary on rule 1.3.23, Jayāditya cites part of a verse (3.14) from Bhāravi's Kirâtârjunīya(see Kielhorn [1885a: 327], K. B. Pathak [1931: 247]). Bhāravi s date is set at the end of the sixth century (P. V. Kane [1961: 119-20], Dasgupta - De [1962: 178]), so that the earliest the Kāśikā can be dated is the end of the sixth to the early seventh centuries. This tallies with I-Tsing's statement (Takakusu [1896: 175]) that Jayāditya died about 660.[448] The lower limit to be set for the Kāśikā involves a consideration of Jinendrabuddhi's date.

Concerning Jinendrabuddhi's dates, one thing is certain: he antedated Haradatta, who refers to him,[449] so that he must be dated earlier than the eleventh century (see below). Moreover, Kaiyaṭa probably knew the Nyāsa,[450] which again shows Jinendrabuddhi is to be dated at earlier than the eleventh century (see note 344). How much earlier has been the object of debate. A verse in Māgha's Śiśupāla-vadha[451] is important. As is well known, the verse involves two meanings for a series of adjectives, depending on whether they are construed with *rāja-nīti* 'king's policy' or *śabda-vidyā* 'knowledge of grammar'. The adjectives are: *anutsūtra-pada-nyāsā, sad-vṛttiḥ, san-nibandhanā, apaspaśā.* With reference to the knowledge of grammar these mean, respectively: 'which includes a nyāsa that does not depart from the sūtras by adding words', 'which includes a worthy vṛtti', 'which includes a worthy basic text', and 'which is devoid of the paspaśā'. In his comments on this verse Mallinātha directly says that the Nyāsa is Jinendrabuddhi's Nyāsa, the vṛtti is the Kāśikā-vṛtti, the basic text is the Mahā-bhāṣya, and the paspaśā is the introductory section of the Mahā-bhāṣya. Modern scholars generally agree on all of these identifications except the Nyāsa. Some scholars agree with Mallinātha; thus K. B. Pathak (1897-1900: 305; 1909-14a: 31), P. V. Kane (1909-14: 92; 1961: 147), S. C. Chakravarti (1918: introduction, p. 3; 1919-25: I: introduction, pp. 22-23). Others have objected to identifying the nyāsa mentioned here with Jinendrabuddhi's work. Kielhorn (1908a) objected principally because he considered Jinendrabuddhi later than Haradatta. But this view is not proper (see note 449). Another objection raised is that there was more than one grammatical commentary called *nyāsa*, so that the word *nyāsa* in the Śiśupāla-vadha verse need not refer to Jinendrabuddhi's work specifically; thus S. K. De (1923: 47; 1960: 48),[452] and most recently Yudhiṣṭhira Mīmāṃsaka (1973: I: 506).[453] At least one of the supports for this objection, namely that Sāyaṇa referred to several Nyāsas in his Mādhavīya-dhātu-vṛtti (see section IV.4), was eliminated by K. B. Pathak (1912: 235-36), who showed that, when Sāyaṇa refers to such a work using the term *nyāsa* alone, he means Jinendrabuddhi's commentary. Liebich (1930: 363) strongly opposed S. K. De, noting that the Nyāsa par excellence was Jinendrabuddhi's.[454] I think this opinion is worthy of support. The Nyāsa in question must be a commentary on a Pāṇinīya text. For it is the Mahā-bhāṣya which has an introductory section called *paspaśā*. Now, it is true that there were other texts called *nyāsa* and that Bhartṛhari referred to such a text (see note 453). But the most famous Nyāsa of Pāṇinian grammar after Bhartṛhari was clearly Jinendrabuddhi's. It seems probable to me, therefore, that Māgha did indeed refer to Jinendrabuddhi's work.[455]

If this is accepted, the question then involves Māgha's date. He is cited by the mid-ninth century poetician Ānandavardhana (see P. V. Kane [1909-14: 91]), so that he must be dated earlier than 850. It seems reasonable to put Māgha's date at about 750 A. D.[456] This would indicate a date of about 700 for Jinendrabuddhi, although there is obviously some conjecture involved.[457] Consequently, the Kāśikā is probably to be dated in the seventh century, a date generally accepted by modern scholars.

The date of Haradatta has also been the object of some disagreement. K. B. Pathak (1931: 251) assigned Haradatta to the thirteenth century because, according to Pathak, no reference is made to Haradatta's work in grammatical works before then.[458] This dating, though accepted by Renou (1940a: 29), cannot be maintained. Dharmakīrti (see section IV.3.1.1) refers to Haradatta by name (see M. Rangacharya [1916-27: I: ix, II: 157]). In addition, Śaraṇadeva (see section IV.2.2.5) quotes the Rūpâvatāra and mentions Dharmakīrti in his Durghaṭa-vṛtti, composed in 1172 (see Gaṇapati Sastri [1909: 30, 72 (rules 24, 175)]). Since Haradatta is posterior to Kaiyaṭa, to whom he probably refers (Yudhiṣṭhira Mīmāṃsaka [1973: I: 394-95]), he is probably to be dated at some time between 1000 and 1100. S. K. Belvalkar (1915: 40) dated him at ca. 1100, Yudhiṣṭhira Mīmāṃsaka at ca. saṃvat 1115 (A. D. 1058/9). He is possibly to be put at a still earlier date (see section IV.3.1.1).

Apart from the articles already mentioned, there have not appeared in recent years many studies devoted exclusively to the Kāśikā or its commentaries. K. V. Abhyankar (1966) discussed one of the examples given in the Kāśikā on 1.1.4, but without reaching a definite conclusion. The question was then taken up by Ojihara (1968), who showed that the example to be accepted for the text is *parṇaṃ na veḥ* 'like the wing of a bird'.[459] R. S. Bhattacharya has discussed differences of interpretation in the Kāśikā and the Mahā-bhāṣya (1954e), and (1966cc) examples given in the Kāśikā on 2.1.6, 6.1.77 and 6.2.14. Ram Gopal (1966) briefly discussed Vedic quotations in the Kāśikā (and in the Siddhânta-kaumudī [section IV.3.2]), ending with a plea for critical editions with these citations given correctly. Vedic citations in the Kāśikā (and the Siddhânta-kaumudī) were again taken up by Mahesh Dutt Sharma (1967), who also (1971b: 54-6) has given a list of citations from the Mahā-bhārata in the Kāśikā.

2.2. *Other running commentaries.*

2.2.1. *The Bhāṣā-vṛtti.*

The Bhāṣā-vṛtti of Puruṣottamadeva, who also commented on the Mahā-bhāṣya (see note 347), is a commentary comparable to the Kāśikā in its method of paraphrasing rules, but less detailed. Moreover, this is truly a *bhāṣā-vṛtti* 'commentary on rules which pertain to the bhāṣā' (see section III.1.5.8a): rules which apply to Vedic usage are omitted. In addition, Puruṣottama considers accentual rules Vedic also, and omits commenting on them, although not all accentual rules were restricted to Vedic by Pāṇini. The Bhāṣā-vṛtti was commented on by Sṛṣṭidhara (ca. 1650) in his Bhāṣā-vṛtty-artha-vivṛti, the beginning and end of which were cited by S. C. Chakravarti (1918: introduction, pp. 11-19).[460]

The Bhāṣā-vṛtti was edited by S. C. Chakravarti (1918), and more recently Dwarikadas Shastri (1971) has produced another edition, which is useful for its indices.[461]

Puruṣottama shows reverence for the Kāśikā and the Bhāga-vṛtti (section IV.2.2.4); he finishes his work with a verse (S. C. Chakravarti [1918: 735], Dwarikadas Shastri [1971: 522]) in which he says that one who intends to comprehend the final views (*siddhânta*) of the Kāśikā and the Bhāga-vṛtti should ponder over his own work, the Bhāṣā-vṛtti. In his commentary on rule 8.3.5, Puruṣottama mentions Kaiyaṭa (see section III.2.2.1 with note 344) and also refers to Maitreya-rakṣita (see section IV.4) in his Laghu-paribhāṣā-vṛtti (K. V. Abhyankar 1967: 127, paribhāṣā 34). He is himself quoted by Śaraṇadeva (section IV.2.2.5) and by Sarvānanda in his commentary on the Amara-kośa, the Ṭīkā-sarvasva, written in 1159/60 (see D. C. Bhattacharya [1922: 203], Kali Charan Shastri [1947: 901-02; 1956: 97], Yudhiṣṭhira Mīmāṃsaka [1973: I: 405]). He is therefore generally placed in the early twelfth century; See S. C. Chakravarti (1918: introduction, pp. 2-5), Nitti Dolci (1938b: xvi-xvii), Yudhiṣṭhira Mīmāṃsaka (1973: I: 405).

2.2.2. *The Mitâkṣarā.*

The Vyākaraṇa-mitâkṣarā of Annambhaṭṭa, who composed a commentary on Kaiyaṭa's Pradīpa (section III.2.2.1), is a simple commentary[462] in which rules are paraphrased with examples to illustrate them. The text has been edited by Jagannāthasvāmy Āryavaraguru and Bhaṭṭanātha (1903-16).

2.2.3. *The Śabda-kaustubha.*

The Śabda-kaustubha of Bhaṭṭojī Dīkṣita, edited by Vindhyeśvarī Prasāda Dvivedī - Gaṇapati Śāstrī Mokate (1917), Gopāla Shastri Nene (1929) and Gopāla Shastri Nene - Mukund Śāstrī Puṇtamkar (1933), is an incomplete work which covers chapters 1, 2, 3.1 - 3.2, and 4 of the Aṣṭādhyāyī. Though Bhaṭṭojī here paraphrases each rule and gives examples to illustrate its application, this is by no means a vṛtti comparable to the Kāśikā or the Bhāṣā-vṛtti. Bhaṭṭojī goes into great detail concerning possible interpretations of rules and notes the opinions of predecessors. He himself tells us this in the introductory verses to his work. After doing obeisance to the three sages Pāṇini, Kātyāyana and Patañjali, to his wise predecessors who established final views, principal among them Bhartṛhari, and to his father Lakṣmīdhara, he notes that he will extract from the ocean which is the Mahā-bhāṣya the kaustubha jewel of grammar (*śabda-kaustubha*), and then says: grasp effortlessly from this work the meaning, in its entirety, which is gotten with great effort after considering many other works. Bhaṭṭojī's reference here to the Mahā-bhāṣya, together with the fact that the work is divided into āhnikas (see section III.2.1 with note 341), led Haraprasāda Shāstrī (1931: xxvi-xxvii) to say that this was really a commentary on the Mahā-bhāṣya. This is not acceptable. Were the Śabda-kaustubha a commentary on the Mahā-bhāṣya, one would expect Bhaṭṭojī to have commented only on those rules to which were devoted separate discussions in the Mahā-bhāṣya. But he does indeed comment on other rules also. Bhaṭṭojī's reference to the Mahā-bhāṣya and other predecessors is immediately explainable in terms of the character of his work. The work is syncretic, treating of views propounded by predecessors, including, of course, the great source of such views, the Mahā-bhāṣya. Moreover, Bhaṭṭojī was an innovator who disagreed with a great many of the views held by earlier Pāṇinīyas. Most scholars (e.g., Belvalkar [1915: 47], Yudhiṣṭhira Mīmāṃsaka [1973: I: 486]) consider the Śabda-kaustubha a commentary on the Aṣṭādhyāyī, and I think this is correct.

Bhaṭṭojī's literary activity probably took place during the last half of the sixteenth century and the early seventeenth century. These are the dates adopted by P. K. Gode (1941: 199), who (1940) discussed the question thoroughly and considered opinions of others.[463]

2.2.4. *The Bhāga-vṛtti.*

The Bhāga-vṛtti of Vimalamati[464] is known only from quotations in other texts. These citations have been collected and edited, with comments, by Yudhiṣṭhira Mīmāṃsaka (1964/5). The apparent reason for the name of the work ('vṛtti [composed] in parts') is (Yudhiṣṭhira Mīmāṃsaka [1964/5: introduction, p. 3]) that Vimalamati separates Vedic and non-Vedic rules, to be considered separately.[465] The Bhāga-vṛtti adheres more closely than other vṛttis to the Mahā-bhāṣya (Yudhiṣṭhira Mīmāṃsaka [1964/5: introduction, p. 3]).

Vimalamati is cited as disagreeing with interpretations given by Jayāditya, one of the authors of the Kāśikā (section IV.2.1); see Yudhiṣṭhira Mīmāṃsaka (1964/5: 26-27 [rules 5. 1. 132, 5. 2. 13]). This would indicate that the Bhāga-vṛtti postdates the Kāśikā. Because of this, K. C. Chatterji (1931: 415-18) dated it at between 850 and 1050. S. P. Bhattacharya (1947) put it at about 1000, and Renou (1940a: 30) gave as its probable date the end of the ninth century because Vimalamati cites Māgha (see Yudhiṣṭhira Mīmāṃsaka [1964/5: 4, rule 1.1.15], and above, section IV.2.1) and is cited by Maitreya-rakṣita (section IV.4). The ninth century seems reasonable and would receive support from a possible reference to a view of Vimalamati's in Kaiyaṭa's Pradīpa (Yudhiṣṭhira Mīmāṃsaka [1964/5: 10-11]).[466]

2.2.5. *The Durghaṭa-vṛtti.*

Though it bears the title *vṛtti*, the Durghaṭa-vṛtti of Śaraṇadeva is not a full commentary of the type exemplified by the Kāśikā. The purpose of the work was stated concisely by Gaṇapati Sastri (1909: English preface, p. 1): "The work has been so named, as it is an exposition (*vṛtti*) reconciling those Lakshyas (forms of words) and Pāṇini's Sūtras which appear difficult to reconcile (*durghaṭa*) with each other." Śaranadeva takes up about 500 rules, together with particular forms, and proposes interpretations whereby the rules account for the forms.

The text was edited by Gaṇapati Sastri (1909) and later by Renou (1941-56), who also translated the text, traced citations, and contributed a study of the author, his work, and its sources (1940a: 45-75). In an introductory verse (Gaṇapati Sastri [1909: 1]), Śaraṇadeva says he composed his work in 1095 of the Saka era (A. D. 1172, Gaṇapati Sastri [1909: English preface, p.2]).

3. REORDERED COMMENTARIES

3.1. *Commentaries which do not treat all rules.*

3.1.1. *The Rūpâvatāra.*

The earliest extant fully reordered commentary on the Aṣṭādhyāyī is the Rūpâvatāra by the Ceylonese Buddhist Dharmakīrti. This work, which was edited by M. Rangacharya (1916-27), is divided into sections called *avatāra*, hence its name. It is also divided into two major parts. The first deals with definition rules (*saṃjñâvatāra*), sandhi rules (*saṃhitâvatāra*), operations on and conditioned by nominal endings (*vibhakty-avatāra*), indeclinables (*avyayâvatāra*), feminine affixes (*strī-pratyayâvatāra*), kāraka rules and affixation rules pertinent to them, compounds (*samāsâvatāra*), and taddhita affixation (*taddhitâvatāra*). The second part, called *dhātu-pratyaya-pañcikā*, deals with rules introducing post-verbal affixes. The organization is, in general, similar to that of the *Siddhânta-kaumudī* (see section IV.1). However, Dharmakīrti omits Vedic and accentual rules and does not devote a special section to uṇ-ādi affixes.[467] The rules treated are very briefly paraphrased, with examples. Dharmakīrti also refers to the views of predecessors (see below).

The Rūpâvatāra is quoted by the Jaina grammarian Hemacandra, whose dates (1088-1172) are known, and by Maitreya-rakṣita (section IV.4), as well as Śaraṇadeva (section IV.2.2.5); see Gaṇapati Sastri (1909: 71 [rule 175]), S. C. Chakravarti (1918: introduction, p. 1), Renou (1940a: 34 n. 1), Kali Charan Shastri (1956: 90), Yudhiṣṭhira Mīmāṃsaka (1973: I: 525). These facts support a date of about 1100. Yudhiṣṭhira Mīmāṃsaka (1973: I: 396, 524) puts Dharmakīrti at approximately saṃvat 1140 (A. D. 1083/4). However, there is some inscriptional evidence which would indicate that the Rūpâvatāra was included in the grammatical curriculum of schools established by the king Rājendra Coḍa in the eleventh century (see Haraprasāda Shāstrī [1931: xcv - xcvi], Nilakantha Sastri [1934]). On the basis of this evidence, the Rūpâvatāra could be placed in the tenth century.[468] This would require putting back the dates assigned to Haradatta (section IV.2.1) and Kaiyaṭa (see note 344).

3.1.2. *The Prakriyā-kaumudī.*

The Prakriyā-kaumudī of Rāmacandra is the earliest kaumudī[469] work which has been fully edited, with a complete Sanskrit commentary.[470] A commentary, called Prasāda, was written on it by the author's grandson Viṭṭhala.[471]

Both of these were edited by K. P. Trivedi (1925-31).

Like the Rūpâvatāra, the Prakriyā-kaumudī does not treat all the rules of the Aṣṭādhyāyī. It contains a brief section on Vedic rules (K. P. Trivedi [1925-31: II: 700-15]), supplemented in his commentary by Viṭṭhala (K. P. Trivedi [1925-31: II: 716-35]), who also supplied comments on accentual rules (K. P. Trivedi [1925-31: II: 736-91]). But even Viṭṭhala's suppletions do not account for all rules. Ādyāprasāda Miśra (1966: 149-55) has given a list of rules not supplied by Viṭṭhala.

Not only does Rāmacandra include in his work vārttikas and parts of vārttikas, he also countenances views of non-Pāṇinian treatises; see K. P. Trivedi (1925-31: I: xxxiii-xxxiv), Ādyāprasāda Miśra (1966: 115-22). Further, Rāmacandra uses sectarian examples, unlike earlier vṛttis, but in accord with the later custom of Bhaṭṭojī (section IV.3.2, see Ādyāprasāda Miśra [1966: 26-26], Mahesh Dutt Sharma [1971: 52-53]). For example, he uses examples such as *hariṃ bhajati* '. . . is devoted to Hari' instead of the neutral *kaṭaṃ karoti* '. . . is making a mat.'

Rāmacandra is generally dated at about the end of the fourteenth and the beginning of the fifteenth century; see K. P. Trivedi (1925-31: I: xliv-xlv), Renou (1940a: 34 n. 1), Ādyāprasāda Miśra (1966: 16-17), Yudhiṣṭhira Mīmāṃsaka (1973: I: 528-29).

The Prakriyā-kaumudī, its background, composition and method, have been studied recently by Ādyāprasāda Miśra (1966).

3.2. *The Siddhânta-kaumudī, its commentaries and abridgements.*

The most complete kaumudī work (see note 469), and the most prominent in India, is the Siddhânta-kaumudī of Bhaṭṭojī Dīkṣita.[472] This popular text has been edited many times[473] and translated into English (Vasu [1905-07], see also P. V. Nāganātha Śāstrī [1963]). Bhaṭṭojī composed an autocommentary on this work, the Prauḍha-manoramā (see Gopāla Shastri Nene [1939], Sitaram Shastri [1964], V. L. Joshi [1966]), which has been translated into Marathi (Wadegaonkar [1945-64]). Both the Siddhânta-kaumudī and the Prauḍha-manoramā were commented on by others also.[474] One of the commentaries on the former, the Bāla-manoramā of Vāsudeva Dīkṣita (early 18th century), goes into great detail explaining derivations and is thereby most useful to beginners (*bāla*, lit. 'child'). The Tattva-bodhinī of Jñānendrasarasvatī[475] is a terser, more scholarly and demanding commentary, essentially a distillation of the Prauḍha-manoramā. Neither of these two commentaries includes the accentual and Vedic rules, on which Jayakṛṣṇa[476] commented in his Subodhinī.[477] All of these are included in the edition of the Siddhânta-kaumudī by Giridhara Śarmā Caturveda and Parameśvarānanda Śarmā Bhāskara (1958-61); the edition by Gopāla Shastri Nene (1958-61) lacks the Tattva-bodhinī. Another commentary on the Siddhânta-kaumudī is the Śabdêndu-śekhara of Nāgeśabhaṭṭa (late 17th to 18th centuries).[478] This has a longer and a shorter version. The former, the Bṛhac-chabdêndu-śekhara, was recently edited by Sitaram Shastri (1960) and has no known commentary. The shorter version, the Laghu-śabdêndu-śekhara – commonly referred to simply as the Śekhara – was edited in full by Rāmaśāstrī Mānavallī and Bhāradvāja Nārāyaṇaśāstrī (1887).[479] This text has a good number of commentaries, among them some written by modern paṇḍitas, which have been published with parts of the text; see Gopāla Shastri Nene (1925), Nandkishore Shastri (1936), Sudāmā Miśra Śāstrī - Sadāśiva Śāstrī Joshi (1938).

The Prauḍha-mano-ramā was, as I noted, also the object of commentaries. One, the Bṛhac-chabda-ratna, was edited recently by Sitaram Shastri (1964). This edition includes also the Laghu-śabda-ratna, edited earlier by Gopāla Shastri Nene (1939) with the commentaries of Bhairava Miśra (late 18th century, see M. S. Bhat [1959a]) and Nāgeśa's student Vaidyanātha Pāya-guṇḍa as well as Gopāla Shastri Nene's own modern comments.[480] A critical edition of the Bṛhac-chabda-ratna was begun by V. L. Joshi (1966).

There has been some controversy concerning the authorship of the Laghu-śabda-ratna. Traditionally, the Bṛhac-chabda-ratna is attributed to Hari Dīkṣita, Nāgeśa's teacher, and the Laghu-śabda-ratna is considered to have been composed by Nāgeśa but attributed by him to his teacher Hari Dīkṣita. K. V. Abhyankar (1951) argued that both of these commentaries were composed by Hari Dīkṣita. He proposed that Hari composed first the longer (*bṛhat*) version and then later wrote the shorter (*laghu*) version, in which he incorporated views from Nāgeśa's Laghu-śabdêndu-śekhara. However, V. L. Joshi presented (1964) evidence in favor of the traditional view. Abhyankar (1964) then restated his position. I do not think he was able to refute Joshi's evidence. Certainly, it is difficult to get around the fact that the Laghu-śabda-ratna disagrees with the Bṛhac-chabda-ratna (V. L. Joshi [1964: 309-28]) and that Nāgeśa's own student Vaidyanātha, at the beginning of his commentary called Prakāśa on the Laghu-śabda-ratna, does obeisance to his teacher Nāgeśa, whom he qualifies as having composed this commentary (V. L. Joshi [1964: 7]). M. S. Bhat (1965) also upheld the traditional attribution against Abhyankar.

The Siddhânta-kaumudī was also abridged by Varadarāja (17th century, see P. K. Gode [1950]), who composed a medium version,[481] a short version[482] and a supershort version called Sāra-siddhânta-kaumudī. The last was edited for the first time, with an English translation, by Devasthali (1968a).

Bhaṭṭojī's interpretations of Pāṇini are styled *navya* 'new' in contrast to those of earlier Pāṇinīyas.[483] Among the ancients (*prâñcaḥ*) whom he attacks vigorously for their views are Rāmacandra and Viṭṭhala (see section IV.3.1.2, K. P. Trivedi [1925-31: I: xxxiv-xxxvii]). Moreover, Bhaṭṭojī disagreed publicly with his teacher Śeṣakṛṣṇa, an act of temerity for which he was viciously attacked by Jagannātha Paṇḍitarāja. K. C. Chatterji (1935d) devoted a short paper to this. Some of the innovations introduced by Bhaṭṭojī have been the subjects of individual studies. Venkitasubramonia Iyer (1970b) and A. N. Jani (1971, 1972) have discussed Bhaṭṭojī's interpretation of rule 1.2.32 (see note 233). V. L. Joshi (1957) discussed Bhaṭṭojī's view that the root *nij* 'clean' forms two kinds of presents: *nenekti* and *niṅkte* (3rd sg.). He concluded that the acceptance of the second type was a mistake, first made by Kṛṣṇalīlaśuka in his comments on the Daiva (see section IV.4), followed by Sāyaṇa in his Mādhavīya-dhātu-vṛtti, who was in turn followed by Bhaṭṭojī. K. Kunjunni Raja (1962) noted that the form *prârthayanti* 'they ask', inflected in the active instead of the middle, resulted from a misquotation of a verse from the Raghu-vaṃśa.

An incorrect reading of a rule from the phiṭ-sūtras (section III.1.4.2a) in many editions of the Siddhânta-kaumudī was discussed by Śānti Bhikṣu Śāstrī (1954). Mahesh Dutt Sharma (1971a; 1972) has treated two readings in the Siddhânta-kaumudī which he thinks are incorrect, and suggested corrections. The same author (1971b: 52-3) has commented on the use of sectarian examples used in the Siddhânta-kaumudī (see also Mangala Deva Shastri [1947], and above, section IV.3.1.2) and traced quotations which appear therein (1971b: 59-64). Most recently, Bhīmasena Śāstrī (1973) has discussed some examples of errors in the Bāla-manoramā on the Siddhânta-kaumudī.[484]

4. COMMENTARIES ON VERSIONS OF THE DHĀTU-PĀṬHA.

Pāṇini's dhātu-pāṭha (section III.1.3.5) is known only through its commentaries.[485] The full texts of three commentaries are available: the Kṣīra-taraṅgiṇī of Kṣīrasvāmin, the Dhātu-pradīpa of Maitreya-rakṣita, and Sāyaṇa's Mādhavīya-dhātu-vṛtti.[486] The first was edited by Liebich (1930) and subsequently by Yudhiṣṭhira Mīmāṃsaka (1957/8). The Dhātu-pradīpa was edited by S. C. Chakravarti (1919), and Sāyaṇa's commentary was edited by Ananta Sāstrī Phadake and Sadāsiva Śarmā Śāstrī (1934) and more recently by Dwarikadas Shastri (1964). Both these editions made use of the earlier editions by Bhāradvāja Dāmodara Śāstrī (1897) and Mahādeva Śāstrī and K. Rangācārya (1894-1903).

The Kṣīra-taraṅgiṇī and the Dhātu-pradīpa are fairly brief works in which roots are listed and forms given, with references to appropriate rules. Except for the initial section of each work, there is not a great deal of disquisition The Mādhavīya-dhātu-vṛtti, on the other hand, is a very expansive work in which all types of derivatives – verbal and nominal – of roots are discussed, with extensive disquisitions concerning details of derivation.

Kṣīrasvāmin preceded Maitreya-rakṣita, who rejected some of his views (see Yudhiṣṭhira Mīmāṃsaka [1957/8]: introduction, pp. 32-33; 1973: II: 91-93]). Further, Kṣīrasvāmin is mentioned by Vardhamāna (e.g., Eggeling [1879-81: 454]) and Hemacandra (see Yudhiṣṭhira Mīmāṃsaka [1973: II: 90-91]). This establishes that Kṣīrasvāmin can be dated at no later than the early twelfth century, a dating already suggested by Liebich (1930: 201-04). Yudhiṣṭhira Mīmāṃsaka (1973: I: 89-93) presents evidence which leads him to date Kṣīrasvāmin at no later than saṃvat 1100 (A. D. 1043/4). Maitreya-rakṣita's date is not known. As noted above, however, he is doubtless posterior to Kṣīrasvāmin. Moreover, he is cited by Śaraṇadeva (section IV.2.2.5). Hence, he probably dates from the mid-twelfth century; for discussions of the evidence see D. C. Bhattacharya (1922: 203), Liebich (1930: 360), Kali Charan Shastri (1947: 1956), Yudhiṣṭhira Mīmāṃsaka (1973: I: 393, 399). Sāyaṇa is known to have lived in the fourteenth century.

There is another commentary, the Daiva of Deva, on which Kṛṣṇalīlaśukamuni composed a commentary, the Puruṣa-kāra.[487] The aim of the Daiva, which is not a full commentary on the whole dhātu-pāṭha, is to show the purpose of listing separately and with different markers roots which are homophonous.

Considerable work has been done on comparing the different versions of the dhātu-pāṭha as commented on in the above works in order to arrive at something close to a critical edition of the dhātu-pāṭha (see section III.1.2.2) And the commentaries on the dhātu-pāṭha have been brought in to some extent in discussions touching on the so-called fictitious roots contained in the dhātu-pāṭha (see section III.1.5.8c). However, there has been little extensive work done concerning the details of what each commentator says, how he argues, and how he is related to other commentators. I have already noted V. L. Joshi's paper (1957) on the root *nij* (see section IV.3.2). Palsule (1957b) considered details of what different commentators say concerning the root *tṛph* (*tṛmph*) 'be pleased'.

V. EVALUATIONS OF COMMENTARIES.

Each Pāṇinian commentator, whether old, new of ultra-new (see section IV. 3.2. with note 483), approached Pāṇini's grammar with certain assumptions and aims. It is assumed that the rules of the grammar have to account for

Sanskrit usage, of whatever epoch (see section III.2.5.3). It is also assumed that these rules should be as concise as possible, containing no superfluous statements, and fully consistent with each other. The essential aim is to arrive at an interpretation of each rule which meets these requirements. In the process of scrutinizing rules, it may be considered that a given statement or part of it is not truly necessary, so that it can be eliminated. However, one must show that modified rules will account for the same desired results as the original rules. Moreover, each commentator has at his disposal techniques of interpretation (see section III.2.6.2). Finally, the assumption is made that each successive teacher of the trio Pāṇini, Kātyāyana, Patañjali is more authoritative than previous ones (Kielhorn [1876a: 52, note], Śrīkṛṣṇamācārya [1971]), since he has been able to consider the arguments and evidence of previous teachers.

Such assumptions and aims carry with them some obvious requirements. If Kātyāyana or Patañjali suggests a given interpretation for a rule, he must justify that interpretation: the rule so interpreted must not only account for desired results, it must also be consonant with what Pāṇini does, as seen from other rules. In addition, a later commentator such as Bhaṭṭojī or Nāgeśa must consider in detail what his predecessors said in order to accept or reject given conclusions. Nor can he merely reject a certain opinion; he must present arguments based on the grammar, on usage, and on statements of older authorities such as Kātyāyana and Patañjali. This leads to very long discussions such as found in commentaries like the Śabda-kaustubha or the Prauḍha-mano-ramā. Some such discussions might strike a modern student as petty hairsplitting.

Some modern authors have indeed taken the position that much commentatorial discussion is such petty hairsplitting, useless for an appreciation of Pāṇini. I think it worthwhile to consider such claims.

Pāṇini's rule 1.3.3 (*hal antyam*, see section III.1.5.3c) provides that a final (*antya*) consonant (*hal*) of an item is classed as *it*, a marker. The term *hal* used in this rule is itself an abbreviation formed by rule 1.1.71 (*ādir antyena sahêtā*, see section III.1.5.3c with note 214). There is a problem here. The term *hal* used in 1.3.3 is formed by 1.1.71, but for 1.1.71 itself to take effect to form this term, *l* must be a marker (*it*). This is the fault called *iterêtarâśrayatva* 'mutual dependency'. Pāṇini should not be guilty of such circularity. Hence, Pāṇinīyas beginning with Kātyāyana make suggestions on how 1.3.3 can be interpreted to avoid the circularity.[488] Kātyāyana first suggests an addition to the grammar, whereby *l* is made a marker separately, and then goes on to suggest an interpretation which achieves the same results. Patañjali notes two additional suggestions. Kaiyaṭa himself suggests an interpretation of Kātyāyana's first statement whereby this does not really require an addition to the grammar. Bhaṭṭojī makes an additional suggestion. And

Nāgeśa considers all the suggestions made, rejecting some and noting which one is finally acceptable. Of such suggestions and discussions K. C. Chatterji (1935c: 23) said, "It did not however occur to the commentators that Pāṇini does not care a *hal* for defects like *itaretarāśrayatva* . . . , etc. In a book containing 4,000 rules which are conspicuous for their brevity is it surprising that there should be certain violations of logical order? "

As I have noted (see section III.1.5.3e), rule 3.1.2 (*paraś ca*) is a heading whereby units introduced by subsequent rules and classed as affixes (*pratyaya*) occur after (*para*) the items to which they are introduced. Rule 3.2.16 (*careṣ ṭaḥ*) introduces *ṭa* (= *a*) to the root *car* 'go about', and this should occur after the root in derivatives such as *kuru-car-a* 'who goes about in the Kuru country'. Now, rule 1.1.46 (*ādy-antau ṭa-k-itau*, see note 160) provides that an item marked with *ṭ* or *k* respectively occurs as the initial (*ādi*) or final (*anta*) part of the unit to which it is introduced. The affix *ṭa* is marked with *ṭ*. If the metarule 1.1.46 were to apply with 3.2.16, then, one would derive **-acar* instead of *-car-a.* The question at hand is: can 1.1.46 apply in affixation rules? Kātyāyana and Patañjali (Kielhorn [1880-85: I: 113.16 - 114.16]) discuss the question thoroughly[489] to see how, in terms of the grammar, 1.1.46 can be kept from applying in affixation rules. Of this discussion, R. Rocher (1967: 582) says: "In such a chapter [headed by 3.1.1, 2], paribhāṣā-sūtra I. 1, 46 should not be taken into consideration, as is clear from an internal analysis of the Aṣṭādhyāyī. Whatever Kātyāyana's reasons may have been to object to that situation and whatever solutions he may have proposed to solve the alleged difficulty, they are interesting only as far as Kātyāyana himself is concerned; they are not relevant to the internal structure of the Aṣṭādhyāyī."

Another problem treated in the Mahā-bhāṣya on 1.1.46 is the following. Rule 3.3.92 (*upasarge ghoḥ kiḥ*) introduces *ki* (= *i*) to a root such as *dhā*, when this is construed with a preverb (*upasarga*), to form a derivative such as *ādhí* 'thought, care' (〈 *ādhā-i*). The genitive-locative dual form of *ādhi* should be *ādhy-óḥ*, accented as shown. Rule 6.1.174 (*udātta-yaṇo hal-pūrvāt*) provides that an ending such as *-os* has a high-pitched vowel if it occurs after a semivowel (*yaṇ*) which has replaced a high-pitched vowel (*udātta*) and which is preceded by a consonant (*hal-pūrva*): *adhí-os* → *ādhy-ós.* But rule 6.1.175 (*nôṅ-dhātvoḥ*) negates (*na* 'not') what is provided by the preceding rule if the ending occurs after a semivowel which has replaced the feminine affix *ūṅ* or a vowel which is part of a root. Now, if 1.1.46 were to apply with 3.3.93, the element *i*, marked with *k*, would be introduced as the final part of the root: *ādhi* 〈 *ādhāi.* Consequently, 6.1.175 would apply to prohibit the accentuation *ādhyóḥ.* Here again, Kātyāyana and Patañjali discuss how this can be prevented. Of this Rocher (1967: 583) says: "However, does paribhāṣā-sūtra I. 1, 46 actually say that a suffix becomes part of the root? In our opinion, it merely states that an element marked with the exponent *k* takes place at the end, not that it becomes the final part of the root. The text of the paribhāṣā-sūtra, taken by itself could be interpreted in . . . [this] way . . . , if only this interpretation did not go against the most basic trends of the Aṣṭādhyāyī. One of the major achievements of the Hindu grammarians is their precise separation of forms into prefix, root, suffix, ending, etc. It is most unlikely that in such a grammar the suffix *i* in *ā-dhā-i* should be regarded as a part of the root."

Thus K. C. Chatterji dismisses a commentatorial argument as petty and is willing to admit that Pāṇini could commit elementary blunders. Rocher considers that what Kātyāyana has to say in a discussion is of no value for an understanding of the Aṣṭādhyāyī. Instead, she prefers a study of the internal structure of the Aṣṭādhyāyī and has recourse to a general trend.[490] On the surface, Rocher's argument seems plausible. However, a more careful look reveals problems. Rocher appears to be saying that, even if rule 1.1.46 applied together with 3.3.93 to derive *ādhi*, no problem would result, as can be seen from a basic trend of Pāṇini's grammar. But the question is not one of basic trends. It is true that Pāṇini's basic system involves introducing affixes to units (see section III.1.5.1a). It is also true, however, that an augment marked with *ṭ* or *k* is, in Pāṇini's system, treated as part of the unit to which it is introduced. For example, the compound *agni-ci* 'who has heaped a (sacrificial) fire' receives (by 6.1.71) the augment *tuk* (= *t*). The derivation of the form *agni-citam* (acc. sg.) involves introducing the ending *am* after *agni-cit*. Such an ending is introduced after a nominal base (by 4.1.1, see section III.1.3.3d with note 60). Now, the augment *t* is here marked with *k*. If, by 1.1.46, this is merely introduced at the end of *ci*, so that one derives *agni-ci-t*, the *t* is not part of a nominal base. Hence, the ending *am* cannot now be introduced after this sequence, since the nominal base after which the ending is to be introduced is separated from this by *-t-*. If, however, *t* is indeed introduced as part of the base, all is in order. Consequently, if one allows 1.1.46 to apply with 3.3.93, one must suffer one of two consequences: either the *i* affixed to *ādhā* is not part of the root, in which case the *t* added to *agni-ci* also should not be part of the nominal base; or the *t* added to *agni-ci* is part of the base, in which case the *i* affixed to *ādhā* too should be part of the root. Of course, one can argue that the derivation of *ādhi* involves an affixation. But this is precisely the point: 1.1.46 should not apply in such an affixation. And the Mahābhāṣya discussion touches on this very point: how does one avoid letting 1.1.46 apply in affixation rules? The discussion is both pertinent and important. For Pāṇini's grammar is a set of related rules, and one must know how these rules are related, how they apply to account for correct results. As for Chatterji's statement, it too misses the point. Commentators had a very good reason for concerning themselves with such problems. It is a datum that Pāṇini described Sanskrit through a set of consistent rules. Given his adeptness at composing a set of nearly 4,000 rules, one should indeed not expect him to commit elementary blunders.

In sum, I think any blanket rejection of commentatorial arguments as hairsplitting or irrelevant is mistaken. One has to distinguish between interpretational stratagems which are ultimately incompatible with Pāṇini's own statements and interpretations which are compatible with Pāṇini's statements and the method they reflect. It may be true that in some cases Bhaṭṭojī has "crushed the life out of Pāṇini's Aṣṭādhyāyī and presented us with the dry bones in fantastic garb."[491] Yet it is also illusory, I think, to believe that a modern can know what Pāṇini intended to be the interpretation of any given rule without first knowing all the rules and how they are related and coming to grips with precisely the kinds of problems treated in the Mahā-bhāṣya and the works of later commentators. In considering these later commentators, one is faced with a qualitative and historical difference among claims. Later commentators are at once the inheritors of their predecessors' ideas and also independent thinkers. If, then, such a commentator chooses as correct one of alternative solutions suggested in the Mahā-bhāṣya, the modern scholar has to ask, as did Nāgeśa, what makes this acceptable and other solutions unacceptable. This involves two major questions: is a suggestion under consideration compatible with what was said in the Mahā-bhāṣya, and is it ultimately compatible with what Pāṇini did?[492] Blanket rejection of given commentators or of a formalistic attitude is, I think, both unjustified and off the mark. For such commentators, who knew Pāṇini's work far better than we, intended what any other student of Pāṇini's should intend: to interpret his statements and test them.

VI. TREATISES ON SEMANTICS AND PHILOSOPHY OF GRAMMAR.

1. INTRODUCTION.

Questions of general linguistic and philosophical import were already treated fairly extensively in the Mahā-bhāṣya (see section III.2.6.3), and these discussions were the bases for later elaborations. There are later Pāṇinīya treatises in which such issues are dealt with in full. Not only are the issues considered, but the view of other schools of thought are also given detailed.

attention. The three major Pāṇinīya treatises on semantics and philosophy of grammar are Bhartṛhari's Vākya-padīya (section VI.2), Kauṇḍabhaṭṭa's Vaiyākaraṇa-bhūṣaṇa, and Nāgeśa's Vaiyākaraṇa-siddhânta-(laghu-)mañjūṣā (section VI.3).

The following are typical questions discussed. An utterance (*vākya*) conveys a meaning (*artha*). But what is it that we call a *vākya*? Is it a single entity over and above component elements which one assumes make up an utterance or is it merely the sum of these components? Similarly, is the meaning conveyed by an utterance something distinct, over and above the supposed meanings of component items or is it somehow related to the meanings of these components?[493] And if the latter, are we to say that each component first conveys its particular meaning and that these meanings are then somehow related or should one posit that each member of an utterance conveys only a meaning qua related to the meanings of other elements?[494] Moreover, different schools operate with what one may call paraphrases. It is agreed by followers of various schools of thought that an utterance such as *devadattaḥ pacati* 'Devadatta is cooking' refers to a person named Devadatta and cooking, which are here related. It is also agreed that a sentence *pākaṃ karoti devadattaḥ* (lit. 'Devadatta is doing cooking') is a paraphrase of the previous sentence, equivalent to it. However, each such sentence is analyzed in terms of relations among relata, and different schools adopt different paraphrases which convey what they consider the verbal cognition (*śābda-bodha*) which results from a sentence. The different paraphrases here accord with what is considered the proper analysis of sentences. The grammarian considers that the principal qualificand (*mukhya-viśeṣya*) of any sentence is an action (*kriyā*), denoted by a verb, qualified as being brought about by different participants. Followers of the school of logic called Nyāya, on the other hand, consider the principal qualificand to be what is denoted by a nominative form; a sentence states predications of it (see section III.1.5.7a). And a ritualist (Mīmāṃsaka) of the major school of ritual exegesis considers that the principal meaning of an utterance is the act of bringing about (*bhāvanā*), denoted by verb endings. These views are discussed from various vantages, including epistemology and grammar. Another question dealt with is this. It is accepted, at least for the purposes of grammar, that components of utterances, such as verb roots and nominal bases, have some meaning. Should one, then, consider that a verb such as *pac* 'cook' denotes both an action (*kriyā*) and its result (*phala*) or only an action or a result, the other meaning being attributed to other elements of utterances. Similarly, should one consider that a noun such as *go* 'cow, bullock' denotes only a substance, only a generic property (*gotva* 'bovinity'), a substance qualified by such a property, or more? And what is a substance? Indeed, is one justified in assuming, except in so far as grammatical usage is concerned, that there are substances distinct from their properties? Again, one speaks of actions (*kriyā*) and time (*kāla*), but should one really assume the existence of something called time as distinct from actions? Such questions were dealt with over centuries, each subsequent discussant building upon the arguments of his predecessors.

Several general works on Indian semantic views are available, among which two are especially noteworthy. K. Kunjunni Raja (1969) gives a clear summary of major positions. Though Kunjunni Raja does not enter into details concerning the arguments advanced in support of different views, his presentation is lucid and trustworthy. B. Bhattacharya (1962) also presents the major views on important topics, with extensive references to, and citations from, the texts. Both works are well written and clear. The same cannot be said of the book by R. C. Pandey (1963), a critique of which was made by Staal (1966c). Two other general works still worth consulting are P. C. Chakravarti's books of 1930 and 1933, which, though diffuse in their treatment, are full of materials. A more recent extensive treatment of the subject, with reference to views not only of grammarians but also of other Indian schools is the work of Kapila Deva Dvivedi (1951). Of a more restricted scope is Gaurinath Shastri (1959), the major emphasis of which is on Bhartṛhari. However, Gaurinath Shastri also discusses at length and with extensive references general questions and the views espoused in various schools. The more recent work of Rāma Sureśa Tripāṭhī (1972) is also concentrated on Bhartṛhari but gives information regarding other views.[495]

2. BHARTṚHARI.

2.1. *The Vākya-padīya: editions and translations.*[496]

The major text on semantics and philosophy of grammar in the Pāṇinian school is Bhartṛhari's Vākya-padīya.[497] This, together with the Mahā-bhāṣya, is the basic work for later treatments of topics in the treatises of Kauṇḍa-bhaṭṭa and Nāgeśa. Not only this, the Vākya-padīya is also referred to extensively in later treatises of many schools.[498]

The text is composed in verses (*kārikā*) and divided into three parts (*kāṇḍa*): the Āgama-samuccaya ('compendium of traditional teaching') also called the Brahma-kāṇḍa, the Vākya-kāṇḍa, and the Pada-kāṇḍa or Prakīrṇa-kāṇḍa ('miscellaneous part'). The third part is further subdivided into fourteen sections called *samuddeśa* in which are treated: generic properties (*jāti*), substance (*dravya*), relation (*sambandha*) between items and their meanings, substance again (*bhūyo-dravya-samuddeśa*), properties (*guṇa*), spatial concepts (*dik*), kārakas (*sādhana*), action (*kriyā*), time (*kāla*), the concept of person (*puruṣa*), number (*saṃkhyā*), the semantics associated with active and middle endings (*upagraha*), gender (*liṅga*), derivatives such as compounds (*vṛtti*, see note 263).[499] The last kāṇḍa is considered by both commentators and most modern scholars to be lacking sections originally included therein.[500] The term *vākya-padīya* was used to refer to the first two kāṇḍas and the term *trikāṇḍī* to refer to the whole work.[501]

The following commentaries on the Vākya-padīya are extant: the Vṛtti on the first and second parts, the latter fragmentary;[502] the Ṭīkā on the second part, usually attributed to Puṇyarāja;[503] Helārāja's Prakāśa on the third kāṇḍa. In addition, the Vṛtti on the first section itself has a commentary, the Paddhati of Vṛṣabhadeva.[504]

The first edition of the Vākya-padīya (Rāmakrishṇa Śāstrī Paṭavardhana et al. [1884-1937]) was by no means critical and was severely criticized by Charudeva Shastri (1930: 630) for this.[505] In the last forty years, however, a considerable amount of work has been done towards producing a good edition of the text and its commentaries. Rau (1962; 1964) gave a survey of manuscript materials. More recently (1971), he has provided a survey of manuscripts together with a bibliography of printed editions, translations, and articles on the Vākya-padīya.[506] Charudeva Shastri (1934; 1939/40) edited the first kāṇḍa with the Vṛtti and excerpts from Vṛṣabhadeva's commentary as well as part of the second kāṇḍa (verses 1-184) together with part of the Vṛtti and the Ṭīkā.[507] The third kāṇḍa, from the last part of the seventh samuddeśa (verse 3.7.156 in Abhyankar - Limaye [1965]) through the thirteenth samuddeśa was edited with Helārāja's commentary by Sāmbaśiva Śāstri (1935). L. A. Ravi Varmā (1942) edited the remainder of the third part.[508] The text of the first kāṇḍa with the Vṛtti and full Paddhati was subsequently edited by K. A. Subramania Iyer (1966a), who has also edited (1963a; 1973) the third kāṇḍa with the Prākāśa.[509] Sanskrit commentaries have also been composed by modern scholars. The first kāṇḍa was commented on by Dravyeśa Jhā (see Sītārāmācāri [1926/7]), Narain Datt Tripathi (see Avadh Bihari Mishra [1937]), Sūryanārāyaṇa Śukla (see Sūryanārāyaṇa Śukla - Rāmagovinda Śukla [1961]).[510] Raghunātha Śarmā (1963, 1968) has edited both the first and second kāṇḍas – the first with the full Vṛtti, the second with part of it – together with his commentary Ambā-kartrī, and is in the process of completing his commentary on the rest of the Vākya-padīya (see Raghunātha Śarmā [1974]). The text of the verses alone was edited by Abhyankar and Limaye (1965).[511]

The number of verses, especially in the first kāṇḍa, differs from edition to edition; editors differ concerning whether certain verses are to be treated as part of the Vākya-padīya or citations in the Vṛtti.[512] Rau (1971: 10-14) has provided a concordance of the editions of Rāmakrishṇa Śāstrī Paṭavardhana et al., Charudeva Shastri, Abhyankar - Limaye, Subramania Iyer, Sāmbaśiva Śāstrī, and Ravi Varmā.

In the last dozen years several translations have been made of parts of the Vākya-padīya. Śānti Bhikṣu Śāstrī (1963) translated the verses of the first kāṇḍa, with annotations. Biardeau (1964b) and K. A. Subramania Iyer (1965a) have translated into French and English respectively the verses and Vṛtti of the first kāṇḍa.[513] The first part has also been translated into Marathi (V. B. Bhāgavat [1965]). In addition, Satyakāma Varmā (1970) has edited this kāṇḍa with a trilingual commentary. Raghavan Pillai (1971) edited and translated the first two kāṇḍas, and K. A. Subramania Iyer (1971a) has translated the first part of the third kāṇḍa. The most recent translation is the English rendering of the Kāla-samuddeśa by P. Sarveswara Sharma (1972), who has also translated Helārāja's commentary on this section.

2.2. *Authorship of the Vṛtti.*

It is universally accepted that Bhartṛhari composed not only the Vākya-padīya verses but also a commentary on part of the Mahā-bhāṣya (see section III.2.2.1).[514] Concerning the Vṛtti on the Vākya-padīya's first and second kāṇḍas (section VI.2.1), there is a difference of opinion. This is attributed to Harivṛṣabha in manuscripts,[515] and some maintain that this is Bhartṛhari – commonly referred to as Hari –, others that the Vṛtti was not composed by Bhartṛhari himself. The major arguments for concluding that the Vṛtti was composed by Bhartṛhari himself are as follows. The Vṛtti does not record variant readings of verses, but later commentators do. Later authors consider the verses and Vṛtti to form a single work. Further, there are striking similarities in thought and expression between the Tripādī (section III.2.2.1) and the Vṛtti.[516]

Biardeau (1964b: 2-21) summarized Charudeva Shastri's evidence (see note 516) and then discussed materials which she considered indicate that the kārikās and the Vṛtti cannot be attributed to the same author. Her principal argument concerns alleged doctrinal differences between the two. For example, Biardeau (1964b: 8-9) notes that the Vṛtti on the first verse of the Vākya-padīya makes of Bhartṛhari an adherent of the view that all things are evolutes of brahman in the sense that brahman remains unchanged, the vivarta doctrine. However, argues Biardeau, there is nothing in the Vākya-padīya to show that Bhartṛhari was an adherent of this doctrine as opposed to the doctrine of pariṇāma, wherein the original actually changes into the evolutes. Biardeau (1964a: 260) notes that these arguments are valid for the Vṛtti on the second kāṇḍa. She is cautious, however, warning the reader (1964b: 5) that these arguments are to be taken with a grain of salt. K. A. Subramania Iyer (1965a: xxix-xxxvii; 1969: 29-36) presents both Biardeau's arguments and others which might be considered to militate against accepting that Bhartṛhari composed the Vṛtti. However, he concludes that the evidence is not sufficient to require disregarding the traditional view. One of the arguments advanced against attributing the Vṛtti to Bhartṛhari is that the commentary sometimes gives different interpretations for a single verse. However, Aklujkar (1972), who has vigorously argued for accepting that the Vṛtti is Bhartṛhari's, has noted (1972: 185), I think correctly, that "In the case of all these instances, a careful reading of the *Trikāṇḍī* and its ancient commentaries will reveal that what seem to be different explanations are also statements of different theses and thoughts acceptable to Bhartṛhari on different levels and in different contexts . . ."

2.3. *The dates of Bhartṛhari and his commentators.*

It was once believed, on the basis of a statement by I-Tsing, that Bhartṛhari had lived in the seventh century A. D.[517] By the end of the nineteenth century, however, scholars had begun seriously to doubt this (see Sadhu Ram [1952: 137], cf. Liebich [1930: 266-80]). And by 1927, Sarup had published Skandasvāmin's commentary on the Nirukta (section III.3.2.1), in which the Vākya-padīya is cited (Sarup [1927b: 28; 1934: 409]). Now, Skandasvāmin is probably to be placed towards the end of the fifth century,[518] so that Bhartṛhari's date has to be earlier than the seventh century. In 1936, C. Kunhan Raja noted (1936: 293-94), "From the mention of Vasurāta as the teacher of Bhartṛhari found in the commentary of Puṇyarāja to stanzas 486 and 489 in kāṇḍa II, the date of Bhartṛhari has to be fixed in the fifth century." It was then confirmed that Bhartṛhari's date could be set no later than the end of the fifth century. For he is cited by the Buddhist logician Dinnāga (Jambuvijaya [1951a: 29; 1951b: 334-35], Rangaswami Iyengar [1951], Frauwallner [1961: 334-35]). Frauwallner proposed the following dates: Dinnāga: ca. 480 - 540 A. D., Vasurāta: ca. 430 - 490, Bhartṛhari: ca. 450 - 510.[519] Other scholars have proposed evidence to set Bhartṛhari's date even earlier. Bhartṛhari is referred to in the Dvādaśāra-naya-cakra of the Jaina logician Mallavādin as reconstructed by Jambuvijaya (Jambuvijaya [1951a: 26, 30; 1951b: 332, 335; 1966: 242, Sanskrit introduction, p. 22 n. 6]). Traditionally, Mallavādin's date is put at 357/8 A. D. (Jambuvijaya [1951a: 26; 1951b: 332]). This would put Bhartṛhari in the fourth century.[520] This and other evidence concerning Bhartṛhari's date has been summarized by Sadhu Ram (1952),[521] J. M. Shukla (1966: 277-81),[522] and Yudhiṣṭhira Mīmāṃsaka (1973: I: 361-68).[523] In view of the evidence, it must be accepted that Bhartṛhari lived no later than the fifth century A. D.[524]

K. Sāmbaśiva Śāstrī (1935: introduction, p. 4) claimed that Helārāja was a direct disciple of Bhartṛhari. However, K. Madhava Krishna Sarma (1943a) presented evidence disproving this. L. A. Ravi Varmā (1942: introduction, pp. 4-6) attempted to show that Helārāja was contemporary with or posterior to Kaiyaṭa. But Swaminathan (1967, especially pp. 30-31) and later P. Sarveswara Sharma (1972: 9-12) have given evidence to show that Kaiyaṭa refers to views of Helārāja. Kanti Chandra Pandey (1963: 166-67) proposed that Helārāja, son of Bhūtirāja, was a teacher of Abhinavagupta, which would place him in the tenth century. This accords with the evidence noted, and has been accepted by P. Sarveswara Sharma (1972: 12). K. A. Subramania Iyer (1969: 40) also considers Helārāja an elder contemporary of Abhinavagupta.

Liebich (1930: 267) and K. Sāmbaśiva Śāstrī (1935: introduction, p. 4) considered Puṇyarāja also a direct disciple of Bhartṛhari. However, K. Madhava Krishna Sarma (1942: 410-12) argued against this opinion. For Puṇyarāja note that part of the third kāṇḍa of the Vākya-padīya was lost due to a break in the tradition or to neglect (cf. section VI.2.1), hence he could not have been a student of Bhartṛhari.[525] To date, however, no scholar has been able to propose a definite date for Puṇyarāja (see Ruegg [1959: 63 n. 1], K. A. Subramania Iyer [1969: 41-42]), though it is probable that he is later than Helārāja (Aklujkar [1974: 183]).

No definite date has been set for Vṛṣabhadeva either (see K. A. Subramania Iyer [1966: xvi-xvii; 1969: 44-45]).

2.4. *Studies on the doctrines set forth in the Vākya-padīya.*[526]

In the last fifteen years, several independent works have appeared in which are treated Bhartṛhari's views on language and philosophy: Gaurinath Shastri (1959 Biardeau (1964a), K. A. Subramania Iyer (1969), Satyakāma Varmā (1971b), Rāma Sureśa Tripāṭhī (1972). In addition, a recent dissertation (Aklujkar [197 has been devoted to the topic.[527] Subramania Iyer's book, a distillation of decades of study of the Vākya-padīya, is at present the fullest treatment of this work and the thoughts it expounds.[528] Subramania Iyer's (1969),

Aklujkar's (1970b) and Rāma Sureśa Tripāṭhī's (1972) studies are elaborate summaries of what Bhartṛhari says, with extensive references to the text of the Vākya-padīya and its commentaries.[529] Biardeau's presentation of some of Bhartṛhari's major ideas, to which she has devoted a large part of her work (1964a: 251-442), is couched in the broader background of theories concerning language, epistemology and cosmology held by other Indian thinkers, that is, a general Indian context. Gaurinath Shastri (1959) also deals in some detail with views of other Indian thinkers, though his focal point is Bhartṛhari. In addition, summaries of Bhartṛhari's thought appear in Ruegg (1959: 57-93), J. M. Shukla (1966: 283-96), Raghunātha Śarmā (1971).

Basic to Bhartṛhari's general philosophy[530] is the concept of brahman, the ultimate being, whose very essence is speech (*śabda*)[531] and from whom evolves (*vivartate*) all that there is.[532] Grammar (*vyākaraṇa*), as a means of discriminating correct (*sādhu*) from incorrect (*asādhu, apabhraṃśa*, see Subramania Iyer [1964]) usage, is a means of attaining ultimate release (*apavarga*), what we call salvation.[533] For, through the use of correct forms (*sādhu-prayoga*) one achieves merit (*dharma*), and through the knowledge of correct usage one gains the insight that speech in its essence is not differentiated. One thus reaches a stage of speech which is not dispersed (*avyatikīrṇa*), which is the source (*prakṛti*) of evolved speech (*vāg-vikāra*), and which is called *pratibhā* or *paśyantī* ('seeing', see below). And finally one reaches the ultimate (*parā*) source (*prakṛti*) of all evolutes, namely brahman (see Subramania Iyer [1966a: 47.6 - 48.4; 1969: 143-45]). Grammar is thus the cure for the stains which affect speech (*vāṅ-malānāṃ cikitsitam*) – that is, incorrect usages – and the door to salvation (*dvāram apavargasya*, Subramania Iyer [1966a: 47.4]).

The ultimate principle is thus speech. And speech is central to all cognition: there is no cognition which does not involve language (Subramania Iyer [1966a: 188.3]). Moreover, language is inherent in man (see Brough [1953b: 171], Biardeau [1964a: 317-18], Kunjunni Raja [1969: 148], Matilal [1971: 30-31], Aklujkar [1970b: 41-42]).

The principal features of Bhartṛhari's theory of language are fairly well known. In the second kāṇḍa of the Vākya-padīya he considers various possible conceptions of what it is that one calls an utterance or sentence (*vākya*),[534] and also what one is justified in considering the meaning (*artha*) of such an utterance. The view he ascribes to is that an utterance is a single, unanalysable, entity. All analysis of a sentence into lesser meaningful elements, down to bases and affixes, is a convenient fiction valid only in terms of abstracted constructs such as those used in a set of rules meant to describe usage, but not valid with respect to actual usage. The meaning of a sentence is also indivisible, over and above any meanings one might attribute to abstracted components, and not a sum of these meanings. For, the abstracted components of a sentence have no independent meanings in situations of actual usage, where one communicates by means of sentences. These components are only assumed meaningful in a context such as a grammar. Bhartṛhari therefore distinguishes (Subramania Iyer [1966a: 64.1-2]) between two types of linguistic units (*śabda*) and, correspondingly, their meanings (*padârtha*). Items are either such as are explained (*anvākhyeya*) by grammarians or such as are posited to convey (*pratipādaka*), in terms of grammatical rules, the items of actual usage. Correspondingly, meanings are either of a fixed character (*sthita-lakṣaṇa*) or such as are abstracted (*apôddhāra-padârtha*). Bhartṛhari recognizes (Subramania Iyer [1966a: 68.5-6]) that, in addition to the sentence, some take syntactic units (*pada*) as the unit to be analysed. Moreover, he notes (Subramania Iyer [1966a: 74.4 - 74.5]) that there are differences of opinion regarding what particular meanings should be ascribed to units such as bases and affixes through the use of anvaya and vyatireka (see note 152).

The indivisible sentence and its equally indivisible meaning are respectively called *vākya-sphoṭa* and *pratibhā.*[535] A sphoṭa is an unanalysable entity, without parts. It is not a sound or a conglomerate of sounds. For sounds serve only to manifest (*vyañj*) a sphoṭa. It is units called *sphoṭa* which make up the linguistic system a speaker has in his intellect and whereby he communicates.[536]

Although, as I noted, Bhartṛhari grants primacy to the sentence as a unit of communication, it is nevertheless a fact that speakers – whether or not they be grammarians – also accept the reality of lower units such as bases, affixes and single sounds. Bhartṛhari also accepts that these have a place in a linguistic scheme, though, as units abstracted from the sentence, they have a lesser right to primacy. Here again, the sounds which one perceives are only the means of manifesting systematic units. Bhartṛhari speaks of sounds manifesting not only sentential units but also syntactic units (*pada*) and sound units (*varṇa*); see Aklujkar (1970b: 86-88, 226-28). Each of these systematic units is a sphoṭa manifested in communication by articulated sounds.[537]

Like Kātyāyana before him (section III.2.6.3) and indeed like every other Pāṇinīya, Bhartṛhari took as a basic premise that the relation between a linguistic unit (*śabda*) and its meaning (*artha*) is fixed and permanent (*nitya*). He also considered various possible ways in which a unit and its meaning can be related.[538] One may say that an item is naturally related to its meaning through the relation called *yogyatā* 'fitness'. As certain organs (eyes, ears, etc.) are naturally fit for playing a part in different cognitions

– one sees with one's eyes, hears with one s ears – so a given item is naturally connected with a given meaning. To be sure, this does not preclude that there is also a convention (*samaya*). But this is only an accompaniment (*upādhi*): it serves as a means to convey the natural relation in the case of items the meanings of which are not well known to one, and this only the first time one learns this relation. In addition, an item and its meaning are related as cause and effect (*kārya-kāraṇa-bhāva*): one uses an item to convey a meaning and the item causes in the hearer a cognition of that meaning. At the base of this relation is another: one identifies the item and its meaning.

In accord with the above, Bhartṛhari operates with several levels of speech (*vāc*).[539] There are, to begin with, the actual perceptible stretches of sound which a speaker utters and a hearer grasps. This is the level of scattered, sense related speech (*vaikharī vāk*). But these stretches of sound result from articulatory efforts which themselves result from a speaker's wishing to express something, and they produce in the hearer a cognition of that meaning. At the next level, called *madhyamā* 'middle', such utterances exist as potential utterances in the intellect of speakers, without actual sequence. At the next level, called *paśyantī* 'seeing', all sequentiality is absent. This level has two aspects. There is a paśyantī level at which there is a distinction among speakers: some have a system of correct usage, others not. There is also a highest (*parā*) paśyantī speech at which all distinctions are obliterated. Here there is no longer any difference between designator and designated: all is one, that is, one comes back to brahman.

The single concept of Bhartṛhari's general theory of language which, more than ony other, has attracted attention is sphoṭa (see note 536). To Brough (1951: 32-34) belongs the merit of stressing that sphoṭa is not a mysterious entity, as some scholars had thought before. In Brough's opinion (1951: 34), "The *sphoṭa* then is simply the linguistic sign in its aspect of meaning-bearer ..." His view was accepted by Kunjunni Raja (1956; 1969: 100-01). On the other hand, S. D. Joshi (1967a: 40) has just as unequivocally said, "In the context of meaningful speech-unit, Bhartṛhari has never used the term *sphoṭa*." In my opinion, both positions require modification. Clearly, Joshi's thesis (1967a: 29, 35, 39-40) that for Bhartṛhari a sphoṭa is never a meaningful unit is untenable, as K. A. Subramania Iyer (1969: 157-58) has pointed out. The source of this difficulty is evident: Joshi has not recognized that Bhartṛhari also uses the term *śabda* with reference to systematic units, including those which are meaningful (see note 537). However, Joshi's thesis, if modified, becomes acceptable. For Bhartṛhari's sphoṭa is not uniquely a meaning-bearing unit. As Joshi (1967a: 46) recognized, the term *varṇa-sphoṭa* is used with reference to a sound unit of the language system (see also Aklujkar [1970b: 9]). This cannot be accommodated to Brough's thesis. The source of this problem is also evident. For, Brough's exposition of sphoṭa was heavily influenced by later Pāṇinīyas. And indeed they did say that a sphoṭa is uniquely a meaning bearer. To them the term *sphoṭa* itself means 'an item which denotes a meaning (*vācaka*)'; a sphoṭa is a unit from which a meaning is made known (lit. 'bursts'), so that a varṇa-sphoṭa too is necessarily meaningful. But in the view of such later Pāṇinīyas the term *varṇa* does not mean 'sound unit' in this context; it denotes a unit lower than a word, namely a base or an affix.[540]

Several studies have been devoted to other particular topics of Bhartṛhari's system, many of them by K. A. Subramania Iyer. He has discussed Bhartṛhari's views on gender (*liṅga*, 1945, 1971), his concept of action (1950-51: 175-78; cf. 1969: 326-43) in connection with Yāska's disquisition on the meanings of verb forms (1950-51: 167-69) and the Mahā-bhāṣya discussion regarding verb roots (1950-51: 169-75), Bhartṛhari's statements concerning the semantics associated with active and middle verb forms (1953-54; cf. 1969: 344-53), his views on the primary (*mukhya*) and secondary (*gauṇa*) meanings of words in given contexts (1968) and the relations between words and their meanings (1967), and, most recently, Bhartṛhari's exposition of taddhita forms involving comparison (1974). Some of these topics have been studied by others also, with differences in emphasis. V. A. Ramaswami Sastri (1952b: 184-87) treated Bhartṛhari's views on mukhya and gauṇa usages. Kunjunni Raja (1957) discussed some aspects of Bhartṛhari's views regarding verbs and nouns and also elliptical sentences (1958: 30-31). Bhartṛhari's discussion concerning coreferential (*samānâdhikaraṇa*) items was treated by Kapil Deva Shastri (1964b), who also devoted two papers to Bhartṛhari's treatment of utterances involving comparison (1964c; 1965) and one to Bhartṛhari's interpretation of a famous Vedic verse (1966). And M. S. Narayana Murti (1972a) has discussed what Bhartṛhari says regarding points of view about rule 1.2.52. One particular Vākya-padīya passage, in which Bhartṛhari presents an argument of Audumbarāyaṇa concerning the classification of linguistic items into four types, has been treated by Brough (1952). On this question see also Sköld (1926b: 121), Strauss (1927a: 111-13), Simonsson (1961), Sreekrishna Sarma (1962: 186-77). Most recently, Matilal (1973) has studied Bhartṛhari's views on what constitutes a substance (*dravya*) and the status of substances and properties (*guṇa*), in the context of other treatments of this topic, including discussions in the Maha-bhaṣya.

2.5. *Evaluations of Bhartṛhari and his commentators.*

It is generally agreed that Bhartṛhari deserves his reputation for his insights into language. There has, nevertheless, been some disagreement on how one should evaluate him. In particular, should one approach him as a linguist or as a philosopher, through his commentaries in addition to the Vākya-padīya and the Tripādī or through these alone?

Satyakāma Varmā (1964) has, he tells us (1964: 9), attempted to present Bhartṛhari's Vākya-padīya as a work on linguistics. Varmā also considers that one must understand Bhartṛhari from his own words, without the "misinterpreting" commentaries (1964: 229), of which only the Vṛtti is at all trustworthy (1964: 1). However, Satyakāma Varmā's own interpretations of Bhartṛhari's words do not always inspire confidence. K. A. Subramania Iyer (1969: 48-50) has given a brief but good critique of some of Varmā's interpretations. Nevertheless, Varmā's work serves to focus on the two points noted above.

Biardeau (1964a: 260-61) states her viewpoint clearly: the earliest known commentary on the Vākya-padīya, the Vṛtti of Harivṛṣabha, is later than Bhartṛhari and modifies his views (see section VI.2.2). Therefore, one can learn Bhartṛhari's views only from the Vākya-padīya itself.[541] On the other hand, Aklujkar (1970b: 7, 115 n. 4) notes that Bhartṛhari's views can be ascertained only from a study of his entire work and says, "It seems to me that Bhartṛhari's ancient commentators carried out this task meticulously or received a highly authentic tradition concerning the views Bhartṛhari held, for I have not noticed a single instance in which the view they single out as Bhartṛhari's view from a plurality of views does not agree with the indications available in the *Trikāṇḍī.*" I think the second position is more fruitful. We should make use of the principle of charity. Assuming that commentators meant to abstract from Bhartṛhari's work the views which could be ascribed to him correctly, one should compare in detail what is said in the Vākya-padīya and its commentaries as well as in the *Tripādī.* These studies are of course intimately related also with studies to determine the authorship of the Vṛtti (section VI.2.2).

Biardeau (1965: 229) has also argued strongly against considering Bhartṛhari's views and Indian semantic views in general only in the context of general linguistics, without couching these views in their Indian background and in the context of other Indian systems. This point is, I think, well taken in part. Certainly Bhartṛhari's theory of language fits, as one should expect, into his general philosophy, and a total system of ideas has to be treated in its context. On the other hand, there is no denying that Bhartṛhari did indeed have a theory of language, which one has the right to consider as just that (cf. Kunjunni Raja [1969: vi-vii]). As long as studies on Bhartṛhari's views concerning language take his total system into account and do not hastily and falsely draw superficial comparisons, they simply represent a particular emphasis and a valid one. Such a valid comparison is made in Ganguli **(1963)**, a work I consider brilliant, in which the author has perceptively used Bhartṛhari's theory of language to discuss issues important to modern semantic and logical theories.

3. LATER SEMANTIC TREATISES.

3.1. *Introduction.*

As I noted earlier (section VI.1), there are two major works on semantics and philosophy of grammar in the Pāṇinian tradition after Bhartṛhari, the Vaiyākaraṇa-bhūṣaṇa of Kauṇḍabhaṭṭa (17th century, see P. K. Gode [1954]) and the Vaiyākaraṇa-siddhânta-(laghu-)mañjūṣā of Nāgeśa.[542] Like Bhartṛhari before them, Kauṇḍabhaṭṭa and Nāgeśa take up views of systems other than the Pāṇinian. Unlike Bhartṛhari, however, they are polemical. They devote a great deal of effort to refuting other views, thereby establishing that only the positions maintained in the Mahā-bhāṣya and the Vākya-padīya are correct. Kauṇḍabhaṭṭa directly says in an introductory verse (K. P. Trivedi [1915: 1, verse 4]) that his purpose is to show that the views of Pāṇinīyas are alone supported by correct arguments, whereas the statements of commentators on Nyāya and Mīmāṃsā, who have distorted the correct views, are not supported by such argurnents. This polemic is justified in the following context. Neither logicians of the Nyāya school nor Mīmāṃsakas composed grammars of their own. Nevertheless, they accepted verbal transmission (*śabda*) as a correct means of knowledge. And the Mīmāṃsakas had to set forth a theory of sentence structure and meaning in accord with their analyses of Vedic passages in connection with ritual usage. To justify their own analyses, then, Naiyāyikas and Mīmāṃsakas accepted as valid Pāṇinian statements, but reinterpreted them to make them accord with their own particular views.

Kauṇḍabhaṭṭa's work is divided into sections called *nirṇaya* ('final determination, ascertainment') dealing with: the meanings of verb roots (*dhātv-artha*), the meanings of L-suffixes and the affixes which replace them (*lakārârtha*),[543] the meanings of nominal endings (*sub-artha*), the meanings of nominal bases (*nāmârtha*), the meanings of compounds (*samāsa-śakti*), the relation between linguistic items and their meanings (*śakti*), the meanings of the negative particle *na* (*nañ-artha*), the meanings of particles (*nipātârtha*), the meanings of affixes such as the one contained in the action noun *pāka* 'cooking' (*bhāva-pratyayârtha*), the meanings of affixes such as that contained in the derivative *aindra* 'for the god Indra' (*devatā-pratyayârtha*), the unmarked or neutral singular (*abhedaikatva-saṃkhyā*),[544] the use of particular number affixes depending on the speaker's intention (*saṃkhyā-vivakṣā*), the meanings of affixes such as that contained in the absolutive *kṛtvā* 'having done' (*kṛtvā-pratyayâdīnām-artha*), sphoṭa (cf. section VI.2.4). Many of the same topics are treated in the Vaiyākaraṇa-siddhânta-laghu-mañjūṣā by Nāgeśa, though in a different order and with different emphases. Nāgeśa not only goes about refuting the views of non-Pāṇinīyas, he also argues against views espoused by Kauṇḍabhaṭṭa and his uncle Bhaṭṭojī Dikṣita.

The Vaiyākaraṇa-bhūṣaṇa is, in the first instance, a commentary on verses (*kārikā*) contained in the Vaiyākaraṇa-siddhânta-kārikā or Vaiyākaraṇa-matônmajjana[545] composed in part by Kauṇḍabhaṭṭa's father's (Raṅgojībhaṭṭa) brother Bhaṭṭojī Dīkṣita. This text contains, in addition to kārikās by Bhaṭṭojī, also verses by Bhartṛhari and others (S. D. Joshi [1960: ix-xi]).

Kauṇḍabhaṭṭa also composed an abridged version of the Vaiyākaraṇa-bhūṣaṇa, the Vaiyākaraṇa-bhūṣaṇa-sāra, in which the essence (*sāra*) of the views and arguments contained in the longer work are presented without all the long and complicated detailed considerations of many other views. The Vaiyākaraṇa-siddhânta-laghu-mañjūṣā is, as the title indicates, a short (*laghu*) version of a longer treatise, the Vaiyākaraṇa-siddhânta-bṛhan-mañjūṣā. In addition, there is a still shorter version, the Parama-laghu-mañjūṣā.[546]

3.2. *Editions, translations, and studies.*

Kauṇḍabhaṭṭa's Vaiyākaraṇa-bhūṣaṇa was edited by Rāmakrishṇa Śāstrī Paṭavardhana (1900) and subsequently by K. P. Trivedi (1915). The latter edition includes explanatory notes. However, these are not very helpful. They expatiate on matters which any student capable of approaching this difficult treatise should already know, and omit discussion of details concerning what is meant in laconic statements which are indeed in need of comment. Such comments are important because there is no Sanskrit commentary on this text. Neither of the two editions traces the very large number of quotations from a great many sources. The Vaiyākaraṇa-bhūṣaṇa-sāra has been edited several times, with various commentaries.[547] Sadāśiva Śāstrī Joshi's edition (1939) contains the Darpaṇa of Harivallabha (ca. 1770-1790, S. D. Joshi [1960: xvi]), the Bhairavī of Bhairava Miśra (late 18th century, M. S. Bhat [1959a]), and the Bhūṣaṇa-vyākhyā of Kṛṣṇamitra (ca. 1750, Sadāśiva Śāstrī Joshi [1939: introduction, p. 5]). The Kāśikā of of Harirāma Kāle[548] was published with the Vaiyākaraṇa-bhūṣaṇa-sāra by K. P. Trivedi (1915). More recent commentaries have also been written on this treatise: the Saralā of Gopāla Shastri Nene (Rāma Prasāda Tripāṭhī [1952]), the Śāṅkarī of Śaṅkara Śāstrī Mārulkara (1957), the Prabhā of Bālakṛṣṇa Pañcolī (Tārakeśvara Śāstrī Caturvedī [1947]), the Bhaimī of Bhīmasena (1969). There is also a fragment of an older commentary, the Laghu-bhūṣaṇa-kānti by Mannudeva (S. D. Joshi [1960: xvi], Yudhiṣṭhira Mīmāṃsaka [1973: II: 419]).

Nāgeśa's Bṛhan-mañjūṣā has not been edited. The Laghu-mañjūṣā was edited in its entirety by Mādhava Śāstrī Bhāṇḍārī (1925) together with two commentaries, the Kalā by Nāgeśa's student Bālambhaṭṭa (Vaidyanātha) and the Kuñjikā of Kṛṣṇamitra, who also commented on the Vaiyākaraṇa-bhūṣaṇa-sāra. This edition is not very good. In one place (p. 40), part of the text is missing, and citatīons, of which there are thousands, are not traced. A better edition of part of the text, with the editor's own commentary, has been made by Sabhāpati Śarmā Upādhyāya (1963).[549] The Parama-laghu-mañjūṣā was edited by Sadāśiva Śāstrī Joshi (1946) with his commentary and notes based on the Laghu-mañjūṣā. Another edition was more recently produced by K. P. Shukla (1961), with his own commentary. Neither edition makes any pretense at being critical.

There is no full translation of any of these texts. However, annotated translations of two sections of the Vaiyākaraṇa-bhūṣaṇa have been made recently (M. M. Deshpande [1972b], J. A. Gune [1974]), and one section of the Vaiyākaraṇa-bhūṣaṇa-sāra was earlier translated with annotations (S. D. Joshi [1960]). But none of these has been published.[550]

In a recent substantial work, Veluri Subba Rao (1969) has treated the major views dealt with in these treatises.[551] In addition, he has given (1969: following p. 258) charts representing the relations of members of sentences and their meanings according to Pāṇiniyas, Nyāya logicians and the major school of Mīmāṃsā. Ruegg (1959: 5-140) devoted a short section to a brief characterization of Nāgeśa's work. In addition, the introductions to the translations noted above contain discussions of particular topics. S. D. Joshi (1960: xxix-lxviii) gives a brief sketch of semantic thought in India, an analysis of the dhātv-artha-nirṇaya section of the Vaiyākaraṇa-bhūṣaṇa-sāra, and a summary of major views concerning sentence analysis. M. M. Deshpande (1972b: 1-124) takes up the major views concerning the meanings of nominal bases, and J. A. Gune (1974: 1-95) discusses views held concerning the meanings of L-suffixes and the endings which replace them.

VII. LITERARY WORKS ILLUSTRATING GRAMMATICAL RULES.

Various poetic works were composed in which was illustrated the application of grammatical rules. Such works are known as *kāvya-śāstra.*[552] The most famous of these works, illustrating Pāṇini's rules, is the Bhaṭṭi-kāvya (V. N. Joshi - W. L. Paṇsīkar [1928]).[553] Recently, Satya Pal Narang (1969: 85-96) has studied the Bhaṭṭi-kāvya's illustrations for sections of Pāṇini's grammar and their arrangement. He also discusses what later commentators have to say on usages found in the Bhaṭṭi-kāvya.

Let me note finally that such literary works are still being composed. Rāma Śaraṇa Śāstrī fairly recently composed a prose work, the Kathā-kallolinī, illustrating Pāṇini's rules in the order of the Siddhânta-kaumudī (see Gayācaraṇa Tripāṭhī [1961]).

VIII. A SUMMARY OF TRENDS.

In previous sections I have considered research according to the topics treated therein; only in the course of discussing these topics have I indicated changes of interest and emphasis. To close this work, let me now summarize quite briefly major trends of research, as I see them, reflected in the work treated.

Pāṇinian scholarship in the nineteenth century[554] was – understandably, since fully usable editions had not been made yet of the most important texts – preoccupied principally with the establishment of texts, especially of the Aṣṭādhyāyī and the Mahā-bhāṣya (see sections III.1.2, III.1.3.3, III. 2.3, III.4), and with the following questions which these texts gave rise to: the relations between Patañjali and Kātyāyana and Pāṇini (see section III. 2.5); the chronology of these authors, their places of origin, and related questions of realia (see section III.3); the language reflected in the Aṣṭādhyāyī, its relation to the language of other texts, especially Vedic, and the compatibility of Pāṇini's description with the facts attested in these texts (see sections III.1.5.6a, 8). These are still topics of discussion.[555] However, some issues which provoked lively controversy in the nineteenth century have been fairly well settled thanks to the work of R. G. Bhandarkar, Liebich and, especially, Kielhorn, certainly the towering European figure of this time, who established a definitive edition of the Mahā-bhāṣya, thus putting to rest some questions which had been provoked by an insufficient knowledge of this text.

Kielhorn also began the modern study of certain technical devices used by Pāṇinīyas in interpreting Pāṇinian rules (see section III.2.6.2) and produced an edition of Nāgeśa's collection of metarules, the Paribhāṣêndu-śekhara (see section III.1.3.7), together with a translation which has been called (Thieme 1957a: 47) "the comparatively easiest and safest way to grasp the principles of the method of the indigenous Pāṇini interpretation" for scholars who do not have the advantage of studying with modern Indian Pāṇinīyas. Moreover, the study of metalinguistic terminology also attracted the attention of scholars early on (see section III.1.5.3). However, it was not until Whitney, himself an eminent linguist who had his own views regarding language and grammars, attacked Pāṇini, claiming his grammar was both inaccurate and ill-conceived (see sections III.1.5.6a, 1.5.7c, 1.5.8), that modern scholars had seriously to consider in detail Pāṇini's grammar from the point of view of theory, of how a grammar should be composed and what it should accomplish. Yet Whitney's attacks on Pāṇini's theoretical stance did not provoke equally sophisticated responses (see section III.1.5.7c). For, though scholars such as Böhtlingk and Liebich were, to a large extent, able to refute Whitney's claims of factual error in the Aṣṭādhyāyī, they appear not to have been able to answer satisfactorily the other question Whitney raised, namely whether any one in his right mind would have chosen to compose a grammar as Pāṇini did. It is true that Liebich, whose scholarly productivity continued from the late nineteenth century on into the twentieth, produced excellent expositions of the technical apparatus of Pāṇini's system (Liebich 1919a; 1920a]), but I think it was with Buiskool's work (1934, 1939) that Whitney's claim was effectively refuted, though silently and only in part: Buiskool's exposition of the last three quarter-chapters of the Aṣṭādhyāyī, wherein rules are extrinsically ordered (see sections III.1.5.2a, b), shows with admirable clarity how carefully and well elaborated Pāṇini's work was. It was also in the first half of the twentieth century that Pāṇini came to be fully appreciated by a linguist with his own sophisticated views of language and grammar who also was sufficiently versed in the intricacies of the Aṣṭādhyāyī to appreciate the genius behind it. This was Bloomfield. Nevertheless, Bloomfield did not make Sanskrit grammar his principal pursuit, indeed he devoted very little of his scholarly energies to this area. It is in fairly recent times that Pāṇini's work has become the object of intensive investigation from the point of view of linguistic theory and technique (see section III.1.5.7b). Of course, scholars have all along devoted themselves to studies of the Aṣṭādhyāyī (see section III.1.5), its commentaries (see sections III.2, IV) and related treatises.[556] Yet I think it proper to speak of a new emphasis in recent times. This trend has been accompanied by an ever increasing interest in Pāṇinīya works on semantics and philosophy of grammar, especially Bhartṛhari's

Vākya-padīya (see sections III.2.6.3, VI).[557] These interests and emphases have given rise to similar controversies. With regard to Pāṇinian grammar: to what extent is it licit to see therein detailed parallels to certain modern linguistic theories (see sections III.1.5.7b, c)? And with respect to the Vākya-padīya: to what extent is one justified in seeing therein parallels to modern theories in general linguistics and philosophy of language (see section VI.2.5)? The question of degree is, of course, all important: it would be simplistic to give an absolutely positive or negative answer to either of these questions.[558]

I think it would be equally simplistic to draw a hard and fast line between philological and linguistic or systematic approaches to Pāṇini and Indian grammarians in general. It is, of course, possible to approach the texts from different angles: one might be interested principally in historical and cultural facts to be gleaned from them or in philosophical ideas treated therein or in grammatical methods presented in them. All these approaches are in fact reflected in the research which has been carried out. Once, however, one enters into the particular subject matter of the Pāṇinian grammatical system or Pāṇinīyas' treatments of semantic questions, the immediate task at hand is to understand what an author like Pāṇini or Bhartṛhari has said and why he has said it in a particular way. These questions are, or course, not always susceptible of easy answers. However, I think everyone will agree on a point concerning an elementary level of understanding: in order to understand what an author such as Pāṇini has said in one given place, one should compare what he says elsewhere in his work. Especially is this true in the case of Pāṇini, who explicitly defines technical terms and states metarules valid in his treatise. Such philological work, leading to what one may call the literal understanding of any given rule, is, I think one must agree, a necessary preliminary to any systematic study in the simple sense that one cannot study systematically what one does not know an author to have said. On a more sophisticated level, one may then ask what an author such as Pāṇini has said and why he has said it in a particular way in the sense of asking what theoretical stance these statements reflect. Now, it is a known fact that there are other Indian grammarians, whose statements made to describe essentially the same linguistic facts as are accounted for by Pāṇini's rules differ in interesting ways from these rules. One may, then, approach the question of Pāṇini's theoretical stance by seeking to understand precisely how his rules operate and comparing this system with those of other Indian grammarians. And in doing this one is assisted by the abundant commentatorial literature (see section V), which, when used judiciously, is illuminating. On the other hand, one could procede directly to understanding Pāṇini's theoretical stance in terms of particular points of view with which one is most familiar, such as modern theories. Of course, the two approaches are not incompatible. It would be naive to claim that any modern understands such issues except in the light of his own background and preconceptions, at least to an extent. And it is well known that Pāṇinīya commentators themselves are not beyond interpreting Pāṇinian statements in terms of views they themselves evolved. However, it seems arrogant to claim that only the light of modern methods can elucidate Pāṇini. It would, I think, be more accurate to say that some recent developments in linguistics have made some linguists more favorably disposed to methods which Pāṇinīyas have been expounding, elucidating, and building upon for centuries.

By the same token, I think it would be ill-advised to contrast some modern studies of Pāṇini and Pāṇinīyas with studies carried out by what are called traditional scholars – paṇḍitas – whether they express themselves in Sanskrit or another language. The traditional scholar, though he may not be conversant with modern theories, is, if he is good, as fully entitled to the respectful attention of linguists and philosophers as anyone engaged in these studies: he has a full command of the techniques of Pāṇinian grammar and is able to expound them with lucidity.

I say this because the recent emphasis noted above could possibly lead to facile sharp demarcations which, in my opinion, would be both unjustified and destructive. Yet the evidence of research being carried out encourages one to think this will not occur. On the contrary, the renewed interest in Pāṇinian studies witnessed in recent years should ultimately lead a fuller appreciation of Indian grammarians and the incorporation of their views into the mainstream of intellectual history. For, as I have noted, work in Pāṇinian studies is proceeding on various fronts: editing of texts, translation, studies of various aspects of the ideas propounded in these texts, and the particular uses of language made to set forth these ideas, together with historical studies of the relations among various authors and schools and their ideas. In sum, I think one can rightly see in these studies a continuity and community of endeavor which promises to be fruitful:

pradhānaṃ ca ṣaṭsv aṅgeṣu vyākaraṇam pradhāne ca kṛto yatnaḥ phalavān bhavati

PART 3:

FOOTNOTES AND INDEX

FOOTNOTES

1. Yudhiṣṭhira Mīmāṃsaka places Pāṇini and other early authors at extremely early dates which are not susceptible of universal acceptance. Best overlooked also are his diatribe against western linguists (1973: I: 14) and his insistence on contrasting Indian views and the views of westerners and their adherents, with chauvinistic tones.
2. Note that Colebrooke (1803) contains a remarkably well informed compilation of Sanskrit grammarians.
3. At the time I was writing this work the seventh volume of Abhyankar Abhyankar was not available to me for detailed consultation.
4. There are two recent popularizations by Rāmalāl (1970) and Vohrā (1971), neither of which makes any pretense at being a scholarly treatment of Pāṇini or Patañjali.
5. B. Ghosh's survey (1945) of pre-Pāṇinian grammar, based on Liebich (1919b) (see Ghosh [1945: 334 n. 1]), is vague and contains generalizations such as: "But the mind of primitive man is always engrossed with the *whole* of the sentence idea . . ." (1945: 334), "The earliest grammatical discoveries were . . . almost accidental . . ." (1945: 337).
6. The page references given are to sections covering studies of Pāṇini specifically; additional references appear in other sections also.
7. These abstracts are not always precise. For example, Dandekar's abstract of Cardona (1970b) (Dandekar [1946-73: 3: 173, number 42]) says, "[Pāṇini] did not know the ritual intimately, but Pāṇini was primarily a very astute grammarian." Cardona's statement (1970b: 209) is: "This does not, of course, mean that Pāṇini did not know the ritual intimately; his own statements prove the contrary. It does show, however, that, quite aside from his being a product of his environment he was also a very astute grammarian.' I have, nevertheless, used Dandekar's abstracts where original articles were not available to me, assuming such lapses to be infrequent.
8. For example, R. Rocher (1965a) is listed (Salus [1971: 7, number 91]) as written by R. Rocher and R. Debels; L. Rocher and R. Debels (1958-60) is listed (Salus [1971: 8, number 93]) as written by R. Rocher and published in *AIONSL*.
9. For discussions concerning the language described by Pāṇini see section III.1.5.7.

10. I use here the term 'rule' only as a convenient word to render the Sanskrit *sūtra.* On the types of rules contained in the grammar see section III.1.5.2c; on the term *lakṣaṇa* "rule" see section III.1.5.1a. For a discussion of the precise number of rules contained in the Aṣṭādhyāyī according to different authors see K. Madhava Krishna Sarma (1968: 1-3). On additions made to the text see section III.1.3.3.
11. A sūtra is normally a verbless statement in which one is to understand the verb "be"; see Cardona (1970c: 219 n. 4). Recently Bahulikar (1972: 44; 1973: 96-97) has discussed the possible reasons for the use of the sūtra style. She notes approvingly a suggestion made by D. H. H. Ingalls that this style arose when writing was introduced and because of a "scarcity of writing material at that period." A similar suggestion was made by Goldstücker (1861: 25-26).
12. These groups of sounds are arranged in subsets to allow the use of abbreviational terms such as *ac* "vowels' to refer to sets of sounds (see section III.1.5.3c). According to tradition, this catalog of sounds was handed down to Pāṇini by the lord Śiva (*mahêśvara*).
13. For example, *sarvâdi* '*sarva* etc.', *juhoty-ādi* '(the verb) *hu* etc.', *gavâśva-prabhṛti* '*gavâśva* etc.', *adi-prabhṛti* '(the verb) *ad* etc.', *kaḍārāḥ* '*kaḍāra* etc.' refer to sets of items by using *ādi* 'first', *prabhṛti* 'starting with . . . ', and the plural; see V. B. Bhāgavat (1969).
14. The term *gaṇa* 'group' is also used to refer to sets of items in the dhātu-pāṭha.
15. One must consult 1.1.71 (*ādir antyena sahêta*, see section III.1.5.3c with note 214) to know that *ac* denotes a set of vowels and 1.3.3 (*hal antyam*, see section III.1.5.3c) to know that the *c* of *ac* is a marker. To know that the vowels *a, i, u, ṛ* etc., denoted directly by *ac*, themselves denote sets of vowels, rule 1.1.69 (*aṇ-ud-it savarṇasya câpratyayaḥ*, see section III.1.5.4b with note 240) has to be consulted. The term *vṛddhi* denotes *ā, ai, au* by 1.1.1 (*vṛddhir ād aic*). The genitive and locative forms *acaḥ, ñ-ṇ-iti* are interpreted by 1.1.49 and 1.1.67 (see section III.1.5.3c with note 217). In addition, the term *ac* in 7.2.115 denotes not merely vowels but a presuffixal base ending in a vowel, which cannot be known without consulting 1.1.72 (*yena vidhis tad-antasya*). This provides that a term X used to state an operation for Y, which X qualifies, denotes the unit Y ending in X. The heading 6.4.1 (*aṅgasya*) is valid in 7.2.115, so that this states an operation on a presuffixal base (*aṅga*) ending in a vowel. Further, 1.1.52 (*alo'ntyasya*) must be consulted to see that the substituend in 7.2. 115 is the final vowel of such a base. And 1.1.50 (see section III.1.5.4a) must be consulted to know which of the vowels denoted by *vṛddhi* replaces a particular substituend. A translation like Böhtlingk's, though it looks faith-

ful to the original Pāṇinian statement, fails to show that metarules and definitions indeed apply together with rules which they serve to interpret (see section III.1.5.2c).

16. Commentaries such as the Kāśikā or the Bhāṣā-vṛtti (see sections IV. 2.1, IV.2.2.1) do not constantly supply all crossreferences simply because they assume a knowledge of the major rules which have to apply in given cases.

17. I do not agree with all of Shefts' translations, but I do not enter into details here.

18. Gaṅgādatta Śāstrī (1950-62) also composed a Sanskrit commentary on the rules.

19. These are editions published without commentary. The dhātu-pāṭha is known as transmitted by commentators, for which see section IV.4.

20. Note that the gaṇa-pāṭha text published by Böhtlingk (1887a) and S. C. Chakravarti (1918) has no claim to great antiquity; on this see Birwé (1961: 460-62).

21. But not always. For example, Böhtlingk (1887a: *212*) does not note that Pāṇini uses the term *upapada* in two values, one technical, the other not (see Cardona [1973d: 52; 1973e: 217 n. 31]). Böhtlingk (1887a: *196*) does distinguish two values of the term *adhikaraṇa* ('locus of an action' and 'thing referred to'), but he also says, "uneig[entlich] auch so v[iel] a[ls] Lokativ" (similarly 1887a: *217*, sv. *karaṇa*, "auch so v. a. Instrumental). He cannot give a textual reference for such a usage because Pāṇini does not so use the term.

22. For example, the term *gati* is given (Pathak - Chitrao [1935: 246]) together with the label *pā*[ribhāṣika]*ś*[abdaḥ], indicating that the entries are instances of this term used technically, but not all the entries listed here meet this qualification. See also Pathak - Chitrao (1935: 247 [sv. *guṇa*], 249 [sv. *gha*]), to mention only a few cases where there is some mixup of entries.

23. Katre's work suffers from a considerable number of errors of commission and omission, some of which are dealt with in Cardona (1973d).

24. To a great extent I think Thieme's point is well taken. However, I do not think Thieme's insistence (1958: 23-24) on the etymological meanings of items is fully justified. Pāṇini, Kātyāyana and Patañjali make abundantly clear how they use particular terms. At best, the assumedly original etymological meaning can serve a historical purpose: to show a historical development of certain meanings. It should not, however, be used to show in what value Pāṇini etc. used particular terms.

25. Fortunately, this contains references both to the rules by number and to pages, so that one corrects the other, since there are many errors.

26. Kielhorn's purpose in compiling this was to demonstrate that the Śākaṭāyana grammar in question was not the work of the Śākaṭāyana of old; see section III.1.3.2b.
27. Possibly in a broad sense, including observers of differences in usage. Of course, even observations of such differences imply grammatical awareness.
28. For this view see sections III.2.6.3, VI.2.4 and note 163.
29. This is a phrase which conveys the meaning of the derivate *āpiśalā* (*brāhmaṇī*) '(a Brāhmaṇa woman) who studies Āpiśali's grammar', as noted by Patañjali (Kielhorn [1880-85: II: 205.3]).
30. Patañjali does not actually cite the rule, which is quoted by later commentators as *dhenor anañaḥ*. For this and other rules of Āpiśali cited in commentaries see Yudhiṣṭhira Mīmāṃsaka (1973: I: 139-40).
31. For other views ascribed to Śākaṭāyana see Yudhiṣṭhira Mīmāṃsaka (1973: I: 164-67).
32. On such pre-Pāṇinian terminology see Kielhorn (1887c: 101) [who is skeptical concerning the value of Kātyāyana and Patañjali's attributions], Mangala Deva Shastri (1926) [who is, I think, too quick to accept that texts such as the prātiśākhyas are all pre-Pāṇinian, see section III.3.2], V. S. Agrawala (1940-41; 1960; 1963a: 346-49), Giridhara Śarmā Caturveda (1965), M. D. Balasubrahmanyam (1966a, c).
33. For the view that Pāṇini was the first Indian ever to compose a true grammar see section III.3.2.1.
34. Edited by Raghu Vira (1934) and Yudhiṣṭhira Mīmāṃsaka (1967/8). The text has again been printed, with an English translation and an introductory essay, by van Nooten (1973). Let me mention in passing that van Nooten's work, in which Yudhiṣṭhira Mīmāṃsaka's edition is not mentioned, is inferior to the latter. For example, the introductory section of the text contains what is in effect a table of contents. In Yudhiṣṭhira Mīmāṃsaka's edition (1967/8: 13) this reads in part: *sthānam idaṃ karaṇam idaṃ prayatna eṣa dvidhânilaḥ sthānaṃ pīḍayati* "This is a point of articulation, this an articulator, effort is twofold (internal and external), the wind (breath) strikes a point of articulation." Van Nooten reads . . . *prayatna eṣa dvidhânilasthānaṃ pīḍayati* and translates (1973: 422), "This process, then, . . . strikes the point where the wind divides in two [the velic?]." Van Nooten has apparently invented a new term, *dvidhânila-sthānam*, which he cannot justify.
35. Van Nooten (1973: 409) also considers the text old. I say "which would definitively prove otherwise" because there are usages in the text which make me suspect the treatise is not as old as has been claimed. Thus, 1.17-18 (Yudhiṣṭhira Mīmāṃsaka [1967/8: 2]) use the terms *et, ait, ot, aut* to refer to *e, ai, o, au*. Kātyāyana and Patañjali (Kielhorn [1880-85: I:

22.1-24]) discuss whether these vowels should be listed in the śiva-sūtras as they are given or with *t* after them, making them terms interpreted by 1.1.70 (see section III.1.5.3c with note 215). It is possible to suspect that the Āpiśala-śikṣā has adopted one of the alternatives discussed in the Mahā-bhāṣya. But I cannot prove this at present.

36. There is no evidence for claiming that Pāṇini referred to Indra, as was pointed out by B. N. Krishnamurti Sarma (1932).

37. Which he puts at nearly 10,000 B. C.

38. I am not competent to judge this last issue; see Vedachala Iyer (1933), P. S. Subrahmanya Sastri (1934). Nor am I sufficiently acquainted with Tolkāppiyar's work to judge the validity of studies such as J. D. Singh - K. Doraswamy (1972).

39. Yudhiṣṭhira Mīmāṃsaka (1965/6b: 22-26) rather harshly attacked western scholars who do not accept the antiquity of the Kāśakṛtsna-dhātu-pāṭha, saying (1965/6b: 22): "It is the nature of western scholars that they deny, without proper reason, the validity of such an ancient text, found suddenly and by which their false assumptions are shown to be wrong (pāścātyānāṃ viduṣāṃ prāyeṇaiṣa svabhāvo vartate, yat te tādṛśaṃ sahasôpa-labdhaṃ prācīnaṃ grantham, yena tair udbhāvitānāṃ mithyā-dhāraṇānāṃ khaṇḍanaṃ jāyate, vinaiva pramāṇaṃ 'kūṭo'yaṃ granthaḥ' ity uktvâpalapanti)." He went on to try to show that the Kātantra-dhātu-pāṭha is an abridgement of the Kāśakṛtsna-dhātu-pāṭha; see also Yudhiṣṭhira Mīmāṃsaka (1973: II: 29-32).

40. On the question whether Pāṇini borrowed from prātiśākhyas see section III.3.2.2.

41. A brief survey of major views appears in Birwé (1966: 1-4).

42. Similarly Keith (1920: 424) and, earlier, Whitney (1893b: 254); see section III.1.5.6a.

43. The use of several terms (*chandas, mantra, nigama*) assumedly promiscuously to refer to Vedic; see Pawte (1935: 66) for a like view.

44. Yudhiṣṭhira Mīmāṃsaka (1973: I: 220-22) is also of the opinion that Pāṇini's grammar had three recensions: an eastern recension which was the basis for the Kāśikā's comments (section IV.2.1), a northern recension on which commented Kṣīrasvāmin (section IV.4) and other Kashmiris, and a southern recension on which Kātyāyana composed his vārttikas. He also maintains that each of these recensions had a longer and a shorter version.

45. It has also been argued that rules suffered corruption. S. P. Chaturvedi (1942) considered that the original reading of 7.1.90 – which is cited as *goto ṇit* in the Mahā-bhāṣya – was *oto ṇit* and said (1942: 79), "A slight corruption in the reading of the s[ūtra] has been taken to be a genuine reading by the commentators." A. N. Jani (1963) also considered that the

rule was originally *oto ṇit* and suggested that the *g-* developed as a transition between the *ṅ* of the previous rule (7.1.18: *puṃso'suṅ*) and the initial vowel of 7.1.90; see also section III.1.3.3f.

46. This gives as ready made (see section III.1.5.2c) the following derivatives: *adhyāya* 'section of a text', *nyāya* 'means of reaching a conclusion', *udyāva* 'mixture', *saṃhāra* 'destruction', *ādhāra* 'substrate', *āvāya* 'that on which one weaves'. According to the Kāśikā, the rule also accounts for *avahāra* 'taking down' (see below).

47. The rule is thus read in the Siddhânta-kaumudī (section IV.3.2), rule number 3301.

48. For discussions on this use of *ca* see note 377.

49. I assume here that the commentary was composed by Candragomin, as accepted by most scholars. I cannot discuss this issue here; the most recent study on the subject is by Birwé (1968).

50. Such genitive forms are interpreted by rule 1.1.49; see section III. 1.5.3c with note 217.

51. R. S. Bhattacharya (1966c: 74-75) gives rule 6.1.163 (*citaḥ*) as an example. If *citaḥ* is interpreted as the genitive singular of *cit*, the rule provides that the final (*anta*, 6.1.159) vowel of an item marked with *c* (*c-it*) is high pitched (*udātta*, 6.1.159). Now, the derivatives *bahu-bhuktá* 'almost eaten', *sarvakaíḥ* 'by all', which contain the affixes *bahuc, akac*, marked with *c*, should be accented as shown. But it is not the entire derivate which is marked with *c*, only the affix. To provide for the proper forms, Kātyāyana states (Kielhorn [1880-85: III: 104.2]) that the rule should apply to a unit marked with *c* along with its base (*saprakṛteḥ*). One of the alternative solutions suggested by Patañjali (Kielhorn [1880-85: III: 104.6-7]) is this: consider that *citaḥ* is the nominative of a derivative of *cit*, containing an affix *a* and meaning "which contains an item marked with *c*". Further, this is considered a statement in accord with early grammars (*pūrva-sūtra-nirdeśa*): the nominative is used to refer to an operand instead of the genitive. Bhattacharya's example is not proper to the extent that what is involved is simply an operand, not a substituend in particular. On this example see also Kielhorn (1887c: 101).

52. On this usage and the discussions it has lead to see section III.1.5.3e.

53. R. S. Bhattacharya (1966c: 75) cites two examples which I do not discuss here; see below for the use of the same argument by others.

54. Sköld (1926a: 32) earlier went so far as to suggest that the entire corpus of Pāṇinian rules was originally metrical, a view impossible to maintain (see V. S. Agrawala [1963a: 19-20], Birwé [1966: 3 n. 1]).

55. Note that very similar principles have again been set forth by Yudhiṣṭhira Mīmāṃsaka (1973: I: 230-35).

56. Pawte cited two rules (7.2.70, 6.1.75) as illustrations.
57. Pawte (1935: 99) also cited as evidence the use of synonyms, for example, *vā, vibhāṣā* and *anyatarasyām,* all meaning 'optionally'. This has been refuted by S. D. Joshi - J. A. F. Roodbergen (1971: 159-61); see also note 58.
58. He also takes up apparent conflicts of rules with the metarules 1.1.66 (see my note 217), 1.1.46 (see my section V), 1.1.70 (see my note 215), 1.4.2 (see my section III.1.5.2b); see Birwé (1966: 16-30, 40-63). He also accepts (1966: 36-39, 89-91), as did others (e.g., R. S. Bhattacharya [1966c: 79-81]) that the use of endingless forms and synonyms such as *vā, vibhāṣā* (see my note 57) indicates different authorship.
59. Scharfe suggests that dual forms in *-os* which Birwé treated as genitives used in ablative value (see below) should be interpreted as Vedic ablative forms. He refers to Wackernagel - Debrunner (1930: 55-56) for support. However, this is not very satisfactory, since, as Wackernagel - Debrunner (1930: 56) note, the Vedic evidence for such ablatives in *-os* is not substantial.
60. 4.1.1: *ṅy-āp-prātipadikāt* 'after (items ending in affixes denoted by) *ṅī, āp* (and after) nominal bases.' The ablative form *ṅy-āp-prātipadikāt* is construed with the term *para* of 3.1.2 (see section III.1.5.3e). 4.1.1 is to be understood as applying with subsequent rules. 4.1.66: *ūṅ utaḥ* '(The item) *ūṅ* (is introduced after a nominal base ending in) *u*.' Subsequent rules, through 4.1.72, introduce the same affix after items ending in *u*-vowels.
61. *sv-au-jas-am-auṭ-chaṣ-ṭā-bhyāṃ-bhis-ṅe-bhyāṃ-bhyas-ṅasi-bhyāṃ-ṅas-os-ām-ṅy-os-sup.* This simply introduces the basic nominal endings generally. Rules such as 2.3.2 (note 159) apply to introduce triplets of these endings under particular conditions.
62. Earlier, Pawte (1935: 63) considered a series of nipātana rules (8.3.90-95) and concluded that they were irregular, hence not composed by Pāṇini. Pawte's objections were met by R. S. Bhattacharya (1966f). Renou (1955: 110) proposed, cautiously, that nipātana rules might have been added to regular rules; but see section III.1.5.2c.
63. However, Bahulikar (1972: 113-14) admits that this is only a suggestion, open to further consideration; this proviso applies to her other suggestions.
64. This is one of 47 instances cited by Birwé (1966: 31-34), who, unlike Pawte and R. S. Bhattacharya before him, assumes that rule 1.1.67 applies to interpret the ablative forms of affixation rules; see section III.1.5.3e.
65. *dhinvi-kṛṇvyor a ca.* The roots *dhiv, kṛv* are marked with *i*, so that they unconditionally receive an infixed augment *n*. Hence, Pāṇini here refers to the roots as *dhinv, kṛṇv.*
66. See also R. Rocher (1967: 584), who similarly rejects Birwé's reasoning concerning 3.1.80.

67. 6.1.101 (*akaḥ savarṇe dīrghaḥ*) provides that *a, i, u, ṛ, ḷ* (*ak*) vowels and homogeneous (*savarṇa*, see section III.1.5.4a with note 234) sounds following them are both replaced by a long vowel (*dīrgha*). This rule comes under the heading of 6.1.84 (see note 172). In the section headed by the last rule, another heading is valid, 6.1.85 (*antâdivac ca*), whereby the single replacement is treated like the final unit of the preceding and the initial unit of the following item.

68. For a brief survey of some of the suggestions made see Birwé (1966: 2-4).

69. Who considered only 1.2.56-57 unoriginal.

70. Who considered 4.2.81, 1.2.51 rules of other teachers, but 1.2.53 Pāṇini's.

71. Palsule was also willing to consider the Mahā-bhāṣya discussions on these rules interpolations.

72. "Besides, the sūtras . . . (IV - 2 - 81), . . . (IV - 2 - 82), . . . (I - 2 - 51), . . . (VII - 1 - 18), . . . (VII - 3 - 105) and . . . (VII - 3 - 120) are considered to be the *sūtras* of his [Pāṇini's] predecessors."

73. For example, T. Venkatacharya (1959: 96), "Pāṇini in his aphorisms from 1. 2. 51 to 1. 2. 57 shows his difference from his predecessors." Similarly, Krishnaswami Iyangar (1972: 7-9).

74. For other suggestions of corruption in the text see note 45. On sūtras considered transferred from the gaṇa-pāṭha see section III.1.3.5c.

75. Cf. V. S. Agrawala (1945: 104), "The text of the sūtras has come down to us almost intact."

76. Who also discusses (1941: 213-15; 1968: 33-36) the legend according to which the śiva-sūtras were transmitted to Pāṇini by Śiva and the source of this legend.

77. These are accompanied respectively by the glosses *vimocane* 'bind' and *prasravaṇe* 'urinate'; e.g., *sūtrayati* 'makes . . . a sūtra', *mūtrayati* 'urinates',

78. For the roots and the sūtras see Böhtlingk (1887a: *83*), S. C. Chakravarti (1919: 150-51), Liebich (1920a: 25; 1930: 195), Yudhiṣṭhira Mīmāṃsaka (1957-58: 317-18), Dwarikadas Shastri (1964: 571-2).

79. Kielhorn (1880-85: II: 34.8): *tat karotîty upasaṃkhyānaṃ sūtrayaty-ādy-artham.*

80. But some of the sūtras included in the dhātu-pāṭha were known at least by the time of Patañjali; see, for example, Kielhorn (1880-85: II: 38. 24-25), Vedavrata (1962-63: III: 102). On sūtras included in the gaṇa-pāṭha see note 91.

81. "The root *bhū* occurs in the meaning 'being' " or "The root *bhū* occurs when the meaning 'being' is to be denoted."

82. A Sanskrit version of Yudhiṣṭhira Mīmāṃsaka's summary as it appeared

in the first edition of this volume (pp. 45-51) is given by Dwarikadas Shastri (1964: introduction, pp. 4 - 8).

83. 1.3.1: *bhūv-ādayo dhātavaḥ* "(The items) *bhū* etc. (listed in the dhātu-pāṭha, are called) roots (*dhātu*)."

84. Similarly, Charudeva Shastri (1957-58). Kiparsky - Staal (1969: 108), on the other hand, first assumed that these entries were original and said, "This might indicate that the lexical entries of the *Dhātupāṭha* should be viewed as a set of lexical insertion rules . . ." However, they then went on to admit (1969: 108 n. 10a) that the entries probably were not original. More recently, Ananthanarayana (1972) appears to accept that roots in the original dhātu-pāṭha were accompanied by meaning entries, though no arguments appear in the summary of his paper.

85. Kielhorn (1880-85: I: 256.11-12) [on 1. 3. 1 vārttika 7]: *vapiḥ prakiraṇe dṛṣṭaś chedane câpi vartate.*

86. *Ataḥ yahāṃ jin dhātv-arthoṃ ko dṛṣṭa kahā jātā hai, ve dhātu-pāṭha meṃ paṭhita haiṃ athavā dhātu-pāṭha meṃ dekhe gae haiṃ, aur jin ke liye vartate kā prayoga kiyā hai, ve loka meṃ vyavahṛta haiṃ, yahī abhiprāya is vacana kā hai.*

87. On cosignifiers (*dyotaka*) see note 152; the actual term *dyotaka* is not used here.

88. According to Pawte; but see below.

89. Pawte (1935: 14-15, 18-19). Pawte (1935: 19-31) gave other arguments which I cannot deal with here.

90. An order which Whitney (1884: 296) characterized as "wholly artificial and unsystematic." See Shefts (1961: 2) for a discussion.

91. Like the dhātu-pāṭha (see note 80), the gaṇa-pāṭha too contains some sūtras. Some of these were known to Kātyāyana and Patañjali as sūtras pertaining to this text, others, identical with vārttikas of Kātyāyana, are definitely post-Pāṇinian. See Birwé (1961: 18, 30), Kapil Deva Shastri (1967: 266-67), Cardona (1973a: 95 n. 26).

92. Kātyāyana and Patañjali speak of the gaṇa-pāṭha as a text propounded by Pāṇini, as has been noted, for example, by P. S. Subrahmanya Sastri (1960: xvi-xviii).

93. 1.1.27: *sarvâdīni sarvanāmāni* '(The items) *sarva* etc. (are called) *sarvanāman.*'

94. 7.2.102: *tyad-ādīnām aḥ* "*a* (occurs instead of the final sound) of *tyad* etc. (when there follows an ending [*vibhaktau* 84])." Rule 5.3.2. (*kiṃ-sarvanāma-bahubhyo'dvy-ādibhyaḥ*) is a heading (section III.1.5.2c) whereby affixes of subsequent rules are introduced after pronominals other than *dvi* 'two' etc. but including *kim* (interrogative), which is part of the subset *dvi* etc.

95. In this interpretation, *vibhāṣā jasi* 'optionally before *jas*' is considered to recur (anuvṛtti, see sections III.1.5.2c, 1.5.3g) in 1.1.34-36 from 1.1.32.
96. But only *pūrvāḥ kuravaḥ*, where *pūrva* is used to name a particular people (the eastern Kuru) and their area.
97. See also Ojihara (1959). Later Ojihara (1963a) retrenched and noted (1963a: 846 = (25)) that this previous position no longer seemed satisfactory to him. Birwé (1961: 26) argued against P. S. Subrahmanya Sastri, who stated (1960: xvii) that Kātyāyana's vārttikas did not show what Pawte had claimed. Birwé (1966: 163) has also claimed that three other rules, 6.1.156, 8.3.99-100 were taken from gaṇa-sūtras. I do not discuss this claim here.
98. He considered (1927: 270) that *vibhāṣā jasi* should not recur in 1.1.34-36; see note 95 above.
99. And also Ojihara's early view; see note 97 above.
100. Certainly Scharfe's claim (1971a: 49) that *pūrva* etc. "are stated in I 1 34 - 36 to be such pronouns only in the nominative plural – and that only optionally . . ." goes against the facts of Sanskrit.
101. In this list Abhyankar includes some definitions and headings (see section III.1.5.2c). This is justified to the extent that such rules, like metarules, do not apply independently but only in conjunction with other rules.
102. See K. V. Abhyankar (1967a: 6 n. 1) for a list of paribhāṣās given in vārttikas.
103. There are earlier editions (see, for example, the bibliography under Renou [1952]) which I do not consider here.
104. See K. V. Abhyankar (1960: preface, opposite p. 6). It is noteworthy that in this list showing the student-teacher descent since Nāgeśa one European appears: Kielhorn.
105. The composition of Sanskrit commentaries on the Paribhāṣêndu-śekhara continued into the twentieth century; see Rājanārāyaṇa Śāstrī (1943), Umeśa Miśra Śarmā (1968).
106. Buiskool considered the prātiśākhyas pre-Pāṇinian; on this question see section III.3.2.
107. Paribhāṣās 4-5 of the Paribhāṣêndu-śekhara: *anekântā anubandhāḥ, ekântāḥ*.
108. Paribhāṣêndu-śekhara, paribhāṣā 7: *nânubandha-kṛtam anej-antatvam* "An item's not ending in (a vowel denoted by) *ec* is not brought about by a marker." Paribhāṣās 6 (*nânubandha-kṛtam anekâltvam*) and 8 (*nânubandha-kṛtam asārūpyam*) further state that a marker does not make an item polyphonous (*anekâl*) or serve to make two items such as *aṇ, ka* (= *a*) dissimilar (*asarūpa*).

109. Number 71 of the Paribhāṣêndu-śekhara: *prātipadika-grahaṇe liṅga-viśiṣṭasyâpi grahaṇam.*
110. In rule 4.1.1; see note 60 above.
111. Kielhorn (1880-85: II: 192.3): *ṅy-āb-grahaṇam anarthakaṃ prātipadika-grahaṇe liṅga-viśiṣṭasyâpi grahaṇāt.*
112. In the pañca-pādī version; see below.
113. The earlier edition by Böhtlingk (1844) was a reprint of the rules as published previously in Calcutta; see Böhtlingk (1844: preface, p. 2).
114. Pade emphasized (1958: x) that according to Nāgeśa Śākaṭāyana was the author of ancient uṇ-ādi-sūtras, not of the present pañca-pādī treatise.
115. 3.3.1: *uṇ-ādayo bahulam* "*Uṇ* etc. (occur) variously", 3.4.75: *tābhyām anyatrôṇ-ādayaḥ* "*Uṇ* etc. (are introduced when there is to be denoted a participant in an action) other than those two (namely sampradāna and apādāna)." For the kāraka terms *sampradāna*, *apādāna* see section III.1.5.5c.1 with note 273.
116. In such cases Patañjali commonly avoids the problem by noting that such nominal bases derived with uṇ-ādi suffixes as give rise to dispute are treated as underived (*avyutpanna*); see Vedavrata (1962-63: III: 309 n. 1) for some references.
117. And earlier by K. G. Subrahmanyam and T. R. Chintamani in articles not accessible to me; see Renou (1940a: 17 n. 1).
118. K. Madhava Krishna Sarma (1941a: 400-01) also pointed out that some of the affixes which appear in the extant uṇ-ādi treatises were not known to Kātyāyana and Patañjali.
119. Similarly R. S. Bhattacharya (1952: 168), M. D. Pandit (1963a: 63-67), Krishnaswami Iyangar (1972: 18), Ramanuja Tatacharya (1972b: 27).
120. The -*ṣ* of *phiṣ* is replaced by *ṭ* in word-final position and before *s* by regular sandhi alternation.
121. This is provided by 6.1.158: *anudāttaṃ padam eka-varjam* 'Excepting one vowel, a pada (see note 151) has no high-pitched vowel.'
122. These provisions are made in 3.1.3: *ādy-udāttaś ca* '(Items introduced by sybsequent rules not only occur after the units to which they are introduced but) also have a high-pitched first vowel,' 3.1.4: *anudattau sup-pitau* 'Nominal endings (denoted by *sup*) and items marked with *p* have no high-pitched vowel.'
123. This is known as *sati śiṣṭaḥ svaraḥ* 'A pitch taught when there is another (which is cancelled by the former).' It can be shown that this erasure procedure was accepted by Pāṇini, though I cannot discuss the details here.
124. Kielhorn also showed (1866: introduction, pp. 11-15) that the earlier view, according to which the author of the phiṭ-sūtras was an easterner, was based on insufficient evidence.
125. Thus in Kielhorn's edition. Devasthali (1967: 49) prefers the reading

sphig-antasya, with the term *sphik* instead of *lup*, both denoting a zero replacement.

126. Kielhorn (1880-85: III: 87.5-6) [on 6. 1. 123]: *na tv idaṃ lakṣaṇam asti prātipadikasyâdir udātto bhavatîti/ idaṃ punar asti prātipadikasyânta udātto bhavatîti.*

127. See also Thieme (1935c) [especially pp. 415-16] on the question of the gender of *śiśira* for Pāṇini, the compound *hemanta-śiśira-* 'winter and cool season' and the Vedic rules pertaining to this.

128. Liebich (1928: 51) [paribhāṣā 74], K. V. Abhyankar (1967a: 48) [paribhāṣā 73]: *liṅgam aśiṣyaṃ lokâśrayatvāl liṅgasya.*

129. Yudhiṣṭhira Mīmāṃsaka proposed his arguments for this view in the first edition of the second volume of his history (pp. 226-27), and Vedavatī accepted his view.

130. Yudhiṣṭhira Mīmāṃsaka (1973: II: 254-55) also attributes such gender treatises to pre-Pāṇinians.

131. He cites (1973: II: 256) one passage from Haradatta's Pada-mañjarī (see section IV.2.1).

132. 1973: II: 256: *kātyāyana ke vārtika aur patañjali ke vyākhyāna kī pāṇinīya liṅgânuśāsana ke aviśiṣṭaṃ liṅgam, avyayaṃ kati-yuṣmad-asmadaḥ (antima prakaraṇa) sūtroṃ ke sāth tulanā karne se spaṣṭa hai ki kātyāyana aur patañjali is pāṇinīya liṅgânuśāsana se paricita the.*

133. The so-called Pāṇinīya-śikṣā is actually two distinct works in several versions; see section III.1.4.4a.

134. The last scholar suggests (1967/8: introduction, p. 6; 1973: III: 63) that the versified śikṣā is based on the śikṣā in sūtra form. However, he gives no substantiating arguments.

135. This text excludes the introductory verse noted above.

136. 1.1.8: *mukha-nāsikā-vacano'nunāsikaḥ* 'A sound pronounced through the mouth and the nose together (is called) *anunāsika.*' Ghosh referred to this as rule 1.1.9, which I have corrected in the citation.

137. In fact, Pāṇini's rule (8.4.1: *ra-ṣābhyāṃ no ṇaḥ samāna-pade*) states explicitly only that *n* is replaced by *ṇ* after *r* and *ṣ*; *ṛ* is not directly stated as a left context. To allow the rule to provide for the replacement after *ṛ* also one must either make an addition to the rule or assume that *r* denotes also the consonant contained in vocalic *ṛ*.

138. *aco'spṛṣṭā yaṇas tv īṣan nema-spṛṣṭāḥ śalaḥ smṛtāḥ/ śeṣāḥ spṛṣṭā halaḥ prôktāḥ.*

139. However, J. D. Singh later (1972a: 92 n. 7) notes that scholars differ and says, "But anyway it is one of the oldest śikṣās." He does not, however, discuss evidence.

140. The classification of spirant as *īṣad-vivṛta* is in fact adopted in the

Āpiśala-śikṣā (Yudhiṣṭhira Mīmāṃsaka [1967/8: 3]), the Madhya-siddhânta-kaumudī and the Laghu-siddhânta-kaumudī (see section IV.3.2) and suggested in the Mahā-bhāṣya; see Cardona (1965a: 226-27).

141. For a description of how the editor came to establish the textus amplior see Yudhiṣṭhira Mīmāṃsaka (1967/8: introduction, pp. 9 - 10; 1973: III: 67-68).

142. For this text see K. C. Chatterji (1953-61: II: 394-95), Yudhiṣṭhira Mīmāṃsaka (1967/8: 24-26). In view of the strong accusation made by Ghosh I quote his own words (1938: xlvii). After noting that statements found in works of other grammarians need not have been borrowed from this śikṣā, Ghosh says, "For this borrowing might well have occurred the other way round, that is the author of the D[ayānanda] P[honetic] S[ūtras] might have culled his materials from sundry sources such as the Mahābhāṣya and the Varṇa-sūtras of Candragomin."

143. Similarly, Yudhiṣṭhira Mīmāṃsaka (1973: I: 238, III: 64).

144. Pāṇinīya-śikṣā 3.6-7 (Yudhiṣṭhira Mīmāṃsaka [1967/8: 12; 1973: III: 74]): *īṣad-vivṛta-karaṇā ūṣmāṇaḥ, vivṛta-karaṇā vā.*

145. This is also the order in the Āpiśala-śikṣā, 1.19 (Yudhiṣṭhira Mīmāṃsaka [1967/8: 2]); see section III.1.3.2a.

146. Pāṇinīya-śikṣā 1.21 (Yudhiṣṭhira Mīmāṃsaka [1967/8: 11; 1973: III: 73]).

147. This appears to be the opinion also of van Nooten (1973), who believes (1973: 409) " . . . that the *Āpiśali-śikṣā*, or one very much like it, fulfilled this function [of providing phonetic descriptions] as a phonetic complement to the grammar in the formative stages of Indian linguistic theory." Van Nooten goes further and appears to consider the sūtra version of the Pāṇinīya-śikṣā none other than the Āpiśala-śikṣā, since he refers (1973: 420 n. 11) to the latter as having been "published by Raghu Vira 1931 and again 1933." This is a possibility to be considered. Indeed, Raghu Vira (1934: 225) appears to have held this opinion. But one has also to consider the differences between the two texts pointed out by Yudhiṣṭhira Mīmāṃsaka (1967/8: introduction, pp. 7-8; 1973: III: 65-66). Van Nooten alludes neither to such differences nor to Yudhiṣṭhira Mīmāṃsaka's edition; see also above, note 35.

148. Charudeva Shastri (1967: 107) stressed a cardinal tenet of Pāṇinīyas, namely that the grammar follows correct usage: it is an explanation (*anuvyākhyāna*) of such usage; see also R. S. Bhattacharya (1966x), Jānakīprasāda Dviveda (1969).

149. These uses of *lakṣaṇa* and *lakṣya* were considered by Staal (1961: 122-24), whose exposition is the basis for Al-George (1971). Al-George asks why Kātyāyana and Patañjali use these terms in this way, takes up rules where

Pāṇini himself uses *lakṣaṇa*, and concludes (1971: 217) that "In all these subordinations the content of the protasis or its equivalent is called *lakṣaṇa* 'sign', because it is expressing [sic] an antecedent of the content expressed by the main clause." Al-George goes on (1971: 218-20) to bring in logical statements of the type *tasmin sati tad bhavati* 'If A then B.' According to him, this is the basis of the use of *lakṣaṇa* 'rule'. See also, in a similar vein, Al-George (1969). There is a more obvious reason, noted above. In his Darpaṇa on the Vaiyākaraṇa-bhūṣaṇa-sāra (see section IV.3.2), Harivallabha says (Sadāśiva Śāstrī Joshi [1939: 80]): *lakṣyate'nvākhyāyate sādhu-śabdo' 'nenêti lakṣaṇaṃ sūtram* 'A lakṣaṇa is a sūtra; (and the latter is thus termed) for this reason: it is that by which correct speech is characterized, that is, explained.'

150. See Thieme (1932: 236-37), R. S. Bhattacharya (1966r), Cardona (1970c).

151. 1.4.14: *sup-tiṅ-antaṃ padam* "An item terminating in a nominal ending (*sup*) or a verb ending (*tiṅ*) (is called) *pada*."

152. For example, 3.4.69 (*laḥ karmaṇi ca bhāve câkarmakebhyaḥ* [*kartari* 67]) provides that L-suffixes (to be replaced by verb endings and participial affixes) are introduced after roots if an agent (*kartṛ*) or an object (*karman*) is to be denoted and, after roots which, in given derivations, denote objectless actions (*akarmaka*), if an action (*bhāva*) is to be denoted. Particular meanings are assigned to bases and affixes. For example, according to Pāṇinīyas a root such as *pac* 'cook' denotes the complex of actions (*kriyā*, *vyāpāra*) which lead to a result, softening (*viklitti*) of food, and this result also. An ending such as *ti* in *pac-a-ti* ' . . . cooks, is cooking' denotes an agent and a number (*saṃkhyā*). One of the methods for arriving at such meaning assignments is the technique of anvyaya and vyatireka, concurrent present and absence: if item I (e.g. *pac*) occurs, meaning M is understood and if I is absent, M is not understood (see Cardona [1967-68]). Pāṇinīyas recognize not only items which denote (*vācaka*) meanings assigned to them but also cosignifiers (*dyotaka*), items which, without denoting meanings attributed to them, have to be used with other items in order that the meanings of the latter be expressed. For example, a base such as *deva* is considered to denote either a god or a goddess. If it is used in the latter meaning, the affix *ī* is introduced after it as a cosignifier of femininity: *devī*.

153. For example, 2.3.31 (*enapā dvitīyā*) introduces a second triplet nominal ending, that is, an accusative ending, after a nominal base which is construed with an item containing the affix *enap* (= *ena*); *dakṣiṇena grāmam* 'south of the village'.

154. For example, 3.2.118 (*laṭ sme*) provides that the L-suffix *laṭ* is introduced after a root if the action denoted by it is referred to the past and the particle *sma* is used.

155. Pāninīyas here use the term *svârtha* 'meaning (*artha*) of (the item) itself (to which is added an affix)'.
156. Scharfe (1971a: 26 n. 27) states, "It is remarkable that Pāṇini has not recognized tenses and moods as separate categories." It is to be noted that Pāṇini operates with different L-suffixes introduced under various meaning conditions in addition to the general one noted in note 152 above. For example, *laṭ* is introduced when an action is referred to the present (3.2.123, see section III.3.1.4 (c)) and also, under particular syntactic co-occurrence conditions, when an action is referred to the past (see note 154); *liṅ* is introduced when modalities such as command are denoted.
157. These morphophonemic rules are of course not limited to padas.
158. There are also derivatives of the types *rāja-puruṣa*, *aupagava*, that is, compounds and taddhita derivatives, which are obligatory (*nitya*). For example, from a string *kumbha-as kāra-s* one derives only the compound *kumbha-kāra* 'pot-maker', not also an alternative string *kumbhasya kāraḥ*, since *kāra* does not occur as an independent item. Again, a compound such as *khaṭvârūḍha* meaning 'intemperate' and not merely 'who has climbed (*ārūḍha*) into bed (*khaṭvā*)' is obligatory: the pejorative meaning conveyed by the compound is proper to it.
159. By rule 2.3.1 (*anabhihite*), a heading (see section III.1.5.2c) whereby affixes are introduced by subsequent rules if what is to be denoted is not otherwise denoted (*anabhihita*); on this see D. M. Joshi (1971). For example, 2.3.2 (*karmaṇi dvitīyā*) states that a second triplet ending (*dvitīyā*), that is, an accusative ending, is introduced after a nominal base if an object (*karman*) is to be denoted. This serves to introduce *am* in (3) but not in (4), where *laṭ* has been introduced to denote an object.
160. In addition, Pāṇini recognizes elements introduced as initial, final and internal elements of other items. By 1.1.46 (*ādy-antau ṭa-k-itau*), elements marked with *ṭ, k* respectively are introduced as initial (*ādi*) and final (*anta*) parts of items. And by 1.1.47 (*m-id aco'ntyāt paraḥ*) an element marked with *m* occurs after (*para*) the last (*antya*) vowel (*ac*) of the item to which it is introduced. Pāṇinīyas call the elements so marked, other than affixes, *āgama* 'augments'. Scharfe (1971a: 21 n. 9) says, "Pāṇini did not have the category of *āgama*." While it is true that Pāṇini himself did not call these elements by this name, he did indeed recognize augments, as noted.
161. Among the affixes subject to replacement are abstract elements, the L-suffixes; see note 152 and below.
162. Note that a zero replacement of an affix has a particular status. When an affix is replaced by zero (*pratyaya-lope*), the operation which would apply in its presence (*pratyaya-lakṣaṇam*) still applies (1.1.62: *pratyaya-lope pratyaya-lakṣaṇam*). For example, the *-n* of *rājan* 'king' is deleted if is

pada-final, as in *rājā* (nom. sg.). This deletion should also apply to *rājan* in the compound *rāja-puruṣa*, in which the element *rājan-* derives from *rājan-as*, a pada (see note 151). After the ending *as* is deleted, the remaining *rājan* is still treated as a pada.

163. This obviates the objection made by W. S. Allen (1955: 111), that Pāṇini might have been confused in his use of the terms *sthānin* and *ādeśa* and that linguists are naive in speaking of substituend and replacement as prior and subsequent elements at a single stage. As long as one recognizes what is at issue, there is no harm in stating, on a level of grammatical operations, that X is replaced by Y (see R. S.Bhattacharya [1966q: 214]). The distinction noted is also pertinent to a question of philosophical import to Pāṇinīyas (see section III.2.6.3). Patañjali discusses in the Mahā-bhāṣya (e.g., Kielhorn [1880-85: I: 75.8-14]) the question whether items are permanent, fixed (*nitya*) or subject to production and modification. Under the former view, it is impermissible to consider that a part of an item is replaced. Hence, Patañjali concludes that one should consider an entire item to occur in place of another whole item. Staal (1969: 503) has accepted this without further comment. However, a comment is required. As Kaiyaṭa (see section III.2.2) notes (Vedavrata [1962-63: I: 244]), this is not strictly reconcilable with what Pāṇini actually says. In deriving a causative such as *dāpi* from *dā* 'give', Pāṇini provides for the final augment *p* to be added to *dā.* Under the view now espoused, one would consider that the entire element *dāp* occurs instead of *dā*, thus eliminating a distinction which Pāṇini makes between substitution and augmenting. Therefore, notes Kaiyaṭa, though one can take the position stated by Patañjali in order to defend a philosophical stand, on the level of grammatical operations (*prakriyā*) one recognizes, albeit as a construct (*prakalpita*), that there are indeed augments added to items. Similarly, a statement "X → Y" is also merely part of a grammatical procedure. On the question of substitution and the Mahā-bhāṣya passage referred to above see also Thieme (1955a: 661 n. 3).

164. There are some general treatments by J. D. Singh (1971a, b; 1972; 1974a, b), in which the author attempts to cover very much ground in a very short compass.

165. It should be noted that the chart illustrating this (Joshi [1969: between pp. 24 and 25]) is cumbersome and does not clarify sufficiently how the system works. Note also that although Joshi uses terms such as "deep structure" he gives them very particular values in his own context (1969: 17 n. 11). S. D. Joshi (1968) has also discussed two views considered by Pāṇinīyas in connection with derivations, namely that rules apply primarily with respect to padas (see note 151) alone (*pada-saṃskāra*) and that they apply to derive padas in the context of utterances (*vākya-saṃskāra*).

166. Note that M. D. Pandit's other paper of 1963 contains a section entitled "Pāṇini's principles of derivation" (1963a: 62-67), which deals, however, with Pāṇini's views as opposed to those of etymologists (see section III.1.4.1b).
167. This section is headed by rule 2.1.3 (*prāk kaḍārāt samāsaḥ*), whereby items derived by subsequent rules are called *samāsa* 'compound'.
168. This section is headed by 2.3.1 (see note 159).
169. The heading for this section is 3.1.1: *pratyayaḥ* '(Items introduced by subsequent rules are called) *pratyaya* "affix".' This translation only conveys the result of what Pāṇini provides. Actually, the heading is considered to recur in subsequent rules, each of which then provides for introducing an element which is then termed *pratyaya.*
170. 3.1.91: *dhātoḥ* '(After) a root'; 4.1.1 (see note 60); 4.1.76: *taddhitāḥ* '(Items introduced by subsequent rules are called) *taddhita.*'
171. 6.1.1: *ekâco dve prathamasya* 'Two (elements) for the first monosyllabic part (of an item)'; 6.1.2: *aj-āder dvitīyasya* ' . . . for the second part of an item which begins with a vowel.' The environments in which this doubling applies are given in subsequent rules. Note that my using 'for' does not imply that substitution is involved, though I cannot here enter into details concerning the interpretation of these rules.
172. 6.1.84: *ekaḥ pūrva-parayoḥ* 'One (element) in place of a preciding and following items.'
173. 6.4.1: *aṅgasya*, 8.1.16: *padasya*; the genitive forms *aṅgasya* 'of a presuffixal base' and *padasya* state operands and relata.
174. This section begins with 8.2.1 (*pūrvatrâsiddham*), whereby rules of this section are treated as nonexistent (*asiddha*) relative to what preceding (*pūrvatra*); see also section III.1.5.2b.
175. R. Rocher (1965-66: 79) also appealed to memorization as a pedagogic reason for the extreme concision of rules. Bahulikar (1972: 4-5; 1973: 76-77) countered that one cannot make such a claim so baldly since we do not know precisely what pedagogic methods were followed at Pāṇini's time.
176. On rules considered together though not stated together in the grammar see section III.1.5.2c.
177. That is, a technical term introduced by a rule which follows. On this section see M. S. Narayana Murti (1967).
178. By 1.4.2: *vipratiṣedhe paraṃ kāryam.* On kāraka classification rules in this section see below, section III.1.5.5c.
179. Note that an operation includes also the assignment of a technical name (*saṃjñā*) to an item, thereby assigning that item to the category named by the technical term.
180. This was also accepted by Birwé (1966); see below.

181. Birwé (1966: 63): "Regeln wie VIII. 3, 32 scheinen zu beweisen, dass Fälle von Konflikten ausserhalb des Abschnittes I. 4, 1 - II. 2, 38 der Aṣṭādhyāyī vorhanden sind. Dies spricht m. E. für die einheimischen Grammatiker, die die Regel I. 4, 2 auf die gesamte pāṇineische Grammatik anwenden."

182. In the most recent paper on this topic Godse (1973) accepts without hesitation the view that *para* in 1.4.2 should be interpreted as meaning 'desired'.

183. Rama Nath Sharma (1972; forthcoming) discusses how rules, by virtue of terms contained in them, relate to other rules in which these terms are defined.

184. This holds also for headings, on which see below.

185. For opinions concerning this recurrence see section III.1.5.3g.

186. 1.3.11: *svaritenâdhikāraḥ* 'That which is characterized by a svarita is an adhikāra,' that is, a recurring item, to be understood in subsequent rules. I have specified "of the type 3.1.1" because headings such as 2.1.3 (note 167), which contain *prāk* 'before', were not marked with svarita.

187. Renou (1955: 124-26) briefly discussed the major headings and concluded (1955: 126) that Pāṇini's varied headings entitle one to suppose that he drew from various sources. But the very short exposition hardly warrants such a major claim.

188. In rule 1.1.56: *sthānivad ādeśo'nal-vidhau*, on which see recently Yaśapāla (1966), Cardona (1970d: 233-34).

189. V. L. Joshi (1971) has suggested that it would be as well to treat as borrowing some items which Pāṇinian commentators consider ready made forms.

190. On pre-Pāṇinian terms such as *auṅ* see section III.1.3.1.

191. *ṭi* denotes that part of an item which begins with its last vowels; *ghu* denotes a set of roots which have the shapes *dā, dhā*; *bha* refers to a unit followed by certain affixes beginning with a vowel or *y*.

192. Rules 1.2.51-57 are as follows. 1.2.51: *lupi yuktavad vyakti-vacane*, 52: *viśeṣaṇānāṃ câjāteḥ*, 53: *tad aśiṣyaṃ saṃjñā-pramāṇatvāt*, 54: *lub yogâprakhyānāt*, 55: *yoga-pramāṇe ca tad-abhāve'darśanaṃ syāt*, 56: *pradhāna-pratyayârtha-vacanam arthasyânya-pramāṇatvāt*, 57: *kālôpasarjane tulyam.* Now, the term *pañcālāḥ* 'place where the Pañcālas live' is derived as follows. To the genitive *pañcāla-as* is affixed *aṇ* (= *a*) to form (by 4.2.69: *tasya nivāsaḥ*) a derivative meaning 'the place of habitation (*nivāsa*) of . . .' The affix is then replaced by zero if the derivative is used to refer to a district (*janapada*, 4.2.81: *janapade lup*). 1.2.51 provides that where such a replacement by zero (*lup*) has applied, the gender (*vyakti*) and number (*vacana*) of the derivative are like those of the original base (*yuktavat*). Hence, *pañcālāḥ*

'Pañcāla country' is masculine plural. According to 1.2.52, qualifiers (*viśeṣaṇa*) of such derivatives also are treated in this way unless they are generic terms; e.g., *pañcālāḥ bahv-annāḥ* 'The Pañcāla country (is) rich in food' but *pañcālāḥ janapadaḥ* 'The Pañcāla country (is) a district.' 1.2.53 then states that what has been said in the previous rules (*tat* 'that') is not to be taught (*aśiṣya*). The reason for this is that the normal understanding (*saṃjñā*) of such terms is authority (*pramāṇa*) enough. The grammar does not have to teach that *pañcālāḥ* 'Pañcāla country' is masculine plural; this is a fact of the language which people know about such area names. Moreover, says 1.2.54, the deletion of an affix such as *aṇ* by a rule like 4.2.81 also does not have to be taught. For a name like *pañcālāḥ* is not understood etymologically: it is not necessarily understood to convey a relation (*yoga*) between the Pañcālas and the place. And (1.2.55), if one assumed that it is on the authority of such a connection that *pañcālāḥ* and such names referred to given areas, then these terms would not be used with reference to areas in which Pañcālas etc. were not living; yet they are. 1.2.56-57 take up a separate topic. The grammar also need not teach how the meaning of a given item is the principal (*pradhāna*) meaning of a certain type of compound or that a base and an affix together denote the meaning of the latter (e.g., *pāc-aka* 'cook-er'). For this is understood from another authority (*anya-pramāṇa*), namely usage. Similarly (1.2.57), the grammar need not give definitions of time (*kāla*) terms such as *adya* 'today' or state that by *upasarjana* is meant a subsidiary item, this for the same reason. In his comments on 1.2.53, Patañjali takes the term *saṃjñā* to mean here 'understanding' instead of 'name' (Kielhorn [1880-85: I: 229.7-8]: *saṃjñānaṃ saṃjñā*).

193. On 1.2.51-57 see also T. Venkatacharya (1959: 96-97). On 1.2.52, see M. S. Narayana Murti (1972a: 49-54).

194. The name of a particular type of compound; see section III.1.5.3b.4.

195. See Cardona (1969: 30) and below, section III.1.5.5b.3.

196. Pāṇini's grammar is therefore known as *akālakaṃ vyākaraṇam* 'grammar in which terms denoting time are not defined'. Laddu (1964; 1969) has summarized what commentators say regarding this and suggested other explanations, which he regards as more plausible; for example, that *akālaka* might mean 'spotless'. I think the traditional explanation is preferable. There is a parallel for such a characterization. Candragomin avoids using technical terms such as *vṛddhi*, so that his grammar is characterized as *asaṃjñakaṃ vyākaraṇam* 'grammar lacking technical terms' (see Kielhorn [1886b: 246]).

197. Aryendra Sharma et al. (1969-70: I: 46): *pradhānaṃ samāse kiṃcit padaṃ pratyayas tavyâdiḥ/ tābhyām artha-vacanam arthâbhidhānam anena prakāreṇa bhavatîti pūrvâcāryaiḥ paribhāṣitam: pradhānôpasarjane . . . pradhānârthaṃ saha brūtaḥ, prakṛti-pratyayau sahârthaṃ brūtaḥ iti* 'By *pradhāna*

is meant here a certain member of a compound; an item such as *tavya* is an affix; previous teachers stated metarules saying that these expressed meanings in a certain way: . . . '

198. Aryendra Sharma et al. (1969-70: I: 46): *ihânye vaiyākaraṇāḥ kālôpasarjanayoḥ paribhāṣāṃ kurvanti* 'Other grammarians state a metarule regarding time words and upasarjana.'

199. It is probable also that Pāṇini was conservative with regard to both successors and some predecessors in his use of terms like *ṭi* (see note 191); see Cardona (1969: 26-30).

200. I consider here only individual articles on particular terms. These and other terms are of course dealt with in the general lexica referred to in section III.1.2.3.

201. And of *sthāna* 'place (of tentative occurrence)', on which see also Thieme (1958: 41-48).

202. Renou (1941-42: 153 n. 2 [Staal (1972: 462 n. 75)]) accepted the Pāṇinīya interpretation that *vyakti* here means 'gender'.

203. Scharfe is certainly in error when he claims (1965: 243) that the suffix of the derivative *kaṭabadarī* ('town near the Kaṭabadarī') is added to the base and not to a genitive form of the base. The rule involved is 4.2.70 (*adūrabhāvaś ca* [*tasya* 69]). This introduces an affix after an item which is a value of *tasya*, the genitive singular of *tad* 'that' used as a variable. Hence, 4.2.70 introduces an affix after a genitive form to yield a derivative meaning 'situated not far from . . . '

204. On phonologic terminology in general see, in addition to the lexica noted in section III.1.2.3, W. S. Allen (1953). Thieme (1957c: 665) expressed serious reservations about Allen's interpretations and translations such as 'glottis' for *kaṇṭha* (lit. 'throat'). I do not think Thieme's point is well taken with regard to this particular term. Indian phonetic texts speak of aperture and closure of the *kaṇṭha-bila* (lit. 'throat hole') associated respectively with lack of voicing and voicing. This is so clearly correct and in accord with what is known about glottal aperture and closure, that the use of 'glottis' is in order.

205. The possible interpretations of *āsya-prayatna* are discussed briefly in Cardona (1965a: 227 n. 6); see also sections III.1.4.4b, III.1.5.4a.

206. And also to denote the replacement of these semivowels by these vowels.

207. Al-George (1968) has taken up the term *vyañjana* 'consonant', used by Kātyāyana and others (see Thieme [1958: 44], Cardona [1969: 9]) and concluded (1968: 13) that the term refers to a "sign" which implies a vowel. Al-George has also read logical relations into the use of this term. The term *guṇa*, used by Pāṇini to denote vowels *a, e, o* and also in the meaning 'part' was discussed by Chitari (1965), who considered that the term had three

meanings: 'quality', 'distinguishing attribute' and 'equal portion'. She concluded that Pāṇinīyas fused the first two. Earlier this term and the concepts associated with it were discussed by K. A. Subramania Iyer (1942).
208. Note that, in verse 5 of his Vaiyākaraṇa-siddhânta-kārikā (see section VI.3.1), Bhaṭṭoji Dīkṣita declares (*vyāpāro bhāvanā saivôtpādanā saiva ca kriyā*) that one and the same thing, an action, is what is denoted by the different terms *vyāpāra, bhāvanā, utpādanā, kriyā.* The terms were used in particular values by followers of other schools.
209. Agrawala (1940–41) dealt briefly with pre-Pāṇinian terms equivalent (or nearly equivalent) to Pāṇini's L-suffixes; see section III.1.3.1.
210. The translations given in parentheses are Shefts' (1961: 13).
211. He also treats the term *āmreḍita*, which Pāṇini uses to denote the second element of a sequence of two syntactic items (*pada*, see note 151) arrived at by doubling under given conditions; e.g., *puruṣaḥ*^{1} *puruṣaḥ*^{2}, where *puruṣaḥ*^{2} is termed *āmreḍita.*
212. Rule 1.2.42: *tatpuruṣaḥ samānâdhikaraṇaḥ karmadhārayaḥ* 'A tatpuruṣa whose constituents refer to the same thing (is called) karmadhāraya.'
213. I have used this term to translate Pāṇini's term *it.* Various other translations have been used by different scholars; for example, 'stummer Laut' (Böhtlingk [1887a]), 'exposant' (Renou [1942: 93]), 'exponent' (R. Rocher [1967: 582-83]), 'determinative' (Scharfe [1971a: 20]).
214. 1.1.71: *ādir antyena sahêtā* 'An initial item together with (*saha*) a final (*antya*) marker (*it*) (forms a term denoting itself and all intervening items).'
215. 1.1.70: *ta-paras tat-kālasya* "(A vowel) followed by *t* (is a term denoting sounds) which have the time duration of it (the vowel followed by *t*)." This *t* is not a true marker (*it*), deleted by 1.3.9 (see above). Nevertheless, its use in the Aṣṭādhyāyī makes it appropriate to treat this here.
216. See Cardona (1973e: 207-08). Commentators such as Patañjali escape objection to such usages by saying that the sūtras are Veda-like in their behavior (*chandovat sūtrāṇi bhavanti*); see R. S. Bhattacharya (1966e: 96), Cardona (1969: 39-40). R. S. Bhattacharya (1966e: 98) suggested that such usages are correct merely by virtue of Pāṇini's having employed them and that Patañjali's appeal to the principle that the sūtras of the grammar are Veda-like is not apposite.
217. As provided by the following metarules. 1.1.66: *tasminn iti nirdiṣṭe pūrvasya* '(A locus) stated by a locative form (is that which conditions an operation) on what precedes (it);' 1.1.67: *tasmād ity uttarasya* '(What is stated using) an ablative form (is that which conditions an operation) on what follows (it);' 1.1.49: *ṣaṣṭhī sthāne-yogā* 'A sixth triplet ending (that is, a genitive ending, is to be understood to denote the) relation (of occurring)

in a place of tentative occurrence (unless another relation is known from a context).' I have read a great deal of interpretation into these translations, though I cannot here enter into a detailed discussion. Note that Pāṇini uses forms such as locatives in other values these forms have in normal Sanskrit also; for example, he uses a locative absolute construction. One particular usage is the locative denoting a cause (*nimitta*) of an operation. Commentators speak of a *nimitta-saptamī* in such cases as the condition for an operation on an item does not have actually to occur after that item. Recently, Gonda (1974) has taken up the term *nimitta.* He does not, however, concentrate on problems of interpreting Pāṇinian rules, preferring to seek a basic meaning for the term *nimitta.*

218. A similar view has been expressed by Wezler (1969: 119); see section III.1.3.7.

219. 2.3.29: . . . *dik-śabda . . . yukte* (*pañcamī* 28) '(Fifth triplet endings are introduced after items) when (they are) connected with words which denote directions . . .'

220. But not Pāṇinīyas, who do not make this rule apply with affixation rules (see below).

221. I do not agree fully with any of the authors noted. For example, Palsule (1970: 3; 1973: 312-13) says of 1.1.68 that "for obvious reasons, this statement was unnecessary." More recently, Wezler (1969: 232-41) and Scharfe (1971a: 41-43) have again taken up 1.1.68 together with the Mahābhāṣya discussion concerning it. I disagree with much of what they say and plan to take up the topic on another occasion.

222. In 1.1.44 (*navêti vibhāṣā*), which defines *vibhāsā* 'optionally' as denoting the meaning of *na vā.*

223. *tad asyāṃ praharaṇam iti krīḍāyām* '(The affix *ṇa* [= *a*] is introduced after an item which is a value of the nominative) *tad* (to form a derivative meaning) "is a weapon in . . ." (provided the locus in question is) a game.'

224. See Cardona (1973e: 216 n. 25) and above, note 217. Paraphrases such as those given in section III.1.5.3d are of course proper so long as one is aware of the details.

225. *tataś ced vivakṣā* 'If (a speaker) wishes to express (the given meaning and have it understood) from that (derivative).' On vivakṣā see section III. 2.6.2.

226. Namely a discussion of Cardona's view (1969: 29) that Pāṇini is conservative in his use of abbreviatory terminology.

227. See also Faddegon (1936: 49-50), Buiskool (1939: 24), S. P. Chaturvedi (1946: 109), Vidya Niwas Misra (1966: 31, 33).

228. I have modified Bahulikar's punctuation; this occurs in a rhetorical question.

229. As far as I can tell, Bahulikar has not discussed this rule.
230. Pāṇini did have to introduce some modifications, which required his marking explicitly an item to be considered to recur; see Cardona (1968a: 450).
231. Renou also considered this a remarkable fact ("fait singulier").
232. "Cette énonciation *ex abrupto* dénote l'enseignement oral, qui exigeait des formes simples, clairement évocatrices, tranchant avec le style technique des explications usuelles. Ces verbes scandent pour ainsi dire les sections assez difficiles à retenir pour l'étudiant, qui décrivent l'emploi des suffixes secondaires; ce sont comme de petites têtes de chapitre d'allure 'frappante'."
233. 1.2.31 (*samāhāraḥ svaritaḥ*) defines the term *svarita* as denoting a vowel which contains a combination (*samāhara*) of high and low pitches. 1.2.32 (*tasyâdita udāttam ardha-hrasvam*) goes on to specify that such a svarita vowel has high pitch on that part of it starting from the beginning which lasts for the duration of half a short vowel, that is, half a mora. I have given the usual interpretation of 1.2.32. Bhaṭṭoji Dīkṣita (section IV 3.2) gives a different one. Venkitasubramonia Iyer (1970b) and A. N. Jani (1971, 1972; cf. 1974) have discussed this rule and pointed out respectively that Nārāyaṇabhaṭṭa and the Kāśikā are closer in their interpretations to the view of earlier Pāṇinīyas than is Bhaṭṭojī.
234. 1.1.9: *tulyâsya-prayatnaṃ savarṇam.* 1.1.10 (*nâj-jhalau*) then states that a vowel (*ac*) and a consonant (*hal*) are not (*na*) savarṇa with each other.
235. According to some descriptions, vowels and spirants are distinguished by their types of articulation; see section III.1.4.4b with note 140.
236. Called *bāhya-prayatna* 'external efforts' by Pāṇinīyas; see W. S. Allen (1953: 22-26).
237. There is, nevertheless, a possible problem. Since 1.1.69 takes effect after 1.1.9-10 have applied, the last rule will not prevent a consonant such as *h* from denoting a sound such as *ā*. For now 1.1.10 states only that a vowel denoted by *ac*, that is, one of the vowels listed in the śiva-sūtras, is not homogeneous with a consonant. And the śiva-sūtras list only short *a* etc. This problem is taken up by M. M. Deshpande (forthcoming d), who, however, does not reach definitive conclusions.
238. Chatterji corrected Siddheshwar Varma (1929: 7), who believed that Pāṇinīyas considered *ṛ* and *ḷ* naturally homogeneous.
239. See Cardona (1965a: 228-32). Among the treatises which do state replacements of the type *h* → *j* are the prātiśākhyas, which describe such morphophonemic operations in terms of modifications of sounds; see sections III.1.5.1a (end), III.3.2b.
240. *aṇ-udit savarṇasya câpratyayaḥ* '(A sound denoted by the term) *aṇ* or

a sound marked with *u* (is a term denoting not only itself but) also sounds homogeneous (with it), provided the sound is other than an affix.' The abbreviation *aṇ* denotes vowels and semivowels listed in the śiva-sūtras.
241. To refer to vowels of a given length, Pāṇini uses a vowel followed by *t*, so that *at* denotes short *a* vowels, *ā* denotes long *ā* vowels; see section III.1.5.3c with note 215.
242. I have outlined these above as I see them.
243. W. S. Allen (1962) also refers to Pāṇini in passing during his discussion of sandhi. On a different level, V. L. Joshi (1965) has made a plea that sandhi alterations be observed in a sentence only where the sense requires this.
244. There is another paper by this author, entitled "The śiva-sūtras and the Sanskrit alphabet", which was unavailable to me; see R. N. Dandekar (1946-73: 2: 99 [number 37]).
245. There is also a paper by A. N. Jani (1966), which is of peripheral interest, dealing with how a musical text made use of the śiva-sūtras in modified form.
246. See, for example, Thieme (1935a: 104, 108; 1957b: 265).
247. Major views are summarized in Cardona (1969: 31-32). Breloer (1929: 27; 1935-36: 142, 144) held a view particular to him and which Thieme (1935a: 111) showed to be untenable; see also Cardona (1969: 34 n. 83).
248. There is some room for argument concerning whether Pāṇini ever had to refer to nasalized semivowels using terms such as *y*. This is discussed by M. M. Deshpande (forthcoming b).
249. Sköld (1926a: 19-20) claimed that the sound *l* was not necessary to close a set, but he was refuted by Thieme (1930: 550-51).
250. See Breloer (1935-36: 147-48), C. Kunhan Raja (1957: 68-69), Vidya Niwas Misra (1966: 59), Scharfe (1971a: 28-29).
251. The initial string for sentence (3) of section III.1.5.1a would be *devadatta-s odana-am pac-laṭ*, with the suffix *laṭ* not yet replaced by an ending.
252. It has, nevertheless, to be emphasized that this is actually a fiction. Affixes such as *laṭ, am* are introduced to denote an agent and an object in the derivation of a sentence such as (3) of section III.1.5.1a, and things are agents and objects relative to actions, so that the rules which introduce these affixes obviously treat of syntax in the context of derivations involving relations between actions and participants in them.
253. 3.2.123: *vartamāne laṭ*; see sections III.2.6.3, III.3.1.4 (c) for the Mahā-bhāṣya comments concerning what is meant by *vartamāna* 'current'.
254. Rules 3.4.77 (*lasya*) and 3.4.78 (*tip-tas-jhi-sip-thas-tha-mib-vas-mas-tātāṃ-jha-thās-āthāṃ-dhvam-iḍ-vahi-mahiṅ*) provides for an L-suffix to be

replaced by a group of basic endings, which are then themselves subject to replacements. The L-suffix *laṭ* is also replaced by the participial affixes *śatṛ* (= *at*), *śānac* (= *āna*) under particular conditions; see section III.1.5.7b.
255. Endings such as *ti* are called *sārvadhātuka.* Rule 3.1.68 (*kartari śap* [*sārvadhātuke* 67].) provides that *śap* is introduced after a root if this is itself followed by a sārvadhātuka affix which denotes an agent (*kartṛ*).
256. 3.2.111: *anadyatane lan*; see section III.3.1.4(b) for part of the Mahābhāṣya discussion on this.
257. 3.4.100: *itaś ca* (*nityam ṅitaḥ* 99, *lopaḥ* 97) 'Zero also obligatorily replaces the *i* of an ending which derives from an L-suffix marked with *ṅ*.'
258. 3.2.110: *luṅ* (*bhūte* 84) '(The L-suffix) *luṅ* (is introduced after a root if the action denoted by it is referred to) the past.'
259. 3.1.43: *cli luṅi* '(The affix) *cli* (is introduced after a root which is followed by an ending which has replaced) *luṅ*;' 3.1.44: *cleḥ sic* '*sic* (occurs) in place of *cli.*'
260. Some of van Nooten's interpretations of rules are not acceptable. Scharfe (1971a: 27 n. 29) pointed out one such case, where van Nooten (1967: 894) spoke of "an imprecision on the part of the great grammarian" Pāṇini.
261. Chaturvedi (1935a: 6) also objected to Pāṇini's having stated replacements such as *sthā* → *tiṣṭha* instead of treating certain present stems such as *tiṣṭha* (*tiṣṭhati* 'is in place') as reduplicated root forms. However, he did not discuss the reasons behind Pāṇini's procedure.
262. Let me note in passing that here again (cf. note 260) some of van Nooten's interpretations are hardly acceptable. For example, he says (1970a: 14), "Depending on the number of items referred to, the user attaches the labels singular, dual, or plural to the stem by the following rules: 1. 4. 21 *bahuṣu bahuvacanam* 'In referring to many, the name is plural'; 1. 4. 22 *dvyekayor dvivacanāikavacane* 'In referring to two and one, the name is dual and singular, respectively.' " But the terms *ekavacana, dvivacana,* and *bahuvacana* here refer to sets of affixes, which are allowed to occur respectively when one, two, or many things are denoted.
263. Composition and taddhita affixation are two kinds of what Pāṇinīyas call *vṛtti.* K. V. Abhyankar (1971) has recently discussed the different kinds of vṛtti to be recognized.
264. This is provided by rule 2.1.1: *samarthaḥ pada-vidhiḥ* 'An operation involving padas (is to apply only to such padas as are) semantically and syntactically related.' For discussion of the exact import of this rule and what is meant by *samartha* see the references given below.
265. "Pāṇini opferte also hier – vielleicht mit schwerem Herz – die Wissenschaftlichkeit dem praktischen Bedürfnis."
266. The rule which serves to derive *śāka-prati* (2.1.9: *sup pratinā mātrârthe*)

comes under the heading of 2.1.5 (*avyayībhāvaḥ*), whereby compounds derived by subsequent rules are classed as avyayībhāva.

267. By 1.1.41 (*avyayībhāvaś ca* [*avyayam* 37]) an avyayībhāva compound is classed as an avyaya. 2.4.82 (*avyayād āp-supaḥ*) provides that feminine affixes denoted by *āp* and nominal endings (*sup*) are replaced by zero after avyayas.

268. Narayana Murti (1971) dealt with a compound type directly provided for by Kātyāyana but not by Pāṇini, the type *vāg-arthāv-iva* 'like word and meaning'. Both he and Hariścandramaṇi Tripāṭhī considered commentatorial arguments.

269. This is in accord with one of the usual interpretations of commentators, who say that *vyaṃsaka* means 'rogue' (*dhūrta*). But commentators themselves differ on the precise analysis of this compound.

270. That is, alternating (*anitya*, cf. note 158) derivatives formed with affixes to which are assigned meanings also denoted by items in equivalent strings, as distinct from the type *tatra* (see section III.1.5.1a), where the affix is redundant (*svârthe*, see note 155).

271. Such derivatives are formed by rules under the heading of 4.1.82: *samarthānāṃ prathamād vā.*

272. Taddhita derivations are also the topic of Wezler (forthcoming b).

273. The kāraka categories apādāna and sampradāna do not, as defined by Pāṇini's rules, correspond to any single general semantic notion. For example, the apādāna category includes points of departure (1.4.24, see below), an object of fear, and several others.

274. For general discussions of kārakas see P. C. Chakravarti (1930: 213-80), R. S. Bhattacharya (1966h), Charudeva Shastri (1969-73: I: 1-78).

275. Whitney (1893a: 171): "Pāṇini does not take up the cases as forms of nouns, setting forth the various uses of each, after our manner; he adopts the vastly more difficult and dangerous method . . ."

276. These are terms used by one or the other of these scholars.

277. See, in a similar vein, R. Rocher (1965-66: 83-84; 1966: 115).

278. Al-George's view is based, in part, on an overextension of an opinion expressed by Renou; see section III.1.5.7a.

279. Hence, and because Pāṇini's kāraka categories are not defined in purely semantic terms, Cardona referred to them as syntactic categories. Since, as noted already in Cardona (1967b), the kāraka categories do indeed have to do with semantics – they link semantics and grammatical expressions – Cardona later (1969: 3) referred to them as syntactico-semantic categories.

280. On the question of levels see section III.1.5.5c.2.

281. For summaries of studies on Pāṇini's kāraka categories see Rogers (1969: 1-29), Cardona (1974b: 279-80). The most recent paper dealing

with Pāṇini's kāraka system is by J. D. Singh (1974c).

282. Rocher (1964a) dealt only with rules 1.4.49-50, 54.

283. He has also misrepresented Pāṇini. In connection with the apādāna category (see note 273), Sinha says (1973: 31) that the different concepts can be correlated with a single kāraka: "In fact this is precisely what is done in Pāṇini's grammar. These concepts are notionally different from each other no doubt but semantically they all have just one 'meaning'." He goes on (1973: 32): "The 'semantic value' or 'meaning' of the kāraka in question thus remains constant and unequivocal throughout its uses. This indeed is the import of Patañjali's discussion on *apādāna* kāraka." This is confused. I assume that by "one meaning" Sinha means point of departure, the semantic correlate of apādāna as defined by 1.4.24. Patañjali and later Pāṇinīyas do indeed assume that this is the meaning common to all apādānas. But Patañjali also directly states in the Mahā-bhāṣya that rules 1.4.25 and following can be dispensed with under this view. Later Pāṇinīyas consider these rules mere expatiations on 1.4.24. Sinha has not shown that Pāṇini too considered that a source of fear, for example, was a mental point of departure and that *bhī* 'be afraid' meant 'depart from mentally in fear'

284. For example, rule 2.3.12 (*gaty-artha-karmaṇi dvitīyā-caturthyau ceṣṭāyām anadhvani*) states that either second or fourth triplet endings (accusative or dative endings) are introduced after a nominal when there is to be denoted an object (*karman*) of an action denoted by a verb meaning 'move', provided that actual movement is involved and the object in question is not a path (*adhvan*); e.g., *grāmaṃ gacchati, grāmāya gacchati* '... is going to the village.'

285. On the order of kāraka classification rules see Rogers (1969: 200-02), Cardona (1970a: 43-44; 1974b: 233-37).

286. This and other possibilities were set forth by Bhartṛhari (section VI.2), Vākya-padīya 3.7.130; see Subramania Iyer (1963a: 333-34).

287. Which I consider in detail in a forthcoming paper.

288. 1.4.55: *tat-prayojako hetuś ca* '(That kāraka) which instigates it (the kāraka classed as agent by the preceding rule) is also (called) *hetu* (in addition to *kartṛ*).'

289. In the second value, the term *hetu* is an akṛtrimā saṃjñā (see section III.1.5.3a).

290. See also R. S. Bhattacharya (1953c: 132). Note that Bhattacharya dealt with more general distinctions made among kinds of agents, for example, between skilled agents and others.

291. This distinction is important for Pāṇini's derivation of what in western grammar would be treated as embedded sentences; see section III.1.5.7b. S. D. Joshi (1974: 262 with note 1) has accepted Kiparsky and Staal's scheme, but he has not given evidence to justify it.

292. See S. D. Joshi (1966b: 20-21). On the four-fold distinction among nouns (*nāman*), verbs (*ākhyāta*), preverbs (*upasarga*), and particles (*upasarga*) found in other treatises see recently Ruegg (1959: 24), S. D. Joshi (1966b: 19-20). There is another categorization of items as generic words, words denoting qualities, action words, and words used ad libitum, occasionally; on this see recently Ruegg (1959: 38), Cardona (1973a: 86, 92 n. 5).
293. Note that Pāṇini does recognize explicitly that items denote qualifiers and qualificands; he uses the terms *viśeṣaṇa* and *viśeṣya*, respectively, for these.
294. The Pāṇinian concept of coreference (*sāmānâdhikaraṇya*) is discussed in Cardona (1973d: 47-49; 1974b: 289-91 [note 56]). The semantic counterpart of this is a relation called *abheda* (lit. 'non-difference') by Pāṇinīyas, which obtains between the denotata of coreferential items; this has been discussed recently by Viśvanātha (1967), Cardona (1973d: 49; 1974b: 247-49, 253-54).
295. Vidya Niwas Misra (1966: 112) states, "Pāṇini did not explicitly define the term *Vākya* (sentence) but he has through the devices of . . ." However, none of the devices noted subsequently can be said truly to define a particular stretch of utterance as a sentence.
296. See Kunjunni Raja (1957a; 1958; 1961; 1964; 1969: 149-224), Gaurinath Shastri (1959: 172-87), B. Bhattacharya (1962: 128-87).
297. See Gaurinath Shastri (1959: 92), Ruegg (1959: 36), Matilal (1966: 377-78), Cardona (1973a: 93 n. 8), Devasthali (1974: 207-11).
298. For brief expositions of the Mahā-bhāṣya passage where this is brought up, as well as the use of a definition of a vākya in rule 8.1.28 see K. Madhava Krishna Sarma (1940f: 85-87), Cardona (1967b: 213-13), Devasthali (1974: 211-14).
299. M. D. Pandit (1973) has discussed the place of formal and nonformal features in Pāṇini's grammar. Among the latter are semantics. Pandit considers it a paradox that Pāṇini take semantics into consideration despite the fact that, in his opinion, commentators note that meaning is not taken into account (1973: 180-81). But this apparent paradox rests on a misunderstanding of the intent of rule 1.1.68 (see section III.1.5.3f).
300. I use here "correct sentence" in a particular way: a sentence which is a means of conveying a correct knowledge.
301. For recent discussions of these conditions see Kunjunni Raja (1957a; 1969: 157-87), Matilal (1966: 382-84).
302. More recently, M. D. Balasubrahmanyam (1971: 25-26) has interpreted rule 3.1.123 in a way which suggests Pāṇini's use of the Śata-patha-brāhmaṇa, but this is only a suggestion. Van Nooten (1968) discussed a passage from the Mahā-bhāṣya trying to show Kātyāyana's way of interpreting Pāṇini so

as to have him account for facts of the White Yajur-veda.

303. Recently, Ramasharma (1971) argued that Pāṇini's rule 5.1.62, which serves to derive the term *cātvāriṃśa* (*brāhmaṇa*), refers thereby directly to the Aitareya-brāhmaṇa. This is not generally accepted, as can be seen from the literature cited by Ramasharma. R. S. Bhattacharya (1966n) argued, on the basis of rule 7.4.38 and its commentaries, that Pāṇini knew also a Kaṭha branch of the Ṛg-veda.

304. Pāṇini uses terms such as *chandas, mantra, nigama*; see below.

305. I mention here also V. P. Limaye (1969) as something of a curiosity. The author suggests additions to Pāṇini's rules in order to let the grammar account not only for Vedic facts but also for Iranian forms.

306. See also Gopāla Śāstrī (1966), S. K. Gupta (1968). Shiva Narayana Shastri (1968a) discussed forms of the verb *kṛ* 'make, do' and suggested that Pāṇini allows a first-class present of this verb for Vedic. Note that Siddheshwar Varma (1950) is not really a study of Vedic rules: Varma considered Kātyāyana's and Patañjali's comments on accentuation and contrasted them with the views of later Pāṇinīyas, whom he considered in error.

307. The rule is 3.4.88: *vā chandasi* 'Optionally in sacred literature.' This is usually interpreted as follows. 3.4.87 (*ser hy ap-ic ca*) provides that the ending *si* (2nd sg.) is replaced by *hi* if it derives from the L-suffix *loṭ*, and the replacement is not marked with *p*, unlike the substituend *sip*; e.g., *punīhi* 'purify' (2nd sg. imperative). 3.4.88 then states that in sacred literature the replacement *hi* is optionally treated as not marked with *p*. In Palsule's interpretation, 3.4.88 provides that *hi* only optionally replaces *si*.

308. Another area of study, the validity of which is not so apparent (see Renou [1969: 493 n. 30]), is the compilation of un-Pāṇinian forms in texts of varying antiquity and styles: Kulkarni (1943a, b, c; 1943-44; 1950-51), V. D. Gokhale (1956-57), N. Sen (1950; 1951; 1952-53; 1955; 1956), H. C. Sil (1960-61; 1966), Satyavrat (1963, 1964), Śivaprasāda Bhāradvāja (1968).

309. M. D. Pandit (1971) also upholds the usefulness of Pāṇini's rules in the interpretation of Vedic texts.

310. See also Siddheshwar Varma (1950) [note 306 above].

311. Renou (1955: 130): "Ces attestations suffisent à montrer que la notion du genre était présente dans l'Aṣṭādhyāyī dans toutes les circonstances où elle pouvait avoir quelque valeur normative, où elle n'était simple effet de l'arbitraire lexical." It would have been well to emphasize that Pāṇini mentions "feminine" when this is required by operations. On the various possible meanings which the term *strī* can have in rules see Cardona (1968a: 452).

312. For Scharfe's view regarding this term and *vyakti* see section III.1.5.3b.1.

313. The import and interpretation of individual rules are also dealt with in

translations and studies of the Mahā-bhāṣya (sections III.2.1-2).
314. Cardona (1969: 26-28) also contrasts Pāṇini's procedure of introducing L-suffixes subsequently replaced by endings with the procedure of other grammars, in which endings are directly introduced.
315. A small study of the Mugdha-bodha was made by K. C. Chatterji (1935b), and more recently Ojihara (1971) has begun a comparative study of the Pāli grammar Sadda-nīti.
316. Earlier, K. C. Chatterji (1934c) had sketched some of the arguments advanced by adherents of Mīmāṃsā and Nyāya against the views held by grammarians. More recently, Frauwallner (1959) argued that the Mīmāṃsā view that sounds are eternal (*nitya*) resulted from the influence of grammarians, the sphoṭa concept in particular (see section VI.2.4). Influence of grammarians has also been assumed as the impetus for Buddhist thinking on language; see recently P. S. Jaini (1959), who discusses (1959: 95, 105-07) the Vaibhāṣikas rejection of the notion of sphoṭa. Another general study is that of de Smet (1960), who considers views of grammarians, Mīmāṃsā and Śaṅkara.
317. Devasthali (1942: 91-93) argued that Śabara did not know the Mahā-bhāṣya. P. V. Kane (1945) then rebutted him, presenting evidence to show that Śabara did indeed know the Mahā-bhāṣya; see also K. Madhava Krishna Sarma (1944-45: 81-82).
318. This remark is less than appropriate. For Pāṇini uses the term *karman* in two values: 'object of an action' and 'action'; the latter is a nontechnical value (see above, section III.1.5.3a).
319. See section III.1.5.7b for Staal's view regarding the contrast between Mīmāṃsā and Pāṇinian grammar.
320. Gonda (1973) is not a systematic study of this topic, despite the title of the paper. The author considers loosely connected topics and some rules in order to emphasize that Pāṇini was aware of linguistic questions and was subtle and precise in his description. More pertinent is the study by Toporov (1961), in which the author takes up questions such as analysis by substitution, the positing of morphologic units, and zero. In what follows the emphasis is on syntactic aspects, since this is the area of Pāṇini's system which has in recent times most attracted the attention of scholars interested in comparing Pāṇini's and modern systems. Quite recently, however, attention has been paid to Pāṇini's phonologic (morphophonemic) rules as compared with the description of the same Sanskrit phenomena in terms of generative phonology. Sag (1974) has argued, convincingly I think, that Pāṇini's description of the phenomena usually ascribed to the effects of Grassmann's Law is correct: Pāṇini posits as basic forms not diaspirate roots such as *dhugh* 'milk' but roots with single aspirates, *duh* etc.;

in particular environments diaspirate forms (*dhugh* etc.) are introduced. In Sag's opinion, Pāṇini's description accurately reflects the historical fact that Grassmann's Law was, at an early stage of Indic, severly restricted in its application. This paper has given rise to a controversy: E. Phelps attempts, in a paper to be published in *Linguistic Inquiry*, to prove that Pāṇini's description is improper, and Sag plans to rebut Phelps in a paper to appear in the same journal. It is noteworthy that the question of basic forms engaged scholars already almost a century ago: Böhtlingk (1890) argued in favor of the Pāṇinian system, wherein there are basic forms such as *dus* instead of *duṣ*.

321. Zgusta (1969) viewed Vidya Niwas Misra's work (1966) unfavorably but approved of Staal's, though he disagreed with the latter in details. Some of Zgusta's own suggestions are, I think, unacceptable. For example, he considers (1969: 413-15) affixation rules such as 3.1.68 (see my note 255) and says (1969: 414): "Indeed, the only way how [sic] we can understand the sūtra [3.1.68] is to take *kartar* as relating to the morphologic category which expresses the relation in question most frequently and translate 'A non-passive verb has a thematic vowel *-a-*'." But see note 255 above. Let me note in passing that P. S. Subrahmanya (1972) operates with what he calls deep structure. However, I cannot tell from the summary precisely what he intends.

322. On the above, cf. Cardona (1967b: 214): "That he then introduced the semantic correlations directly in the definitions of the grammatical *kāraka* terminology is of interest. For in doing so Pāṇini accounted quite neatly for relations among sentences – though, note, not between positive and negative or declarative and interrogative – and the interrelations of paradigmatic case forms."

323. And to have been influenced by Pāṇinian ideas. On this topic the most recent paper is by Rogers (forthcoming).

324. See also Franke (1892) and K. C. Chatterji (1934d) for studies of a particular construction.

325. "Das Sanskrit, welches Pāṇini lehrt, ist syntaktisch so gut wie identisch mit der Sprache der Brāhmaṇa's und Sūtras . . . " He went on to note some differences.

326. Franke's reasoning was less than lucid, as Whitney (1893a: 175) noted.

327. Renou's statement (1955: 114) that the rules in which Pāṇini states *bhāṣāyām* 'in the bhāṣā' are numerically insignificant and most often without real linguistic significance is, in my opinion, too sweeping. On *bhāṣa* see also R. S. Bhattacharya (1953d).

328. Cited approvingly by Whitney (1884: 282 [Silverstein 1972: 290]), with disapproval by Liebich (1891: 44).

329. Whitney (1893a: 173): "No one, certainly, would think of denying that Pāṇini observed and described with remarkable acuteness and to the best of his ability. Nor, again, I should think, that he described an actual language – 'an' rather than 'the', for just what language he was dealing with is one of the disputed points."(1893a: 176): "nor do I see that any one has the right to say that Pāṇini's speech was not a living one."
330. This view was shared by, among others, Grierson (1893) and Aufrecht (1875).
331. Ideas similar to these appeared already in Benfey (1852: 71-77); see also Bendall (1889: 253 with note 2).
332. Note that, in his discussion of rule 3.1.1 (see note 83), Kātyāyana says that this rule is stated and roots are listed in the dhātu-pāṭha so as to prevent classing as a root (*dhātu*) an element such as appears in the form *āṇapayati* 'command' (Skt. *ājñāpayati*), that is, middle Indic elements; see Kielhorn (1885c), Palsule (1961: 213).
333. D. N. Shastri (1967: 299-300) also claims that some of Pāṇini's statements are poor. After noting that Pāṇini treats the root *gam* 'go' as transitive, he says, "It can easily be shown that to hold this root to be transitive is erroneous." But D. N. Shastri has apparently forgotten rules like 2.3.12 (see my note 284).
334. On this see K. A. Subramania Iyer (1964a), Periveṅkateśvara Śāstrī (1971: 38-39), Rāmānārāyaṇa Tripāṭhī (1971: 70), and below, section VI.2.4.
335. This is the correct rendition of *darbha-pavitra-pāṇi*, as was noted by T. Venkatacharya (1959: 91).
336. Wezler (forthcoming a) has entered the controversy on the side of Scharfe.
337. For example, rule 1.1.1 (*vṛddhir ād aic*) is analyzed into the components *vṛddhiḥ, āt, aic*; see Yudhiṣṭhira Mīmāṃsaka (1973: I: 434).
338. For example, by bringing in metarules and by anuvṛtti (see section III.1.5.2c).
339. For a brief survey of authorities mentioned in the Mahā-bhāṣya see Kielhorn (1887c). Pāṇinian commentators themselves refer to commentaries some of which are considered to predate Patañjali; see S. C. Chakravarti (1919-25: I: introduction, pp. 8-9), Yudhiṣṭhira Mīmāṃsaka (1973: I: 439-58). On the characteristics of a vṛtti, see also R. S. Bhattacharya (1955b: 124-26).
340. He also claimed (1947: 339) that when a rule is not directly discussed in the Mahā-bhāṣya the Kāśikā's examples can be considered traditional; similarly, S. M. Katre (1968-69: I: preface, p. 10). Others have appealed for more caution; see Thieme (1956: 16 n. 38), Cardona (1973d: 43 n. 2).
341. Which is divided into sections called *āhnika* 'day's study'; on the

number of āhnikas (85) and the number of rules to which are devoted independent discussions (1701) see Vedavrata (1962-63: I: introduction, pp. 3-4).

342. The preserved text begins with a lacuna and ends with the seventh āhnika (Kielhorn [1880-85: I: 132.7]).

343. Note that later commentators cite statements, apparently from Bhartṛhari's commentary on the Mahā-bhāṣya, on sections after the first three quarter-chapters; see Yudhiṣṭhira Mīmāṃsaka (1973: I: 376-79).

344. Raghavan (1950) showed, on the basis of a citation from the Pradīpa in the Alaṅkāra-sarvasva of the poetician Ruyyaka, that Kaiyaṭa's lower limit is 1150 A. D. Yudhiṣṭhira Mīmāṃsaka (1973: I: 393-96) discusses evidence for Kaiyaṭa's dating and places him at saṃvat 1090 (A. D. 1033/4). Renou (1940a: 24-25) also considered the eleventh century a proper date for Kaiyaṭa, and this is the generally held opinion. It is possible that Kaiyaṭa is to be dated somewhat earlier, see section IV.3.1.1.

345. Late 17th to 18th century; on Nāgeśa's dates see P. V. Kane (1930: 453-56), P. K. Gode (1955). Nāgeśa is also called Nāgojībhaṭṭa. The former is the Sanskrit version, the latter the Marathi version.

346. See also the bibliography under Mahā-bhāṣya for an anonymous edition recently published. A list of editions of the text appears in Vedavrata (1962-63: I: introduction, pp. 2-3). Of historical interest are an early partial edition with English translation by Ballantyne (1856), part of which was made known earlier by Müller (1853), and the Benares edition of 1872, which was the basis for Weber's study of 1873 (see Weber [1873d: 293]).

347. The commentaries are respectively by Rāmacandra Sarasvatī (16th century), Īśvarānanda (16th c., but also attributed to Rāmacandra Sarasvatī), Nārāyaṇa (post-Nāgeśa), Śivarāmendra Sarasvatī (17th c.); see Narasimhacharya (1973: introduction, pp. xiv-xix), P. S. Filliozat (1973: vi-vii). D. C. Bhattacharya (1943) gave some fragments from other commentaries, among them one on the Mahā-bhāṣya by Puruṣottamadeva (see section IV.2.2.1). A rich survey of commentaries and supercommentaries on the Mahā-bhāṣya is given by Yudhiṣṭhira Mīmāṃsaka (1973: I: 359-433).

348. Note that Pathak - Chitrao (1928) list inflected verb forms but nominals in their stem forms.

349. Herein he established criteria (pp. 7-29) and then tested them (pp. 29-46)

350. The arguments concerned involve stylistics and comparisons of passages, a discussion of which would require extensive citation from the texts, so that I pass these over without comment.

351. They have been conveniently collected in Vedavrata (1962-63: II-V).

352. Similarly, S. C. Chakravarti (1919-25: I: introduction, pp. 7-8), Haraprasāda Shāstrī (1931: xviii).

353. There is a work called Śloka-vārttika-vyākhyā(na) by Rājarudra, in which śloka-vārttikas have been collected and commented on. Through the kindness of Professor V. Raghavan I obtained a copy of this from the Government Oriental Manuscripts Library, Madras. I plan to edit this together with a study of the śloka-vārttikas in a subsequent volume.
354. Vākya-padīya 2.478-484 in the edition by Abhyankar and Limaye (1965: 56-57). These and the subsequent final verses of the second book of the Vākya-padīya were published, together with Puṇyarāja's commentary, by Kielhorn (1874b); on the verses in question see also Thieme (1956: 18-20), Raghunātha Śarmā (1968: 74), Raghavan Pillai (1971: 145-46, 188-89).
355. Vyāḍi is mentioned in the Mahā-bhāṣya, which also refers to the Saṃgraha, a work considered to have consisted of 100,000 ślokas (or equivalent to this in length); see R. S. Bhattacharya (1954b), Thieme (1956: 18 n. 44), Yudhiṣṭhira Mīmāṃsaka (1973: I: 275-91).
356. Rāja-taraṅgiṇī verses 1.176, 4.488; see Kielhorn (1875), Böhtlingk (1900), Liebich (1930: 247, 270-72), Thieme (1956: 20 n. 48).
357. This is usually taken to refer to the Mahā-bhāṣya, but Thieme (1956: 19 n. 45) argued for considering the ṛṣi to be Pāṇini.
358. Earlier, Goldstücker (1861: 237-38 with note 279) had dealt with these verses. Instead of *viplāvite*, he read *vilāvite*, which he translated 'cut into pieces'. He also translated *grantha-mātre* as 'preserved in one copy only'.
359. And to Burnell, who believed (1875: 91-92) that the Mahā-bhāṣya "... is not in its original form."
360. Böhtlingk (1875a, b) maintained a similar view, but his conclusion was based on the erroneous supposition that Kātyāyana's aim was to attack Pāṇini and Patañjali's purpose to defend Pāṇini against Kātyāyana; see section III.2.5.1. On the use of the term *ācārya* to refer to respected predecessors, not one's teacher, see P. V. Kane (1942).
361. See K. B. Pathak (1931-32), S. P. Chaturvedi (1941), R. S. Bhattacharya (1954a), Laddu (1966). Palsule (1949) considered a passage interpolated because he considered the rule discussed therein also interpolated; see section III.1.3.3f.
362. This scholar argues as Kielhorn did, but does not, as far as I can see, mention him.
363. But the last scholar also holds that Kātyāyana belonged to a school different from Pāṇini's; see note 364.
364. This is none other than the Aindra school (see section III.1.3.2c). Other scholars also maintain that Kātyāyana followed the Aindra school as opposed to Pāṇini, who was an adherent of the Māheśvara school, for example, Vedpati Mishra (1970: 60, 68).

365. A similar view was earlier expressed by K. Madhava Krishna Sarma, who (1940e: 204) contrasted Kātyāyana the theorist with Patañjali, who "... does not countenance unnecessary theorization."
366. See also R. G. Bhandarkar (1885 [= 1927-33 1: 159-60], 1895 [= 1927-33 3: 14-15]. On the use of participial forms for finite perfect forms see also Thieme (1963).
367. See Böhtlingk (1887a: xviii n. 2), Kielhorn (1885: 186), Thieme (1956: 22), R. Rocher (1968a: 277). On language differences see also Lévi (1906-08).
368. K. Madhava Krishna Sarma (1940f: 83) also argued that there were two new sentence types which developed in the time between Kātyāyana and Patañjali.
369. This is also the view of Laddu (1966), according to S. D. Joshi (1969: viii n. 22). Earlier, S. P. Chaturvedi (1940c: 60) had contrasted Kātyāyana, who, like Pāṇini, "never lost touch with the 'changing' aspect of the language" with Patañjali, who had a scholastic attitude.
370. See R. G. Bhandarkar (1873c [= 1927-33 1: 126-29], 1876), Kielhorn (1876a: 52-53), Shefts (1961: 17). Siddheshwar Varma (1963) has given a general survey of the way rules are discussed and other general aspects concerning the Mahā-bhāṣya.
371. When a name is used in an example, the name first chosen is Devadatta, then Yajñadatta is used as an additional name. S. Sen (1952-53, 1953) has gathered together the examples in which the first name is used.
372. Some of these techniques have been mentioned in the course of previous discussions: see section III.1.5.2b (*para* interpreted to mean 'desired'), 1.5.3a (interpretation of terms as anvartha-saṃjñā), 1.5.3g (maṇḍūka-gati), 2.6.1 (yoga-vibhāga), note 186 (sūtras considered to be Veda-like).
373. Vārttika 5 on 3.2.1. In connection with this Kaiyaṭa notes the following (Vedavrata [1962-63: III: 221]). The grammar is an explanation (*anuvyākhyāna*) of correct usage, of items which are perennial (*nityānāṃ śabdānām*), and serves to show that such items are correct. In normal usage, items such as *āditya-darśa* are not used to signify the meanings conveyed by sentences such as *ādityaṃ paśyati.* Hence, there is no need for the grammar itself to account for such an item. Nor will the grammar be used to infer that such an item is correct.
374. For another case where Pāṇini does not consider pertinent in the context of his rules a distinction which is both semantically and syntactically relevant see section III.1.5.7b.
375. I assume Pāṇini was indeed aware of this distinction, as he was aware of other comparable distinctions such as the one between animate and other agents; see section III.1.5.7b.

376. On vivakṣā in relation to syntax (kāraka categorization) see Charudeva Shastri (1963b), Cardona (1974b: 237-38, forthcoming e).
377. This applies also to other interpretational devices. For example, later commentators such as the authors of the Kāśikā (section IV.2.1) interpret *ca* 'and, also' in some rules as being used to include what is not actually stated in the rules (*anukta-samuccayârtha*). Patañjali does not do this; see Kielhorn (1887e: 251), Böhtlingk (1887c), Bühler (1887: 18-20).
378. See Venkatarama Sarma (1966-67). A general survey of such philosophical discussions was supplied by P. C. Chakravarti (1926: 478-94), who (1926: 428) characterized Patañjali as "a philosopher of no mean order." Another, more recent, general survey of these topics was made by B. Bhattacharya (1956), who treated: the relation between word and meaning (52-55), perception (55-57), grammatical gender (57-59), substance and attribute (59-63), the duality of ātman (external and internal self, 63-64), perception and inference (64-65).
379. Patañjali also uses the term *sphoṭa* twice in the course of discussions concerning sounds (see P. C. Chakravarti [1930: 98-99], K. Madhava Krishna Sarma [1943b: 28-31], Brough [1951: 34-37], Ruegg [1959: 50], S. D. Joshi [1967: 13-20]). On Bhartṛhari's concept of sphoṭa see section VI.2.4. One of the Mahā-bhāṣya discussions concerns rule 8.2.18 (*kṛpo ro laḥ*), which provides that the *r* which appears in forms of the root *kṛp* 'arrange' is replaced by *l*. It is asked how one can let the rule provide for replacing *ṛ* by *ḷ* to provide forms such as the participle *kḷpta*. One suggestion made is that the rule refers to sphoṭas only. Brough (1951: 37) and Ruegg (1959: 50) claimed this shows that for Patañjali *ṛ* and *ḷ* belonged to the same phoneme. This is not in accord with commentators, who I think are correct here. According to them, what is meant is that the rule now states a type for both the substituend and the replacement: the *r* and *l* referred to in the rule include the *r* and *l* which occur in *ṛ*, *ḷ*; see Cardona (1968c: 449).
380. The view that items are fixed has a consequence for grammatical procedures; see section III.1.5.1a with note 163.
381. Connected with this question is the other one whether the objects considered signified by items are themselves permanent (*nitya*) or not. Note that I have used here the term "type" to render Sanskrit *ākṛti* in a manner neutral with respect to the arguments concerning what this word meant to Patañjali (see below).
382. As commentators have noted, this view has affinities with the theories of Sāṃkhya-yoga. Jacobi (1911: 27) considered the views put forth in the Mahā-bhāṣya crude with respect to the Sāṃkhya-yoga theories. Later, a formal definition of grammatical gender was proposed: that is masculine which is referred to by *ayam* 'this' (nom. sg. masc.), that is feminine which

is referred to by *iyam* (nom. sg. fem.), and that is neuter which is referred to by *idam* (nom. sg. nt.); see Sadāśiva Śāstrī Joshi (1946: 110-11).
383. Pāṇinīyas also had a formal definition of a thing: anything in the range of a pronoun (, which is used as a variable) is a thing; see K. A. Subramania Iyer (1963a: 187 [Vākya-padīya 3.4.3]).
384. On the basis of this passage it was also claimed that what one refers to as time is merely actions which characterize other actions.
385. I mention in passing P. C. Chakravarti's (1926: 738-42) treatment of what he termed scientific theories in the Mahā-bhāṣya. This is not a very satisfactory discussion. For example, Chakravarti treats as scientific some things which are more folk beliefs, as illustrated by examples such as *gomayād vṛściko jāyate* 'A scorpion is born of cow dung.' This was pointed out by K. C. Chaṭṭopādhyāya (1927).
386. According to Nāgeśa (Vedavrata [1962-63: I: 15]), these Bhrāja verses were composed by Kātyāyana.
387. For additional studies see section III.3.
388. For surveys of views see Liebich (1891: 1-8), Winternitz (1920: 383), de la Vallée Poussin (1930: 35-42, 199-202), V. S. Agrawala (1963a: 458-78).
389. See also Goldstücker (1861: 227), Kielhorn (1885b: 186-87), Lüders (1919: 744 [1940: 473]). Burrow's assertion (1955: 48) that Pāṇini's date "is most commonly fixed in the fourth century B. C." met with a strong negative reaction from Thieme (1955b: 429).
390. Bad or spoiled barley (*duṣṭo yavaḥ*) according to Kātyāyana (4.1.49 vārttika 2).
391. Similarly, Lévi (1890: 236 n. 1). Note that it has not always been assumed that *yavana* was used in Sanskrit only to refer to Greeks; see, for example, Rajendralal Mitra (1874).
392. N. N. Das Gupta (1936) argued that Pāṇini got his knowledge of Yavanas from Yavana settlements near Gandhara before Alexander. Das Gupta (1936: 357) considered that these were Yavanas of Sogdiana and set Pāṇini's dates at between 479 and 327 B. C.
393. C. V. Vaidya (1930: 151-52) also pointed out that rule 2.1.70 does not show that Pāṇini postdated the Buddha. Vaidya (1930: 153-4) noted in addition that rule 8.2.50 (*nirvāṇo'vāte*), which gives the item *nirvāṇa* 'extinguished', cannot be used as evidence to show that Pāṇini was pre-Buddha either. M. S. Bhat (1959b) argued differently to place Pāṇini after the Buddha. He equated the Pauṣkarasādi mentioned by Kātyāyana in his third vārttika on 8.4.48 with Pokkharasāti of Buddhist literature. According to Bhat, Pauṣkarasādi was a pre-Pāṇinian teacher contemporary with the Buddha.
394. Haraprasāda Shāstrī (1931: xiv-xvi) also rejected the Kathā-sarit-sāgara

story as evidence. However, he accepted as evidence a statement in the tenth century work on poetics, Kāvya-mīmāṃsā, according to which Pāṇini was one of a series of scholars examined at Pāṭaliputra. He placed Pāṇini's time at somewhere in the fifth century.

395. In the latter passage Yudhiṣṭhira Mīmāṃsaka has conveniently gathered together the available passages cited from the poem Jāmbavatī-vijaya, attributed to Pāṇini.

396. Goldstücker did not, however, fully understand the passage. For further discussions concerning this passage see R. G. Bhandarkar (1887a, b, 1919 [= 1927-33 1: 317]), Kielhorn (1887a), Ludwig (1893). The most recent study of this passage is Buddha Prakash (1969).

397. He read *mādhyamikān* in example (2) and accepted (1861: 230-31) that *mādhyamika* here referred to the followers of the Buddhist school. This reading caused a great deal of mischief before Kielhorn finally established the reading *madhyamikām* (see note 401). *Mādhyamikān* still appears in example (2) as cited in the Kāśikā in the editions of Śobhita Miśra (1952), Nārāyana Miśra (1969-72), Aryendra Sharma et al. (1969-70).

398. In his Hāthigumpha cave inscription, Khāravela speaks of a Yavana king who fled to Mathurā. Konow (1923: 35) was among those who read his name as Dimita. He concluded that Patañjali's Yavana was Demetrios, so that Patañjali's date could be the early second century B. C. But this is highly conjectural and has not been accepted generally; see Sircar (1965: 216 n. 5) and Sadhu Ram (1972: 38, 62), where full bibliographic references are given.

399. Mazumdar (1925: 218) considered that Menander's date was not so well established.

400. Bhandarkar actually wrote *puṣpamitram.* I do not consider here the details concerning the name of the king.

401. However, Bhandarkar still wrote *mādhyamikām.* Kielhorn (1878) established the reading *madhyamikām.* G. S. Gai (1960) gave further archaeological evidence for Kielhorn's view that this was the old name for the town Nagarī in Rajasthan.

402. Weber was obviously pertinacious. He was also not in full control of the materials he used. As an example of this trait, let me cite Weber's interpretation of 3.2.123 vārttika 1. This reads *pravṛttasyâvirāme śiṣyā bhavantȳ avartamānatvāt.* The form *śiṣyā* is a nominative singular feminine, in accord with *bhavantī*, a term denoting present endings. Weber translated (1873d: 309): "sie sind zu belehren (über den Gebrauch des Praesens auch) bei Nichtvollendung einer begonnenen (Handlung), weil dieselbe nicht vor sich geht." He considered the sandhi form *bhavanty* a third plural present ('they are') and the sandhi form *siṣyā* to be a form of the nominative plural masculine *śiṣyāḥ.*

403. Liebich (1899: 312) first proposed to read *ajayad gupto hūṇān*, but Kielhorn (1903) corrected to the reading shown and accepted later by Liebich (1930: 264-67).
404. See Shambhu Nath Tripathi (1956: 112 [rule 2.2.92]). This example is of interest also because V. S. Agrawala (1953b: 181) suggested an emendation to *aruṇad menandro mathurām* 'Menander besieged Mathurā.' He proposed to consider this an old example, giving a direct reference to Menander. But I see no evidence to support this conjecture.
405. Yudhiṣṭhira Mīmāṃsaka (1973: I: 337-50) discusses just about all the evidence one can find in the Mahā-bhāṣya and other texts to establish Patañjali's date. He accepts that Patañjali was a contemporary of Puṣyamitra. However, he thinks the date of the latter is considerably earlier than is usually accepted.
406. This opinion was tentatively accepted by Renou (1953d: 91); see also Frauwallner (1960: 111). But Renou (1957a: 35) characterized Patañjali as "datable du 3me s. avant J. C." and (1957a: 114 n. 526) referred to 3.2.111 vārttika 2. Perhaps "3me s." is a misprint.
407. Another issue which has engaged scholars should be mentioned here although its resolution does not contribute directly to the precise dating of Patañjali. According to Pāṇinīyas such as Nāgeśa, Patañjali was the author not only of the Mahā-bhāṣya but also of the Yoga-sūtras and the medical work Caraka-saṃhitā. Some modern scholars have argued that the author of the Mahā-bhāṣya was not the same as the author of the Yoga-sūtras. Jacobi (1911: 25; 1931: 87-88) and Renou (1940b) held this position, arguing on the basis of language and style (see also Woods [1914: xii-xvii]). Jacobi was opposed by Liebich (1919a: 7-9; 1921: 57-60), Renou by P. V. Kane (1962: 1397-98); see also Puri (1957: 12-15), Prabhudayāla Agnihotrī 1963: 53), Yudhiṣṭhira Mīmāṃsaka (1973: I: 335-37). Fairly recently, Janáček (1958: 100) concluded that Jacobi's (1931: 87-88) appeal to a statistical method with respect to the use of vocabulary in the texts in question proves nothing and that the question has not yet been answered satisfactorily. I have no definite opinion on this question. K. Madhava Krishna Sarma (1944-45: 76-79) argued against another traditional identification, namely that Patañjali – who is considered to have been Śeṣa, Viṣṇu's serpent – was identical with Śeṣanāga, the author of the philosophical text Paramârtha-sāra.
408. *Devānāṃ-priya* literally means "beloved of the gods" or "the gods' own" (Hara 1969). There have been several studies devoted to this term, especially with regard to the question of how it later came to mean "fool"; see Kielhorn (1908: 504), S. P. Chaturvedi (1935), Dasaratha Sharma (1950), Hara (1969), Palsule (1969), Buddha Prakash (1970).

409. In his eighth vārttika on 2.1.69, Kātyāyana states that an additional provision should be made for a group of compounds, the first of which is *śāka-pārthiva.* The members of the compound are considered to refer to the same thing (*samānâdhikaraṇa*), which is shown by letting an item which would follow the first member be deleted. Thus, *śāka-pārthiva* = *śāka-bhojī pārthivaḥ* 'king (*pārthiva*) who eats (*bhojin*) vegetables (*śāka*).'
410. V. Bhattacharya (1921) suggested evidence to support Jayaswal's view, namely the use of *bhojin* in the meaning 'principal' (*pradhāna*).
411. Kātyāyana is traditionally identified with Vararuci. In the Mahā-bhāṣya (Kielhorn [1880-85: II: 315.8]) a poem composed by Vararuci (*vāraruca kāvya*) is referred to, but no indication is given that this Vararuci was considered to be Kātyāyana. There is also a liṅgânuśāsana composed by Vararuci, whom Franke (1890b: 52) considered quite old – contemporary with Vikramāditya. In addition, there is a work, the Nirukta-samuccaya (Yudhiṣṭhira Mīmāṃsaka [1965/6c]), attributed to Vararuci, which deals with the interpretation of Vedic verses in the etymological tradition. Yudhiṣṭhira Mīmāṃsaka (1965/6c: introduction, p. 3) puts this Vararuci also at a time before Vikramāditya, because he is prior to Skandasvāmin (see note 518). There is, in addition, a work called Vāraruca-saṃgraha (Gaṇapati Sastri [1913]), in which are set forth, in verse form, kārakas and their expression, compounds, taddhita derivatives, and verbal derivatives. Gaṇapati Sastri (1913: English preface, p. i) accepted that this Vararuci was probably the contemporary of Vikramāditya. Finally, there is a Prākṛta grammar, the Prākṛtaprakāśa (Cowell [1868]), attributed to Vararuci. The identification of any of these with Kātyāyana is uncertain; see Pischel (1900: §32), Nitti - Dolci (1938a: 11-12). On Kātyāyana and the Vājasaneyi-prātiśākhya see note 430.
412. S. P. Chaturvedi (1940c) argued, on the basis of Pāṇini's vocabulary, that his language was old enough to warrant one's putting him about the ninth century B. C.; see also C. V. Vaidya (1930: 159). Keith (1945) argued that Chaturvedi's assumption was not necessary and that Pāṇini could be put at about 350 B. C. Chaturvedi (1950) then replied to Keith, but without undue insistence on his own earlier proposal.
413. Moreover, it is doubtful in the extreme that there even was an eastern school of grammarians at Pāṇini's time; see section III.1.3.1.
414. Weber (1873d: 317-18) tried to argue, unsuccessfully, that the statement *yathā laukika-vaidikeṣu* was not part of a vārttika. More recently, Satyakāma Varmā (1971a: 180) has again doubted that this was a vārttika of Kātyāyana, but without solid evidence.
415. Rajendralal Mitra (1883) and Kielhorn (1883: 227, 1886d) gave evidence to show that it does not; see also S. K. Belvalkar (1915: 33), Yudhiṣṭhira Mīmāṃsaka (1973: I: 334-35). Lévi (1925: 199-200) tried to reconcile the

Kāśikā's statement that Gonarda was eastern with the view that Patañjali was referred to by the term *gonardīya* and his own view, based on Pāli texts, that Gonarda was in Mālvā.

416. This passage was also considered by R. K. Mookerji (1935), who concluded that the part of India Patañjali knew well had a trade route or highway from Sāketa to Pāṭaliputra.

417. See Prabhudayāla Agnihotrī (1963: 55), Ramākānta Misra (1966: 78). Puri (1957: 15-18), who gives a summary of earlier work, is noncommittal. The passage treated by Bhandarkar is dealt with again in a forthcoming paper by Scharfe, who agrees with Bhandarkar. Let me note in passing that Yudhiṣṭhira Mīmāṃsaka (1973: I: 335) considers Patañjali a Kashmiri.

418. Note that Goldstücker (1861: 220-21) devoted some space to refuting what he considered to be Müller's view as expressed earlier (Müller [1859: 163]), that Yāska came after Pāṇini. However, Müller (1869: introduction, pp. 4-5) himself later said that this was a misunderstanding due to careless expression on his part. I mention this because Müller's careless wording caused later authors also to devote space to refuting his alleged view; see Shiva Narayana Shastri (1969a: 69; 1972b: 66).

419. Müller did consider that Pāṇini's rule 1.4.109 (*paraḥ saṃnikarṣaḥ saṃhitā* 'The maximum drawing together of sounds is called *saṃhitā*') was taken from the Nirukta (1.17, Sarup [1927a: 40]). But this cannot be claimed definitively unless there is supporting evidence.

420. Mehendale (1968: 1-2) too has recently rejected 2.4.63 as evidence for Yāska's priority to Pāṇini. But he also accepts Sköld's view that this rule was interpolated (see section III.1.3.3e).

421. Keith (1914: clxx) attacked Liebich for this. But Keith's argument was no argument at all; he did no more than cite others, whose view he accepted.

422. This concerns rules 5.1.63 (*tad arhati*, see section III.1.5.5b.3), 66 (*daṇḍâdibhyo yat*), whereby is derived *daṇḍya* 'who merits punishment' (*daṇḍam arhati*). For Thieme's opinion see below.

423. I have omitted Thieme's argument that Yāska's use of *karman* at the end of a compound meaning "having the meaning . . . " is a hybrid use which presupposes Yāska's knowledge of Pāṇini's term *karman* "object" A full discussion of this would require extensive citation of texts.

424. Such arguments were already proposed by Satyavrat Sāmaśramī (1890), according to Giridhara Śarmā Caturveda (1954: 22-23), who also showed them to be unacceptable.

425. He also deals with Yāska's and Pāṇini's knowledge of various texts and persons.

426. This is the conclusion I have reached also in a paper which considers

all the evidence in detail, and which I have not published because of the lack of decisive results.

427. Texts dealing with rules for relating the analyzed Vedic texts (*pada-pāṭha*) with continuous texts (*saṃhitā-pāṭha*) by means of rules and which also treat general phonetic matters.

428. Lüders (1894: 1) considered the Taittirīya-prātiśākhya the oldest, but Liebich (1919b: 38, 45-46) thought the Rk-prātiśākhya and the Vājasaneyi-prātiśākhya were the oldest. Siddheshwar Varma (1929: 21, 27) treated the Ṛk-prātiśākhya as the most ancient, but Thieme (1958: 41) claimed that the Vājasaneyi-prātiśākhya is the oldest. My own view is that the Ṛk-prātiśākhya is probably the most ancient in its present form, since it shows less influence of Pāṇinian methodology than the others.

429. Goldstücker (1861: 198). Goldstücker (1861: 186-213) is reproduced in Venkatarama Sarma (1935: 123-55).

430. Thieme, in accord with Goldstücker (1861: 194), accepted that Kātyāyana was the author of both vārttikas on Pāṇinian rules and the Vājasaneyi-prātiśākhya, which he composed later. Thieme's opinion was criticized by Keith (1936: 742), to whom Thieme (1937-38) responded. K. Madhava Krishna Sarma (1941-42: 230) also held, like Keith, that the two works were by distinct authors. I have not reached a definite conclusion of my own on this issue. On Kātyāyana and Vararuci see note 411.

431. B. Ghosh (1938: 389): "But Max Müller has given us good reasons to believe the work [the Ṛk-prātiśākhya] in its earliest form was composed by Śākalya, the author of the Padapāṭha of the Ṛksaṃhitā."

432. See Liebich (1919b: 41), Siddheshwar Varma (1929: 28), Thieme (1935c: *22* n. 3), Ruegg (1959: 42 n. 2), Cardona (1969: 13 with note 32, 32). The fact that certain rules of these treatises can be shown to have been borrowed from Pāṇini does not, of course, prove that the entire treatises are post-Pāṇinian. This is a difficult question indeed. Liebich (1919b: 41) cautiously said only, "für dieses Sūtra [the Vājasaneyi-prātiśākhya rule equivalent to Pāṇini 1.1.49] besteht daher die Wahrscheinlichkeit, dass es aus der Aṣṭādhyāyī nachträglich in das Vāj. Prāt. geraten ist . . ." K. Madhava Krishna Sarma (1941-42: 91) also admitted such borrowing, but argued that the Vājasaneyi-prātiśākhya as a whole was earlier than Pāṇini.

433. Thieme (1935c: *22*): "Dass das Prātiśākhya den Ausdruck *sthāna* in diesem Zusammenhang vermeiden wollte, dürfte die Veranlassung gewesen sein, dass es Pāṇinis Anschauung von der grammatischen Substitution durch die von Verwandlung ersetzt hat . . ."

434. For further discussions on this issue see Whitney (1862: 579-80), Vishva Bandhu (1923: 24-32), Sūrya Kānta (1939: 27-30, notes pp. 26-27), Giridhara Śarmā Caturveda (1954: 8-18). The last mentioned is an excellent survey of the evidence.

435. Agrawala (1939; 1943; 1946; 1947; 1953a). For other articles, which I have not been able to obtain, see R. N. Dandekar (1946-73: 1: 62, 2: 94-95). Such studies continue to attract scholars; recently, C. Ramachari (1968) devoted a paper to a study of artisans reflected in the Aṣṭādhyāyī.
436. On patronymics see also Dange (1970a) and V. N. Gokhale (1939), who treated Pāṇini's taddhita rules (section III.1.1.5b. 3 above) not only as they reflect the patronymic system but also with regard to other matters such as geographic details.
437. On Vedic texts see section III.1.5.6a.
438. Shiva Narayana Shastri (1969a: 73) also refers to the bhikṣu-sūtras as a Vedānta text, but R. K. Mookerji (1969: 231) calls this a text of rules for mendicants.
439. Amalananda Ghosh (1935) studied smṛti passages in the Mahā-bhāṣya, citing passages from the latter and their parallels in smṛti texts. Ghosh was also cautious, noting that it is not possible to know whether Patañjali used the actual smṛti texts or only the sources of these. On Sircar's view that Patañjali's knowledge of a wide variety of literary compositions indicates a relatively late date see section III.3.1.4.
440. Since the main emphasis of the present work is Pāṇini and his successors as grammarians, I have not entered into discussions concerning details of realia.
441. I am of course speaking of commentaries which we have, not of earlier commentaries which possibly existed; see section III.2.1.
442. See Belvalkar (1915: 36), Yudhiṣṭhira Mīmāṃsaka (1973: I: 459-60). Ojihara (1961-62) studies details of disagreements in the comments of the two authors. D. C. Bhattacharya (1922: 190-91) gave evidence from the Nyāsa (see below) showing that Jayāditya commented also on the last three chapters.
443. These vārttikas are not always given in the commentary at the same place where Kātyāyana stated them. For example, the two vārttikas given in the Kāśikā on 3.1.110 are vārttikas 1-2 on 3.1.124. Moreover, the vārttikas are frequently cited in a version different from Kātyāyana's. For example, after citing and paraphrasing with examples vārttika 4 on 3.2.171, Patañjali says (Kielhorn [1880-85: II: 135.11]) *apara āha* 'someone else says', and gives another version. It is this which appears in the Kāśikā on 3.2.17. Vedpati Mishra (1970: 144-54) has taken up some of the variations in vārttikas as they appear in the Kāśikā.
444. The Nyāsa was commented on in the Anunyāsa of Indumitra and the Tantra-pradīpa of Maitreya-rakṣita, neither of which has been published; see S. C. Chakravarti (1919-25: I: introduction, pp. 19-21), K. C. Chatterji (1931b), Renou (1940a: 28 with note 3, 29 with note 1), Raghavan (1945), Yudhiṣṭhira Mīmāṃsaka (1973: I: 507-20). The last gives a survey of other commentaries and supercommentaries on the Kāśikā.

445. For example, Śobhita Miśra (1952), Nārāyaṇa Miśra (1969-72). For bibliographic information on other editions, which were inaccessible to me, see Birwé (1973: 440).
446. There was an earlier edition of the Pada-mañjarī published in the Pandit; see Birwé (1973: 441) for details.
447. Liebich (1892: I) himself makes this claim.
448. As for Vāmana, he is not identical with the poetician Vāmana who lived in the 8th to 9th centuries; see Müller (1880: 305), M. Sen (1934), P. V. Kane (1909-14: 92; 1961: 147).
449. See K. B. Pathak (1909-14a: 26-31), S. C. Chakravarti (1919-25: I: introduction, p. 23), Yudhiṣṭhira Mīmāṃsaka (1973: I: 504). Kielhorn (1908a: 502) believed Jinendrabuddhi had copied from Haradatta, but this view was disproved by K. B. Pathak (1909-14a: 26-29; 1931: 250) and later generally given up (see Renou [1940a: 27 with note 6]). I know of only one scholar recently to have accepted Kielhorn's view, U. P. Shah (1960: 9 n. 5).
450. For evidence see K. B. Pathak (1931: 246-47), S. C. Chakravarti (1919-25: I: introduction, p. 21), Yudhiṣṭhira Mīmāṃsaka (1973: I: 505).
451. Śiśupāla-vadha 2. 112: *anutsūtra-pada-nyāsā sad-vṛttiḥ san-nibandhanā/ śabda-vidyêva no bhāti rāja-nītir apaspaśā* 'A king's policy does not prosper without spies even if (in carrying it out the king) take no step contrary to rules set down, properly support dependents, give gifts for services, just as the knowledge of grammar does not shine forth as complete (if one does) not (know) the paspaśā, . . .'
452. De also gives bibliography on this issue.
453. The most important detail to note in the present context is that Bhartṛhari, in his Tripādī (see section III.2.2.1) refers to a Nyāsa (Abhyankar - Limaye [1969: 233.18]), as has been noted by Yudhiṣṭhira Mīmāṃsaka (1973: I: 388).
454. The objection had little effect: S. K. De (1960: 48) later merely repeated what he had said earlier. Note that the same kind of problem arises concerning the poetician Bhāmaha's reference to a Nyāsa. But this particular reference is more important to other issues, so that I pass it by; see P. V. Kane (1961: 117-18) for an excellent summary of arguments and bibliographic information.
455. For additional bibliography on this question see Renou (1940a: 28 n. 1), Dasgupta - De (1962: 188 n. 1).
456. K. B. Pathak (1909-14a: 31) put Māgha at the end of the eighth century, but P. V. Kane placed him in the first half of the eighth century (1909-14; 1961: 147). However, part of Kane's argument is based on assuming a date no later than 700 for Jinendrabuddhi. Kielhorn (1906) discussed an

inscription in which king Varmalāta's date is given as saṃvat 682 (A. D. 625). Now, at the end of the Śisupāla-vadha, Māgha gives his lineage and notes that his grandfather had been minister of a king whose name appears in editions variously as Varmala, Dharmanābha, etc. Kielhorn proposed that the name was Varmalāta, the very king of the inscription. Hence, he also proposed to put Māgha in the second half of the seventh century. This has also been proposed by Yudhiṣṭhira Mīmāṃsaka (1973: I: 463-64). However, I do not think the evidence in question is strong enough to make this definitive.

457. D. C. Bhattacharya (1922: 193-94) placed Jinendrabuddhi in the ninth century for the following reasons. Jinendra cites variant readings of a verse cited in the Kāśikā on 1.1.75; in his comments on 1.1.1 and 7.1.6, Jinendra appears to refer to other, earlier commentaries on the vṛtti.

458. Similarly, D. C. Bhattacharya (1922: 195 n. 1) claimed that Haradatta could not be earlier than the twelfth century because he was first quoted in a thirteenth-century work.

459. This is the reading given by Aryendra Sharma et al. (1969-70). Other editions (Śobhita Miśra [1952], Dwarikadas Shastri - K. P. Shukla [1965-67], Nārāyaṇa Miśra [1969-72]) read *parṇaṃ nayeḥ*.

460. No complete edition of this has been published, as far as I know. Renou (1940a: 31 n. 1) referred to a partial edition which was inaccessible to me.

461. These have some lacunae. For example, Kaiyaṭa and Śrutapāla are not listed, though they are mentioned in the commentary on 8.3.5.

462. Of course the proviso regarding such simple commentaries applies here (see section IV.2.1).

463. Earlier, R. G. Bhandarkar (1883-84 [= 1927-33 2: 147]) had said that Bhaṭṭojī flourished in the mid-seventeenth century. Aufrecht (1891) pointed out that Bhaṭṭojī was definitely teaching before 1620. Yudhiṣṭhira Mīmāṃsaka (1973: I: 487) gives his dates at about saṃvat 1570-1650 (A. D. 1513-94).

464. S. C. Chakravarti (1919-25: I: introduction, pp. 13-14) attributed the work to Bhartṛhari, but Haraprasāda Shāstrī (1931: xxxvii) characterized Chakravarti's arguments as "absolutely unconvincing." K. C. Chatterji (1931) showed that the work should be attributed to Vimalamati; see also O. P. Rangaswami (1937). S. P. Bhattacharya (1946: 284-87) suggested that the author of this was Indumitra (see note 444), but this has not been accepted; see Yudhiṣṭhira Mīmāṃsaka (1973: I: 470).

465. In view of this characteristic, I have considered the Bhāga-vṛtti here and not immediately after the Kāśikā, where it belongs chronologically.

466. Yudhiṣṭhira Mīmāṃsaka (1973: I: 471) adopts an earlier dating: saṃvat 702-705 (A. D. 655-659). He does so on the basis of the statement by

Sṛṣṭidhara that the Bhāga-vṛtti was composed on the order of king Śrīdharasena. This dating does not accord with the citation from Māgha unless one accepts an earlier date than usual for the poet.

467. He also omits the two rules in which Pāṇini refers to uṇ-ādi affixes (see note 115). Nevertheless, Dharmakīrti does mention uṇ-ādi affixes and cites some uṇ-ādi-sūtras (see Rangacharya [1916-27: II: 165, 290]).

468. This is the date given by Ādyāprasāda Miśra (1966: 12). Rangacharya (1916-27: I: Sanskrit introduction, pp. vii-xiv), after discussing evidence, concluded only that Dharmakīrti had to be put somewhere after the ninth and before the thirteenth centuries. In his English preface (p. v), however, he set Dharmakīrti's date in the late twelfth century.

469. This title is used because, like the moonlight (*kaumudī*), which takes away darkness and cools, so do these works dispel ignorance while not involving the great effort necessary to understand works like the Mahā-bhāṣya and its commentaries.

470. Between the Rūpâvatāra and the Prakriyā-kaumudī there was another work, the Rūpa-mālā, which has been edited recently (Keśava Deva Pāṇḍeya [1973]). On this work and its author, Vimalasarasvatī, see Belvalkar (1915: 44), K. P. Trivedi (1925-31: I: xxx-xxxiii), Yudhiṣṭhira Mīmāṃsaka (1973: I: 527).

471. On other commentaries see Belvalkar (1915: 45-46), K. P. Trivedi (1925-31: I: L-LIV), Ādyāprasāda Miśra (1966: 123-30), Yudhiṣṭhira Mīmāṃsaka (1973: I: 529-34).

472. For Bhaṭṭojī's dates and his Śabda-kaustubha see section IV.2.3; for his Vaiyākaraṇa-siddhânta-kārikā see section VI.3.1.

473. For example, Paṇsīkar (1913), Mohanvallabh Pant (1962), B. K. Pancholi (1966), and the editions noted below. There is no use trying to give an exhaustive survey of editions, since this text is so popular. A Sanskrit - Hindi lexicon of examples for rules in the Siddhânta-kaumudī has been compiled by Rādhāramaṇa Pāṇḍeya (1966).

474. A full survey of commentaries is given by Yudhiṣṭhira Mīmāṃsaka (1973: I: 535-42). See also P. K. Gode (1951).

475. According to Yudhiṣṭhira Mīmāṃsaka (1973: I: 412), Jñānendra was a contemporary of Bhaṭṭojī. Yudhiṣṭhira's basis for this is the story popular in Varanasi that Bhaṭṭojī requested Jñānendra to compose a commentary on his work. Other scholars (e.g., Belvalkar [1915: 48], C. Kunhan Raja [1947: 88]) assign him to the early eighteenth century. The Tattva-bodhinī was itself commented on by Jñānendra's student Nīlakaṇṭha; see Yudhiṣṭhira Mīmāṃsaka [1973: I: 536].

476. Posterior to Nāgeśa, on whose commentary on the phiṭ-sūtras he commented.

477. For commentaries on the phiṭ-sūtras and the liṅgânuśāsana as included in the Siddhânta-kaumudī see sections III.1.4.2a, III.1.4.3a.
478. On Nāgeśa's dates and the name Nāgojī see note 345.
479. No other complete edition of this is available to me.
480. Another relatively modern commentary on the Laghu-śabda-ratna is the Citra-prabhā of Hari Śāstrī (see Tata Subbaraya Sastri [1932]), born about 1811.
481. The Madhya-siddhânta-kaumudī. This has been edited various times, for example, Nārāyaṇa Rāma Ācārya (1950). The text with a modern Sanskrit commentary and a Hindi paraphrase has been edited by Sadāśiva Śāstrī Joshi and Rāma Candra Jhā (1960).
482. The Laghu-siddhânta-kaumudī, edited various times (e.g., Nārāyaṇa Rāma Ācārya (1948). Ballantyne (1849) edited the text with an English translation, see also V. V. Mirashi (1928).
483. The terms *navya* 'new' and *prāñc* (or *prācīna*) 'old' are relative. To Nāgeśa, Bhaṭṭojī's views are the latter, and for Bhaṭṭojī the views of Rāmacandra are old. S. P. Chaturvedi (1940c: 61) suggested a fourfold division of Pāṇinīyas into *prācīnatara* 'extremely ancient', *prāñc* 'ancient', *navya* 'new' and *navyatara* 'ultranew'.
484. There is a late and syncretic commentary on Pāṇini's rules by Viśveśvara Sūri, the Vyākaraṇa-siddhânta-sudhā-nidhi (Dadhi Rāma Śarmā et al. [1914-24]), in which are discussed in considerable detail not only the interpretations of individual rules but also the views of Naiyāyikas and Mīmāṃsakas, in addition to those of earlier Pāṇinīyas. Viśveśvara Sūri refers, among others, to the works of Bhaṭṭojī and Kauṇḍabhaṭṭa (e.g., Dadhi Rāma Śarmā et al. [1914-24: 37]). Another recast of Pāṇini's grammar is the Prakriyā-sarvasva of Nārāyaṇabhaṭṭa (1560-1666, see Venkitasubramonia Iyer [1947: vii-x; 1972: 20-23], opposed to Kunjunni Raja [1946]). This incorporates metarules not included in the Aṣṭādhyāyī, which Nārāyaṇa took from the Sarasvatī-kaṇṭhâbharaṇa of Bhoja (eleventh century), as well as uṇ-ādi rules, so that I have not treated it here as strictly within the purview of Pāṇinīyas. Venkitasubramonia Iyer (1972) has provided a very good survey of Nārayaṇabhaṭṭa's work and its sources. For editions of the Prakriyā-sarvasya not yet fully edited, see page 320 of this survey. Nārāyaṇabhaṭṭa also admitte the propriety of non-Pāṇinian forms (see Sreekrishna Sharma [1965]).
485. There is no available ancient commentary on the Pāṇinian gaṇa-pāṭha (section III.1.3.6); see Kapil Deva Shastri (1967: 43-45), Yudhiṣṭhira Mīmāṃsaka (1973: II: 152-61). The most important available work devoted exclusively to a gaṇa-pāṭha is Vardhamāna's Gaṇa-ratna-mahôdadhi (edited by Eggeling [1879-81]), but, as is well known, this is not a commentary directly on Pāṇini's gaṇa-pāṭha (see Eggeling [1879-81: ix], Birwé [1961: 478-90]).

Vardhamāna's work was composed in saṃvat 1197 (A. D. 1140) according to a verse (Eggeling [1879-81: 480]) which does not occur in all manuscripts. Modern scholars have accepted the twelfth century as his date (see Renou [1940a: 14], Yudhiṣṭhira Mīmāṃsaka [1973: II: 180]).
486. There were other commentators, among which Bhīmasena is of special interest (see section III.1.3.5b). Yudhiṣṭhira Mīmāṃsaka (1973: II: 80-107) gives a survey of commentators.
487. Yudhiṣṭhira Mīmāṃsaka edited the text (1962/3), which had previously been edited by Gaṇapati Sastri (1905). The former (1957/8: introduction, p. 36; 1962/3: introduction, pp. 3-4) has given evidence from which to infer that Deva postdated Maitreya-rakṣita. Kṛṣṇalīlāśukamuni cites Hemacandra (Yudhiṣṭhira Mīmāṃsaka [1962/3: introduction, p. 6]) and is quoted by Sāyaṇa in his Mādhavīya-dhātu-vṛtti (e.g., Dwarikadas Shastri [1964: 110, under root number 207]), which establish his limits.
488. The various arguments given to support different suggestions and reject others are too lengthy and complex to be summarized here.
489. Part of this discussion was summarized by Birwé (1966: 16-18). However, Birwé's treatment is unsatisfactory, since he leaves out the most important part of the discussion. I treat this in a forthcoming paper on the evaluation of Pāṇinian commentators.
490. Note that I have singled out Chatterji and R. Rocher in this context only because they have been particularly articulate in their views. Others have argued in similar fashion. One example will suffice here. As I have noted (see note 12), Pāṇini arranged his śiva-sūtras so as to form abbreviations denoting sets of sounds. Now, there are two śiva-sūtras which are closed by the same marker, *ṇ*: the first (*a i u ṇ*) and the sixth (*laṇ*). Accordingly, there are two possible abbreviations: *iṇ*$_1$ referring to *i* and *u* vowels and *iṇ*$_6$ referring to all vowels and semivowels excepting *a*. Rule 8.3.57 (*iṇ-koḥ*) is a heading valid in subsequent rules, among them 8.3.59 (*ādeśa-pratyayoḥ*). This provides that *s* is replaced by the retroflex *ṣ* if it is a replacement (of a root initial *ṣ*) or the initial of an affix and occurs after certain sounds, among them those denoted by *iṇ*. The rule should apply to provide not only forms such as *agniṣu, vāyuṣu* (locative plurals of *agni* 'fire', *vāyu* 'wind') but also *pitṛṣu* (*pitṛ* 'father') and others, where *s* is preceded by *ṛ*. Hence, *iṇ* here should be *iṇ*$_6$. One might consider that *iṇ* is ambiguous, so that it could be interpreted as *iṇ*$_1$. This would be a fault. However, as Patañjali notes (Kielhorn [1880-85: I. 35.11-12]), Pāṇini does not really use *iṇ* ambiguously. When he does wish to refer to *i* and *u* vowels alone, he uses another term; thus, in 1.2.26, he uses *vī* to refer to these sounds. Hence, Pāṇini's procedure shows that *iṇ* in a rule such as 8.3.59 is uniquely *iṇ*$_6$. Millonig (1973: 425) has argued that Patañjali's claim is unacceptable. Since Pāṇini often uses pratyāhāras which refer to more sounds

than are actually pertinent to a given rule, Millonig claims, he could have used *iṇ* for 1.2.26, so that one does not know why he used *vī* here. What Millonig has not noted is that, if *iṇ* were used in 1.2.26, it could there be interpreted as $iṇ_6$, so that the rule would provide for wrong results. Moreover, though it is true that Pāṇini does indeed use abbreviations which refer to more units than are directly pertinent to a given rule, he does so only where the additional units are neutral with respect to the operation in question, so that no wrong results are provided by the rule. In effect, by using *vī* in 1.2.26 (and *yvoḥ* in 6.4.77), Pāṇini as much as tells us that he does not use *iṇ* ambiguously. The rest of Millonig's arguments meant to show that commentators are useless are equally untenable.

491. K. C. Chatterji (1935b: 1). Chatterji (1956-57) also pointed out some instances where later commentators misused Pāṇinian rules and vārttikas.

492. Thieme (1957a) is a beautiful study of just such questions with regard to the Mahā-bhāṣya, Kaiyaṭa, Bhaṭṭojī and Nāgeśa.

493. I say "supposed" (Sanskrit *prakalpita*) because, for Pāṇinian grammarians such as Bhartṛhari, a sentence is indeed a single entity, with a single meaning, and components and their meanings are posited for grammatical purposes.

494. These views are respectively called *abhihitânvaya-vāda* ('doctrine of relation of meanings denoted independently') and *anvitâbhidhāna-vada* ('doctrine of denoting related meanings'), on which see Gaurinath Shastri (1959: 172-287), Sreekrishna Sharma (1959), B. Bhattacharya (1962: 158-87), Kunjunni Raja (1969: 189-213).

495. The papers by Siddheshwar Varma (1925, 1926) and Aklujkar (1970a) are very sweeping overviews which do not enter into details. Burrow (1936) is a short summary only.

496. On Bhartṛhari's commentary on the Mahā-bhāṣya see section III.2.2.1; for other works attributed to him see section VI.2.2 with note 514.

497. Note that I use here this title instead of Trikāṇḍī (see below) because it is the more commonly used one.

498. A good repertory of citations from the Vākya-padīya is given in Abhyankar - Limaye (1965). The repute of this work was such that many verses were attributed to Bhartṛhari which are not found in manuscripts of the Vākya-padīya; see Abhyankar - Limaye (1965) for a collection of these. Sadhu Ram (1956: 53-59) considered, contrary to others, that eight of these verses were part of the original text. R. S. Bhattacharya (1966jj) has discussed the citation of verse 3.2.12 by **Medhātithi** in his commentary on the Manusmṛti (see also Abhyankar - Limaye [1965: 245]).

499. A detailed table of contents of the Vākya-padīya was compiled by J. M. Shukla (1966: 192-98).

500. See Charudeva Shastri (1930: 632), Aklujkar (1969: 548), K. A. Subramania Iyer (1969: 7-8). Aklujkar (1969: 548 n. 5) and Subramania Iyer (1969: 8) disagree with Sadhu Ram (1956: 71-79), who argued that two of the sections in question did not originally belong in the third kāṇḍa.
501. See Kielhorn (1883: 227), Gaurinath Shastri (1956: 72), Aklujkar (1969: 547-55), Yudhiṣṭhira Mīmāṃsaka (1973: II: 399-400). Aklujkar argues against those who considered the term *Vākya-padīya* proper as referring to the entire work (e.g., Charudeva Shastri [1934: Sanskrit introduction, pp. 7-8]) and suggests (1969: 552-53) an explanation for the use of this title with reference to the first two kāṇḍas. Yudhiṣṭhira Mīmāṃsaka (1973: II: 400) claims this title refers only to the second kāṇḍa, a view he held earlier, in the first edition of this volume of his history (p. 349). Aklujkar (1969: 547 n. 2) rightly notes that this opinion has no support.
502. There are two manuscripts of this, one in the Government Oriental Manuscripts Library, Madras, the other in the Śrī Hemacandrācārya Jaina Jñānamandira at Patan (Gujarat). I owe my awareness of the second to Ashok Aklujkar.
503. Aklujkar (1974) has recently set forth evidence to support the proposition that this was composed by Helārāja. In the first edition of the Vākya-padīya (see below), the commentary printed for the verses of the first kāṇḍa was attributed to Puṇyarāja. Charudeva Shastri (1930: 636-44; 1934: Sanskrit introduction, pp. 18-26) demonstrated that this was a false attribution and that the commentary there printed was an abbreviated version of the Vṛtti. Nevertheless, some later scholars still referred to this commentary as Puṇyarāja's (e.g., Brough [1951: 45 n. 1], S. D. Joshi [1960: xxvi]). On this topic see also K. A. Subramania Iyer (1963b: *gha*, 1965a: x) and Aklujkar (1972: 181 n. 1c), who gives extensive references.
504. It is also known that Helārāja composed a commentary called *Śabdaprabhā* on the first kāṇḍa as well as a commentary on the second and that one Phullarāja composed comments which appear where Helārāja's commentary on the third kāṇḍa has gaps (twice); see K. A. Subramania Iyer (1969: 36-38), Aklujkar (1974: 178-79, 183-84). Moreover, according to I-Tsing a commentary on the last kāṇḍa was composed by Dharmapāla; see Frauwallner (1961: 134-35), Aklujkar (1969: 549 n. 7), Yudhiṣṭhira Mīmāṃsaka (1973: II: 407).
505. Charudeva Shastri (1930: 632-34) also supplied some corrections; see also Satyavrat (1966: 42-45). Rau (1962: 374) was more charitable to this edition, calling it a pioneer work.
506. Rau gives brief critical comments on editions, which I shall note below.
507. Charudeva Shastri (1939/40) was not authorized for publication by the editor; see Aklujkar (1969: 555 n. 32).

508. Rau (1971: 48): "Die Trivandrum-Editoren bleiben hinter *CĀRUDEVA-ŚĀSTRĪ* . . . an Gewissenhaftigkeit weit zurück."
509. Of Subramania Iyer (1963a) Rau says (1971: 49), "Dies bedeutet ohne Zweifel einen Fortschritt gegenüber der Trivandrum Edition, aber keineswegs eine wirklich befriedigende Lösung der Aufgabe." On the other hand, in elaborating his edition of 1966, Subramania Iyer has, according to Rau (1971: 49), made use of just about all the manuscript materials available.
510. Concerning the last, Subramania Iyer (1963b: *ca*) has noted that the Bhāva-pradīpa commentary, though very learned, does not always convey what Bhartṛhari meant, as reflected in the Vṛtti.
511. Rau (1971: 49) characterizes this as without the slightest critical value.
512. Sadhu Ram (1956: 59-71) attempted to show that as many as 35 of the verses considered citations in the Vṛtti by Charudeva Shastri (1934) should be treated as parts of the Vākya-padīya. Aklujkar (1971c) has recently studied the number of verses in the first kāṇḍa.
513. Biardeau's is, in general, a more literal translation than Subramania Iyer's, though both take some liberties in the case of difficult passages. For example, Biardeau (1964b: 27) translated the second half of the fifth verse cited in the Vṛtti on 1.1 (*aṅgārâṅkitam utpāte vāri-rāśer ivôdakam*) as follows: "comme des fragments de charbon dans une flambée, ou de l'eau dans l'océan." Subramania Iyer (1965a: 2) translated somewhat more closely: "like the waters of the ocean, which are impregnated with heat at the time of dissolution." Wezler (1974) has objected to both translations. However, his own suggestion, that *utpāta* here means 'sunrise' is, I think, unacceptable. I think the usual meaning of this word, namely portent, is quite proper here: 'like the waters of the ocean, which, when there is a portent (such as a falling star [*ulkā-nirghāta*]), appear as though marked with embers.'
514. He is also known to have composed a work called *Śabda-dhātu-samīkṣā*, not extant; see K. Madhava Krishna Sarma (1940b), K. A. Subramania Iyer (1969: 9-10). In addition, the Bhaṭṭi-kāvya (see section VII) and three centuries of verses (*śataka-trayī*) have been attributed to him. For discussions of these topics see K. A. Subramania Iyer (1969: 10-14), Satyapal Narang (1969: 16-19) (who gives references), Yudhiṣṭhira Mīmāṃsaka (1973: I: 370-71). On Bhartṛhari's works see also J. M. Shukla (1966: 190-208).
515. Various explanations have been suggested to account for the name Harivṛṣabha; see Charudeva Shastri (1930: 635), Ramakrishna Kavi (1930: 235 n. 2), K. A. Subramania Iyer (1965a: xviii). The most recent suggestion was made by Aklujkar (1972: 182 n. 2b), who reviewed and rejected earlier proposals.
516. See Charudeva Shastri (1930: 634-36, 644-45; 1934: Sanskrit introduction, pp. 16-17), Swaminathan (1963), K. A. Subramania Iyer (1965a:

xvi-xxix, 1969: 16-29), Aklujkar (1972: 183 n. 4), Yudhiṣṭhira Mīmāṃsaka (1973: I: 369-70). V. P. Limaye (1966: 228) also suggested that the reference to Dhyāna-kāra in both the Vṛtti and the Tripādī might point to common authorship. K. Madhava Krishna Sarma (1942: 407-09) suggested other evidence which is inconclusive (see Aklujkar [1972: 188 n. 13]).

517. See Sadhu Ram (1952: 137 n. 6) for references to scholars who held this view. More recently against I-Tsing's dating see Brough (1973: 259). This late date is still given in some recent reference works (e.g., K. V. Abhyankar [1961: 269], *sv. Bhartṛhari*).

518. This dating depends on the dating of Skandasvāmin's pupil Harisvāmin and the interpretation of a verse by the latter in which he gives the date of composition of his commentary on the Śata-patha-brāhmaṇa; see Sarup (1934: 54-65, 1937). S. L. Katre (1948) interpreted the verse differently and put Skandasvāmin in the first century B. C., a date accepted by Yudhiṣṭhira Mīmāṃsaka (1965/6c: introduction, p. 3). Venkatasubbiah (1936: 203) doubted that Harisvāmin was Skandavāmin's pupil, and C. Kunhan Raja (1936: 296) doubted that the citation from Bhartṛhari was in the commentary of Skandasvāmin instead of Maheśvara's.

519. Frauwallner's dates have been accepted by K. A. Subramania Iyer (1969: 2). Ruegg (1959: 64) considered it probable that Bhartṛhari should be placed at about the beginning of the sixth century and agreed (1959: 4 n. 1) with Nakamura (1955), who placed Bhartṛhari at about 450 to 500 A. D.

520. There is one factor which could cast doubt on the early date proposed by Jambūvijaya on the basis of Mallavādin's work. Mallavādin refers to Praśastapāda (Jambūvijaya [1961: 148]). If Praśastapāda is considered a predecessor of Diṅnāga, the early date for Bhartṛhari is in order. However, if he postdates Diṅnāga, then the early date for Mallavādin, and consequently for Bhartṛhari, is cast into doubt. I cannot discuss details of this question here.

521. Sadhu Ram (1952: 151) put Bhartṛhari in the third century at the latest.

522. Shukla (1966: 281) concludes that Bhartṛhari lived in the middle of the fourth century.

523. Yudhiṣṭhira Mīmāṃsaka (1973: I: 359) gives Bhartṛhari's date as prior to saṃvat 400 (A. D. 343/4).

524. Incidentally, since Bhartṛhari himself mentions Candra (see section III. 2.4), the latter's date cannot be so late as Lévi (1903) claimed in speaking against Liebich (1899), who put Candra at about 450.

525. This argument of course presupposes that Puṇyarāja composed the ṭīkā on the second kāṇḍa; see note 503.

526. A brief survey of scholarship in this area is supplied by Staal (1969: 517-21).
527. I have not seen Sreekrishna Sharma's dissertation (1954), hence cannot speak of its contents.
528. Subramania Iyer devotes special sections to summarizing Bhartṛhari's views on: universals and substances (1969: 228-63), qualities (264-73), spatial concepts (274-82), kārakas (283-325), action (325-43), person and aspect (344-53), gender (359-70), and complex formations (*vṛtti*, 371-401). He has not, however, devoted a special section to time (*kāla*), on which see J. M. Shukla (1953), Satyavrat (1958), P. Sarveswara Sharma (1972: 12-39) and Rāma Surésa Tripāṭhī (1972: 205-44), who also deals with other topics treated by Subramania Iyer.
529. Subramania Iyer devotes almost 150 pages (1969: 405-562) to textual citations, and Aklujkar's notes, where he has given references to texts, take up 165 pages (1970b: 115-279).
530. Bhartṛhari's philosophical views have been treated by Biardeau (1964a: 251-355) and K. A. Subramania Iyer (1969: 69-146). In addition there are other, shorter, contributions: Gaurinath Shastri (1956, 1968-69), Sreekrishna Sharma (1962), V. Anjaneya Sarma (1965). Nakamura (1960) surveyed Bhartṛhari's general views in a study which was later criticized by Aklujkar (1971a) for being based on an insufficient understanding of the Vākya-padīya.
531. Gaurinath Shastri (1959: 54-57; 1968-69) has discussed the śabda-brahman ('speech brahman') doctrine in contrast to the doctrine of absolute monism, with special emphasis on the concept of vivarta (see note 532 and section VI.2.2). He has also (1939) dealt with the logician Jayanta's critique of the śabda-brahman doctrine and its attendant linguistic views (see also Ruegg [1959: 88-89]). On the śabda-brahman doctrine see also Hārāṇacandra Śāstrī (1937), Haridatta Śāstrī (1971). Rāmaprasāda Tripāṭhī (1971: 133-37) has briefly treated Bhartṛhari's views on creation, on which see also Rāmanārāyaṇa Tripāṭhī (1971: 72-74).
532. Bhartṛhari's concept of vivarta (see section VI.2.2. and note 531) was also studied by Hacker (1953: 13-21), who saw Buddhist influence therein. Ruegg (1953: 273-5), on the other hand, saw in this a development of a view found mentioned in the Mahā-bhāṣya, according to which it is not linguistic elements which undergo changes but ones cognition of them. There has been some discussion concerning whether Bhartṛhari himself was a Buddhist, a view espoused by K. B. Pathak (1890-94: 344-45). This opinion has been shown to be incorrect; see Charudeva Shastri (1930: 645-47; 1934: Sanskrit introduction, pp. 3-7), V. A. Ramaswami Sastri (1936-37, 1937, 1938), K. Madhava Krishna Sarma (1940a, 1940c [where he translated 13 verses of the first kāṇḍa of the Vākya-padīya to show that Bhartṛhari was an intuitionist]), Biardeau (1964a: 255-56), and, most recently, Nakamura

(1972). Several studies have been devoted to Bhartṛhari's mastery of Mīmāṃsa thought and techniques; see V. A. Ramaswami Sastri (1952a; 1955-56; 1958), Swaminathan (1961).

533. See K. A. Subramania Iyer (1964a; 1969: 57-59, 146). In the last passage, he differs from Biardeau (1964a: 268), who said, "... ce salut reste indéfini ..."

534. See P. C. Chakravarti (1930: 128), Ruegg (1959: 83-88), Kunjunni Raja (1964), and above, section III.1.5.5c with note 296.

535. The last term is usually translated "intuition, flash of insight"; see Aklujkar (1970b: 15-16) for a discussion. Aspects of the concepts vākya-sphoṭa and pratibhā have been treated by Gopinath Kaviraj (1924: 13-21), P. C. Chakravarti (1930: 100-06, 135-36), Gaurinath Bhattacharya (1937: 100-03, 108-11), K. A. Subramania Iyer (1940; 1969: 181-204), Brough (1952: 75-76; 1953: 164-73), K. C. Pandey (1963: 712-14); Biardeau (1964a: 316-22, 400-11), Raghunātha Śarmā (1964d); see also the references given in note 536.

536. Bhartṛhari's concept of sphoṭa has been the object of many studies, some detailed discussions, others summary expositions; see P. C. Chakravarti (1930: 100-06), Ramaswami Sastri (1932-33), K. A. Subramania Iyer (1935, 1947, 1965b; 1966b: 12-26; 1969: 147-80), Gaurinath Bhattacharya (1937: 13-33), Heimann (1941), Brough (1951), Kapila Deva Dvivedi (1951: 349-98), Kunjunni Raja (1956; 1969: 116-27), Gaurinath Shastri (1959: 102-35), K. C. Pandeya (1960-61), Herman (1962-63), Biardeau (1964a: 359-400), T. N. Dave (1966), Īśvara Namputiri (1967: 342-45), S. D. Joshi (1967a: 20-55), Kapil Deva Shastri (1967), Svāmī Dayānanda (1969: 591-93), Aklujkar (1970b: 8-14), Periveṅkateśvara Śāstrī (1971), Rāmanārāyaṇa Tripāṭhī (1971: 71-72), Viśvanātha Miśra (1971). Abegg (1914) and Liebich (1923) treated the sphoṭa concept as set forth in the 14th century compendium Sarva-darśana saṃgraha. See also note 316 above.

537. Bhartṛhari also used the term *śabda* 'linguistic item' as a synonym of *sphoṭa*; see Aklujkar (1970b: 120 n. 30).

538. On these relations see Biardeau (1964a: 420-38), K. A. Subramania Iyer (1967, 1969: 204-18), Aklujkar (1970b: 104-05).

539. On these see Ruegg (1959: 79-81), Biardeau (1964a: 321-25), K. A. Subramania Iyer (1969: 144-45), Aklujkar (1970b: 67-75), Rāma Sureśa Tripāṭhī (1972: 44-48). Note that Bhartṛhari did not recognize an absolute fourth level called *parā vāk* 'supreme speech', which was recognized by later thinkers, especially in the Kashmir Śaiva school of thought. On this see Ruegg (1959: 80-81), K. C. Pandey (1963: 625-26), Biardeau (1964a: 322-25), K. A. Subramania Iyer (1969: 69-70), Rāma Sureśa Tripāṭhī (1972: 48-50).

540. Nāgeśa, Sphoṭa-vāda (V. Krishnamacharya [1946: 5]): *tatra sphuṭaty artho'smād iti sphoṭaḥ/ vācaka iti yāvat* 'Sphoṭa (is so called) because (it is that)

from which a meaning bursts; (it is) tantamount to "meaningful (item)".'

541. Biardeau (1964a: 261 n. 1) remarks that she has not used the Tripādī because the one manuscript of this is poor, which could indicate that there was not a very lively tradition connected with Bhartṛhari.

542. There are other relatively late works dealing with semantics, such as the Vṛtti-dīpikā of Kṛṣṇabhaṭṭa (Gopinath Kaviraj [1930]), and later treatises on Nyāya and Mīmāṃsā deal extensively with detailed problems of semantics. More particularly, there is a series of works devoted to sphoṭa (see section VI.2.4) such as the Sphoṭa-candrikā of Kṛṣṇabhaṭṭa Maunī (Gopāla Shastri Nene [1929]), the Sphoṭa-siddhi of Bharata Miśra (K. Sāmbaśiva Sastri [1927]) and the Sphoṭa-siddhi-nyāya-vicāra (Gaṇapati Sastri [1917]). Two such works are expecially noteworthy. One of the most famous is not by a Pāṇinīya at all, the Sphoṭa-siddhi of Maṇḍana Miśra, which has been edited with the Gopālikā commentary (Rāmanātha Śāstrī [1931]) and translated into French (Biardeau [1958]) and English (K. A. Subramania Iyer [1966b]). Nāgeśa also devoted a special work to this topic, the Sphoṭa-vāda, edited with his own commentary and a superb introduction by V. Krishnamacharya (1946).

543. A large part of this section is devoted to discussing precisely what constitutes an injunction (*vidhi*).

544. In a compound such as *rāja-puruṣa* (see section III.1.5.1a), the number associated with the denotatum of the first member is not specified; a form such as *rāja-puruṣaḥ* (nom. sg.) can correspond to *rājñaḥ puruṣaḥ, rājñoḥ puruṣaḥ*, or *rājñāṃ puruṣaḥ* (' . . . of a king', ' . . . of two kings', ' . . . of many kings'). Pāṇinīyas accept that the compound derives from *rājan-as puruṣa-s*, with the singular affix *as*. However, this affix is here not treated as introduced on condition that one thing is to be denoted. Instead, it is associated with singularity which encompasses all numbers. This is called *abhedaikatva-saṃkhyā* 'singularity of nondifferentiation'. In other words, Pāṇinīyas operate here with an unmarked singular and allow for the ambiguity of first members of compounds at the source of derivation.

545. On the second title see S. D. Joshi (1960: ix). Joshi (1960: xvii-xviii) has noted that the Vaiyākaraṇa-matônmajjinī, which had earlier been considered a commentary on the Vaiyākaraṇa-bhūṣaṇa-sāra, is actually a commentary on this text by Bhaṭṭojī's student Vanamāli Miśra.

546. This text shows deviations from the Laghu-mañjūṣā with respect to some opinions. Kapil Deva Shastri (1974) doubts that the sections in question are actually Nāgeśa's. He also remarks (1974: 299 n. 1) that he has in press a study of the Parama-laghu-mañjūṣā and is engaged in producing a critical edition of the Laghu-mañjūṣā.

547. A conspectus of editions appears in S. D. Joshi (1967a: 233-34).

548. Harirāma states (K. P. Trivedi [1915: 608]) that he composed his work in (presumably saṃvat) 1854 (A. D. 1797).

549. Kapil Deva Shastri is engaged on a critical edition of the text, see note 546.
550. Ruegg (1959: opposite table of contents) notes that he produced a French translation of the first section of the Parama-laghu-mañjūṣā. This too has not been published.
551. Subba Rao includes other materials, but this is his major emphasis.
552. For a survey of such works see Yudhiṣṭhira Mīmāṃsaka (1973: II: 423-56). A good collection of literary passages to illustrate Pāṇini's rules was compiled by Vīrarāghavācārya (see T. Chandrasekharan [1954-55]). For studies of un-Pāṇinian forms in literary texts see note 308.
553. Such literary works are not uniquely related to Pāṇini's rules. Nārāyaṇabhaṭṭa composed such a poem illustrating his Prakriyā-sarvasva (see Venkitasubramonia Iyer [1970]). On Bhartṛhari's possibly being the author of the Bhaṭṭi-kāvya see note 514.
554. I take this as a starting point because it is in the nineteenth century that one sees published research on the range of issues noted below by scholars who both knew the Indian grammarians and made their findings public in the way this is usually understood in modern times. A selection of writings about Pāṇini prior to Colebrooke appears in Staal (1972: 4-32). Let me note, nevertheless, that coupling the terms 'Pāṇinian scholarship' and 'the nineteenth century' as I have done could reasonably be considered objectionable. For, it cannot be denied that Pāṇinīyas such as Nāgeśa (sections III.1.3.7, III.2.2, IV.3.2) could be as critical as any modern scholar in treating questions of common interest (see section V). Moreover, it can be maintained that there has been a continuous tradition of Pāṇinian scholarship dating from Bhaṭṭojī Dīkṣita (sections IV.2.2.3, IV.3.2) to this day. Nāgeśa was a student of Hari Dīkṣita (section IV.3.2), Bhaṭṭojī's grandson, and the teacher - student lineage from Nāgeśa and his student Vaidyanātha Pāyaguṇḍe continues through modern scholars such as K. V. Abhyankar. Kielhorn belongs in this lineage (see K. V. Abhyankar [1960: chart opposite p. 6 of the introduction]). Not only was Liebich Kielhorn's student, but a living scholar, Thieme, links up to Kielhorn through Lüders, who wrote his dissertation (Lüders [1894]) under Kielhorn and was Thieme's direct teacher. Note finally that I refer in this section to recent dissertations not mentioned earlier, since these presumably reflect what established scholars in the field deem topics worthy of further investigation.
555. See the sections referred to. In addition, there are dissertations on pre-Pāṇinian grammars (Tika Rama Panthi [1967]), pre-Pāṇinian terminology in Pāṇini (Saroja V. Bhate [1971]), Kātyāyana and Patañjali and their relations to each other (Rāmasureśa Tripāṭhī [1960], Satī Prasāda Miśra [1965], Sudarshan Kumari Arora [1969]), un-Pāṇinian elements in epic Sanskrit

(Veena Bhatnagar [1973]; see note 308).

556. In addition to the works considered in the sections shown, there are dissertations dealing with indeclinables (Sītārāma Śukla [1966]); rules relative to padas (Ramanath Sharma [1971]), *iṭ* augmenting (Paik [1973]), and accentual features (Vāma Deva Miśra [1968], M. D. Balasubrahmanyam [1969]); and studies on the uṇ-ādi-sūtras (Ram Awadh Pandey [1963], Kaushi Ram [1971]), śikṣā (Madhukar Phatak [1969]), the Mahā-bhāṣya (Insler [1963]), the Kāśikā (Prajñā Devī [1969], Athlekar [1974]), Haradatta and the Pada-mañjarī (D. K. Kharwandikar [1973]), Bhaṭṭojī Dīkṣita (Surya Kanta Bali [1971]), and Nāgeśa (Dharmadhikar Vidyadhar [1966]).

557. In addition to the works mentioned in these sections, there are dissertations by Satyavrat (1955), Naradeva Shastri (1968b), Suśīla Candra Miśra (1968).

558. For my own opinions see the sections referred to.

INDEX

The following is an index of names of modern scholars only. Since the present volume is a survey of research and volume 2 of my work will include complete indices of rules and commentatorial passages, I have not included these here.

Entries of the index are accompanied by two sets of numerals. The first refer to pages of the bibliography and the critical survey. The second refer to numbered footnotes. These are preceded by the symbol 'N' and separated from the former by a semicolon.

Some works listed as forthcoming appeared in the interval between the time I submitted the final manuscript and the time proofs became available. Particulars concerning these are given within square brackets at the end of appropriate entries. Limitations of space preclude my including any discussion of what is said in articles and books thus referred to. Such limitations also preclude my adding here new works by authors not already listed in the bibliography. Note, finally, that I have also made some necessary corrections within brackets appended to entries of the index.